STATISTICS

Measuring Sustainable Development

INTEGRATED ECONOMIC, ENVIRONMENTAL AND SOCIAL FRAMEWORKS

OECD

ORGANISATION FOR ECONOMIC CO-OPERATION AND DEVELOPMENT

ORGANISATION FOR ECONOMIC CO-OPERATION AND DEVELOPMENT

Pursuant to Article 1 of the Convention signed in Paris on 14th December 1960, and which came into force on 30th September 1961, the Organisation for Economic Co-operation and Development (OECD) shall promote policies designed:

- to achieve the highest sustainable economic growth and employment and a rising standard of living in member countries, while maintaining financial stability, and thus to contribute to the development of the world economy;

- to contribute to sound economic expansion in member as well as non-member countries in the process of economic development; and

- to contribute to the expansion of world trade on a multilateral, non-discriminatory basis in accordance with international obligations.

The original member countries of the OECD are Austria, Belgium, Canada, Denmark, France, Germany, Greece, Iceland, Ireland, Italy, Luxembourg, the Netherlands, Norway, Portugal, Spain, Sweden, Switzerland, Turkey, the United Kingdom and the United States. The following countries became members subsequently through accession at the dates indicated hereafter: Japan (28th April 1964), Finland (28th January 1969), Australia (7th June 1971), New Zealand (29th May 1973), Mexico (18th May 1994), the Czech Republic (21st December 1995), Hungary (7th May 1996), Poland (22nd November 1996), Korea (12th December 1996) and the Slovak Republic (14th December 2000). The Commission of the European Communities takes part in the work of the OECD (Article 13 of the OECD Convention).

Foreword

The term "Sustainable Development" seemed to take life with the Brundtland Commission Report of 1989. Indeed the definitions and analysis offered in that Report still enjoy wide acceptance.

Members of the OECD agree that Sustainable Development stands on three pillars: economic, social and environmental. And, in fact, the aims of the OECD, as set forth in its Convention drafted some 44 years ago, targeted Sustainable Development. The first part of Article I reads:

> *to achieve the highest sustainable economic growth and employment and a rising standard of living in Member countries, while maintaining financial stability, and thus to contribute to the development of the world economy;*

This squarely addresses the economic and social dimensions of Sustainable Development. The OECD has pursued those aspects of Sustainable Development with determination since that time, and the spectacular growth of OECD economies, complemented by social safety nets, public health, education and so on, bears testimony to the success of the OECD in implementing Sustainable Development within the framework of the two pillars.

But what of the third pillar, the environment? It was not mentioned in the Convention and this should not be a surprise because 44 years ago, it was not on the public agenda. We hardly spoke of the environment until Rachel Carson woke us up in 1962 with her seminal work "Silent Spring"! Once again, the OECD was out in front when in 1970 Secretary-General Emil Van Lennep established the Environmental Directorate and the very first intergovernmental committee dealing with the environment. In fact, Gro Harlem Brundtland chaired the first OECD Ministerial meeting on the environment in 1974.

So it was in the early 1970s that the OECD began to address all three pillars of Sustainable Development, some 19 years before the Brundtland Commission Report. Does this mean that nothing has changed and that for the OECD it is business as usual? Not at all. The broad interdisciplinary reach of the OECD enables it to address, in an informed and thoughtful way, the trade-offs that arise when the policies supporting the different pillars inevitably clash. For years the OECD examined the trade-offs between economic growth and the social dimension of Sustainable Development. However, the trade-offs between environmental policies and the other two pillars have not been as evident, except perhaps in specific sectors such as fisheries. In order to give decision-makers a rational basis for choices across the full range of economic, social and environmental policies, we need a clear framework to identify and, where possible, measure the trade-offs. Otherwise the whole exercise on Sustainable Development would be of little value.

This volume contains a wide range of papers that can help policy makers and statisticians to understand how to address the measurement of Sustainable Development and develop useful tools to support forward-looking decisions. We are still a long way from having internationally comparable statistical tools for Sustainable Development, but with the analysis and the comparison of good national and international practices, the OECD aims to shorten this process, according to its original mandate.

Donald Johnston

Secretary-General

OECD

Table of Contents

Accounting Frameworks for Sustainable Development:

What Have We Learnt?

Enrico Giovannini

Chief Statistician of the OECD and Director of the Statistics Directorate

Over the last decade, there has been an increasing attitude, both at the national and international level, to complement policy documents and statements with statistical information (for example, describing past and current tendencies in the economy, the society, etc.) and to set quantitative targets for the policy itself. This attitude has obliged statisticians to face new challenges and develop new concepts and new statistical data sets for meeting policy needs. On the other hand, media and the civil society are also demanding more information to assess current trends and evaluate results of various policies.

The case of Sustainable Development (SD) is no exception and several actions have been undertaken over the last decade by international and supranational organisations (UN, OECD, EU, etc.) to measure trends in economic, social and environmental phenomena related to SD. Well known measures of economic growth (i.e. gross domestic product in real terms) have been analysed in conjunction with several measures of social and environmental variables, in attempt to provide an overall evaluation of the sustainability of current trends both in developed and in developing countries.

In particular, the initiative launched several years ago by the United Nations Commission for Sustainable Development to design a set of SD indicators has been followed by similar attempts carried out by the OECD and, more recently, by the European Commission. These projects have a common aim to draw up lists of indicators able to inform policy makers and public opinion about changes in historical paths of economic, social and environmental phenomena, without trying to summarise this complexity in a single (composite) measure of sustainability[1]. In addition, proposals have been put forward by research institutes, academics and a few international organisations to assess the overall "sustainability" of single countries' positions and trends, helping both policy makers and public opinion (mainly through media) to assess past policies and design future actions.

All these developments have stimulated national statistical authorities and other data providers to design new theoretical frameworks and to enlarge the coverage of statistics, mainly on social and environmental phenomena. They have also contributed to the improvement of the quality and frequency of evidence-based policy debates, despite the fact that policy makers have never reached an agreement on a single set of indicators (or other measures) to be used for comparing countries' performances. The difficulty in

---

1. See Hass and others (2002) for a review of these proposals and initiatives.

achieving an agreement reflects the difficulty in defining such a broad concept, the diversity of national approaches and policies to sustainable development and the lack of a theoretical foundation to some initiatives aimed to measure sustainability. Although long and accurate debates have taken place regarding the measurement of SD, no clear consensus has been reached on this issue[2]. In particular, many users are still looking for a fully integrated view of economic, social and environmental domains and tools for evaluating overall trade-offs between different policy options; questions to which indicators alone are not able to provide fully satisfactory answers.

A possible way to, at least partially, overcome these problems is the development of accounting frameworks, encompassing economic, social and environmental phenomena. The OECD has been working on the measurement of SD since the 1980s and several publications have been devoted to illustrating the various options and efforts made by national and international bodies in this respect[3]. In particular, in September 1999, the first OECD workshop was organised on frameworks for measuring SD, where several approaches were analysed[4]. More recently, in the context of the "2001-2003 horizontal project on sustainable development" and to integrate the work already done in the area of economic, social and environmental indicators, the OECD decided to organise a second workshop on accounting frameworks in order to compare more concrete experiences already available in member countries and in other international organisations. Looking at the quantity and the quality of the papers presented to the workshop one could say that this initiative was very timely and useful, and the richness of contributions demonstrated the feasibility of these approaches.

The OECD workshop on "Accounting Frameworks for Sustainable Development", organised by the Statistics Directorate in co-operation with other Directorates, was held on 14-16 May 2003. The meeting was attended by more than 70 experts, representing 19 OECD Member countries, 4 International Organisations and several OECD Directorates. Deputy Secretary General Berglind Ásgeirdóttir opened the meeting and chaired the final session on main conclusions of the workshop. During the three days, 22 papers were presented; (all available documents - including presentations - are available on the OECD web site **www.oecd.org/std** under Statistical Methodology - Publication and Documents - Events, Conferences, and Meetings).

What did we learn from this workshop? I was asked to answer this question during the final session. Therefore, what follows is my personal viewpoint and does not necessarily represent the consensus view of all participants, even if brief comments expressed by some delegates on my presentation allow me to say that, at least, no major disagreements were expressed in regards of these summary remarks.

As previously stated, the quality of papers was very good and I will not try to cover all aspects discussed during the workshop. Therefore, I will concentrate my remarks on the five following topics:

---

2. The difficulty in agreeing on indicators is also, and mainly, due to the fact that the indicators chosen by different countries to measure SD are closely tied to their national plans and strategies.

3. See OECD (1998), (2000), (2001a).

4   See OECD (2001b). These approaches include developments of the traditional national accounts system, construction of synthetic measures of sustainability such as "genuine savings", physical measures of material flows, and selections of indicators based on variants of the "pressure, state, response" model. The workshop also discussed a number of initiatives undertaken within the OECD to monitor trends in the sustainability of specific sectors and sub-national areas.

- The state of the art in accounting frameworks;

- Strengths and weaknesses of various approaches;

- Statistical/analytical issues;

- Institutional issues;

- Statistical policy recommendations for national statistical authorities and international organisations.

First of all, I would like to stress the importance, for analytical and policy purposes, of the increasing coverage of national accounts. Originally, national accounts were developed to deal with economic phenomena, but nowadays one has to recognise a clear tendency towards the extension of national accounts frameworks to other domains, such as environmental and social domains[5]. This extension has been done both in theoretical terms and in practice[6]. In this respect, a very important milestone, after the publication of the 1993 version of the System of National Accounts (SNA), was achieved in 2003 with the publication of the handbook on "Integrated Environmental and Economic Accounts (SEEA)". On the other hand, the work undertaken in the context of the Leadership European Group on "Social Accounting Matrices" represents an important contribution to the practical inclusion of social aspects in national accounts.

The SEEA handbook (jointly published by the United Nations, the OECD, the International Monetary Fund, the European Commission and the World Bank) contains an overview of various ways to put into operation the original definition of SD proposed by the Brundtland Commission. In particular, three main approaches are identified (see United Nations and others, 2003):

- the three-pillar approach;

- the ecological approach;

- the capital approach.

The first approach must contain no single focus (or object) of sustainability, but instead all economic, social and environmental systems must be simultaneously sustainable in and of themselves. Central to the ecological view of SD is the notion that economic and social systems are sub-systems of the global environment. Therefore, it follows that sustainability in the economic and social spheres is subordinate to sustainability of the global environment. Finally, the capital approach borrows the concept of capital from economics, but broadens it in a variety of ways to incorporate more of the elements that are relevant to the sustainability of human development. In doing so, it takes concepts from the physical sciences (especially ecology and geography) and from the non-economic social sciences and integrates them within a framework based on capital.

Each of these views needs specific measurement tools. The SEEA and other methodological work done by international organisations and individual researchers represent important contributions. Equally important is the extensive work undertaken in several OECD countries to implement these approaches and provide policy makers and

---

5. It is worth noting that R. Stone proposed the development of an integrated social and economic set of accounts in 1948.

6. See, for example, E. Giovannini (1995).

public opinion with concrete tools to evaluate the interaction between economic, social and environmental phenomena. The workshop offered an impressive view of the relevance and the quality of this work: several experts were surprised by the number of projects carried out in several countries to implement "national accounts-type" frameworks. In a sense, *the first thing that I learned* from the workshop is that a large number of good practices are already available and that these practices are more numerous and advanced than expected when we planned the organisation of the workshop. These experiences were not very well-known at an international level and/or widely recognised as concrete ways for evaluating SD trend and policies. From this point of view, the workshop was an ideal opportunity to share experiences and to create a better network among experts in this field, confirming the key role that the OECD can play in this respect.

The second thing that I learned from the workshop is that there are various approaches to developing integrated national accounts-type frameworks (INATF). These approaches are characterised by different degrees of complexity, flexibility and cost. In particular, there are some limitations on the flexibility of extensive INATFs and the costs necessary to implement them are quite high. Clearly, a good design of the overall scheme (covering economic, environmental and social dimensions) is a necessary prerequisite for minimising costs, but the use of multiple classifications to capture specific phenomena can expand very quickly the breakdown of the accounts and, thus, the cost for estimating very detailed statistical figures. From this point of view it is worth noting that all experiences presented during the workshop tried to integrate two dimensions (economic-environmental, economic-social), but there were no approaches which aimed to integrate all the three domains at once.

On the other had, one must recognise that INATFs were not originally developed to address SD policy issues. In particular, a "vision" of INATFs capable of encompassing all three dimensions of SD is not yet available. Nevertheless, is it quite clear that INATFs can (and should) be used for addressing SD issues. On the other hand, it is not completely clear if they can perform better than other approaches (i.e. indicators), if they are cost-efficient and if they can successfully meet user needs. To answer these questions it can be useful to try to draw a rough "quality profile" of various available approaches. In particular, the following table attempts to summarise my personal quality profile[7], using quality dimensions used for developing the "Quality Framework for OECD Statistics". I will refer here to three main approaches to statistics for sustainable development: the first includes large integrated national-"accounts-type frameworks and indicators" (input-output, environmental accounts, social accounting matrices, etc.); the second, here defined as "other accounting aggregates" includes simpler approaches aimed to measure the depletion of capital (genuine saving approach, footprint approach, etc.); and the third includes sets of "stand-alone indicators". It is quite clear that these three tools are not completely independent. In particular, accounting frameworks and indicators sets can be seen as complementary and mutually supporting tools. For example, indicators can be calculated on the basis of data obtained from various types of sources (including accounting systems) and accounting frameworks can lead to the calculation of highly coherent indicators. However, in the following table I will try to highlight main differences among the three approaches, more than their linkages.

---

7.   Under the heading "other accounting frameworks" I included an approached based on "genuine saving", the "footprint" approach, etc.

Indicators	Integrated national accounts-type frameworks and indicators	Other accounting aggregates	Stand-alone
Relevance	++	++	+++
Accuracy	+++	+	++
Credibility	+++	+	++
Timeliness	++	++	+++
Accessibility	++	+++	++
Interpretability	++	++	++
Coherence	+++	+	+
Cost-efficiency	+	++	++

I do not have here the opportunity to explain all details of my personal evaluation and I do not want to give the impression that one must necessarily choose only one approach, but I would like to stress how some dimensions can be evaluated very differently by various groups of users. For example, the way in which the dimension of "relevance" is evaluated by different users can substantially vary according to their institutional roles. For example, I would say that an individual ministry would be much more interested in sectoral indicators of sustainability in order to check if its specific acts are pushing the country in the right direction. On the contrary, the prime minister's office (and perhaps the Ministry of Treasury) would be more interested in using complex INATFs to simulate the overall impact of individual policies, in addition to indicators highlighting key trends/issues. Finally, public opinion would be more interested in "headline" indicators or other accounting frameworks able to summarise in "one number" (or in a few figures) the situation of the country *vis-à-vis* SD. In other words, the way in which institutions involved in SD issues are organised at the national level can strongly influence the direction of the statistical research and the implementation of theoretical models, as well as the use of statistical tools. Therefore, the *third thing that I learned* is that, looking at national experiences, there is a strong link between the way in which political responsibilities for SD are allocated to various bodies and the development of statistical tools for measuring SD trends and for evaluating SD policies. In particular, countries which invested more in developing complex INATFs are those where statistical systems are quite centralised and where national statistical offices have a strong role and reputation in terms of analytical studies.

Papers presented at the workshop made clear that there are several important statistical issues to be addressed to successfully implement frameworks for measuring SD. In particular, in terms of tools developed to evaluate the interaction between the economic and the environmental dimensions, the main issues concern the coherence between concepts and classifications adopted in national accounts and in "basic" statistics; the linkage between physical and monetary units, and the availability of basic information on environmental phenomena (an issue to which society has placed great importance in terms of concern for its sustainability). In the area of economic-social dimensions, it is quite clear that "Social Accounting Matrixes" were not precisely developed for analysing SD issues. Thus the most appropriate classifications to this purpose have still to be developed, as well as a consensus view on how to measure the human and social capital (and its distribution between social groups). In addition, the availability of basic information about the social dimension of sustainability is quite limited and new approaches should be developed to take into account the role of public services and services provided within households. In this respect, an interesting idea could be the development of accounts based on the time-use.

Several statistical/analytical issues still need to be addressed. For example, in some cases the role of subjective perceptions could be taken into account to complement "objective" measures of certain phenomena. The linkage between accounting frameworks and SD indicators should be reinforced (in particular, reinforcing the analytical soundness of some indicators), as well as the co-operation between statisticians and experts involved in the development of models to capture behaviours and predict future tendencies. Finally, it seems quite clear that input-output type statistics and general equilibrium-type models are complementary and that better accuracy and timeliness of the former can improve substantially the quality of results drawn from the latter.

In conclusion, *the fourth thing that I learned* is that a long list of statistical and analytical issues is still pending and that better identification of an international research programme in this area could greatly help both statisticians and analysts in their work. From my perspective, one of the priorities should be the design of a "minimum set of integrated accounts" capable of addressing the most relevant issues raised by policy makers and civil society in debates related to SD. In fact, today there are so many alternatives to developing accounting frameworks that it is not easy to identify the best way to proceed. Therefore, this proposal would help countries to focus their statistical efforts for SD purposes, minimising the amount of resources involved and improving the international availability of comparable data.

As previously mentioned, institutional arrangements can be fundamental in promoting statistical work, both at national and international levels. In particular, the institutional environment, directly or indirectly, influences (among other things) the consensus on the knowledge base to be developed through statistical tools, the division of labour among public bodies involved in statistical activities, the level of funding for statistical activities and the relationships between statistical agencies and public opinion. In this respect, policy makers and analysts have to understand that the involvement of statisticians from the early beginning in measurement issues is an asset, especially in domains (like SD) multidisciplinary in nature and characterised by a high degree of complexity. This is *the fifth thing that I learned* and I hope that this message can be clearly sent to experts working both at the OECD and in capitals.

In conclusion, considering the technical, institutional and organisational issues analysed during the workshop, I would like to suggest the following *recommendations to national statistical authorities*:

- To promote the development of a coherent statistical approach to SD, including both indicators and frameworks, each national authority should elaborate its own "strategic view" on statistics for SD, encompassing technical issues, organisational aspects and communication initiatives[8]. This strategy should be presented to and discussed with policy makers (both the government and the parliament) and other national data providers. In particular, the involvement of bodies (ministries, regions, etc.) other than the national statistical office is fundamental in decentralised statistical systems.

- SD is a long-term issue. Therefore, medium-long term investments in specific statistical domains must be carefully planned, but a roadmap with concrete intermediate deliverables should be established from the beginning. Policy makers

---

8. The SEEA could serve as a guide to countries wishing to elaborate such a view, at least as far as relationships between economy and environment are concerned.

and public opinion need more information on economic, social and environmental dimensions according to an integrated view, and they cannot accept to wait for years to have something (even provisional) from official statisticians.

- To meet the needs of different groups of users, both indicators and frameworks are useful and the overall planning should take into account the possible interaction between these tools. Indicators can be also very important for capturing the attention of policy makers and media, but accounting frameworks provide a much more solid and integrated structure and statistical base for evaluating existing trade-offs between various policies and deriving related indicators.

- The respective roles of national accountants (in charge of accounting frameworks) and other "sectoral" statisticians need to be clarified and the interaction between the two groups maximised, identifying specific targets for each of them. Both groups can bring a fundamental contribution to the understanding of SD issues, but they need to establish a continuous and fruitful technical and scientific dialogue, a behaviour that, in some national statistical systems, cannot be taken for granted.

- The interaction among national statistical offices (NSOs) of different countries should be increased, both at technical and strategic levels. In many instances, SD issues are multi-country in nature and the statistical description of these interactions must be agreed upon by various countries. This is not true only in the European Union context, but also in other areas of the world.

- National statistical offices should be more involved in analytical projects, including those devoted to building models. The partnership between NSOs, on one hand, academics and other researchers, on the other, can be very fruitful for all parties. For example, statisticians can better define analytical needs and develop more sophisticated tools able to meet them; analysts can devote more energy to learning about the reliability of available figures and adapt their tools to new statistics to be developed. In the case of SD, where several "dimensions" are involved, this dialogue is even more important than in other fields.

- Statisticians have to speed up the process of developing statistics for SD. There is also an increasing need to simplify the sets of indicators developed over the last decade and enhance the internal coherence and analytical soundness of available information. Statisticians must contribute to this effort, by improving the interpretability and accessibility of statistics for SD.

Similarly, I would like to identify the following *recommendations for international organisations*:

- International authorities should help national statistical offices to address:

  - technical issues, especially those concerning environmental and social accounts, and their harmonisation at international level;

  - the linkages between various economic, social and environmental dimensions;

  - relationships between indicators and accounting frameworks;

  - the design of an overall strategy for developing national account-type frameworks able to produce statistics that cover SD issues in a coherent and integrated way.

- International organisations should improve their co-ordination on the subject and should develop a first programme for collecting data produced through accounting frameworks for SD analyses. In addition, they could launch joint communication initiatives to inform policy makers and the media about new statistical developments in this area, as well as to promote the actual use of new statistical products in decision making and policy analysis.

- A better dialogue should be established at the international level between policy makers and statisticians, to help the former express clear and coherent needs, and the latter meet these needs developing and implementing new international standards.

- International organisations directly involved in policy analyses linked to SD issues should foster the dialogue between analysts and statisticians, and ensure that the latter are involved as appropriate in projects carried out for analytical and policy purposes.

From the OECD perspective, the Organisation should pursue these initiatives, in close consultation with member countries and other international organisations. The presentation to its stakeholders, in 2004, of main results achieved in the context of the horizontal project on sustainable development represents an ideal opportunity in this respect. In addition, the agreement just achieved with the Statistical Division of the United Nations, the Statistical Division of the UN Economic Commission for Europe and Eurostat to launch (in the context of the Conference of European Statisticians) a steering group on statistics for sustainable development, represents an important step toward a better co-operation at international level and can ensure an adequate follow-up to these conclusions.

References

HASS J.L., BRUNVOLL F., HOIE (2002) "Overview of Sustainable Development Indicators used by National and International Agencies", *OECD Statistics Working Papers*, 2002/2. OECD, Paris.

GIOVANNINI E. (ed.) (1995) "Social Statistics, National Accounts and Economic Analysis", Proceedings of the International Conference in Memory of Sir Richard Stone, *Annali di Statistica*, Serie X, Vol. 6, Istituto Nazionale di Statistica, Roma, Italy.

OECD (1998) *Environmental and Sustainable Development Indicators*. State of the art in Member countries. Informal contributions, OECD, Paris

OECD (2000) *Towards Sustainable Development: Indicators to Measure Progress*. Proceedings of the Rome Conference, Rome, Italy, 15-17 December, OECD, Paris

OECD (2001a) Sustainable Development: Critical Issues, OECD, Paris

OECD (2001b) Frameworks to measure Sustainable Development: An OECD Expert Workshop, OECD, Paris

UNITED NATIONS AND OTHERS (2003) *Integrated Environmental and Economic Accounting 2003*, available at http://unstats.un.org/unsd/environment/seea2003.htm

Opening Remarks "The Role of the OECD"

B. Ásgeirsdóttir

Deputy Secretary-General, OECD

Why OECD countries need to lead the work on sustainable development?

Our Ministers have recognised that OECD countries "bear a special responsibility for leadership on sustainable development worldwide, historically and because of the weight they continue to have in the global economy and environment". It was agreed in Johannesburg that now is the time to move from words to action. The priorities for action are clear: *We need to achieve more sustainable consumption and production patterns, to increasingly decouple environmental pressure from economic growth, to ensure sustainable management of natural resources, and to work together in partnership to reduce poverty.*

But these are easier said than done. In some areas there are major obstacles hampering the necessary policy reforms, resulting in a distinct "implementation gap" between policy advice and action. The result of this "implementation gap" has been deterioration in some environmental conditions, and the continuance of poverty, hunger and disease as defining characteristics of the lives of so many. Most of the challenges that remain relate to either the protection of global public goods, such as biodiversity or a stable climate, or to continuing inequalities between countries or peoples in terms of development, poverty reduction, and access to basic good and services such as energy and clean water and other ecosystem services.

One of the areas where OECD countries can show leadership is to increase the coherence and integration of their own policies, and to take the necessary steps either unilaterally or in co-ordination with others to overcome some of the obstacles to policy reform. This includes integrating sustainable development concerns across Ministries, and ensuring that existing policies do not work against each other. For example, OECD countries are the largest donors of overseas development assistance (ODA), but at the same time have policies in place to protect and subsidise their own national industries often at the expense of developing country economic opportunities. In fact, it is probable that in many instances the development benefits of official aid are swamped by the effects of trade distorting subsidies and other barriers to trade. OECD country support to domestic production – particularly in the sectors of agriculture, fisheries and energy – amount to roughly 6-7 times the amount of ODA provided to developing countries. Not only do many of these subsidies lead to economic distortions and environmental damage in OECD countries, but together with other barriers to trade they represent a loss of an estimated US$ 43 billion a year to developing country trading partners.

OECD is working together with its member countries to identify and establish more coherent policies for sustainable development, and to overcome some of the obstacles – such as the fear of a loss of competitiveness – which block policy reform. As an interdisciplinary Organisation, the OECD is particularly well suited to supporting countries in their efforts to increase coherence across the full range of public policies affecting sustainable development. But policy prescriptions are not enough. Success boils down to a question of will! For that we depend on political leadership.

OECD also plays an important role in reinforcing political will by monitoring country progress towards sustainable development. Monitoring progress helps countries to identify the effectiveness of the policies they are using both to achieve nationally agreed objectives and to implement their international commitments; it also facilitates peer review and peer pressure as tools to encourage countries to implement appropriate policies effectively. OECD's unique system of country surveys helps to foster good governance by ensuring accountability in government policies using the peer review system and by sharing best practices in policy experience amongst countries.

As you may know, the OECD has been actively promoting policy analysis and prescriptions for sustainable development since 1998. In particular, to respond to the mandate received by OECD Ministers in 2001, a horizontal project was launched, involving national and international organisations, to identify measurement, analytical and policy issues. The project brought to the attention of policy makers and civil society the need for a more integrated view of economic, social and environmental dimensions of the development, proposing policy prescription to enhance sustainable development.

One of the issues raised in the project concerned is measurement problems. This meeting aims to analyse models developed in the field of accounting frameworks for sustainable development, as well as projects launched in a few OECD countries to extend the national accounts schemes to environmental and social phenomena.

Following the mandate given by Ministers in 2001, OECD has been working to better incorporate reviews of sustainable development policies and performance in our country economic surveys. Having agreed upon a list of sustainable development indicators, each Economic and Development Review of OECD countries will include a new section assessing the country's performance. This is a new departure for OECD as an Organisation, and an important one to ensure transparency and accountability in moving towards sustainable development. This new activity will not replace the comprehensive environmental performance reviews which will continue to be undertaken for all OECD member countries over a 5-6 year cycle.

The OECD is also doing new, groundbreaking work on environmentally harmful subsidies and environmental taxes. Work in both areas is linked to accounting frameworks for sustainable development.

What is the OECD doing on the social pillar of sustainable development?

Work on the social aspects of sustainable development analyses the links between environmental and social changes and on balancing progress between the various dimensions of sustainable development.

Environmental issues have historically driven much of the discussion on sustainable development. More recently, however, social aspects have also come to the fore, both at international and domestic level. The social and economic needs of the poorest countries were as much a part of the agenda of the 2002 World Summit on Sustainable Development as the environmental themes that dominated the Rio Earth Summit 10 years earlier. At the same time, several OECD countries are more fully integrating some of the social challenges they face – the fight against poverty and exclusion, the importance of providing all individuals with the skills required to compete in more flexible labour market, the special needs of groups such as children and ethnic minorities – in their national sustainable development plans or strategics.

OECD work on the social aspects of sustainable development is pursuing two main tracks. The first looks at some of the direct links between environmental and social conditions. The OECD Environmental Strategy for the First Decade of the 21st Century, which was adopted by Environment Ministers in May 2001, identified the social and environmental interface as one of its five objectives. Under the heading of "enhancing the quality of life" Environmental Ministers called for measures to limit the adverse environmental effects of urbanisation and spatial development; to address disparities in exposure to environmental threats and policies; to increase awareness of environmental threats; and to promote participation in decision making and access to justice on environmental matters. OECD activities that are contributing to better understanding the relations between environmental and social conditions include special chapters in individuals OECD Environmental Performance Reviews, analysis of the employment and distributive effects of environmental policy, and work on environmental democracy and education.

The second track of OECD work takes a broader perspective of the social aspects of sustainable development, and looks at the role of social protection systems in creating more inclusive societies. Such systems include not only government programmes such as unemployment or child welfare payments, but also support provided by families, communities and firms. Each has an important role in promoting more inclusive societies, reducing poverty, protecting individuals against a range of risks, and facilitating structural adjustment. However, sustaining the performance of these institutions over time requires confronting a range of persistent pressures (such as lower fertility rates, changing family structures, weaker community ties, migration pressures, widening inequalities, and persistent poverty and exclusion) that are putting at risk their capacity to deliver results.

The OECD has looked at how various pressures affect social protection systems over the lifecycle of individuals. It discusses ways of reducing the possibility of conflicts between social, economic, and environmental trends, and stresses that social protection systems are essential not only in industrialised countries, but also in developing and transition economies, where the existence of adequate and extensive social safety nets will affect the pace and sequencing of economic and environmental reforms.

There is a need to improve accounting frameworks to measure sustainable development and to address information gaps that remain in many areas. Currently available statistics are not capable of giving an integrated view of various dimensions of sustainable development, nor fully taking into account in a transparent way all the subsidies arising from policies. There is a lack of integration between the three dimensions of sustainable development and policy-makers have difficulties in evaluating trade-offs between alternative policies through the use of different sets of indicators. This meeting will analyse models that have been developed for sustainable development, as well as projects launched in a few OECD countries to extend the national accounts schemes to environmental and social phenomena. In addition to technical issues, this meeting will also address the problem of establishing institutional set-ups for promoting the dialogue between statisticians and policy makers in this field.

While the OECD is using available information to support policy analysis, information gaps remain daunting in many areas. Major gaps standing in the way of progress relate to scientific information, specific indicators, and underlying data. It is important that throughout the OECD, the organisation continues to address these gaps in order to better inform policy debates and to help overcome obstacles to policy reform.

The difficulty in achieving an agreement on this issue can be partially due to the lack of theoretical foundation of some initiatives aimed to measure sustainability. Although long and accurate debates took place on the measurement of sustainable development, one can say that no clear consensus has been found on this issue. In addition, users are looking for "integrated" views of economic, social and environmental domains and tools for evaluating trade-offs between different policy options, questions to which indicators are not able to provide fully satisfactory answers.

A possible way for overcoming these problems is the development of accounting frameworks to provide a fully integrated view of economic, social and environmental phenomena and looking at some experiences developed by some OECD countries, the integration of traditional input-output matrices with more recent proposals concerning environmental and social accounting models appears a very attractive solution. In addition, projects carried out by international organisations over the last few years (i.e. the development of the System of Economic and Environmental Accounts and studies on Social Accounting Matrixes) provided not only coherent and well established methodological frameworks, but also a new impetus to the implementation of such frameworks in OECD countries.

What is the strength of the OECD for the work on sustainable development?

The strength of the Organisation and the value added of its work on sustainable development are its holistic approach based on economics and the multidisciplinary nature in which the work is carried out. These stem from the OECD's ability to bring together decision-makers across the whole range of policy communities, including through peer review processes. The OECD provides governments with a forum in which to identify emerging issues and analyse, discuss and develop public policies. The OECD also acts as facilitator and, through multi-stakeholder co-operation, helps to move the sustainable development agenda forward. Governments are not the only ones that can move SD forward; the business community has an important role to play. One example of this is the work to promote the environmental component of the Guidelines for Multinational Enterprises.

Rather than continuously refining the definition of "sustainability", the OECD focuses on those components of the sustainable development concept that it regards as particularly relevant and where it has a clear comparative advantage. In 1998, the OECD Ministers agreed to interpret "sustainable economic growth" as including social and environmental, as well as economic, considerations. While the environmental intensity in some economic sectors has declined in recent years (i.e. some environmental pressures have been decoupled from economic growth), the increased scale of economic activity at world scale is resulting in a net degradation of the global environment.

Conclusion

Few people question the Brundtland Commission definition of sustainable development, namely "development that meets the needs of the present without compromising the ability of future generations to meet their own needs". Within societies, the luxuries of one generation are often the needs of the next. But that is not true of the health of the biosphere upon which all of us, rich, less rich and poor, depend. This means sound and effective management of the global commons which takes us far beyond our individual country reviews.

In both instances the OECD has a key role to play by carrying out new, groundbreaking work on environmentally harmful subsidies, environmental taxes and decoupling indicators. The 30 OECD countries need to take lead on sustainable development, and that if they work together to achieve sustainable development, other countries would follow. The OECD also provides a forum for exchanging views and policy experiences among countries, and for working together to develop the right framework conditions and monitoring systems to facilitate the implementation of global sustainable development.

After the work already done in the area of indicators for sustainable development, the OECD decided to organise this workshop on accounting frameworks for comparing experiences already available in member countries and looking at the quantity and the quality of the papers one could say that this initiative has been absolutely necessary and timely. The results of this workshop will be presented to OECD Committees active in this field and I hope that the contributions presented during these three days will push policy makers to support further the implementation of accounting frameworks for sustainable development.

The Role of Institutions in Building Frameworks to Measure Sustainable Development: The Canadian Experience

R. Smith

Statistics Canada

Introduction

This paper focuses on the institutional arrangements that have led recently to a proposal for a national set of environment and sustainable development indicators for Canada.[1] The indicators are to be derived from an improved environmental information system, including an expanded set of national accounts with new measures of natural, human and, in principle, social capital. The paper describes the players involved in identifying the indicators, the origins of the initiative, the process by which it unfolded and the institutional lessons learned.

The players involved

Three federal institutions were central in this initiative: the National Round Table on the Environment and the Economy (NRTEE), the federal environment ministry (Environment Canada) and the federal statistical agency (Statistics Canada). The latter two need no special introduction here, but the former, being somewhat unique, deserves a brief introduction.

The NRTEE, established in 1994, is a publicly funded, independent agency of the Government of Canada. Its mandate is to act as a catalyst in the identification, explanation and promotion of the principles and practices of sustainable development. It carries out this mandate in all sectors of the economy and all regions of the country. Given the breadth of sustainable development, the NRTEE is obliged to break its work into manageable pieces. It does so by focusing on those critical, yet relatively unexplored, questions lying at the intersection of the environment and the economy.

As an arm's length agency, the NRTEE offers a neutral forum wherein all stakeholders can openly and freely discuss and debate critical issues and co-operate to find solutions. Through its efforts, the NRTEE contributes to a balance that promotes economic prosperity for all Canadians while preserving the environment for the benefit of current and future generations.

The NRTEE comprises 25 decision makers and opinion leaders from across the nation and all sectors of society. These distinguished Canadians are appointed for three-

---

1.   The opinions expressed here are those of the author and should not be taken to represent the official position of Statistics Canada. The author wishes to thank Claire Aplevich of the National Round Table and the Environment and the Economy for providing background material for this paper.

year renewable terms by the Prime Minister. Their efforts are supported by a Secretariat of approximately 28 professional and support staff located in the nation's capital. The Secretariat, headed by a President and Chief Executive Officer, provides managerial, analytical, communication and administrative services to the NRTEE members and their task forces and committees.

The NRTEE's activities are organized into programs, each overseen by a task force of NRTEE members and representatives from the community at large. Task forces commission research, conduct national consultations, identify areas of agreement and disagreement and recommend measures to promote sustainability. Their recommendations are reviewed in plenary session before public release. The full membership meets quarterly to review progress of existing programs, establish future priorities and launch new programs.[2]

Genesis of the environment and sustainable development indicators initiative

On a roughly annual basis, the Government of Canada prepares a budget that sets out where and how taxpayers' money will be collected and invested. The budget is the official blueprint for the Government's economic agenda. The Minister of Finance and his officials are responsible for its preparation and delivery to Parliament, usually in the month of February.

In response to funding requests from Environment Canada and the NRTEE leading up to the 2000 federal budget, the Minister of Finance announced in February 2000 that "the federal government will provide $9 million over the next three years to the National Roundtable on the Environment and the Economy and to Environment Canada to develop environmental and sustainable development indicators in collaboration with Statistics Canada."[3] In his presentation to Parliament, the Minister noted that "as we move to more fully integrate economic and environmental policy, we must come to grips with the fact that the current means of measuring progress are inadequate." He went on to say that "in the years ahead, these environmental indicators could well have a greater impact on public policy than any other single measure we might introduce."[4]

Following the budget announcement, the funding provided was split equally between the NRTEE and Environment Canada for work on complementary projects. Environment Canada was to investigate the possibilities for creating an improved system for basic environmental information in Canada, a system seen to be essential to development of the indicators. The NRTEE was to focus specifically on the development of the indicators requested by the Minister.

What follows here is focused on the latter of the above initiatives, as the indicators work is most closely related to the topic of the workshop for which this paper has been prepared. Given the very close relationship of the two initiatives, a summary of the initiative led by Environment Canada is provided in a text box below.

---

2. Further information about the NRTEE and its membership can be found at www.nrtee-trnee.ca.

3. Department of Finance Canada, 2000, *The Budget Plan 2000: Better Finances, Better Lives*, Ottawa. (Available at www.fin.gc.ca.)

4. The Honourable Paul Martin, 2000, *The Budget Speech 2000: Better Finances, Better Lives*, Ottawa. (Available at www.fin.gc.ca.)

The ESDI Initiative: process and recommendations

In response to the request from the Minister of Finance, the NRTEE launched the *Environment and Sustainable Development Indicators (ESDI) Initiative* in the fall of 2000. The basic premise adopted for the initiative was that society must better account for those economic, environmental and human assets that are necessary to sustain a healthy society and economy, now and in the future. Collectively, these assets represent the nation's capital stock. It is this stock that must be maintained if development is to be sustainable.[5]

To lead the ESDI Initiative, the NRTEE assembled a 30-member Steering Committee. Members included representatives from organisations involved in developing sustainability indicators, non-governmental organisations, academia, government, business and financial organisations. From the outset, the NRTEE collaborated closely with Statistics Canada and Environment Canada to ensure the credibility and relevance of its recommendations.

The ESDI Initiative unfolded in three phases:

- Phase 1 (September 2000 to March 2001) focused on the development of the capital approach on which the initiative was based. Statistics Canada played a key role at this stage as primary author of the conceptual framework.[6] Reviews of existing indicator initiatives were also undertaken. A major event during this period was a National Conference on Sustainable Development Indicators held to review the proposed capital framework and discuss the path forward. Some six hundred people attended, demonstrating an unexpected level of interest in the initiative.

- Phase 2 (April 2001 to June 2002) was devoted to identifying potential indicators. Much of this work was conducted by advisory groups of experts focused on identifying possible indicators of natural and human capital. From the lists prepared by these groups, the ESDI Steering Committee selected a draft set of core indicators. A second national conference was convened to review the proposed core indicators at the end of phase 2.

> Box: *The Canadian Information System for the Environment*
>
> At the same time as the NRTEE undertook preparation of a national set of environment and sustainable development indicators, Environment Canada considered the possibilities for preparing an improved environmental information system for the nation. A high-level task force was struck to recommend a preferred approach to constructing this Canadian Information System for the Environment. Its final report, delivered in October 2001, included a number of recommendations, the most fundamental of which was the creation of a distributed network of environmental databases linked together via the internet.[1] Environment Canada has since made considerable headway in implementing this vision and is currently seeking funding for a major investment in that regard. Clearly, once fully established, this system will be of great value in the preparation of the indicators requested by the Minister, in addition to serving many other ends.
>
> [1]   Task Force on a Canadian Information System for the Environment, 2001, *Sharing Environmental Decisions*, Ottawa. (Available at www.ec.gc.ca/cise.)

---

5.   For details of the capital approach adopted by the ESDI Initiative, see Smith, R., 2003, "A Capital-based Sustainability Accounting Framework for Canada," also prepared for the OECD meeting on Accounting Frameworks to Measure Sustainable Development, Paris, 14-16 May, 2003.

6.   See Smith, R., C. Simard and A. Sharpe, 2001, *A Proposed Framework for the Development of Environment and Sustainable Development Indicators Based on Capital*, Paper prepared for The National Round Table on the Environment and the Economy's Environment and Sustainable Development Indicators Initiative. (Available at www.nrtee-trnee.ca.)

- Phase 3 (July 2002 to March 2003) involved further review of the recommendations, technical refinement and initial feasibility testing of the proposed indicators, and the development of long-term recommendations linked to data collection and reporting.

The final report of the ESDI Initiative, *Environment and Sustainable Development Indicators for Canada*, was released in early May 2003.[7]

Recommendations of the Initiative

The NRTEE concluded that, at present, Canada has insufficient data on its natural and human capital assets and on the linkages among environmental, social and economic issues. Canada, like most other developed countries, relies heavily on macroeconomic indicators such as the Gross Domestic Product to support economic decision making. These indicators provide only a partial view of the factors that affect development and they do not account for the full costs and benefits of economic decisions.

To remedy this asymmetry, the NRTEE recommended a small set of easily understandable indicators to track the state of natural and human capital:

- an **Air Quality Indicator** to track the exposure of Canadians to ground-level ozone (O_3) and, eventually, other pollutants

- a **Freshwater Quality Indicator** to provide a national measure of the overall state of water quality as measured against major objectives for water use in Canada (*e.g.*, water for drinking, aquatic habitat, recreation and agriculture)

- a **Greenhouse Gas Emissions Indicator** to track Canada's total annual emissions of greenhouse gases

- a **Forest Cover Indicator** to track changes in the extent of Canada's forests

- a **Wetlands Cover Indicator** to tracks changes in the extent of wetlands in Canada, and

- a **Human Capital Indicator** to track the percentage of the workforce with educational qualifications beyond the secondary school level.

The NRTEE has recommended that Statistics Canada publish these new indicators annually and that the Minister of Finance incorporate them in the annual federal budget statement. Such indicators will provide a better basis for assessing the interactions between the economy, the environment and society and will improve Canada's ability to measure its progress.

Recognizing that indicators are most effective when supported by detailed information, the NRTEE has also recommended improving and expanding the data systems required to report on capital. Specifically, it proposes that the federal government expand, in a stepwise manner, the System of National Accounts to include new accounts covering natural, human and social capital. So that the basic data needed to construct these accounts are available, the NRTEE has recommended expanding and improving data collection, particularly in the environmental domain. This would include investments in improved scientific monitoring systems, more thorough use of existing administrative data and the expansion of environmental surveys. Clearly, the improved environmental

---

7.   Available at www.nrtee-trnee.ca.

information system proposed by Environment Canada (see text box) would be the target for much of this investment.

The path forward

Following delivery of the NRTEE's final report to the Government, the Minister of the Environment was asked to report to the Prime Minister and his Cabinet with advice on an appropriate government response to the recommendations. At the time of writing, this response is awaited.

Institutional lessons learned

One of the clearest lessons to emerge from the ESDI Initiative is the value of a well-funded, effective third-party organization like the NRTEE. Its role in both stimulating the Government of Canada to explore the possibility of creating sustainable development indicators and in bringing together key stakeholders in a neutral, positive forum to discuss ideas and chart a path forward has been paramount. Had the NRTEE not existed to fill this role, a government ministry would have been required to do so. Given ministries' roles of advocating policy in specific domains, their ability to seek and find common ground on a question as broad as sustainable development is somewhat compromised. Without such an advocacy role, the NRTEE is able more easily to engage its partners in open and free debate of the sort needed to resolve the complex issues surrounding sustainable development.

One key activity of the NRTEE in promoting sustainable development – and one that was crucial in this initiative – is its *Greening of the Budget* submission. This is an annual set of recommendations that outlines the ways in which the federal government might better integrate economic, social, and environmental considerations into its budget. In the fall of 1999, the NRTEE submitted its recommendations for Canada's 2000 federal budget to the Minister of Finance. Included in that submission was a recommendation that the federal government support Canadian capacity in the area of "applied sustainability economics," including the development of national sustainability indicators. This recommendation caught the attention of the Minister of Finance at the time and was instrumental in the subsequent funding allocation that brought the ESDI Initiative to life. The fact that it was, somewhat uniquely, the Minister of Finance himself who requested the work with certainly contributed to the level of interest and participation the initiative ultimately enjoyed.

The value of building national environmental statistical capacity has also been demonstrated by this initiative. Statistics Canada has been active in environmental accounting for over 10 years and, despite having relatively few data and a modest budget, it has developed a core competency in the field. Its accounting framework is well established conceptually and the accounts developed so far have demonstrated their utility in a number of applications. They are published periodically along with a related set of 10 indicators under the title *Econnections: Linking the Environment and the Economy*.[8]

In addition to its environmental accounts, the agency conducts a set of four household and business environmental surveys. These surveys provide a sound foundation that could be rapidly expanded if required to respond to the need for sustainable development

---

8.   Statistics Canada, 2000, Econnections: Linking the Environment and the Economy – Indicators and Detailed Statistics, 2000, Catalogue no. 16-200-XKE, Ottawa.

information. The experience gained in designing and running them is a valuable component of the agency's environmental capacity. Environmental surveys are, in many ways, different from their social and economic counterparts and it can require several years to "get it right" when running them. Not only are respondents unaccustomed to providing environmental data, but the individuals who traditionally complete survey forms (comptrollers and accountants) are often unfamiliar with the questions asked on environmental surveys. This means that other individuals must be targeted with the questionnaires. Developing frames for environmental surveys is challenging as well, in part because industrial classifications are not structured with environmental concerns in mind.

The agency has also invested considerably in the capacity to conduct spatial environmental analysis. This includes acquiring the computer hardware, software and know-how needed to work with spatial data and building the necessary databases of spatially referenced economic, social and environmental data. Given the highly localized nature of environmental phenomena, the ability to compile and manipulate such data is fundamental.

The strength of this overall statistical program has benefited Statistics Canada greatly in the ESDI Initiative, both in terms of the credibility that comes with a demonstrated track record and in terms of its ability to respond to the conceptual and empirical questions posed by other participants. At this point it is not clear what role Statistics Canada will play ultimately in building Canada's sustainable development information system. Regardless of the role, the agency believes it is well prepared.

Clearly, building a truly robust and useful sustainable development information system is beyond the grasp of any single organisation. Perhaps more than any other topic faced by governments today, sustainable development cuts across traditional institutional, policy and intellectual boundaries. Addressing it will require the simultaneous and co-ordinated efforts of scientists, policy developers, managers, politicians and, of course, society in its broadest sense. It goes without saying that achieving the level of mutual trust and commitment required to bridge the gaps between the "stovepipes" that persist in bureaucratic institutions is challenging. One such challenge particularly evident from Statistics Canada's involvement in the ESDI initiative is the difficulty in finding common language and shared viewpoints between natural and social scientists. The latter tend to approach the issues surrounding sustainable development from an anthropocentric perspective, while the former tend to be more bio-centric in their views.[9] Thus, the concept of capital, which has its roots in the anthropocentrism of the economics tradition, resonates more fully with social scientists than natural scientists. This tension has been evident in Canada, with fewer natural scientists stepping up to embrace the concept than social scientists.

A related challenge has been that of defining a clear information role for Statistics Canada with respect to sustainable development. Unlike in the social and economic domains, where Statistics Canada has a long and broad tradition as a provider of neutral, policy-relevant information, the agency has never played a large role in informing environmental policy. The same can be said of most statistical agencies worldwide. Although many statistical agencies do provide environmental information and some,

---

9.   There are, of course, exceptions to these general tendencies. The author, for one, is a natural scientist who believes sustainable development is meaningful only when interpreted from an anthropocentric viewpoint, even though his ethical framework is more closely aligned with the bio-centrists.

including Statistics Canada, have done so for 25 years or more, they are still, relatively speaking, newcomers in the field. Much longer and more fully developed is the role of ministries of agriculture, forests, mines, fisheries and environment in this regard. Not only have such organisations provided environmentally relevant information for much longer than statistical agencies (some for over 100 years), they generally have much broader professional capacity for doing so. Statistical agencies tend not to employ large numbers of the natural scientists typically required for environmental data collection, especially collection of the complex physical data required to monitor environmental quality. All this means that statistical agencies, much more so than in the social and economic domains, can offer only a portion of the environmental information needed for a sustainable development information system.

In Statistics Canada's experience, defining and gaining acceptance of the statistical agency's portion of this work is challenging. Two points that have surfaced in Canada during the discussions related to the ESDI Initiative are the responsibility for the preparation of the indicators themselves and the potential conflict between "public-right-to-know" and the traditional statistical commitment to confidentiality of individual data. On the former point, it is evident that there is some reluctance on the part of those scientists whose job it is to collect basic physical data on, for example, air quality to relinquish to Statistics Canada the role of compiling those same data into an aggregate indicator. On the latter point, the potential conflict for the agency is with an approach that is increasingly popular with those in the environment domain wherein pollution data are reported for specific polluting establishments.[10] The challenge is reconciling this approach with the iron-clad guarantee of confidentiality that is the hallmark of every statistical agency in the western world, including Statistics Canada. These debates are on-going at this time and exploring them in their full detail is beyond the scope of this paper. The lessons learned by Canada in resolving them should ultimately be of interest to other countries faced with similar challenges. Documenting the nature of these debates more fully is a task the author hopes to tackle in the near future.

---

10. This approach began with the *Toxic Release Inventory* in the United States and has since been adopted in a number of other countries, including Canada.

Accounting for Sustainability

K. Hamilton

World Bank

Introduction

When the Brundtland Commission offered its famous definition of sustainable development–"to meet the needs of the present without compromising the ability of future generations to meet their own needs"–it presented many challenges to policy-makers. Not least among these is the question of how we measure progress towards sustainable development. Without indicators to guide policy, commitments to achieving sustainability risk being no more than fine words on paper.

Since the time of the Brundtland Commission there has been a worldwide effort to develop indicators of sustainable development – Box 1 highlights some of the principal approaches. A rough grouping of these approaches would include:

- Extended national accounts – the UN System of Environmental and Economic Accounts; the World Bank's measure of adjusted net savings; the genuine progress indicator / index of sustainable economic welfare.

- Biophysical accounts – the ecological footprint.

- Unweighted indices – the living planet index; the environmental sustainability index.

- Weighted indices – environmental pressure indices by theme.

- Eco-efficiency – resource flows in total and per unit of GDP.

- Indicator sets – as published by the UN Commission for Sustainable Development and many countries.

The question of what constitutes a good indicator is by now well understood. The OECD (1994) established selection criteria for *environmental* indicators under three broad headings – policy relevance, analytical soundness, and measurability – but these criteria are broadly applicable to other indicators as well:

- Policy relevance:

  – Indicators should be easy to interpret.

  – They should show trends over time.

  – They should be responsive to changes in underlying conditions.

  – A threshold or reference value should be established, against which conditions can be measured.

Box 1. **Indicators of Sustainable Development**

Measuring sustainability is fundamental to achieving sustainability. Selected examples of indicators of sustainable development include:

UN System of Environmental and Economic Accounts A framework for environmental accounting.

Genuine Saving – World Bank. Change in total wealth, accounting for resource depletion and environmental damage.

Genuine Progress Indicator – Redefining Progress, and *Index of Sustainable Economic Welfare* – UK and other countries. An adjusted GDP figure, reflecting welfare losses from environmental and social factors.

Ecological Footprint – Redefining Progress, WWF and others. A measure of the productive land and sea area required to produce renewable resources and sequester carbon emissions.

Living Planet Index – WWF. An assessment of the populations of animal species in forests, fresh water and marine environments.

Environmental Sustainability Index – World Economic Forum. An aggregate index spanning 22 major factors that contribute to environmental sustainability.

Environmental Pressure Indices – Netherlands, EU. A set of aggregate indices for specific environmental pressures such as acidification or emissions of greenhouse gases.

Resource Flows – World Resources Institute. Total material flows underpinning economic processes.

UN Commission for Sustainable Development – Prototype SD indicator sets for individual countries.

- Analytical soundness:

  – Indicators should be well-founded in technical and scientific terms.

- Measurability:

  – Indicators should be calculated from data that are readily available or available at reasonable cost.

  – Data should be documented and of known quality.

  – Data and indicators should be updated at regular intervals.

A particular issue with respect to sustainability indicators is that they must be capable of integrating a large variety of factors. This is because the question of sustainability is strongly linked to the extent of substitutability between the range of assets underpinning the development process. There are no sustainable diamond mines, for example, but there can be sustainable diamond mining countries – if they can transform the proceeds of diamond extraction into other productive assets.

This suggests the following as desirable criteria for choosing sustainability indicators:

- There should be an underlying framework which permits the user to understand how different indicators are interrelated.

- There should be a numeraire that permits the aggregation of disparate information.

- Aggregate indicators constructed using the numeraire should have clear interpretations with respect to sustainability.

- Conversely, the component parts of an aggregate indicator should be linked to policy levers.

These criteria clearly favour the accounting approaches to indicator construction highlighted above and, to a lesser extent, weighted indices such as the Environmental Pressure Index work in the Netherlands and the EU. A key indicator derived from monetary environmental accounting is the World Bank's measure of adjusted net saving, described below[1].

Net saving and sustainability

Much of the early effort on environmental accounting focused on the measure of a 'green GNP,' motivated by a concern that traditional measures of national product measured the goods but not the 'bads' associated with economic activity – see, for example, Ahmad and others (1989) and Lutz (1993). It can be argued that it is fundamentally important to have better measures of income, in particular to ensure that consumption of assets is not treated as income. More recent research, however, has concentrated on the linkages between wealth and sustainability rather than income measurement.

There is a basic plausibility to the notion that the sustainability of development is intrinsically linked to the evolution of national wealth. Pearce and Atkinson (1993) were the first to explore this empirically, measuring net savings rates adjusted to reflect environmental depletion and degradation for over 20 countries.

Recent theoretical work has derived the precise linkage between saving effort and development prospects – Hamilton and Clemens (1999) establish this for economies on an optimal growth path, while Dasgupta and Mäler (2000) show how a suitable definition of shadow prices for assets permits the extension of the theory to non-optimal economies. There are two basic results linking levels of saving (defined as the change in real wealth, excluding capital gains) and development prospects.

First, if adjusted net savings are positive at a point in time, then the present value of social welfare along the development path is increasing. This implies, of course, that a development path where net saving is everywhere positive is also one where the present value of social welfare is always increasing. To answer the question of whether prospects for social welfare are improving, therefore, it is sufficient to measure net saving.

Second, if adjusted net saving is negative at a point in time, then not only is the present value of social welfare declining, but the level of social welfare over some interval in the future along the development path must actually be lower than current social welfare. This is equivalent to saying that the economy is on an unsustainable path. Negative net saving is therefore an indicator of unsustainability.

The critical factor in turning theory into practice with regard to these extensions to national accounts is that a sufficiently broad range of assets must be included in the saving measure. This implies that simply 'greening' the accounts to include natural

---

1. Wackernagel *et al.* 2001 look at net saving and the ecological footprint as complementary approaches to measuring sustainability.

resource depletion and pollution damages, for instance, is not sufficient: at a minimum some accounting of human capital is required, and ideally accounting for social capital and technological change should be included as well.

Empirical work on the measurement of net saving has been published by the World Bank since 1999 in the *World Development Indicators*[2]. Table 1 presents the summary estimates of net saving for 1999.

Table 1 - **Adjusted net savings, 1999, % of GDP (US$)**

	Gross domestic savings	Consump-tion of fixed capital	Energy depletion	Mineral depletion	Net forest depletion	Carbon dioxide damage	Education expenditure	Adjusted net savings
Low income	20.3	8.3	3.8	0.3	1.5	1.4	2.9	7.8
Middle income	26.1	9.6	4.2	0.3	0.1	1.1	3.5	14.3
Low and middle income	25.2	9.4	4.1	0.3	0.4	1.2	3.4	13.3
High income	22.7	13.1	0.5	0.0	0.0	0.3	4.8	13.5
East Asia and Pacific	36.1	9.0	1.3	0.2	0.4	1.7	1.7	25.2
Europe and Central Asia	24.6	9.1	6.0	0.0	0.0	1.7	4.1	11.9
Latin America and Carib.	19.2	10.0	2.8	0.4	0.0	0.4	4.1	9.6
Middle East and N. Africa	24.2	9.3	19.7	0.1	0.0	1.1	4.7	-1.3
South Asia	18.3	8.8	1.0	0.2	1.8	1.3	3.1	8.3
Sub-Saharan Africa	15.3	9.3	4.2	0.6	1.1	0.9	4.7	3.9

Source: World Development Indicators 2001

The accounting underlying this table is as follows:

Adjusted net saving	=	Gross domestic
	-	Consumption
	-	Energy depletion
	-	Mineral depletion
	-	Net forest depletion
	-	CO2 damage
	+	Education

Depletion is measured as total resource rent, the difference between world prices and the economic cost of production – this likely over-estimates depletion, particularly for countries with high reserves to production ratios. Energy depletion includes crude oil,

---

2.   Adjusted net saving was referred to as 'genuine' saving in early editions of the *World Development Indicators,* as well as in Hamilton and Clemens (1999).

natural gas and coal, while mineral depletion includes bauxite, copper, iron, lead, nickel, phosphate, tin, zinc, gold, and silver. Net forest depletion represents the excess of harvest over natural growth. Damages[3] from CO2, a global pollutant, are deducted on the assumption that countries have the right not to be polluted by their neighbours. Important resources not included owing to data availability include fisheries, subsoil water, agricultural soils and diamonds. Data availability also precludes measures of urban air pollution damages.

Education expenditures are treated as an addition to saving effort in Table 1 (rather than as consumption in standard national accounting). However, owing to the wide variability in the effectiveness of government education expenditures, these figures cannot be construed as the value of investments in human capital. The accounting for human capital is also incomplete because depreciation of human capital is not estimated.

Looking at income groupings, the broad picture that appears in Table 1 is one of moderately high net savings rates in middle and high income countries, and significantly lower rates in low income countries. This is partly explained by lower gross savings in low income countries. However, net saving is also depressed in low income countries owing to relatively high CO2 damages (as a per cent of GDP), high levels of net forest depletion, and relatively low education expenditures.

Turning to regional groupings, the polar cases are East Asia and Pacific, with robust levels of net saving (but recall that urban air pollution damage is excluded) at 25% of GDP, and Sub-Saharan Africa, where the net saving rate is about 4%. Given the caveats about the treatment of education expenditures above, it is likely that net savings in Sub-Saharan Africa are negative in aggregate. Of the developing regions, Eastern Europe and Central Asia have relatively high net savings rates, while these rates are more modest in South Asia and Latin America and the Caribbean. Negative net saving is recorded for the Middle East and North Africa, owing to the heavy dependence on oil exports in the region, but there is a likely upward bias in the depletion estimates for the oil economies.

Figure 1 scatters net savings rates against income levels (on a logarithmic scale) in order to display an important relationship at the country level. As expected, there is a general upward trend in this figure, with higher income countries achieving higher levels of net saving. Perhaps the most important observation is that nearly half the poorest countries, those below a GDP per capita of $1000, have negative net savings.

Measuring net saving tells us whether *total* wealth is rising or falling in a country. However, population growth rates are significant in most developing countries, which suggests that development prospects are better measured by the change in wealth per capita. Box 2 presents research results on such a calculation for 90 countries in 1999. As expected, factoring population growth into the savings equation results in many more countries facing an unsustainable future, as evidenced by declines in wealth per capita.

Policy implications of adjusted net savings

As theory suggests, net savings figures can indicate whether, in aggregate, development prospects are rising and whether an economy is on a sustainable path. The empirical results suggest that in many countries an important policy goal must be to

---

3.   Fankhauser's (1995) estimate of $20 per tonne of carbon emitted is used.

increase net savings. The policy levers to achieve this can be applied at the level of the different assets that constitute total national wealth. This story of the development process as management of a portfolio of assets was featured in previous work by the World Bank (World Bank 1997).

The range of policy levers available to boost savings can be inferred from the components of saving appearing in Table 1. The questions that policy makers should pose include the following:

- To what extent do monetary and fiscal policies boost gross saving rates? Government dissaving, in particular, can be an important part of this question.

Figure 1: **Adjusted net savings rates vs. GDP per capita, 1999 (US$)**

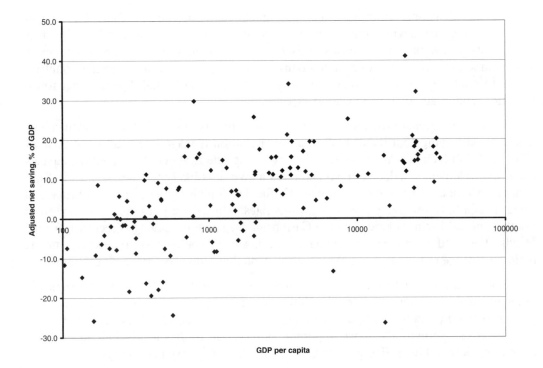

Source: derived from World Development Indicators 2001

- Do natural resource policies encourage over-exploitation? If resource royalties are not captured, or if tenure is insecure (or non-existent, as in an open-access fishery), then resource exploiters have a strong incentive to boost extraction rates above efficient levels.

- Do pollution policies encourage emissions beyond socially optimal levels? Well-crafted pollution policies will push emissions to the level where marginal damages and marginal abatement costs are equalized. Many of the newly industrialized countries exhibit pollution levels significantly above this level.

- Are sufficient resources committed to education expenditures? Are these expenditures effective?

As noted above, the assets accounted in Table 1 are limited by data availability. Additional policy questions surround investments in other assets, such as health capital (are all children immunized, for example) and knowledge and technology (are appropriate levels of R&D being funded).

Box 2. **Estimating changes in wealth per capita**

In countries where there is significant population growth, the sustainability question revolves not around the evolution of total wealth, but rather around changes in wealth *per capita*. If population growth rates are taken as exogenous, a simple formula makes this clear:

$$\Delta\left(\frac{K}{P}\right) = \frac{K}{P}\left(\frac{\Delta K}{K} - \frac{\Delta P}{P}\right)$$

The formula says that the change in wealth per capita is just equal to total wealth per capita (K is wealth, P population) times the difference between the percentage increase in total wealth and the percentage increase in population. This is the correct measure of net saving in an economy with a growing population, and the prospects for sustainability and the present value of social welfare per capita depend upon the sign of this measure.

Hamilton (2002) provides estimates for roughly 90 countries of both an extended measure of net saving (ΔK) and of total wealth K in order to measure the change in wealth per capita. One of the key results of this analysis is shown in the figure below, which scatters the change in wealth per capita as a percent of total wealth per capita against population growth rates.

Figure 2: **Percentage change in wealth per capita vs. population growth 1999**

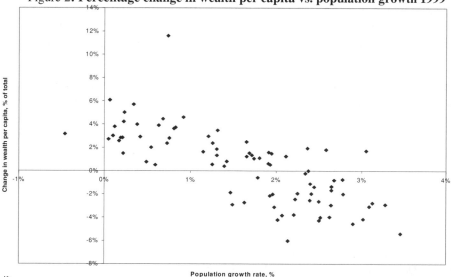

Source: Hamilton

These estimates suggest that over 30 countries are experiencing declining wealth per capita; the great majority of these have population growth rates greater than 1.5% per year. For comparison, the projected population growth rate in Sub-Saharan Africa to 2015 is 2.3%.

Achieving higher net saving levels is clearly important. This mobilizes resources for development. But a critical issue concerns the *effectiveness* of the investments that are made out of savings. If governments, in particular, are investing in 'white elephant' projects with low rates of social returns, then each dollar of saving is not producing one dollar of productive assets – overall wealth is growing more slowly than its potential.

The fundamental policy message that derives from the savings analysis is therefore: boost net savings through a combination of macro and sectoral policies, and boost the effectiveness of public investments, particularly in critical assets like human capital.

Broad conclusions on sustainability indicators

Box 1 highlighted a broad range of indicator efforts that aim, more or less directly, at assessing progress towards sustainability. It was argued above that without an integrating framework and a numeraire that permits weighting and aggregating across disparate elements of the economy and the environment, the ability of many of these indicators to measure progress towards sustainability is limited. However, selected biophysical indicators may be an essential complement to the monetary accounting-based indicators.

The argument for complementary indicator sets revolves around the limits to substitutability between produced and natural assets. If certain natural assets provide critical services and have no practical substitutes (the ozone layer is a good example), this may restrict the usefulness of monetary accounting in the limit. In particular, if the nature of some environmental problems is that catastrophic changes in the state of the system can occur with little warning that a limit is being approached, then the usual rising marginal damage curves that underlie monetary accounts may not be measurable.

Pearce and others (1996) argue that the net saving indicator is most useful for that part of nature which is deemed to be exploitable. Biophysical indicators on the extent of preservation of critical natural assets can complement the saving indicator. Unsustainability is signalled when either the savings rate turns negative or loss of critical natural assets occurs.

There are good reasons beyond the measurement of sustainability for extending national accounting systems. This argument is made forcefully by Nordhaus and Kokkelenberg (1999) in *Nature's Numbers*, the report to the US National Research Council on environmental accounting. But for many developing countries the combination of low saving effort, high resource depletion, high population growth, and ineffective public investments, particularly in education, means that the sustainability question is vital.

References

Ahmad, Y.J., El Serafy, S., and Lutz, E., (eds), 1989, *Environmental Accounting for Sustainable Development*, The World Bank, Washington.

Dasgupta, P., and K-G Mäler (2000), Net national product, wealth, and social well-being. *Environment and Development Economics* 5, Parts 1&2:69-93, February and May 2000.

Fankhauser, S., 1995. Valuing Climate Change: The Economics of the Greenhouse. London: Earthscan

Hamilton, K., and M. Clemens, 1999. Genuine Savings Rates in Developing Countries. *World Bank Economic Review* 13:2, 33-56.

Hamilton, K., 2002. Sustaining Per Capita Welfare with Growing Population: Theory and Measurement. Presented to the World Congress on Environmental and Resource Economics, Monterey, June 24-27, 2002. Environment Dept., the World Bank.

Lutz, E. (ed), 1993, *Toward Improved Accounting for the Environment*, The World Bank, Washington.

Nordhaus, W., and E. Kokkelenberg eds., 1999, Nature's Numbers: Expanding the National Economic Accounts to Include the Environment. Washington: National Academy Press.

OECD, 1994. Environmental Indicators–OECD Core Set. Paris.

Pearce, D.W. and G. Atkinson,1993. Capital theory and the measurement of sustainable development: an indicator of weak sustainability. *Ecological Economics* 8: 103-108.

Pearce, D.W., K. Hamilton and G. Atkinson, 1996. Measuring Sustainable Development: Progress on Indicators. *Environment and Development Economics* 1 (1996): 85-101.

Wackernagel, M., K. Hamilton, J. Loh and J. Sayre, 2001. Accounting for Sustainable Development: Complementary Monetary and Biophysical Approaches. The World Bank (mimeo).

World Bank 1997. *Expanding the Measure of Wealth: Indicators of Sustainable Development.* ESD Studies and Monographs No. 17. Washington: The World Bank.

World Bank, 2001. *World Development Indicators 2001.* Washington: The World Bank.

Sustainable National Income and Multiple Indicators for Sustainable Development [1]

B. de Boer, Statistics Netherlands, Voorburg

R. Hueting, Foundation SNI Research, The Hague

Abstract

Developing indicators for sustainable development is discussed in the context of a view on sustainability based on experiences with environmental economic modelling. This view coincides with an explanation of a specific indicator, sustainable national income (SNI).

The goal of publishing the SNI is to put into perspective the significance of gross national product (GNP) in political opinion-forming and policy-making. We summarise the place of both indicators in economic theory. To this end, sustainability is defined as non-declining welfare. This is almost equivalent to a non-declining volume of national income, or non-declining availability of environmental functions (possibilities to use our physical surroundings). The relevant environmental economic aspects of sustainability are thus incorporated in the SNI. Social aspects are limited to the conditions that employment and income distribution must remain unaffected and a subsistence level of income must be guaranteed. Sustainability thus defined takes the form of a development path that can be achieved in future if at least two conditions are satisfied: people must have dominant preferences for sustainability and blockages, such as the prisoner's dilemma, must be overcome by some form of concerted action. The sustainable path used here is the path with maximum non-declining income under current technology, which is the SNI. This path is not instantaneously achievable, but the difference in income between the actual path and this sustainable path is a measure of the current degree of unsustainability of the country considered. Moreover, under the assumed preferences the SNI is an improved monetary welfare measure in comparison to standard national income.

A calculation method for the approximation of this theoretical SNI has been set-up by dividing the theoretical model in separate approximate steps involving no feedback loops. First, the state of the environment on the sustainable path with maximum production (income) is estimated for each environmental problem taken into account. Second, this state is transformed in maximum allowable levels of emissions and the other forms of use of the environment, such as land use, by employing a model for each environmental problem. Third, these so-called sustainability standards are used as constraints in a dedicated general economic equilibrium model which maximises national income, thus producing the approximate SNI in the year considered. This model reduces the use of the

---

1. The authors wish to thank Dr. Reyer Gerlagh of the Institute for Environmental Studies at the Free University in Amsterdam for his valuable input.

environment down to the imposed sustainability standards by employing changes in production and consumption processes, varying from adding technical appliances via process adaptations to shifting production capacity to environmentally less damaging activities. The SNI can increase and its distance to GNP can decrease by technological progress.

Indicators of sustainable development

Like most of our colleagues, we characterise the system of our concern as the interacting social, economic and environmental subsystems of the world, a country or a region. The interactions between these subsystems can be described by variables representing human or physical actions (flows) from one subsystem to another and reactions. Actions and reactions can be investments, changes in employment, changes in types of use of the environment by economic activities such as resource use and emissions, et cetera. The reactions are to a large extent determined by characteristics of the stocks (the state, the condition) of the environmental, social and production-consumption subsystems, labelled as the stocks of natural, human and produced capital. Variables representing these (re)actions and characteristics of stocks can be labelled action and state variables, or flow and stock variables. The central question is apparently, how to measure whether the system is heading for sustainability, in other words, whether it tends towards sustainable development?

An approach to sustainable development

The question how to measure sustainable development can of course only be answered after having stated what one means by sustainability. Pezzey (1994) for instance inventoried a large variety of definitions. Yet, the theory these authors developed inspired us to make a cautious delimitation of the concept that might be useful in developing indicators. We do so by making use of some insights that we gathered from working with environmental economic theory on sustainability, more specifically from the theory of sustainable national income (SNI), and give some practical examples, including the application of the SNI. The following reasoning depicts our view on sustainability.

The interdependence of the environmental, social and production-consumption subsystems makes sustainability a characteristic of the system as a whole: the social subsystem cannot be sustainable while the environmental subsystem is not (the opposite holds true in the short term but not in the long term, see Hueting, 2003), and so on. It follows directly that the system's behaviour (or development) is either sustainable or it is not.

The development (or behaviour) of the social-economic-environmental system can be said to be sustainable if the development does not threaten the existence of the system itself, nor the elements and characteristics of the system that people (as elements of the system) want to preserve for whatever reasons. A sustainable development therefore requires the preservation of vital elements and characteristics of the system. These essential variables include human health and vital environmental functions *i.e.* possibilities to use our physical surroundings (specifically to withdraw space, substances and organisms and to emit substances) (Hueting 1980, Pezzey 1994, Goodland 1995 and Hueting and De Boer 2001). Examples are the function 'air for physiological functioning of humans, plants and animals (breathing)' of air, the function 'drinking water' of water and the function 'soil for raising crops' of soil. It is clear that a sustainable development according to this "definition" is not unique, but that does not need to be a problem.

From the above it follows rather directly that a development is sustainable if the essential variables are constant or increasing, *i.e. never decreasing*. However, this condition results in a group of sustainable balanced development paths (such as path *s* in Figure 1) which generally do not coincide with the actual development path (*a* in Figure 1) at any time instant. Therefore, this type of sustainable development path generally cannot take-off from the actual development path immediately. This is why a sustainable balanced growth path can only be attained by an infeasible leap or approached in the course of time via a transition path.

Feasible transition paths (such as *f* in Figure 1) from the actual development path *a* to a sustainable balanced growth path such as *s* generally exist. On such a transition path, the essential variables gradually converge to a never-decreasing pattern on a sustainable balanced growth path such as *s*, but they never reach the path exactly. In stability theory, however, a transition path to a stable path is considered stable itself. Therefore, a transition path such as *f* may be considered a sustainable development as well, although the essential variables have diminished to sustainable levels only at the end of path *f*. [2]

A development of the social-economic-environmental system includes the reactions of people and their governments to their perceptions of this development, so an unsustainable development might turn into a sustainable one, or *vice versa*. This makes sustainability a time-dependent criterion. At first sight it might seem odd that the whole system's survival would be at stake in a certain period and not in the next period, or *vice versa*, while the system still exists. The reason is that the system is dynamic and threats to its existence are therefore not immediately effective and may consequently be averted before they would become effective. So, a development of the social-economic-environmental system can be called sustainable if the extrapolation of the development into the future with the best of our knowledge shows that all essential variables converge to non-decreasing patterns or close ranges around those patterns. Therefore, if the development changes, it may also change from being unsustainable into being sustainable, or *vice versa*.

---

2. Stability theory shows that the group of sustainable development paths can be broadened further. Like a stable path, a path may still considered sustainable if it ultimately stays circling within a constant range around the balanced growth path *s*, where this range should of course be acceptable according to the preferences of the people. Thus, stochastic fluctuations, stable limit cycles and limited chaotic system behaviour around the balanced growth path may be incorporated in the sustainability concept. We shall not use this extended sustainability concept here.

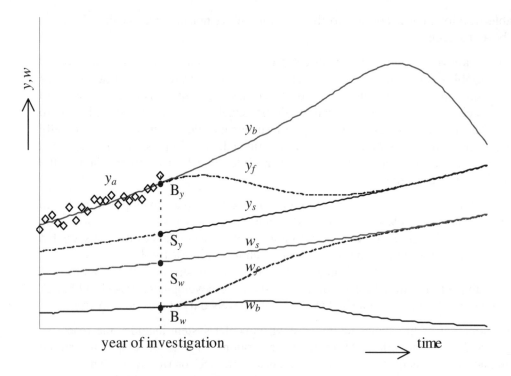

Figure 1. Actual standard national income observations (y_a, fictitious example) compared with the net national income (y) and a welfare indicator (w) on three optimal paths, calculated with a dynamic environmental economic model. The business-as-usual path (index b) approximates the actual path (index a) by assuming incomplete expression of preferences for the environment. These preferences are assumed to be completely expressed on the infeasible sustainable path (index s) and the feasible transition path (index f). The points B_y and B_w indicate the levels of national income y and the welfare measure w on the business-as-usual path b in the year of investigation; S_y and S_w are the corresponding points on the infeasible sustainable path.

Sustainability clearly puts society in control: the system is not autonomous but human decisions are vital for it's the continuation of its existence. People may threaten the system's survival, including that of people in the future, by maintaining an unsustainable development, and only people can turn it into a sustainable development.

The well-known definition in the report "Our common future" (WCED, 1987) summarises the reasoning so far quite well by saying that the world economic development is sustainable if it takes care of the needs of the present generation without damaging the possibilities of future generations to satisfy their needs.

Some conditions to sustainable development indicators

The next step is how to develop from these still rather abstract notions a set of indicators for the "degree of", "distance to" or "movement towards" sustainability of actual system development.

From stability theory it also follows that the notion of a set of stable or sustainable paths defines at each time instant a region of initial points of these paths, the border of which can be considered as the sustainability boundary (Perrings, 1996). This boundary consists of points of no return. If a point on the actual development path at a certain time lies within the sustainability boundary of that moment, a sustainable balanced development path still can be reached and the actual development still can be deemed sustainable. This elegant concept could be turned into a great instrument along with a satellite accounting system monitoring the actual developments of the (most important) essential physical or monetary action (flow) and state (stock) variables. It could even be used to develop sustainability indicators. Unfortunately, the assessment of this boundary must be considered practically impossible and practical criteria for sustainability must be developed.

To that end, consider a set of action and state variables of the social-economic-environmental system. What makes these variables sustainability indicators? Of course, the variables must be calculated correctly in accordance with the conventions of the system of national accounts. It can then be established for instance whether a variable is increasingly "uncoupled" from the growth of production. But even if such uncoupling is observed, it still cannot yet be established whether this fact guarantees sustainable development if it is not clear in which direction the variable must change to this end. For instance, remaining at the same level can be insufficient to attain sustainability because of the persistent and cumulative character of the burden. In such cases only a slowing-down of the deterioration would have been attained. It is therefore paramount to have a notion of the closest sustainable balanced growth path of the system as a whole (*s* in Figure 1), *i.e.* the set of sustainable levels of all monitored variables that is the closest to the actual situation. Because this dictates in which direction and at what pace the variables must change. Only then, can one judge if the monitored development is a sign of a transition towards sustainability (such as *f* in Figure 1). More importantly, only then can one see whether sustainability is still far away or relatively close for the essential variables.

The sustainable levels of the essential action and state variables are mutually dependent and must in theory be estimated by modelling the whole system. Below we give an example of how this can be done. From this exercise it follows that certain action and state variables must change with certain rates at least in order to achieve that other state variables reach sustainable levels. For example, the (equivalent) emission of greenhouse gases (an essential action variable) should be reduced with a rate of at least about 0.5% of last year's emission each year world-wide during the next centuries in order to prevent unsustainable global warming (temperature at ground level is an essential state variable). That is, according to a set of different global warming models. These conditions to the rates of change of some key action or state variables are even less accurate than the estimates of the sustainable levels of these variables, but they provide important additional information for judging the "degree" of sustainability of the monitored course of these in the course of time.

Summarising, we propose to judge the degree of sustainability of the actual development by comparing the actual levels and the development of the monitored variables with the levels they must ultimately attain on an estimated sustainable path. From this comparison may follow demands on the rates of change of some variables. Such a sustainable path is the one corresponding with maximum sustainable national income, the SNI.

Sustainable national income

We illustrate the process just explained using the calculation of the sustainable national income (SNI) according to Hueting (1980) and Hueting and De Boer (2001), performed by the Institute for Environmental Studies in co-operation with Statistics Netherlands for the statistical years 1990 and 1995; see Verbruggen *et al.* (2000), Hofkes *et al.* (2002) and Gerlagh *et al.* (2002).

The SNI is defined as the maximum attainable national income under absolute preferences for sustainability, while technology and societal essential variables as employment remain as observed, except the size of the population. The reasons for these choices are:

- the SNI is designed to show the trade-off between production and the sustainable levels of environmental functions (the levels to which the environment can be used), taking the effects of changing technology and sectoral employment into account

- the effects of expected *future* technological progress and of expected *future* population growth on *present* sustainable national income must not be incorporated in the SNI

- effects of reaching sustainability on employment and other social variables, and thus on national income, are not incorporated in the SNI, because these effects cloud the indicator

- many societal essential variables *may* correlate positively or negatively with the level of production and the levels of environmental functions, and may therefore be monitored separately (Goodland 1995, Hueting 2003).

- the size of the population is an essential element in the ultimate sustainable state and it is therefore an outcome of the SNI calculation (although family planning was not used as one of the measures to attain sustainability in the practical calculations).

The income maximisation selects only one sustainable balanced growth path as the vehicle for the SNI and as the goal of transitions to sustainable development. We illustrate this below. Further, we explain how this path is approximated for essential variables and how the SNI is calculated.

Theoretical environmental-economic model

Like before, we start with the theory, in which we use a reliable model of the relevant processes in production, consumption and the environment. Remember that we assume all societal elements to be constant, except population size. The model takes care of the interactions, the resulting volume and price changes and consequently maximises national income properly.

The interactions in production and consumption are taken care of by production functions and welfare functions, at least one function per activity, where each function has multiple inputs. The use of the environment, or possibilities to do so, appear in both the production and the welfare functions. The model simulates the changes of state and action (flow) variables in the economy, the environment and society in their mutual dependence. The model has time dependent solutions, which form a path in variable space vs. time. We discuss those paths by means of two important aggregate output variables, plotted on the same vertical axis. One of them is the volume of national income as a measure of production and consumption, the other one is a welfare measure.

The model can produce different paths by providing it with different inputs. A crucial input is the structure of the preferences for using the vital functions of our physical surroundings for increasing production in the short term on the one hand and for safeguarding these functions in the long term on the other. This welfare function can – for a large part – only be assumed, because these preferences can be measured only very partially (Hueting 1980, Hueting and De Boer 2001).

One may assume for instance that the people prefer the actual state of affairs in production, consumption, society and the environment. If the parameters of the model are estimated (calibrated) well, the model approximates the present development of national income (path *a* in Figure 1) by path *b*. Far extrapolation of path *b* might indicate a collapse of welfare and income because of depletion of vital environmental functions.

Assumed stronger preferences for the environment produce a model path with lower income, but higher welfare, and a probably postponed collapse.

If dominant preferences for sustainable use of the environment are assumed, two paths may be calculated.

If the state of the environment as well as the technical and other measures in the economy are optimised directly in the first year of calculation so as to maximise SNI, the sustainable balanced growth path (*s* in Figure 1) will be calculated. Its characteristic is that environmental functions do not decline in future due to their use for production and consumption, because this use is limited. The sustainable path starts from an already sustainable state. The initial point lies on the 'permanently' sustainable path with maximum income (the SNI), here called *the* sustainable path. As no transition occurs following the initial state, it is a 'balanced growth' path. The path is infeasible in that it cannot be reached directly, but only by a transition path as just mentioned. Again the availability of environmental functions will not decrease on this path, but now national income does not decrease either. It may increase, but in theory, "as far as the model reaches into the future", this national income never decreases (technically, the collapse is shifted to infinity). Moreover, because national income is still maximised under the presumed preferences, this sustainable development path produces *the* sustainable national income.

If the state of the environment and the technical and other measures in the economy are chosen as they are in the first year of calculation, the model produces a theoretically feasible transition path (*f* in Figure 1), departing from the actual development path in that year. During the transition, environmental functions will not be exhausted beyond the levels reached in the sustainable equilibrium, but income will drop gradually when more and more measures are taken to reach the equilibrium.

One could ask how it is possible that we assume strong preferences for sustainability, while it is obvious that currently the world follows a non-sustainable development path. It is obvious, however, that individuals generally do not have the power to prevent large-scale damage to the environment. It is also obvious that, when they have the power to change their conduct in a sustainable way, they have objections to being the first ones to take such steps, even if they have strong preferences for the result. This is because it would cause them disproportional costs, while they expect the effect to be close to zero because they doubt that others will follow suit (prisoner's dilemma). Because of the existence of these and other 'blockages' (or 'barriers'), it suffices to assume one set of preferences to explain both the actual development where the blockages are effective and the assumedly preferred more environmentally benign path where the blockages are overcome (Hueting and De Boer 2001). This construction has the additional advantage that the comparison of national income on both paths is less problematic than with two different welfare functions.

The distance between the sustainable path and the actual development path in terms of national income is the distance to sustainability we have to bridge as a country in terms of the required opportunity costs. If we recalculate the expected future SNI trajectory in each year or each couple of years with the same model on the basis of new information on production, consumption and environmental protection technology, the starting point of the trajectory provides the SNI of that year in the statistical sense. The SNI's at these starting points in the consecutive years of calculation form the time series of SNI we are looking for (Figure 2).

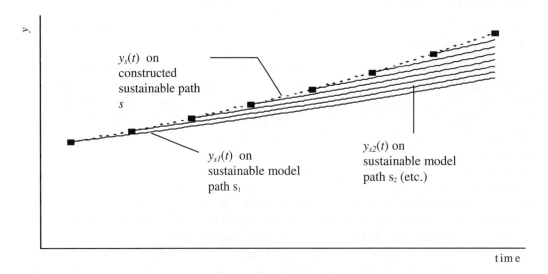

Figure 2. Construction of the unfeasible sustainable path s and the corresponding sustainable national income y_s. In the calculation of the sustainable national income according to Hueting, technological progress is *ex ante* assumed zero on each model path. In that case national income on these paths ($y_{s1}(t)$, $y_{s2}(t)$ et cetera) are constant and their graphs are horizontal lines (not shown in the figure). National income on the *ex post* constructed sustainable path s, however, may still rise due to technological progress.

Practical SNI model approach

Generally, a sufficiently accurate integral economic-environmental model is so large and complex that a sustainable solution providing the SNI cannot be found. Therefore, we have decided to approximate the sustainable path by using a set of models that co-operate in a sequential fashion, without the mutual feedback that would make the model collection generally valid.

The case of sustainable development, however, offers a possibility to make this simplification without generating a large error. Remember that the necessary condition for sustainability is that environmental functions are maintained forever, at the lowest levels of availability that enables the environment to stay supporting these levels. Put less technically, we seek the maximum levels of use of the environment that may be sustained forever, in other words, levels above which the very possibilities to continue with this use would disappear in the future. Three conditions are set up that are assumed to hold if the environment is used sustainably. These conditions must be satisfied both in the present and in the future.

The first condition is that the extinction of biological species at the global level may not be accelerated by human influence. The second condition is that any changes in the state of the environment may have only a minor, acceptable impact on human health. The third condition is that vital environmental functions must be present all over the world; that is, not equally spread but within reach for human use. These three conditions impose bounds on the acceptable variation in the state of the environment, however imprecise. Think of maximum allowable pollutant concentrations, minimal ozone column, maximum global warming et cetera. We call these bounds sustainability standards for *the state* of the environment.

These bounds to the state of the environment are used as inputs in models of the environmental problems concerned, such as the use of natural resources and space, climate change, acidification, eutrophication, dispersion of harmful substances and desiccation. Iteration with such a model yields limits to the use of the environment by production and consumption mentioned before. We call these limits sustainability standards for *the use* of the environment, and they are actually approximations of the use of the environment on the sustainable path (which we cannot compute directly). The standards represent both the assumed preferences for sustainable use of the environment (the vertical demand line in Figure 2.7, Hueting and De Boer 2001) and the knowledge we have of the 'behaviour' of the environment under (or close to) that sustainability, however approximate this knowledge sometimes may be. Table shows the most important standards as developed in the project.

Table 1. **Sustainability standards for the Netherlands, 1990**

Environmental Theme	Units	Emission	Sustainability standard	Required Reduction (%)	
Greenhouse effect	Billion kg CO_2 equivalents/yr	254.5	53.3	201.2	(79.1%)
Ozone layer depletion	Million kg CFC 11 equivalents/yr	10.4	0.6	9.8	(94.2%)
Acidification	Billion acid equivalents/yr	40.1	10.0	30.1	(75.1%)
Eutrophication	Million P-equivalents/yr	188.9	128.0	60.9	(32.3%)
Smog formation	Million kilograms NMVOC/yr	527.1	240.0	287.1	(54.5%)
Fine particles	Million kilograms/yr	78.6	20.0	58.6	(74.6%)
Dispersion to water	Billion AETP-equivalents/yr	196.8	73.5	123.3	(62.7%)

CFC 11: chlorofluorocarbon 11
NMVOC: volatile organic compounds excluding methane
AETP: aquatic ecological toxicity potentials
kg AETP-equivalents: kg 1,4-dichlorobenzene

These standards are used as inputs to a dedicated applied general equilibrium model (AGE) of the country's economy. We have chosen to use a static model; this means that the dynamics of production and consumption, caused by changes in capital stocks and so on, are neglected. Again, this assumption is acceptable by virtue of the intended comparison between the actual development path and the permanent sustainable development path. The model calculates the sustainable equilibrium of the maximum national income in the year involved. This maximum is the - practically approximated - sustainable national income.

In this general equilibrium model, it is necessary to make additional assumptions *e.g.* regarding time scale, regarding reactions to price changes due to internalisation of costs to eliminate environmental burdens and regarding what will happen to international trade when all the countries in the world simultaneously take sustainability measures (which is one of the – logical – basic assumptions of the SNI estimate). This too introduces uncertainty margins in the results. Of course, these margins do mean that there are different possible results, but principally that different SNI's do not exist.

The SNI in combination with standard NI indicates the distance to sustainability as it develops in time, or in other words, as an indicator of how far we live beyond our means, or how fast we proceed in correcting it. This distance can decrease by an increase of SNI because of technological progress and by changes in production and consumption patterns.

Numerical results

Table 1 presents the macro-economic results for SNI variant 2 in comparison with the reference net national income (NNI) situation, for 1990. SNI2 assumes that world market prices change proportionally as domestic prices when world-wide sustainability constraints are implemented. SNI1 assumes the world market prices do not change; this variant, which is in 1990 42,5 % lower than NNI, is not presented in the table. SNI2 is 56% below NNI in the base situation. In Table 1 income is partitioned by sectors. The row entry 'Other VA' in corresponds to the capital and abatement sector, and to taxes and emission permits paid for directly by consumers. SNI has to be corrected for double counting, which describes the part of value added spent on reduction of dehydration and on soil clean up.

Table 1. **Macro-economic results (billion euros)**

Variant 2 : Fixed Trade Patterns	NNI, 1990	SNI2, 1990	
National Income	**213.0**	**94.2**	**(-56%)**
Agricultural Production	7.6	16.0	(111%)
Industrial Production	61.8	46.7	(-24%)
Services Production	128.9	27.2	(-79%)
Other VA	14.8	14.9	(1%)
Double counting	0.0	-10.7	

At first sight perhaps remarkably, we find the sharpest decrease in value added in the services sector, which is the sector with the lowest burden on the environment. The industrial sector with its much greater burden on the environment decreases far less. The agricultural sector with its intensive use of natural resources even shows an increase in value added. This can be explained as follows.[3] The labour productivity in the latter sectors decreases substantially because environmentally benign production methods require more labour per unit of output. This leads to an increase in real prices and consequently to an increase in value added per unit of output. However, the increase in prices causes a relatively small decrease in the total output of the sectors because of the low price elasticity of the demand (change in demand resulting from change in price), especially for food. In the services sector real prices increase far less, because the production of services such as culture, education and the administration of justice cause much less of a burden on the environment. However, the price elasticity of the demand for these products is much higher than for products such as food and shelter. This causes a decrease in the value added of the services sector, mainly caused by a move of labour from this to the other sectors.

This course of affairs is exactly what could be expected according to the theory on which the SNI is based (e.g. Hueting and De Boer 2001). This theory is in line with standard economic theory and with the conventions of the System of National Accounts (SNA). According to this theory both income distribution and employment level will remain unaltered when the costs of decreasing environmental burdens are – gradually – internalised in the products (remember that the infeasible leap to sustainability in the

---

3 .   Another explanation is possible as well; see Gerlagh *et al.* (2002) and Hofkes *et al.* (2002).

model will in reality take quite some adaptation time, otherwise substantial frictions will occur). The assumption of unaltered income distribution and constant employment level (see above) seems to be logical and realistic. Because of the price rise of the environment burdening products the income ratio (the ratio of the values added) between (1) the workers in the sectors producing these products and (2) the workers in the services sector can remain unaltered. Because of this and because of the difference in the price elasticity of the demand, workers in the services sector can move to the other sectors, so that the overall employment level can remain constant.

The just described mechanism will not occur in SNI1, because in SNI1 in the rest of the world relative prices of environmentally burdening and not burdening products remain unaltered, so that the Netherlands can import environmentally burdening products cheaply from abroad. This also explains why SNI1 is higher than SNI2. However, another process occurs in SNI1, affecting domestic prices of imported and exported goods and causing effects analogous to the effects occurring via the mechanism just described in SNI2, be it to a limited extent (Figure 3).

Figure 3. **Break up of income in value added, from NNI to SNI1.**

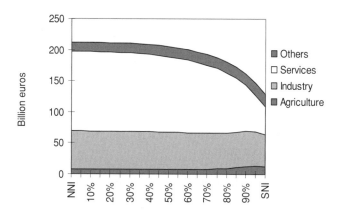

A trend decomposition for 1990 - 1995

The SNI-indicator has been calculated for the Netherlands for 1990 and 1995. For each year, the calculated value of SNI is sensitive to various assumptions, so that for a set of possible assumptions, we find a range of SNI values, as opposed to a unique point calculation. Yet, since assumptions typically affect the calculated SNI value in about the same way for different years, the trend between the two periods will be less sensitive to the assumptions, as the following figure portrays.

Figure 4. **Trends for NNI, SNI1, and SNI2 (different assumptions on trade).**

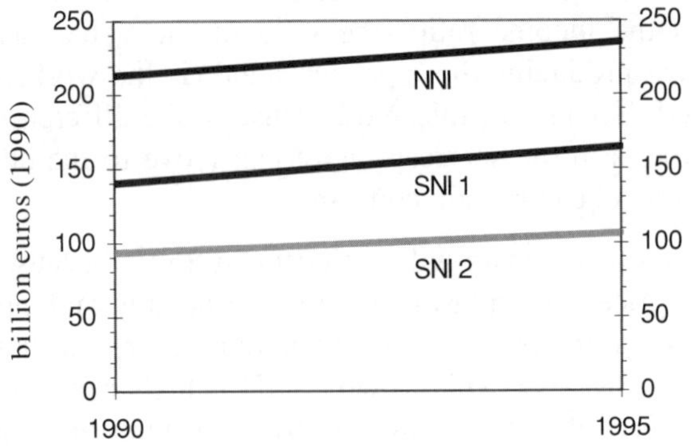

We explain this picture by decomposing the changes in the SNI into a scale effect, a composition effect, an emission effect, and a technology effect (Table 3). Whereas NNI increased by 10.4% over the period 1990-1995, SNI (variant 2) increased by 13.9%. The table shows that the increase in sustainable income is mainly due to (i) the composition effect, that is the change in the structure of the Dutch economy, with a slightly decreasing share for industries and an increasing share for services, and (ii) an emission effect, that is a decrease in the emission intensity of all sectors, on average. An extensive trend analysis is given in Hofkes *et al.* (2002). It falls beyond the scope of this presentation.

Also, we notice that we cannot claim that the economy has become more sustainable, though SNI grew faster than NI, since the gap between NI and SNI increased, in absolute terms, from 135 to 146 billion euros. To become more robust, we would need to extend the trend analysis to, at least, a ten-year period.

Table 3. **Decomposition of changes in NNI and SNI2 (billion euros, 1995 prices).**

	NNI		SNI2	
1990	242.8		107.4	
Scale effect	268.4	(+10.5%)	110.1	(+2.5%)
Composition effect	268.4		113.1	(+2.7%)
Emission effect	268.4		122.8	(+8.6%)
Technology effect	268.4		122.2	(–0.5%)
1995 relative to 1990	268.4	(+10.5%)	122.2	(+13.9%)

Note: The 1995 values are corrected for inflation between 1990 and 1995 of 14%.

Concluding comments

The main emphasis of the research was on the construction of an applied general equilibrium (AGE) model to calculate a sustainable national income indicator for the Netherlands. We have been successful in the sense that we have shown that an AGE model can be extended with a list of environmental themes, and that abatement costs can be included explicitly in the model to account for the costs associated with emission reduction measures.

Our calculations indicate that climate change, caused by emissions of greenhouse gases, is currently the most pressing environmental issue, in terms of costs involved to meet the sustainability standards. Whether the gap between net national income and the

SNI level will increase or decrease over time largely depends on the greenhouse gas policies that will be implemented in the coming years.

There are still many improvements and refinements to be made to our modelling analysis. Without being exhaustive, we recall some features that deserve special attention. First, the coverage of relevant environmental functions (themes) can be extended. For the Netherlands, land use and waste disposal beg for inclusion. Moreover, there is need for a discussion about what level of resource use can be called sustainable. We also note that the list of environmental themes included is biased to 'sink' functions of the environment, as opposed to the environmental 'source' functions associated with forests, mineral deposits, topsoil, fish stocks, and water resources. Our focus is typical for current Dutch environmental concerns. If the calculations would be repeated for other countries, one should consider including other natural resources. For many poorer countries, the sustainable use of the environmental 'source' functions is of more immediate importance then the sustainable use of the 'sink' functions.

Second, the modelling of international trade can be worked out further. Third, the information on technical options of abatement and their costs needs to be kept up to date. Fourth, in the present model, emissions are linked to outputs. Part of the emissions can better be linked to certain types of inputs, for instance, CO_2 emissions to fuel inputs. Modelling emissions through links with (fuel) inputs will allow a better reflection of substitution possibilities. Fifth, the model might benefit from a differentiation of the abatement cost curves between sectors and a differentiation of the expenditure effects of technical abatement. In short, changing and modifying assumptions that underlie the SNI calculations means that a whole gamut of sensitivity analyses can be done.

Though sensitive to several assumptions and qualifications, we have a measure of the part of income that depends on an excessive use of resources. For the Netherlands, for 1990, we calculated that about half of its income could be attributed to resource use that exceeds a sustainable level. In the midst of the many theoretic analyses on sustainable income levels, policy makers may find it useful to have a numerical result.

Presenting an SNI does, in our view, not rule out disaggregated indicators on the pressure and the state of the production and consumption system, society and the environment. On the contrary, these indicators add considerable detail and explanation to an aggregated indicator such as SNI, just like the detailed results of an SNI calculation do. In fact, many of those indicators are used in an SNI calculation. However, the discussion on the obtained results points out that the SNI should always be compared to the actual NI. Likewise, disaggregated indicators for the actual environmental pressure and state can in our experience only have meaning as sustainability indicators if they are compared with the relevant sustainability standards, however roughly these are estimated.

References

Gerlagh, R., Dellink R., Hofkes M.W., and Verbruggen H., 2002, "A measure of sustainable national income for the Netherlands", *Ecological Economics* 41:157-174.

Goodland, R., 1995, "The concept of environmental sustainability", Ann. Rev. Ecol. Syst. 26, 1-24.

Hofkes, M.W., R. Gerlagh, W. Lise, and H. Verbruggen, 2002, *Sustainable National Income: a trend analysis for the Netherlands for 1990-1995*, IVM report R-02/02, Institute for Environmental Studies, Amsterdam, the Netherlands.

Hueting, R. 1980, *New Scarcity and economic growth*, North-Holland, Amsterdam (Dutch edition 1974)

Hueting, R. 2003, "Sustainable National Income, a Prerequisite for Sustainability". In: Bob van der Zwaan and Arthur Petersen (ed.*), Sharing the Planet, Population – Consumption – Species, Science and Ethics for a Sustainable and Equitable World.* Pugwash, Eburon Academic Publishers, Delft.

Hueting, R., and B. de Boer, 2001, "Environmental valuation and sustainable national income according to Hueting". In: E. C. van Ierland, J.van der Straaten, and H.R.J. Vollebergh (editors), *Economic Growth and Valuation of the Environment, a Debate*, Edward Elgar, Cheltenham, UK, pp. 17-77.

Perrings, C., 1996, "Ecological resilience in the sustainability of economic development". In: S. Faucheux, D. Pearce and J. Proops, *Models of sustainable development*, Edward Elgar, Cheltenham, UK, pp.231-252.

Pezzey, J., 1994, *Theoretical essays on sustainability and environmental policy*, Ph.D.-thesis, University of Bristol, Bristol.

UN, 1993, Integrated environmental and economic accounting, United Nations, New York.

Verbruggen, H., Dellink R.B., Gerlagh R., Hofkes M.W., and Jansen H.M.A., 2001, "Alternative calculations of a sustainable national income for the Netherlands according to Hueting". In: E. C. van Ierland, J.van der Straaten, and H.R.J. Vollebergh. (editors), *Economic Growth and Valuation of the Environment, a Debate*, Edward Elgar, Cheltenham, UK, pp. 275-312.

WCED, 1987, *Our common future*, World Commission on Environment and Development, Oxford, New York.

Accounting for Sustainable Development: Complementary Monetary and Biophysical Approaches

K. Hamilton, World Bank

J. Loh, WWF International

J. Sayre, Redefining Progress

T. Thouvenot, WWF France[1]

M. Wackernagel, Global Footprint Network

Summary

This Working Paper explains the utility of combining monetary accounts with biophysical accounts to track progress towards sustainability.

Monetary accounts capture information on the assets that contribute to a nation's wealth, on the assumption that safeguarding wealth is indispensable for maintaining economic vitality. Biophysical accounts consider the uses of domestic and global natural capital, on the assumption that maintaining economic vitality depends on basic ecological services such as renewable and non-renewable resources, waste absorption, and stable climate conditions.

Used in tandem, these two measurements provide policymakers with detailed intelligence on economic and ecological viability. Such an approach can also illuminate the relationship between national and global sustainability, and identify policy responses.

Protecting the Wealth of Nations

When the Brundtland Commission offered its famous definition of sustainable development - "to meet the needs of the present without compromising the ability of future generations to meet their own needs"[2]- it presented several challenges to policymakers. Not least among these is the question: how do we measure progress towards sustainable development?

In the wake of the Brundtland Commission's report sustainable development has been interpreted as a three dimensional concept which combines economic, social, and ecological perspectives. The foundation for this concept is a set of assets that underpin

---

1. World Wide Fund for Nature International (WWF), Avenue Mont-Blanc, 1196 Gland, Switzerland, jonathan@langleycourt.co.uk.

2. World Commission on Environment and Development (WCED, chaired by Gro Harlem Brundtland), 1987. *Our Common Future*. Oxford University Press, New York.

and support the development process. These may be divided into the following broad categories:

- *Physical capital:* economic assets such as buildings, machines and infrastructure that are the economist's usual concern.

- *Social capital:* people's skills and abilities as well as the institutions, relationships, and norms that shape the quality and quantity of a society's social interactions.

- *Natural capital:* natural resources, both commercial and non-commercial, and ecological services which provide the requirements for life, including food, water, energy, fibers, waste assimilation, climate stabilization, and other life-support services.

If the per capita value of these assets declines, economists conclude that future social well-being will be less than current well-being[3]- a development path that is not sustainable. Pearce *et al.*[4] call this *weak* sustainability. While this represents the core of sustainability, this requirement is limited in practice by the difficulty of determining the values of these assets. Monetary values can be assigned for assets traded on a market such as timber or cereals. But for other natural assets, determining an accurate price can be elusive. More importantly, even if values can be determined for natural capital assets, they may not signal that certain ecological limits are being breached in an irreversible manner, with serious consequences for human welfare.

Pearce *et al.* offer a way out of this conundrum by introducing the concept of *strong* sustainability. *Strong* sustainability recognizes that there are natural assets (which are frequently global) that do not have substitutes - for example the ozone layer - whose loss would entail serious harm to human beings and nature. *Strong* sustainability therefore requires that some critical amount of the non-substitutable natural capital be preserved, independent of any increases in value of other social or physical assets.

Any meaningful analysis of sustainability would therefore need to pay attention to both concepts of sustainability. This can be accomplished by complementing purely monetary assessments (measuring in dollars or Euros), which are useful for documenting core aspects of weak sustainability, with biophysical ones (measuring in tones, hectares or joules) effective for tracking strong sustainability.[5]

Using monetary and biophysical accounts in tandem

To illustrate the usefulness of combining monetary and biophysical accounts for tracking progress towards sustainable development, this Working Paper draws together two particular approaches which are currently under active development.

3. P. Dasgupta, and K-G Mäler, 2000, Net National Product, Wealth and Social Well-Being, *Environment and Development Economics* Vol. 5 No.1&2, p69-93.

4. David Pearce, Anil Markandya and Edward Barbier, 1989. *Blueprint for a Green Economy*. Earthscan Publications, London.

5. Monetary accounts are capable of dealing with many aspects of strong sustainability, provided there is scientific information to support the construction of marginal damage curves. The practical difficulties in establishing these damage curves however, may be more limiting than the theoretical ones. The theoretical limits refer to situations where the loss of welfare is arbitrarily large for a small change in the state of a resource (i.e. where the marginal damage curve is literally vertical). In such cases, the monetary accounting approach breaks down.

Monetary asset accounts

Monetary asset accounts analyze to what extent the wealth of a nation is increasing or decreasing per citizen,[6] thereby informing about progress on 'weak sustainability.' Table 1 highlights the results of such monetary accounting in per capita terms for selected countries. It details first the components of depletion and degradation of the environment - the value of depletion of minerals and mineral fuels, the value of *net* depletion of forests (i.e. where harvest rates exceed natural growth rates), and the global damage incurred when CO_2 is emitted. The sum of these figures is a crude monetary measure of depletion and degradation. This sum is juxtaposed with figures on net domestic saving - the amount of GDP that is not consumed by households and governments, less the value of depreciation of produced assets.

Comparing net saving to total depletion and damage provides an initial assessment of sustainability. It answers the question of whether countries are depleting their natural assets faster than they are building up produced assets. It provides a less than complete picture, however. Some elements of what the national GDP accounts consider to be consumption, such as education expenditures, are clearly not; some natural assets, such as soils, are not accounted for in the World Bank figures owing to problems of data availability, as well as analytical issues.

A major omission in the comparison of net saving to total depletion and damage is the effect of population growth. This is shown as the final entry in Table 1. To take Zimbabwe as an example, the suggestion from the table is that net wealth actually increased by $4 per capita in 1997. However, this somewhat larger sum of national wealth has to be shared among a Zimbabwean population that has grown by 2.1% over the course of the year, which produces a decline in wealth per capita of $36. The intuitive conclusion to be drawn from this result is that the percentage increase in total wealth was substantially less than the percentage increase in total population.

Table 1: **Monetary asset accounts**: Results from 6 selected countries (measured in 1997 US dollars, 1997 data). The table provides estimates of annual change in value of some main national assets, including the impact of demographic growth on per capita wealth.

Depletion, damage, and saving effort – Selected countries, in 1997$ per capita (1997 data)

	Australia	Chile	Indonesia	Netherlands	Pakistan	Zimbabwe
Mineral and fuel depletion	-411	-335	-61	-26	-9	-24
Net forest depletion	0	0	-6	0	-7	-3
CO2 damages	-94	-22	-7	-57	-4	..
Total depletion and damage	-505	-358	-73	-83	-20	-26
Net domestic saving	2108	678	237	4041	15	30
Effect of population growth	-832	-220	-68	-517	-54	-36

Source: World Bank estimates, derived from World Bank (1999) and Hamilton (2002).

---

6. Kirk Hamilton, 2000. *Genuine Savings as a Sustainability Indicator*, World Bank, Washington. Kirk Hamilton, 2002. *Sustaining per capita welfare with growing population: theory and measurement.* Presented to the 2nd World Congress on Environmental and Resource Economics, Monterey CA, June 24-27, 2002. Kirk Hamilton, 2002. *Sustaining per capita welfare with growing population: theory and measurement.* Presented to the 2nd World Congress on Environmental and Resource Economics, Monterey CA, June 24-27, 2002.

Biophysical accounts of natural capital

Biophysical natural capital accounts measure sustainability by evaluating to what extent humanity's demands on the biosphere, in terms of renewable and non-renewable resource consumption and waste production, exceed nature's capacity to renew itself.[7] They are derived from material accounts[8] and the biological productivity[9] literature and assess, for any given activity, the biologically productive area required to produce the resources and to absorb the waste of that activity, using prevailing technology. [10] Such biophysical accounts, therefore, provide a measure of strong sustainability.

Table 2 provides an outline of the results, providing key data for the same set of nations as in Table 1. The first section of the accounts captures the biological productivity of the nation - the supply of ecological services within its own borders. The second section documents the nation's uses of natural capital in various categories - its demand on ecological services. All results are presented in the same common units: global hectares - standardised hectares with world-average biomass productivity.[11] As Table 2 shows, in some cases nations' demand on nature is smaller than their domestic supply, and in some cases it is larger.

It is worth noting that a distinct advantage of the biophysical approach is that it offers a broader, more global perspective on sustainability. This is important, because many of the environment-related issues of sustainability do not respect national borders. In this context, Table 2 sheds light on some of the biophysical difficulties inherent in measuring sustainable development. According to this analysis, the Earth provides 1.9 hectares of bioproductive space per world inhabitant. In contrast, the average consumption of the world citizen requires 2.3 global hectares, or 1.2 times more. This means that, currently, it takes the biosphere 1.2 years to regenerate what humanity consumes within one year. CO_2 is responsible for almost half of the impact: it would take about 1.0 global hectares per person to either sequester the excess CO_2 or produce the same energy with plant matter. As demand (consumption) exceeds supply (biocapacity), the world's natural capital is being depleted. Examples are deforestation, freshwater scarcity, fisheries decline, or CO_2 accumulation in the atmosphere.

For countries, the accounts can reveal specific vulnerabilities. Take the example of Australia. This country is endowed with 41 hectares of land per inhabitant, of which 33 are biologically productive, and 11.4 hectares of fisheries. This biocapacity corresponds

---

7.   Mathis Wackernagel, Larry Onisto, Patricia Bello, Alejandro Callejas Linares, Ina Susana López Falfán, Jesus Méndez García, Ana Isabel Suárez Guerrero and Ma. Guadalupe Suárez Guerrero, "National Natural Capital Accounting with the Ecological Footprint Concept", *Ecological Economics*. June 1999 Vol.29 No.3, p 375-390.

8.   E. Matthews, et al., 2000. *The Weight of Nations - Material Outflows from Industrial Economies,* World Resources Institute, Washington D.C.

9.   Peter M. Vitousek, Paul R. Ehrlich, Ann H. Ehrlich, and Pamela A. Mateson, 1986. "Human Appropriation of the Products of Photosynthesis." *BioScience.* Vol.34 No.6. p368-373.

10. Parts of this area can be located all over the world. Its size depends not only on the amount of resources used, but also on the efficiency by which the resources are harvested and processed.

11. Each global hectare represents the average regenerative capacity of each of the 11.4 billion biologically productive hectares on the planet. These 11.4 billion bioproductive hectares, including 2.0 billion hectares of coastal areas and upwelling zones, host over 90 percent of the world's bioproductivity. The remaining 39.5 billion hectares that make up the surface of planet Earth - such as Antarctica, the Sahara desert or the deep oceans - provide hardly any biomass production and are host to little life.

to merely 14.6 global hectares per Australian, primarily due to water scarcity. In contrast, Australia's vast transportation infrastructure, large share of

Table 2: Biophysical natural capital accounts: Results from 6 selected countries and the world (with demand on nature measured in 'global hectares', 1999 data). The upper part of the table provides estimates of the biological capacity available in the country by adjusting the land and sea area of a country for its biomass productivity. Hence the biocapacity can be expressed in the common units of 'global hectares.' The lower part of the table documents the use of biocapacity in various subcategories.

	Australia	Chile	Indonesia	Pakistan	Nether-lands	Zimbabwe	World
Population (in millions)	19	15	209	152	16	12	5,978
Supply							
Physical land area (ha/cap)	41.1	5.0	0.9	0.5	0.2	3.4	2.2
Multiply by % of land bioproductive (%)	80%	42%	85%	44%	85%	100%	70%
Add physical area of bioproductive sea (ha/cap)	11.4	1.5	0.9	0.0	0.5	0.0	0.4
= Total bioproductive area (ha/cap)	44.1	3.6	1.7	0.3	0.6	3.4	1.9
Multiply by relative bioproductivity* (-)	0.33	1.17	1.09	1.44	1.24	0.42	1.00
Total biocapacity supply (global ha**/cap)	14.6	4.2	1.8	0.4	0.8	1.4	1.9
Demand (in global hectares** per capita)							
Agriculture	2.3	0.9	0.3	0.3	0.9	0.4	0.6
Forest products	0.6	0.7	0.3	0.1	0.5	0.4	0.3
Fish products	0.3	0.4	0.2	0.0	0.3	0.0	0.1
Built-up area	0.1	0.2	0.1	0.1	0.2	0.0	0.1
CO_2 emissions (and nuclear power)	4.3	0.8	0.3	0.2	2.9	0.5	1.1
Total biocapacity demand *(global ha**/cap)*	7.6	3.1	1.1	0.6	4.8	1.3	2.3

Source: Redefining Progress, based on primary data from UN agencies, as also reported in the *Living Planet Report 2002*[12]
Definitions: * = 'relative bioproductivity' indicates by which factor national ecosystems are more productive per hectare than world average
** = 'global hectares' are hectares with world average biomass productivity
coal energy, and high consumption of animal products boosts its demand on nature to an equivalent of 7.6 global hectares per Australian.

The same accounts applied to Zimbabwe reveals a somewhat different picture. For this country, the accounts show 3.4 hectares of land per Zimbabwean. However, due to water scarcity and poor soils, the biomass productivity of these hectares is low. Hence these 3.4 hectares per person correspond to only 1.4 global hectares per Zimbabwean– these are hectares with global average bioproductivity. This biocapacity is nearly equal to the 1.3 global hectares required for producing the resources and absorbing the waste associated with the consumption of an average Zimbabwean.

A variety of sub-indicators can be drawn from the national biophysical accounts. For example, they can show how much of the biological capacity (in various ecosystems

---

12.   For more details, consult: World-Wide Fund for Nature International (WWF), UNEP World Conservation Monitoring Centre, Redefining Progress, Center for Sustainability Studies, 2002. *Living Planet Report 2002*, WWF, Gland, Switzerland.

categories) is used for producing all the goods and services of a country, or how much biological capacity is supplied from local sources and how much is imported or exported. Or they can track how efficiently nations use their resources in order to determine the contribution of technological improvements to mitigate the impact of human activities.

Monetary and Biophysical Accounting as Complements

One of the key advantages of monetary accounting is the presumption that 'a dollar is a dollar' - that is, one dollar's worth of two different goods can be presumed to yield the same amount of well-being to the consumer. This does not, however, negate the importance of information on physical quantities. Information on physical scarcity (reserves of minerals for example) is often critical in determining economic efficiency. It is this measure of physical scarcity which permits the owner to maximize the value of a mine. Biophysical information on stock sizes and growth rates for living resources, to give another example, similarly sets the basic conditions for optimal harvest of these resources.

Both accounts provide national averages - but could with more research also generate data about sectors and income groups. While nations are never homogeneous, national average figures as provided by the two accounts offer nevertheless important information for national policy making. For instance, many economic policies, such as monetary and fiscal instruments, social policies such as education, or environmental policies such as pollution standards or resource rents are national in scale.

Biophysical and the monetary accounts are also complementary with regard to scale. Monetary accounts are powerful at the micro level from households up to nations, but have limitations at the global level. At the global level, biophysical measures can better capture trans-boundary effects and the health of the planet as a whole. For instance embedded carbon flows can be factored into a country's biophysical profile. In contrast, global monetary aggregates are often bereft of meaning. To take just one example, global average income per capita is roughly $6000, a figure that masks enormous disparities in income.

Biophysical accounts, in contrast, while useful at the global level, may be less helpful to policy makers at the household level. At the global scale they can address critically important questions. For example, by what amount does global emission of CO_2 exceed the ability of terrestrial and aquatic systems to absorb it? Or, what are the productivity trends of the world's natural capital assets? For most households, however, the income figures of the monetary asset approach will be perceived to be more relevant than numbers on local biomass productivity.

Limitations of the Current Accounts

Both frameworks share one significant limitation: the amount of internationally comparable data available at the national level that is reliable and relevant to the accounts. Some data sets are improving, such as land-use and bioproductivity data collected by UN organisations such as the Food and Agriculture Organization. Other areas remain poorly documented. For instance, owing to data limitations the monetary environmental accounts published by the World Bank do not include important resources such as soils, subsoil water, and fisheries, and most local pollutants. Work is underway to improve this situation.

As mentioned, monetary accounts face the further challenge of how to include assets that cannot be reliably priced, and how to reflect critical thresholds of assets where the marginal damage curves may be close to vertical, meaning that substitutes for the asset are of such prohibitive cost as to be nil for all practical purposes. The ozone layer is such an asset.

Biophysical accounts are faced with another set of difficulties. For example, biologically productive land and water accounts are biased towards living resources. Non-renewable inorganic resources (such as ores) are only included in the accounts in so far as their use compromises biocapacity.

Since the biophysical accounts analyzed here avoid exaggerating human impact, human demands on nature that are not sufficiently well documented are excluded. The resulting estimates of excess demand over supply are therefore, conservative. In addition, secondary functions provided by areas already included in the accounts, such as freshwater collection, pollination, or waste absorption of biological waste are not added to the accounts a second time. Hence, the presented biophysical accounts will be insensitive to a reduction in freshwater use or water pollution.

Furthermore, since biologically productive land and water accounts focus on the regenerative biological capacity, they exclude emissions which nature cannot break down. This makes the accounts insensitive to contamination through heavy metals, radioactive materials and persistent organic compounds, or to irreversible losses of assets such as biodiversity. These aspects need to be tracked separately.

Nevertheless, by exploiting more of the existing data sets, both accounts can become more robust and comprehensive.[13]

It is also worth recording that one important area which continues to require further work is the international science which underpins many of the data sets. After all, unlike most economic data, environmental variables are not linear. Thus, scientific study is critically important to advance data sets on sustainability. While the level of scientific knowledge on issues like climate change is very high, establishing thresholds of irreversibility for a whole range of other global environmental issues remains a pressing priority. It is clear, that such scientific research would help guide and support the further development and improvement of monetary and biophysical accounting.

Policy Implications

When used in tandem, the two accounts provide policymakers with a wealth of information. Taken together can provide the *tools for policymakers* by addressing specific

---

13.   Even with presently available data, both accounts have the potential to be fine-tuned and expanded. For example, the monetary asset accounts can include more existing data from valuation research, and could become more comprehensive if more valuation of core natural and social assets become available. Taking advantage of more comprehensive data sets that have recently become available, the biophysical natural capital accounts can become more sensitive to agriculture, fisheries and forestry. They could also improve with further research that would:

- Strengthen the data sets on built-up areas, embodied energy and resources in traded products (particularly as production chains globalize), and embodied energy and resources in services such as tourism;

- Reduce uncertainties about the global carbon cycle and ecosystems productivities,

- Collect more quantitative data on the link between freshwater withdrawal and impact on biocapacity as well as the bioproductivity damage of stratospheric ozone depletion, persistent pollutants, and climate change.

concerns relevant to sustainability: how a nation's wealth is changing over time, and what amount of biological capacity it is using. In particular, this tool can assist in identifying the cost of depleting natural capital assets; the cost of demographic growth; the intensity of use of local ecosystems which links directly to pressure on biodiversity; and the distribution of resource use among nations.

In the case of a non-OECD country such as Pakistan, the monetary measurement reveals that the country depletes minerals and energy at 9 dollars a year per Pakistani, and forest harvest exceeds natural growth by a similar amount. CO_2 damages per capita are in the range of other low-income countries. As a result, total depletion and damage more than offset net saving effort. But even without adjusting net savings for natural capital depletion, the per capita loss of wealth due to population growth far exceeds the savings rate. At the same time, a biophysical measurement documents that out of the 0.5 hectares land area per Pakistani, only 0.2 are biologically productive. Due to their intensive use and productive soils, these areas correspond to the biocapacity of 0.4 global hectares. Despite modest consumption levels, the average Pakistani's demand for ecological services of 0.6 global hectares still exceeds the nation's capacity, depending on imports of ecological services and depletion of natural capital stocks. (See Table 3 for similar summary of other countries).

Table 3: **Interpreting selected countries with both accounts.**

	Accounting for Nations' Change in Wealth (measured with the monetary accounts)	Accounting for Nations' Use of Ecological Capacity (measured with the biophysical natural capital accounts)
Australia	Australia is a major producer of minerals and mineral fuels, reflected in resource depletion of $411 per capita per year. Dispersed population and dependence on coal lead to high CO_2 damages per person. Domestic saving rates per person of over $2100 are relatively low for its income level, while wealth loss owing to population growth is higher than for most other high-income countries.	Australia is endowed with 41 hectares of land per inhabitant, of which 33 are biologically productive, and 11.4 hectares of fisheries. This biocapacity corresponds to merely 14.6 global hectares per Australian, primarily due to water scarcity. In contrast, Australia's vast transportation infrastructure, large share of coal energy, and high consumption of animal products boosts its demand on nature to an equivalent of 7.6 global hectares per Australian.
Chile	Chile is a leading producer of copper, resulting in an annual $335 depletion per capita. CO_2 damages are typical for their income level. Domestic saving effort is strong, more than compensating for the per capita wealth loss owing to population growth.	Chile controls 5.0 hectares of land and about 1.5 hectares of productive sea area per citizen. These areas have a biocapacity of 4.2 global hectares per Chilean. This is 1.1 global hectares greater than the 3.1 global hectares needed to regenerate what the average Chilean consumes. Within Chile, resource consumption is unequally distributed: the wealthiest 20 per cent consume resources at the level of average U.S. citizen.
Indonesia	Indonesia, a major oil exporter, depletes $61 of mineral and energy resources a year for each of its 200 million inhabitants. Forest use exceeds natural growth at a rate of $6 a year per Indonesian. CO_2 damages are at a similar level. The savings effort is strong, more than offsetting the per capita wealth loss owing to population growth.	The 0.7 hectares of bioproductive land per Indonesian have the capacity of 1.6 global hectares due to the country's high humidity and fertile soils. Fisheries contribute nearly 0.3 additional global hectares. In contrast, all the resource uses combined correspond to 1.1 global hectares per Indonesian, or slightly more than half of its maximum capacity.
Pakistan	Pakistan depletes minerals and energy at $9 a year per citizen. Forest harvest exceeds natural growth by a similar amount. CO_2 damages per capita are in the range of other low-income countries. Total depletion and damage more than offset net saving effort, but are overshadowed by the loss of per capita wealth owing to population growth.	Out of the 0.5 hectares land area per Pakistani, only 0.2 are biologically productive. Due to their intensive use and productive soils, these areas correspond to the biocapacity of 0.4 global hectares. Despite modest consumption levels, the average Pakistani's demand of 0.6 global hectares still exceeds the nation's capacity, making it dependent on imports of ecological services and depletion of natural capital stocks.
Netherlands	The Netherlands depletes its energy resources at moderate per capita levels, while its CO_2 damages per person are notably lower than those of Australia (partly owing to higher population density). Savings effort is strong, far exceeding the reduction of per capita wealth due to population growth.	Fertile soil, humid climate, and intensive land use boost the actual 0.2 hectares per Dutch person to an equivalent of 0.6 global hectares. Productive fisheries bring this total to 0.8 global hectares. Still, the Dutch demand exceeds this biocapacity six fold. The gap between biocapacity and demand is bridged with imports.
Zimbabwe	Zimbabwe has moderate levels of mineral depletion at $24 per person, and forest harvest (mostly for fuel wood) exceeds natural growth. Total depletion roughly offsets the saving effort, leaving the country substantially poorer in per capita terms once the effect of population growth is included.	Due to water scarcity and poor soils, the 3.5 hectares of land per Zimbabwean is only worth 1.4 global hectares. This about the same as the 1.3 global hectares necessary to maintain the resource flow of the average Zimbabwean.
World	Rough calculations[14] suggest that there is a slight net increase of total wealth per person across the globe. However, this global average masks the fact that estimated declines in wealth per capita are sizable in roughly 30 countries.	The Earth offers 1.9 (global) hectares of bioproductive space per world citizen. In contrast, the average world citizen demands 2.3 global hectares. The difference indicates liquidation of the world's natural capital (such as forest depletion, fisheries decline, or CO_2 accumulation in the atmosphere).

These accounts also offer *a common platform for comparing significant sustainability issues* by tracking them in each accounting system with a common measurement unit. For example in the case of Pakistan, the accounts identify major sustainability concerns: forest overuse, population growth, as well as overall biocapacity constraints in the face of already low levels of resource consumption for average Pakistanis. Using a common framework allows analysts to address issues in concert rather than in isolation, and helps to identify possible synergies and trade-offs.

---

14. For details, see Kirk Hamilton, 2002. *Sustaining per capita welfare with growing population: theory and measurement.* Presented to the 2nd World Congress on Environmental and Resource Economics, Monterey CA, June 24-27, 2002.

In addition to providing a country analysis and highlighting critical issues, the two accounts also assist in *identifying policy priorities*. With limited budgets, be they financial or biological, difficult trade-offs are inevitable. Comprehensive frameworks such as the approach presented in this paper help explore the implications of such choices and assist policy makers to prioritize competing needs.

Furthermore, such a complementary approach also supports the *development of policy responses*. The accounts offer platforms for designing policy packages that produce multiple benefits and address the needs of a variety of sectors and the responsibilities of several agencies. They can, for instance assist in the development of environmental policy prescriptions such as improving the pricing of resources and pollutants by capturing, *inter alia*, royalties on mineral and energy extraction, and by enforcing property rights. Such policies improve the efficiency of environmental services[15] since they reduce incentives to overexploit resources or to pollute indiscriminately.

The natural capital accounts support policy interventions that aim at reducing human use of nature to a level that can be sustained by nature. Since overall use is determined by four factors–population levels, people's consumption patterns, the eco-efficiency with which consumption items are produced, and the robustness of natural capital stocks to withstand degradation - each becomes an area for policy intervention. The tools are the same. For example, policies aimed at reducing carbon intensity include carbon taxation, fuel taxation, trading of carbon emissions and sequestration, and subsidies to technologies that are less carbon-intensive. These policies can complement efforts to improve the monetary accounts of a country, for example where reducing carbon emissions also reduces local air pollution and its associated costs.

In summary, used in tandem, these two measures help track a country's progress toward sustainable development, highlight critical issues and identify policy responses. As a consequence, they not only illuminate the relationship between national and global sustainability, but also help improve policymaking for sustainable development.

Notes

Environment Department, The World Bank, 1818 H St. NW, Washington DC 20433, U.S.A., khamilton@worldbank.org

The Global Footprint Network is advancing the science of sustainability. It increases the effectiveness and reach of the Ecological Footprint by strengthening the Footprint community, standardising the tool, and building wide support for bringing human demands in line with Earth's limited resources. More on the science behind the Ecological Footprint with examples of how it has been used to advance sustainability can be found on the website www.FootprintNetwork.org.

Mathis Wackernagel: Global Footprint Network, 1050 Warfield Ave, Oakland, CA 94610-1612 USA; Tel: +1-510-839-8879; Fax: +1-510-834-9202; Mathis@FootprintNetwork.org; www.FootprintNetwork.org

Redefining Progress, 1904 Franklin Street 6th floor, Oakland CA 94610, U.S.A.

WWF is the world's largest and most experienced independent conservation organisation. It has 4.7 million regular supporters and a global network active in 96 countries. www.panda.org

15.   Efficient pollution policies aim at investing in pollution abatement up to the point where the marginal cost of abatement begins to exceed the marginal cost of pollution damage.

A Few Remarks on Methodological Aspects Related to Sustainable Development

I. Pierantoni

ISTAT, Italy

Introduction[1]

Over the last few years, environmental and economic literature has focused on a) how and at which rate natural renewable and non-renewable resources should be exploited, b) depletion in environmental quality caused by pressures generated by anthropic activities (pollution, waste and undesired residuals), c) sustainable development as a long run concept, which implies combining lasting development with conditions in social and environmental dimensions in line with intergenerational equity. SD is a complex and multi-domain issue, which has to combine efficiency, equity and intergenerational equity on economic, social and environmental ground.

SD definitions can be borrowed from current literature and/or political documents. Available concepts and related theories regarding SD can help understand the main elements in SD definitions, thereby ensuring that the main questions regarding these definitions and other theories can be outlined in order to select the indicators and frameworks required in SD strategy.

Main Elements Categorising the Definition of Sustainable Development

The term "sustainability" can be both elusive and have different meanings depending on the specific reference literature or the context in which it is used.

In the past, studies on sustainable development mainly focussed on the conditions ensuring optimal consumption - that could be maintained in the long run and did not deplete generated capital - according to technical progress and the growth rate of the population (the optimal rate of consumption was equal to growth rate of population plus growth rate of technical progress).

In relation to the issue of sustainability in economic development, we must combine the standard solution to problems regarding scarcity for living generations with the solution to problems regarding intergenerational equity, which is a dynamic optimisation problem. If present generations deplete the stock of capital, then future generations will have less growth than present generations.

---

1. I would like to thank Mr. E. Giovannini, who provided useful comments on an earlier draft of the paper, and Mrs R. Montgomery for her interesting comments during an e-mail exchange. I want to quote here the experiences carried out in 2001, inside the Friends of the Chair Advisory Group on development indicators of the United Nations Statistical Commission, Expert Group on Environment and Energy, with Maila Puolama, Hilary Hillier and other experts of other countries.

There is a mainstream in environmental economics literature in which SD has been analysed as part of this conceptual theoretical framework, subsequently ensuring that definitions for capital and environmental functions are crucial.

When sustainability is associated with development (economic development), it can be interpreted as the conditions under which durable economic development are consistent with environmental conditions that will not deplete the options of future generations (see Chapter 3a below). This definition implies that environmental changes have a specific relationship with an economic process (production or consumption) and that the change will produce effects in the long run given technical progress and the population growth rate.

In order to measure this definition of SD we need indicators and to look for relations among these dimensions. Both the economy and the environment affect the sustainability of development; they are "constraints" on durable development and the existence of links is consequently a condition to the suitability of the SD indicator.

There are also other interpretations of sustainability. Sustainability can be defined in relation to only one dominion (environmental or social), therefore involving the sustainability of some natural processes or sustainability related to social phenomena. This interpretation focuses on an impact analysis and does not necessarily identify a long run analysis, although there are cases in which long run analyses have been undertaken. In this case, links between the phenomena in question and long run economic growth are not necessary.

In relation to certain issues, sustainability involves studying the conditions under which an ecosystem may or may not remain resilient, which implies a choice in terms of time and space. In other cases, sustainability may mean a generic ability of society to cope with a problem, even if the problem does not relate to long run effects or solely relates to living generations.

A number of aspects in mono-dimensional definitions may be useful in relation to SD. How can the concept of mono-dimensional sustainability (i.e. resilience of an ecosystem) be encompassed within a multidimensional SD definition? Can this always be considered as a constraint within the dynamic optimisation problem? Is the critical natural capital the right concept through which to identify the natural environment, which performs important and irreplaceable functions?

There is some confusion between the three-dimensional framework and the mono-dimensional framework of SD. In these two cases, sustainability may have different meanings and therefore involve short run and long run policies, indicators related to short run effects and others regarding long run effects. This causes some confusion when selecting the indicators to measure progress in niche and SD policies.

The need to identify links between indicators is only strong when we adopt the multidimensional framework for SD, *i.e.* sustainable economic development in line with environment conditions that do not deplete natural resources for future generations. In the second and more general interpretation, sustainability relates to specific problems within a specific dimension and therefore links with economic development may be very weak.

Another approach towards SD focuses on the intrinsic values in natural resources - which are providing utilities for people and may therefore be utility function arguments - and on the environment as input for production processes (see Chapter 3b below). A dominant decision-maker, with this approach, has to select which potential different environmental stocks or environmental functions to encompass within the welfare function.

Using a welfare function may imply predominance of present generations over future generations, given that the current status quo is the starting point and that results may be influenced by the preferences of now alive generations (and their standard of life). Consequently, there are problems relating to constraints on resources and to intergenerational equity and how to select the weights to attribute to the utilities of different generations (present and future). This implies solving a problem with social choice, in other words how to select an objective function to be maximised in inter-temporal planning.

Approaches based on cardinal utilities (see Chapter 3d) are related to individualistic categorisations and provide definitions of needs and individual valuations.

The approach related to Sen's theory of development like freedom and of need like individual "capabilities" (see Chapter 3c), underlines more wide interpretation of social capital and human capital.

At the international level, the most well-known general definition is that provided in the Bruntland Report (World Commission on Environment and Development, 1987). The essential element in this definition is the ability of present generations to meet their own needs without compromising the ability of future generations to meet their own needs. "Ability" may have different meanings. It may relate to the "availability" of options (i.e. production and consumption, different social and environmental functions) for both individuals and society in general.

Whatever contents are chosen and before selecting possible needs, the concept of ability recalls different concepts of capital; therefore, according to this more general definition, we have to adopt larger definitions of capital than those more frequently included in production functions. The following different types of capital should be considered: a) economic capital, b) human capital – knowledge, know-how, health, security, c) environmental capital – natural renewable and non-renewable resources, ecological functions, d) social capital - culture, institutions, the efficiency and quality of institutions, co-operative behaviours, trusts, and social norms.

Finally, which more appropriate variables for representing the "living conditions" of individuals could be used to reply to the question, "What elements are needed to maintain stability in current society and all future societies?" Could the reply create a link between all different approaches to analysis? Which could be a definition of stability and, then, is stability always a positive value? This once again implies solving a problem regarding social choice.

The four stocks of capital (social, human, environmental and economic) are always crucial variables within all these definitions of SD. As these capitals may be partially complementary and policies may relate to more than one type of capital, links between the four stocks must be found via the various dimensions (social, economic and environmental) and which of these links are more important must be identified; the relative importance or priority must obviously be assessed according to specific criteria.

Dealing with these problems and assessing them within the various approaches could provide us some tools for solving the complex task of deciding from which indicators and which framework we have to choose, as well as when we need a system of indicators estimated using basic statistics and when we need indicators based on accounting frameworks when looking for more effective solutions.

A round-up of existing literature on Sustainable Development

The previous chapter provided a synthesis of the principle elements categorising definition of SD according to more relevant literary approaches to SD, which will be now described. The introduction of exhaustible natural resources in development theory has imposed some limits, which may be compensated by technological innovation, substitutability with manufactured capital and returns to scale. These limits may be analysed within different theoretical approaches by which exhaustibility problems have been analysed.

Growth models and exhaustible natural resources

Using a Cobb-Douglas production function with natural resources, Stiglitz (1974a) concluded that, given some assumptions, optimal development paths are possible even with exhaustible natural resources; the choice among alternative optimal paths is related to paths which have different growth rates, whereby paths with high rates of resource utilisation have low growth rates in the long run. He subsequently dealt with the topic of whether optimality can be obtained on a perfect market without having future markets, in other words whether markets can cope with social costs (Stiglitz 1974b).

Twenty-five years ago, Solow (1974) dealt with the problem of intergenerational distribution of optimal accumulation of capital. Introducing exhaustible natural resources using a Cobb-Douglas production function does not change the results, assuming that the substitution elasticity of natural resources and capital goods is at least unitary. It is therefore feasible to indefinitely maintain a constant per-capita consumption rate, given the exhaustible natural resources. The present generation may use the finite stock of resources but must increase the renewable capital stock in order to retain the overall (natural plus man made) capital stock. A sustainable path can be maintained if this is done optimally. The direct substitutability between production factors through the technical substitute of natural resources ensures that the level of production and, subsequently, the level of consumption may be maintained.

Solow (1986) looked for a rule to solve the problem regarding how consumption of natural resources should be allocated over time to ensure intergenerational equity. In a very simplified model, the solution is to reinvest the rent from resources in real capital, thereby imposing aggregate capital stock to be constant at different periods in time. This will guarantee a flow of constant consumption[2]. The Hotelling rule[3] - a rule for inter-temporal efficiency - and the Hartwick rule[4] - a specific investment policy - will ensure that a constant stream of consumption will be maintained from some date onwards. The flow of man-made capital will offset the efficient decline in employing exhaustible natural resources. Results involving a growing labour force and technological progress

---

2.   He assumes a very simple society that produces current output under constant return to scale using labour (supply of labour is constant), the services of a stock of capital and withdrawals from a given stock of non renewable resources (there is no technological progress).

3.   The Hotelling Rule means that the shadow value of a unit of non extracted natural resource should increase at the same rate as the current marginal product of man-made capital at any given time.

4.   The Hartwick Rule means that society must invest the competitive rents from current use of exhaustible resources in man-made capital goods at any given time (see Hartwick 1977).

are more complicated; technological progress must grow at a faster rate than the population, otherwise present generations will be entitled to consume more.

These initial models are based on production functions where there are exhaustible natural resources in addition to labour and man made capital. The substitutability between renewable and non-renewable resources is a crucial aspect of this problem. More recently Solow (1997) wrote that resource scarcity and limits to future development deriving from such scarcity depend on the substitutability of resources in production processes, which depends on the necessity of natural resource in production function, the cost of replacing non-renewable natural resources with capital or renewable natural resources and technical progress, which may allow replacement of natural resources with man-made capital. The role of this substitution in reducing pollution, dematerialising products or disseminating recycled goods in production functions is essential.

Intrinsic values of natural resources and intergenerational equity

In the contribution from Beltratti-Chichilnisky-Heal (1994), natural renewable resources have an intrinsic value and not just instrumental relevance. When the stock is relevant - *i.e.* climate, diversity of species etc. -, natural resources are welfare function and aggregate production function arguments, whereby they are considered as stocks and not flows as occurred in previous models. This ensures that these stocks have a value both when they are protected and when utilised within production processes.

Alternative growth paths are assessed in this model via an objective function, whereby utilities have two components. The first component derives from a discounted integral of utility functions over time of consumption and environmental resource from zero to infinite time, whereas the second is the lower limit in an infinite sequence of utility values for the long run, whereby T is approximate to infinite (the long run behaviour of utility values). These two components are weighted by complementary weights; one of which has the utilitarian discounted criteria when the weight on long run behaviour is zero, while-values between 0 and 1 ensure that the ability to generate welfare is also considered in the very long.

This problem is solved by maximising a utility function constrained by capital accumulation, resource renewability, initial conditions and non-negativity conditions in capital stock, environmental stock and consumption.

The discounted utilitarian solution (in the extreme case when the weight on very long run utilities is zero) in this model shows that consumption of goods must be proportional to regenerative ability of environment in a stationary state. This rule allows the higher level of consumption to be retained indefinitely, thereby ensuring future generations access to essential natural resources through its proportionality to the regenerative capacity of the environment.

When society only worries about very long run consumption and environment values, the solution - called "sustainable preference" - derives from the marginal transformation rate and marginal substitution rate tangent point between consumption and environment through stationary states (tangency point between the indifference curve and regeneration function of the environmental resource). Authors call this configuration the "Green Golden Rule", as it captures the highest indefinitely-maintainable utility level. Solutions to intermediate cases (positive values for both weights) require much more complex mathematics.

The associated axioms underlying the approach are an interesting aspect in this kind of welfare function, *i.e.* where a positive weight is assigned to the limiting properties of a growth path. One of these is non-dictatorship - neither present nor future generations must assume a role of dictatorship[5].

The welfare function in this approach includes the intrinsic value of environment and the production function the instrumental value of environment. From the point of view of a dominant decision-maker, it is essential that the relevant component in the possible values is defined. The following possible values apply:

- direct use value (utility deriving from immediate and direct consumption),

- indirect use value (utility deriving from retaining ecological functions, which give benefits)

- option values (utility derived from the possibility of consumption in the future, when some conditions will be achieved),

- existence values (utility derived from the simple existence of a species, also without any possible use of them),

- bequeath (or inheritance) value (utility derived from living values to future generations).

- This approach involves coping with the problem of assessment and valuation of non-market goods.

Development like freedom and need like capabilities

Sen's theory is pertinent here, as he opens human and social capital, and therefore economics, to contributions from different sciences. Sen categorises individual preference definitions through the concept of capabilities and functionings. These innovations have influenced U.N. works and the list of sustainable indicators for the development of developing countries. Although Sen's thoughts can be more directly applied to developing countries - where there is less freedom and less freedom of choice - developed societies require more thorough analysis in terms of policies in order to identify an operative definition of freedom (and of rights) and to measure this.

The relevant factors are substantial freedom and an individual's capabilities to personally decide what has value (see Sen, 2000a). This implies that not only possessing goods is relevant, but also the personal characteristics that allow them to use goods for their own purposes. Sen distinguishes between "functionings" - which comprise everything that an individual may wish to be or do and which he/she attributes a value (being fed, being healthy, being respected, etc.) - and "capabilities" - which are a number of alternative combinations of "functionings" that an individual is capable of doing. Capabilities are the substantial freedom to combine functioning and reflect real freedom to choose and real outcomes.

A validation of this thought implies that freedom has more operational contents from the viewpoint of politics, which allow us to measure capabilities and their relationship

---

5.   Non-dictatorship from present generation means that "it should not be possible to determine the ranking of any two utility streams by looking only at finite numbers of their components. Non dictatorship of the future means that the ranking of two utility streams should not depend only on their limiting properties, but should be sensitive to their characteristics over finite horizons", Beltratti et al (1994), pages 149-150.

with functioning[6]. A person may have free access to a right, but not wish to have access to it; but without access one has to demonstrate that there is access but no desire to do so. A lack of desire must however be explained, as it could depend on few opportunities (education, quality of family relations, etc.).

Basically, capabilities are directly related to the well-being and freedom of individuals and have an indirect role in influencing social change and economic development or production, where they overlap the more well-established (or consolidated) concept of human capital. The indirect relation derives from the individual dimension of capabilities and the collective dimension of social change and economic development. The theory regarding and valuation of human and social capital may be widened through capabilities and statistics on capabilities, as these are not simple concepts to define and difficult to measure. Phenomena to value the consistency of social and human capital may be described through capabilities; these insights could help ensure more stable societies today. A more stable society today could be a necessary condition to ensure sustainable economic development in the long run.

Cardinal utilities and the theory of happiness

The aim of some EU member state experiences with sustainable development is to retain happiness in present and future generations. This evokes more recent theories - some of which were also developed in relation to statistics - with roots in a theory prior to welfare (Bentham utilitarianism). According to standard theory, the values found by individuals on the market relating to goods and services (price and quantity) provide all the information required in terms of utility, thereby ensuring they can assess the effects of various policies via the relative social well-being functions on offer. According to theories of happiness, the opinions of individuals regarding their own satisfaction gives a wider measure of individual utilities and the more valuable aspects of their living conditions.

In this context it is possible to quote Van Praag contributions (see 1968, 1971, 1994) and the happiness theory (see Ng 1977, 2000, and for a more recent survey on this issue see Frey B. S., Tutzer L. 2000).

In Van Praag approach, subjective judgements on levels of satisfaction may be measured through surveys, where individuals are asked to value the utility received from a budget in terms of goods from a cardinal viewpoint. Each reply associates a pair of goods (i.e. income and air quality) with a quality level of utility. Under certain assumptions[7] and once a specific utility function has been selected, the utility quantity (one per score) and the marginal substitution rate between income and air quality can be estimated. The marginal substitution rate between income and air is estimated by calculating the relationship between the marginal air quality utility and the marginal income utility, thereby leaving the initial overall utility unchanged.

---

6.   A discussion on normative foundations of Sen's theory and on his theory for public policy are in Balestrino A., Carter I. (eds) (1996), and more recently in Review of Political Economy, (2002), 14, 4, *"Symposium on Amartya Sen's Capability Approach"* (see Pressman S. - Summerfield G., and Gasper).

7.   In Van Praag approach the assumption is related to the capacity of individuals to minimise the inaccuracies of answers, in such a way that differentials of preferences between levels of satisfaction are the same. Individuals have to assign to scores of satisfactions the two amounts of goods which together are corresponding to a qualitative judgement mapped on a standardised utility scale. (i.e. amount of revenue per month and a qualitative noise level)

Another way to estimate the intensity of subjective preferences is by running multiple cross-section regressions by matching different survey results, in other words those relating to the satisfaction of people with regards to certain social and economic aspects relevant to lifestyle and well-being.

While ordinalism is appropriate to theory regarding consumer demand, it is not appropriate in certain issues such as social choice theory, the optimal population, valuation of life, choice regarding risks, etc. Ng writes that satisfaction in preferences and desires are less important than happiness, as they contribute towards happiness; "...happiness/unhappiness is good/bad in itself and no other thing is so in itself" (Ng 2000, page 54-55) and "the use of happiness gives us the appropriate criterion to judge the desirability of changes or policies in the presence of preference changes" (Ng 2000, page 56). Interpersonal comparisons of utilities are not value judgments but "subjective judgments of fact and that economists are more capable in making those judgments of fact closely related to their field of study" (Ng 2000, page 82).

The happiness theory provides good insights into economic policy at the micro level when the weak Pareto-improving condition fails to understand trade-offs between different conditions (to hold a job or to be unemployed) and to value the effect on individual well-being of the quality of governance or of components in social capital on an aggregate level (for a survey see Frey B. S., Tutzer L., 2002).

It therefore follows that empirical research and statistical surveys providing the opportunity to estimate implicit or contingent prices may be very useful in increasing the meaning and informative contents in these approaches. Some empirical research has been conducted (see Van Praag 1971, Dagenais 1977, Nese 1993, Pierantoni 1994 e 1996, Welsch 2002, Bjornskov 2003).

The Van Praag approach may be considered as a contingent valuation. It involves a survey based on questionnaires. The person responding to the questions is asked to associate a level of quality for resources with a level of monthly income, which together provide an opinion regarding quality that can be represented on a standard utility scale. Opinions regarding quality are classed "terrible, bad, very unsatisfactory, a little satisfactory, satisfactory, very satisfactory, more than satisfactory, very good, excellent". There is very little difference between one level and another to ensure that individuals are forced to limit imprecision when replying, thereby ensuring that the differentials between different levels are the same. For a survey of the main problems related to a contingent valuation method, see Mitchell R. C., Carson R. T. (1989).

The happiness theory was applied using different survey results within regression models. Welsch, (2002) makes an empirical application of the Ng approach; he uses aggregate measures on environmental quality in estimates with cross-section data coming from survey on subjective well-being. Matching this data with per-capita revenue and other explicative variables, he estimates the marginal substitution rate (MSR) as a partial derivative of happiness on the pollution agent and of happiness on revenue. The marginal substitution rate from pollution on revenue is the quantity of additional revenue that has to be given to a representative individual for an additional quantity of pollution. The slope for the indifference curve regarding for revenue and pollution is thereby calculated, given a level of revenue and a level (in quantity or in quality) of natural resource; the estimated MSR obviously derives from specification of the utility function. This approach may not provide an appropriate or econometrically significant specification for the model or hypothesis.

Another less common application of the happiness theory regards the effect of income distribution on happiness. The results of a study comparing European and USA valuations are of interest. Inequality has a negative and statistically important effect on happiness in Europe but not in the USA; therefore people are more sensitive to inequality in Europe than in USA, where the perception of higher social mobility may explain the lower level of dissatisfaction in inequality[8].

Are these approaches useful to the issue of SD? They are most certainly useful for analysing well-being, as they provide tools that can be used to understand the intensity of preferences and assess present generations, embedding cognitive processes and the individual attitudes to risks; surveys are the main tool for eliciting preferences, values and happiness and this kind of survey should ensure initial integration between social and economic determinants in observed behaviours and intensity of preferences at the micro-level. In relation to future generations, these approaches can provide indirect tools to solve the problem of sustainable development. Surveys could be used to discover opinions regarding SD and different policy options, however this could also be encompassed in welfare analyses of current generations and thereby satisfy the need for knowledge in a decision-maker concerned with the utilities (and possible reactions or voting behaviour) of his/her electors.

Can this approach be related to an analysis of SD? If a dominant decision-maker decides to respect and promote or maintain happiness of current and future generations, then this aim could be related to an SD issue. This is obviously a problem regarding social choice. Retaining the happiness of present and future generations may be interpreted as aiming to maintain a given relationship between the happiness of current and future generations. This implies that a decision-maker moves along the same social indifference curve on a map of indifference curves, through which a combination of private and public consumer goods is designed. This relationship does not imply the same mix of goods, but a mix of goods that takes future generations onto the same social curve, in other words the set of points giving the same level of utility. The facts that needs are endogenous means that certain needs that may be judged as necessary for all present and future generations should be selected.

Marginal substitution rates (MSR) estimated through these approaches are considered "subjective" values, as they are based on individual choices related to implicit markets; they can help identify demand prices as opposed to objective prices, whereby the latter are determined through balanced supply and demand without externalities.

Panel surveys on different aspects regarding private and public goods and services - which are possible sources of "happiness" - should be used to test the possible task of SD in terms of maintaining the happiness of different generations. These methodologies are experimental; they have not been tested through official surveys with comparable samples and sample surveys may help understand the relationship between results deriving from different types of experimental methodologies. These values (compensative surplus or willingness to pay) are embedding subjective aspects behind demand - which may not be fully explored in surveys or available time series and consequently be biased; finally these are individual values, which should be aggregated in order to give social values.

In conclusion, these approaches must be used according to their potential informative added value. They produce measures that are considered subjective; they are useful for

---

8.   This research by Alberto Alesina, Di Tella and MacCulloch is quoted in Frey B. S., Tutzer L. (2002).

exploring present well-being and sources of happiness. They can thereby provide better knowledge on needs and help social accountants to decide the conceptual framework of social accounts and the important resources and uses to assess.

Finally, these approaches provide estimates that can support SD strategy, but that are less useful as a direct indicator of SD. We have to explore in more detail how and if maintaining happiness across generations can be considered an SD issue, while avoiding overlapping with welfare analysis.

Another point to highlight is that these approaches (together with other approaches described in Freeman 1976 and Braden Kolstad, 1991 and not discussed here as they do not involve SD issues) provide money measures useful inside development models - when environment is an argument in utility and production functions - and ensure that the social costs of specific policies within a Cost-Benefit Analysis approach can be estimated. Marginal substitution rates (MSR) estimated via these approaches can be used to estimate the social values of resources or pollution, which are to be retained or preserved for future generations. These values correct market values when there is a market with externalities or provide goods without a market (i.e. public goods) a price.

It is useless to remember that a good assessment of conditions and changes in the environment following pressures from humans and not human activities are required to use these approaches. Improving a system for the assessment of social and environmental goods and services and capitals is essential to improvement in valuation processes.

Ecological economics and criticism to the mainstream

Ecological economics has made a number of criticisms regarding mainstream theories over the last few years, which place the very foundations of these theories in doubt.

Some criticism made in the Seventies above all focused on limits imposed by physical conditions on economic activities[9]. They were mainly related to the principle of conserving the mass balance (Boulding 1966). A cowboy economy involves an open system with non-exhaustible resources and in which waste produced by output may be freely disposed, whereas a "spaceman" economy comprises a closed system in which limited and continuously circulating resources must be used very carefully. It is believed that these uses should be minimised to guarantee conservation of the mass balance.

This criticism could be overcome if scrap and waste were entirely recycled and thereby completely re-used. However, this argument cannot overcome the second law of thermodynamics. Entropy grows continuously in a closed system, until "thermic death" occurs. Entropy grows with growing economic activity. Extensive recycling inevitable implies extensive energy consumption, which will deplete energy stocks from the earth (oil, coal, etc.). Energy stocks used today are lost to future generations, whereas direct sun energy could be put to better use and therefore avoid such losses. These points are supported by Georgescu-Roegen (1971). However, if sun energy flows are expected to weaken and subsequently die when the sun becomes a nova, all energy stocks could finish with the end of the earth - so why maintain goods that are doomed to finish anyway for future generations? The possible answers to this must explore the time dimension of the predicted end of the earth and of the possible life-span of energy stored in the earth (coal, oil, etc.).

---

9.   For a survey see Paladini R. (1991) and   Stern D. J. (1997).

Technical progress can obviously provide extensive support and be used as an antidote to catastrophic predictions. As far as checking dissipative or economising behaviour of the economy are concerned, Material Balances of the Economy are the right tool and the right answer to Georgescu-Roegen points.

Other criticisms focused on limits of substitutability between different inputs in production functions and on limits of utilitarian approaches, and violations of axiomatic postulates of neo-classical utility theory in some empirical applications (see Stern 1997). This led to the creation and development of a number of experimental studies on preferences, attitudes and choices[10].

Limits to substitution in consumption between goods or between gains and losses have indirect implications on sustainability, as more goods provide utility but cannot be substituted at all or under extreme limits. When there are limits on substitution between goods, an indifference curve and a utility function cannot be estimated and this problem affects some of the approaches discussed in the previous chapter (see Ng 1979) Utility is not defined when there are lexicographic preferences and one good is preferred and not substituted by any other goods (normally this is known as a *non-satiety condition*). In this case one point - representing a combination between a private and an environmental good - provides utility and no other point will give the same utility, but more or less utility. This is the case in which no depletion of an environmental good will be accepted in exchange for a higher private good when - given the private good - the environmental good decreases, the utility also decreases, thereby ensuring that an indifference curve and an utility function cannot be estimated. Some studies of contingent valuation highlight these aspects. This condition affects models based on the intrinsic values of environment for the component that is considered not substitutable.

Criticism relating to limits in substitutability in production deny the basic conclusion of previous growth models, which led to the conclusion that constant aggregate capital should be tracked in long run. The objective behind conserving aggregate capital is based on the assumption that there is indifference regarding the composition of capital - in other words economic or natural capital. Some natural resources are exhaustible and, if exploited at a higher than endogenous rate of regeneration - in view of current technology - they will exhaust rapidly and become unavailable for future generations. Losses in exhaustible natural resources are causing irreversible damage to future generations, as they will have fewer options than current generations. The extent of such losses depends on the environmental functions satisfied by resources. Some functions are primary and not modifiable - at least in the short run - whereas others are secondary and still others depend on relevant technology (fuel carbon may be necessary in a certain period and no longer in another).

When preferences are lexicographic or there is no substitutability between production factors, then natural capital or some basic environmental functions are considered necessary and must not be changed. However, this also means that the composition of capital is relevant and that a number of conditions in the ecological or environmental dimension must also be included in a definition of sustainable development. Development is therefore sustainable when it can ensure a future level of consumption that is indefinitely maintained, taking into account the shortness of exhaustible resource stocks

10. See Subjective Expected Utility in Von Neumann J., Morgenstern O. (1974); for analysis of violations of postulates and for other developments see Kahneman D., Tversky A. (1989); Viscusi W. K. (1989); Smith V. K. (1992).

and that it has to retain natural capital stock within some quantity or quality levels, which are defined according to given thresholds.

When it is impossible to assume that there is indifference regarding the composition of aggregate capital (i.e. between economic and natural capital), then strong sustainability is assumed and constraint must be adopted to ensure that exhaustible resources can be retained in long run. In this case, strong sustainability in economic development may be constrained by the carrying capacity (maximum size of a population that a habitat can support for a certain amount of time within long run equilibrium) and resilience (the capacity of natural systems to absorb perturbations without changing structure) of systems.

Strong Sustainability

According to contributions from ecological economics (see Daly 1997, Rao 2000)[11], limits may be set to a greater or lesser extent. The important point here is that strong sustainability may impose total absolute limits (natural capital must be kept constant) or lower limits (natural capital must be maintained within a given threshold) according to carrying capacity or resilience rules.

In biological and ecological processes, the resilience of a system is its capacity to absorb disturbances to a system. Loss of resilience is related to thresholds beyond which a system changes and suffers irreversible losses (i.e. gas emissions with long atmospheric residence, desertification of soil, loss of species through high pollution). Damage irreversibility means that such loss is irreversible. There are many causes for perturbation, which can lead to the development of phenomena with non linear behaviour and, therefore, to irreversible losses. Non-linear development of effects means that not all types of diffusion can be forecast and irreversibility of losses means that losses cannot be repaired.

This uncertainty regarding cause-effect relations explains why limits cannot always be identified.

The concept of carrying capacity is important to SD, as it measures the maximum extent of a population that can be supported by a habitat over a certain period and in a long-term balance context. There are different definitions of carrying capacity that we will not discuss at this point.

Definition of different types of capital and their inter-relations, assessment of capital in physical quantities and definition of goods and services provided via capital in physical quantities are essential with strong sustainability. The knowledge of possible thresholds can help to understand which type and how much capital must not be changed by current generations.

The following functions are relevant in terms of ecological capital:

- the capacity to supply resources that can be used in production processes and consumption activities,

- the capacity to receive waste from production processes and consumption without damaging ecosystems,

---

11.   See also the review "Ecological Economics", March 2003, v. 44, n.2-3, which offers a Special Section to the issue "Identifying Critical Natural Capital", with contributions on frameworks and on experiences.

- the capacity to maintain the health of the ecosystem via services necessary to survival (climate, radiation effects, protection through the troposphere ozone), the capacity to provide goods and services for leisure, free time, actual consumption or options regarding consumption and to maintain human health.

Definition of a threshold implies a micro-level analysis or a spatial analysis. When a threshold can be embedded in models, it can be used as a criteria in selecting indicators (the existence of a threshold is a proxy of relevance) and a criteria in monitoring the time trends for some environmental changes (we monitor overcoming of the threshold). The direction of changes could - but does not always - verify whether or not a system is approaching the overcoming of a threshold.

Previsions and Monitoring: Which Tools for Which Tasks?

Sustainability can be monitored through basic statistics, indicators, indices and indicators deriving from satellite accounts (environmental and social) integrated with economic accounts, although all to different levels of effectiveness. Monitoring is the final stage in a more complex decisional process beginning with other activities.

To begin with, *i.e.* in environmental issues, we require an organised network of scientists and good progress in the knowledge of ecosystem resilience and carrying capacity with regards to non-linear behaviour in the most important environmental phenomena. We require a forecasting model (a number of forecasting models) on economic growth (i.e. growth in GDP and growth in energy demand) to ensure quantification of changes and identification of the possible changes in direction with environmental phenomena. A number of variables are essential to ensuring appropriate previsions, *i.e.* technical coefficients of production and technical factors of emissions for sources and processes.

Technology and economic previsions can be used to assess changes in a number of specific pressures and the feasible target that could be set for these.

Due to the uncertainty of scientific knowledge in certain areas, this track may not be followed for all issues. Currently, this has been done with regards to atmospheric pollutant emissions according to the Kyoto protocol.

In this case it is possible to monitor the yearly aggregate values through indicators on total emissions for pollutants and processes and/or through indicators on emissions related to NACE branches from satellite accounts (NAMEA on air emissions).

A monitoring tool kit may be diversified and flexible according to timeliness and accuracy criteria. Indicators may relate more to time monitoring given a specific target. Building up an environment account calls for more time, however these types of indicator are of a higher quality and provide more detailed information (i.e. emissions related to branches) that can be used in comparisons with other countries. Choosing indicators or environment account indicators implies a trade-off timeliness-accuracy.

Environment accounts and national accounts certainly aim to provide statistics that can be used in forecasting models and the models required to estimate possible targets. In this stage of a decision, it is important that the most accurate statistics possible are available. Detailed relevant statistics are required more than timely up-dating to ensure good operative models.

In view of this timeliness/accuracy trade-off, approaches that provide and implement complementarily between indicators and indicators that are selected within account frameworks should be adopted when selecting SD indicators.

In view of the complexity in environmental and some social phenomena, the real problem is whether or not indicators can substantially highlight such difficulties. Could this doubt also relate to environmental (social) accounting based indicators? If trade-offs between different policies should be estimated -which they certainly should -, then complex models are required to ensure that the results of policies can be assessed and that these can be compared with forecasts.

Weak and strong sustainability: which indicators?

Weak and strong sustainability is a categorisation linked to economic and environment domains, related to limits imposed on natural capital.

Weak sustainability - as generalised using *older development models* - leads to the assumption that indicators showing declining amounts in time-series of exhaustible natural resources can be misleading and must be read alongside indicators of other types of capital. Declining natural resources do not really represent a poorer capital for future generations when economic capital increased, but merely that we leave a different distribution of overall capital and that growth is - and will be - positive. Reduction in a number of specific stocks is not particularly important in relation to the approaches set forth in Chapter 3a. Under the hypothesis of weak sustainability, other types of capital (human or environmental capital) and technological innovation must be assessed, as this may change the composition of capital stocks through quantity-related aspects, although above all through quality-related aspects. Indicators regarding technological innovation that relate to both productive (economic capital and human capital) and environmental aspects (environmental capital) are required.

Micro-level analyses are essential to all these cases, as these illustrate whether or not and where there is substitution in input factors, as well as the main trade-offs between different types of capital.

According to the approach involving the *intrinsic value of resources*, more indicators may be used to monitor SD-related aspects. Indicators relating to capital stocks and indicators relating to demand aspects are thereby required. The environmental functions that are important to individuals or those (or how much of them) that the dominant decision-maker decides to retain for future generations must be identified within this approach. The environment functions relating to ecological capital are relevant in this perspective. More relevant services relate to consumption (recreational goods and services, aesthetics pleasure and free time services for immediate consumption or for optional uses), services required for survival (climate, radiation effects, ozone laying protection), sink functions and provision of production inputs and raw materials.

These services or goods may be assessed using different metrics. Some assessments are really very difficult, as the relative uncertainty is linked to the cause or the intensity of the effects of the real phenomena. Finally, valuation may be rather complex, as non-market goods are not exchanged at real values but at implicit values; under certain conditions, limits on substitutability in consumption do not allow definition of an implicit value.

In relation to these problems, environment accounting cannot avoid the difficulties related to uncertainties, but may divide the assessment phase from the valuation phase. This clear distinction is useful from both a technical and a political viewpoint, as problems - and progress in solving problems related to these phases - may be very different.

According to the approaches involving *cardinal utilities and the happiness theory*, indicators must be linked to individual satisfaction of needs or to the normative needs that will supposedly be maintained indefinitely. This implies that indicators related to the happiness of current generations that are encompassed inside a welfare analysis are required.

Under the assumption of weak sustainability, the list of possible indicators includes assessment of resources (different types of capital, types of services provided by ecological functions) and assessment of outcome or goods and services provided via economic and environmental activities. With more general definition of SD, SD indicators are more similar well-being indicators or structural indicators. Time series of these different indicators may illustrate opposite trends and indicators do not help understand whether or not there is a trade-off between aims.

Strong sustainability implies definition of critical natural capital, which depends on specific ecological problems and resilience thresholds; as far as the social functions of natural capital are concerned, not all of these should be entirely maintained for present and future generations, which is a choice left to the public. A dominant decision-maker will have to select which components of capitals and which functions provided by capitals will be constrained by some given quantitative or qualitative threshold. These choices and decisions may be framed through micro-economic analysis and/or spatial analysis. With strong sustainability, decreasing values for natural resources indicate depletion in capitals for future generations. As there is no reason to believe that all natural capital must be retained for the future, the assessment of different resources must be followed by a valuation process comprising various steps, whereby metrics may be a quantity as numeraire or money values. Basic statistics and indicators may implement accounting frameworks, which are suitable to record these stocks and flows within a conceptual model. In this case too, the opposing trends of indicators may only be interpreted once the trade-off between the objectives of policies is understood[12].

How to link social, economic and ecological concepts when measuring development sustainability

In this chapter, the possible links between social, economic and ecological concepts in sustainable development (SD) are discussed according to elements that categorise the various definitions of SD, which were identified in Chapter 2.

SD may be monitored by using basic statistics, indicators and indicators calculated using an accounting framework (economic, social and ecological).

Indicator systems are usually selected according to specific criteria (OECD: policy relevance and usefulness for the user, analytical soundness, measurability). Users become the public decision-maker responsible for adopting policies focussing on sustainability,

---

12. For a description of capital approach see Statistics Canada (2001). About critical natural capital see: Ekins P., Folke C., De Groot R. (2003); Ekins P., Simon S., and others (2003); Deutsch L., Folke C., Skanberg K. (2003); Chiesura A., De Groot R. (2003); Ekins P. (2003).

which must be monitored. Issues to deal with are so identified according to policy relevance.

The indicators that originate in accounting frameworks must also satisfy these criteria, however these indicators are established in the conceptual model with which the accounting framework was created. The economic theory (macroeconomic), for example, is the reference outline for national economic accounting, whereas the economic facts and economic system structure and operation are subjected to observation. There has recently been considerable development in integrated environmental and economic accounting[13]. By means of a system of satellite accounts, the National Matrix of Environmental Accounting (NAMEA), Material flow accounts and EPEA have been implemented.

The statistics produced with accounting frameworks refer to the short-term - maximum one year - and are *ex post* values. By means of this data, *i.e.* with national economic accounts, analysts (both Keynesians and monetarists) shall use macroeconomic models to study the possible relations of cause and effect among the variables.

Despite the different levels of consolidation, comprehensiveness and flexibility in these accounting frameworks, they did not arise on the incidental boost of political decision-makers; they supply tools for monitoring macro-policies and incorporate both the quality and statistical and thematic consistency that are part of an account system. The links among the variables forming an account constitute the foundations of the account system.

The sets of indicators for SD are usually subdivided in issues/themes and sub-themes, related to policies chosen by politicians, who represent prevailing user needs. This implies selecting the most suitable indicators to represent the sustainability concept adopted by public decision-makers, based on specific criteria. In this case the links among the various selected indicators and phenomena that those indicators represent are implicit in choices made by public decision-makers, in the interaction between the policies and their effects. The list of indicators used as monitoring tool might reveal - *ex post* - some inconsistencies in the adopted policies and reasons for the choices in terms of desirable (or undesirable) variations. In order to test these results, however, it is not as necessary to find descriptive relations between policies and domains, which the policies belong to, so much as to have a picture of the causal relations between the resulting phenomenon and their determining factors.

The Resource-Outcome approach proposed by the OECD constitutes a middle course between indicators derived from basic statistics and indicators derived from accounting frameworks. This approach is based on a set of indicators, whose core lies in the definitions of various types of capital and the outcomes resulting from the policies. This approach is complementary (see OECD 2001) to accounting frameworks related results; its main quality is its speedy manner of supplying statistics that can then be changed by the more accurate statistics deriving from accounting frameworks.

There are numerous interactions between the various domains that depend on the kind of phenomena observed, the time horizon in which the phenomenon is analysed and placed in relationship to each other and the uncertainty of the system of knowledge related to the origins of some phenomena (natural, physical, etc.). What are the most important interactions in SD and what links can best represent them?

---

13.   For Italy see the other paper "Integrated Environmental and Economic Accounting in Italy" in this meeting.

Various contents can be ascribed[14] to the term 'links', such as:

- the descriptive aspects of the phenomena connecting the various domains (social, economic, ecological) in order to better describe them as they occur; accounting frameworks are important to this outcome, since they are created according to conceptual outlines related to the links between the domains, however they are generally made on a yearly basis;

- causal relations between the variables that ascertain a phenomenon; basic statistics, indicators and accounting systems are all useful in supplying statistics to create and develop ways of forecasting and providing statistics for gaining in-depth knowledge of the possible relations among the variables. Whether the phenomenon is mono-domain or multiple-domain, a model is required to accurately interpret the meaning of variations contrary to the various indicators or to estimate trade-offs among the objectives;

- orders of priority among the various indicators that might better portray the SD or might be more or less shared in their essential normative meaning. In the experience of international organisations, various operations in this direction were conducted using indicators and indicators from accounting frameworks.

Good describers of the origins of a phenomenon and how it develops are required to provide in-depth knowledge of this phenomenon. Such knowledge helps manage short-term policies, structural policies and extremely long-term policies. In all three cases, representing a complex and multiple-domain phenomenon, an accounting framework can help a public decision-maker decide, or a statistician choose the most representative indicators and the analyst to choose most appropriate models, thereby ensuring that monitoring activities are more accurate.

When the indicators require orders of priority, these must be made according to a criterion that captures the essence of SD. This means knowing the structure of the phenomenon and its relationship to SD and thereby ensuring that the best possible indicator is chosen. In this case, accounting frameworks are a possible - but not the only - tool; for example, accounting frameworks are unsuitable when the phenomenon involved refers to a very limited territory, whereas accounting frameworks could prove too expensive when the relative phenomenon is not very complex in its nature and in its distribution.

Phenomena for which the relations of causality are to be identified must be modelled. In this case, basic statistics, indicators and accounting frameworks are all useful tools. They supply information to ensure long-term forecasts and to define long-term targets that require monitoring on a yearly basis. Accounts such as Input/Output tables and NAMEA also supply valuable information (technical coefficients of production, technical coefficients of emissions, etc.)

How important is defining the links between the variables in the various concepts in relation to sustainable development? This can be better understood by looking at the most important factors that categorise sustainable development in the various theoretical approaches.

---

14.   Here there is a widening of hints given by Steurer A. (2003), in his last paragraph "Possible steps towards sustainable development statistics".

According to the most restrictive definition, development is sustainable when the growth rate of consumption equals the sum of the development rate of the population plus the development rate of technical progress. Under these conditions, the economic capital grows at the same rate. The time span considered is long-run and includes existing and future generations.

The variables in this case belong to economic and social domains, whereas the links involve economic development, factors of production, labour and economic capital factors, innovations and the existing and estimated populations. These links among the variables are well described in national economic accounts, as they are, and by standard, macro-economic equations. More data about the population and its characteristics could increase the complexity of the model, and could be supplied by using indicators and eventual Social Matrix Accounts.

When durable economic development is associated with the use of economic and ecological capitals, the environment domain is added to the social and economic domains. The condition of substitutability among production factors (economic capital and natural capital) is necessary in order to sustain the production level; in order to have distribution among generations of optimal accumulation of capital, the total capital endowment of a country (economic capital and natural capital) must be preserved for existing and future generations.

Using this definition of sustainability, economic development is also the reference term for defining links among the variables as well as among the various domains. The most relevant variables are the endowment of capital stocks that influence development, rates of economic and natural capital accumulation, quality variations and maintenance activities.

Under this definition of SD, natural resources are considered for their instrumental value in production factors, hence for their capacity to produce income and wealth. This capacity may be limited by qualitative depletion of natural resources, an effect that can be generated on highly polluting production activities, consumption or individual behaviour that causes the release of undesired solid, gaseous or liquid waste in the environment.

Economic accounting provides, depending on their state of implementation, a good description of relations among economic macro-level aggregates. Integrated environmental and economic accounting can describe relations between economic and ecological aggregates. The interaction among social aspects is mostly entrusted to basic statistics and the indicators are calculated using these. The indicators that may be selected using this approach should represent the stocks and variations of capital stocks, and indicators related to activities that most significantly influence the levels of future development or are influenced by development.

Monitoring coherent indicators, using this definition of SD, may involve basic statistics, indicators and indicators deriving from accounting frameworks. When the object of policies is to identify the trend of a phenomenon (e.g. total emission quantity), monitoring can be made by estimating the emissions supplied by the various countries. When there is an international agreement defining an objective for a certain period of time, monitoring involves verifying the variations with respect to that target. When the objectives are more specific to certain economic sectors or specific processes, monitoring carried out by means of indicators based on accounting frameworks has a better quality. In general, one can say that, where the phenomenon observed is complex and is created through interaction between decisions and production, consumer choices observed on markets and individual and social behaviour, it is always necessary to represent it first by means of a conceptual model that exemplifies the relationships, and then choose the indicator that best represents it.

Integrated accounting frameworks should be used in approaches in which the sustainability of development is based on a relationship with aggregate capital stocks. However, this means that the survey activity in basic statistics and resources specifically used for this purpose must be improved. Indicators continue to be the main monitoring tool used to date for some primary resources (land, forests, rivers, etc.)

Relationships that have been identified to date are expanded in the approach to SD, which also takes into consideration the intrinsic value of the environment and intergenerational equity. As in previous cases, significant links are established between economic and quality development and the quality of asset stocks and ecological services supplied to the different generations. The environment as a function of well-being broadens the list of possible SD indicators to choose from, since this is a question of ecology and services supplied by it. The existence of a costraint in the use of natural resources is considered in this approach. To this end one must clearly express which rules could link economic and ecological concepts within a context of sustainable development. According to Daly (1990) and Rennings-Wiggering (1997), these rules can be briefly described as follows:

- the exploitation or collection rate of renewable resources must equal the regeneration rate;

- the emission rate of wastes must equal the carrying capacity of the ecosystem in which waste is disposed;

- non-renewable resources should be exploited in an almost sustainable way, depleting them at the same rate as the implementation of renewable substitutes.

How do these rules help us understand which indicators to choose? Can they influence the setting up of ecological accounts and the ratios that are established among the variables? Or are they useful as guidelines in order to read - *ex post* - the meaning of the indicators collected to monitor the policies?

Indicators should measure the effective trends against the given targets in using natural resources. To this end it is necessary to define the primary resource and its functions, the elements of the damage that are to be considered and the possible reference standards.

Remaining on the subject of weak and strong sustainability, one must understand when there are critical thresholds of ecological functions and critical loads of depositions. It is necessary to understand if and when going beyond these thresholds will cause serious and irreversible damage in the nearer or more distant future. This kind of indicator expresses itself in quantity and according to metrics typical of the observed phenomenon.

This approach relies heavily on official statistics - it actually requires statistical knowledge of all the assets and services (in terms of quantity and prices, where they exist) provided by the environment, *i.e.* those that immediately refer to economic activities and, hence, to development, those with a weak or no reference to development or those merely linked to individual or collective preferences and attitudes. In this case, strong investments in social and economic investigations alongside integration of ecological data are required. Given the current status of know-how, the interaction among different scientifically based knowledge is still low; this does not reinforce arguments of sustainable development that are not strongly dependent on the interaction between economic growth and other domains.

The indicators can help measure partial phenomena that are not yet integrated into a system of conceptual relations with the three main domains in question. More specifically in relation to this meaning, indicators are more useful in representing the intrinsic value of the environment, which is an argument in welfare function. The public decision-maker is responsible for identifying the most significant ecological utilities to be preserved for present and future generations and the indicators may be a suitable tool for measuring them. There is a problem of the unit measure for each of these assets and utilities, however, this being a matter of indicators, there is no problem of how to make these measurements comparable, or at least not until the decision is taken to adopt the indexes.

Accounting frameworks may be more immediately appropriate to represent the instrumental value of the environment according to their degree of implementation, however the valuation problem regarding comparability between the various unit measurements of stocks and capital flows remains.

According to the happiness theory and Sen's theory of capabilities, emphasis is mostly placed on individual utilities and on "needs" and individual capabilities, respectively. This results in a more generic definition of SD and makes it more difficult to distinguish between policies and/or analysis of welfare from the policies and/or analysis of sustainable development. These approaches do not generally consider the long-term period required by the subject of sustainability to growth. The problem of intergenerational equity is not a prominent aspect for the happiness theory. Sen treats the subject of inequality quite clearly (see Sen 2000b); he connects inequality with the heterogeneity of human beings and the many variables, based on which inequality may be defined. According to Sen, the problem of equity is analysed from the point of view of equalisation of capabilities among individuals that may permit the reduction of the differences. Differences in human capital and social capital create inequality in society and can influence development. Since Sen embraces all of the possible links between economic, human, ecological and social capital, from the perspective of an individual, application of his approach in an SD context may cause confusion, while inside welfare politics can be very innovative. More in depth analysis should be devoted to all possible contents of human capital inside well-being, and then it will be more evident how these results can help SD analysis.

Any operation that improves the level of health of the population could be interpreted as "maintenance activity" of the human capital in current society, in as much as this can be traced back to SD. However, could any human activity whose negative externality is the loss of human life be included within actions addressed to pursuing sustainable development? The weakening of links to economic development as well as a long time period, and the vastness of possible definitions of normative need, which make the concept of "ability to satisfy needs" operational, make the choice of indicators more complicated and the process of political decisions to implement plans and programmes for sustainable development more expensive and perhaps less effective. Some social problems can be so important that they have to be coped with immediately and without having a too long time horizon; in this case it is more effective the adoption of welfare politics, to be monitored through structural indicators.

Sen also takes the merit for having indicated the link existing between the development and existence of fundamental rights for individuals, *e.g.* freedom. This assertion is very important in developing countries, whereas the problem in developed countries is identifying the number of rights that are compatible with lasting development. Perhaps this query should be analysed within the potential in-depth examinations of definitions of social capital.

In this case, official statistics could reply by offering statistics rather than accounting frameworks when the rights in question are essential and do not lead to special distributions in terms of social classes, otherwise complex and defined conceptual forms would certainly be necessary to support the indicator.

It is without a doubt that the official statistics and the scientific community should work on better definitions of social capital, of rights, of human capital. Activities should be carried on looking for indicators on social capital and on human capital, not only in their instrumental values, at national and at a local level; links with growth could be verified comparing statistics in areas where growth could be jeopardised.

In a context involving analysis of sustainability, another possible interpretation of these theories may be based on the role of the different types of capital. The distribution of capital (economic, ecological, social, and human) influences well-being and, thus, pre-establishes the fundamental values on which civil societies are based. Policies that preserve the integrity of the various forms of capitals, that allow for a more equal distribution of them and increase the well-being of living generations, reinforce the stability of today's societies. When current societies become more stable, future societies could also be stable. This interpretation concentrates the attention on existing generations and links among the significant variables are identified within market mechanisms and the non-market choices made today. Future generations shall inherit the results of this "stability". Up to what point can the stability of a society be considered a positive value to be preserved indefinitely? This is not a statistical problem, but a definition of social stability could help the work of statisticians.

Since these approaches expand the subject of observation, possible links may be very different. Interactions between domains may be defined through micro-level analysis of behaviour or be based on common relations among macro-level aggregates, when they refer to situations that can be observed on actual markets. A more in-depth exploration is required, where the phenomena refer to intangible goods. The relations with these approaches have their foundations in happiness and individual capabilities; hence, they are based on phenomena that are not very long-term; they may have more complex definitions due to the subjective nature of the phenomenon and possible scanty knowledge of the determining factors of individual choices. Here it is important to remember that accounting frameworks do not measure well-being (even if there is a relationship between GDP and well-being) and satellite accounts were created to record the interactions among macro-level economic aggregates and ecological and social phenomena, whereas Sen's theory and happiness theories cannot be immediately traced to that structure.

Obviously the positive influence of theories that introduce more subtle definitions of types of capital may supply valuable factors towards improving the use of satellite accounts. In this sense official statistics could find an additional urge to define human capital in more detail and try to better define and measure the possible contents of social capital.

According to the definition of SD in the Bruntland Report, the fundamental factors are the need and "ability of different generations to meet their own needs". This is a very generic definition that recalls a multiple-domain definition of SD. With this definition the choice of indicators should be based on criteria, representing the concept "ability to meet their own needs". This certainly refers to the various forms of capital and, consequently, a time reference related to different generations.

The "needs" to which this definition refers are of a normative nature and important to both current and future generations. Since it is improbable that all needs can be preserved indefinitely, the problem lies in choosing which needs are so relevant as to require the maintenance of the ability of various generations to supply themselves with such needs. These needs should undoubtedly have features that make them independent from the cultural and historical reference period, thus there should be a few basic needs, essential towards the human and ecological survival of the planet.

With this interpretation of SD, many interactions may be pinpointed:

- in economic development, given the instrumental value of the various types of capital;

- in well-being, given the direct, intrinsic value of these types of capital and the functions they fulfil;

- in investment activities, with which environmental, social, human and economic capitals are preserved and improved in terms of both quantity and quality. Such capitals will have positive and/or negative effects on economic growth and on well-being of current and future generations.

Inside this definition, the entitlements (health care system, pensions and social security system) are originating the question if future generations (born and not yet born) will be able to pay these actual entitlements for unhealthy people or for retired people. As far as needs are concerned, causes of death and relevant diseases can have impacts only on now born generations, or they could imply some negative effects lasting in the future (i.e. when death is strongly related to some age brackets or when there is a specific spatial dimension of the phenomenon). As far as education and levels of education are concerned, indicators could be chosen thinking to relations with economic growth and to relations with social aspects. I.e. actual growth could originate an early school dropping out in full employment areas and this phenomenon could cause negative effects on future growth (a low quality of labour market). A low social development, *i.e.* in disadvantaged social groups, could cause a negative attitude to studies, which will give less opportunity to future earnings and, in some areas, to future growth.

In this case, the demand for official statistics can be quite diversified. Where the attention is concentrated on type of capitals, accounting frameworks or indicator systems that imply complex conceptual models are required. Where types of needs are concerned, the tool to use depends on the complexity of the need, on its distribution over space and time. An accounting framework could be not necessary for measuring, *i.e.,* the life expectancy of a population.

On the other hand, it is always necessary to make a distinction between statistics necessary to forecasting models and statistics necessary inside monitoring activities. Much information is required to measure the compatibility of a pension system with economic growth and the growth rate of the population. This information includes the life expectancy of the female and male population, the growth rate of GDP, the growth rate of the average wage, the growth of the population, the rate of the active population and the yield of production factors. In order to measure whether a health system is compatible with economic growth and the growth rates of the population and does not create problems for financing future generations, accounting frameworks supply better quality data for forecasting models[15]. If monitoring is to concern large aggregates, the use of indicators derived from statistics on expenses is sufficient. If the monitoring is to concern specific aspects of health policies, the accounting frameworks can give more accurate, better quality data. This consideration is valid for all the types of policies that one can think of within an SD context.

Final conclusions

The sustainability of development is a rather complex issue. It implies a decision-making process, where the decision maker is giving his own targets and is choosing his own interpretation of sustainability he wants to reach. So SD cannot be based on objective bases. It is strongly linked to political decisions. What can be led inside more defined track is the process of decision-making. This implies to have a good tool kit for all the process: forecasting models, monitoring process and models useful to verify results of politics and trade-offs between given aims.

In almost all theoretical approaches discussed the choice of the shape of utility functions and of production functions is a judgment value. It is a "strong" hypothesis also to have the present or current situation (of a developed country) like reference point, while framing the inter-temporal dynamic optimisation.

The relevant interpretations of SD, in the more recent literature, see

- growth models and the optimal development path with exhaustible natural resources, with their emphasis on economic capital and on natural capital,

- a model encompassing the intrinsic values and the instrumental value of natural resources and intergenerational equity, with an emphasis on economic capital, on environmental capital and on different services provided by natural stocks,

- Sen's theory of development like freedom and of need like individual "*capabilities*", with an emphasis on social capital and on a more wide interpretation of human capital,

- approaches based on cardinal utilities and on the theory of happiness, which provide definitions of needs and individual valuations,

- ecological economics and criticism to the mainstream, which are focussed on limits imposed by physical conditions on economic activities and on some very foundations of economic theory (limits on substitutability between different inputs in production functions and limits to substitution in consumption)

- strong sustainability, which imposes total absolute limits or lower thresholds on natural capital stock according to carrying capacity or resilience rules.

The integrated analysis (economic, social and environment and their interplays) of SD involves a by step process. Sustainability can be monitored through basic statistics, indicators, indices and indicators deriving from satellite accounts (environmental and social) integrated with economic accounts, although to different levels of effectiveness.

---

15. There is a general approach called "generational accounting" which can be used to analyse several long term problems of fiscal policy, in order to verify their compatibility with the expected demographic evolution, and has been also applied to immigration policy; see Coda Moscarola F. (2003).

Monitoring is the final stage in a more complex decisional process beginning with other activities.

Linkages between the different domains of SD can be descriptive relations of the variables, or causal relations between the variables that ascertain a phenomenon, or orders of priority among the various indicators that might better portray the SD. Indicators and indicators derived from accounting frameworks are based on descriptive relations; but they can be used in order to look for causal relations between the variables, inside models.

The existence of links can help to understand which is the best tool of monitoring and which should be the investments of official statistics.

Indicators are more useful for timely information, for more general information, where linkages between different dimensions are more limited and obviously when accounting frameworks are not available. Indicators derived from accounting frameworks are the best tool of monitoring when decision-makers need a specific knowledge of trends (i.e. emissions related to a NACE branch, specific aspects of health), when SD tasks are more strongly related to capital endowments and growth. When SD is defined through different types of needs, the tool to use depends on the complexity of the needs and its distribution.

The "Driving force, Pressure, State, Impact, Response" is a conceptual model, representing a chain of descriptive environmental relations; it has been useful in selecting indicators of SD inside environmental dominion and in defining an overlapping area with social and economic dominions. It is less useful in order to represent other social or economic phenomena.

Efficiency, equity and intergenerational equity can be monitored by indicators and accounting frameworks if all is "going better". If some indicators show improvements and other show worsening it is necessary to measure the trade-off between aims; in this case indicators and accounting frameworks provide information necessary to dynamic modeling.

Our scientific and statistical apparatus are far from adequate to perform all necessary elaboration, but official statistics made and are making progress.

References

Balestrino A., Carter I. (eds) (1996), Functionings *and Capabilities: Normative and Policy Issues*, a special issue of "Notizie di Politeia", 43/44.

Beltratti A., Chichilnisky G., Heal G. (1994) Sustainable Growth and the Green Golden Rule, in Goldin I., Winters L. A. (eds) *The Economics of Sustainable Development*, Cambridge University Press.

Bjornskov C. (2003) The Happy Few: Cross-Country Evidence on social Capital and Life Satisfaction, KYKLOS, vol. 56, fasc. 1, 3, 16.

Boulding K. E. (1966), The Economics of the Coming Spaceship Earth, in H. Jarrett (ed) Environmental Quality in a Growing Economy, Baltimora, Johns Hopkins Press.

Braden J. B., Kolstad C. D. (eds) (1991) *Measuring the Demand for Environmental Quality*, Amsterdam, Elsevier Science Publishers B. V.

Chiesura A., De Groot R. (2003) Critical natural capital: a socio cultural perspective, Ecological Economics, 44, 2-3, pag. 219-232.

Coda Moscarola F. (2003) Immigration Flows and the Sustainability of the Italian Welfare State, Politica Economica, XIX, 1, 63-90.

Dagenais D. L. (1977) Evaluating Public Goods from Individual Welfare Functions, European Economic Review, 9, 123-149.

Daly H. E. (1990) Towards some operational principles of sustainable development, Ecological Economics, 2, 1-6. Daly H. E. (1997) Georgescu-Roegen versus Solow/Stiglits, Forum, Ecological Economics, 22, pag. 261-266;

Deutsch L., Folke C., Skanberg K. (2003) The critical natural capital of ecosystem performance as insurance for human well-being, Ecological Economics, 44, 2-3, pag. 205-218. Ekins P. (2003) Identifying critical natural capital: Conclusions about critical natural capital, Ecological Economics, 44, 2-3, pag. 277-292

Ekins P., Folke C., De Groot R. (2003) Identifying critical natural capital, Ecological Economics, 44, 2-3, pag. 159-164.

Ekins P., Simon S., and others (2003) A framework for the practical application of the concepts of critical natural capital and strong sustainability, Ecological Economics, 44, 2-3, pag. 165-186.

Freeman A. M. III (1976) The *Benefits of Environmental Improvement. Theory and Practice*, Resources for the Future, Johns Hopkins University Press, London.

Frey B.S., Tutzer L. (2002) What Can Economists Learn from Happiness Research?, Journal of Economic Literature, v. XL, June, 402-435.

Gasper D. (2002), Is Sen's Capability Approach an Adequate Basis for Considering Human Development?, *"Symposium on Amartya Sen's Capability Approach"*, Review of Political Economy, (2002), 14, 4, pages 435-462.

Georgescu-Roegen N. (1971), The Entropy Law and the Economic Process, Cambridge, Mass, Harvard University Press.

Hartwick J. M. (1977) Intergenerational Equity and the Investing of Rents from Exhaustible Resources, American Economic Review, v. 67, 5, 972-974.

Kahneman D., Tversky A. (1989) Prospect Theory: An Analysis of Decision under Risk, in "Econometrica", 47, 2, pp.263-291.

Mitchell R. C., Carson R. T. (1989) Using Surveys to Value Public Goods: the Contingent Valuation Method, Resources for the Future, Washington, D.C.

Nese A. (1993) La valutazione dei beni ambientali, in Economia Pubblica, 11, 523-531.

Ng, Yew-Kwang (1977) A Case for Happiness, Cardinalism, and Interpersonal Comparability, Economic Journal, 107, 1848-1858.

Ng, Yew-Kwang (1979) *Welfare Economics*, The MacMillan Press Ltd.

Ng, Yew-Kwang (2000) *Efficiency, Equality and Public Policy with a Case for Higher Public spending*, MacMillan Press LTD.

OECD (2001) *Sustainable Development. Critical Issues*, Paris, ISBN 92-64-18695-6.

Paladini R. (1991) Economia ed Ecologia, in Pierantoni I. (ed) *Ambiente e azione pubblica. Metodi e Strumenti di Intervento*, Quaderni per la ricerca, Serie Studi/24, Istituto di Studi sulle Regioni, Consiglio Nazionale delle Ricerche, Roma.

Pierantoni I. (1994) La valutazione delle risorse ambientali il caso dell'aria, report on the convention between ISPE and the Ministry of the Environment

Pierantoni I. (1996) *Domanda di ambiente e valutazione contingente: lo status quo della ricerca ed il caso dell'aria,* in Economia, Società e Istituzioni, LUISS, VIII, n. 3.

Pressman S., Summerfield G., Sen and Capabilities, *"Symposium on Amartya Sen's Capability Approach"*, Review of Political Economy, (2002), 14, 4,pages 429-434

Rao P. K. (2000) *Sustainable Development*, Blackwell Publishers, Oxford.

Rennings K., Wiggering H. (1997) Steps towards indictors of sustainable development: linking economic and ecological concepts, Ecological Economics, 20, pag. 25-36.

Sen A. (2000a) *Lo sviluppo è libertà*, Economia, Oscar Saggi Mondadori.

Sen A. K. (2000b) *La diseguaglianza. Un riesame critico*, Il Mulino, Bologna.

Smith V. K. (1992) Environmental Risk Perception and Valuation: Conventional versus Prospective Reference Theory, in Bromley D. W., Segerson K. (eds) *The Social Response to Environmental Risk*, Boston, Kluwer.

Solow R. M. (1974) Intergenerational Equity and Exhaustible Resources, The Review of Economic Studies, vol. XLI, Symposium on the Economics of Exhaustible Resources, 29-45.

Solow R. M. (1986) On the Intergenerational Allocation of Natural Resources, Scandinavian Journal of Economics 88(1), 141-149.

Solow R. M. (1997) Reply – Georgescu Rogen versus Solow/Stiglitz, Ecological Economics, 22, 267-268.

Statistics Canada (2001) A proposed approach to sustainable development indicators based on capital, paper submitted to Joint ECE/Eurostat Work Session on Methodological Issues of Environment Statistics (Ottawa, Canada, 1-4 October 2001). Stern D. J. (1997) Limits to Substitution and Irreversibility in Production and Consumption: A Neoclassical Interpretation of Ecological Economics, Ecological Economics, 21, 197-215

Steurer A. (2003) "The use of National Accounts in developing SD Indictors", Second Meeting of the ESS Task Force on Methodological Issues for Sustainable Development Indictors, 3-4 February 2003, DOC.SDI/TF/018/04.1(2003).

Stiglitz J. (1974a), Growth with Exhaustible Natural Resources: Efficient and Optimal Growth Paths, The Review of Economic Studies, vol. XLI, Symposium on the Economics of Exhaustible Resources, 123-137.

Stiglitz J. (1974b), Growth with Exhaustible Natural Resources: The Competitive Economy, The Review of Economic Studies, vol. XLI, Symposium on the Economics of Exhaustible Resources, 139-152

Van Praag B.M.S. (1968) *Individual Welfare Functions and Consumer Behaviour*, Amsterdam, North Holland.

Van Praag B.M.S. (1971) The Welfare Function of Income in Belgium: an Empirical Investigation, European Economic Review, 2, 337-369.

Van Praag B.M.S. (1994) Ordinal and Cardinal Utility: an Integration of the two dimensions of the Welfare Concept, in Blundell R.- I. Preston - I. Walker (eds) *The Measurement of Household Welfare*, C.U.P., 86-110

Viscusi W. K. (1989) Prospective Reference Theory: Toward an Explanation of the Paradoxes, in "Journal of Risk and Uncertainty, 2, pp. 235-264.

Von Neumann J., Morgenstern O. (1974) *Theory of Games and Economic Behaviour*, Princeton University Press, Princeton.

Welsch H. (2002) Preferences over Prosperity and Pollution: Environmental Valuation based on Happiness Surveys, *KYKLOS*, vol. 55, fasc. 4, 473-494.

World Commission on Environment and Development (1987), *Our Common Future* (The Bruntland Report), Oxford: Oxford University Press.

Aspects of Sustainability: The Australian Experience

B. Dunlop

Australian Bureau of Statistics

Introduction

This paper discusses the concepts of sustainable development and the main conceptual frameworks that are relevant to measuring sustainability in Australia. It also outlines a number of statistical initiatives across the social, economic and environment fields that are providing insights into aspects of sustainability.

As the national statistical agency, the Australian Bureau of Statistics (ABS) plays a leading role in the national collection and reporting of information about the various dimensions of life in Australia. While a number of other agencies also have important roles in providing information on issues such as sustainability, the main focus of this paper is on ABS work that can inform the sustainability debate and decision-making processes.

Concepts of sustainable development

In 1992 the Council of Australian Governments released *The National Strategy for Ecologically Sustainable Development* (NSESD). The concept of ecologically sustainable development is described in this document as 'development that improves the total quality of life, both now and in the future, in a way that maintains the ecological processes on which life depends'. This broad concept has helped to guide the development of measures of sustainable development in Australia.

The strategy commits all levels of government to a package of core objectives and guiding principles that have social, economic and environmental dimensions. For example, the three core objectives are:

- to enhance individual and community wellbeing and welfare by following a path of economic development that safeguards the welfare of future generations;

- to provide for equity within and between generations; and

- to protect biological diversity and maintain essential ecological processes and life-support systems.

A number of alternative views of sustainable development are outlined in the latest draft (2002) of the United Nations *System of Integrated Environmental and Economic Accounting* (SEEA) which has been used by ABS to guide the development of Australia's environmental accounts. The SEEA considers that the most widely accepted concept is 'development that meets the needs of the present without compromising the ability of future generations to meet their own needs'. But it notes that there is widespread divergence of thought about what 'needs' should be covered and how they should be measured.

ABS has identified six alternative views of how the concept described in SEEA could be operationalised:

- Preservation of national wealth.

- Rising per capita income and rising levels of wellbeing: ensuring that the welfare and quality of life of the population continues to rise.

- Strong sustainability: never using renewable resources in excess of their natural regeneration

- Weak sustainability: replacing any natural resources used with alternative resources of an equal value.

- Resource efficiency: using natural resources prudently and efficiently.

- Target dependent sustainability: not consuming certain resources beyond a critical level and not using sink functions beyond their assimilative capabilities.

The NSESD concept, with its wide focus elaborated through objectives, could be seen as embracing all of these views and more. For example:

- it has a stronger emphasis on the need to protect biological diversity and maintain essential ecological processes and life-support systems; and

- it covers intra-generational equity issues that can be obscured when sustainable development is looked at from a 'whole of population' perspective.

A number of reports aimed at assessing sustainable development or addressing particular sustainability issues have been produced by Australian government agencies. For example:

- *Are We Sustaining Australia: A Report against Headline Sustainability Indicators for Australia*, a periodic report by Environment Australia, which measures performance against the core objectives of NSESD using a range of indicators, first released in 2001.

- *State of the Environment Report*, a five yearly report coordinated by Environment Australia, first issued in 1996 with the second issue in 2001.

- Implementation of Ecologically Sustainable Development by Commonwealth Departments and Agencies, a report by the Productivity Commission in 1999.

- *The Intergenerational Report*, a five yearly report by the Treasurer and first issued in 2002.

ABS has also produced various reports that include measures and analysis relating to aspects of sustainability. For example:

- *Measuring Australia's Progress*, published in 2002 and discussed later in this paper.

- Environmental accounts on a range of topics (Water, Energy and Greenhouse Gases, Minerals, Environment Protection Expenditure), also discussed later in this paper.

- Compendium or thematic publications (e.g. Environment by Numbers, Australia's Environment Issues and Trends, Australian Social Trends, Education Indicators, etc).

Key frameworks and their relevance to measuring sustainability

There are several key conceptual frameworks used by the ABS in producing economic, environment and social statistics. The internationally endorsed *System of National Accounts* (SNA) provides the conceptual base for the Australian national accounts. It also provides detailed international standards that are used in compiling a wide range of other economic statistics. As previously noted, the United Nations *System of Integrated Environmental and Economic Accounting* (SEEA) is being used to guide developments in Australia's environment statistics. For social statistics, the ABS *Measuring Wellbeing* framework describes their scope and conceptual base and sets out an integrated system for their description, development and analysis. ABS has also recently developed a framework of indicators to measure and analyse national progress. These indicators were presented in the ABS publication *Measuring Australia's Progress*.

Each of these frameworks is relevant to measuring sustainability, as explained in the following paragraphs.

The system of national accounts

The System of National Accounts (SNA) is a well-established methodology for producing a coherent, consistent and integrated set of macro-economic accounts that cover all aspects of economic activities. The most recent version of the SNA was issued in 1993 by the Commission of the European Communities, International Monetary Fund, Organisation for Economic Co-operation and Development and World Bank.

The SNA consists of a number of flow accounts -- covering production, income and accumulation -- and a balance sheet account. It is the balance sheet account that is most relevant to the issue of sustainability. The balance sheet shows, at a point in time, the value of an economy's assets and liabilities; the difference between the two equalling net worth. By looking at balance sheets for different points in time, it can be established how an economy's net worth is changing over time. If net worth is increasing (or at least remaining constant), then it could be said that an economy is operating sustainably. This analysis is improved if the balance sheets are prepared in real/volume terms and the ABS produces both sets of data on an annual basis (we are not aware of any other country that does so).

But there are significant limits to the use of balance sheets as an indicator of sustainability. First, only assets that are considered to be "economic" are included on the balance sheet. For an asset to be included on an SNA balance sheet it must be (a) under the control of an institutional unit and (b) capable of delivering economic benefits to the owner. The value assigned to the asset is the (market) value of these economic benefits. While this means that some assets that are "environmental" in nature - such as land, sub-soil assets and forests - are included, other environmental assets such as the air and (for the most part) water are not included. Therefore the harmful effects of economic activity on these assets are not reflected in the balance sheet. Furthermore, for those environmental assets that are included on the balance sheet, only their economic values are recorded. This means, for example, that depletion of sub-soil assets is reflected on the balance sheet, but changes in bio-diversity within forests are not.

Second, balance sheets provide no information about human capital. They do not show, for example, whether there is an increase (or perhaps even a decrease) in the levels of educational attainment within a community. Nor do they show whether people are living longer, or whether they are more or less healthy.

Third, the balance sheets do not show the impacts of economic activity (and other influences) on what might broadly be termed "social capital". This type of capital, which can be difficult to describe, could be influenced by things such as crime rates, the levels of unemployment, income inequality, the extent of volunteerism, and the ability of persons to participate in a full range of socio-economic activities. It is clear that there could be externalities from economic activity that has (potentially both positive and negative) impacts on these dimensions. But it is possible that these dimensions may also be affected by non-economic influences.

Of the flow measures available in the national accounts, both income and saving are relevant to the issue of sustainability. But as for balance sheets, no allowance is made for either positive or negative impacts on environmental, human or social capital in deriving the income or saving measures. Even though the economic aspects of environmental assets are reflected on the balance sheet, the economic depletion of these assets is not reflected in income, and hence saving, measures in the system. Furthermore, certain influences on economic wealth, such as the impact of natural disasters and discoveries, are not reflected in the system's income and saving measures.

Of course, the limitations of the SNA in providing a comprehensive measure of sustainability are well recognised. (Indeed the SNA makes no pretence to providing such a comprehensive measure.) But the core framework can be re-cast or extended to provide more information on sustainability, particularly to the extent that sustainability is affected either directly or indirectly by economic activity. This is normally achieved through the development of satellite accounts.

There are two types of satellite accounts. In the first type, the underlying concepts of the SNA are not changed, but classifications etc are altered to give a greater focus on a particular type of economic activity, such as that associated with tourism, environmental expenditure, or health expenditure. In this type of satellite account, non-economic measures, such as life expectancies in the case of a health satellite account, can be introduced in such a way that the relationships between economic activity and the non-economic measures can be studied. In the second type of satellite account, the SNA concepts are altered, but in such a way that they can be linked back to the "core" concepts. This type of satellite accounting enables, for example, a more comprehensive treatment of environmental assets, or the specific recognition of human capital as an asset, or the treatment of 'unpaid' activities such as household work and voluntary work as production. The main difficulty with constructing the second type of satellite accounts is the problems associated with assigning monetary values to activities that are essentially non-economic in nature.

The system of integrated environmental and economic accounting (SEEA)

The purpose of SEEA is to:

- explore how sets of statistical accounts can be compiled which will permit investigation and analysis of the interaction between the economy and the environment; and

- enlarge the scope of the SNA in order to develop a coherent, comprehensive accounting framework which allows the contribution of the environment to the economy and the impact of the economy on the environment to be measured objectively and consistently.

Only by integrating the economic and environmental dimensions can the implications for environmental sustainability of different patterns of production and consumption be examined or, conversely, can the economic consequences of maintaining given environmental standards be studied.

The SEEA accounting system contains four categories of accounts which cover both flows and stocks, in physical and monetary terms, as well as adjustments to the SNA. Wherever possible SEEA uses the same definitions and classifications as the SNA so that environmental and economic data can be fully integrated and easily analysed and modelled. This is not the case with International Energy Agency and Intergovernmental Panel on Climate Control standards and classifications for compiling energy balances and greenhouse gas accounts (which, for example, do not use standard industrial classifications and whose data can not be readily reconciled and modelled with other economic data).

The latest draft (2002) of SEEA notes that it can serve as at least a partial framework for measuring the most common interpretations of the concept of sustainable development. As noted earlier, ABS has summarised these interpretations into six alternative views. Each view, and the usefulness of SEEA for informing the view, is discussed below.

Preservation of national wealth

The welfare of future generations is to a large extent determined by the capital base of a country, how well capital is used and whether capital is being built up or eroded. The capital base can be considered to comprise the traditional measures of capital covered by the SNA (produced assets, non-produced assets and financial assets and liabilities) as well as other aspects of wealth.

SEEA describes techniques for valuing two aspects of wealth not covered by the SNA. These are:

- quality of the environment from a human perspective (including the aesthetic and health dimensions that are components of the amenity of the environment); and

- biological diversity, essential ecological processes and life-support systems and the service functions that the environment provides (including sink functions).

By providing these additional valuation techniques and by embracing a broader concept of what constitutes assets and wealth, SEEA provides an enhanced basis for considering whether national wealth is being maintained.

Rising per capita income and rising levels of wellbeing

Rising per capita income in real terms is regarded by some as evidence of sustainable development. However, the many other important aspects of wellbeing also need to be measured to provide a comprehensive picture that adequately informs this view of sustainable development.

A common measure of change in material living standards and aspects of economic wellbeing is real net national disposable income per capita, or alternatively GDP per capita. SEEA describes a variety of adjustments that can be made to national income or product measures, some using non-market valuation techniques and modelling, to enhance the usefulness of the measures for sustainability analysis.

One such adjusted measure which is gaining wider acceptance and which uses market valuations is 'depletion adjusted net domestic product' (dpNDP). This accounts for the reduction in national wealth associated with decreases in the stock and value of natural resources (such as sub-soil assets and native forests). Other measures include 'damage adjusted net national income' (daNNI), which treats damage to human health (for example) as a decrease in welfare and something that income should be adjusted for (even though there is no absolute value placed on welfare); and 'environmentally adjusted net domestic product' (eaNDP) which uses a maintenance cost approach to try to estimate what the accounting entries would have been for the same level of economic activity if all the costs associated with maintaining the environment and preventing degradation had been incurred and internalised within market prices.

Strong sustainability (never using renewable resources in excess of their natural regeneration)

The SEEA framework includes natural resource accounts for minerals, energy, water, biological resources (timber, fish, etc), land and soil. These accounts can be used to assess whether there is any depletion and degradation of resources taking place and thus whether economic activity associated with the various natural resources is being undertaken in a sustainable manner. In this context, depletion is viewed purely in quantitative terms (e.g. ensuring that there is no decrease in hectares of forest, tonnes of fish biomass, etc). Degradation can involve assessments of changes in water quality or soil fertility (as examples).

Weak sustainability (replacing any natural resources used with alternative resources of an equal value)

Measures of 'weak' sustainability can be derived from the national balance sheet, produced in Australia by the ABS as part of the standard national accounts. The trends in the different components of the balance sheet and national net worth show whether decreases in one asset class (e.g. the value of timber or sub-soil assets) are being balanced by increases in the value of other asset classes within the SNA boundary (such as produced assets or financial assets). It is interesting to note that, in the Australian context, the quantity (and value) of economically exploitable sub-soil assets has risen over the last decade because of new discoveries and improvements to technology.

Resource efficiency: using natural resources prudently and efficiently

In this view of sustainable development the requirement is that non-renewable resources should be used prudently and efficiently, with care that the same function is available to future generations. Physical flow accounts described in SEEA can be used to assess:

* whether a country is becoming more material and energy intensive or less (and how its production functions and efficiencies change with new technology and compare with international counterparts);

* to what extent renewable resources are being substituted for non-renewable resources; and

- to what extent recycling is taking place.

Some of this analysis may require standardising for population differences and the impacts of differing patterns of international trade.

Target dependent sustainability: Not consuming certain resources beyond a critical level and not using sink functions beyond their assimilative capabilities

The notion here is that countries (or indeed the planet) should have targets beyond which they should not consume certain resources or pollute or degrade the environment. Examples of this are energy self sufficiency targets; greenhouse gas emission targets associated with the Kyoto protocol; air and water quality targets; and targets associated with preservation of biodiversity (such as kangaroo populations, percentages of the area of biodiversity regions set aside for national parks, etc). The SEEA framework of accounts can be used to produce measures to inform judgments about such targets and to monitor performance against the targets.

ABS well-being framework for social statistics

The broad framework ABS uses to develop and organise its social statistics program was published in *Measuring Wellbeing: Frameworks for Australian Social Statistics* (ABS Cat. no. 4160.0) in 2001. This framework describes the scope of social statistics and the linkages both within this field of statistics and with economic statistics. It also describes commonly used definitions, classifications and counting rules and where relevant is consistent with national accounting standards. Its systematic approach supports the identification and analysis of data needs and helps to ensure that a comprehensive and well balanced array of data items are collected across the social statistics program. It also facilitates integration across the social and economic fields, particularly in areas such as economic resources and work.

The concept of wellbeing is central to the framework. This multifaceted concept recognises a range of fundamental human needs and aspirations, each of which can be linked to an area of social concern. These needs and aspirations are the focus of government social policy and service delivery, and are reflected in many of the structures of government. While the framework does not discuss the concept of sustainable development, it does recognise links between wellbeing and sustainability. As noted earlier, these links are explicit in the NSESD approach to defining sustainable development and one of the SEEA views also focuses on wellbeing and how it changes over time.

Key dimensions

A number of key areas of social concern form one dimension of the framework. The areas identified are: Population; Health; Family and community; Education and training; Work; Economic resources; Housing; Crime and justice; and Culture and leisure. Each of these areas has its own more detailed framework, or set of frameworks, and is explored through a series of questions:

- How does this area relate to wellbeing?

- What are the key social issues that need to be informed?

- What groups are at risk of disadvantage?

- What are the social and economic transactions that affect individual wellbeing?

- What detailed frameworks relate to this area?

- What definitions, classifications and units of measurement will result in effective social indicators?

- What data sources relate to this area?

Another dimension of the framework focuses on a variety of population groups which are of special interest to the community and to governments. These groups include, for example, older people, children, youth , families with children, the unemployed, lone parents, people with disabilities, carers, recipients of various government benefits, low income earners, Aboriginal and Torres Strait Islanders, and people whose language background is other than English.

These two basic dimensions of the framework are brought together in the form of a matrix showing areas of social concern by population groups. The scope of social statistics in Australia is broadly defined by reference to this matrix and the relationship of its elements to the various aspects of human wellbeing, both at the level of the individual and for society as a whole. The ABS aims to provide information about the elements of this matrix over time through its work program activities.

Sustainability is one of the themes that flow through many of the social issues identified for each area of concern. For example, sustainability is discussed in relation to population growth and population ageing; city growth; the increasing costs of the health system; the changing nature of work (such as growth in part-time and casual employment); trends in savings patterns and their retirement income implications; and the changing distribution of economic resources between 'richer' and 'poorer' households. Through a focus on measuring and analysing changes over time in the various aspects of wellbeing, the framework can assist in the systematic description and development of indicators relating to sustainable development.

Application of the broad framework

A practical illustration of the analytic application of the framework is the annual ABS publication *Australian Social Trends*. It is structured according to the framework's areas of concern and draws on a wide range of data, sourced from both ABS and other agencies, to present a contemporary picture of Australian society. For each area of concern it provides a set of national and State/Territory indicators which describe how key aspects of wellbeing have been changing over time and how circumstances differ between geographic areas. It also provides comparisons with other countries.

The framework has been central to ABS work in social statistics for many years and has evolved to accommodate changing perspectives and information needs over that time. Its flexibility suggests it will maintain its value well into the future. While very different from the accounting frameworks used in describing the economy and the environment, it has performed an important complementary role as an integrating tool in social statistics.

Detailed frameworks for particular fields of social statistics

Detailed statistical frameworks have been developed, or are under development, for each area of social concern to support analysis of particular social issues. These map the conceptual terrain for that area and provide, along with detailed statistical standards, the foundations on which integrated statistical datasets can be built. Frameworks of this kind have been developed and published for areas such as health, labour market, learning, and household income, expenditure and wealth. Frameworks are also under development in areas such as social capital, crime and justice, and sexual assault.

Measuring Australia's progress

In April 2002 ABS released a new publication, *Measuring Australia's Progress* (MAP), which attempts to answer the question *Is life getting better in Australia?* It uses a suite of indicators to consider some of the key aspects of progress and how they are linked with one another. The publication does not claim to measure every aspect of progress that is important. Nor does it consider all of the many different ways that parts of Australia and groups of Australians are progressing. But it does provide a national summary of many of the most important areas of progress, presented in a way which can be quickly understood.

Progress and sustainability are intimately linked. However, suitable measures of sustainability have not yet been agreed or developed for many of the different aspects of progress. Recognising this, the publication does not enter into any direct discussion of sustainability. For some areas of progress it does report on whether levels of capital are being maintained but the primary focus is on whether various aspects of life - environmental, social and economic - are improving.

Design of the publication involved choosing a presentational model, identifying the dimensions of progress, selecting the indicators that would give statistical expression to those dimensions, and deciding on a more compact subset of headline indicators. With no definitive national or international approach to measuring progress, three possible presentational models were considered: the one-number approach; the integrated accounting framework approach; and the suite of indicators approach. The ABS settled on the indicators approach as its preferred model. In our view this approach strikes an appropriate balance between the simplification of the one-number approach and the complexity of the accounting approach. It also avoids some of the measurement issues associated with the other two approaches.

Progress dimensions

The framework within which the indicators were developed and organised has 3 broad dimensions, covering the economy, society and the environment. Each of these broad dimensions contains a number of finer dimensions. For example, the society dimension has separate dimensions for key areas of social concern - health, education and training, work, economic disadvantage and inequality, housing, crime, and social attachment. It also has separate dimensions for other expressions of or influences on social progress, specifically communication and transport, culture and leisure, and governance, democracy and citizenship.

Decisions on which indicators to present within each dimension were made after reviewing thousands of potential indicators and assessing them against a number of criteria. For some dimensions of progress (e.g. social attachment), it was not possible to compile an indicator that satisfied all of these criteria. In such cases proxy measures were used as interim indicators pending further statistical development work.

A wide ranging consultation process, along with advice from numerous experts, helped the ABS choose the areas of progress and the best indicators to measure each area.

Of the 90 indicators chosen, 15 were selected for the headline set. Deciding on the headline set was easier for the economic dimension of progress than for the social and environmental dimensions. For example, it was not possible to select just a couple of indicators to encapsulate progress across the key areas of social concern, so separate headline indicators were included for each area. As a result, the headline suite shows 2 economic dimensions, 7 social dimensions and 6 environmental dimensions.

Headline dimensions	Headline indicators	Supplementary indicators
Health	Life expectancy at birth	Proportions of people surviving to ages 50 and 70; Infant mortality rate; Burden of disease
Education and training	People aged 25–64 years with a vocational or higher education qualification	Education participation rate for those aged 15–19; Year 7/8 to Year 12 apparent retention rate
Work	Unemployment rate	Extended labour force underutilisation rate; Long-term unemployment rate; Retrenchment rate; Casual employees; People in part-time jobs; People in jobs with longer hours (50 hours a week or more); Average hours per week, full-time workers
Biodiversity	Extinct, endangered and vulnerable birds and mammals	
Land clearance	Annual area of land cleared	
Land degradation	Salinity, assets at risk in areas affected, or with a high potential to develop, salinity	
Inland waters	Water management areas, proportion where use exceeded 70% of sustainable yield	Water diversions: Murray–Darling Basin; River condition (biota) index; Net water use; River environment index
Air quality	Fine particle concentrations, days health standards exceeded, selected capital cities	Highest one hour averages of SO2, selected regional centres; Days when ozone concentrations exceeded guidelines, selected capital cities; Consumption of ozone depleting substances
Greenhouse gases	Net greenhouse gas emissions	Total greenhouse gas emissions (including land clearance); CO2-e emissions, net, per capita and per $ GDP
National wealth	Real national net worth per capita	Real national assets and liabilities per capita; Real net capital stock per capita; Economically demonstrated resources (minerals and energy) per capita; Real net foreign debt
National income	Real net national disposable income per capita	Real Gross Domestic Product per capita ; Proportion of the population in work; Terms of trade
Economic disadvantage and inequality	Real equivalised average weekly disposable income of households in the second and third deciles of the income distribution	Real equivalised average weekly disposable income of groups of higher income households; Children without an employed parent; Real equivalised weekly disposable income of households at selected income percentiles; Ratios of income of households at selected income percentiles; Share of total income received by households in low and high income groups; Gini coefficient; Proportion of households with income below both the half mean and half median income of all households
Housing	*No headline indicator*	Households with housing affordability problems; Households with insufficient or spare bedrooms
Crime	Unlawful entry with intent and assault (victimisation rates)	Homicide rate; Imprisonment rates
Social attachment	No headline indicator	Attendance at live performances; Participation in organised sports; Voluntary work; Marriage and divorce rates; Persons living alone; Waking-time spent alone; Homelessness; Suicide and drug-related death rates (indicators in the *Work* dimension are also relevant)

Commentary that accompanies the indicators discusses trends in progress over the last 10 years or so together with differences within Australia and the factors influencing change. The publication also discusses how some of the dimensions of progress are linked with one another, either through trade-offs or reinforcements. The ABS has been careful to explain that overall progress should not be assessed by simply counting the numbers of areas getting better and subtracting those getting worse. It also acknowledges that some analysts will assign greater importance to some aspects of progress than to others.

It is possible to arrange the set of indicators in different ways to display progress from different analytic perspectives. For example, the publication discusses how the indicators can be grouped into broad categories of wealth. Four categories of wealth are identified: human capital, natural capital, produced and financial capital; and social capital.

Future measurement and reporting of progress

ABS is continuing to develop the framework and suite of progress indicators, in consultation with government, academic, community and other representatives. The outcomes of this work will be reflected in the second edition of the publication in early 2004. Various changes to the publication, including giving more prominence to the area of *governance and citizenship*, elevating the *productivity* dimension to headline status, and combining the dimensions of biodiversity, water and land into one overarching dimension - the *natural landscape* - are being discussed. ABS also intends giving a more detailed articulation of MAP's underlying framework, and including feature articles on aspects of progress, including one comparing Australia with other OECD members.

Environmental accounts

ABS has produced several environmental accounts:

- Energy and Greenhouse Gas Emissions Accounts, Australia 1992-93 to 1997-98

- Water Account for Australia, 1993-94 to 1996-97

- Fish Account, Australia 1997

- Mineral Account, Australia 1996

- Environment Protection Expenditure, Australia 1995-96 to 1996-97

- Environment Expenditure, Local Government, Australia 1999-2000

In addition to these accounts the annual National Balance Sheet which ABS produces includes three natural resources: land, subsoil assets (minerals and fossil fuels) and native standing timber (see ABS Cat. No. 5241.0.40.001).

The second edition of the water account will be published later this year (2003). New editions of the energy, minerals and environment protection expenditure accounts are planned but the earliest any of these could be ready is 2005. Beyond this the ABS aims to produce land use and forest accounts, but these are still embryonic.

The environmental accounts can be used to assess some of the six broad interpretations of sustainability put forward in regard to the SEEA. In this part of the paper we use data from the energy and greenhouse gas emissions accounts to demonstrate how aspects of sustainability can be assessed. For example, in terms of national wealth, the account shows that net present value of energy resources was $76 billion in 1998, with natural gas and black coal accounting for 70% of total value (see Table 1 below). The estimated value of energy assets has doubled since 1992-93, mainly as a result of increases in the net present value of these two products. By this criterion energy resources have been a positive contributor to changes in national wealth, and usage of these resources has therefore been sustainable.

Table 1. **Net Present Value of Energy Assets (millions of dollars)**

Resource	1992	1993	1994	1995	1996	1997	1998
Black coal	3,282	8,164	7,830	12,824	11,706	16,363	25,019
Brown coal	169	288	428	488	541	663	659
Uranium	2,187	1,962	1,631	1,535	1,532	1,642	1,909
Crude oil	13,385	15,646	17,909	18,031	16,644	14,546	12,821
Condensate	2,575	3,196	3,399	4,292	4,553	5,496	5,501
Natural gas	14,770	18,597	20,247	25,476	26,384	28,424	27,904
LPG	1,253	912	1,168	1,682	1,851	2,244	2,090
Total energy assets	**37,621**	**48,765**	**52,612**	**64,328**	**63,211**	**69,378**	**75,903**

Source: ABS Cat. No. 4604.0

The energy accounts can assess strong and weak sustainability. Australia has an abundance of fossil fuel and mineral reserves (see Table 2 below). While strong sustainability is theoretically impossible to achieve given that these resources regenerate over geological timescales (hundreds of millions of years), in practice discoveries and new technology mean that additional economically viable resources become available. Sustainability can be assessed by looking at the stock of energy resources and at what rate they are being used. In 1998, the expected life spans of the demonstrated black and brown coal resources were calculated at over 200 and 700 years respectively.

Table 2. **Demonstrated sub-soil energy assets, 1998**

Resource	Economic Demonstrated Resource(a) (Petajoules)	5 year lagged moving average of resource life (Years)
Black coal	1,379,700	258
Brown coal	398,670	744
Crude oil	8,880	9
Natural gas	53,040	48
Condensate	7,141	33
Liquefied petroleum gas	4,576	45
Uranium	285,290	131

(a) Refers to that part of demonstrated resources for which extraction is expected to be profitable over the life of the mine given current prices and costs.
Source: ABS Cat. no. 4604.0

One example of target dependent sustainability is the promoting of greater use of renewable energy, with the aim of achieving greenhouse gas reductions. The energy account shows that in 1997-98, renewable energy sources provided a little under 6% of Australia's domestic energy requirements. Government initiatives have set a mandatory target for electricity retailers to source an additional two per cent of their electricity from renewable energy sources by 2010. Future accounts will be able to assess progress towards this target.

The relative efficiency of industries with regard to energy use and production of greenhouse gases can be assessed by looking at the energy account data in combination with other economic data, for example energy use per dollar of production or greenhouse gas emissions per dollar of production.

Other approaches and measures related to aspects of sustainability

A number of other developments underway in ABS will also assist research, discussion and decision-making on sustainability issues. These developments include national and sector balance sheets expressed in nominal and real terms; satellite accounts on various topics; measures of human capital; a framework and indicators of social capital; a framework and indicators of a knowledge-based economy and society; and improved measures of the distribution of household income and wealth.

National and sector balance sheets

The national income, expenditure and product accounts, input-output tables and national and sector balance sheets complete the Australian System of National Accounts. The sets of accounts form an integrated system in that income, production and expenditure transactions ultimately lead to changes in the stock of Australia's economic assets and liabilities recorded in the balance sheets. At the same time, economic assets recorded in the balance sheets provide the capital service inputs into current and future production, so they are an important determinant of the level of our current and future incomes and consumption. The balance sheets therefore provide important information on the sustainability of the economic system. If the stock of assets and net worth are increasing over time it would indicate that income levels into the future can at least be maintained.

The ABS has published a comprehensive set of national and sector balance sheets since 1995 (data are available back to 1989). These include the value of produced and non-produced assets and financial assets and liabilities. Estimates of the stock of non-produced (natural resource) assets are described as "experimental" because of the indirect method in which the values for some natural resources (sub-soil assets and forests) are derived. Nevertheless, they are regarded as reasonable indicative estimates of the value and trends in Australia's natural resources over time. The accumulation and revaluation accounts track the determinants of year to year changes in the value of assets and liabilities. Changes in values result from new capital formation less consumption of fixed capital (depreciation), the discovery (or renewals) of natural resources less their depletion, financial transactions, and revaluations of assets and liabilities due to price change.

Real/volume balance sheets at the national level (not by institutional sector) were released for the first time in 2001. They are designed to remove the effect of price changes in order to allow the analyses of changes in the value of Australia's assets, liabilities and net worth over time free of the direct effects of inflation. While volume estimates for the major categories of produced assets have been available for many years in Australia's national accounts, the focus of the new work was on volume estimates for stocks of non-produced, non-financial assets and real estimates of financial assets and liabilities, so as to derive an estimate of 'real' net worth. These estimates are also described as "experimental" because, like incomes, financial assets and liabilities cannot be decomposed into price and volume components so it is impossible to derive conventional volume indexes for them. Instead, they are deflated by a broad based price index in order to measure changes in the purchasing power of financial assets and liabilities over a designated numeraire of goods and services, and are referred to as "real" estimates.

Satellite accounts

The 1993 version of the System of National Accounts (SNA93) provides for a set of "satellite accounts" that develop certain fields of analytical interest as an adjunct to the core national accounts. They may explore certain areas in more detail, adopt different scopes or concepts or link physical and monetary data. They have the status of being compatible with the national accounts concepts and definitions, and therefore have direct linkages to and have the associated statistical integrity of that system. Many of these accounts can be seen to relate directly or indirectly to aspects of economic and social sustainability. Work undertaken to date in the ABS is outlined below.

Unpaid work and household satellite accounts

Households can obtain goods and services by purchasing them in the market or they can produce them themselves using their own capital and labour. The former are fully captured in the national accounts while by convention the latter are only partially captured. The own-account production of all goods used for own consumption or capital formation is included as are housing services provided by owner occupied dwellings, but all other services produced in the household for own use such as cleaning, food preparation, servicing and repair of goods, caring and instruction of children are excluded. The value of volunteering services provided to others is also excluded from the value of production and consumption. While SNA93 explicitly recognises that these activities are within the concept of economic production, for a variety of reasons they are excluded from the production boundary defined for the national accounts.

In order to properly compare consumption per capita or standards of living between communities or nations it is clear that the production/consumption boundary should be redrawn to include the production of all services for own use. Even within a nation intertemporal comparisons over a long time period can be distorted as economic activity moves across the production boundary over time. The tendency for households to purchase from the market what they used to provide for themselves (such as cleaning services, takeaway food) is reflected as a growth in the level of GDP even though the production and consumption of those services may not have increased overall.

Australia, like a number of other countries has put considerable effort into measuring the value of unpaid work (and own consumption and capital formation). Time Use Surveys have been conducted for 1992 (pilot survey) and 1997 and it is proposed to collect time use data from households again in 2005-06. The value of unpaid work has been compiled for 1992 and 1997 using input methods and it proposed that the valuation work be updated whenever new time use data become available. The results have been released as a "satellite account" to the national accounts. The ABS would also like to investigate the possibility of interpolating between and extrapolating from benchmarks and some work has already been undertaken to investigate the demographic *versus* behavioural influences behind changes in time use patterns. There is also a longer term aim to integrate the work into a more substantial satellite account for household production.

Non-profit institutions satellite account

Non-profit institutions (NPIs) play an important role in the provision of welfare, social and other services in Australia. They are an important part of the social fabric because of the wide community involvement through donations and volunteering. The output and value added of non-profit institutions are already included in the national accounts, but in Australia each is indistinguishable in the accounts. Market services are valued in the usual way whereas non-market services are valued 'at cost'. However as mentioned above, the value of volunteer services provided to and by NPIs is excluded from the national accounts. An NPI satellite account brings together all of the market and non-market transactions of NPIs into an account, including an estimate for the value of volunteer services.

The ABS released a satellite account for NPIs in 2002. It is planned to update the account some time in the future.

Tourism satellite account

For many countries, tourism is a key source of income now and into the future. Actions which may damage the tourism potential of a country can have significant implications for the sustainability of their economies, or conversely actions to promote tourism potential can be an important source of future economic growth. Countries that are reliant on tourism for a significant proportion of their income may also be vulnerable to world events outside their control.

"Tourism" is not an industry in the national accounts or industry accounts more generally as it refers to the status of the customer as a visitor rather than the good or service produced. Because of this it is not possible to compile a comprehensive set of economic statistics for tourism by direct collections. Instead, the output and value added of the tourism industry has to be modelled within the supply and use tables of the national accounts system. This is what is referred to as a tourism satellite account.

The ABS has produced a tourism satellite account for each of the years from 1997-98 with the latest update in progress for 2001-02.

Environmental satellite account

Environmental satellite accounts focus on the interaction between the environment and the economy. As discussed earlier in this paper, SEEA provides a framework for such accounts and ABS work in this area is being guided by that framework.

In the context of the national accounts, the criticism is often made that the concept of income does not account for the run down or addition to environmental assets resulting from the economic process i.e. it is not a sustainable concept of income. ABS has published experimental estimates of income adjusted for the depletion of natural resources in a satellite account context (see the June quarter 2002 issue of *National Income, Expenditure and Product*, ABS Cat. No. 5206.0). While this represents progress towards a concept of sustainable income it still falls short of an ideal concept as it does not include a deduction for the damage of environmental assets more generally.

Other satellite accounts

ABS has also made progress in scoping and developing frameworks for some other satellite accounts that touch on aspects of the sustainability issue. At the present time, a substantial amount of work has been completed on the development of frameworks for satellite accounts on information and communication technology (ICT) and on education and training. Some early work has also been undertaken to scope a sport and recreation satellite account. The first of these accounts is designed to provide information on the supply and use of ICT products in the economy and is an important indicator of a nation's connection to the "new economy". The rapid growth in the production and use of ICT products is thought to be an important factor in the strong, low inflationary growth in some countries over the past decade or so. A pilot study has been undertaken with a view to compiling a more substantial ICT account for 2002-03.

Education and training and sport and recreation satellite accounts would focus on aspects of the development and maintenance of human and social capital. As is the case for the other satellite accounts, they would aim to group together common activities that may be spread across a number of conventional industries and to use the supply and use framework to integrate the data. There is also the potential to extend the SNA production boundary by developing new concepts such as treating education and training as an input to the production of own-account human capital. While a detailed framework has been developed for education and training and some thought is being given to sport and recreation, resources are not available to proceed further with the compilation of these accounts at the present time.

Household income and wealth distribution measures

ABS is undertaking a major program of work to upgrade its measures of household income, including measures of income distribution across the population and over time. It is aiming to improve the methodology for collecting, deriving and presenting these measures and provide greater comparability with data on income benefits from administrative sources. In undertaking this work, consideration is also being given to implementing the recommendations of the Canberra Group on household income statistics and to improving the measurement of an extended income concept - final income - which adjusts disposable income (private income plus direct government benefits less direct taxes) to include the net effect of indirect government benefits and indirect taxes. Investigations are also proceeding into the treatment of non-cash income and salary sacrificing across a range of surveys with the aim of clearer delineation of the income concept being measured and more accurate and consistent reporting in social and economic settings.

A strategy to provide measures of the changing composition and distribution of wealth across Australian households is also being implemented. These measures will be consistent with the measures of household income and relatable to national accounting measures. Bringing the distributional data for income and wealth together will provided deeper insights into how economic disadvantage and inequality of households are changing over time. As part of this strategy, in September 2002 ABS released a paper *Experimental Estimates of the Distribution of Household Wealth, Australia, 1994-2000*, which reported the findings of a study that melded a range of existing data sets to construct experimental wealth data dissected by household characteristics. ABS is also planning a six yearly direct collection of data on household wealth in conjunction with its household income and expenditure surveys, starting from 2003-04.

Human capital measures

Discussions about sustainability often consider whether a nation is preserving its capital stock. As indicated earlier, human capital - the knowledge, skills and attributes embodied in people - is often considered to be one of the four broad types of capital stock (alongside social, natural, and produced and financial capital).

Later in 2003 the ABS plans to release a working paper *Measuring the Stock of Human Capital for Australia*, which will include the first official estimates of the dollar value of a key dimension of Australian human capital. The estimates are calculated using the 'lifetime labour income' approach. Using this method, we measure the stock of human capital as the discounted present value of expected lifetime labour market income. Expected income streams are derived by using cross-sectional information on labour income, employment rates and school participation rates. This approach is also able to account for the effect on human capital formation of current schooling activities – that is, it can account for additional human capital embodied in those individuals who are still participating in formal education and who anticipate improved employment and income prospects as a result.

Using the Population Census data for 1981, 1986, 1991, 1996 and 2001, the study provides five snapshots of age-earnings profiles for four categories of educational attainment for both men and women over the twenty year period. Based on these age-earnings profiles, the study derives per capita measures of lifetime labour market incomes for each age/sex/education cohort, and applies these per capita measures to the number of people in the corresponding cohort. It then aggregates across all cohorts to estimate human capital stock.

The estimates are confined to people aged 25 to 65 years. Separate estimates, for that age range, will be given both for the population and for those people in the labour force.

Social capital framework and indicators

In Australia, social capital has emerged as an area of considerable interest to policy makers, social analysts and researchers. This interest has led to a demand for measures of social capital to enlarge understanding of society, its functioning and social wellbeing and to inform policy development and research. Measures of social capital have the potential to provide additional explanatory variables for social outcomes that the current range of socioeconomic and demographic indicators may not adequately explain. ABS has been undertaking a range of investigation and development work in this field.

The initial work has focussed on understanding, describing and defining social capital in the context of other types of capital (natural, produced and financial, and human) and as a contributor to wellbeing. Following consultation with stakeholders, ABS is using the definition of social capital adopted by the OECD to guide its work.

Current effort is centred on developing and refining a framework covering the different dimensions and components of social capital in a way that will facilitate their measurement, and on developing indicators that capture these elements. A range of ABS and non-ABS collections are being analysed for potential indicators and to identify data gaps. A paper describing the framework and defining the indicators will be published later this year. Data items to support priority indicators will be specified for inclusion in an ABS survey to be conducted in 2005-06.

Knowledge-based economy and society (KBE/S) framework and indicators

In August 2002, the ABS released a discussion paper, *Measuring a Knowledge-based Economy and Society - An Australian Framework*. The proposed ABS framework draws on work done by a number of organisations and individuals. In particular, it builds on work of the APEC (Asia-Pacific Economic Co-operation) Economic Committee and the OECD Growth Project.

ABS proposes a KBE/S framework model with five dimensions. Three core dimensions, "innovation and entrepreneurship", "human capital" and "information and communications technology", provide the focus of the framework and define the key characteristics of a KBE/S. In addition, there are two supporting dimensions: a "context" dimension and an "economic and social impacts" dimension. The context dimension is very broad and incorporates a number of background elements and preconditions, such as business environment and effectively functioning markets. The dimension on economic and social impacts is included in the framework on the presumption that a KBE/S has an impact on the economy and society.

Within each dimension are characteristics. A characteristic is an aspect of a dimension which has been used to both further describe the dimension and to give it some structure by splitting it into more understandable elements.

Finally, statistical indicators provide quantitative measures of characteristics. In the proposed framework, an indicator is defined as a single figure or a small data set showing a broad dissection (for instance by broad industry, age group etc). Where possible, time series and/or internationally comparative views will also be shown.

The next phase in the KBE/S project is to populate the framework with statistical data and to disseminate those data. The discussion paper sought comment and feedback on several aspects of the framework, including the relevance and range of indicators proposed. Considerable feedback has been received and, overall, the comments indicate that the published framework is acceptable as a working basis for organising statistics across this very wide-ranging area.

Our intention is to gradually build up a KBE/S statistical data product over time rather than attempt to cover all possible indicators in the first release. Development of indicator data for the product is reasonably well progressed and ABS is aiming for a first release around June 2003.

Conclusion

A range of different approaches are proving useful for analysing sustainability issues in Australia. Some of these approaches are based on accounting frameworks. Others are based on frameworks that provide measures of the changing levels of wellbeing or indicators addressing a particular theme or topic. No single approach adequately covers all dimensions of interest. Particularly in the social field, a variety of approaches are needed to support research and evidence-based decision-making. The suite of indicators approach has been of particular value in bringing the social, environmental and economic dimensions together to provide an overall perspective on national progress in Australia over the last decade.

References

Australian Bureau of Statistics 2003, *Measuring Learning in Australia: A Framework for Education and Training Statistics*, Cat. no. 4213.0, ABS, Canberra

Australian Bureau of Statistics 2002, *Australian Social Trends, 2002*, Cat. no. 4102.0, ABS, Canberra

Australian Bureau of Statistics 2002, *Education and Training Indicators, Australia*, Cat. no. 4230.0, ABS, Canberra

Australian Bureau of Statistics 2002, *Social Capital and Social Wellbeing*, Discussion Paper, ABS, Canberra

Australian Bureau of Statistics 2002, *Potential Development of Education and Training Satellite Accounts*, Scoping Paper, ABS, Canberra

Australian Bureau of Statistics 2002, *Measuring a Knowledge-based Economy and Society* - an Australian Framework, Cat. no. 1375.0, ABS, Canberra

Australian Bureau of Statistics 2002, *Measuring Australia's Progress*, Cat. no. 1370.0, ABS, Canberra.

Australian Bureau of Statistics 2001, *Measuring Wellbeing: Frameworks for Australian Social Statistics*, Cat. no. 4160.0, ABS, Canberra

Australian Bureau of Statistics 2001, *Labour Statistics: Concepts, Sources and Methods*, Cat. no. 6102.0, ABS, Canberra

Australian Bureau of Statistics 2001, *Energy and Greenhouse Gas Emissions Accounts, Australia*, 1992-93 to 1997-98, Cat. no. 4604.0, ABS, Canberra

Australian Bureau of Statistics 2000, *Unpaid Work and the Australian Economy, 1997*, Cat. no. 5240.0, ABS, Canberra

Australian Bureau of Statistics 2000, *Australian National Accounts: National Balance Sheet, 1999-2000*, Cat. no. 5241.0.40.001, ABS, Canberra

Council of Australian Governments 1992, *National Strategy for Ecologically Sustainable Development*, Commonwealth of Australia, Canberra

Harrison and Vardon 2002, *Environmental Accounting: Concepts, Practices and Assessment of Sustainable Development,* 46th Annual Conference of the Australian Agricultural and Resource Economics Society, Canberra

A Capital-based Sustainability Accounting Framework for Canada

R. Smith

Statistics Canada

Introduction

This paper presents a proposed approach to the creation of a measurement system for sustainable development.[1] The system uses an expanded notion of capital as its conceptual framework. Its analytical framework is that of the System of National Accounts (SNA).

The paper is divided into four sections. The first discusses an interpretation of sustainable development based on welfare and how capital can be used to frame this interpretation. Next, the concept of capital is explored in more detail as it applies to the environment. This is followed by a description of a system of environment accounts based on capital proposed recently by Statistics Canada. A brief discussion of issues for further exploration concludes the paper.

A welfare interpretation of sustainable development

The term sustainable development has been the subject of much discussion since its popularisation in the Brundtland Commission's famous 1987 report *Our Common Future*.[2] Regrettably, for all this discussion the world has yet to reach a consensus on its meaning. A necessary first task in any work on sustainable development is, then, to state clearly how the concept is interpreted for the purposes at hand. The interpretation here is as follows.

First, **development** is assumed to be the on-going increase in human welfare. Welfare, in turn, is assumed to be a function of consumption of goods and services (products) that generate utility for the consumer. Both marketed and non-marketed products are assumed to generate utility for consumers. Thus the terms "consumption" and "consumer" are used more broadly here than is typically the case. Consumption takes place whenever an individual (a consumer) benefits from the enjoyment or use of *any* good or service, regardless of the price paid for it.

Human welfare is assumed to have no upper limit; that is, it is always possible to find a new pattern of consumption that will generate a higher level of welfare than that which exists at the moment. It is assumed, however, that consumption of some products results in external effects that, beyond certain levels, will lead to utility-decreasing reductions in

---

1.   The opinions expressed here are those of the author and should not be taken to represent the official position of Statistics Canada. The author wishes to thank Karen Wilson and Martin Lemire of Statistics Canada for providing helpful comments.

2.   World Commission on Environment and Development, 1987, *Our Common Future*, Oxford: Oxford University Press.

the availability of other products. For example, the consumption of manufactured goods may result in the release of pollutants that reduce the capacity of the environment to provide key ecosystem services. Therefore, it is only exceptionally true that development can occur in the long run simply by increasing overall consumption levels following their current pattern. It is almost inevitable that this will result in excess consumption of some products and reductions in the availability of others. Rather, for development to occur **sustainably**, it is necessary to recognize situations in which the increased utility derived from the consumption a particular product is not outweighed by the loss in utility from an associated decrease in the availability of another product.

Put another way, development can only be sustainable when human activities do not broadly and persistently undermine the capacity of certain essential systems to provide welfare-increasing consumption opportunities. Three such systems can be identified: the environment, the economy and society. Each one provides products that are fundamental to human development. Each is fragile and subject to perturbation from human activities and each is inter-related with the others. If welfare is to continually increase, each of these systems must be maintained in and of itself. It is not conducive to sustainability that consumption of the products from one system diminishes the capacity of the other systems.

Yet it is not assumed here that each of these systems must be maintained unchanged. Rather, substitution possibilities are assumed between the systems. That is, consumers can choose to consume more of the products offered by one system (say, the economy) and fewer of those offered by another system (say, society) while maintaining or enhancing their overall welfare. Such substitutions have taken place throughout history and will no doubt continue in the future. The extent to which they will take place is a function of human values, information with which to assess tradeoffs, political factors and many other variables that are beyond discussion here. While it is taken for granted that such substitutions will occur, the possibilities for welfare-increasing substitutions are not assumed to be without limit (this point is taken up again later in the paper).

Capital as a conceptual framework

When economists speak of the capacity of the economic system to generate products on an on-going basis, they refer to its *capital stock*. This stock comprises tangible goods such as machinery, equipment, buildings and infrastructure and intangible items such as computer software and specialized knowledge. Capital goods (or assets) such as these are required today in order that production take place tomorrow. Economists have identified several general characteristics of such goods. First, it is not the goods themselves that are of value, but the services they offer. Second, they tend to depreciate over time; that is, the quality of the services they produce generally declines as the goods age. For this reason, economic production is not sustainable in the long-term unless there is continual investment to replace capital goods as they wear out.

Many researchers have noted that it is not just machinery, equipment and the like that share the characteristics of capital goods. They note that elements of all three essential systems mentioned above (the economy, the environment and society) have value for the services they render to humans and are subject to deterioration unless maintained. These elements, it is argued, qualify for treatment as capital just as much as more traditional goods.

The most widely studied of these relatively newly recognized forms of capital is the labour force, which is now commonly accepted in the academic literature to comprise a stock of *human capital*. Human capital has been defined as "the knowledge, skills, competences and other attributes embodied in individuals that are relevant to economic activity".[3] Its flow corollary is the labour services that are used in the economy. The investments needed to maintain it are education and, somewhat more controversially, healthcare and on-the-job training.

More recent and less well-studied from a capital perspective are **natural capital** and **social capital**. Natural capital is the term used increasingly to describe those elements of the environment that yield resource materials and ecosystem services. Unlike other forms of capital, no explicit human investment is required to maintain natural capital. Rather, what is needed is that human impacts on the environment are limited so that they do not represent a *disinvestment* in natural capital.[4]

Social capital is a more recent term that describes the capacity of societies to generate trust, faith, tolerance, ingenuity and other human qualities that are essential for development. The investments needed for its maintenance are the creation and maintenance of effective public institutions and processes.

It is argued here that this emerging, broadened concept of capital represents the most suitable conceptual framework for the development of a sustainable development information system. To begin with, there exists a well-developed body of thought around the concept of capital that provides clear guidance on *what* such a system should measure. Of paramount importance is identification and measurement of the capital goods (or assets) that provide the service flows necessary for development. Along with measurement of these assets, measurement of the factors that lead to their increase (investment) and decrease (depreciation) is essential to the capital approach.

As much as the approach provides guidance on what should be measured, it also dictates what *not* to measure. For one, measurement of current consumption is not required. While consumption is an important indicator of current welfare, it says nothing about the possibilities for sustaining welfare in the future.

Also excluded is measurement of the individual elements that comprise assets (for example, the individual pulleys, bolts and gears that make up a machine or the individual species that make up an ecosystem). These elements do not, in and of themselves, generate service flows. Only when combined in the form of a functioning asset do they do so. Measurement of the complete asset itself is, therefore, all that is required from the capital perspective.

It is important to underline the extent to which this guidance on what and what not to measure simplifies building a sustainable development information system. Each of the three systems essential to development is extraordinarily complex and the number of variables that could possibly be measured for any of them is enormous. Measurement of them all is, obviously, out of the question. Some means is required of identifying a manageable set. In the absence of a theoretical framework as a guide, the selection of variables would be subjective and may tend toward a large set since nothing would

---

3.   Organisation for Economic Co-operation and Development, 1998, *Human Capital Investment – An International Comparison*, OECD: Paris, p. 9.

4.   It must be noted that the 1993 SNA includes several categories of tangible non-produced assets that would fall under the heading of natural capital, although that term is not used in the SNA. These include certain land areas, proven sub-soil mineral and fossil fuel reserves, certain non-cultivated biological assets and certain water resources. In general, these are recognized as assets in the SNA only insofar as they are privately held and profitable under current price and technology conditions.

constrain the number chosen. With the notion of capital as a guide however, it is relatively straightforward to determine the variables that must be measured; that is, those related to the extent of assets and their increase and decrease. Moreover, the number of variables (assets) that requires measurement is sufficiently constrained that the practical problem of building the information system is manageable.

A second strength of the capital approach is its close alignment with the notion of inter-temporal justice inherent in sustainable development. The Brundtland Commission emphasized the importance of meeting the needs of present generations while protecting the right of future generations to meet their own needs. Similarly, economists and accountants have always argued that a portion of current income must be set aside for investment in new capital goods to replace those that wear out. It is, they note, the responsibility of current consumers to forego some consumption so that future consumers will inherit at least the same possibilities for economic production as are enjoyed today.

As noted earlier, sustainable development requires maintenance of the welfare-generating capacity of not just the economic system but of the environmental and social systems too. From a capital perspective, this simply means extending the economic concept of investment from the economic domain to the environmental and social domains. While the nature of what can be considered investment in the environmental and social domains is quite different from that in the economic domain, the notion is nonetheless useful in guiding the creation of a sustainable development information system.

A final strength of the capital approach is the familiarity to the average citizen of its practical implications, if not its theoretical underpinnings. Nearly all people understand that they must maintain their homes, their belongings, their finances and, indeed, their bodies if these things are to continue to provide them with the security, income and health that are essential to a good life. If presented with the notion that nations must similarly maintain their economies, their natural environments and their social structures to ensure long-term development, most people would intuitively grasp the importance of doing so. For this reason, it seems reasonable to contend that they would comprehend without difficulty a system for measuring sustainability based on capital.

To summarise, development is assumed here to be a function of the consumption of goods and services provided by three essential systems, the economy, the environment and society. It is sustainable when the ability of these systems to provide products over the long term is not widely and persistently compromised by human activities. The elements of the systems that ensure their long-term ability to provide products are labelled assets, a term borrowed from the economic literature. The concept of an asset is considerably broadened here to include not just the produced assets of the economy (machinery, equipment, buildings, etc.), but elements of all three systems that are of value for the services they offer and are subject to deterioration. This expanded notion of capital is useful as a basis for a sustainable development information system because it offers explicit guidance on what (and what not) to measure, it aligns well with the inter-temporal aspect of sustainable development and it is intuitively understandable for average citizens.

The next section expands on one of the three categories of capital, natural capital, to demonstrate how the theoretical framework can be operationalised in terms of measurable variables.

The environment from a capital perspective

The environment contributes to human welfare through the provision of both material and service flows. The materials it provides include metals and minerals, biological products (*e.g.,* timber), water and fossil fuels. The service flows range from the assimilation of waste materials to the regulation of the global climate. They are defined broadly here to include pure utility flows; for example, the psychic enjoyment of wilderness.

According to the capital approach, the great complexity of the environment and humankind's relationship to it can be simplified by focussing on the distinct stocks of natural resources and individual ecosystems that are the source of these material and service flows. These stocks and ecosystems are the environmental assets that contribute to welfare and must be included in the measurement of sustainability. Collectively, they are labelled *natural capital*.

It is important to note that the adoption of the economic term capital by no means limits the consideration of the welfare benefits of the environment to economic benefits alone. On the contrary, although economic benefits are part of what natural capital offers, they are just a subset of the complete range. The complete range can be grouped into two broad categories: use benefits and non-use benefits.

Use benefits are, as the name implies, associated with the active human use of an environmental asset. For a use benefit to be realised, people must be engaged in activities that depend upon a current-period flow of either a material or a service from the environment. Use benefits can be further divided into two sub-categories: direct-use benefits and indirect-use benefits.

- **Direct-use benefits** include those derived from the use of the environment as a source of materials, energy or space for human activities. Also included are the benefits associated with non-consumptive uses of the environment, such as recreation. Some direct-use benefits are clearly economic in nature since they manifest themselves in the context of economic activity (the value of resource extraction for example). Others are non-economic; that is, they provide benefits for which there is no associated transaction in the marketplace. The benefits derived by humans from the aesthetic appreciation of the environment are an example of non-economic direct-use benefits.

- **Indirect-use benefits** are those associated with human use of the services provided by ecosystems. They do not derive from the active use of ecosystems themselves, but rather from the passive use of services that ecosystems render free of charge. They include the benefits humans derive indirectly when they enjoy the clean air and water, stable climate and protection from the sun's damaging ultra-violet radiation afforded by ecosystems. By their nature, indirect-use benefits are always non-economic, as there is never any market transaction associated with the indirect use of the environment.

The second broad category of environmental benefits is that of **non-use benefits**. These are derived from the continued existence of elements of the environment that may one day provide *use* benefits for those currently living or for generations to come. An example is the benefit derived from maintaining a rain forest to protect sources of genetic material for development of drugs or hybrid agricultural crops in the future. As with indirect-use benefits, non-use benefits are purely non-economic.

The categories of natural capital

Three main categories of assets provide the environmental benefits listed above: **renewable and non-renewable resource stocks** (*i.e.,* sub-soil resources, timber, fish, wildlife and water), **land** and **ecosystems**. Each of these plays a different role in terms of its contribution to environmental welfare and each is subject to differing impacts from human activity.

Non-renewable resources: Non-renewable resources represent stocks from which materials can be withdrawn for use in human activity. These materials provide direct-use benefits as inputs into industrial processes and in private activities. Because sub-soil resources do not have the capacity to renew themselves, except in geologic time, these resources are subject to permanent depletion as the result of use. They do not play an important role in ecosystems, so their use does not inherently lead to a qualitative degradation of the functioning of the environment. In practice however, the exploration and development activity required to make these resources available can cause significant degradation of the environment, not to mention the degradation of the environment at the local, regional and even global scale that can result from the *use* of resources once extracted.

Renewable resources: Renewable resources (trees and other plants, fish and wildlife and water) also represent stocks from which materials can be withdrawn for use in the economy. Unlike sub-soil resources, these resources can renew themselves under appropriate conditions. If withdrawals within a given period are less than or equal to natural renewal, there need be no depletion as a result of human use. Of course, withdrawals are not always less than renewal, so depletion can and does occur. Fish resources are an obvious example. Aside from the possibility of depletion, renewable resources are also subject to qualitative degradation as a result of human use. Qualitative degradation does not necessarily reduce the absolute size of renewable resource stocks, but makes them less productive or less valuable. This degradation can be the result of harvesting activities (*e.g.,* changes to the natural age- and species-distribution of forests, unintended mortality of non-target fish species); of pollution impacts (*e.g.,* acid rain); and of disturbance from urbanisation, agriculture, recreation and other land use changes. This degradation can negatively affect welfare because of reductions in use benefits (*e.g.,* lower quality material supplies, reduced aesthetic value) or non-use benefits (reduced options for the future).

Land: When land is considered as natural capital, it is with reference to its role in the provision of space.[5] Land benefits humans in two ways from a spatial perspective. First, there are the direct-use benefits associated with the occupation of land for human purposes (dwellings, transportation infrastructure, agriculture, recreation). Second, there are the indirect-use benefits associated with the services of the ecosystems that occupy land areas.

Land area is, of course, not subject to quantitative depletion (at least not yet – climate change may change this if sea levels rise sufficiently). Nor is it subject to qualitative degradation in the same way as renewable resources. However, land areas of specific types can be augmented or diminished as a result of changes in the way in which land is used. For example, increasing use of land for urban purposes necessarily means reduced

---

5.   Soil is not a part of land in this respect, although it clearly does fit within the framework of natural capital. It could be treated either as a natural resource stock or, more reasonably, as a component of terrestrial ecosystems.

use of land for other purposes (agriculture, recreation, wildlife habitat, etc.) in areas around growing cities.

It is not clear *a priori* whether a given change in land use represents a net benefit or loss for human welfare. Clearly, at the margin it is generally assumed that decisions regarding land use are made such that the more highly valued use wins out over the less highly valued. There are two reasons to suspect that this assumption might not always be true in the long run. First, it may be that decisions that are sensible at the margin from a private perspective do not make sense in aggregate from a societal perspective. Clearly, a farmer with 100 hectares of land on the edge of a major city may see very clearly that his land is valued much more highly for housing than it is for crop production. However, when one recognizes that most good farmland is found near settled areas, one sees that the private decision to convert farmland to subdivisions may not make sense from the broader perspective of food security. Second, the framework used for valuing land in land-use decisions generally recognises only private, direct-use values. If indirect-use and non-use values were brought into the equation, the decision might look different.

Ecosystems: Ecosystems (*e.g.*, forests [as opposed to trees]; oceans, lakes and rivers [as opposed to the fish in them]) provide flows of unpriced services that are used by humans in a variety of ways. The waste assimilation services of rivers, for example, are used by industries and households alike to absorb waste products that would otherwise have to be disposed of by another means at a cost. Ecosystems are subject to both quantitative depletion through human activities (*e.g.*, the conversion of forests into urban land) and to qualitative degradation *via* the same mechanisms just mentioned for renewable resources.

The treatment of ecosystems as capital is the most difficult of the three forms of natural capital. In theory, the correct approach is to observe the services that are provided by ecosystems and to estimate the benefits that these services provide to humans. A list of the major services provided by ecosystems would include cleansing of fouled air and water; the provision of productive soil; the provision of biodiversity; the provision of a predictable and relatively stable climate; the protection from incident solar radiation; and the provision of reliable flows of renewable natural resources.

Even if we can identify what the major ecosystem services are, we cannot observe them directly, just as we cannot observe the transportation service that an automobile provides. In the latter case, economic theory suggests that the discounted value of the services rendered by the automobile over its life is equivalent to the price established for it in transactions between buyers and sellers in a free market. While this theory is useful in understanding the valuation of produced capital goods, it is of little practical value in measuring ecosystems that are not bought and sold.

One possible approach to measuring ecosystems is to consider the quality of their service *outcomes*. The list of major ecosystem services given above translates naturally into a list of outcomes that are more or less observable and that could be used as the basis for measuring ecosystems as capital. For example, the service of waste assimilation has a corresponding outcome of clean air and water. If the outcomes of ecosystems services are constant over time (*e.g.*, air quality does not decline) then one can conclude that the natural capital – that is, the ecosystems – that provide these outcomes are intact. Obviously, the measurement of ecosystem service outcomes is by no means straightforward. Nevertheless, it is argued here that it offers a proxy for ecosystem services that is practically applicable.

Substitution of natural capital

Fundamental to the capital approach is the notion that different forms of capital are substitutable with one another. According to the theory, natural capital should be replaceable with either produced or human capital in any particular human endeavour without reducing the welfare the activity yields. There is diverging opinion on the extent to which this is actually the case. In one school of thought, the possibilities for substituting natural capital with other forms of capital are indeed assumed to be very great if not limitless. In another, they are assumed to be limited to specific cases. The implications of these two viewpoints for the way in which natural capital is measured are great.

If the possibilities for replacing natural capital with other forms of capital are essentially limitless then there is a compelling need to measure natural capital commensurably with produced and human capital. Only when all forms of capital are measured using the same yardstick is it possible to meaningfully compare welfare trade-offs when one form of capital is used in place of another. For all practical purposes, the only common yardstick available for this purpose is money. A sustainable development information system founded on this interpretation of the capital approach would require that all natural capital be measured in monetary terms. This would be problematic in practice, as monetary valuation of the environment is an underdeveloped field. Many forms of natural capital can not be credibly valued given existing methods.

The opposite viewpoint is that the possibilities for substitution of natural capital are limited. Many forms of produced and human capital are seen to be of value only when combined with natural capital; for example, a fishing fleet is essentially worthless unless combined with healthy fish stocks to exploit. Other forms of natural capital are seen to provide services essential to human welfare for which there exist no known substitutes. Examples of this type are few. Global atmospheric systems that provide protection from solar radiation and climate regulation are two. True wilderness, with its matchless psychic value, is another.

The position taken here is that possibilities for the substitution of natural capital are significant but not unlimited. They range from a very high degree of substitutability for traditional natural resources (minerals, metals and fuels) to effectively no substitutability for global systems like the atmosphere.

That substitution of traditional natural resources is possible is readily demonstrated clearly by the many instances in which human ingenuity has arrived at means of making better use of, or even eliminating the need for, certain natural resources. A sawmill is a simple example. Much more efficient use of timber is made if it is cut with a blade than with an axe and, so, sawmills allow more production from the same amount of wood. In other instances, technology has allowed substitution of a relatively rare form of natural capital with one that is superabundant. Fibre optic cable has replaced much of the copper wire that used to be required for communications cables, to cite a popular example.

Of course, there is no certainty that the past will be a reliable guide to the future, but the historical record does give reason to believe that humans will continue to find means of substituting traditional natural resources with produced or human capital. This implies the need to measure these resources in monetary terms, as well as in physical terms, so that the welfare implications of their drawing down can be compared against increases in other forms of capital.

At the other end of the substitution spectrum are examples of natural capital for which no substitute has been found or is likely to be found. As already mentioned, these are relatively few in number but extraordinarily important in contributing to human welfare. The best examples are global atmospheric systems that control climate and regulate radiation reaching the earth. We know of no way of directly substituting for these systems; sunscreen is at best a *partial* substitute for *some* of the services of the ozone layer. If their functioning is reduced, the best we can do is hope to adapt to the changes. Since the loss of irreplaceable forms of natural capital leads inevitably to welfare declines, sustainability demands that such losses be minimized.

Measurement of irreplaceable environmental assets is best undertaken in physical terms. Monetary valuation is not necessary since they are not substitutable by other forms of capital and, therefore, there is no reason to want to directly compare stocks of these assets with stocks of produced or human capital assets. Stocks of irreplaceable natural capital assets must be evaluated in and of themselves.

Factors that affect natural capital

To this point, the discussion has focused on what natural capital is and how it relates to other forms of capital. A fuller treatment of the factors that influence the availability of natural capital is required to complete the discussion and point the way to operationalisation of the approach.

To begin with, it is important to recognize that natural capital is affected by both natural and human processes. Each has the ability to both augment natural capital and cause its decline. Natural processes were, of course, responsible for the creation of natural capital in the first place and it is natural processes that ensure the growth of renewable resources and the functioning of ecosystems. Natural processes are also responsible for the loss of certain forms of natural capital; for example, pest infestations can reduce the quality and quantity of trees across large tracts of forests. An information system founded upon capital would certainly want to measure the impact of such events on environmental assets, even though the events are largely out of the control of humans.

Of much greater interest from a policy perspective are the impacts of human activities, as it is here that the control levers are mainly found. As noted earlier, human activities affect natural capital either through depletion or degradation. Depletion is the result of natural resource exploitation and land use change. Degradation can also be the result of resource exploitation and land use change, but also, importantly, of the introduction of waste products into the environment. Each of these processes is discussed briefly below.

Exploitation of non-renewable resources: By definition, stocks of non-renewable resources are finite and any use of them today necessarily reduces the amount available for use tomorrow. The practical consequences of such depletion are not so straightforward however. First, not all non-renewable natural resource stocks are known. Thus, when we compare depletion against stocks to calculate reserve lifetimes, we are comparing it against only that portion of the theoretically available stock that we actually know to exist. Of course, known stocks are subject to change – sometimes dramatic change – as a result of exploration activity. Thus, the theoretically appropriate depletion concept is one net of new discoveries.

Second, some non-renewable resources are superabundant even if strictly speaking finite; sand and gravel is an excellent example. Economic theory says that these resources derive value mainly from their location rent; that is, the value attributable to them from their proximity to a source of demand. Distant stocks of such resources have no value. Other non-renewable resources that are not superabundant may nevertheless be sufficiently abundant that, in theory, their use today need not preclude any foreseeable future use. Some would argue that many metallic ores are in this category and that any future demand for these ores will be met simply by devising means of extracting deeper reserves.

The final complicating factor with respect to depletion of non-renewable resources is that not all resources are gone forever once they are extracted and used in the economy. Specifically, it is possible in theory to reuse metals an infinite number of times through recycling. Of course, in practice some use of metals is dissipative and leads to irrecoverable losses, so complete recycling is never possible. Nonetheless, it is wrong to consider the stock of metal available for the future as just that found in underground ore; the "above-ground inventory" has to be considered as well. In the case of non-renewable energy resources, this is not at all true and all use leads to irreversible loss of the high grade, stored energy.

Exploitation of renewable resources: Exploitation of renewable resources need not lead to losses in natural capital provided that the rate of exploitation is equal to or less than the rate of natural growth. While true in a logical sense, this commonly accepted notion neglects the tension between renewable resources as inventories of raw material and the same resources as integral parts of functioning ecosystems. Old growth forest, for example, can be viewed as an extremely valuable source of high grade timber or as a special type of forest ecosystem offering very significant indirect-use and non-use benefits. To a large extent, realising the value of old-growth forests as raw material sources precludes realising any value as unique ecosystems and *vice versa*. An information system founded on capital would want to provide information relevant to evaluating old growth forests from both of these perspectives.

Even in the case where exploitation of a renewable resource does not lead to any quantifiable change in the size of the stock, there may well be qualitative changes that will affect its value as natural capital. For example, when a mature timber tract is clear-cut it is normally the case that nature will, left to its own devices, restock the land with trees. However, the natural way of things is such that the replacement trees will be of a different species than those that were cut. So-called "transitional species" will tend to dominate in the early years. These may be of lower value as natural capital for a variety of reasons: they may be less valued as material inputs; they may be less rich in terms of supporting biodiversity; or they may be less attractive from an aesthetic perspective. Only after many decades, or even centuries, will the forest begin to resemble that which it replaced. Given that the average rotation age for cutting in managed forests is less than 100 years, once mature timber tracts are cut, we may never again see them as they would exist in their undisturbed state.

Land-use change: Land-use change refers to human-induced changes in the functions that land areas are allowed to fulfil. It normally involves physical restructuring of the land surface in some way; for example, through removal of vegetation, soil or rock; modification of slope; or damming of waterways to create reservoirs. As noted above, land area itself cannot be depleted or degraded in the same way as other forms of natural capital. However, land-use change does lead to increases and decreases in specific categories of land. An increase in land used for urban purposes can only come at the expense of land used previously for some other end. Equally importantly, land-use change can lead to degradation of other forms of natural capital (particularly ecosystems). The construction of transportation corridors can disrupt wildlife habitat and breeding patterns, for example.

Emission of wastes: The final and most complex way in which human activity impacts natural capital is through the emission of wastes.[6] The impact of wastes is mainly felt in terms of degradation in the capacity of ecosystems to provide the service outcomes we rely upon. Excessive introduction of wastes can, for example, overcome the assimilative capacity of the environment and reduce its supply of clean air and water.

Understanding the relationship between waste emissions and the degradation of natural capital is extremely complex. There is no explicit guidance offered on this point in capital theory. It is properly the domain of the environmental sciences and this speaks to the need to engage scientists in identifying the most important waste emissions to measure in a sustainable development information system. Although some wastes are obvious, others may not be.

From a policy perspective, waste emissions represent important levers of control and, therefore, it would be imperative that the information system measure them as fully as possible. Of great importance would be linking waste emissions data with data from economic information systems so that the full force of our economic understanding can be brought to bear in studying the costs and benefits of reducing waste emissions.

Operationalising the approach – A proposed set of environmental accounts

The foregoing has laid out the conceptual framework for a sustainable development information system based on capital with a particular focus on the environmental component of the system. It is now a relatively simple matter to describe a system of accounts that could be used to operationalise the approach. Such a system has been proposed recently by Statistics Canada as the basis for a national set of environmental and sustainable development indicators.[7] It comprises three broad components: Natural Capital Asset Accounts, Material and Energy Flow Accounts and Environmental Protection Accounts.[8]

The accounts described below do not represent Statistics Canada's first foray into the field of environmental accounting. Indeed, a limited version of this system of accounts has been produced on an occasional basis since 1997.[9] Those familiar with the recently revised UN handbook on integrated environmental and economic accounting (commonly

---

6. Wastes in this context include all gaseous, solid and liquid materials rejected into the environment from human activity.

7. For a discussion of the process that led to the development of this proposal see Smith, Robert B., 2003, "The Role of Institutions in Building Frameworks to Measure Sustainable Development: The Canadian Experience", also prepared for the OECD meeting on Accounting Frameworks to Measure Sustainable Development, Paris, 14-16 May, 2003.

8. Additional details on this proposed set of accounts are available from the author.

9. See Statistics Canada, 2000, Econnections: Linking the Environment and the Economy – Indicators and Detailed Statistics 2000, Catalogue No. 16-200-XKE, Ottawa, and Statistics Canada, 1997, Econnections: Linking the Environment and the Economy – Concepts, Sources and Methods of the Canadian System of Resource and Environmental Accounts, Catalogue No. 16-505-GPE, Ottawa.

known as the SEEA)[10] will note that the system corresponds closely to the accounting framework of the SEEA.

Natural Capital Asset Accounts

The proposed Natural Capital Asset Accounts will provide estimates of Canada's key natural capital stocks (natural resources, land and ecosystems) and the annual changes in these stocks due to natural and human processes. These accounts will in all instances present physical estimates of the extent and quality of natural capital. In addition, to the degree possible, stock estimates will be presented in monetary terms so that they are directly comparable with the estimates for other forms of capital included in the national accounts. The accounts will be compiled at a minimum at the national level; where appropriate, sub-national estimates will also be presented using ecologically and politically defined spatial units.

The Natural Capital Asset Accounts will form the basis for the estimation of several new macro aggregates. Most importantly, they will be the source of the estimates of the value of natural capital that will be included in an expanded estimate of national wealth. In addition, a variety of aggregate measures in physical terms will be possible, including, for example, life length of remaining proven energy and mineral reserves, ratio of remaining proven reserves to total reserves, ratio of harvested forest area to total forest area, and so on. These aggregate measures will reveal the extent to which stocks of natural capital are being depleted (or not) in the course of economic development.

The Natural Capital Asset Accounts will comprise 1) Subsoil Asset Accounts, 2) Biological Resource Asset Accounts, 3) Land and Terrestrial Ecosystem Asset Accounts, 4) Water and Aquatic Ecosystem Asset Accounts, and 5) Atmospheric Asset Accounts. Each of these is described briefly in the Annex to this document.

Material and Energy Flow Accounts

The proposed Material and Energy Flow Accounts will describe the annual flows of materials and energy between the Canadian environment and economy and within the Canadian economy itself. In addition, flows between the Canadian environment and the rest of the world economy and environment will be tracked. Such flows will include intentional imports and exports of materials and energy as well as unintentional transboundary movements of materials in air and water currents. These accounts will be measured in all cases in physical units and, where possible, in monetary terms as well. They will be compiled at the national and provincial levels at a minimum and, where possible, sub-national estimates will also be presented using ecologically defined units. For a limited number of highly important material flows (for example, energy and greenhouse gas flows) accounts will be compiled on a quarterly basis.

The Material and Energy Flow Accounts will be structured using the same detailed classification of producers, commodities and consumers found in the Input-Output Accounts. In this way, the data on material and energy flows will be easily combined with the corresponding economic data on production and consumption. Based on this combination, indicators will be calculated describing the extent to which the economy

---

10. United Nations, European Commission, International Monetary Fund, Organisation for Economic Co-operation and Development and World Bank, 2003, *Integrated Environmental and Economic Accounting 2003*, ST/ESA/STAT/SER.F/61/Rev.1 (Final draft), New York: United Nations (http://unstats.un.org/unsd/environment/seea2003.pdf).

exerts demands on the environment as a source of raw materials and as a sink for waste materials. This combination of economic and environmental data has substantial potential for the study of dematerialisation (that is, the de-coupling of economic growth with growth in the throughput of material and energy), a goal which is considered by many as a cornerstone of sustainable development.

The Material and Energy Flow Accounts will comprise 1) Energy Flow Accounts, 2) Raw Material Flow Accounts, 3) Recycled Material Flow Accounts, 4) Water Use Accounts, 5) Greenhouse Gas Emission Accounts, 6) Air Pollutant Emission Accounts, 7) Water Pollutant Emission Accounts, and 8) Solid Waste Emission Accounts. Each is described briefly in the Annex.

Environmental Protection Accounts

The proposed Environmental Protection Accounts will show the transactions within the economy that are concerned with protecting, improving and managing the environment by business, government, households (including individuals) and trade with the "rest of the world." The accounts will provide statistical information on society's response to environmental problems in terms of expenditures and revenues related to protecting the environment. In addition, the production and consumption of environmental goods and services will be tracked. These accounts will be measured in all cases in monetary units and updated annually. They will be compiled at the national and provincial/territorial levels[11] at a minimum; where appropriate, sub-national estimates will also be presented using ecologically defined units.

The Environmental Protection Accounts will comprise 1) Environmental Revenue and Expenditure Accounts, and 2) Supply and Use Accounts for Environmental Goods and Services. Again, each is described briefly in the Annex.

Conclusion

An argument has been set forth for the adoption of a capital approach as the foundation for a sustainable development information system. A number of its advantages have been outlined, the conceptual framework has been described in detail as it applies to the environment and it has been shown to be operationalisable in a system of accounts. In the author's opinion, the approach offers the greatest promise for creating robust, policy-relevant information for sustainable development.

At the same time, questions inevitably remain in such a new field. A few of the more urgent and interesting are noted below.

Given the need to measure many forms of capital using money as the yardstick, additional work to develop valuation techniques is urgently required. At the moment, only a fraction of the environmental assets that should be measured in monetary terms can be monetized with existing techniques. As a starting point, research on the valuation of fisheries, water, recreational land use and environmental waste assimilation services is required.

The question of substitution deserves more careful attention. It has been argued here that some environmental assets provide essential and irreplaceable services and,

---

11. Canada is a federation comprising 10 provinces and 3 territories. Control over natural resource management and environmental quality rests largely with the provincial and territorial governments.

therefore, ought not to be considered substitutable. Many would disagree. To better reveal the nature of this disagreement and attempt to resolve it, a fuller exploration of ecosystem services and the interpretation of "substitution" in the context of these unpriced and, sometimes, unrevealed flows would be helpful.

Finally, the ethical foundation of the capital approach offers a rich set of issues for debate. Many would find the strongly anthropocentric perspective of the approach indefensible. The notion that environmental assets have value only, or even mainly, because of the services they provide for humans would be rejected from almost any other perspective. Certainly, most true environmentalists would find it unacceptable. Yet there is not necessarily a wide gulf between the anthropocentric and eco-centric moral views when it comes to the need to preserve environmental services. It is possible from both perspectives, albeit by different routes, to conclude that fundamental environmental services must be preserved. The possibilities for such convergence are worthy of further exploration.

Annex – Detailed descriptions of the proposed environmental accounts

Natural capital asset accounts

Subsoil asset accounts – The Subsoil Asset Accounts will present estimates of Canada's stocks of fossil fuels (coal, crude oil/tar sands and natural gas) and metallic and non-metallic minerals. Estimates will be provided for proven and probable reserves (in physical and monetary terms) and, where possible, the estimated total reserve base (in physical terms only).

Each year the accounts will record the opening and closing stock levels of each resource and show how these levels can be reconciled through changes due to extractions, additions and (in the case of the monetary estimates) revaluations. A constant stock level measured at the beginning and at the end of a year will mean that additions to the resource stocks through new discoveries offset depletion of existing assets during that period.

Biological resource asset accounts – The Biological Resource Asset Accounts will present estimates of the size and characteristics (*e.g.*, age structure, species mix) of commercially and non-commercially exploited biological stocks (forests, fish populations, terrestrial wildlife). For each year, the accounts will record the opening and closing stock levels of each resource and show how these levels can be reconciled through changes in stock level due to extractions, additions and (in the case of the monetary estimates) revaluations. A constant stock level measured at the beginning and the end of a year will indicate that annual harvesting and other losses are offset by annual growth.

Land and terrestrial ecosystem asset accounts – The Land and Terrestrial Ecosystem Asset Accounts will describe Canada's land area from a number of perspectives. Estimates will be provided at a detailed geographical scale for land cover (what is found on the surface of the land), land use (what purpose or purposes the land is put to), land capability (the potential of the land for use in agriculture, recreation, settlement, etc.).

The accounts will include a land use change matrix that will portray how Canada's land use changes over time. This will allow, for example, tracking of the conversion of ecologically important land types such as wetlands to other uses.

To the extent possible, the Land and Terrestrial Ecosystem accounts will include estimates of the monetary value of Canada's land areas. Geographic information system (GIS) technology will be used to document and store information in a consistent spatial frame.

Water and aquatic ecosystem asset accounts – The Water and Aquatic Ecosystem Asset Accounts will describe Canada's water resources and aquatic ecosystems quantitatively and qualitatively. Estimates will be provided for the quantity of water held in surface water bodies and groundwater aquifers for each drainage basin in the country.

Estimates will also be provided of the annual rate of water renewal in each basin. The quality of water by major water body will be recorded in a set of water quality accounts. Estimates of the value of Canada's water stocks will be presented where possible.

The Water and Aquatic Ecosystem Accounts are the companion to the Land and Terrestrial Ecosystem Asset Accounts in that they use GIS technology as an integrating platform to bring relevant information on water availability and use into one common spatially referenced database.

Atmospheric asset accounts – Atmospheric Asset Accounts will present estimates of the quality and, where possible, the value of Canada's atmospheric systems (quantitative estimates of these systems are generally not meaningful). The accounts will integrate micro-data from Canada's air quality monitoring networks into a spatial framework consistent with Statistics Canada's population data. This will allow the estimation of a population-weighted air quality indicator for urban areas in Canada. The accounts will also provide the ability for users to easily access time series data on air quality for individual urban areas.

Material and Energy Flow Accounts

Energy Flow Accounts – The Energy Flow Accounts will describe the supply and use of energy commodities in the Canadian economy. Estimates will be provided for business, government and household use of fossil fuels, electricity and alternative energy forms in physical and monetary units. Estimates will also be provided for our international trade in energy commodities. The estimates will be provided nationally and for each province/territory on a quarterly basis.

Raw Material Flow Accounts – Raw Material Flow Accounts will describe the supply and use of virgin raw materials (timber, fish, other biological resources, metals, non-metallic minerals) in the Canadian economy. Estimates will be provided in physical and monetary units for business, government and household use of these materials, as well as for our international trade in them. The estimates will be provided nationally and for each province/territory on an annual basis.

Recycled Material Flow Accounts – The Recycled Material Flow Accounts will describe the flows of recycled materials within the Canadian economy. The accounts will measure both the flows of waste materials that are diverted from disposal back into the economy through an organized recycling programme (such as the blue box programme used for most households) and the flows of scrap materials that are recycled because of their positive economic value rather than the existence of a recycling programme. The estimates presented in the accounts will be broken down to the greatest extent possible by type of material. The accounts will be expressed in physical units and, where prices exist for specific recycled materials, in monetary units. The estimates will be provided nationally and for each province/territory on an annual basis.

Water Use Accounts – The Water Use Accounts will describe the supply and use of water in the Canadian economy. The supply of water will be measured separately for groundwater and surface sources, and municipal supply will be recorded separately from self-supplied water. The use of water will be recorded for several different purposes (irrigation, cooling, other industrial processes, institutional use, household use and exports). These accounts will detail supply and use of water at both the provincial and drainage basin levels on an annual basis. Estimates will be made in physical units and, where possible, in monetary units.

Greenhouse Gas Emission Accounts – The Greenhouse Gas Emission Accounts will describe the emissions of greenhouse gases from business, government and household activity in Canada. In addition to presenting estimates for each of the main greenhouse gases, the accounts will make use of global warming potentials to express all emissions in terms of carbon dioxide equivalents. The accounts will be expressed initially in physical units only. If and when a programme of domestic emission trading is implemented, research will be conducted into the use of the price of emission certificates as the basis for valuing the carbon content of emissions. The estimates will be provided nationally and for each province/territory on a quarterly basis.

Air Pollutant Emission Accounts – Air Pollutant Emission Accounts will describe the emissions of polluting substances into the air from business, government and household activity in Canada. The pollutants measured will include those responsible for acid rain and urban smog and others considered dangerous to the health of humans and/or plants and animals (*e.g.*, pesticides). In addition to measuring the emissions into the Canadian atmosphere from domestic activities, the accounts will detail the flow of pollutants to Canada from foreign sources (and *vice versa*) as a result of long-range transport in air currents. The accounts will be expressed initially in physical units only. Research will be undertaken to determine if suitable methods and data sources can be found to assign monetary values to the flows of air pollutants in Canada. The estimates will be provided nationally and for each province/territory on an annual basis.

Water Pollutant Emission Accounts – The Water Pollutant Emission Accounts will describe the disposal of polluting substances into waterways from business, government and household activity in Canada. The pollutants measured will include those responsible for eutrophication and excessive oxygen demand as well as those considered dangerous to the health of humans and/or plants and animals (*e.g.*, heavy metals). In addition to measuring the emissions into Canadian waters from domestic activities, the accounts will detail the flow of pollutants to Canada from foreign sources (and *vice versa*) as a result of long-range transport in surface water. The accounts will be expressed initially in physical units only. Research will be undertaken to determine if suitable methods and data sources can be found to assign monetary values to the flows of water pollutants in Canada. The estimates will be provided nationally and for each province/territory on an annual basis.

Solid Waste Emission Accounts – The Solid Waste Emission Accounts will describe the generation and disposal of solid wastes from business, government and household activity in Canada. The accounts will include estimates for the flows of both hazardous (*e.g.*, spent nuclear fuel) and non-hazardous solid wastes. To the greatest extent possible the waste flows will be broken down by type of material. The accounts will be expressed initially in physical units only. Research will be undertaken to determine if suitable methods and data sources can be found to assign monetary values to the flows of solid wastes in Canada.

Environmental protection accounts

Environmental Revenue and Expenditure Accounts – Environmental Revenue and Expenditure Accounts will provide a detailed breakdown of the revenues associated with the production of environmental goods and services and the expenditures by businesses, governments and households for the purpose of complying with environmental regulations or agreements. Expenditures on capital goods will be recorded as well as current expenditures on goods and services, labour and other primary inputs. Business expenditures will be tracked on industry-by-industry basis and government expenditures by level of government. The accounts will also track the transactions between sectors of the economy related to taxes, subsidies, licenses, fines and fees that have an explicit environmental basis as well as expenditures for a variety of environmental purposes (*e.g.*, pollution abatement, site reclamation, resource management), environmental research and development expenditures (*e.g.*, climate change technologies), and the rate of adoption of environmental technologies.

Supply and Use Accounts for Environmental Goods and Services – The Supply and Use Accounts for Environmental Goods and Services will measure the production and consumption of goods and services related to the protection of the environment. Environmental goods and services include technologies used in sustainable production (end-of-pipe versus change-in-process approaches), products and services that reduce or prevent environmental damage or risk, minimize pollution and resource use (*e.g.*, "green" consumer products) as well as those activities related to natural resource management and adaptation to environmental problems. The accounts will present the supply from producers of environmental goods and services on an industry-by-industry basis as well as the disposition of this supply between intermediate demand and investment by industries, final household and government demand, and exports. Imports will also be tracked in order to give a complete accounting of the domestic use of these goods and services.

The accounts will be structured using the same classification of producers, commodities and consumers found in the Input-Output Accounts. This means the accounts will provide an estimate of the total supply of environmental goods and services as well as an estimate of the value added of environmental goods and services in the Canadian economy. These data can be directly linked to other national account aggregates in order to measure trends in the "environment industry" (*e.g.*, measure of capital turnover and its relationship to investment decisions in environmental protection).

A Framework for Estimating Carbon Dioxide Emissions Embodied in International Trade of Goods

N. Ahmad

Science, Technology and Industry Directorate, OECD

Executive summary

Efforts such as the Kyoto Protocol to reduce emissions that may be linked to climate change focus on six green house gases of which carbon dioxide is by far the largest by volume, representing about 80% of the total emissions of these six gases. Almost all carbon dioxide is emitted during the combustion of fossil fuels and OECD countries account for over half of the total carbon dioxide emission in the world while an additional four countries (Brazil, China, India and Russia) together account for a further quarter of the global total. Many policies designed to reduce these emissions set emission reduction goals based on some previous level (*e.g.* 1990 in the case of Kyoto for many countries) which is used as a benchmark for success and compliance to the protocol.

Concurrent with this, many of the more advanced economies, such as those that constitute the membership of the OECD, have undergone considerable change, becoming increasingly service oriented and increasingly dependent on developing economies for manufactured goods. Between 1995 and 2000 OECD exports to the rest of the world grew by 7% in nominal terms, whereas imports from the rest of the world to the OECD grew by 47%. As a result, by 2000, the OECD trade deficit with the rest of the world stood at $340 billion compared to a broad balance in 1995 (a deficit of 4 billion $US). Detailed trade figures show that imports of goods that require significant energy to produce them are part of this change in the pattern of trade. For example, OECD exports of metals to the rest of the world stood at 50 billion $US in 1995, with imports standing at $55 billion. By 2000 however OECD exports to the rest of the world fell to $40 billion whereas imports rose to $62 billion. The rise of China as a key trading partner for many OECD countries is a key factor behind this shift: China's share of EU, Japanese and US imports rose from 3%, 5% and 3% in 1990 to 6%, 14% and 8% in 2000. China is now the leading steel producer in the world. At the same time, carbon dioxide emissions from developing economies have trebled over the last three decades, far outpacing the growth in developed economies. China's emissions alone increased by 25% over the period from 1990-2000.

The objective of this paper is to describe an analytical framework that can be used to explore what role trade in manufactured goods by OECD economies has had on their CO_2 emissions, mainly by creating an indicator that estimates the emissions associated with the *domestic consumption*[1] of these economies as a complement to the more common

---

1. Analogous to total domestic final demand where emissions from household and government final consumption and investment, including changes in business inventories are calculated regardless of the fact that the goods being consumed where imported or produced domestically.

indicator of emissions associated with *domestic production*[2] of emissions; such as that used in the Kyoto Protocol. In brief the concept of *consumption* excludes emissions associated with exports and includes emissions generated in the production of imports by tracing these imports back to their place of origin and estimating their emissions based on the production processes used to create them. It does this by developing an analytical framework, based on input-output tables, that attempts to measure the indirect carbon dioxide requirements of economies by measuring carbon dioxide emissions, from fossil fuel-use, embodied in imports and exports both directly and indirectly. The results of the study for 24 Countries, responsible in 1995 for 80% of global emissions and global GDP, will be presented in a forthcoming paper planned for completion in June 2003[3]. Given the aggregation used of the input-output tables used in this proposal, it is not envisaged that the analysis will be sufficient to allow specific policy measures to be developed, however by presenting emissions on the basis of *domestic consumption* it is possible to have a better understanding of the possible causes of changes in emissions in any particular country, allowing an assessment of the impact of industrial change on global emissions.

The paper contains six sections. Section 1, which presents some background to the Kyoto Protocol, and growth in CO_2 emissions more generally; Section 2 which describes the methodology, and introduces the notion of embodied emissions; Section 3, outlining the planned data sources; Section 4, listing the key assumption used; Section 5, describing some potential applications, by extending the methodology in Section 2; and Section 6, which provides some concluding remarks.

Introduction

CO₂ Emissions – Background

The Intergovernmental Panel on Climate Change (IPCC), created in 1988 to assess the scientific, technical and socio-economic information relevant to anthropogenic emissions, established in its second report in 1995 a link between these emissions and climate change, stating that "the balance of evidence suggests a discernible human influence on global climate". The release of this report culminated in the adoption of the Kyoto Protocol to the United Nations Framework on Convention and Climate Change (UNFCCC) in December 1997.

The Kyoto Protocol (Box 1) set out a framework for measuring and reducing these emissions, and, acknowledging that economies are at different stages of development and that developed economies produce the majority of GHG emissions, encourages developed and transition economies, (known as Annex I[4] countries), to take the lead in limiting their emissions. Non-Annex I countries, made up largely of developing economies, are also

2. Where the emissions from only domestically produced products for household and government final consumption and investment, including changes in business inventories are included as well as emissions associated with the production of products destined for export

3. Nadim Ahmad and Andrew Wykoff - *Carbon Dioxide Emissions Embodied in International Trade of Goods* - OECD, Science Technology and Industry Directorate working paper.

4. Annex 1 countries: Australia, Austria, Belarus, Belgium, Bulgaria, Canada, Croatia, Czech Republic, Denmark, Estonia, Finland, France, Germany, Greece, Hungary, Iceland, Ireland, Italy, Japan, Latvia, Liechtenstein, Lithuania, Luxembourg, Monaco, Netherlands, New Zealand, Norway, Poland, Portugal, Romania, Russian Federation, Slovakia, Slovenia, Spain, Sweden, Switzerland, Turkey, Ukraine, UK, US. Not all Annex 1 countries have ratified or acceded to the Kyoto convention.

encouraged to reduce emissions but, given their different stages of economic development, have no emissions targets.

Six types of GHGs are recognised in the Protocol: carbon dioxide (CO_2), Methane (CH_4), Nitrous Oxide (N_2O), Hyrdofluorocarbons (HFCs), Petroflorcarbons (PFCs) and Sulphur Hexafluoride (SF_6). Chief amongst these is CO_2 from fossil fuel combustion, making up about 80% of total GHG emissions (Table 1), and, which has increased by over two-thirds over the last three decades and 10% since 1990 (Figure 2).

Table 1. **GHG Emissions of Annex I countries and the contribution of CO_2, 1999**

Source Category	Total GHG emissions (Gt CO_2- eqt)	Contribution to total GHG emissions %	Share of CO_2 in each source category
Fuel Combustion	11.4	80.0	98.2
Fugitive Fuel	0.4	3.0	14.3
Industrial Processes	0.7	4.9	50.5
Agriculture	1.2	8.3	n/a
Other	0.5	3.8	n/a
Total	14.2	100.0	n/a

Source: UNFCCC, *Report on national greenhouse gas inventory data from Annex I parties for 1990 to 1999*, FCCC/SBI/2001/13, 25 October 2001, and FCCC/SBI/13/Corr.1 Excludes Belarus, Croatia, Romania, Liechtenstein, Lithuania, Russia, Slovenia, and Ukraine for which 1999 inventories were not available.

Table 2 provides a breakdown of the contribution made by different sectors to total domestic emissions in 24 selected countries,[5] with a detailed breakdown of the manufacturing sector to illustrate the importance of the metals and chemicals industries.

Emissions from electricity generation make-up about one-third of total global emissions from fossil fuel combustion, although the contribution of electricity differs significantly by country depending on the fuel sources used for electricity generation. The electricity industry in France for example, which generates most of its electricity using nuclear fuel sources, is responsible for only about 5% of total domestic emissions, compared to about 50% in Australia, Denmark, Greece, and Poland.

Emissions from transportation and manufacturing contribute about 20% each but, again, the contribution differs significantly by country. For example, emissions from transportation and manufacturing contributed 23% and 16% respectively of total Annex I emissions in 1995 compared to 14% and 32% in non Annex I economies,[6] although the contribution of transportation in non-Annex I economies is likely to increase as they develop. Importantly, as will be demonstrated, a significant share of total CO_2 emissions is emitted during the production process of final goods and services, directly by the (final good) producing industry, or indirectly by other industries supplying intermediate goods or services (*e.g.* electricity and transportation) to the (final good) producing industry.

---

5. The 24 countries, with the year Input-Output tables are available shown in parentheses, are Italy, (1992); India (1993); Greece (1994); Australia, Czech Republic, Finland, France, Germany, Japan, Korea, Netherlands, Poland, Spain, UK, (1995); Brazil (1996); Canada, Denmark, Norway, US, China: (1997); Hungary, Sweden, Russia, (1998).

6. Indeed even within Annex I economies significant differences exist, for example transportation was responsible for only 6% of the Czech Republic's emissions from fuel combustion in 1995 but about 30% in the US. For manufacturing however the position is reversed, 31% in the Czech Republic and 12% in the US.

Figure 1. **CO_2 emissions from fossil fuel combustion 1971-2000, Mt CO_2**

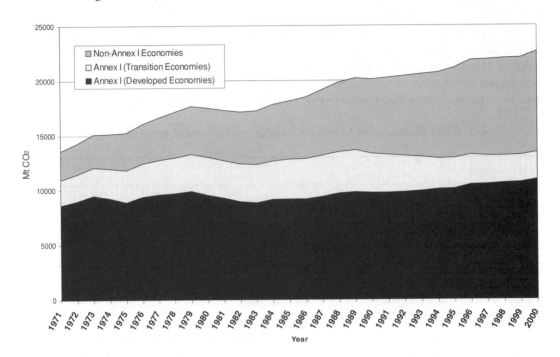

Annex I, Transition Economies: Belarus, Bulgaria, Croatia, Czech Republic, Estonia, Hungary, Latvia, Lithuania, Russia, Slovakia, Slovenia and Ukraine.

Source: IEA

Annex I countries as a whole have increased CO_2 emissions from fossil fuel consumption by just over 1% since 1990. Although this is broadly consistent with the Kyoto objective of stabilising emissions in 2000 at 1990 levels, this reflects significant reductions in emissions by Annex I transition economies. Indeed, excluding transition economies, emissions in Annex I countries (Annex II[7] parties) grew by over 10%. However this is significantly less than the growth in emissions from non-Annex I economies, which have more than trebled over the last three decades. This largely reflects the fact that non-Annex I countries are made up of mainly developing economies in the process of increasing industrialisation, leading inevitably to higher GHG emissions compared to their relatively low recent levels. Over this period the share of total emissions by non-Annex I economies is estimated[8] to have increased from under 20% to over 40%.

Growth in International Trade, 1990-2000

Between 1990 and 2000 the share of emissions from non-Annex I economies increased from just over 30% to just about 40%. Emissions in China alone increased by 0.7Gt CO_2, [representing 3¼% of total global emissions in 2000, (22.7Gt CO_2)]. Much of this increase reflects the production of goods for export to Annex I and OECD economies. In fact in 2000, China, accounted for over 8% of all goods imported into the

---

7.   Annex II parties: Annex I parties excluding transition economies.

8.   Pre-1990 Estimates for Former Soviet Union and Yugoslav Republics Annex I parties assume that shares in 1990 for each country, as a percentage of the total emissions in the FSU or FYR, are unchanged.

US, 14% of imported goods in Japan, and 6% of goods in the EU; significantly higher than in 1990 (3, 5 and 3%).

Moreover between 1995 and 2000 OECD exports to the rest of the world grew by 7% in nominal terms, whereas imports from the rest of the world grew by 47%. And so, by 2000, the OECD trade deficit with the rest of the world stood at $340 billion compared to a broad balance in 1995 ($4 billion, deficit). At the detailed level the trade figures show that imports of GHG-intensive goods rose dramatically. For example OECD exports of metals to the rest of the world stood at $50billion in 1995, with imports standing at $55 billion. In 2000 however exports to the rest of the world fell to $40 billion whereas imports rose to $62 billion. In non-metallic mineral products (cement etc), the OECD's trade surplus has fallen from $3 billion in 1995 to zero in 2000 as import growth outpaced export growth (45% compared to 17%). In fact, even in those areas where OECD economies can be expected to have a competitive edge, imports from the rest of the world outpace exports. Taking Hi-Tech[9] industries as a whole, imports from the rest of the world have grown by 84% since 1995; more than double OECD export growth (41%), meaning that by 2000 a trade surplus of $33 billion in 1995 had become a trade deficit of $16 billion.

The fact that the Kyoto Protocol restricts emissions only in Annex I countries, but not elsewhere, means there is scope for Annex I countries to reduce domestic emissions without adjusting final demand patterns or finding more carbon efficient production methods to respond to these patterns. This is because they can import more of the goods from non-Annex I countries (whether intermediate or final demand) needed to meet final demand, rather than produce them domestically. This may have a negligible impact on global emissions but, as Annex I economies tend to use less carbon intensive production processes than non-Annex I economies, global emissions could well be higher.[10]

The concern for policy makers is that by imposing additional costs, such as taxes on fossil fuel use, the Kyoto protocol may inadvertently encourage such outcomes.[11] This will work to reinforce the long-term trend of the declining share of manufacturing in developed economies, which increasingly import the manufactured goods they once produced from non-Annex I countries.

Carbon-Intensities

The potential importance of this issue is not generally known. No comprehensive data set has yet been developed, which would allow trends in CO_2 emissions associated with trade flows to be monitored, or an empirical assessment of the supposition that production processes in developing economies are more carbon-intensive than those in developed economies. It is difficult to prove this conclusively without detailed data on emissions in equivalent production processes.

---

9. Hi-Tech industries are defined as ISIC Revision 3 industries 30, 32, 33, 2423 and 353.

10. This argument has been made by A. Wyckoff & J.M. Roop, The embodiment of carbon in imports of manufactured products, 1994, Energy Policy March 1994; Munskgaard & Pedersen, CO_2 Accounts for Open Economies: Producer or Consumer Responsibility, Energy Policy 29, 2001.

11. Academics, government agencies and increasingly businesses have criticised the Protocol because it does not actively encourage economies to increase the production of goods (and so emissions) where their production processes are amongst the least carbon-intensive in the World. Carbon-intensive sectors such as steel and oil production have been singled out. See for example:
http://www.rautaruukki.fi/rr_web/rr_icc.nsf/allByID/B875E4982B1504CEC2256BA400357680.
& *http:// www.ifc.org/ogmc/docs/proceedings/BernardTRAMIER.pdf*.

One common way of examining the carbon-intensity of economies, overall, is to compare CO_2 emissions as a per cent of GDP in a common currency, *e.g.* US$. However, largely because of its aggregated nature, this comparison can be misleading in the context of assessing production processes since it assumes that:

- Prices for goods and services across countries are the same. For goods traded internationally this may be true but for services this is rarely so. Economies with cheap services relative to other countries tend to have lower GDP levels (when converted to a common currency) and thus higher economy-wide carbon-intensities.

- Economies produce, relatively, the same basket of goods, which is rarely the case. Economies with abundant natural mineral resources for example tend to have industries that either extract or exploit these resources and export much of their output. So for example economy A, with a higher proportion of carbon-intensive industries producing goods for export, than economy B, will tend to have higher economy-wide carbon-intensities even if all manufacturing processes are as carbon-intensive as those in economy B.

- A significant proportion of emissions are emitted directly by households, mainly for transportation, or indirectly by consuming electricity for household consumption for example. Higher emissions by the household sector in one economy relative to another will in turn lead to higher economy wide emissions although production processes may be equivalent.

Figure 2 below tries to compensate for the last bullet-point by excluding emissions from transportation, since much of these are related to the household sector (or exports), any emissions from electricity generation related to household consumption of electricity, and any other direct emissions from the household sector. It shows emissions in 50 countries/regions, responsible for over 95% of CO_2 emissions from fossil fuel consumption in 1995; showing global share of emissions for each country/region. It shows that Australia has the highest emissions per US$ of GDP of all Annex II economies but still significantly less than the ratios in Annex I Transition economies and most non-Annex I countries with significant shares of global CO_2 emissions. For example Australian ratios, on this basis, are about one-tenth the size of China's and Russia's and about one-twentieth of Ukraine's.

Australia's position as the most carbon-intensive of Annex II economies partly reflects the fact that electricity generation in Australia is relatively carbon-intensive (coal being the primary source) but also the fact that it exports a relatively high proportion of carbon-intensive products; which the comparison below does not adjust for. The relative position of non-Annex I economies however and Annex I transition economies is affected by differences between actual exchange rates and exchange rates adjusted for purchasing power parities. Figure 3 reproduces the comparison in Figure 2 but with GDP adjusted for purchasing power parities.

In this comparison the position of non-Annex I and Annex I transition economies relative to Annex II economies is much closer, indeed, on a PPP basis, ratio's fall in nearly all of these economies, relative to ratios calculated using actual exchange rates. For example China's ratio is only roughly double that of Australia's, Russia's three times Australia's and Ukraine's about 5 times as much. The actual position of China relative to Australia is likely to fall somewhere in between these two ratios (2 to 10 times as much).

What these charts say about the relative carbon-intensities of production processes in each country however is difficult to deduce but they do support the supposition that they are more carbon-intensive in non-Annex I and transition economies. Given this likelihood the concern that by imposing additional costs on production in Annex I economies, such as taxes on fossil fuel use, the Kyoto protocol may inadvertently lead to increases in global GHG emissions warrants scrutiny. A comparison of emissions generated directly and indirectly to meet total final domestic demand in economies can give some indication of the size and importance of this issue; in other words by estimating emissions embodied in imports and exports.

Identifying the influence of incentives arising from the Kyoto Protocol on these emissions and trade flows would require an empirically based behavioural model. Equilibrium models such as the OECD's GREEN model have attempted to establish the possible size of changes in global (CO_2) emissions (by measuring carbon-leakage) that might occur in response to policy or price changes, and these have tended to suggest that this was not likely to be significant. However these models require a number of behavioural assumptions, whose empirical basis is limited, that restrict the confidence with which conclusions can be drawn. Moreover since the GREEN model was developed the world has changed a great deal, in a way that would have been difficult to predict back then: in particular the collapse of centrally planned economies, the increasing importance of China and, especially since the creation of NAFTA, Mexico,[12] as producers and exporters of manufactured goods.

This paper proposes the use of input-output (IO), bilateral trade, and IEA CO_2 emissions' data to develop data, which can serve as a starting point for an empirical assessment of this issue. The methodology is explained in Section 2. A forthcoming paper detailing the results of this work is planned for June 2003. In the longer term, as a time series of IO tables is developed, it is envisaged that the scope of this methodology can be extended to determine not just the size and importance of embodied emissions at a fixed point in time but, also, whether the growth in emissions generated by domestic production has decoupled from the growth in emissions generated (whether domestically or abroad) to meet total domestic (final) demand. Moreover the development of a time series and more recent IO tables can be used as updated inputs into general equilibrium models such as GREEN and GTAP.[13]

---

12. Mexico is not an Annex I country and Mexico's shares of US and Canadian imports have increased from 6% and 1% in 1990 to 11% and 3% respectively.

13. Global Trade Analysis Project, Purdue University: *http://www.gtap.agecon.purdue.edu/*.

Table 2. **Direct CO_2 emissions from fossil fuel combustion by sector as a percentage of total emissions**

INDUSTRY	ISIC CODE	AUSTRALIA	CANADA	CZECH REP.	DENMARK	FINLAND	FRANCE	GERMANY	GREECE	HUNGARY	ITALY	JAPAN	KOREA
AGRICULTURE, ETC.	01-05	1.4	2.0	2.6	3.9	3.1	2.4	0.7	3.8	2.9	2.0	3.0	2.2
MINING, EXTRACTION, REFINING	10-14, 23	6.6	12.7	1.8	4.0	3.1	5.4	3.6	3.6	3.8	4.7	5.1	2.9
FOOD, BEVERAGES, TOBACCO	15-16	1.1	0.0	1.3	2.7	1.1	2.1	1.0	1.3	1.5	1.2	0.7	1.1
TEXTILES, LEATHER, FOOTWEAR	17-19	0.2	0.0	1.0	0.1	0.2	0.4	0.2	0.5	0.2	0.9	0.6	1.4
WOOD AND PRODUCTS OF WOOD AND CORK	20	0.1	0.2	0.2	0.1	0.7	0.0	0.1	0.0	0.1	0.0	0.0	0.1
PULP, PAPER PRINTING AND PUBLISHING	21-22	0.6	2.4	0.9	0.3	5.3	1.3	0.9	0.3	0.4	0.9	1.4	1.1
CHEMICALS	24	1.5	4.2	1.7	0.6	2.0	5.8	4.3	0.5	3.8	5.8	3.5	5.6
OTHER NON-METALLIC MINERAL	26	1.8	0.8	2.7	2.7	3.7	2.4	2.4	6.1	2.6	4.8	3.2	4.7
IRON AND STEEL	271 + 2731	3.6	2.9	8.9	0.2	6.7	5.5	3.7	0.5	3.5	3.4	6.5	1.3
NON-FERROUS METALS	272 + 2732	4.6	0.6	0.1	0.0	0.2	0.5	0.3	1.6	0.4	0.2	0.6	0.2
OTHER METAL PRODUCTS, MACHINERY EQPT	28-32	0.2	0.0	1.3	0.7	0.5	1.3	0.8	0.0	0.7	1.6	0.8	0.7
MOTOR VEHICLES, TRAINS, SHIPS PLANES	34, 35	0.1	0.0	0.5	0.1	0.2	0.1	0.4	0.0	0.2	0.0	0.0	0.4
OTHER MANUFACTURING AND RECYCLING	25, 33, 36-37	0.0	4.2	8.8	0.4	0.1	2.2	0.5	1.1	0.1	0.5	3.2	2.8
ELECTRICITY, GAS, WATER	40-41	**46.4**	**21.5**	**41.8**	**51.9**	**36.0**	**5.4**	**32.3**	**49.8**	**41.0**	**25.7**	**28.6**	**20.9**
TOTAL INDUSTRIAL PRODUCTION		*68.3*	*51.5*	*73.5*	*67.8*	*62.9*	*34.6*	*51.4*	*69.0*	*61.3*	*51.8*	*57.4*	*45.3*
CONSTRUCTION	45	1.1	0.6	1.6	0.8	0.2	0.7	0.3	0.1	0.1	0.1	1.5	0.3
TRANSPORT USE		24.1	29.3	6.0	20.5	20.3	35.4	19.5	23.1	14.8	26.1	21.4	21.5
NON-TRANSPORT SERVICES	50-52, 62, 64-99	1.2	7.6	2.0	1.6	0.1	9.3	5.7	0.8	7.1	0.0	6.0	12.4
NON-TRANSPORT RESIDENTIAL		2.3	8.9	9.0	8.5	11.0	14.8	14.8	6.3	14.4	17.0	6.6	5.7
AUTO-PRODUCERS NON-SPECIFIED		1.7	0.9	5.3	0.7	4.3	4.5	6.7	0.6	1.1	4.3	6.3	12.5
OTHER NON-SPECIFIED		1.4	1.2	2.5	0.1	1.2	0.7	1.7	0.2	1.3	0.8	0.9	2.3

INDUSTRY	NETHER-LANDS	NEW ZEALAND	NORWAY	POLAND	SPAIN	SWEDEN	UK	US	BRAZIL	INDIA	CHINA	RUSSIA	WORLD
AGRICULTURE, ETC.	5.4	2.6	6.0	4.0	2.3	2.8	0.5	0.9	5.3	0.2	2.7	1.4	1.9
MINING, EXTRACTION, REFINING	9.2	5.1	36.4	4.2	5.9	4.3	7.3	5.0	8.5	3.0	5.1	3.3	5.6
FOOD, BEVERAGES, TOBACCO	1.8	0.3	1.4	2.4	1.9	1.5	1.4	1.0	1.7	0.4	2.0	0.5	1.1
TEXTILES, LEATHER, FOOTWEAR	0.2	0.0	0.1	0.7	0.8	0.2	0.4	0.2	0.6	0.9	1.3	0.0	0.6
WOOD AND PRODUCTS OF WOOD AND CORK	0.0	0.0	0.2	0.3	0.1	0.2	0.0	0.2	0.0	0.0	0.2	0.1	0.1
PULP, PAPER PRINTING AND PUBLISHING	0.5	0.0	2.0	0.7	1.1	3.2	1.0	0.9	1.5	0.8	1.0	0.0	0.9
CHEMICALS	8.6	7.7	4.3	3.6	4.7	3.8	3.5	3.2	6.4	5.3	6.2	2.7	4.5
OTHER NON-METALLIC MINERAL	1.0	0.0	3.4	3.2	5.0	2.2	1.1	1.1	3.7	3.9	8.5	0.9	3.0
IRON AND STEEL	3.5	5.8	7.3	5.2	3.7	5.4	2.9	1.6	8.8	10.6	9.3	6.5	4.7
NON-FERROUS METALS	0.1	0.0	0.6	0.4	0.4	0.5	0.3	0.4	2.2	0.1	0.9	0.7	0.5
OTHER METAL PRODUCTS, MACHINERY EQPT	0.6	0.0	0.4	0.9	0.5	0.8	0.6	0.5	0.0	0.2	1.9	0.4	0.7
MOTOR VEHICLES, TRAINS, SHIPS PLANES	0.1	0.0	0.2	0.4	0.4	0.5	0.5	0.3	0.0	0.0	0.5	0.0	0.2
OTHER MANUFACTURING AND RECYCLING	0.2	12.6	0.1	0.0	0.6	1.1	1.6	0.2	1.9	8.2	1.0	0.4	0.4
ELECTRICITY, GAS, WATER	26.4	11.3	0.6	47.5	28.9	15.0	32.8	36.7	3.8	40.2	38.6	34.7	32.1
TOTAL INDUSTRIAL PRODUCTION	*57.7*	*45.5*	*62.7*	*73.5*	*56.2*	*41.6*	*53.9*	*52.3*	*44.4*	*73.7*	*79.1*	*51.8*	*56.2*
CONSTRUCTION	0.4	1.0	0.3	0.3	0.1	0.0	0.4	0.0	0.0	0.0	0.4	0.2	0.4
TRANSPORT USE	16.9	43.9	36.6	6.9	31.0	40.5	23.5	29.6	43.2	13.3	5.8	12.7	20.2
NON-TRANSPORT SERVICES	1.6	5.2	3.0	2.0	2.2	7.1	4.6	4.2	1.2	0.0	2.0	0.6	3.2
NON-TRANSPORT RESIDENTIAL	11.8	1.8	3.0	12.6	5.9	7.9	14.2	6.9	6.4	6.0	9.0	9.3	8.8
AUTO-PRODUCERS NON-SPECIFIED	3.2	1.5	0.8	4.3	3.1	2.0	1.4	5.8	2.6	6.3	0.7	24.2	9.7
OTHER NON-SPECIFIED	8.4	1.0	-6.3	0.5	1.6	0.8	1.9	1.3	2.3	0.6	2.9	1.1	1.1

Notes: Italy, 1992; India 1993; Greece 1994; Australia, Czech Republic, Finland, France, Germany, Japan, Korea, Netherlands, Poland, Spain, UK, 1995; Brazil 1996; Canada, Denmark, Norway, US, China: 1997; Hungary, Sweden, Russia, 1998.

Source: IEA.

Figure 2. **Direct CO_2 emissions from fossil fuel combustion in industrial production (excluding transportation emissions and emissions to produce household electricity) % of GDP, (Kg CO_2 per $US), 1995, and shares of global emissions, %**

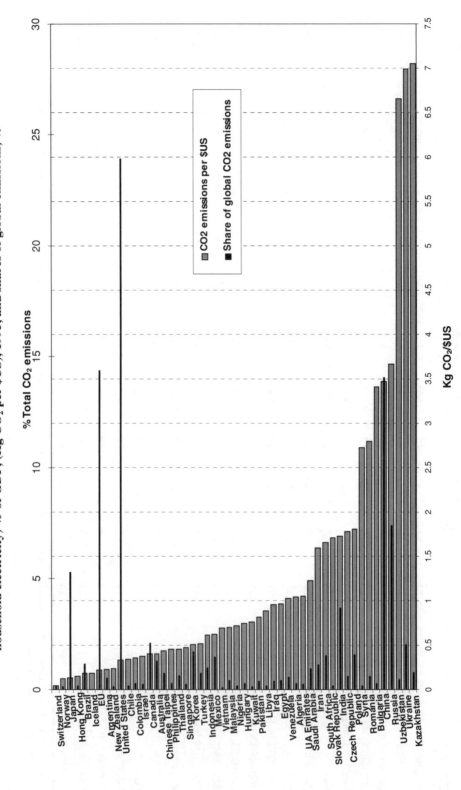

Source: IEA.

Figure 3. **Direct CO_2 emissions from fossil fuel combustion in industrial production (excluding transportation emissions and emissions to produce household electricity) % of GDP, (Kg CO_2 per $US, PPP 1995)**

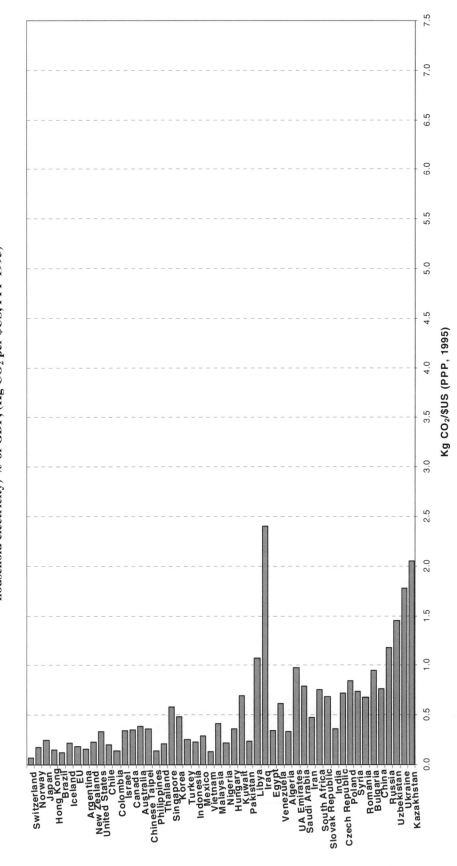

Kg CO_2/$US (PPP , 1995)

Source: IEA.

MEASURING SUSTAINABLE DEVELOPMENT: INTEGRATED ECONOMIC, ENVIRONMENTAL AND SOCIAL FRAMEWORKS – ISBN-92-64-02012-8 © OECD 2004

Methodology

Embodied emissions

The schematic below provides a very simple exposition of how changes in production patterns can impact on domestic emissions figures, without necessarily changing global emissions, and introduces the concept of "embodied " emissions. It shows a hypothetical production process required to build a motor car from start to finish, beginning with metal ore extraction, in country "*W*". Emissions generated during each process are shown, so one unit of coal and mineral ore extraction required to build one car results in "*A*" direct GHG emissions and "*A1*" other (indirect emissions), which, for ease of understanding we will assume to be emissions related only to the generation of electricity. Note that, in this example, direct GHG emissions are only generated by the extraction (*e.g.* flaring) and steel production (*e.g.* coke burning) industries. Therefore, total emissions directly generated by the five processes shown below are equal to "*A + B*", and indirect use of electricity has led to emissions of "*A1 + B1 + C1 + D1 + E1*". Total economy emissions generated directly and indirectly for one car produced in "*W*" are therefore equal to the sum of all 7 emissions.

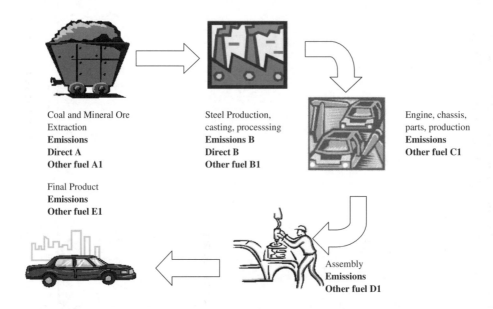

Coal and Mineral Ore
Extraction
Emissions
Direct A
Other fuel A1

Steel Production,
casting, processsing
Emissions B
Direct B
Other fuel B1

Engine, chassis,
parts, production
Emissions
Other fuel C1

Assembly
Emissions
Other fuel D1

Final Product
Emissions
Other fuel E1

Now consider what happens if coal and mineral ore extraction operations move to Country "*X*", Steel Production to Country "*Y*" and engine, chassis and parts production to Country "*Z*", with "*W*" in effect merely assembling motor cars for consumption by domestic consumers (and exports). In this scenario emissions in "*W*" fall to "*D1 + E1*" but global emissions remain unchanged (assuming the productive efficiency in each country is the same). Note too that as a result of the changes in production, emissions related to electricity generation have also fallen in "*W*".

In this way it can be seen that measure of emissions embodied in total final domestic demand in economy "*W*" (irrespective of whether emissions are directly generated in economy "*W*" "*X*" "*Ý*" or "*Z*") can serve as a complement to the more conventional measure based on direct emissions in economy "*W*". This measure is referred to as *domestic consumption* in the remainder of this paper (see Box 1 below).

Box 1. **The Kyoto Protocol**

The text of the Protocol to the UNFCCC was adopted at the third session of the Conference of the (188) Parties to the UNFCCC in Kyoto, Japan, on 11 December 1997; it was open for signature from 16 March 1998 to 15 March 1999 at United Nations Headquarters, New York. By that date the Protocol had received 84 signatures. Those Parties that have not yet signed the Kyoto Protocol may accede to it at any time and it enters into force 90 days after the date on which not less than 55 Parties to the Convention, incorporating Annex I Parties which accounted in total for at least 55% of the total carbon dioxide emissions for 1990 from that group, have deposited their instruments of ratification, acceptance, approval or accession. At present (March 2003) 106 Parties to the Convention have deposited these instruments, incorporating 43.9% of Annex I emissions in 1990, see below. "Annex I" Parties to the convention were called upon to adopt policies that would return GHG emissions to 1990 levels (with a few exceptions) by the year 2000, and in the medium term, for greenhouse gas (GHG) emissions to be reduced by at least 5% by 2008-2012 (the commitment period) compared to 1990 levels, see below.

Table Box 1. **Annex I Parties: 1990 CO_2 Emissions, Reduction Commitments, and Ratification Status**

Party	1990 CO_2 Emissions (Gg)	% of Annex I emissions in 1990	Ratification, Acceptance Accession, Approval	Reduction commitment % of base year period
Australia	288 965	2.1		108
Austria	59 200	0.4	Ratified	92 (87)
Belgium	113 405	0.8	Ratified	92 (92..5)
Bulgaria	82 990	0.6	Ratified	92
Canada	457 441	3.3	Ratified	94
Croatia				94
Czech Republic	169 514	1.2	Approval	95
Denmark	52 100	0.4	Ratified	92 (79)
Estonia	37 797	0.3	Ratified	92
Finland	53 900	0.4	Ratified	92 (100)
France	366 536	2.7	Approval	92 (100)
Germany	1 012 443	7.4	Ratified	92 (79)
Greece	82 100	0.6	Ratified	92 (125)
Hungary	71 673	0.5	Accession	94
Iceland	2 172	0.0	Accession	110
Ireland	30 719	0.2	Ratified	92 (113)
Italy	482 941	3.1	Ratified	92 (93.5)
Japan	1 173 360	8.5	Acceptance	94
Latvia	22 976	0.2	Ratified	92
Liechtenstein	208	0.0		92
Luxembourg	11 343	0.1	Ratified	92 (72)
Lithuania				
Monaco	71	0.0		92
Netherlands	167 600	1.2	Accession	92 (94)
New Zealand	25 530	0.2	Ratified	100
Norway	35 533	0.3	Ratified	101
Poland	414 930	3.0	Ratified	94
Portugal	42 148	0.3	Approval	92 (127)
Romania	171 103	1.2	Ratified	92
Russian Federation	2 388 720	17.4		100
Slovakia	58 278	0.4	Ratified	92
Slovenia			Ratified	92
Spain	260 554	1.9	Ratified	92 (115)
Sweden	61 256	0.4	Ratified	92 (104)
Switzerland	43 600	0.3		92
Ukraine				100
United Kingdom	584 078	4.3	Ratified	92 (87.5)
United States	4 957 022	36.1	(Will not be submitted for ratification)	93

Source: UNFCC. (The EU as a group are committed to an 8% reduction, the figures in parentheses are the individual national rates allocated through an EU agreement. Source EEA.)

The policy instruments encouraged by the Protocol to achieve these commitments are varied, for example: taxes on the use of fossil fuels and energy (electricity); fiscal measures encouraging the use or development of cleaner technology; protection and enhancement of GHG sinks and reservoirs; progressive reduction of market imperfection and fiscal incentives in GHG emitting sectors that run counter to the Kyoto objective; and emissions trading permits, allowing ratifying countries to sell permits if actual emissions fall below their individual targets set out in the Protocol. The Protocol also encourages the transfer of cleaner technology between countries by providing emissions credits for such transfers. Two mechanisms exist, 1) the Joint Implementation Mechanism (JIM), which gives emission credits to Annex I parties that implement emission reduction projects, or increase removals by sinks, in other Annex I countries (operative from 2008), and; 2) Clean Development Mechanisms, which are similar to JIMs but concern transfers between Annex I and non-Annex I countries (from 2000).

The principle of *domestic consumption* measures is that the total emissions related to the production of the car should be allocated to the final consumer, since they gain the utility and to some extent initiated the production process via their demand. With this measure total *domestic consumption* of GHG emissions is the same wherever production occurs. In effect the emissions directly and indirectly generated at each step of the production process are "embodied" in the product sold. Therefore one unit of coal and mineral ore, contains "*A + A1*" of embodied emissions, one unit of processed steel embodies "*A + A1 + B + B1*" of emissions and so on.

Calculating these estimates is non-trivial. At each stage of production it requires the estimation of emissions related to electricity generation, for example, to be "embodied" within each unit of output sold (in fact it requires emissions embodied in all intermediate inputs, not just energy, to be re-embodied at each stage of production). These embodied emissions subsequently need to be traced across all economies, from Country "*X*" through to "*W*".

The OECD has assembled the basics of the accounting framework needed to provide indicative estimates of these measures: Input-Output tables (representing the production process), bilateral trade data and IEA CO_2 emissions (from fossil fuel combustion) data (see Section 3). A number of assumptions are needed in conducting an analysis of this nature. Because the aim of the study is primarily to establish the importance of embodied emissions and, in particular, to determine whether they warrant specific policy measures, the emphasis will be to use assumptions that produce conservative estimates of embodied emissions, biased downwards, so as not to exaggerate the need for specific policy measures (see Section 4).

The approach is to calculate, for each country (W):

1. CO_2 emitted during the domestic production of manufactured goods and embodied within:

   a. Manufactured goods and services consumed in country (W), (and exports of services).

   b. Exports of manufactured products from country (W).

2. CO_2 emitted (by other countries) during the production of manufactured goods for export to country (W), and embodied within:

   a. Manufactured goods and services consumed in country (W) (and exports of services).

   b. Exports of manufactured products from country (W).

In this way it is possible to define the following aggregates for country (W):

- *Domestic consumption* of CO_2 emissions = (1.a) + (2.a)

- Domestic production of CO2 emissions = (1.a) + (1.b)

- Total exports of embodied emissions = (1.b) + (2.b)[14]

- *Total imports* of embodied emissions = (2.a) + (2.b)

---

14. Often referred to as re-exported emissions in the remainder of this report. This includes emissions embodied in imports that are directly (re) exported with no additional processing and emissions embodied in imports used in the process of producing exports. Note the double accounting nature of imports and exports which both include this emissions component.

- Net trade balance in embodied emissions = (1.b) – (2.a).

The Input-Output Framework

Let the production function (input-output table) at a point in time for a country be defined as *A,* with components, a_{ij} that represent the ratio of domestic inputs from industry *i* to the output of industry *j* (known as the Leontief matrix) where *n* is the number of industries, and industries 1 to k (< n) are manufacturing. Further let the import matrix (with dimension k*n) be defined as M_c, with components m_{cij} representing the ratio of manufactured imports from industry *i* in country *c* (the exporting country) to the output of domestic industry *j* at *f.o.b.* prices. Total CO_2 consumed within this economy (assuming no imports of services) can be shown to be equal to:

$$(\text{I}) \qquad E*(I-A)^{-1}D \quad +\sum_{c}^{w} {}^{m}E_c* \{M_c*(I-A)^{-1}*D +{}^{m}D_c\}$$

$$\qquad\qquad (1a) \qquad\qquad (2a)$$

Where *E* is a 1*n vector of the ratio of CO_2 emissions per monetary value of domestic output by industry with zero entries for all service industries; *D* is an n*1 vector of domestic consumption[15] of domestic production; $^{m}E_c$ is a 1*k vector of CO_2 emissions per unit of country *c* exports (converted into the importing country's currency), and known here as the export emission ratio (emission factor); and $^{m}D_c$ is an n*1 vector of imports from country *c* directly purchased as domestic final consumption (not intermediate). *W* is the total number of exporting countries.

The first term in equation (I) can be shown to be equivalent to (1a) above, (domestic emissions consumed domestically), and the second term can be shown to be equivalent to (2a) above, (imported embodied emissions in manufactured products consumed domestically).

One important point to note is that $^{m}E_c$ includes both domestically produced and imported emissions. The "j"th component of which can be shown to be equal to:

$$(\text{II})_d \qquad\qquad {}^{m}E_{cj} = \; z_j/(Exp_{jj} + \sum^{w} {}^{m}Exp_{djj})$$

$$(\text{III})_d \qquad Z =[E*(I-A)-1Exp \; + \; \sum^{w} mEd*\{Md*(I-A)-1*Exp +mExpd\}]$$

$$\qquad\qquad (1b) \qquad\qquad (2b)$$

Where *Exp* is a n*k matrix with components exp_{ij}, where exp_{ii} = exports by domestic industry *i* in country c, and all other entries are zero, and $^{m}Exp_d$ is an k*k matrix, where exp_{dii} exports of imports from country d by country c of product *i* and all other entries are zero; (For most countries all entries of $^{m}Exp_d$ are zero).

The first term in equation (III) can be shown to be equivalent to (1b) above, (domestic emissions embodied within manufactured exports) and the second term to be equivalent to (2b), (imported emissions embodied within manufactured exports). It should be evident from equations (II) and (III) that the export emission ratio $^{m}E_c$, involves an iterative

---

15. "Domestic consumption" includes household and general government final consumption, investment including changes in inventories, and exports of services but not exports of manufactured products (ISIC 1-40).

process, since it is a function of the export emission ratios in other countries, which are in turn dependent on ^mE_c. In this study this iterative process was started by setting (2b) above in equation (III) to zero.[16]

Data

Three datasets are available for this study: input-output tables, international trade flows in manufactured products, and estimates of CO_2 emissions from fuel combustion by industry and country. Estimates of CO_2 emissions from fuel combustion, embedded within the imports and exports of manufactured goods, agricultural products, mining and quarrying and electricity, are calculated for each country. In this way it is possible to show CO_2 emissions' generated by total final domestic demand (households, government, investment, inventory changes), *domestic consumption* of embodied emissions, as a complement to the more conventional measures based on *domestic production.*

A number of studies have attempted to investigate CO_2 emissions using this approach,[17] most however assume that imported goods are produced in other countries using the same production processes as goods produced domestically. But, at least, for developed economies, this approach is likely to underestimate the significance of trade on global emissions embodied in traded goods. This mainly reflects the fact that goods made in developing economies are likely to be more carbon-intensive than the same goods made in developed economies. This study plans to overcome any bias by taking technical coefficients from input-output tables (to reflect production processes) in 24 economies (see below) representing over 80% of world GDP (source World Bank, 2001 data) and CO_2 emissions from fuel combustion (source IEA).

Input-Output Tables

Input-Output tables for 24 countries are available for use in this study: Australia 1994/95; Brazil 1996, Canada 1997; China 1997, Czech Republic 1995; Denmark 1997; France 1995; Finland 1995; Germany 1995; Greece 1994; Hungary 1998; India 1993, Italy 1992; Japan 1995 and 1997; Korea 1995; Netherlands 1995 and 1997; New Zealand 1995/96, Norway 1997; Poland 1995; Russia 1998, Spain 1995; Sweden 1998; UK 1995; and US 1997. All Tables are produced on an ISIC Revision 3 basis.

Most of these tables have been produced by the OECD Secretariat, largely by converting existing country supply and use tables, and are under continued development. This transformation process uses varying degrees of assumption depending on the country, and the aim is to reduce the scale of these assumptions, as more data becomes available.[18]

The OECD input-output tables are produced on a 41 industry-by-industry basis but for the purposes of this analysis they have been collapsed to a 17-industry basis,

---

16. It is interesting to note that the same results could be achieved by defining an input-output table with dimension (n*w) by (n*w), where w is the number of separate countries (or regions) defined in the system, and where sales of services across countries (imports of services) are set to zero.

17. Indeed some environmental measures already incorporate this principal, for example the "ecological footprint" and the Montreal Protocol on Substances that deplete the Ozone Layer (see, *http://www.unep.org/ozone/montreal.shtml*).

18. *The OECD Input-Output database,* paper presented to 14th International Conference on IO Techniques – Montreal, October, 2002

described in Table 3 below. Because the industry classification for those industries where significant direct emissions occur (electricity, metals, chemicals) is the same in both the 17 and 41 industry classification the sensitivity of thc results to the level of aggregation is not expected to be significant, although this will be tested.

Table 3. **Industry Classification**

Industry	ISIC Revision 3 Industries
AGRICULTURE, HUNTING, FORESTRY AND FISHING	01-05
MINING AND QUARRYING AND PETROLEUM REFINING	10-14, 23
FOOD PRODUCTS, BEVERAGES AND TOBACCO	15-16
TEXTILES, APPAREL AND LEATHER	17-19
WOOD AND WOOD PRODUCTS	20
PULP, PAPER, PRINTING AND PUBLISHING	21-22
CHEMICALS	24
OTHER NON-METALLIC MINERAL PRODUCTS	26
IRON AND STEEL	271 2731
NON-FERROUS METALS	272 2732
FABRICATED METAL PRODUCTS, MACHINERY AND EQPT	28-32
MOTOR VEHICLES, TRAINS, SHIPS PLANES	34, 35
PLASTICS, OTHER MANUFACTURING AND RECYCLING	25, 33, 36-37
ELECTRICITY, GAS	40
CONSTRUCTION	45
TRANSPORT AND STORAGE	60-62
ALL OTHER SERVICES	41, 50-99, ex 60-62

IEA CO_2 emissions

The classification of industries shown above is based on the industry classification used in the International Energy Agency's database, where CO_2[19] emissions by each industry group are available. The estimates of CO_2 emissions from fuel combustion are calculated using the IEA energy balances together with default methods and emission factors from *Revised IPCC Guidelines for National Greenhouse Gas Inventories,* using the IPCC Tier 1 Sectoral Approach. For the purposes of this study a number of points should be noted:

- IEA estimates of CO_2 emissions from fuel combustion and countries own estimates may differ, although in general these are not significant. This mainly reflects the fact that countries may have more detailed information on emissions from fuel combustion than is available at the IEA. For example the IEA uses an average net calorific value (NCV) for coal, whereas countries may have specific NCVs for production, imports, exports etc. Equally IEA estimates include emissions from coke inputs into blast furnaces,[20] whereas countries may have included these emissions in the IPCC Industrial Process category, and not the Fuel combustion category used here. IEA fuel data comes directly from IEA Member Countries.

---

19. Further information can be found at *www.IEA.org*. See also IEA's annual publication "CO_2 Emissions from Fuel combustion".

20. In the reduction of iron in a blast furnace through the combustion of coke, the primary purpose of coke oxidation is to produce pig iron and the emissions can be considered as in industrial process, as is the practice in some countries, these emissions are included in fuel combustion emissions in the IEA statistics.

- One industrial sector of IEA data warrants specific mention, *Unallocated Auto-producers*. This sector includes emissions from producers that generate their own electricity or heat, wholly or partly, for their own use as an activity that supports their primary activity. Ideally these emissions should be allocated to the actual ISIC industry where the producers are classified but it difficult to achieve. That said these emissions are not particularly significant in the context of the estimates presented above for most countries (see Table 2). For example, in the US, emissions from *Unallocated Auto-producers* made up about 5% of total emissions in 1997. As manufactured exports make up about 6% of total final demand (of domestic products) in the US, most of the emissions from *auto-producers* can be expected to be embodied within products consumed domestically. Although much depends on which industries are actually responsible for the emissions. The significance of this will be tested in the planned analysis. That said the default position will be to exclude these emissions from the main analysis and thus emissions embodied in imports and exports will be correspondingly lower, ensuring that the general theme of producing conservative estimates will be maintained. For some countries however the size of *auto-producers* is significant, in particular Russia.

- IEA data does not specify which industries have been responsible for transportation emissions; since the emissions data is calculated on the basis of the carbon content of petrel/diesel designated for transport use, supplied into an economy, not by user. Indeed the total figure for emissions related to transportation includes households and not just industries. It is possible to estimate the emissions in each sector by applying carbon coefficients to their purchases of petrol. However this may introduce systematic biases in the results based on the geographical size of countries. The bias comes about because estimates of the value of transportation within imports (which are measured on c.i.f.[21] basis) are not available. If, for any product, emissions from fuel-used in domestic transportation were embodied, but estimates from foreign transportation were not, an inconsistency and potential bias would be introduced. For example it would mean that fuel used in transporting a good from the East-Coast to the West-Coast of the US would be embodied within the good but fuel used in transporting the same good from Spain, say, to the West-Coast would not, and so emissions embodied in US produced goods would appear to be higher, even if the production process in the US was the same as that in Spain. It is possible however to provide illustrative estimates of these embodied emissions, using stylised assumptions which attempt to overcome this bias, and these will be investigated.

- IEA emissions data covers only CO_2 emissions from fossil fuel combustion, responsible for about three-quarters of anthropogenic GHG emissions. Other GHGs might be important for some industries (*e.g.* aluminium production emits PFCs) but these will not be considered in this study.

Bilateral Trade

The OECD Bilateral Trade database[22] shows imports into and exports from 41 countries/regions,[23] by producing country and destination country, for all 2-digit

---

21. C.I.F (cost, insurance, freight) prices show the value of imports at the importing country's frontier, including the insurance and freight charges incurred between the exporter's frontier and that of the importer.

22. *Source:* OECD Bilateral Trade database, Science Technology and Industry Directorate.

products within ISIC 01-40. The countries/regions covered are: All OECD countries, Argentina, Brazil, China, Hong Kong, India, Indonesia, Malaysia, Philippines; Singapore, Thailand, Taiwan, and the Rest of the World (ROW).

There are some data quality issues concerning the bilateral trade database. The first relates to the fact that imports by country A from country B are not always consistent with exports from country B to country A. This is partly because exports are on an f.o.b.[24] basis whereas imports are recorded c.i.f. (this study assumes that 10% of the import value reflects transportation and insurance costs) but other factors play a part too. For example a lot of trade from China goes through Hong Kong, and Chinese data may record this trade as exports to Hong Kong, whereas reporting-importing countries may record the goods as having come from China, not Hong Kong. Equally the bilateral trade data is not always consistent with the equivalent country totals shown in the corresponding input-output tables.

Ideally CO_2 emissions embodied in imports of *services* would also be recorded in the estimates of embodied emissions. The lack of bilateral trade data in services makes it difficult to do this, however, and so, the analysis will focus on emissions embodied in goods. The input-output tables do however contain estimates of trade in services, and so provide a possible starting point for estimating embodied emissions in international trade in services, assuming an internationally common emissions factor for services can be derived or estimated. However in adopting this approach it is important to have estimates of imports by product on an f.o.b. basis; which is rarely the case. Not accommodating for c.i.f./f.o.b. differences is a common error in much of the literature on this subject and is likely to contribute to the general pattern of low total CO_2 emissions embodied in imports, relative to total CO_2 embodied in exports, often recorded in these analyses, since exports of transport services usually have relatively high emissions factors.

Assumptions

The section that follows focuses primarily on the assumptions required to develop the data sources needed in this study. It does not focus on the conventional IO assumptions. One IO assumption that is worth mentioning here however concerns differential pricing, namely that the analysis assumes that goods produced in any country are sold for the same price in the domestic market as abroad and that domestic consumers, whether industries or households, pay the same price for all goods produced domestically. In some key industries, such as electricity, this is rarely the case. Households tend to pay more per KWh of electricity than industries, and this means that estimates of emission factors for manufactured goods are likely to be lower than they would be if it were possible to correct for differential pricing in electricity, as are estimates of emissions embodied in imports and exports.

As stated earlier, the key aim of this study is to establish the significance of emissions embodied in imports and exports and whether it is large enough to warrant policy scrutiny. In this regard it is important to establish that this is so unconditionally. Meaning that, as far as is possible, establishing that the emissions do warrant policy action is not dependent on the nature of assumptions used. As such where assumptions are necessary

---

23. Bilateral trade between non-member countries is not covered however, for example Brazil's exports to Argentina are not shown in the database.

24. F.O.B (free-on-board) prices are valued at the exporter's frontier value.

they will tend to lead to estimates of embodied emissions that are biased downwards. In most cases variant estimates, based on less conservative assumptions, can also be produced to illustrate the sensitivity of the estimates to the assumptions used and thus the conservative nature of the central results.

CO_2 emissions from industrial production only

Because bilateral trade data is only presently available for goods and electricity (ISIC 01-40), the main focus of the study will be on CO_2 emissions used by the industrial production sector (agriculture, mining and quarrying, manufacturing and electricity generation), embodied in imports and exports of goods, and not emissions related to fuel-use for transportation and direct emissions by the service sector, although indicative estimates of these emissions are planned. This means that the estimates presented for imports and exports of embodied emissions will be biased downwards.

Estimating Emission Factors in countries where IO data is not available

For those countries/regions where input-output tables are not available, export emissions' ratios (^mE_c in equation (I) above), will be estimated on the basis of the emissions ratios of countries that are believed to have similar emissions profiles and production processes, except for electricity generation and oil and gas extraction in OPEC countries, (see below). These assumptions are shown below, listing the country where IO data is not available first, followed by its "proxy" country in parentheses and italics.

> Austria – (*emission factors proxied by Germany*); Belgium – (*Netherlands*); Iceland – (*Denmark*); Ireland – (*UK*); Mexico – (*US*); Portugal – (*Spain*); Slovakia – (*Czech Republic*); Switzerland – (*Germany*); Turkey – (*Greece*); Argentina – (*Brazil*); Hong-Kong, Indonesia, Malaysia, Philippines, Singapore, Taiwan, OPEC countries (excluding oil) – (*Korea*); Rest of the World – (US).

Adjusting for differences in electricity generation

In most countries electricity generation is responsible for most CO_2 emissions (Table 2). Moreover the carbon-intensity of electricity generation differs significantly across countries, (Table 4). Because of the significance of electricity emissions and the variance in the carbon-intensity of electricity generation across countries, it is proposed that emission ratios in each country where IO tables are not available will need to be adjusted to reflect known differences in the carbon-intensity of electricity generation. The adjustment is best described by an example. Electricity produced in Germany for example produces nearly 3 times as much CO_2 emissions per KWh of electricity than in Austria. To estimate Austrian emission factors therefore it will be assumed that the production process of each industry in Austria is the same as that in Germany, except that electricity is 3 times less carbon intensive. So, for given unit of Austrian manufactured output, embodied emissions that reflect electricity inputs are three times lower than in Germany. In other words, in equation (I) above, the component for Austrian electricity in vector "E" is one third that of Germany's. All other components of the equation remain the same as their German equivalents.

Table 4. **Electricity emissions (direct)**

Country	Australia	Canada	Czech Rep.	Denmark	Finland	France	Germany	Greece
Mt CO_2 Emissions per TWH	0.75	0.17	0.48	0.42	0.22	0.04	0.43	0.86
Electricity Direct Emissions % of Total Domestic Emissions	*46*	*21*	*42*	*54*	*36*	*5*	*32*	*50*
Country	Hungary	Italy	Japan	Korea	Netherlands	New Zealand	Norway	Poland
CO_2 Emissions per TWH	0.39	0.45	0.32	0.39	0.46	0.08	0.00	0.61
Electricity Direct Emissions % of Total Domestic Emissions	*41*	*26*	*29*	*21*	*26*	*11*	*1*	*48*
Country	Spain	Sweden	UK	US	Brazil	China	India	Russia
CO_2 Emissions per TWH	0.41	0.04	0.50	0.52	0.03	0.75	0.90	0.18
Electricity Direct Emissions % of Total Domestic Emissions	*29*	*15*	*33*	*37*	*4*	*39*	*40*	*34*

Source: IEA.

Gas and Oil – Extraction and Refining

Emission factors for oil and gas extraction for OPEC countries will be separately estimated by taking IEA estimates of direct emissions by the "crude/refined oil and gas" sector in each OPEC country and dividing these figures by the $US value of crude/refined oil and gas output in each country. An average OPEC value can be calculated by weighting emissions by output in each OPEC country.

Although these assumptions are likely to introduce a potential source of error, most trade within the 24 countries studied is conducted within the 24 countries where there is IO data, limiting the extent of errors from this source, see Table 5 below, although because emission factors are likely to differ significantly across countries (Figures 2 and 3), changes in the assumptions might impact significantly on estimates of embodied emissions. This is mitigated however by the fact that the assumptions chosen are deliberately conservative, (*e.g.* using US emission factors as proxies for ROW countries), although it is planned to test the sensitivity of the results to these assumptions by varying the proxy country chosen.

Table 5. **Imports from input-output countries – % of total imports**

Country	Australia	Canada	Czech Rep.	Denmark	Finland	France	Germany	Greece
Imports from (24) IO countries %	78	90	55	83	84	74	69	80
Country	Hungary	Italy	Japan	Korea	Netherlands	New Zealand	Norway	Poland
Imports from (24) IO countries %	74	74	72	80	71	83	84	80
Country	Spain	Sweden	UK	US	Brazil	China	India	Russia
Imports from (24) IO countries %	78	83	72	66	54	67	49	66

As the coverage of the IO database expands so to will the ratios in Table 4 rise. In this context the inclusion of IO tables for high trade, high emission non-member OECD countries, such as Singapore, Malaysia, Indonesia, and Chinese Taipei is as important as the inclusion of other OECD Member countries, such as Mexico, although the importance of each country varies according to the importing country, Mexico for example is very important for the US statistics as are Asian economies to Japan.

Coherence between IEA emissions data and Input-Output tables

The analysis will assume coherence in industrial classifications. Both the IEA data and Input-Output data are based on ISIC rev 3 classifications but it is difficult to ensure, without further investigation, that establishments in both data sets have been allocated consistently.

Bilateral Trade Data – Allocation of imports to industries

Bilateral trade data cannot identify which domestic industries are responsible for imports. This can be estimated using import proportions in the input-output framework for each country. So for example, for country A, if industry A1 imports 10% of total economy imports of product Y, (40% of which comes from country B and 60% from country C), the model assumes that 4% of Y from country B and 6% of Y from country C are imported by industry A1.

Differences in IO years

Because not all input-output tables cover the same year, estimates of emissions embodied in exports from country A to country B in year t, will need to be converted to emissions embodied in imports into country B from country A by assuming that the emission ratio is constant for given volume of output for each product over time. It is planned to use US output price indices at the 41 IO industry level to deflate exports and imports into the appropriate year's prices, adjusted for movements in exchange rates. It is not known whether this will adversely affect the results without further investigation but it seems unlikely that it will; since most IO tables cover the period 95-97 (the smaller the period of time the less likely the change in deflators), and because, for most countries, most trade occurs with countries that have IO tables in the same year. For example the US tables are for 1997, and IO tables with most key trading partners are also available in this year: Canada, China, Japan, as well as Denmark, Netherlands, Norway.

Further applications

Time Series data

In theory it is possible to extend the method used in this section to calculate a time series of *domestic consumption*. The key assumption in applying input-output analysis to *time series* data is that the technology in use and relative prices (hence IO coefficients) remain constant over time. For short periods of time this is not an unreasonable assumption, and where only one year is analysed (the same year as the input-output table) it is not necessary at all (and this is largely the case for the proposed analysis set out in Section 2). For longer periods of time however the assumption becomes increasingly weak; particularly if the period of time covers unusual economic events; such as significant changes in relative prices (*e.g.* oil price shocks); new technology development and adoption etc, and/or unusual political events *e.g.* the move from centrally planned to market economies.

Different countries are likely to be affected to varying degrees by these events/processes but it seems likely that economies in transition and economies in the process of industrialisation are likely to have experienced significant changes in their production functions over the last decade. In this context it seems highly likely that production methods as reflected in IO tables for China, Russia, India, Hungary, Poland, and the Czech Republic have changed considerably over the 1990s. Considerable changes have also occurred in developed economies, for example Denmark's increasing use of renewable energy sources for electricity, or the UK's switch from coal to gas powered generation.

Nevertheless over a relatively short period of time it may be useful to estimate and investigate outcomes on a "business as usual" assumption, assuming stability in IO coefficients. This would provide tentative indications of trends over time provided production processes remain largely unchanged.

Decomposing emission factors using own emission factors

The methodology described above will result in emissions factors that reflect not only the relative carbon intensity of production processes within countries but also the relative importance of trade more generally. For example, imports make up a relatively small proportion of US GDP and so, ceteris paribus, emissions embodied in imports, as a proportion of total domestic emissions, are also likely to be small compared to other countries. One way of isolating the importance of trade from differences in production processes is to estimate the size of embodied emissions in imports if the emission factors for imports are assumed to be the same as those used domestically.

Most studies conducted in this area tend to adopt this approach. Although, as stated earlier, this is likely to underestimate embodied emissions for developed economies. Nevertheless taken together with the approach outlined above estimates based on own-emission factors help to illustrate two points: (1) The importance of trade generally, and in particular whether exported goods are more CO_2-intensive than imports and (2) The importance of the origin of imports. A comparison of estimates produced using both approaches will provide an insight into how carbon-intensive production processes are in each country relative to the average "international intensity"[25] for that country.

As such it will be possible to disentangle some of the factors that underpin estimates of emissions embodied in imports and exports. For example if a country with a (monetary) trade surplus imported the same mix of products as it exported, (and for any given product the emission factor was the same for goods imported and exported), emissions embodied in exports would be higher than emissions embodied in imports;

---

25. The phrase "international *intensity*' is used to describe the average emission factor for total imported goods in any country. This measure will differ for each country since it reflects the mix of products imported by trading partner; which will be different in each country. In essence (for the importing country) this boils down to comparing emissions embodied in imports using the importing country's emission factors and emissions embodied in imports using actual emission factors in each exporting country. If the former is higher this indicates a more carbon intensive production process than the "international' average. An alternative approach to determine this is to examine emissions embodied in exports using both approaches (a different weighting mechanism). Using this method Australia, Canada, and Greece have emission factors close to their "international' average.

entirely reflecting the (monetary) trade surplus. Therefore for any country with a (monetary) trade deficit but with a surplus in embodied emissions (higher emissions embodied in exports than imports), it follows that the mix of exported goods must be more carbon-intensive than the mix of imported goods. On the other hand countries with (monetary) trade surpluses but deficits in embodied emissions must import more carbon-intensive products than they export.

Moreover by comparing estimates of emissions embodied in imports using own-emission factors with estimates of emissions embodied in imports using estimated actual emission factors it will be possible to determine whether the domestic production process is more carbon-intensive than the average "international intensity".

Concluding comments

Emissions in non-Annex I economies are significant and growing at a faster rate than emissions in Annex I economies. Concurrent with this is the decline in the relative size of the manufacturing base in developed economies and a growing dependence in these economies on goods produced in non Annex I economies. The method proposed in this paper is designed to reveal the significance of CO_2 emissions in embodied in imported manufactured goods in OECD economies, providing estimates of emissions based on *domestic consumption* that can be used to complement the *domestic production* measures adopted in the Kyoto Protocol.

The role of Chinese exports in this analysis, (and to a lesser but still significant extent) Russia, may prove significant. For example, trade between China and the OECD, in particular, has increased rapidly over the last ten years (and looks set to continue), if this trend continues, the emissions embodied in imports by the OECD may become significant, if they are not already so. On the other hand any growth in embodied emissions through increased imports could be offset by reductions coming through from technological advances in the production processes in these countries. The large difference in carbon-intensities of non-OECD and OECD economies (Figures 2 and 3) suggest that the scope for reductions through Clean Development and Joint Development Mechanisms is considerable.

It is difficult to predict how embodied emissions in OECD trade are likely to change in the future but it seems more likely than not, that domestic policies predicated on reducing production by domestic industries will exacerbate the growth in imported emissions, since they (inadvertently) provide an incentive to companies to outsource CO_2 intensive production processes to countries with less restrictive GHG reduction regimes, because of competitive forces. If this is done in tandem with a transfer of more efficient production processes, then the impact on global CO_2 emissions may still be downwards but if imports merely displace domestic production the outcome will possibly be different.

Embodied emissions and the importance of international trade in this context are of course not new developments and it is possible that, were the data readily available, and of high quality, emissions' indicators based on consumption may also have been included in the Kyoto Protocol. The fact that they were not probably reflects, in part, the difficulty involved in estimating them, as well as the fact that polices aimed at reducing domestic production of GHGs are more easily effected. The accounting framework illustrated here can be used to complement the Kyoto Protocol and statistical measures giving policy makers an+ insight into the impact of *domestic consumption* on global emissions, as well as providing a vehicle that will facilitate an assessment of the reasons for changes in emissions in any country; for example distinguishing between changes in emissions that occur because of improved (less carbon-intensive) production processes and changes that occur because of increases in imports that displace domestic production.

The analysis described in this paper has already begun and we anticipate that results from this work will be available in the summer of 2003.

Results from the Norwegian Environmental and Economic Accounts and Issues Arising from Comparisons to Other Nordic NAMEA – Air Emission Systems

Julie Hass

Statistics Norway

Abstract

A brief introduction of hybrid accounts (NAMEA), highlighting some of the challenges in developing these accounts, provides background information for the more detailed analysis work presented in the paper. Specific Norwegian uses of the hybrid accounts data for the development of national- and industry-level time series with decoupling and emission intensity indicators are presented. When possible, the factors influencing the developments are identified including the effects of policy. In general, the indicators show that the Norwegian economy is showing weak decoupling and decreasing emission intensities connected to most types of air emissions, however, certain industries are not making progress in these directions. Decomposition analyses show that it is often technology advancements that result in major improvements in industries as well as increases in energy efficiency, but other factors are also important. The time series data also provide evidence that the long-term policy focus for reducing acidification air emissions is reducing these types of emissions. Examples from a Nordic comparison of NAMEA-air data show some of the strengths and weaknesses of hybrid accounts when making international comparisons. One conclusion from the Nordic comparisons was that nationally consistent data are not necessarily internationally consistent because the current national NAMEA-systems are not yet fully harmonized. The Norwegian experience shows that using hybrid environmental and economic accounts (NAMEA) provides consistent, coordinated data and results in more reliable indicators and a more solid foundation for analyses.

Introduction

There are basically two major approaches to combining economic and environmental information. One approach is to convert one type of information into the units of the other in order to allow the information to be combined or added together. The other approach is to keep the different types of information in their original units and link the two data sets together.

The first approach is primarily used when a valuation is calculated for environmental assets or degradation. There are a variety of valuation methods and approaches that are used in these conversion processes. This approach, however, can be sensitive to the estimation methods used (such as the choice of discount rates etc.) and often the criticisms to these conversion approaches can block the regular incorporation of these estimates into environmental and economic statistical systems.

On the other hand, if the environmental data and the economic data are kept in their original units and the two data sets are then linked together, this approach has been successfully incorporated into regular statistical production in a number of countries, for example the Netherlands, Austria and Norway, to name a few. However, the two data sets need to be coordinated and use the same definitions before they can be combined. This can be easier said than done.

Often environmental statistics use a geographic definition whereas, economic statistics use industry categories and an economic definition. Another difference between the two systems can be the definition of a country. For the national accounts, the residence principle is a major criteria for determining which economic activity will be included. However, for air emissions, the definition is often based more on a geographic definition of the country. The differences can be substantial for a country like Norway that has a large ocean transport industry. This industry is included in the economic activity but is excluded from the official national air emissions for reporting to the Kyoto Protocol (although these data are included as supplementary information). Developing industry-based data that uses the same definitions and groupings as the national accounts is the key to developing hybrid accounts.[1]

Hybrid accounts (NAMEA: National Accounting Matrix including Environmental Accounts)

When combining environmental and economic information into hybrid accounts there is, in general, no attempt to convert physical units into monetary units, or *vice versa*, which means that these accounts largely avoid the problems associated with placing a monetary value on the environment but the accounts are flexible enough to include valuation information if this is considered desirable and asset accounts are included in the hybrid accounts. For example, the Netherlands include valuations of their oil and natural gas resources in their NAMEA matrices and Finland includes valuations of their forest and peat resources. Keuning (1996) describes the most important difference between the NAMEA-approach and the SEEA[2] as being the starting points. The NAMEA starts from an expansion of the national accounts substance accounts (input-output tables) whereas the SEEA focuses on an expansion of the standard asset accounts with accounts for non-produced natural assets.

There is a wealth of statistics covering the environment and the economy but it can be a challenge to integrate these sets of information. Often classifications and definitions do not match, so constructing an overall information system for monitoring and analyzing environment and economic trends is important. The NAMEA system is one approach to developing this type of information system. Keuning (1997) advocates the use of the basic principles of the national accounts to a wider range of statistics and in particular with environmental statistics. The system can function as a monitoring tool but also as an analysis framework. Keuning also suggests that analyses based on NAMEA-based information can yield projections and simulations for attributes that have not yet been incorporated into econometric models but have been included in the accounting system.

---

1. Hybrid accounts are also known as NAMEAs which stands for National Accounting Matrix including Environmental Accounts. This terminology was originally coined in the Netherlands. "NAMEA" and "hybrid accounts" are used interchangeably in this paper.

2. SEEA is the abbreviation for System of Economic and Environmental Accounts.

A description of the Dutch NAMEA and about the method for developing this approach can be found in de Haan and Keuning (1996), Keuning, van Dalen and de Haan (1999) and Keuning and de Haan (1998). The accounting system developed by the Dutch is a symmetric social accounting matrix system in which there are the same number of columns and rows and there is a balancing item included in the system to balance the differences in the column and row totals.

The Nordic NAMEAs on the other hand start with the symmetric input-output tables from the national accounts and extend these to include primarily environmental and employment data, resulting in a rectangular shaped system (Hellsten, Ribacke and Wickbom 1999, Hass and Sørensen 1998, Jensen and Pedersen 1998). This differs from the Dutch NAMEA system that is symmetrical or square in shape. The Dutch system is a full social accounting matrix with balancing entries whereas the Nordic approaches only enter detailed emissions across the rows. The Nordic approaches are slightly different from the system in the Netherlands but the most important features of the accounting system are included.

Countries outside the Nordic region have also developed these types of NAMEA environmental accounting systems. See for example, Japan (Ike 1999), United Kingdom (Vaze and Balchin 1996, Vaze 1999) and for a summary of other EU-15 countries plus Norway that have NAMEA systems (Eurostat 1999, 2001).

Norwegian NAMEA

Figure 1 is a schematic of the Norwegian NAMEA matrix. The shaded areas show where there are entries in the matrix. The row "Production according to industry" and the column "Intermediate consumption according to industry" can be shown for approximately 65 different NACE categories. The inner upper left-hand box is the national accounts supply and use table. The column totals and row totals for this area of the accounting system will be equal. This principal is illustrated in the figure by showing the row and column totals by the same letter.

The physical environment and employment data is then added by extending the national accounts supply and use matrix to the right and bottom. In the Norwegian NAMEA system there are eighteen different types of air emissions included in column 9, "Air emission types," and three environmental themes are included in row and column 10, "Environmental themes." The three environmental themes are the greenhouse gases theme, the acidification theme and the tropospheric ozone precursors theme. Combining certain emission types together leads to the calculation of these themes (or indices). See the appendix for the calculation formulae for these themes.

The row and column totals for the emissions data also need to be equal (shown in the figure by "L" and "M"). Areas "J" and "K" are where the emissions data are found according to the NACE industry groups. The data for this analysis have been taken from these areas in the Norwegian NAMEA matrix. The employment and energy data are found in area "N" where this information is also listed according to industry (NACE) groups. Since the row and column totals need to be equal, this provides a check whether the information included in the accounting system is correctly entered. The row and column totals are only additive if the units are the same; in other words, it is not valid to add entries in the economic section together with the entries in the environment section.

Figure 1. **Schematic of Norwegian NAMEA-matrix**

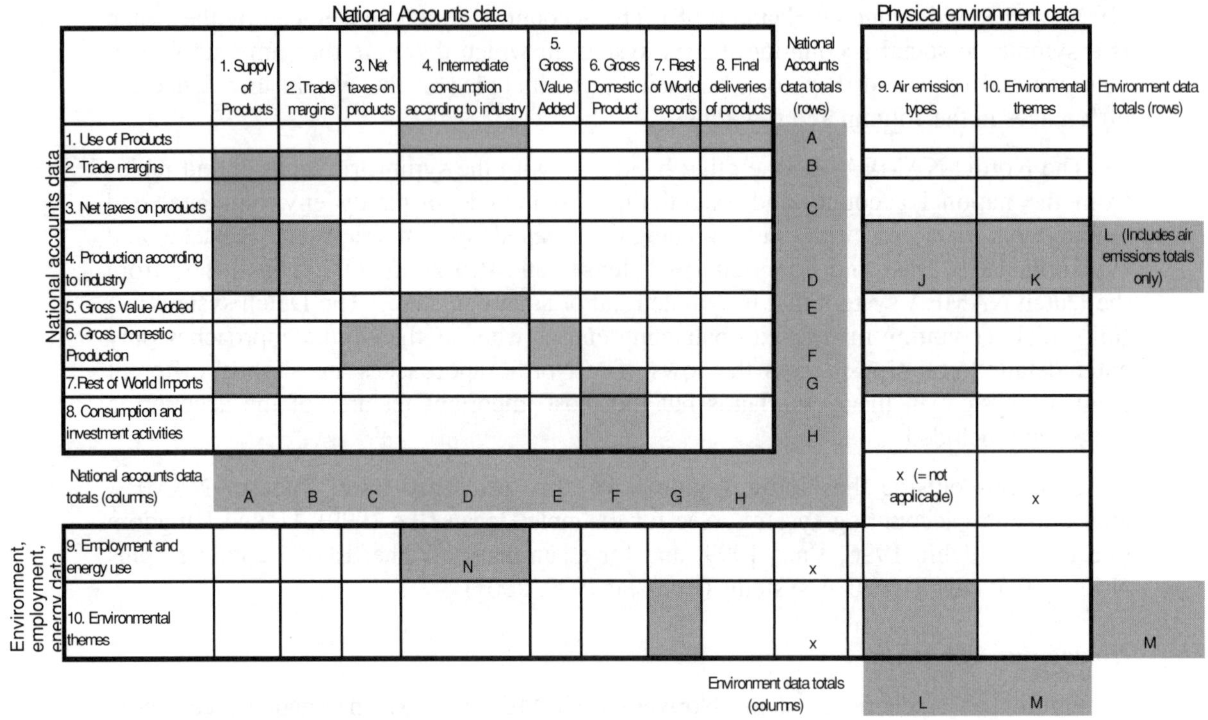

| | National Accounts data | | | | | | | | | Physical environment data | | |
	1. Supply of Products	2. Trade margins	3. Net taxes on products	4. Intermediate consumption according to industry	5. Gross Value Added	6. Gross Domestic Product	7. Rest of World exports	8. Final deliveries of products	National Accounts data totals (rows)	9. Air emission types	10. Environmental themes	Environment data totals (rows)
1. Use of Products									A			
2. Trade margins									B			
3. Net taxes on products									C			
4. Production according to industry									D	J	K	L. (Includes air emissions totals only)
5. Gross Value Added									E			
6. Gross Domestic Production									F			
7. Rest of World Imports									G			
8. Consumption and investment activities									H			
National accounts data totals (columns)	A	B	C	D	E	F	G	H		x (= not applicable)	x	
9. Employment and energy use				N					x			
10. Environmental themes									x			M
Environment data totals (columns)										L	M	

Source: Hass and Skaborg 2000 (adapted originally from Hass and Sørensen 1998).

In this matrix, the emissions from other countries that are deposited within the national borders and the acidification emissions that are transported outside the borders are included under the export and import row and column 7. Because these transboundary data are included, the national totals for the various air emissions could not be taken directly from the matrix system. National totals needed to be re-calculated excluding the import/export data.

The Norwegian NAMEA system includes emissions occurring from ocean transport in row 4, "Production according to industry" (area "J"). When this area is expanded to show all of the 65 NACE groups, ocean transport is found under NACE 61.101 Ocean Transport. It could be argued that these emissions should be shown as exports or outside of the industry section of the matrix since these emissions are not occurring within the national borders. Emissions from international shipping are not included in the EMEP transboundary calculations which are used for import and export estimates of acidification emissions. Denmark (Jensen and Pedersen 1998) shows emissions from international shipping in a separate row that is not part of the industry section of the matrix. There are a number of important issues arising when trying to decide where to include various types of emissions in the NAMEA system and these issues can be important when attempting international comparisons.

The NAMEA system is very flexible and can be adapted to include a variety of environment-related data. Appropriate additional columns and rows are simply added to the matrix to accommodate the new information. Solid waste, energy use, new types of air emissions, water use, land use and environmental protection expenditure are all areas under development in different countries for inclusion in their respective hybrid accounts (see Sørensen, *et al.* (2001) for the latest developments in the Norwegian NAMEA system). In the next section the Norwegian NAMEA-data will be presented, highlighting in particular the different uses of the data in trend analysis and policy evaluation whenever possible.

Norwegian hybrid accounts (NAMEA) for 1990-2001

Results from the Norwegian hybrid accounts show that certain economic activities have a large influence on the economic and environmental trends. Having a time series of data broken down according to industries allows trend changes to be observed as well as the results of some government policies. In this section, the economic, air emission and greenhouse gas intensity trends for Norway as a whole and for selected significant portions of the economy will be briefly presented and discussed.

Economic, air emission and greenhouse gas intensity trends for Norway

Figure 2 shows the economic, air emission and greenhouse gas intensity trends for Norwegian activity (defined in accordance to the residence principle as used in the national accounts). The growth rates for the period 1990-2001* (the data for 2001 are preliminary) for total value added for Norway is higher than the growth rates for all of the different types of air emissions. A pronounced difference is seen with respect to emissions of acidification precursors (NO_x, NH_3, SO_2) which have declined 8% while total value added has increased 46%. The largest change in any of the 18 air emission components included in the Norwegian NAMEA is seen for lead emissions which were reduced by 96% over this same time period.

The emissions profile for Norway is heavily influenced by ocean transport. On average over the 11-year period, ocean transport contributes 19% of greenhouse gas emissions (in CO_2-equivalents), 51% of acidification emissions (in Potential Acid Equivalents) and 31% of tropospheric ozone precursors (in Tropospheric Ozone Forming Potentials). When this sector is removed from the Norwegian economic and emissions profile (see Figure 3), the variation in the trends is reduced and the observed changes are slightly larger.

Ocean transport is an important source of world wide air pollution but is excluded from the Kyoto Protocol and is often not included in discussions regarding international air emissions or indicator definitions. Due to the importance of shipping to the Norwegian economy, Norway has actively worked within the International Maritime Organization (IMO) to encourage improvements in the air emissions from maritime fleets.

In 1987 at the International Conference on the Protection of the North Sea, Ministers of North Sea states agreed to initiate actions to improve quality standards of heavy fuels in order to help reduce marine and atmospheric pollution. And for the Norwegian ocean going fleet, the acidification emissions have been reduced by almost 6% although greenhouse gas emissions are nearly unchanged and tropospheric ozone precursors (especially due to NO_x) have increased.

In 1997 the Protocol of 1997 (MARPOL Annex VI) was adopted which required certain air emission reductions and included establishing the Baltic Sea as a designated SO_x Emission Control area. As of 31 March 2003 there are, unfortunately, only 8 contracting states covering 26% of world tonnage so that the convention has not yet entered into force.

Figure 2. **Economic, air emission and greenhouse gas intensity trends for Norway (total), 1990-2001* (Index 1990 = 1)**[1]

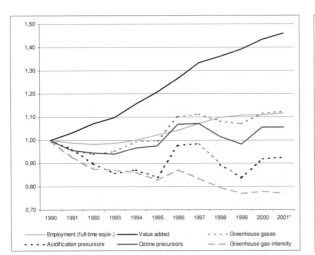

Figure 3. **Economic, air emission and greenhouse gas intensity trends for Norway excluding ocean transport, 1990-2001* (Index 1990 = 1)**[1]

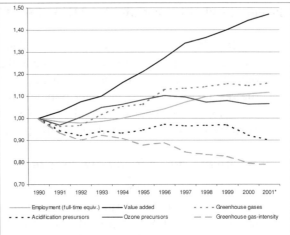

1. Greenhouse gas calculations include only CO_2, CH_4 and N_2O.
Source: National Accounts and Environmental Accounts, Statistics Norway.

1. Greenhouse gas calculations include only CO_2, CH_4 and N_2O.
Source: National Accounts and Environmental Accounts, Statistics Norway.

The trends in the time series figures show that the economic growth in Norway has been greater than the growth in the various air emissions. This is particularly shown by the greenhouse gas-intensity indicator[3] line in the graphs. This downward sloping line shows a reduction in the greenhouse gas intensity of the Norwegian economic activity, in other words, there has been greater growth in the economy than in greenhouse gas emissions. This is a positive development. Some specific reasons for recent changes in CO_2 emissions include lower activity in the ferroalloy (metals) industry, less use of diesel in crude petroleum and natural gas extraction, reduced production of refined oil products and reductions in coastal traffic. With respect to other greenhouse gases, emissions of N_2O (nitrous oxide) have increased from the manufacture of commercial fertilizers, as have emissions of perfluorocarbons (PFCs) from aluminium production.

Identifying more general factors behind the trends in Norwegian air emissions has been done by a decomposition analysis. Bruvoll and Medin (2000 and 2003) have identified 8 factors that have influenced the trends in Norwegian emissions. Their analyses show that, whereas, economic growth alone would have resulted in major emissions increases, this has been counteracted primarily by more efficient use of energy and by the increased use of abatement technologies. In addition, they found that the substitution of cleaner energy for more polluting energy sources, other technological advances and political actions have contributed to the positive trends but to a much lesser degree. As we will see, these factors and others will be important when examining trends in selected industries.

---

3. Calculated as: greenhouse gas emissions in CO_2-equivalents / value added in constant 1995-prices (see Gugele and Roubanis 2003).

Figure 4 shows the importance of various industries with regards to their greenhouse gas emissions stemming from their economic activity in 2000. Again, the transportation sector (including ocean transport) dominates as is shown by the largest portion of the pie diagram (27%). This is also the case for ozone and acidification precursors, 42 and 62% respectively, for this sector. Mining and Quarrying is second in emissions of ozone precursors, contributing 30% of the Norwegian totals, while agriculture, fishing and forestry is second in acidification precursor emissions with 14%.

Figure 4. **Greenhouse gas[1] emissions from emitting sectors. Norway total, %, 2000**

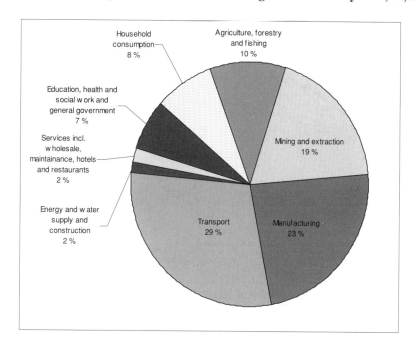

1. Greenhouse gas calculations include only CO_2, CH_4 and N_2O.
Source: National Accounts and Environmental Accounts, Statistics Norway.

In addition to looking at Norway as a whole, the NAMEA hybrid accounts allow for the examination of trends at more detailed industry levels. In the next section of this paper the following sectors are examined in more detail: Mining and Quarrying (including extraction of crude petroleum and natural gas), Manufacturing, Services (including wholesale, maintenance, hotels and restaurants) and Households.

Economic, air emission and greenhouse gas intensity trends for Mining and Quarrying (including extraction of crude petroleum and natural gas)

The Mining and Quarrying industry, which includes the extraction of crude petroleum and natural gas (NACE Section C, divisions 10-14), is a major part of the Norwegian economy and it is also very important in terms of Norway's air emissions. From 1990 to 2001 the value added of this industry has increased 96% and on average accounts for approximately 13% of total value added in Norway. This is a very important industry in Norway but it is also, unfortunately, pollution intensive. The industry's long-term focus on reducing emissions of both greenhouse gases and acidification gases has been encouraged and required by the Norwegian authorities. The results of these efforts can be seen in the divergent trends of these two types of emissions in comparison with the trend in value added for this industry (see Figure 5).

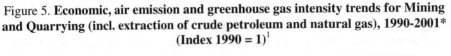

Figure 5. **Economic, air emission and greenhouse gas intensity trends for Mining and Quarrying (incl. extraction of crude petroleum and natural gas), 1990-2001*** **(Index 1990 = 1)**[1]

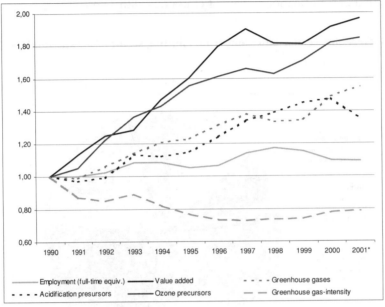

1. Greenhouse gas calculations include only CO_2, CH_4 and N_2O.

Source: National Accounts and Environmental Accounts, Statistics Norway.

There has been a large decrease of SO_2 emissions for this industry between 1990 and 2001; however, there has been an increase in NO_x emissions that at least partially counteract these SO_2 reductions when these are combined into acidification precursors. The growth in use of natural gas for production of electricity on oil platforms contributes to these increased NO_x emissions. In 2001 there has been a major reduction in flaring of natural gas offshore which has led to lower NO_X emissions and which helps explain the sudden drop in the acidification precursors' trend from 2000 to 2001.

The increase in the use of gas turbines for electricity production offshore has also led to increased CO_2 emissions although this has been partially offset by a reduction in flaring (the burning of excess natural gas without energy recovery).

On the other hand, the relatively recent focus of authorities and of the industry on tropospheric ozone precursors, in particular non-methane volatile organics (NMVOCs), has only started to show some positive results. More than 50% of Norway's NMVOC emissions come from evaporation during loading and storing of crude oil offshore. The slight reductions seen in the trend for the ozone precursors in 2001 are due to lower oil production that leads to smaller amounts of crude oil being loaded offshore and the fact that recovery facilities for vapours released during loading have been installed at certain facilities. Even with these improvements, further reductions are necessary if Norway shall meet the emission target set in the Gothenburg Protocol for NMVOCs, 195 000 tons in 2010 (target excludes ocean transport).

The greenhouse gas intensity indicator shows that the trend indicating improvement appears to be reversing. Initially this indicator shows an improvement but, by 1996 this appears to have stalled and since 1999 this indicator has reversed and shows that the situation is actually worsening.

Economic, air emission and greenhouse gas intensity trends for Manufacturing

For well over 15 years the Norwegian authorities have focused on the reduction of acidification emissions from the Manufacturing industry (NACE Section D, Divisions 15-37). The results of this focus can clearly be seen in the downward sloping line for acidification emissions in Figure 6.

On the other hand, the manufacturing industry has been exempt from one of the mechanisms to encourage the reduction of greenhouse gases, specifically the CO_2-taxes on fossil fuels when used in production processes. The trend for greenhouse gas emissions has, in general, increased more than the increases in value added. As the enterprises in the Manufacturing industry become part of the Norwegian greenhouse gas emissions trading system in the next few years, there are expectations that the trends for these gases will also start to go down.

In the later part of the period, value added in the manufacturing industry has levelled out and employment has gone down. This is primarily due to the ferro-alloys industry being in a recession which has consequently reduced production levels.

Figure 6. **Economic, air emission and greenhouse gas intensity trends for Manufacturing, 1990-2001* (Index 1990 = 1)**[1]

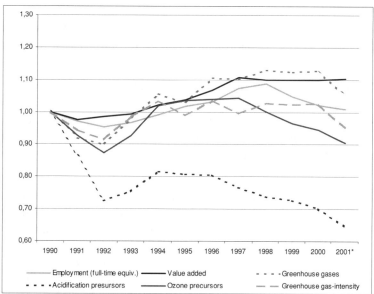

1. Greenhouse gas calculations include only CO_2, CH_4 and N_2O.

Source: National Accounts and Environmental Accounts, Statistics Norway.

Bruvoll and Medin (2000) found that in contrast to all other sectors, the pulp and paper products industry actually had an increase in energy intensity (total energy use in relation to total production). Since they found that for CO_2 emissions, decreased energy intensity was the most important cause for decoupling of economic growth from emissions, the increase in energy intensity for the pulp and paper products industry means that decoupling is not yet in evidence in this case. The variation in the greenhouse gas intensity indicator from 91 to 104% also shows that there is no consistent decoupling in the manufacturing industries as a whole.

Preliminary figures for 2001 show a marked reduction for all emission types in the manufacturing industry. This is primarily due to lower production levels in general in 2001 and in particular to closures in the metals industry. Also in 2000 one of Norway's three oil refineries closed which also means lower emissions levels. Although the greenhouse gases in these figures only include CO_2, CH_4, and N_2O, the national figures reported under the Kyoto protocol show that there has been a major reduction in emissions of SF_6 in 2001 due to the closure of an enterprise engaged in the primary production of magnesium.

Economic, air emission and greenhouse gas intensity trends for services[4]

From 1990 to 2001 the services industries have contributed more and more to the Norwegian economy, measured in value added, than has the manufacturing industry. The services industry accounted for 34% of total value added in 1990, increasing to 40% in 2001. Whereas, the manufacturing industry provided 15.5% of total value added in 1990 and only 11.7% in 2001. The services industry in 2001 had employment (measured in full-time equivalents) of 2.3 times the employment in the manufacturing industry.

During this time period, Norway has been undergoing some changes in the structure of its economy as manufacturing becomes less dominant and the services industries become more important. These general trends are also important to the air emissions profile for the country. In 2000, the services industries contributed only 2% of total greenhouse gas emissions, 1% of acidification emissions and 2.5% of tropospheric ozone precursors.

The trends look particularly consistent and good for acidification precursors and tropospheric ozone precursors with overall reductions of more than 40% over the whole time period (see Figure 7). The changes in greenhouse gas emissions, on the other hand, are relatively small. The greenhouse gas intensity indicator shows a more than 40% improvement, but this may be a bit misleading since this is due primarily to the growth in value added since there has been little change in the greenhouse gas emissions.

The reductions in the acidification and ozone precursors are primarily from mobile sources, which for this group of industries is transportation related. Included in the "services" is also NACE Section G, wholesale and retail trade. Technological improvements to vehicles during the time period 1990-2001 have meant that there have been substantial reductions in certain emissions, specifically NO_x, CO, NMVOC. The reductions in these emissions have counter-acted the increases of N_2O and NH_3 due to the increase in the number of vehicles with catalytic converters. Emissions of CO_2 have not changed to any great degree since the gains in technology have been offset by increases in activity. The reduction in the sulphur content of fuels has lead to lower levels of SO_2 emissions. The reduction of sulphur content in fuels has been a major policy focus of the

---

4.   Includes business services (NACE Section K), Financial intermediation (Section J), hotels and restaurants (Section H), wholesale and retail trade (Section G), supporting activities for transport (Division 63) and post and telecommunications (Division 64).

Norwegian authorities and the reductions in the fuel content has led to lower emission levels of SO_2.

Figure 7. **Economic, air emission and greenhouse gas intensity trends for Services, 1990-2001* (Index 1990 = 1)[1, 2]**

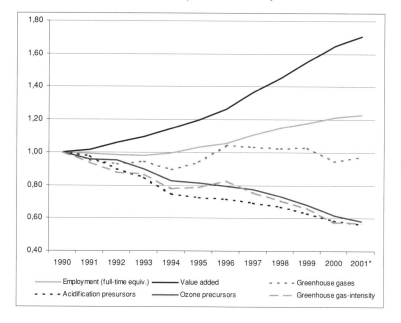

1. Greenhouse gas calculations include only CO_2, CH_4 and N_2O.

2. Includes business services (NACE Section K), Financial intermediation (Section J), hotels and restaurants (Section H), wholesale and retail trade (Section G), supporting activities for transport (Division 63) and post and telecommunications (Division 64).

Source: National Accounts and Environmental Accounts, Statistics Norway.

Economic, air emission, solid waste and greenhouse gas intensity trends for Households

Household activities also contribute to air pollution creation mostly from transportation and heating. There has been more than a 19% increase in private vehicle ownership and use (1.8 million in 1990 to 2.1 million in 2001) which has resulted in increased kilometres driven and an increase in air emissions from private vehicles. The average age of private vehicles is currently 10.2 years. Although the age of vehicles continues to increase there is an increasing number of vehicles with catalytic converters. Vehicles with catalytic converters and that use lead-free gasoline (petrol) have led to drastic reductions in lead emissions but these vehicles have a more mixed effect on other types of air emissions. In particular, NO_x emissions have been reduced however, N_2O (nitrous oxide) emissions have increased due to catalytic converters. During this time period there has been an increase in the use of diesel cars which have higher emissions of CO and CO_2 than cars using petrol (gasoline). Again, the technological improvements in the vehicles used by households have reduced some types of air emissions, but these improvements are however, partially offset by an increase in the kilometres driven by households.

Figure 8. **Consumption, air emission and greenhouse gas intensity trends for Households, 1990-2001* (Index 1990 = 1)**[1]

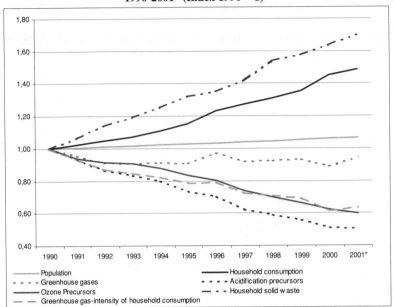

1. Greenhouse gas calculations include only CO_2, CH_4 and N_2O.

Source: National Accounts and Environmental Accounts, Statistics Norway.

Household consumption is used as the most relevant economic indicator for households. Household consumption has increased 49% from 1990 to 2001. Only household waste has increased more (70%) during this period.

The NAMEA-accounts only have direct emissions for households; however, by using input-output (I-O) analyses it is possible to identify some of the indirect emissions corresponding to Norwegian household consumption. In Figure 9, the direct and indirect greenhouse gas emissions for households are shown. The left-hand bar in figure 9 shows the 1997 direct greenhouse gas emissions (in CO_2-equivalents) from households, as can be obtained from the NAMEA-accounts. The right-hand bar shows the results from the I-O analysis.

These results show that household consumption of Norwegian-produced products resulted in substantial emissions, nearly twice that of direct emissions. Eighty per cent of the indirect emissions are connected to deliveries of foodstuffs, beverages and tobacco, transport services and housing, electricity and fuel. This analysis only captures the emissions from products that are produced in Norway and consumed by Norwegian households. The emissions connected to all of the imported products that are purchased by Norwegian households are not captured in this type of analysis. There are many products that are imported into Norway for household consumption; therefore, these results only provide a portion of the picture connected to indirect emissions from household consumption.

Figure 9. **Direct and indirect Norwegian household emissions of greenhouse gases, 1997**

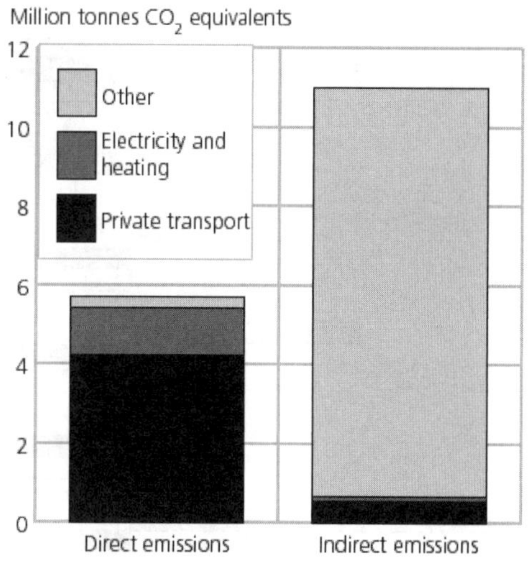

Million tonnes CO_2 equivalents

Source: National Accounts and Environmental Accounts, Statistics Norway.
Reference: Statistics Norway (2001): Natural resources and the Environment 2001, pp. 210-212.

The results from a Swedish study (Wadeskog 2000) were similar in terms of which products were responsible for the majority of indirect emissions. In the Swedish case, the same product groups accounted for 82% of CO_2 emissions in 1995. However, in the Swedish study, the indirect CO_2 emissions were about the same as the direct emissions, whereas the indirect emissions were nearly twice the direct emissions for Norwegian households. This is probably due to the high level of hydroelectricity production in Norway and the high use of electricity for household heating in Norway.

Decoupling factors

Economic activities are often the driving forces that result in increasing environmental pressures. The OECD (2002) has developed the calculation of decoupling factors to give an indication of the degree to which environmental pressures and economic forces are interacting (see Appendix A for calculation information for decoupling factors).

A positive number for the decoupling factor means that the environmental pressure relative to the economic pressure is less in the last period than in the first. This also indicates that there has been a positive environmental development with respect to the economic development. If the increase or reduction in the value added over the period is the same as that in the air emissions, this will result in a decoupling factor equal to zero.

Figure 10 presents decoupling factors for Norway and selected sectors. These factors were calculated using data from 1990 and 2000. Data for 2001 was not used since these are only preliminary figures.

Figure 10. **Decoupling factors[1] for Norway and selected sectors (between 1990 and 2000)**

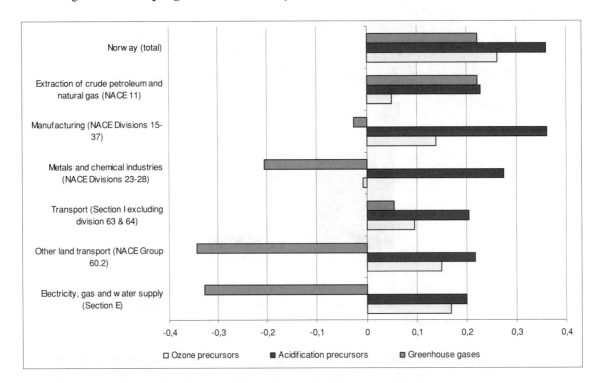

1. Greenhouse gas calculations include only CO_2, CH_4 and N_2O.
Source: National Accounts and Environmental Accounts, Statistics Norway.

For Norway as a whole (including ocean transport), decoupling of the economic growth from all three aggregate types of air emissions appears to be occurring, although this decoupling is rather weak at between 0.2 and 0.4. This is also true for the extraction of crude petroleum and natural gas (NACE 11) but the decoupling for ozone precursors is only very slightly positive.

The manufacturing industries show a stronger decoupling for acidification precursors but for greenhouse gases, this is negative, indicating that the change in greenhouse gas emissions is greater than the change in value added. Negative results are obtained for the metals and chemical industries (NACE Divisions 23-28) with respect to greenhouse gases and ozone precursors. There has been a positive development with respect to acidification emissions in these industries.

For transportation as a whole, including ocean transport, there has been weak decoupling for all three aggregate types of emissions. However, if NACE Group 60.2 (Other land transport) is examined by itself, there is a very strong negative decoupling result with respect to greenhouse gases. This is due to increases in N_2O emissions from vehicles that have catalytic converters and the large increase in activity in land transport in recent years that has over-shadowed the technological improvements related to greenhouse gases. On the other hand, the technological advances and reductions in the content of sulphur in fuels have exceeded the growth in activity in relation to emissions leading to acidification (SO_2, NO_x and NH_3) and the same for tropospheric ozone precursors, but to a lesser degree.

And finally, NACE Section E, Electricity, gas and water supply, also shows a negative result with respect to greenhouse gases. There are very low air emissions from this NACE section due to the predominance of hydropower for the production of electricity and the high use of electricity for heating in Norway. In the past ten years there has been a greater use of energy recovery often from waste incineration which has been used specifically for heating. This has resulted in an increase in the air emissions from steam and hot water supply (NACE 40.30). These slight emission increases have then resulted in a strongly negative decoupling for this section. This is an example of when this decoupling factor may be misunderstood if the reasons for the change and the magnitudes of the change are not examined in more detail.

Norwegian policy evaluation

In the previous sections, the results of Norwegian air pollution policies have been pointed out when it has been possible to identify that these policies have been instrumental in the trend development. There are so many different factors and complex interactions occurring that it is not always possible to isolate the policy factors from the technology, energy efficiency, energy mix, economic and other factors. But having industry based data is necessary in order that analyses, such as input-output and decomposition analyses, can be performed.

An intimate knowledge of the changes in the emissions profiles in each industry is needed to be able to understand the trends, as well as analyses of the total data set to be able to identify the major factors that are influencing the developments over time.

In general, the time series NAMEA data has been used to show that the long term focus of the Norwegian authorities on acidification precursor emissions has shown results in all sectors and especially in the manufacturing sector. The situation with regards to greenhouse gases is mixed. The extraction industry appears to be making some progress but that appears to be reaching diminishing returns in the most recent years and there is little progress to point to in the manufacturing industries in this area. One area of great effectiveness is in the area of reduction in lead emissions. A thorough analysis of Norwegian environmental policy through 1995 is presented in an analysis paper from the Ministry of the Environment (NOU 1995:4 only in Norwegian) and a recent evaluation and comparison of economic instruments in Nordic environmental policy was made by the Working Group on Environment and Economics under the auspices the Nordic Council of Ministers (2002).

Nordic hybrid accounts (NAMEA) comparison

The Nordic NAMEA systems (Norway, Denmark, Sweden and Finland) are structurally very similar although there are some differences with regards to the specific set up of the national accounts input-output table and also where certain types of emissions are shown, such as ocean transport emissions and emissions from landfills (Hass and Skarborg 2000).

To evaluate whether the different NAMEA-systems in the Nordic countries are comparable a study was made of the following six different industries: Agriculture (NACE 01), Manufacture of pulp, paper and paper products (NACE 21), Manufacture of chemicals and chemical products (NACE 24), Manufacture of basic metals (NACE 27), Electricity, gas, steam and hot water supply (NACE 40), and the Transportation sector (NACE 60, 61, 62). See Hass and Skarborg (2000) for the full report. These different industries were chosen because they were of particular importance to the emissions profiles of all four countries.

A number of specific issues needed to be addressed and adjustments made before a comparison could be made with any confidence. Some of these issues were emissions from ocean transport, CO_2 emissions from biofuels, how imports and exports were handled, aggregation issues with regards to the definition of industry groups, allocation differences with respect to emissions, consistency of the time series of data, potential double counting with respect to calculating total energy use and emissions from landfills.

Once these issues were evaluated and the data sets adjusted, a comparison of the different industries in each country was attempted. Some explanations for why there were differences between the countries were also proposed.

Understanding observed differences

Although the Nordic economies are similar in many ways, when comparing environmental and economic variables it becomes clear that the industries have different compositions and different emission intensities. The reasons behind these observed differences can be due to differences in the structure of the industries or it can be differences between the types of activities that are included in the industries. The following two examples illustrate these two different reasons.

Structural differences

Structural differences help to explain the differences between the greenhouse gas intensities in NACE Division 24, Manufacture of Chemicals and chemical products, between Norway and Denmark. Figure 11 shows the greenhouse gas intensities for the four different Nordic countries. Norway has very high emissions per value added when compared to Denmark. This difference can be explained primarily by examining the types of enterprises and production activities that are predominant in the two countries in this NACE division.

In Norway, the emissions from this industry are arising primarily from the manufacture of basic chemicals and agro-chemical products. The production of these types of products results in relatively high levels of air emissions relative to value added.

In Denmark, on the other hand, there is a larger proportion of the value added in this division coming from pharmaceutical enterprises than in Norway. The pharmaceutical enterprises have much lower levels of air emissions and higher levels of value added; this combination makes the Danish chemicals industry appear more efficient, whereas, the reason is due primarily to the structure of the two industries in the different countries and the two very different types of production activities that are classified within the same division.

More detailed levels of industry categories were examined but either the emissions data or the economic data were not available or it did not make sense to break down the categories into smaller groupings due to the high level of integration between enterprises in the different categories.

Figure 11. **Greenhouse gas intensities for NACE 24 (Manufacture of chemicals and chemical products) for Denmark, Finland, Norway and Sweden. CO_2-equivalents tons per value added in 1995 ECU**

Figure 12. **Acidification intensities for NACE 21 (Manufacture of pulp, paper and paper products) for Denmark, Finland, Norway and Sweden. mPAE per value added in 1995 ECU**

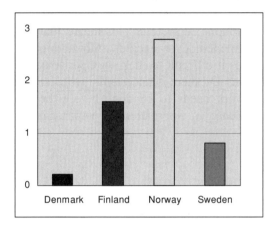
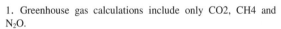

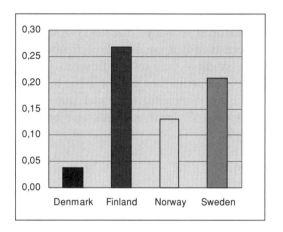

1. Greenhouse gas calculations include only CO2, CH4 and N₂O.

Source: Hass and Skarborg (2000), p. 40, Figure 28.

1. Greenhouse gas calculations include only CO_2, CH_4 and N_2O.

Source: Hass and Skarborg (2000), p. 38, Figure 24.

Differences in activities included

The manufacture of pulp, paper and paper products (NACE 21) is very important to Finland, Sweden and Norway and to a lesser degree to Denmark. This industry has a relatively high level of integration between pulp and paper manufacturing making it impractical to look at more detailed NACE groups since it would be very difficult to develop good economic information for the separate activities. In terms of value added, Finland's industry is the largest of the four, with Sweden a close second.

From Figure 12 it appears that Finland is much less efficient (higher emissions per value added) than Sweden and Norway. This result was a little unexpected since size advantages were expected to be seen for the Finnish industry which would lead to more efficient production systems. However, upon closer examination of the activities included in the Finnish enterprises, it is common that these enterprises own and operate their own power producing plants instead of purchasing power from others. This means that the emissions associated with their secondary activity of power production is also included in this NACE category. This can account for the high emissions intensity in Finland.

On the other hand, some of the differences are due to different types of industrial processes since much of the emissions from this industry are process related. This can be an indication that the processes in Sweden and Norway are more emissions efficient but it is difficult to make this conclusion with any certainty due to the differences regarding the emissions included in the different NACE divisions in the different countries.

Improvements needed for international comparisons

Hybrid accounts have been most widely used in national contexts and the focus has been placed on consistency over time for the national systems. These accounts have proved to be very useful for trend analyses and other types of analyses since tools that are used for predominantly economic analyses, such as input-output analyses, can now be used with the hybrid data. Consistency between the data sets over time at the national level is of primary importance when attempting these types of analyses.

When international comparisons are going to be made, then additional requirements for the data sets need to be met. Although NAMEA accounting systems are being developed in many countries, NAMEA is not yet a harmonized system. This means that there is still a great deal of freedom for countries to include or exclude information according to their own definitions. This freedom makes it difficult to make comparisons between countries since there can be different definitions and there is uncertainty whether you are comparing the exact same things. Further work needs to be done before the NAMEA (hybrid) accounts can be used with confidence in international comparison work.

Conclusions

Having coordinated economic and environmental data will allow for greater consistency in the development of national indicators. It will also provide additional opportunities for analyses to understand the different factors influencing the changes in the environmental profiles of Norwegian industries. The Norwegian Ministry of the Environment has been supportive of the development of these accounts and is interested in using the data more extensively in their policy development and analyses.

The Norwegian hybrid accounts are planned for annual publication (in May) and were established as official statistics in 2002. When the accounts were published in 2002 great interest was shown in the results which resulted in several newspaper articles and an interview on the main evening news of the national television station.

The NAMEA systems in the Nordic countries are similar and provide a rich set of data for analyses and comparisons. Some of the country-specific ways of presenting the data make it difficult to use the data without checking that certain types of information are treated in similar ways. Once these differences are adjusted for, the NAMEA systems do allow for some interesting comparisons to make. Understanding the differences between the countries needs intricate knowledge of both the structure of the industries in the countries and the way that the NAMEAs are developed.

Acknowledgments

Contributions to this work have been made by the members of the Norwegian Economic and Environmental Accounts team at Statistics Norway, and especially, Kristine Erlandsen, Tone Smith and Knut Ø. Sørensen, and by the air emissions statistics group at Statistics Norway. Work at Statistics Norway has been partially funded by the Norwegian Ministry of the Environment and by Eurostat. The Nordic comparison work was largely taken from the work performed during the Nordic NAMEA comparison project which included participation from Veronica Skarborg and Marianne Eriksson (Statistics Sweden), Ole Gravgård Pedersen (Statistics Denmark) and Harri Manninen (Statistics Finland) and was partially funded by the Nordic Council of Ministers.

Contact information

Dr. Julie L. Hass, Division for Environmental Statistics, Postboks 8131 Dep, N-0033 Oslo, Norway.

Tlf: +47 – 21 09 45 15, Fax: +47 – 21 09 49 98, e-mail: julie.hass@ssb.no

References

In *StatBank* you can find detailed Norwegian NAMEA data for all industries and air emission components for each of the available years (currently 1990-2001*). This data is updated annually as part of the regular publication of the *Norwegian NAMEA*.

Bruvoll, A. and H. Medin (2000): Factoring the environmental Kuznets curve: Evidence from Norway. Discussions Papers 275, Statistics Norway.

Bruvoll, A and H. Medin (2003): Factors Behnind the Environmental Kuznets Curve: A Decomposition of the Changes in Air Pollution. Environmental and Resource Economics 24: 27-48.

De Haan, M. and S.J. Keuning (1996): Taking the Environment into Account: The NAMEA Approach. Review *of Income and Wealth,* 42**:2,** 131-148.

Eurostat (1999): Pilot studies on NAMEAs for air emissions with a comparison at European level. Eurostat (Unit B1).

Eurostat (2001): NAMEAs for Air Emissions: Results of Pilot Studies. Eurostat (Unit B1).

Fuglestvedt, J.S., T.K. Berntsen, O. Godal and T. Skodvin (2000): Climate implications of GWP-based reductions in greenhouse gas emissions. *Geophysical Research Letters,* 27:3, Feb. 1, 2000, 409-412.

Godal, O. and J. Fuglestvedt (2000): GWP og misforstått ekvivalens: Kan klimagasser veies sammen? CICERO: *Cicerone,* 1/2000, 15-18.

Gugele, B. and N. Roubanis (2003): Indicators concerning CO_2 and other greenhouse gas emissions. Paper for the Second Meeting of the ESS Task Force on Methodological Issues for Sustainable Development Indicators Meeting of 3-4 February 2003. Eurostat document SDI/TF/023/05 (2003) EN.

Hass, J. (ed.) and V. Skarborg (2000): *Nordic Environment-Economic Indicators: Nordic Natural and Environment Accounts – Part III.* TemaNord 2000:515. Copenhagen: Nordic Council of Ministers.

Hass, Julie L. and Knut Ø. Sørensen (1998): Environmental profiles and benchmarking of Norwegian industries. Results from the Norwegian economic and environmental accounts (NOREEA) project. Statistics Norway: *Economic Survey* 1/98.

Hellsten, E., S. Ribacke, G. Wickbom (1999): SWEEA – Swedish environmental and economic accounts, *Structural Change and Economic Dynamics,* 10, 39-72.

Ike, T. (1999): A Japanese NAMEA. *Structural Change and Economic Dynamics,* 10, 123-150.

Jensen, H.V. and O.G. Pedersen (1998): *Danish NAMEA 1980-1992 (Revised).* Statistics Denmark.

Keuning, S.J. (1996): The NAMEA experience, an interim evaluation of the Netherlands integrated accounts and indicators for the environment the economy. Presented at the International symposium on Integrated Environmental and Economic Accounting in Theory and Practice, Tokyo, 5-8 March 1996.

Keuning, S.J. (1997): SESAME: an Integrated Economic and Social Accounting System. *International Statistical Review,* 65:1, 111-121.

Keuning, S.J. and M. de Haan (1998): Netherlands: What's in a NAMEA? Recent results. In K. Uno and P. Bartelmus (eds.), *Environmental Accounting in Theory and Practice.* London: Kluwer Academic Publishers, 143-156. ISBN 0-7923-4559-2

Keuning, S.J., J. van Dalen, and M. de Haan (1999): The Netherlands' NAMEA; presentation, usage and future extensions. *Structural Change and Economic Dynamics,* 10, 15-37.

Nordic Council of Ministers (2002): *The Use of Economic Instruments in Nordic Environmental Policy 1999-2001.* TemaNord 2002:581. Copenhagen: Nordic Council of Ministers.

NOU (1995:4): *Virkemidler i miljøpolitikken.* Norges Offentlige Utredninger. Oslo: Statens forvaltningstjeneste.

OECD (2002): Indicators to measure decoupling of environmental pressure from economic growth. OECD SG/SD(2002)1/FINAL.

Statistics Norway (2001): *Natural Resources and the Environment 2001. Norway.* Statistical Analyses 47. Oslo: Statistics Norway, pages 210-212.

Sørensen, K.S, J.L. Hass, H. Sjølie, P. Tønjum and K. Erlandsen (2001). *Norwegian Economic and Environment Accounts (NOREEA) Phase 2,* Statistics Norway Document 2001/02.

Vaze, P. (1999): A NAMEA for the UK. *Structural Change and Economic Dynamics,* 10, 99-122.

Vaze, P. and S. Balchin (1996): The Pilot United Kingdom Environmental Accounts, Economic Trends, HMSO, London.

Wadeskog, A. (2000): Hushållen og miljön. *VälfärdsBulletinen* Nr. 1/2000, 14-15.

Appendix A: Conversion factors

The following provides conversion factors and calculation examples of environmental themes and decoupling factors.

Decoupling factors are calculated based on OECD's definition (OECD 2002):

Decoupling factor = 1 – decoupling ratio

where the decoupling ratio is defined as:

$$decoupling\ ratio\ =\ \frac{\left[\dfrac{Environmental\ \Pr essure\ _{last\ period}}{Driving\ Force\ _{last\ period}}\right]}{\left[\dfrac{Environmental\ \Pr essure\ _{first\ period}}{Driving\ Force\ _{first\ period}}\right]}$$

In this paper the environmental pressure was air emissions and the driving force was value added (in constant 1995-basic prices).

Calculation of environmental themes

There is some debate whether it is appropriate to aggregate various types of air emissions into a single entity or theme. This is of particular interest since the Kyoto protocol has established this type of calculation for greenhouse gases using the GWP conversion factors (Godal and Fuglestvedt 2000; Fuglestvedt, *et al.* 2000). In this report, emissions types have been aggregated into three themes to be able to include more information in the calculations.

Greenhouse theme

Type of emissions	Amount of emissions (tons)	*	Conversion factor (GWP)	=	CO_2-equivalents (tons)
CO_2	11 388 060	*	1	=	11 388 060
CH_4	31 686	*	21	=	665 406
N_2O	99	*	310	=	30 690
			Sum		12 084 156

In order to calculate the greenhouse theme, the emissions for each of the compounds that contribute to that theme and the corresponding conversion factors are needed. Each of the emission types are multiplied by the Global Warming Potential (GWP) conversion factor and then added together to give a total. The following is an example using Norwegian data for NACE 11 Crude petroleum and natural gas extraction industry for 2000. This calculation shows that the oil and gas extraction industry (NACE 11) in Norway had emissions of 12.1 million tons CO_2-equivalents in 2000. This calculation only includes the three greenhouse gases, CO_2, CH_4 and N_2O whereas the official method for calculating this theme in Norway is to include all of the greenhouse gases included in the Kyoto agreement. All of these gases and their corresponding conversion factors are listed in the table at the end of this section. The calculation example above would need to be extended to include all of the different gases and not just the three shown in the example for reporting according to the Kyoto Protocol.

Acidification theme

Type of emissions	Amount of emissions (tons)	*	Conversion factor	=	Potential Acid Equivalent (tons PAE)
NOx	59 741	*	1/46	=	1 299
SO2	632	*	1/32	=	20
NH3	0	*	1/17	=	0
			Sum		1 318

The Norwegian emissions data for the three gases that contribute to acidification are reported in tons and this calculation results in tons PAE. The emissions are multiplied by the conversion factors to give potential acid equivalents (PAE) for each emission type. The sum of these values is the acidification potential emissions from the Norwegian crude petroleum and natural gas extraction industry (NACE 11) for 2000.

Tropospheric Ozone Precursors theme

Type of emissions	Amount of emissions (tons)	*	Conversion factor	=	Tropospheric Ozone Forming Potentials (tons TOFP)
NOx	59 741	*	1.22	=	72 884
NMVOC	234 877		1		234 877
CO	7 713	*	0.11	=	848
CH4	31 686	*	0.014	=	444
			Sum		309 053

The Norwegian emissions data for the four gases that contribute to the formation of tropospheric ozone are reported in tons and this calculation results in tons TOFP. The emissions are multiplied by the conversion factors to give tropospheric ozone forming potentials for each emission type. The sum of these values is the ozone precursor emissions from the Norwegian crude petroleum and natural gas extraction industry (NACE 11) for 2000.

Summary table with theme conversion factors

The following table provides the conversion factors for calculating the three environmental themes: greenhouse effect, acidification and tropospheric ozone precursors.

Compound	Conversion factor to CO_2-equivalents using Global Warming Potentials (GWP)* for **Greenhouse theme** – (100 year GWPs)	Compound	Conversion factor to Potential Acid Equivalent (PAE/kg)** for **Acidification theme**
CO_2	1	NO_x	1/46
CH_4	21	SO_2	1/32
N_2O	310	NH_3	1/17
HFC-23	11 700		
HFC-32	650		
HFC-125	2 800	**Assumes complete dissociation. This is not likely under normal conditions but these values provide an upper estimate.	
HFC-134	1 300		
HFC-143	3 800	Compound	Conversion factor to Troposheric Ozone Forming Potentials (TOFP) for **Ozone precursors theme**
HFC-152	140		
HFC-227	2 900	NO_x	1.22
C_3F_8 (PFC-218)	7 000	NMVOC	1
CF_4 (PFC-14)	6 500	CO	0.11
C_2F_6 (PFC-116)	9 200	CH_4	0.014
SF_6	23 900		

*These values are based on atmospheric research and models and the values may change in the future. These are the values published by the IPCC (1995). The IPCC (1989) values were revised upwards. For example, in 1989, the GWP for CH_4 was 11 and the GWP for N_2O was 270.

These values are also published in Statistics Norway's annual publication, "Natural Resources and the Environment" in Appendix Table C1.

Appendix B: Norwegian NAMEA data

Table B-1:

Value added, employment and greenhouse gas, acidification and ozone precursor emissions according to industry groups. 2000.

Table B-2:

Norway's total value added, employment and air emissions (according to components). 1990-2001*

Additional data is available in *StatBank*, the database available on Statistics Norway's website.

Table B-1. **Value added, employment and greenhouse gas, acidification and ozone precursor emissions according to industry groups, 2000**[1, 8]

	Total gross value added[2] Million NOK (1995-constant basic prices)	Employment (full-time equivalent persons) 1 000 full-time equiv.	Carbon dioxide, CO_2 1 000 tons	Methane, CH_4 Tons	Nitrous oxide, N_2O Tons	Greenhouse gases emissions[4] Tons CO_2-equivalents	Nitrogen oxides, NOx Tons	Ammonia NH_3 Tons	Sulphur dioxide, SO_2 Tons	Acidification precursors[5] Tons acid-equivalents	Non-methane volatile organic carbons, NMVOC Tons	Carbon monoxide, CO Tons	Tropospheric ozone precursors[6] Tons NMVOC-equivalents
Totals	991 710	1 974.5	55 016	332 966	18 245	67 664 258	513 312	25 437	83 421	15 262	377 760	581 460	1 072 622
Agriculture, forestry and fishing	25 586	79.3	1 970	99 332	9 592	7 029 005	37 129	23 216	1 069	2 206	3 852	21 191	52 871
Agriculture and hunting	10 845	58.3	506	99 212	9 538	5 546 648	5 313	23 215	190	1 487	2 341	13 389	11 684
Forestry and logging	5 333	5.1	48	13	18	53 521	715	0	19	16	763	1 232	1 771
Fishing	4 455	13.1	1 404	104	35	1 417 058	30 989	0	855	700	724	6 410	39 237
Fish farming	4 953	2.8	11	2	1	11 777	113	1	4	3	24	159	179
Mining and extraction	133 023	26.4	11 942	32 219	138	12 661 730	68 855	0	945	1 526	235 731	8 906	321 165
Mining and quarrying	2 118	3.9	159	346	37	177 500	1 495	0	121	36	249	412	2 124
Oil and gas extraction	127 206	15.4	11 388	31 686	99	12 084 156	59 741	0	632	1 318	234 877	7 713	309 052
Service activities incidental to oil and gas extraction	3 699	7.1	395	187	3	400 074	7 619	0	193	172	605	782	9 989
Manufacturing	117 761	281.4	13 456	28 513	5 781	15 847 217	24 548	558	20 240	1 199	32 416	47 484	67 987
Fish and fish products	3 714	11.6	213	8	2	213 884	463	0	406	23	34	120	612
Meat and dairy products	4 023	15.9	95	4	3	96 011	346	1	43	9	56	259	507
Other food products	10 191	17.1	162	6	3	162 968	284	1	131	10	858	251	1 232
Beverages and tobacco	2 082	6.1	85	2	1	85 386	86	1	36	3	69	164	192
Textiles, wearing apparel, leather	1 855	7.3	26	1	1	26 147	37	0	31	2	331	72	385
Wood and wood products	4 948	15.2	57	15 751	33	398 322	635	0	220	21	2 143	6 884	3 896
Pulp, paper and paper products	8 388	9.4	340	11 629	87	611 067	1 635	0	1 527	83	388	3 515	2 932
Publishing, printing, reproduction	9 753	31.2	44	3	2	45 068	52	2	2	1	5 922	281	6 016
Refined petroleum products, chemical and mineral products	10 629	22.3	4 006	109	30	4 017 618	6 943	1	3 557	262	16 407	520	24 937
Basic chemicals	7 303	8.0	3 112	959	5 602	4 868 362	5 116	547	5 685	321	1 655	32 764	11 515
Basic metals	12 115	14.4	5 023	14	6	5 025 125	8 166	0	8 468	442	1 941	1 157	12 031
Machinery and other equipment n.e.c	28 024	75.1	198	10	5	199 704	338	3	92	10	1 039	641	1 522
Building and repairing of ships	3 504	13.0	26	1	1	26 005	188	0	11	4	595	82	833
Oil platforms and modules	6 901	19.9	15	1	0	14 834	33	0	4	1	5	22	47
Furniture and other manufacturing n.e.c	4 331	14.9	55	12	4	56 715	227	1	28	6	972	753	1 332
Energy and water supply and construction	63 219	144.8	984	200	177	1 043 406	7 323	17	853	187	11 040	5 976	20 634
Production and distribution of electricity	24 945	16.0	34	3	4	35 215	206	2	12	5	58	340	348
Water, steam etc	381	0.3	263	143	28	274 620	1 107	0	643	44	471	664	1 897
Construction	37 893	128.5	687	55	145	733 571	6 010	16	197	138	10 510	4 972	18 390
Wholesale, maintenance, hotels and restaurants	151 043	324.3	482	79	45	498 077	1 702	41	152	44	4 700	6 804	7 525
Wholesale and retail trade, maintenance and repair of vehicles	134 846	270.9	434	70	41	448 240	1 590	36	132	41	4 608	6 138	7 224
Hotels and restaurants	16 197	53.4	48	9	4	49 836	112	4	21	3	92	666	301
Transport	55 880	119.3	19 612	1 317	636	19 837 017	347 323	77	58 799	9 392	18 723	39 885	446 863
Transport via pipelines	12 999	0.7	14	5	0	14 102	37	0	0	1	1	10	48
Railways and trams	1 977	8.1	53	3	18	59 090	726	0	24	17	62	172	967
Other land transport	15 237	46.5	3 119	193	195	3 184 028	21 937	77	319	491	4 791	20 607	33 823
Air transport	5 071	12.7	1 443	33	46	1 458 103	4 992	0	165	114	2 116	5 444	8 805
Ocean transport	18 143	43.6	13 512	976	340	13 637 413	288 172	0	56 783	8 039	10 186	12 308	363 123
Inland water and costal transport	2 453	7.7	1 471	107	37	1 484 281	31 460	0	1 508	731	1 567	1 344	40 097
Services	240 472	312.1	783	237	174	842 213	4 125	184	124	104	10 913	28 680	19 105
Supporting activities for transport	16 046	27.7	183	32	21	190 511	1 593	20	56	38	6 363	3 255	8 664
Post and telecommunications	29 146	38.5	325	124	95	357 227	1 414	103	21	37	2 106	15 882	5 581

	Total gross value added[2] (Million NOK 1995-constant basic prices)	Employment (full-time equivalent persons) (1 000 full-time equiv.)	Carbon dioxide, CO_2 (1 000 tons)	Methane, CH_4 (Tons)	Nitrous oxide, N_2O (Tons)	Greenhouse gases emissions[4] (Tons CO_2-equivalents)	Nitrogen oxides, NOx (Tons)	Ammonia NH_3 (Tons)	Sulphur dioxide, SO_2 (Tons)	Acidification precursors[5] (Tons acid-equivalents)	Non-methane volatile organic carbons, NMVOC (Tons)	Carbon monoxide, CO (Tons)	Tropospheric ozone precursors[6] (Tons NMVOC-equivalents)
Financial intermediation	44 908	45.1	142	50	36	153 889	518	39	23	14	792	5 984	2 083
Dwelling services (households)[7]	59 601	1.2	.	.	.	.	.	.	.	.	.	.	.
Business services etc	90 771	199.6	133	31	22	140 585	600	22	23	15	1 652	3 559	2 776
Education, health and social work	154 536	533.2	613	146	202	678 444	1 432	85	237	44	3 358	13 407	6 583
Education	46 139	149.2	87	14	5	88 627	115	4	47	4	98	714	316
Health and social services	79 264	309.9	291	76	166	344 421	747	49	96	22	2 562	7 687	4 319
Other social and personal services	29 133	74.1	235	55	31	245 396	571	32	94	17	699	5 007	1 947
General government	55 479	153.7	268	162 786	355	3 797 109	1 933	2	95	45	798	752	5 518
Public administration and defense	33 911	99.0	186	14	6	188 335	1 805	1	75	42	776	645	3 049
Water, wastewater and waste, local gov	4 235	3.3	72	162 770	349	3 598 409	116	0	14	3	15	56	2 442
Other service activities, local gov	17 333	51.4	10	2	0	10 364	11	0	6	0	7	51	26
Consumption													
Household consumption	554 023[3]	.	4 904	8 138	1 144	5 430 041	18 940	1 257	908	514	56 229	408 374	124 371

1. NAMEA-values use the National Accounts definition of Norwegian activity, not a geographic definition of Norwegian territory as is used for reporting to the Kyoto protocol and other international air emissions reporting systems.

2. Total gross value added is the sum of value added for the different kind of activities including chaining discrepancies and without the corrections that are needed for calculating GNP (Gross National Product).

3. Household consumption is not included in the calculation for total value added.

4. Greenhouse gases calculations include only CO_2, CH_4 and N_2O.

5. Acidification precursor calculations include NO_x, SO_2 and NH_3 emissions.

6. Ozone precursor calculations include NO_x, NMVOC, CO and CH_4 emissions.

7. Emissions for dwelling services are included in emissions from household consumption.

8. Last updated: 20 March 2003.

Table B-2. **Norway's total value added, employment and air emissions (according to components), 1990-2001***[1]

	1990	1991	1992	1993	1994	1995	1996	1997	1998	1999	2000	2001*
Economic data												
Total gross value added. Million NOK (constant 1995 basic prices)[2]	691 942	713 379	741 269	758 900	799 594	835 001	875 834	922 636	940 806	962 604	991 710	1 010 634
Employment. 1000 full-time equivalent persons	1 778.7	1 757.3	1 748.7	1 756.2	1 779.5	1 816.5	1 851.9	1 906.8	1 953.5	1 967.1	1 974.3	1 983.4
Emissions to air												
Greenhouse gases												
Carbon dioxide – CO_2. 1000 tons	48 638	46 038	45 507	45 913	48 208	48 308	54 571	55 091	53 219	52 302	55 016	55 399
Methane – CH_4. Tons	307 312	311 774	315 763	321 822	325 917	328 657	332 637	335 074	329 645	327 562	332 966	333 435
Nitrous oxide – N_2O. Tons	18 087	17 544	15 328	16 468	16 796	17 057	17 142	16 957	17 832	18 510	18 245	18 318
Acidification precursors												
Sulphur dioxide – SO_2. Tons	141 953	141 539	124 361	114 314	113 979	95 974	116 729	116 212	89 814	77 099	83 421	91 567
Nitrogen oxides – NO_x. Tons	500 283	470 935	441 913	424 256	436 025	433 720	508 257	516 539	486 884	460 002	513 312	508 554
Ammonia – NH_3. Tons	22 589	22 953	24 540	24 283	24 568	26 081	26 538	25 982	25 905	25 481	25 437	24 639
Ozone precursors (also NO_x and CH_4)												
Non-methane volatile organic carbons – NMVOC. Tons	304 640	303 164	330 358	345 602	360 338	375 396	382 032	379 001	362 963	366 115	377 760	386 037
Carbon monoxide – CO. Tons	880 178	811 933	789 622	791 365	777 085	744 951	720 519	684 053	644 085	609 175	581 460	560 887
Heavy metals												
Arsenic – As. Kg	4 416	4 316	4 188	4 215	4 708	3 985	4 444	4 192	4 379	4 223	3 680	3 352
Lead – Pb. Kg	188 359	145 058	127 943	87 730	24 544	22 655	11 451	10 727	10 248	9 123	8 208	7 266
Cadmium – Cd. Kg	1 878	1 806	1 783	1 826	1 386	1 205	1 307	1 316	1 333	1 144	943	908
Copper – Cu. Kg	23 115	20 242	20 431	20 297	18 923	19 665	20 237	20 656	21 387	21 408	20 475	20 771
Chromium – Cr. Kg	15 747	15 694	15 361	14 753	14 260	13 818	14 703	15 441	14 315	13 357	11 522	9 702
Mercury – Hg. Kg	2 236	2 104	1 899	1 539	1 622	1 519	1 688	1 680	1 546	1 543	1 502	1 444
Particulates												
PM10. Tons	73	67	64	70	71	70	73	77	70	67	69	67
PM2.5. Tons	61	56	53	59	61	60	63	66	61	58	59	57
Other emissions												
Polycyclic organic hydrocarbons-PAH-4. Tons	15	14	13	14	14	14	14	14	14	13	14	15
Dioxins. Mg	146 538	113 376	109 778	107 476	106 800	83 235	66 469	58 138	49 519	52 455	51 071	50 596

1. Last updated 20 March 2003.

2. Total gross value added is the sum of value added for the different kind of activities including chaining discrepancies and without the corrections that are needed for calculating GNP (Gross National Product).

Accounting for Sustainable Development: the NAMEA-based approach

M. de Haan and P. Kee

Statistics Netherlands

Introduction

Accounting for sustainable development requires a broadening of scope of the conventional System of National Accounts (SNA; United Nations *et al.*, 1993). This wider perspective is necessary to account for the priceless environmental and social externalities, which are important in a sustainable development context. This paper's focus is on the Dutch National Accounting Matrix including Environmental Accounts (NAMEA; cf. De Haan and Keuning, 1996), which extends the SNA with physical flow accounts. The NAMEA is published by Statistics Netherlands every year. The environmental accounts show the interactions between producer and consumer (household) activities and the natural environment. These interrelationships occur as a consequence of the environmental requirements of these activities: natural resource inputs and residual outputs. These requirements are appointed to these activities when and where they actually take place. This direct recording is consistent with prevailing national accounting practices.

By providing economic and environmental data in a consistent Leontief-type framework, the NAMEA is particularly suited for analytical purposes. This paper discusses various analytical applications that are directly related to sustainability policy issues, such as decoupling environmental pressures from economic growth. The systems approach of the NAMEA allows sustainability issues to be considered from two different perspectives. The first perspective takes the activities of producers and consumers (households) as a reference. The second perspective, which is particularly relevant for open economies, grasps sustainability issues by taking domestic demand for goods and services as the point of departure. This approach shifts the focus from the activities to the goods consumed. This second perspective can be analytically deduced from the first by taking the environmental consequences of international trade into account. Policy measures derived from the first approach are directed towards the sustainable performance of activities on the production side. In the second approach they aim at realizing sustainable consumption patterns or lifestyles. Both perspectives and both kinds of policy measures are of course useful in addressing and enhancing sustainable development.

Another relevant national accounting module is the Social Accounting Matrix (SAM; United Nations *et al.*, 1993, pp. 461-88). A SAM elaborates on the interrelationships between economic and social statistics by incorporating information on labour and households in the national accounts. Expanding the SNA with NAMEA and SAM yields a consistent and linked set of indicators that are useful for analyzing interactions between the different dimensions of sustainability.

This paper proceeds as follows. Section 2 discusses the accounts of the NAMEA. Section 3 presents NAMEA-based analyses of producer and consumer activities and international trade. Section 4 concludes.

The NAMEA

The NAMEA consists of a National Accounting Matrix (NAM) extended with Environmental Accounts. All accounts are presented in matrix format. This format reconciles supply-use tables and sector accounts, creating a comprehensive accounting framework that can be presented at various levels of detail. The economic accounts in the NAM-part of the NAMEA present the complete set of accounts of the SNA. This part, however, is slightly different from standard SNA practices. These differences relate to a regrouping of transactions which accommodate either its linkage to the environmental accounts or enhance a clear representation of transactions that are relevant from an environmental perspective. For example, transactions directly related to environmental management, such as environmental protection expenditures and environmental taxation and subsidies, are explicitly shown in the economic accounts.

The environmental accounts in the NAMEA are denominated in physical units and focus on the consistent presentation of material input of natural resources and output of residuals for the national economy. These inputs and outputs are the environmental requirements of the economy. Environmental requirements generally are not related to market transactions, and therefore they are not represented in the standard national accounts. By the presentation of the economic accounts in monetary terms and the environmental accounts in the most relevant physical units, the NAMEA maintains a strict borderline between the economic sphere and the natural environment. The NAM is extended with two accounts on the environment: a substances account (account 11) and an environmental themes account (account 12).

Substances account

The substances account provides information on the physical exchanges between the economy and the natural environment. It systematically determines the origin (in the column) and destination (in the row) of ten types of pollutants. Table 1 provides a detailed overview of the origin, and table 2 of the destination, of these substance flows in the 1997 NAMEA for the Netherlands.

Table 1 distinguishes between residuals originating from consumers, producers and other sources. Taken together, these outputs constitute the gross emissions by residents. These figures for the emission by residents of a particular country are important for assigning the responsibility of pollution to particular countries. For example, the NAMEA greenhouse gas emissions by residents include emissions resulting from international transport activities. De Haan and Verduin (2000) point out that this measure would be a much better focus in international emission reduction agreements than the usual greenhouse gas inventory, which disregards international transport. A registration by residents is also necessary for linking in a meaningful way the environmental data with the economic data, which are recorded according to the same resident principle.

Table 1. **Detailed presentation of the origin of substance flows in the NAMEA of 1997 (column--account 11)**

	CO_2	N_2O	CH_4	CFCs and halons	NO_x	SO_2	NH_3	P	N	Waste	Natural gas	Crude oil
	11a	11b	11c	11d	11e	11f	11g	11h	11i	11j	11k	11l
	mln kg			*1 000 kg*	*mln kg*						*petajoules*	
EMISSION BY CONSUMERS	36 790	3.53	21.17	45	109.42	2.05	6.77	8.64	115.44	5 120		
Own transport	15 640	3.32	3.99	-	87.61	1.52	-	-	25.50	70		
Other purposes	21 150	0.21	17.18	45	21.81	0.53	6.77	8.64	89.94	5 050		
EMISSION BY PRODUCERS	163 270	69.32	618.58	803	591.09	234.08	180.89	84.49	903.37	10 050		
Agriculture and forestry	9 230	26.32	448.95	5	32.51	1.75	176.50	53.01	612.79	860		
Fishing	3 760	0.88	0.13	-	77.31	63.11	-	-	19.81	110		
Crude petroleum and natural gas production	250	0.02	0.08	-	1.00	0.35	0.15	-	0.50	90		
Other mining and quarrying	1 820	0.01	157.57	-	3.20	0.17	-	-	1.17	100		
Manufacture of food products, beverages and tobacco	4 520	0.07	0.34	20	6.99	0.48	0.23	2.54	15.46	460		
Manufacture of textile and leather products	420	0.01	0.05	-	0.58	0.01	0.01	0.03	1.95	50		
Manufacture of paper and paper products	1 930	0.01	0.08	-	2.18	0.08	0.10	0.82	4.33	360		
Publishing and printing	310	0.02	0.04	-	1.07	0.03	-	-	0.41	90		
Manufacture of petroleum products	11 200	0.07	0.60	-	15.53	52.14	0.02	0.01	5.99	70		
Manufacture of chemical products	22 470	35.06	3.11	231	27.65	12.22	2.77	7.51	19.37	1 980		
Manufacture of rubber and plastic products	250	0.01	0.04	-	0.41	0.01	-	0.02	0.27	90		
Manufacture of basic metals	8 870	0.01	0.09	-	9.35	10.09	0.07	0.17	3.98	110		
Manufacture of fabricated metal products	530	0.03	0.04	-	1.42	0.04	-	0.02	1.33	80		
Manufacture of machinery n.e.c.	380	0.02	0.04	-	1.03	0.03	-	0.07	0.90	80		
Manufacture of electrical equipment	1 140	0.01	0.11	-	1.79	0.35	0.01	0.02	1.10	90		
Manufacture of transport equipment	170	0.01	0.07	1	0.44	0.02	-	-	0.86	70		
Recycling industries	370	-	-	78	0.15	-	-	-	0.00	740		
Manufacture of wood and wood products	80	0.01	0.01	-	0.34	0.01	-	-	1.13	40		
Manufacture of construction materials	3 150	0.02	0.29	-	11.93	3.85	0.50	0.05	5.84	180		
Other manufacturing	300	0.02	0.03	-	0.61	0.04	-	-	1.34	120		
Electricity supply	44 400	0.35	1.23	-	44.33	12.46	-	0.03	21.81	50		
Gas and water supply	50	-	1.95	-	0.15	0.02	-	-	0.03	30		
Construction	1 910	0.40	0.25	225	21.38	1.44	-	2.95	8.83	1 330		
Trade and repair of motor vehicles	660	0.04	0.02	-	1.85	0.06	-	-	0.99	100		
Wholesale trade	1 890	0.30	0.13	6	12.30	0.33	-	0.04	4.22	170		
Retail trade, repair (excl. motor vehicles), hotels and restaurants	2 280	0.04	0.02	11	2.73	0.06	-	0.01	1.51	140		
Land transport	7 560	1.83	0.44	-	87.62	2.31	-	-	27.62	90		
Water transport	6 440	1.51	0.24	-	129.32	57.95	-	-	35.46	610		
Air transport	10 290	0.06	0.11	-	38.63	0.85	-	-	9.82	20		
Supporting transport activities	390	0.05	0.03	1	3.84	0.27	-	-	1.45	50		
Financial, business services and communication	4 030	0.58	0.50	-	20.46	0.67	0.53	-	8.56	510		
Public administration and social security	2 710	0.32	0.12	-	21.88	11.39	-	-	6.22	180		
Education	870	0.04	0.12	-	1.37	0.01	-	-	0.44	70		
Health and social work activities	1 730	0.43	0.22	-	2.03	0.39	-	-	0.62	130		
Sewage and refuse disposal services	5 590	0.72	1.40	225	4.87	1.05	0.02	17.21	76.26	740		
Other services	1 320	0.07	0.11	-	2.82	0.04	-	-	1.00	60		
OTHER DOMESTIC ORIGIN												
Waste dumping sites	960	-	464.06	33	0.31	0.02	-					
Transport differences								6.62	15.66			
Emission by residents	201 020	72.85	1 103.81	881	700.82	236.15	187.66	99.75	1 034.47	15 170		
FROM THE REST OF THE WORLD												
Non-residents in the Netherlands					41.01	12.00	-	-	11.25		.	
Transfer by surface water or air					59.80	70.40	22.10	15.00	313.41			
OTHER CHANGES OF NATURAL RESOURCES											3 364	250
Total = NAMEA colomn total 11	201 020	72.85	1 103.81	881	801.63	318.54	209.76	114.75	1 359.12	15 170	3 364	250

Source: Statistics Netherlands, 2000

Table 2. **Detailed presentation of the destination of substance flows in the NAMEA of 1997 (row-account 11)**

	CO_2	N_2O	CH_4	CFCs and halons	NO_x	SO_2	NH_3	P	N	Waste	Natural gas	Crude oil
	11a	11b	11c	11d	11e	11f	11g	11h	11i	11j	11k	11l
	mln kg			*1 000 kg*	*mln kg*						*petajoules*	
ABSORPTION BY PRODUCERS												
Agriculture								1.09	5.41			
Crude petroleum and natural gas production											2 541	88
Construction								3.00	3.00			
Sewage and refuse disposal services								17.18	109.50	4 460		
TO THE REST OF THE WORLD												
Residents in the rest of the world					282.31	130.70	-	-	79.20		.	
Transfer by surface water or air					411.68	92.15	34.00	16.00	424.51			
CONTRIBUTION TO ENVIRONMENTAL THEMES												
Greenhouse effect	201 020	72.85	1103.81									
Ozone layer depletion				881								
Acidification					107.64	95.70	175.76					
Eutrophication								77.47	737.50			
Waste										10 710		
Changes in natural resources											823	162
Total = NAMEA row total 11	201 020	72.85	1103.81	881	801.63	318.54	209.76	114.75	1359.12	15 170	3 364	250

Source: Statistics Netherlands, 2000

The figures for emissions by residents may differ substantially from those for emissions in the Netherlands. When considering the effects of pollution, the latter data are relevant only for those substances that contribute to regional environmental problems. For substances that exert an effect only on global environmental worries like climate change or ozone layer depletion, a country's perspective is not relevant. This is the reason why emission transfers from and to the rest of the world (ROW) are reported only for the substances that accumulate on a regional scale in the natural environment (tables 1 and 2, columns 11e-11i; data on international waste flows are not yet available). For these substances, table 3 shows the relationship between emissions by Dutch residents and the accumulation of these substances in the Netherlands. The table is derived from tables 1 and 2.

Table 3. **Net emissions by residents and net accumulation on national territory, 1997**

	NO_x	SO_2	NH_3	P	N
	mln kg				
Emissions by consumers	109	2	7	9	115
Emissions by producers	591	234	181	84	903
Emissions by other sources	0	0	–	7	16
Gross emissions by residents	701	236	188	100	1 034
Absorption by producers (-)	–	–	–	21	118
Net emissions by residents	**701**	**236**	**188**	**78**	**917**
Emission transfers from the ROW	101	82	22	15	325
Emission transfers to the ROW	694	223	34	16	504
Net accumulation on national territory	**108**	**96**	**176**	**77**	**738**

Source: Statistics Netherlands, 2000.

Table 3 shows that the emissions to the ROW exceed those from the ROW. This implies that the accumulation on national territory is smaller than the net emissions by residents. This is especially true for NO_x and SO_2 with differences of 85% and 59%, respectively. From tables 1 and 2 it can be seen that the emissions to and from the ROW are dominated by transfers by surface water or air. The exception is the emission of SO_2 to the ROW, which is mainly caused by residents. The substantial emissions of NO_x and SO_2 by residents in the ROW are mainly caused by transport activities, especially by water transport. This is a reflection of the importance of the transport sector for the Dutch economy. Evidence for the significance of this sector can also be found in the (not shown) substantial share of mobile sources in total NO_x and SO_2 pollution by Dutch residents in 1997: 77.1% and 59.9%, respectively.

Environmental themes account

Just as the balancing items of the accounts in the NAM-part of the NAMEA provide important economic indicators, the balancing item of the substances account provides a relevant environmental indicator: the contribution of pollutants to environmental themes. This balancing item equals the total amount of substances originating from the various sources in the column minus the other destinations in the row. For CO_2, N_2O, CH_4 and CFCs/halons this balance is equal to the emission by residents. For NO_x, SO_2, NH_3, P, N and waste it corresponds to the net accumulation on national territory. For natural gas and crude oil it equals "other changes of natural resources", which includes additions to proven reserves, minus "absorption by producers", which registers extractions. The environmental themes were introduced by De Haan *et al.* (1994) to surpass the measurement problems related to the impacts of environmental degradation. The themes-oriented representation of environmental pressures is particularly useful for the formulation of policy goals with respect to these pressures.

The balance in the row of the substances account of the NAMEA is at the same time an element of the column of the environmental themes account. This latter account aggregates with conversion factors the various substances, which contribute to the same theme, into environmental theme-indicators. The environmental themes establish a link between pressures on the environment and its state. They reflect the mechanisms by which specific pressures are related to particular environmental damages. A direct link is often difficult to establish. For example, in the case where the environmental damage manifests itself only if a specific threshold is exceeded. Table 4 shows in bold summary indicators, which are present in the row of the environmental themes account.

The NAMEA contains two environmental themes that address global environmental problems: the greenhouse effect and ozone layer depletion. The greenhouse-effect theme relates to the danger of climate change caused by a concentration of greenhouse gases in the atmosphere. The greenhouse gases include carbon dioxide (CO_2), nitrous oxide (N_2O) and methane (CH_4). The ozone-layer-depletion theme relates to the potential negative effects of a higher exposure to UV-B radiation caused by chlorofluorocarbons (CFCs) and halons. These substances are sometimes also regarded as greenhouse gases, but the evidence is mixed. Table 4 expresses the relative contribution of each greenhouse gas in CO_2-equivalents. The conversion factors for N_2O and CH_4 respectively are 309.315 and 20.996. CFCs and halons are expressed in CFC11-equivalents. The resulting aggregated theme-indicators for the greenhouse effect and ozone layer depletion reflect the contribution of Dutch residents to these global environmental problems.

Table 4. **Environmental theme indicators, 1997**

	Greenhouse effect	Ozone layer depletion	Acidification	Eutrophication	Waste	Change in natural resources
	(CO_2-equivalents)	(CFC11-equivalents)	(acid-equivalents)	(nutrient-equivalents)	(mln kg)	(petajoules)
CO_2	201 020					
$N_2O \cdot 309.315$	22 580					
$CH_4 \cdot 20.996$	23 180					
	246 780					
CFCs and halons		931				
$NO_x \cdot 0.217$			23			
$SO_2 \cdot 0.313$			30			
$NH_3 \cdot 0.588$			103			
			157			
$P \cdot 10$				775		
N				738		
				1 512		
Waste					**10 710**	
Natural gas						823
Crude oil						162
						985

The themes "acidification", "eutrophication" and "waste" relate to internal environmental problems that are caused by the accumulation of pollution on Dutch territory. The acidification theme relates to the damage caused by the deposition of nitrogen oxides (NO_x), sulphur oxides (SO_2) and ammonia (NH_3) in soil and surface water. The eutrophication theme relates to the problem of accumulating nitrogen (N) and phosphorus (P) in soils and subsequently in groundwater and surface water. Acidification and eutrophication are serious threats, for example they endanger ecosystems and the quality of drinking water. The accumulation of waste is a serious environmental problem as well. This theme is restricted to waste consisting of products that have lost their economic use. This kind of waste can be measured in kilograms. Acidification is expressed in acid-equivalents by applying the conversion factors 0.217, 0.313 and 0.588 to NO_x, SO_2 and NH_3, respectively. Nutrient-equivalents, which are assumed to equal 10 kg P or 1 kg N, are taken as the common unit to calculate the eutrophication indicator. The composite theme-indicators for acidification, eutrophication and waste in table 4 are estimates of the accumulation of the relevant substances in the natural environment of the Netherlands.

The theme "change in natural resources" points to the interdependence of economic activities and the depletion of natural resources. Table 4 shows for natural gas and crude oil the balance of extraction and all other changes in proven reserves in petajoules. The summary theme-indicator estimates the net change in the combined proven oil and gas reserves during the reference year.

The NAMEA and policy analyses

The NAMEA is an extension of the SNA that shares a number of key characteristics with the input-output model developed by Leontief (1970). Input-output analysis is a powerful tool for the study of relationships between the economic and environmental variables in the NAMEA. As will be shown below, it is particularly useful as a decomposition methodology. Decomposition is typically helpful in detecting the major driving forces of the periodic changes in the environmental performance of an economy.

Environmental-economic profiles

The respective contributions to the environmental theme-indicators by the consumer's emissions, subdivided by purpose, and the producer's emissions, subdivided by sector, may be straightforwardly compared on the basis of the figures in tables 1, 2 and 4. Next, these pollution shares may be compared to the economic data from the NAM-part of the NAMEA, for example to the corresponding shares in total consumption outlays or value added. This provides an environmental-economic profile, which depicts the environmental and economic role played by the various consumer and producer activities during a year.

With NAMEA-based time series, environmental-economic profiles over time may be constructed. These time profiles may for example address the question how economic change influences pollution patterns. In a times-series analysis on the basis of NAMEA, De Haan (2001) applies an input-output model to decompose the annual change in pollution into changes due to: final demand volume, the structure of production and demand, and eco-efficiency (pollution per unit of output). His results are presented in Figures 1-3. The bold lines show pollution rates – the percentage changes in the level of pollution compared to 1987 levels – as measured by the production-related CO_2- and acid-emissions and solid waste generation using annual data for 1987-1998 (solid waste 1997). The figures also depict the breakdown of the pollution rates among its three components. In all three cases, basically two major forces determined the development of pollution. On the one hand, demand volume strongly triggered pollution rates. On the other hand, pollution rates decreased due to efficiency improvements. The structure effects were less strong and generally led to a decrease in emissions. Overall, CO_2-emissions increased by 20% between 1987 and 1998. Production-related pollution in the cases of solid waste and acidification significantly decreased on balance. Further analysis for CO_2 reveals that the macro decomposition pattern generally applies at the industry level as well, though important differences across industries exist. For example, the manufacturing of chemical products and air transport services together are estimated to account for 8 percentage points of the overall efficiency gain of 12%.

Figure 1. **Decomposition of annual changes in production-related CO$_2$-emissions, the Netherlands, 1987-1998**

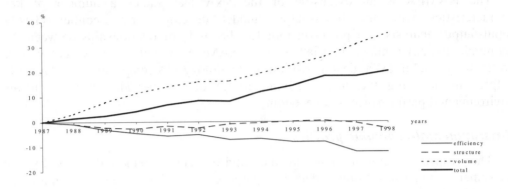

Figure 2. **Decomposition of annual changes in production-related solid waste generation, the Netherlands, 1987-1997**

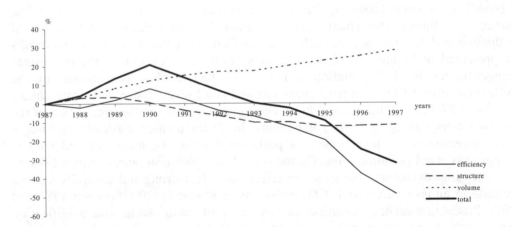

Figure 3. **Decomposition of annual changes in production-related acid-emissions, the Netherlands, 1987-1998**

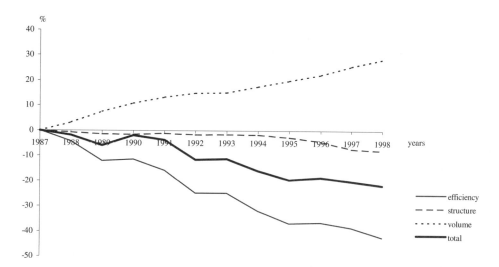

Producer and consumer activities

The NAMEA links the activities of producers and consumers directly to the corresponding environmental requirements. The requirements of government activities are registered in relation to government production and not to consumption. Environmental requirements consist of gross emissions minus the residuals that are reabsorbed into the economic sphere by either waste treatment or recycling, and natural resources. Producer activities are classified by industry. This classification is based on the International Standard Industrial Classification (ISIC). Consumer activities are classified by purpose. Table 1 distinguishes between own account transportation and other purposes. A more detailed NAMEA could provide a further breakdown based on a reconciliation of types of consumption expenditure with kinds of household activities. This matching follows the accounting work on household production.

From the link between the environment on the one hand, and producer and consumer activities on the other, environmental-economic performance indicators can be derived. For example, for production eco-productivity indicators can be calculated that measure production per unit of environmental requirement. Table 5 presents eco-productivity indicators related to CO_2 and to the acidification theme. Eco-productivity steadily increased between 1988 and 1998. This means that the environment was used more efficiently in 1998 compared to 1988. The result was a decoupling of economic growth from environmental pressures. GDP and the emission of CO_2 increased, and the amount of acid decreased during the relevant period.

Table 5. **Eco-productivity measures for production in the Netherlands.**

	1988	1993	1998	1993	1998
				index 1988 = 100	
GDP in market prices (million guilders) in constant (1997) prices	583 399	659 224	750 142	113.0	128.6
Pollution from production					
CO_2 in mln kg	140 620	149 890	166 540	106.6	118.5
Acid-equivalents	350.307	316.798	279.580	90.4	79.8
Eco-productivity					
GDP / CO_2	4.1	4.4	4.5	106.0	108.5
GDP / Acid-equivalents ✕ 1000)	1.7	2.1	2.7	125.0	161.1

Therefore, decoupling with respect to CO_2 was relative (weak), and with respect to acid absolute (strong). Environmental performance indicators may be derived for individual industries or consumer activities as well. For example, eco-efficiency indicators may highlight the environmental efficiency or inefficiency of specific household activities.

International trade

In section 2a we noted that the figures for the emission by residents, which are reported in table 1, are important for assigning the responsibility of pollution to particular countries. This point of view means that the activities of resident producers and consumers, which were addressed in the previous section, are held responsible for the pollution. Alternatively, the responsibility could be assigned to final domestic demand categories. This approach is followed by De Haan (2002). Final domestic demand will be labelled conveniently domestic consumption, but investment is included as well. Part of domestic consumption consists of goods and services from abroad. In this alternative view then, the pollution caused by the production of these import goods in foreign countries should no longer be regarded as these foreign countries' responsibility. Instead, the importing country would be responsible. This means that international trade is viewed as the displacement of environmental requirements: a country's import involves the export of pollution, and *vice versa*.

The international transfer of environmental burdens by a country can be addressed by considering its environmental balance of trade. This indicator is defined as the pollution imported via the export of goods and services minus the pollution exported via the import of goods and services. The emissions that can be attributed to domestic consumption are subsequently given by deducting the environmental trade balance from the emissions by residents. We call this measure environmental consumption. Table 6 presents the Dutch environmental balance of trade and environmental consumption for the substances contributing to acidification and eutrophication. The calculation of these two indicators makes use of input-output methods to relate pollution flows to product flows. The first row shows the figures for the net emissions by residents, which are taken from table 3.

The next three rows reveal that the pollution embodied in exports exceeds the pollution embodied in imports for all substances. This implies that the Netherlands is a net importer of embedded pollutants related to acidification and eutrophication. This can be seen immediately from the positive environmental balance of trade for all substances. A positive balance means that environmental consumption is less than residents' emissions. Put differently, Dutch pollution responsibilities measured by domestic consumption are lower than those measured by the activities of producers and consumers.

Table 6. **The environmental balance of trade and environmental consumption, 1997**

	NOx	SO₂	NH₃	P	N	Acidifica-tion f(1-3)	Eutrophi-cation f(4-5)
	1	2	3	4	5		
	mln kg					acid-eq.	nutr.-eq.
(I) Net emissions by residents	701	236	188	78	917	338	1 701
(II) Environmental balance of trade:	207	105	65	20	244	117	441
- emissions attributed to export	521	239	181	73	854	295	1 585
- emissions attributed to import (-)	313	134	115	53	610	179	1 144
(I) – (II) Environmental consumption	494	131	122	59	673	221	1 260

Table 7. **The environmental balance of trade of the Netherlands for acid pollution, 1997**

	Export	Import	Environmental balance of trade	Composition effect	Trade balance effect
	1	2	3 = 1 – 2 = 3a+ 3b	3a	3b
	acid -eq.				
Belgium and Luxembourg	36.7	24.9	11.8	–0.6	12.3
Denmark	4.1	4.7	–0.6	–2.4	1.8
Germany	80.9	38.8	42.1	15.5	26.6
Finland	2.5	1.7	0.9	0.8	0.1
France	24.5	13.6	10.9	5.8	5.0
Greece	4.4	0.5	3.9	1.9	2.0
Ireland	2.2	2.7	–0.5	0.2	–0.7
Italy	19.3	5.7	13.6	8.0	5.5
Japan	5.3	2.3	3.0	4.7	–1.7
Norway	2.6	2.3	0.3	3.3	–3.0
Austria	3.0	1.3	1.8	0.5	1.3
Portugal	2.1	1.0	1.1	0.8	0.3
Spain	8.1	3.7	4.4	2.7	1.7
Czech Republic	0.5	0.3	0.2	0.0	0.2
United Kingdom	31.3	17.6	13.7	11.8	1.9
United States of America	12.3	12.8	–0.5	3.8	–4.3
Sweden	4.6	3.9	0.7	1.4	–0.7
Switzerland	5.9	1.9	4.0	2.4	1.6
Other countries	45.0	38.9	6.1	17.3	–11.2
Total	**295.3**	**178.6**	**116.7**	**77.8**	**38.9**

Table 8. **The environmental balance of trade of the Netherlands for nutrient pollution, 1997**

	Export	Import	Environmental balance of trade	Composition effect	Trade balance effect
	1	2	3 = 1 – 2 = 3a + 3b	3a	3b
	nutrient -eq.				
Belgium and Luxembourg	183.5	164.9	18.6	−53.2	71.8
Denmark	24.2	16.4	7.8	−0.2	8.0
Germany	470.5	255.6	214.9	51.1	163.7
Finland	8.9	7.3	1.6	1.4	0.2
France	152.4	113.9	38.5	2.5	36.0
Greece	32.8	2.5	30.3	16.4	13.9
Ireland	10.8	19.1	−8.3	−4.2	−4.1
Italy	116.1	32.5	83.6	51.1	32.6
Japan	19.5	7.9	11.6	17.5	−6.0
Norway	7.0	6.6	0.3	8.6	−8.2
Austria	19.2	7.5	11.7	3.8	7.9
Portugal	10.4	9.1	1.2	−0.8	2.1
Spain	42.0	25.5	16.5	6.4	10.1
Czech Republic	3.9	1.6	2.2	0.9	1.3
United Kingdom	163.9	76.9	87.0	77.5	9.5
United States of America	37.9	97.6	−59.7	−38.2	−21.5
Sweden	22.9	19.8	3.1	6.8	−3.6
Switzerland	18.2	7.4	10.8	5.5	5.3
Other countries	241.1	271.9	−30.8	36.7	−67.4
Total	**1 585.2**	**1 144.2**	**441.0**	**189.5**	**251.5**

Environmental trade balances may also be calculated for separate trade partners. Table 7 presents the acid trade balance and table 8 the eutrophication trade balance for the Netherlands with respect to its main trading partners. The first column shows the pollution imported from the countries to which the exports are directed. The second column shows the pollution exported to the countries from which the imports originate. The third column presents net imported pollution from the respective countries. The most important country of origin of net imports of both acid and nutrient pollutants is Germany, followed by the United Kingdom. These two countries account for 36.1% and 11.7% of total net imports of acid pollutants and 48.7% and 19.7% of total net imports of nutrient pollutants, respectively. Italy, France and Belgium/Luxembourg also are relatively important contributors to the positive acidification and eutrophication related environmental trade balance. Columns 3a and 3b, tables 7 and 8, decompose the bilateral environmental trade balances into components due to the composition of trade flows and into components due to the volumes of these export and import flows. These component parts result from an input-output model and respectively are called the composition effect and trade balance effect. The net import of pollutants in the Netherlands is mainly due to the composition effect for those related to acidification and to the trade balance effect for those related to eutrophication. This overall picture, however, does not completely apply to the two most important net exporters of acid and nutrient pollutants to the Netherlands. For Germany the trade balance effect dominates, and for the United Kingdom the composition effect, for both kinds of substances.

The environmental consumption perspective calls for an alternative representation of the origin and destination of pollutants, which is provided by De Haan (2001). Rearranging terms in table 6, we get: emissions by residents + emissions attributed to import = environmental consumption + emissions attributed to export. This identity allocates the pollution by origin (source) on the left hand side to the destination (purpose) of pollution on the right hand side. These destinations consist of final demand categories. The equation follows the "supply = demand" identity of the supply and use tables in the national accounts. Table 9 provides the above set-up for CO_2-pollution in 1990 (col. 1) and 1997 (col. 3). Pollution rates – the percentage change in the level of pollution between 1997 and 1990 – are presented in column 6 of the table. The overall CO_2-pollution rate for the Netherlands was 16%. Looking at the separate origins, we see that the pollution in foreign countries by the Dutch import of goods and services showed the highest rate. The share in total CO_2-pollution of this source increased from 33.5% in 1990 to 35.3% in 1997. Producer and consumer activities experienced identical pollution rates, and hence the first activities' contribution to overall CO_2-emissions remained well above the share of the latter activities. Looking at the separate destinations, the imported pollution by the export of goods and services showed the highest growth rate. Its share in total CO_2-emissions increased by 1.5 percentage points to 48.5% in 1997. The pollution rate of environmental consumption was just below 13%. The rate of its consumption component was significantly higher than its investment component (14% against 2%). This also holds for the respective shares in overall CO_2-emissions.

With input-output analysis, the pollution rates in table 9, column 6, are decomposed into rates due to a demand effect (col. 4) and rates due to a production effect (col. 5). The demand effect captures the effect of a combined change in demand volume and structure. The production effect relates to the effect of a combined change in eco-efficiency and production structure. The second column in table 9 is based on this decomposition exercise by showing the estimated pollution levels in 1997 in the absence of the production effect. The figures in this column are higher than the actual pollution levels for 1997 in column 3. Put differently, the demand effect is positive and the production effect is negative, as can be seen from columns 4 and 5.

Table 9. **Origin and destination of CO_2-pollution, the Netherlands, 1990-1997**

	1990	1997 (disregarding the production effect)	1997	Demand effect	Production effect	Total
	1	2	3	4	5	6
				= (2-1)/1	= (3-2)/1	= (3-1)/1
	billion kg			*%-change*		
Origin						
Domestic						
Production (direct)	145	171	163	18	–6	12
Consumption (direct)	33	41	37	24	–12	12
Rest of the World						
Import (attributed)	89	116	109	30	–8	23
Total	**266**	**328**	**309**	**23**	**–7**	**16**
Destination						
Domestic						
Consumption (direct + attributed)	115	139	132	20	–6	14
Capital formation (attributed)	26	27	27	3	0	2
Rest of the World						
Export (attributed)	125	162	150	30	–10	21
Total	**266**	**328**	**309**	**23**	**–7**	**16**

Conclusion

This paper examines the relevancy of the NAMEA to accounting for sustainable development. The NAMEA extends the SNA with environmental accounts in physical units. The environmental performance indicators, which are derived from this integrated set of economic and environmental accounts, cover important environmental themes. The paper shows that the linked economic and environmental indicators allow monitoring and analyzing a wide range of sustainability issues within one coherent framework. The incorporation into this single accounting system of a SAM, from which social indicators can be derived, provides opportunities for an integral policy analysis of sustainable development.

References

Haan, de M. (2001), "A structural decomposition analysis of pollution in the Netherlands", *Economic Systems Research*, 2, 181-96.

Haan, de M. (2002), Disclosing international trade dependencies in environmental pressure indicators: the domestic consumption perspective, paper presented at the International Input-Output Association Conference, Montreal.

Haan, de M. and S.J. Keuning (1996), "Taking the environment into account: the NAMEA approach", *Review of Income and Wealth*, 2, 131-48.

Haan, de M. and H. Verduin (2000), "De vergelijking van economische baten en milieulasten", *Milieu, tijdschrift voor milieukunde*, 15, 159-66.

Haan, de M., S.J. Keuning and P.R. Bosch (1994), *Integrating indicators in a National Accounting Matrix including Environmental Accounts (NAMEA)*, National Accounts Occasional Papers NA-60, Statistics Netherlands, Voorburg/Heerlen.

Leontief, W. (1970), "Environmental repercussions and the economic structure: an input-output approach", *Review of Economics and Statistics*, 52, 262-71.

Statistics Netherlands (2000), *National accounts of the Netherlands 1999*, Statistics Netherlands, Voorburg/Heerlen.

United Nations, International Monetary Fund, Commission of the European Communities – Eurostat, Organisation for Economic Co-operation and Development, World Bank (1993), *System of National Accounts 1993*, New York.

The New Zealand Experience with Environmental Accounting Frameworks in Measuring Inter-relationships between the Economy, Society and the Environment[1]

C. O'Brien

Statistics New Zealand

Introduction

New Zealand is carrying out an environmental statistical programme to develop natural resource and sustainability measures. Recent work has concentrated on developing natural resource accounts (for forestry, water, energy and fish) and producing a discussion document on New Zealand Sustainable Development Indicators.

This paper discusses the detail of these and other environmental statistics that have been, or will be, released by Statistics New Zealand. The statistical frameworks used for New Zealand's environmental statistics allow for outputs that reveal inter-relationships between the environmental, social and economic dimensions. The paper summarises how well these inter-relationships are being measured in New Zealand environmental statistics, and discusses what may be required to improve the measurement of these inter-relationships in the future.

Initial Selection of Frameworks

For natural resource account development, Statistics New Zealand is using the framework from the System of Environmental and Economic Accounts (SEEA). Statistics New Zealand began developing natural resource accounts from the beginning of 2001. For many of these resources in New Zealand, there are gaps in existing data which natural resource accounts can address.

Statistics New Zealand has released an experimental sustainable development indicator publication. This publication discusses a number of frameworks, but no particular framework has been selected for New Zealand sustainable development indicators. The appropriate framework will be determined after feedback from the initial report is analysed and after consultation with other organisations.

New Zealand's Progress on Natural Resource and Environmental Accounts

The following comments are based on Statistics New Zealand's outputs and expectations as at May 2003. The Statistics New Zealand environmental web page[2]

---

1. Paper prepared by Chase O'Brien and Zane Colville (*Statistics New Zealand*).

2. *http://www.stats.govt.nz/domino/external/web/Prod_Serv.nsf/htmldocs/Environment.*

provides current information on the status of Statistics New Zealand's environmental statistics development. It should be noted that the environment team is not part of the National Accounts Division, although the two groups work closely together.

The natural resource accounts (sections 3.1 to 3.4) and the Environmental Protection Expenditure account estimate (3.5) have all been developed using the SEEA framework. Flow accounts are being estimated as Supply and Use tables. Ecosystems accounts are not being developed at present.

Energy Account

Statistics New Zealand published a physical stock account for energy in November 2002, with a physical flow account to be released in 2003. Monetary accounts will be released later.

The energy physical stock account estimates New Zealand's stock of coal, oil and gas in units of petajoules. The stock account indicates that New Zealand's stock of coal is effectively unlimited (estimated at 1,000 years supply from known existing stocks at current extraction rates), although stocks of the other energy sources are being extracted and consumed at an unsustainable rate. These estimates may be interesting for policy purposes, but were already well known from other external data sources.

The forthcoming energy flow account estimate is likely to provide new information that may be useful for policy analysis and monitoring purposes. The energy flow account will estimate emissions that have been caused by energy generation and use. Other statutory bodies already produce estimates of emissions, but only at a broad industry level. Statistics New Zealand can produce estimates at a greater level of industry detail by the integration of energy physical data with internal data sources such as National Accounts monetary input-output studies.

Other government departments also produce energy statistics using a supply / use approach, although these estimates are physical estimates only, and need to be adjusted to meet the SEEA framework. When the monetary energy flow accounts are produced, this will be the first time that New Zealand energy supply and use data will be available in physical and monetary units, where the data is consistent and comparable over energy sources and time. Together, these tables will allow for more sophisticated analysis of energy use in New Zealand, making possible, for example, estimates of energy use and emissions by industry compared with industry Gross Domestic Product (GDP) and employment. The SEEA notes that these tables overseas have proven to be of great interest to policy makers and the general public, as some countries have found that many of their significant polluting industries are actually quite small in monetary terms.

The Department of Prime Minister and Cabinet (DPMC) published a Sustainable Development "Programme of Action" in January 2003 (DPMC 2003). This report summarised the government's sustainable development priorities, and highlighted the importance of energy and water. New Zealand's energy objectives include security of supply, further development of renewable energy, and that energy use become more efficient and less wasteful. The energy accounts should assist the government in monitoring its success in meeting its energy efficiency objective. Energy efficiency is defined in the report as using less energy for the same amount of production.

The energy account has an economic-environmental focus. The framework and data allows for the relevant economic and environmental data to be integrated relatively easily. While the energy accounts will not directly include social data, the policy uses that the accounts could be used for could have major social implications. For example, successive governments have attempted to ensure that households have secure access to power, partly because "health and wellbeing are affected by the coldness and dampness of many of our homes, which fall below the temperature level recommended by the World Health Organisation" (DPMC, 2003, p. 16).

Forestry Account

Statistics New Zealand has released physical stock and flow accounts for forestry covering the period 1995 – 2000, with a monetary flow account expected to be released in the next few months. A monetary stock account for forestry will be produced later.

The Forestry physical stock account estimates that New Zealand has 2.742 million hectares of timber available for wood supply in 2000, and 5.266 million hectares of timber not available for wood supply. New Zealand's total land area is 26.802 million hectares. The remnants of New Zealand's indigenous forests account for the timber not available for wood supply. Since New Zealand is a signatory to the Kyoto Protocol it will need to monitor the size and other characteristics of its forest resource. The land area covered by indigenous forests has been increasing in recent years due to natural extension, and increased protection of indigenous forests on private land. There are some concerns over degradation of this forest estate however, mainly due to introduced pests such as possums.

Most timber available for wood supply comes from commercial pine forests, although there are some indigenous forests that can be harvested, with restrictions. Forestry products account for a significant proportion of New Zealand's exports (12.2% of exports of goods in 2000). The most notable feature of the commercial forest estate is the large volume of wood that will become available from 2005 on as a large number of pine forests mature at more or less the same time. This phenomenon is known domestically as the "wall of wood". The planted area of commercial forests has been increasing in recent years, although this growth is expected to slow or decline due to low recent returns from logging.

The forestry stock account provides a complete estimate of New Zealand's exotic and indigenous forests, in hectares and cubic metres. Estimates of commercial and non-commercial forests are also provided. The account mainly serves to bring together data that was already available but was scattered over a variety of sources. The accounts therefore provide sustainability measures of forestry that were not readily available previously.

The forestry flow accounts are mainly based on National Accounts annual input-output studies, supplemented with additional volume information not utilised by National Accounts.[3] Both flow accounts were estimated at the same time to ensure that the monetary and physical flow accounts would be consistent with each other and consistent with the already published National Accounts. The flow accounts are expressed in standard volumes, and in roundwood equivalents to better allow for comparisons between different forestry commodities.

The derivation of the forestry account meant that many external and internal data sources were analysed for possible incorporation into the account. Bringing data together

---

3. The National Accounts Division does not produce constant price input-output tables, so the non-use of some volume data in current price input-output analysis is perhaps understandable.

and putting it in a SEEA framework has revealed some inconsistencies in that source data. For example, for the cubic metre estimates for commercial forests in the physical forestry stock account, Statistics New Zealand obtained data for the main components of the stock account (stock levels, harvesting, thinning and growth). Even though all this data came from the same government department, the forestry stock account based on this data could not be balanced. The stock account invariably had a significant residual of the same sign. This indicated a consistent error in the source data. After consultation with the government department concerned, it was decided that the estimate for "growth" was the weakest estimate. The government department responsible for the growth estimate agrees that there is a problem with its estimates and it is reviewing its methodology as a consequence. In the meantime, however, this "growth" estimate has been incorporated into the forestry stock account tables. The forestry stock tables include a balancing item.

The forestry account uses a slightly different forestry commodity classification to that used by National Accounts. The environment team has recommended that the National Accounts revise their commodity classification to be consistent with that used in the forestry account, and discussions are taking place to this end. The commodity classification in the forestry account was utilised after a review of physical data sources and classifications used by the Ministry of Agriculture and Forestry. This classification best reflects domestic industry practice and outputs. The National Accounts uses the Australian and New Zealand Standard Commodity Classification, although this classification can and has been modified by National Accounts when necessary.

At present the forestry accounts mainly have an economic focus. The physical accounts do not as yet contain estimates of residuals, carbon binding, ecosystems, or measures of degradation (although the accounts do contain some residual data *e.g.* sawdust and recognise that other residuals also exist such as black liquor). Statistics New Zealand would like to bring some or all of these environmental measures into future versions of the accounts. Further development of the accounts would therefore very likely provide more detail on the economic-environmental links within forestry.

Water Account

Annual water accounts covering the period 1996-2001 are being developed for New Zealand, but published accounts are unlikely to be available before 2004. The water accounts will be made available on a regional basis and contain data on New Zealand's groundwater and surface water resources. Geothermal water data will not be included in the accounts to be released due to an absence of data.

Although New Zealand generally has an ample supply of water by international standards, water issues have become a concern to government: "freshwater allocation and use, water quality issues, and water bodies of national importance are fundamental elements for New Zealand's sustainable development. There are a number of water-resource management issues that must be addressed for us to sustain our economic growth, natural environment and heritage, and the health and wellbeing of our people" (DPMC, 2003, p. 13).[4] For instance, increased water use by dairy farms has raised concerns as to whether this is economically the best use of water, and has also led to

4.   The "desired outcomes" in the report include maintaining water quality and allocating water in a sustainable, efficient and equitable way.

concerns over degradation of the stock of water.[5] Policy makers in New Zealand have few tools to evaluate these issues, which have economic, environmental and social dimensions.

Regional water accounts are considered to be desirable as many of New Zealand's water issues exist on a regional rather than national basis. New Zealand's geophysical form has a great influence on water quality and availability. In general, the West Coast of New Zealand receives far more rainfall than the East Coast. This is particularly the case in the South Island, where prevailing westerly winds release most of their moisture as rain and snow west of the main divide of the Southern Alps. The eastern slopes of the Southern Alps are in a "rain shadow". The greatest rainfall tends to fall in areas with the least population, while areas with the greatest demand can suffer from water shortages. Hydropower generation accounts for a significant proportion of New Zealand's electricity consumption, but hydropower storage is limited and requires continuous recharging from rivers. The lack of hydro storage mainly arises from the characteristics of New Zealand rivers, which are very short and steep by international standards.[6]

The physical water account development involves collating and compiling water information that has not been collected and presented in a consistent manner in New Zealand before (MFE, 1997, 7.53).[7] The amount of water consumed for irrigation in New Zealand is large but is only known approximately. A 1999 study (LE, 2000) determined that irrigation accounts for 77% of water allocation in New Zealand (with industrial water use and public water supply accounting for the remainder of the allocation). Since this percentage is based on water allocation data it does not necessarily reflect actual irrigation water use. It is often used as a proxy for actual water use, however, in the absence of actual water use data. For the water account, Statistics New Zealand is compiling and estimating data on actual water use by industry, households and irrigation. Given gaps in existing water data, and the current concerns related to water allocation and quality in New Zealand, it is expected that the water accounts will be seen as very useful for policy purposes when they are made available. The accounts would be more useful still if a measure of water quality can be incorporated into the accounts.

The water accounts do not measure water quality, with such measures being too technical and resource intensive for Statistics New Zealand to consider undertaking. Other government departments and local authorities estimate measures of water quality. In the future, water quality could conceivably be integrated into the water account, through the derivation of water quality accounts as described in the SEEA, although the feasibility of this has not been explored. Much New Zealand water is used for hydropower generation and/or irrigation, as well as for human use. All of these significant

---

5.   For example, refer Dave Hansford (31 January 2003). "Are we Reaching the Bottom of the Bucket?" New Zealand Environment, 10-12: "There's only so much water to go round, and as we put more and more pressure on the land to produce grapes and sustain burgeoning dairy herds, we're sucking the country dry". Also refer Geoff Collett (April 5, 2003), "Meridian's Power", The Press, Christchurch: "Meridian Energy needs water to generate much-needed electricity. Farmers and recreational users lay equal claim to the snow-fed waters of the South Island. Is a compromise possible, and is Meridian being too aggressive in protecting its resource"? Many articles in a similar vein have been published in New Zealand in recent months.

6.   This paragraph is mostly derived from MFE (1997). At the time of writing (April 2003), New Zealanders are being asked to reduce their power consumption due to low hydro lake levels.

7.   "Assessing the extent of these effects [of people on water flows and quality] is difficult because most water data are collected by regional councils for local purposes and cannot be readily combined into national statistics."

water uses have varying water quality requirements. Therefore any New Zealand water quality accounts would need to be fairly sophisticated to be useful to policy makers.

Little work has been undertaken on monetary water accounts so far by Statistics New Zealand although some water output is valued in New Zealand, and the National Accounts Division has produced some monetary estimates of water industry output. Linking the National Accounts estimates to the water resource accounts may be difficult, given the regional nature of the water accounts, while the National Accounts are derived at a national level only.

The focus of the water account is primarily economic with some social element, as it illustrates the availability and the allocation of water, but does not have degradation estimates, at least in the initial version of the account.

Fish Account

Statistics New Zealand has released a physical stock account for fish, and a physical flow account should be released in a few months. These accounts have numerous weaknesses and omissions, and their main function is in illustrating what data is currently available to produce a fish account under a SEEA framework, if required.

Most of New Zealand's commercial fish stocks are managed under the Quota Management System (QMS). The fish resource is generally of high commercial quality, but it is limited in size, and would be subject to depletion unless managed carefully. The QMS was introduced in 1986 partly in response to the apparent depletion of New Zealand fish stocks. New Zealand's shore conditions are also suitable for aquaculture production in a number of areas.

The physical stock account development has identified some significant data gaps. Much of the physical data that is available is of too low a quality to use in official statistics, including the data used by the Ministry of Fisheries for QMS modelling. At the same time, the data that is in the fish physical stock account is generally readily available from other data sources. Because of this, and the general belief that the QMS is already working well as a fish management system, some industry participants have questioned the need for the fish stock account.

After evaluating these concerns, Statistics New Zealand has decided not to produce monetary accounts for fish in the immediate future, and the existing physical accounts will not be updated in the future. Monetary fish accounts will only be produced in future if they are required as an input to some broader measure such as environmentally adjusted GDP.

Environmental Protection Expenditure

Statistics New Zealand recently released an experimental set of Environmental Protection Expenditure (EPE) accounts for 2000/01. EPE accounts have been produced for environmental protection activities and natural resource management.

This initial EPE estimate is based on existing administrative data sources and provides estimates of public sector EPE only. Producing a full EPE account in New Zealand would require new surveys or enhancements to existing surveys. Existing commodity collections could also need to be adjusted to collect EPE information. These options all appear to be feasible, although whether these steps are taken depends on the reaction to the initial set of EPE accounts. Funding is required before the accounts can be developed further.

The EPE accounts do not link very well with other Statistics New Zealand outputs such as the National Accounts. The EPE "commodity" does not exist in the commodity classification used by National Accounts. To increase the linkages between the EPE and the National Accounts, the EPE account could be estimated as part of a satellite account (see section 4 below), although at present there are no plans on doing this. At this stage, the New Zealand EPE accounts should be considered to be environmentally focussed with few economic linkages. The EPE accounts provide data that is not available from other data sources, and provides one indicative measure of sustainability. The New Zealand EPE accounts really need to be developed further to be useful for monitoring and policy purposes however.

Satellite Accounts in New Zealand

The National Accounting framework allows for the integration of economic and environmental data via an environmental Satellite account (SNA93, Chapter XXI, D). At present there are no plans for New Zealand to produce a full environmental satellite account, although many of the required elements will be available after the natural resource account development work is completed.

New Zealand has experience with Satellite Accounts from the publication of a Tourism Satellite Account (TSA) (SNZ, 2002b). Producing the TSA has proved to be rather resource intensive for a relatively small national statistical agency, which has implications for the production of an environmental Satellite account. The environment team needs more resources to be able to produce an environmental satellite account. Whether this happens mainly depends on the demand for measures such as an estimate of depletion adjusted Gross Domestic Product.

Although New Zealand has only just begun producing natural resource accounts, the desirability of utilising an extended accounting framework for satellite accounts are becoming apparent. Even though hybrid resource accounts are being produced, it is still difficult for users to aggregate the individual resource estimates to gain an overview of the New Zealand environmental-economic interaction. At present the natural resource accounts are mainly being used for analysis on a resource by resource basis. A satellite approach would make the existing resource accounts far more useful by better integrating the existing estimates and making their links with the economy (and each other) more apparent.

New Zealand Sustainable Development Indicators

An initial report on New Zealand Sustainable Development Indicators (SDI's), called "Monitoring Progress Towards a Sustainable New Zealand", was published by Statistics New Zealand in August 2002. This was the first attempt by Statistics New Zealand to produce sustainable development indicators, although socio-economic indicators had previously been published. The "Monitoring Progress" report is subtitled "an experimental report and analysis", reflecting that the report is very much a discussion document and a starting point for SDI development in New Zealand.

The "Monitoring Progress" report was produced with input from many other New Zealand government departments, including the Ministry for the Environment, Ministry of Social Development, Ministry of Economic Development, The Treasury and the Department of Internal Affairs. Because the "Monitoring Progress" report is intended as a discussion document, the report has not settled on a particular SDI framework. The appropriate SDI framework will be determined after feedback from the initial report is analysed, and after consultation with other government departments.

The indicators selected in the "Monitoring Progress" were chosen after a series of steps. An initial set of indicators were chosen based on UN guidelines and from existing indicators such as the Ministry for the Environment's Environmental Performance Indicators. The set of indicators was compared against criteria to select the final indicators most relevant to sustainable development.[8] The types of capital used in the report are: Environmental capital, Economic capital, Social capital, Human capital, Cultural capital and Institutional capital. All of these types of capital are based on OECD definitions apart from "Cultural capital", which is defined as "the set of values, traditions and behaviours which link a specific group of people together". This was considered to be an integral part of sustainable development for New Zealand. The capital approach was used throughout the report to assist in the analysis of themes[9] in relation to:

The "Monitoring Progress" report therefore includes numerous economic, social and environmental indicators (along with indicators classified to other types of "capital"). Since a specific New Zealand SDI framework has not been determined, however, these indicators have not been "linked" together (to produce such measures as "decoupling" indicators, or a Global progress Indicator, for example). Therefore, while the SDI report provides information on the economic, social and environmental dimensions, at this stage it does not illustrate the inter-relationships between these dimensions. If further development of New Zealand SDI's is supported, it is expected that an SDI framework will be selected that allows for more sophisticated analysis and the linking of economic, environmental and social indicators.

Conclusion

The natural resource accounts mainly have an environmental and economic focus, particularly if the accounts are further developed. The accounts are generally successful in showing the inter-relationships between the economy and the environment for specific natural resources. This is fairly predictable given that SEEA focuses on the environment and the economy (SEEA 2000, 1-2, 1.11). The accounts would be far more useful if they were incorporated into some kind of satellite account.

The New Zealand natural resource accounts have weak links with the social dimension. Also, any likely future developments of the accounts will not improve the situation much. For example, while the industry level statistics in the flow accounts could be linked to employment data, this is arguably fairly peripheral information. A more significant improvement to data with social relevance could be in providing and improving measures of environmental degradation. Statistics New Zealand therefore supports any move to firm up SEEA guidelines on how to measure degradation.

8. The criteria were: indicator recommended by the UN or OECD, accepted as an indicator for New Zealand and published by an official (NZ) agency, technically and analytically sound, relevant, measurable and cost effective, and simple to understand and easy to interpret (p. 93).

9. The themes used in the report are: population, environment and ecosystem resilience, skills and knowledge, living standards and health, consumption and resource use, and social cohesion (p. 93).

Many of New Zealand's natural resources are currently managed in such a way that there is little or no depletion of the resource (forestry and fish). Resources such as energy are being depleted, but information on that depletion is already widely available. Arguably, then, New Zealand may need statistical measures of environmental degradation more than statistical measures of environmental depletion.

The relationship between the environmental, economic and social dimensions may be best illustrated through the use of a more sophisticated SDI framework in New Zealand. It seems unlikely that alternative data sources in New Zealand will provide the necessary social statistics, at least in the short term, and it will be important to choose an appropriate SDI framework.

References

DPMC (2003), Sustainable Development for New Zealand Programme of Action, Department of Prime Minister and Cabinet, New Zealand: *http://www.beehive.govt.nz/ViewDocument.cfm* ?DocumentID = 15944 Programme of Action.

LE (2000), *Information on Water Allocation in New Zealand*, Report No 4375/1, Lincoln Environmental.

MFE (1997), *The State of New Zealand's Environment 1997*, Ministry for the Environment.

SNZ (2002a), *Monitoring Progress Towards a Sustainable New Zealand*, Statistics New Zealand, *http://www.stats.govt.nz/domino/external/web/nzstories.nsf/htmldocs/ Monitoring+Progress+Towards+a+Sustainable+New+Zealand.*

SNZ (2002b), *Tourism Satellite Account 1997-1999*, Statistics New Zealand, *http://www.stats. govt.nz/domino/external/pasfull/pasfull.nsf/web/Reference+Reports+ Tourism+Satellite+Account+1997-1999?open.*

United Nations, International Monetary Fund, Commission of the European Communities-Eurostat, Organisation for Economic Co-operation and Development, World Bank (1993), *System of National Accounts 1993*, New York.

United Nations, Organisation for Economic Co-operation and Development, Statistical Office of the European Communities, World Bank (forthcoming), *System of Environmental and Economic Accounts: SEEA 2000*, Draft for the Statistical Commission, January 2002: *http://www4.statcan.ca/citygrp/london/ publicrev/intro.htm.*

Integrated Environmental and Economic Accounting in Italy

C. Costantino, F. Falcitelli, A. Femia, A. Tudini

ISTAT, Italy

Introduction

The debate on sustainable development is mainly focused, in Italy, on issues related to the interrelationships between the natural system and the economic system. This occurs both in the sphere of political discussion and in the context of related statistical work.

The interaction between economy and environment is taken into account in different contexts by various disciplines. In some cases ecologically sustainable development is addressed by means of methodologies inspired by some accounting vision of the problem at issue, all of which, in recent years in the Italian debate, have used the label "environmental accounting". In fact, this label indicates a variety of activities, which range from institutional ones to business management, from analytical work to measurement exercises; furthermore, they may be focused on macro as well as micro level and may have a national as well as a local perspective.

The first Italian strategy for sustainable development has been explicitly defined with the "Environmental action strategy for sustainable development in Italy" (EASSDI),[1] issued by the Ministry of the environment and adopted by the Inter-Ministerial Committee for Economic Planning in 2002. It includes environmental accounting in a broad sense among the instruments to be used for environmental action and sustainable development. Environmental accounting in a broad sense is also the subject of a bill on environmental accounting (EAB) currently under discussion in the Italian Parliament; this aims at introducing the adoption by the government of planning documents concerning ecological sustainability which are to be linked to those normally adopted for economic planning.

Within environmental accounting envisaged at the strategic and legislative level by the EASSDI and the EAB respectively, a crucial role is attached to integrated environmental and economic accounting developed by Istat, thus indicating a great attention given by the political world to environmental accounting of official statistics. This highlights growing political awareness about the potential of this discipline as a tool for structuring statistical information on economy and environment in a perspective of ecological sustainability. Especially in the context of the EAB it is believed, also, that not only the production of the relevant statistics but even the use of the same statistics in the political debate on sustainable development can be better structured by making use of environmental accounts.

---

1. See Ministero dell'Ambiente e della Tutela del Territorio (2002).

The emphasis put by the EASSDI and the EAB on Istat environmental accounting stems from the perceived capability of Istat environmental accounting to deal with these two dimensions of sustainable development – the economic and environmental ones – in an integrated way.

As a matter of fact, environmental accounting in Italy is strictly linked with work at the international level on this subject, which in turn has been focused on sustainability issues since its very beginning. As a consequence, investigating interrelationships between the economic and environmental dimensions of development has been put at the core of the same work. This has led, as described in the SEEA2003, to the definition of frameworks that are of particular interest for the measurement of sustainable development thanks to the links established between the environmental and economic aspects covered.[2] It should be noted, also, that environmental accounting developed at the international level has been conceived according to main national accounting concepts and definitions, and several modules have been defined as satellite accounts to national accounting. Physical and monetary aggregates stemming from environmental accounting can therefore be used in a modeling context, thus helping economic analysis in an ecological sustainability perspective, as well as facilitating the construction of various measures of sustainable development based on an integrated view of the economy and the environment.

In the following paragraphs, the structure of the above mentioned EAB, its main objectives and the role it envisages for environmental accounting frameworks are discussed (par. 2), as well as the approach followed at Istat in identifying accounting frameworks to measure ecologically sustainable development (par. 3). As far as the Istat approach is concerned, a discussion of the complexity of the interaction between economy and environment emphasises the importance of referring to an analytical framework such as the DPSIR model and highlights a number of basic concepts followed at Istat in identifying a framework for developing environmental accounts (par. 3.1). Then the overall accounting framework, looked at as both a structure for the specific environmental accounts implemented (par. 3.2.1) and as a rationale for the definition of systems of indicators (par. 3.2.2), is discussed, the focus being on the accounting framework's capability to ensure integration of environmental and economic aspects. Some concluding remarks are in paragraph 4.

Environmental accounting frameworks in a bill for introducing sustainable development in government planning

The political debate going on in Italy on environmental accounting in a broad sense emphasises, as anticipated in the previous paragraph, a need of environmental accounting frameworks that are suitable for structuring not only the production but also the use of statistical information in decision taking and policy making for sustainable development.

Such an evolution towards user-oriented frameworks is highlighted by environmental accounting concepts/frameworks that are embedded/envisaged in the above mentioned EAB. This is currently under discussion in the Italian Parliament under the title "Central

---

2. See United Nations, European Commission, International Monetary Fund, Organisation for Economic Co-operation and Development, World Bank (2003).

and Local Government Environmental Accounting".[3] Such bill, which has given impetus to the debate recalled above, is focused on environmental accounting in a broad sense for General Government planning towards an environmentally sustainable development path.

The bill aims at introducing the so called "Documents concerning the ecological sustainability of development" (DESDs from now on) as new planning tools to be approved by Central and Local Government. These documents should include information and targets concerning the environmental dimension of the development in a sustainability perspective; furthermore, they should be approved – by each unit of General Government (*i.e.* State, Regions, Provinces, and Municipalities) – together with the approval of the corresponding financial and economic planning documents.

Besides this *environmental planning tool* – *i.e.* the DESDs – the bill aims at introducing an *environmental information tool* to be approved on a regular basis for supporting the elaboration of the DESDs: such a tool is a system of "Environmental accounts" (EAs from now on) to be adopted by each unit of General Government.

The regular approval of both tools aims at introducing a twofold parallelism:

3. between economic and environmental planning, in practice between financial and economic planning documents on the one hand and the corresponding DESDs on the other hand;

4. between economic and environmental information, in practice between tools which support economic and environmental planning, i.e. economic accounts on the one side and the EAs on the other side.

The bill does not specify the contents nor the frameworks for the DESDs and the EAs it envisages. Nonetheless, the bill gives a number of general criteria and indications to that end.

As far as the DESDs are concerned, the following criteria are pointed out:

- they should contain a selection of results and information provided by the EAs;

- the selection of results and information from the EAs should vary according to the institutional level of General Government by which the DESDs they support are approved;

- the results and information extracted by the EAs should be organised in a way that would allow a comparison with financial and economic planning documents;

---

3. In 1998 a first bill, with a similar denomination, was presented in the Senate, followed by four more bills, almost identical to the first one. Following a common examination process, an amended text based on the first bill was passed by the Senate, but not by the Chamber – the other body of the Italian Parliament – within the period of office of the previous legislature. In 2001 the same text previously passed by the Senate has been presented again and is presently under discussion, again at the Senate. Similarly to what had happened before, three more bills have been presented soon after the reiterated presentation of the first bill. Although these three bills are slightly different from the first one, even in this case a common examination process for all the four proposals has been set up by the Parliament.

- the EAs results and information should be included in the DESDs gradually, taking into account the state of the art and soundness of official statistics environmental accounting.

As far as the EAs are concerned the bill gives the following main indications:

- they are to be produced within the National Statistical System;

- they should describe the interactions between economy and environment, with particular reference to environmental "pressures" and "responses" (environmental expenditures),[4]

- the content and framework of the EAs should vary according to the institutional level of General Government by which they are adopted;

- the content and framework of the EAs should be defined and changed taking into account the state of the art of official statistics in this field at the international and national levels.

The bill also calls for operational frameworks, which, are to be defined subsequently, based on the above criteria and indications, by means of laws by decree to be enacted once the bill is passed.

Despite the fact that the bill at issue has not been passed yet, a number of Local Government bodies have launched experimental projects for developing environmental accounting in a broad sense at the local level. At the present stage very few projects have been finalised. The work in progress shows mainly the following:

- these projects are mainly focused on EAs and not on DESDs;

- in order to develop EAs at the local level, their intention is to make reference to environmental accounting approaches and modules developed within the international and national official statistics context (e.g. the EPEA5);

- most of these projects are in fact exclusively centred on the calculation of environmental expenditures carried out by the Local Government unit; this in practice implies making a re-classification of the public expenditure concerned, based on the budget analysis method. In order to do that a number of projects make reference to the EPEA and in particular to the CEPA classification;

- some projects – in addition to the calculation of environmental expenditures carried out by the Local Government unit – envisage to develop a system of "pressure" and "state" indicators referred to the territory managed by the Local Government unit; such an approach is a sort of hybrid between a micro and a macro one; as a matter of fact, environmental expenditures carried out by the Local Government unit correspond to a micro perspective, while the environmental pressures born and the state of the environment observed in the whole territory managed by the same unit correspond to a macro perspective;

- there is a great heterogeneity in methods and results, although it is the intention of most projects to make reference to standardised international environmental

4.   According to the DPSIR model. See paragraphs 3.1 and 3.2.1 in the present paper.

5.   See Eurostat (1994 and 2002a).

accounting approaches. This may produce a certain level of confusion, to the extent that the content of international definitions, classifications and accounting schemes is changed while keeping the original labels.

The bill described above highlights the demand of environmental accounts coming from policy makers, who are interested in having the support of official statistics in decision taking and planning at the different levels of General Government. One crucial point is that there is a twofold need of user-oriented frameworks; these are:

5. an accounting framework for defining and organising the EAs to be adopted by the different levels of General Government;

6. a framework for identifying and organising within the DESDs of the different levels of General Government the information and results to be extracted from the EAs.

This need of frameworks is also emphasised by the experimental projects launched so far by Local Government units, given the heterogeneous and sometimes confused approaches that are being followed in an attempt to implement the bill on a pilot basis at the local level.

As far as the EAs are concerned, the same experimental projects suggest, in particular, that a user-oriented accounting framework for Central and Local Government units can be defined by selecting and organising relevant components from accounting frameworks and modules developed at the international level within official statistics. While it appears that there is no need of completely new frameworks, the experience made so far also suggests, however, that there is a need of guidelines for a proper application of existing standardised approaches.

The Istat approach to frameworks for measuring ecologically sustainable development

The complex interaction between economy and environment

The successful search for an organic and, to the extent possible, complete statistical description of the interrelationships between the economic and environmental dimensions of development is one of the basic features of environmental accounting. A clear vision of these interrelationships has therefore been considered to be essential since the beginning of work developed at Istat in this field. To that end, a map of the relevant relationships in the technosphere/ecosphere dialectic has been identified in the well-known and internationally agreed-upon DPSIR model.

This model provides a very effective representation of the environmental/economic interaction circuit in a sustainability perspective. As it is described in Figure 1, the model leans on the description of a strong connection between the components that form it: man, with all his activities (driving forces), causes stress (pressures) to the natural environment, whose conditions (state) tend to be modified as a consequence of this stress;[6] wherever these modifications of environmental conditions turn out to be undesirable for man (impact), the anthropic system tends, in turn, to react (response) to the environmental change, to eliminate the causes or the consequences; in turn, when

---

6. The fact that the conditions of the natural environmental are the result of the combined effect of stress produced by the anthropic system and the spontaneous evolution of the natural system is not looked at here.

these responses are intended to eliminate the causes, they retroact more or less effectively on the pressures carried out by man on nature.

Partly due to the heterogeneity of the elements that are included in the DPSIR model (both *between* and *within* the boxes) and partly due to insufficient knowledge of complex interactions, one can not rely on a series of identities that tie all the elements of this environmental/economic interaction circuit in a unique accounting framework. Starting from the DPSIR model, therefore, there is no way to derive from it directly a framework for describing the interrelationships between economy and environment in an accounting fashion.[7]

Nevertheless, the DPSIR analytical framework is seen as an essential reference for developing environmental accounting at Istat in a way that is meaningful in a sustainable development perspective.

Figure 1.   **The DPSIR circuit**

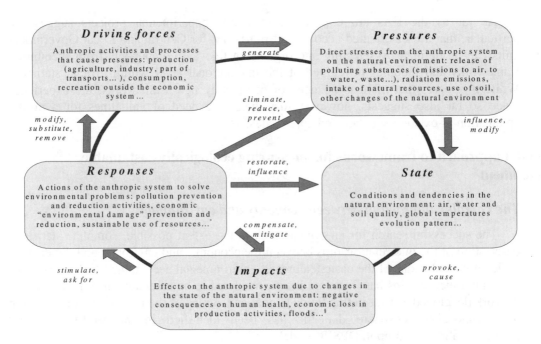

Notes:

§   The social system at large, and not just the economy, is affected by changes in the state of the natural environment. This may be an important source of demand for ecological sustainability policy and may retroact on the economy. To the extent that this occurs, impacts on the social system are accounted for in the environmental/economic interaction circuit even though they do not have, *per se*, an economic or an environmental dimension. Their analysis, however, is not a current task of environmental accounting and integrating them in a common "accounting" framework would require, *inter alia*, a substantial enlargement of social accounting schemes.

°   There are examples of responses aimed at solving environmental problems which are addressed to the social system, *e.g.* information campaigns directed to changing social behaviour as a response to the need for energy saving. They are accounted for in the environmental/economic interaction circuit insofar as they imply economic costs and/or retroact on economic behaviour.

7.   Differently from what can be done, for instance, with the "income circuit" of National Accounting.

The heterogeneity of the different elements included in the DPSIR model stems from the very complexity of the real world. Environmental accounting does not aim at bypassing this complexity by establishing a common unit of measure for all relevant things, *e.g.* by means of monetary values.[8] When the different dimensions of sustainable development are considered, the *reductio ad unum* of the vast variety of phenomena that have to be kept under control for the development to be sustainable may prove hardly satisfactory

Sustainable development is an intrinsically multidimensional concept: to the extent that there is no way to compensate an unsustainable situation in one dimension with a *plus* in another dimension, the requirements to be satisfied for each dimension must be all simultaneously fulfilled. In other words, looking at the overall sustainability of the development, the trade-offs and synergies concerning the choices on mobility and global warming, social security and instruction, income generation and protection of biodiversity cannot be annihilated by weighing and summing up the respective indicators.[9]

Sustainable development and welfare measurement are fields where the complexity of the world irreducibly dominates all reductive approaches. A balance is to be found, therefore, between the need for effective communication and the importance of not hiding important facts. Policy-makers themselves may found advantages from keeping sight on all relevant variables, as opposed to seeing them all reduced at one; in fact, no statistical method can be recommended as a substitute for responsible political choice, for establishing what is better or more necessary.

The recognition that – given the real world complexity – different measurement units need to be simultaneously used in order to have an acceptable description of reality has been one fundamental pillar of the development of Istat environmental accounting since the beginning.[10] Thus, single balance-sheet-like exhaustive accounting schemes deemed capable of measuring at once all crucial aspects of sustainability concerning the technosphere/ecosphere dialectic have not been regarded as the best option.[11] Instead, the primary objective has been to develop, according to an overall accounting framework like that provided by the SEEA2003, a well articulated system of environmental accounts, concerning various aspects and moments of the environmental/economic interaction circuit represented by the DPSIR model and integrated through a common basis of concepts, definitions and classifications.

---

8. See the arguments raised in the SEEA2003 and Costantino (1996). We also regard as important the issue of the very limited substitutability that may occur in the real world. When absolute impossibility of interchange between certain resources occurs – not just between economic and natural ones, but also between different natural resources – this corresponds, on the measurement ground, to an impossibility of establishing exchange ratios between the different resources themselves, if physical or monetary aggregates that have a clear meaning in a sustainable perspective are to be calculated.

9. The fact that a ratio may be calculated at which one resource can be exchanged for another one on actual or hypothetical markets is also relevant: it means that both produced and natural resources may have an economic value. These values, however, may or may not be related to all the functions that natural resources do have in nature according to an ecological sustainability perspective. As a consequence, an "environmentally adjusted" monetary aggregate based on consideration of actual and hypothetical markets may be questionable in such a perspective.

10. See Costantino (1996) on directions for the developing integrated environmental and economic accounting in Italy, which have been adopted in the recommendations given by a Commission set up in 1991.

11. A *fortiori* this is valid when taking into account also other aspects of sustainability.

In this view each specific accounting scheme is supposed to contribute valuably to the measurement of economic/ecological aspects of sustainable development. In practice, the Istat approach is that of a gradual development of the measurement tools, a concentration of efforts on a limited number of environmental accounting modules – the ones most demanded by policy-makers – and on disseminating knowledge on the chosen modules.

A framework for accounts and a rationale for indicator systems

Environmental accounting modules

Work on environmental accounting has been developed at Istat, since the beginning of the 1990s, in response to the need of providing an integrated view of the economic and environmental dimensions of development. This corresponds to a vision of how to measure sustainable development like the one now embedded in the above mentioned EASSDI and the EAB.[12]

While the overall work is developed at Istat in a way consistent with the framework set out with the SEEA2003, the implementation of the specific accounting schemes is consistent with the main work going on in this field within the European Statistical System and is closely linked to the Eurostat statistical programme (Eurostat, 2002b).

Current projects are focused on a number of environmental accounting modules which have been given high priority in a round table organised by Istat and the Ministry of the environment in 2001. The participants in the round table, among which representatives of the central government, welcomed the achievements of official statistics in the field of environmental accounting and supported Istat's current statistical programme in this field. In particular, the round table recommended continuing efforts on modules which Istat had already given high priority such as the Economy-wide Material Flow Accounts (MFA), the National Accounting Matrix including Environmental Accounts (NAMEA) and the Environmental Protection Expenditure Account (EPEA).[13] Later on all these environmental accounting modules have been included in the recommendations that the Eurostat Task Force "European Strategy for Environmental Accounting" has prepared for the Statistical Programme Committee (Eurostat, 2002c).

Considering the DPSIR circuit has been useful, as explained in previous paragraph 3.1, to better understand the complexity of interactions between economy and environment and thus to define the basic Istat approach to environmental accounting. The same rationale has been enlightening in identifying priorities for developing work in this field having in mind ecological sustainability issues.

In the environmental/economic interaction circuit, moments of *direct* interrelationships between the human and the natural systems – *i.e.* those of immediate physical interaction between parts of the two systems – can be identified in the Pressures box and in the State-Impacts arrow. These direct interrelationships are of two different kinds according to their "direction", *i.e.* to whether it is the economic phenomena that causes a change in the environmental conditions (Pressures) or *vice versa*

12. See paragraphs 1 and 2 in the present paper.

13. It is assumed that the environmental accounting modules mentioned here are well known; no presentation of them is made, therefore, in the present paper. As useful references, see Eurostat (2001 for MFA; 2000 for NAMEA; 1994 and 2002a for EPEA).

(State-to-Impacts arrow). All other boxes and arrows identify elements that are indirectly relevant for the actual interactions.

In the current formulation of environmental policy, both nationally and internationally, important objectives relate to environmental pressures.[14] Pressures are indeed the actual scope – though indirect – of policy action. It is important to point out, however, that the use of environmental pressure indicators as instruments for monitoring the effectiveness of societies' efforts towards sustainability should be accompanied by the use of other planning instruments such as state indicators, which tell how much more efforts are still needed, and driving force indicators, which are subject to the direct influence of policy (Responses). A system of driving force and state indicators should therefore be set-up, parallel and connected to that of pressure indicators, in order to create a coherent and complete reference for action.

Since the physical phenomena are a sustainable development issue before and possibly more than their economic consequences, the measurement of Pressures has been given the highest priority within Istat environmental accounting. Besides Pressures, also Responses have been put at the centre of the accounting framework, the former being the targets and the latter the instruments in the immediate reach of policy. The MFA and NAMEA modules cover the Pressures side; EPEA the Responses side. In the middle/long term, the development of balance sheets covering quantitative and qualitative aspects of selected natural assets will enable, *inter alia*, the formulation of environmental policy also in terms of objectives for the state of the environment.

The DPSIR model can also be looked at as a framework in which the statistical tools developed to measure the ecological sustainability of the development can be contained and organised, thus clarifying the positions and the mutual relationships of the elements of the environmental/economic interaction circuit to which the same statistical tools refer. Figure 2 shows the placement of Istat environmental accounting priority modules in the DPSIR map.

Such an intersection between the environmental accounting framework and the DPSIR analytical framework also helps to understand the meaning of the aggregates provided by the environmental accounts developed, maximising the communicability of their results.

As for the kind of the statistical tools to which priority has been given at Istat within environmental accounting, it is possible to identify two complementary approaches: 1) balance-sheet-like accounts for particular aspects, *i.e.* for families of interrelated phenomena that have a common unit of measure and for which some accounting identity can be defined on the basis of *necessary*[15] mathematical relationships; 2) side-by-side measures of environmental and economic phenomena that constitute different aspects or consequences of the same human activities. Both are defined according to the principles of National Accounting; the economic aspects are measured in monetary terms where appropriate, while environmental variables maintain their own units. Both kinds of accounts are present in Istat work on environmental accounting: MFA and EPEA are of the first type, NAMEA is of the second one.

---

14. With respect to this, international negotiations on the emissions of air pollutants are a well-known example.

15. *I.e.* their fulfilment does not depend on the actual behaviour of the systems they represent.

Developing systems of indicators: the case of sector environmental pressure indicators

Environmental accounting is a discipline which not only enables the production of a number of accounting modules; it also provides a framework that can be enlightening when developing, in an ecological sustainability perspective, environmental statistics and indicators.

The possibility of a specific contribution from environmental accounting is currently being considered by the European Statistical System Task Force on Methodological Issues for Sustainable Development Indicators (TF SDI),[16] among whose main tasks there is analysing and possibly developing suitable frameworks for statistical work on indicators of sustainable development (Eurostat, 2002d).

Environmental accounting has been found very useful in methodological work on environmental indicators at Istat, where the discipline has been developed building on both national accounting and environmental statistics expertise. One interesting result of this combination has been the establishment of what here is referred to as an environmental accounting rationale. It is in a sense a way of thinking, which leads to the systematic adoption of main national accounting concepts in the statistical description of interrelationships between economy and environment, while taking stock of methodological achievements in environmental statistics.

Such a rationale has been applied in methodological work on sector environmental pressure indicators. This work started in the 1990s with a project for the sector Tourism carried out jointly by Istat and Statistics Sweden within the Eurostat SIPs,[17]., followed by another project carried out by Istat with the aim of harmonising the results obtained for the different sectors covered by the Eurostat SIPs (Costantino, Femia, 2002).[18]

The two studies, centred on target sectors identified at the political level,[19] refer to human action at large, with no limitation, in principle, to activities covered as such by national accounting statistics; the target sectors overlap among each other to a certain extent. In such context, two contributions stemming from the environmental accounting rationale seem to be of particular interest. One has to do with the need of clearly establishing the boundary between the natural sphere and the sphere of human action; the other one deals with a systematic approach to the consideration of the different human activities generating environmental pressures, investigated by target sector.[20]

16.   See Steurer (2003).

17.   See Cammarrota, Costantino, Fängström (1999).

18.   Both projects obtained financial contribution from the European Commission. The SIPs – Sectoral Infrastructure Projects – were launched by Eurostat in the framework of the European ESEPI action – European System of Environmental Pressure Indices (Commission of the European Communities, 1994).

19.   The different SIPs cover the five target sectors identified as areas of special attention in the 5th Environmental Action Programme for the European Communities – *i.e.* Agriculture, Energy, Industry, Tourism, Transport – plus Waste management.

20.   See Costantino, Femia (2002).

Figure 2.   **Placement of Istat environmental accounting priority modules in the DPSIR map**

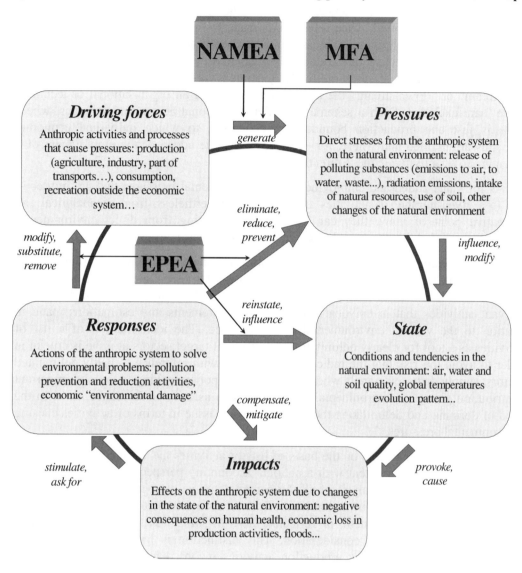

The first point concerns a preliminary step which is to be taken prior to identifying the relevant environmental pressures. The latter are defined in terms of the material/energy flows between the natural system and the anthropic system due to human action, and one should keep in mind, in particular, that wherever a flow is considered as a pressure exerted by the economic system on nature, at the same time there is a boundary line to be considered as crossed by the flow at issue, which is exactly the one between economy and environment. With respect to this, making reference to the SNA[21] concept of production boundary may even help to arrive at a clearer definition of the boundary between the natural sphere and the sphere of human action at large. This boundary should be kept univocal in developing a system of environmental pressure indicators by target

---

21.   Commission of the European Communities, International Monetary Fund, Organisation for Economic Co-operation and Development, United Nations, World Bank (1993).

sector, and consistent among the various sectors under examination that compose the anthropic system. Once the boundary between the natural system and the anthropic system is clearly identified, when reference is made to the environmental pressures of a given group of activity, unless expressly indicated otherwise, these are intended as the flows crossing the boundary that are directly generated by the activities belonging to that group; environmental pressures indirectly generated via other activities that are either "up-stream" or "down-stream" the activities at issue – in an organisational or technical sense – are excluded. Such a scheme is similar to national accounting schemes, where there is just one production boundary in coherence to which individual economic activities are defined and where, for example, the value added or the employment of a given group of activity are those directly generated by it.

As for value added and employment, the environmental pressures that are indirectly due to a given number of activities are important, nevertheless, from an analytical and normative point of view; they can be calculated starting from direct environmental pressures, provided that these are known for all the relevant intermediate steps.[22]

More generally, an environmental accounting rationale may help to define a set of indicators that, while concerning different environmental issues, are brought together to form an organic framework. This can be done, in particular, thanks to a definition of the relevant activities that is univocal for all the measurements and estimations made in relation to the various environmental issues covered. The identification of a list of activities as a tool for clearly delimitating the different target sectors at issue is crucial in order to avoid the risk that the indicators, calculated with reference to badly delimited sectors, supply distorted signals when considered for policy making. A second important contribution given by environmental accounting seen as a rationale relates, then, to the need of defining and delimitating the target sectors at issue in terms of activities causing environmental pressures.[23]

A delimitation of sectors on the basis of lists of activities has been developed at Istat according to criteria consistent with a national accounting perspective.[24] For each target sector, in the systematic analysis of all the human activities that generate environmental pressures a first important distinction has been that between activities recorded as such in the national accounting system, or reflected there in some way, and the other human activities to be taken into consideration. This distinction is basically tantamount to identifying, in addition to the production activities recorded in the national accounts, other possible activities that may or may not have a counterpart in transactions recorded in this system, but which create environmental pressures to be considered in addition to those already associated to production activities. The practical implication of the

---

22. E.g. this can be done via the vertical integration of sectors with the Input-Output technique, at the branch-of-activity level, and with the analysis of the life cycle at the product level.

23. It should be noted that the sectors at issue are to be considered separately but not necessarily unlinked, given possible overlapping such as that between e.g. the Transport and the Energy sectors.

24. The fact that not all dimensions of the definition of a sector can be reduced to the allocation of activities, when speaking of environmental pressures, has not been neglected. Besides the physical flows in which the current functioning of the economic system is substantiated, indeed, there are in each sector accumulated stocks. In general terms, the following criterion has been followed: when it is the existence of stocks that is a cause of environmental pressures, these should be associated only to the sectors using the same stocks (one such case could be that of roads); when it is their construction or dismantling that is a cause of environmental pressures, these should be associated to both the user and the producer (of the construction or dismantlement service) sector.

distinction shown here relates to the fact that the identification of those activities that are not recorded in the national accounts may not be immediate and may require "ad hoc" investigations (no standard classification – such as the NACE for production activities – is available).

Figure 3. **Delimitation and schematic representation of the environmental pressures due to the sector Tourism**

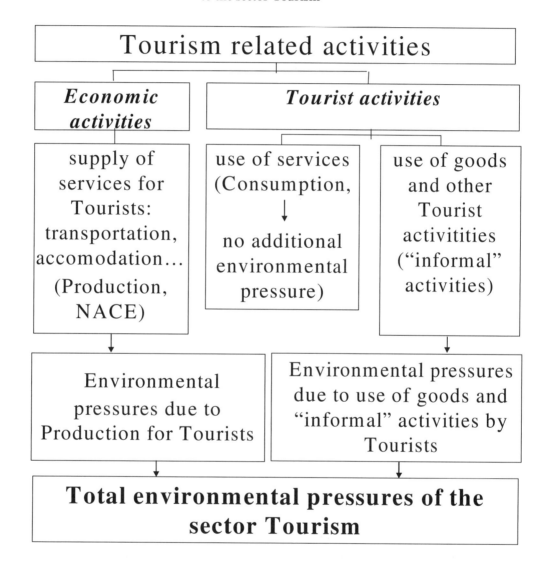

This approach has been introduced by Istat when dealing with the sector Tourism, which is a particularly interesting example to consider.[25] As can be seen from the basic scheme reported in Figure 3, different sets of activities which form the sector Tourism are

---

25. Tourism economic satellite accounting is dealt with in Commission of the European Communities - Eurostat, Organisation for Economic Co-operation and Development, World Tourism Organization, United Nations Statistics Division (2001).

– INTEGRATED ENVIRONMENTAL AND ECONOMIC ACCOUNTING IN ITALY

distinguished.[26] First of all, production activities at the service of tourists, on one side, and tourists' activities, on the other side, are separately identified. Within the latter, furthermore, the use of services supplied to tourists is distinguished from the use of goods and other tourist activities, which form a distinct set of activities with respect to those which immediately involve economic transactions and whose environmental pressures remain attributed to the production sphere.[27] It should be noted that there is concomitance between the purchase and the use by tourists of the services supplied to them by economic activities; as a consequence, the consumption of services provided by the activities included in the NACE Rev.1 does not create separate environmental pressures.[28] The use of services by tourists is not to be taken into account for the delimitation of the sectors, therefore, in addition to the supply of the same services. On the other hand, the use of material goods bought as such – differed in time with respect to the act of purchasing them – may cause, instead, separate environmental pressures, and the same applies to other tourists' activities whose relevance under the environmental profile does not depend on the use of any particular product, such as for instance the lighting of fires in forests; all these activities, therefore, are also to be accounted for in the delimitation of the sectors.

Activities carried out "in the economic system" and "informal activities" exhaust, then, the set of human activities and the union of their respective environmental pressures gives the set of all (anthropogenic) environmental pressures. The distinctions described above have been adopted systematically and applied, as appropriate, to all the target sectors at issue, for the examination of anthropic activities in order to identify environmental pressures caused by them.

Further distinctions have also been made within production activities, by identifying separately principal, secondary and ancillary ones have been distinguished. To that end, the individual items of the European classification of economic activities (NACE Rev.1) have been considered. For each sector, first the activities that provide the principal output have been identified, then the secondary activities that are homogeneous to the principal ones have been added – regardless of the sectors in which they are actually carried out – thus leading to a delimitation of the six sectors which generates ideal groups of homogeneous activities.[29] Finally, some production activities that belong to one of the six sectors – when carried out as principal or secondary activities – can also appear as ancillary activities in other sectors; in such cases they have been identified as well, in order to be properly accounted for.[30]

26. The figure is elaborated starting from a similar figure in the SIP report on the sector Tourism (see Cammarrota, Costantino, Fängström, 1999, mentioned before).

27. In this sense they are labelled here as "informal activities".

28. As a matter of fact, the environmental pressures generated at the time of use of a service (for example, a trip in a taxi) coincide with the ones due to its production, already accounted for among those considered in the relevant sector.

29. The approach followed is the same applied, for example, for the construction of Input-Output tables for homogeneous branches of economic activity.

30. As an example of the importance of doing so, one may consider the case of waste transport, an activity that is explicitly included in division 90 of the NACE Rev.1, "Disposal of solid waste, wastewater and similar": it is advisable to include this activity both in the Transport and in the Waste Management sectors. Whatever the role (principal, secondary or ancillary) of this transport activity in the economic units in which it is carried out, it is under the direct and determining influence of transport policy; environmental pressures coming from

As it is already clear from consideration of the Tourism example, in order to complete the delimitation of the sectors, in addition to identifying the production activities, in some cases the analysis has explicitly taken into account some activities carried out by households, which come under the realm of target sector policies, without being economic activities. Such activities generate environmental pressures that are additional to those put down to the production activities recorded in national accounts. As a matter of fact, these additional environmental pressures are generated either during a consumption phase which is separate from the production of the goods being consumed, or in activities that, as such, do not have any counterpart in terms of production, although their execution contributes – as for example in the case of many recreational activities – to satisfying households' needs.

Concluding remarks

The current debate on ecologically sustainable development in Italy, while focusing on a broad concept of environmental accounting, emphasises how an environmental accounting framework can help to structure even the use of statistical information for decision taking and policy making in a sustainable development perspective.

Such evolution is highlighted in particular by the fact that the bill currently under discussion in the Italian Parliament[31] calls for laws by decree which are supposed to identify accounting frameworks for developing environmental information tools and environmental planning tools as well. Since the former are to be found within environmental accounting of official statistics – supposed to provide the figures for the latter – a crucial step is the use of specific environmental accounting schemes of official statistics, in particular the Istat ones.

As a matter of fact, the main focus of the experimental projects carried out so far in an attempt to implement the bill on a pilot basis at the local level has been on the environmental information tools envisaged in the same bill, *i.e.* the EAs. For these, it appears that there is no need for completely new frameworks, though there is a need of guidelines for a proper application of existing standardised approaches.

In order to identify a suitable overall accounting framework, it has been useful to consider the complex interaction between economy and environment in the light of the environmental/economic interaction circuit. This has been done on the basis of the DPSIR model, which, while not allowing to set a series of identities as *e.g.* in the case of the "income circuit" underlying the system of economic national accounts, nevertheless provides a basic rationale for analysing statistical information on the interaction between the natural and the anthropic systems. Given the complexity of the real world – as well as the concept of sustainable development itself – it has been considered, then, as an acceptable statistical description of the interrelationships between the economic and environmental dimensions of development, one that is obtained by simultaneously using different units of measure, the necessity of which is not necessarily to be by-passed. What is needed is a well articulated system of integrated environmental and economic accounts,

---

this activity should therefore be accounted for (also) in the Transport sector. It is also worthwhile to mention that transport of waste is considered in the chapter "Transport" in the 5EAP.

31. See paragraph 2 in the present paper. As explained there, the bill aims at the regular and simultaneous approval of targets concerning the environmental dimension of the development together with the economic policy targets.

focused on various aspects and moments of the environmental/economic interaction circuit.

The overall framework for environmental accounting has been found, therefore, in the SEEA2003. At present, the major focus is on environmental pressures and responses of society, given the importance attached to these aspects in the formulation of environmental policy; in particular, the MFA and NAMEA modules correspond to the targets and EPEA to the instruments that are in the immediate reach of policy. In the middle/long term, the development of balance sheets covering quantitative and qualitative aspects of selected natural assets will enable, *inter alia*, the formulation of environmental policy also in terms of objectives determined for the state of the environment. An accounting framework tailored in this way is supposed to help users in evaluating trade-offs between alternative policies, by providing them with sets of indicators that are integrated to the maximum extent possible through a common basis of concepts, definitions and classifications.

The environmental accounting approach – in a sense a rationale based both on national accounting and environmental statistics expertise – has been found very useful also in methodological work on environmental pressure indicators related to target sectors identified at the political level.[32] In particular, a substantial contribution has been given, within projects funded in the framework of the European ESEPI action, for a systematic definition of the boundary between the natural sphere and the sphere of human action starting from the national accounting concept of production boundary; furthermore, a systematic approach has been provided for looking at the different human activities that cause environmental pressures to be considered by target sector, based on the distinction between principal, secondary and ancillary activities as well as household activities, and having the environmental pressures directly generated by these activities as the variables to be quantified.

That was an example of how an environmental accounting framework, in addition to being essential for the production of a number of accounting modules, can also be enlightening for developing environmental indicators in a sustainable development perspective. Such an approach may also be considered *e.g.* for the work going on within the European Statistical System Task Force on Methodological Issues for Sustainable Development Indicators.

References

Cammarrota M., Costantino C, Fängström I. (1999) *Joint final report of the sectoral infrastructure project – Tourism*, in Eurostat: "Towards environmental pressure indicators for the EU: an examination of the sectors", Luxembourg.

Commission of the European Communities (1994) Communication from the Commission to the Council and the European Parliament on Directions for the EU on Environmental Indicators and Green National Accounting (COM (94) 670 final), Bruxelles.

Commission of the European Communities, International Monetary Fund, Organisation for Economic Co-operation and Development, United Nations, World Bank

---

32.   See paragraph 3.2.2 in the present paper.

(1993) *System of National Accounts 199,* Brussels/Luxembourg,New York, Paris, Washington, D.C.

Commission of the European Communities – Eurostat, Organisation for Economic Co-operation and Development, World Tourism Organization, United Nations Statistics Division (2001) *Tourism Satellite Account: Recommended Methodological Framework,* Luxembourg, Madrid, New York, Paris.

Costantino C. (1996) *First report of the Commission Istat-Fondazione Eni Enrico Mattei for the study of a system of environmental accounting,* in Musu I. – Siniscalco D. (editors): "National accounts and the Environment", Kluwer Academic Publishers, Dordrecht, The Netherlands.

Costantino, Femia, (2002) Environmental Pressure Indicators – Sectoral Indicators Project: Harmonisation of the SIP results, Eurostat, Luxembourg.

Eurostat (1994), *SERIEE – 1994 Version,* Luxembourg.

Eurostat (2000) NAMEA 2000 for air emissions – Manual, Luxembourg.

Eurostat (2001) Economy-wide material flow accounts and derived indicators, a methodological guide, Luxembourg.

Eurostat (2002a), SERIEE Environmental Protection Expenditure Accounts – Compilation Guide, Luxembourg.

Eurostat (2002b) Environmental Accounts 2002 – Present state and future developments, Eurostat Doc. ACCT/02/01, Luxembourg.

Eurostat (2002c) The European Strategy for Environmental Accounting – Report to the Statistical Programme Commettee, Luxembourg.

Eurostat (2002d) *The Task Force Mandate,* Doc. SDI/TF/002/02(2002), Luxembourg.

Ministero dell'Ambiente e della Tutela del Territorio (2002) *Strategia d'azione ambientale per lo sviluppo sostenibile in Italia,* Roma.

Steurer A. (2003) *The use of National Accounts in developing SD Indicators,* Eurostat Doc. SDI/TF/018/04.1(2003), Luxembourg.

United Nations, European Commission, International Monetary Fund, Organisation for Economic Co-operation and Development, World Bank (2003) *Integrated Environmental and Economic Accounting 2003,* on the web.

The Danish Environmental Accounts with Examples of Its Use

O. Gravgaard Pedersen

Statistics Denmark

Introduction

The current Danish Environmental Accounts include information on energy and water use, emissions to air, environment taxes and subsidies. Physical and monetary asset accounts for the Danish reserves of oil and natural gas are included in the framework as well. The environmental accounts are linked with the Danish national accounts and input-output tables through common classifications and definitions. This facilitates analysis of the interaction between the economy and the environment.

The environmental accounts are used in several ways as basis for analysis, which relates to the discussion of sustainable development. The paper provides varied examples of this use.

In the first section of this paper *the overall structure* of the Danish environmental accounts are described. The section that follows gives examples of the use of the accounts. The first example concerns *indicators for decoupling of economy and environment* and the construction of *industrial profiles*. The second example is about *emissions accounts and structural decomposition analysi*s based on the accounts and input-output modelling. The third example describes how *economy-wide material flow accounts* have been extended to include a breakdown by industries and households in order to make it possible to analyse the economic causes of the material flows. The fourth example, in which the accounts have been used in combination with a national consumer survey, extends the analysis to include also certain *socio-economic aspects* of the interaction between economy and environment. The example shows also how the basic information can be used to construct indices of environmental impacts and how they can be summarised via Data Envelopment Analysis (DEA) to obtain a total *environmental score by income groups and household types*. The fifth example concerns how the energy and emissions accounts are used as basis for the modelling of *how a greenhouse gas reduction strategy effect the economy*.

The first five mentioned examples concern the use of information on flows (emissions, material flows, energy use). Contrary to this, the sixth example concerns information on stocks, namely the *physical and monetary asset accounts* for the Danish oil and natural gas reserves. The example emphasises the importance of having both physical and monetary asset accounts available.

The paper ends up with arguing that first of all it is the consistency, level of detail and classification in the Danish environmental accounts and the subsequent use for analysis that qualifies the accounts in relation to the sustainability discussion - not so much the ability to construct overall aggregate indicators from the accounts.

The Danish Environmental Accounts

Accounts for energy use, water use, and emissions to air

The Danish environmental accounts are constructed as satellite accounts linked with the national accounts and the input-output tables. Basic accounts for energy use, water use, and air emissions are published yearly with a lag of approximately one and a half year in relation to the reference year (i.e. accounts for 2001 is published in May 2003). The basic flow accounts are formed as supply and use tables as described in SEEA 2003.

For the water accounts a distinction is made between surface water and groundwater. For the energy accounts 40 types of energy products are included. The environmental flow accounts are broken down by 130 industries as well as various types of final demand (private consumption, exports etc.). This ensures consistency with the national accounts with regard to classification of activities.

Monetary accounts are constructed complementary to the physical accounts for energy and water. The latter are fully consistent with the physical accounts and they are used as basis for the national accounts as far as the description of the monetary transactions related to energy and water are concerned. In this way, full consistency between the environmental accounts and the national accounts are ensured.

For the air emissions accounts, which are made up in tonnes, eight substances (CO_2, SO_2, NO_x, CH_4, N_2O, NMVOC, NH_3, and CO) are distinguished. For energy related emissions, the accounts include a breakdown of the emissions by the same 40 types of energy, which are included in the energy accounts. Furthermore, all information on emissions is broken down by 130 industries and households.

As a supplement to the basic emissions accounts also accounts for cross-boundary air pollution into and out from Danish territory are given.

Finally, the various substances are weighted into indices for greenhouse gas effect (global warming potential, GWP) and acidification (potential acidification effect, PAE).

Environment taxes and subsidies

The Danish environmental accounts include accounts for environment (related) taxes and subsidies by industries and final demands. Taxes and subsidies are divided into the four groups: Pollution, Energy, Transport and Resources. The environment taxes are defined as taxes, which are based on physical entities with a negative impact on the environment. The environment subsidies are defined as subsidies, which are assumed to reduce the use of physical entities with negative impact on the environment. Especially, the delimitation and selection of environment subsidies are difficult and subject to further considerations and development.

Based on the national accounts´ supply and use tables, environment taxes and subsidies on products are allocated by the industries and final demand categories, which use the products. This makes it possible, for example, to compare CO_2 emissions of an industry to the CO_2 taxes paid by the same industry. Thus, analysis in relation to the Polluter Pays Principle and incentives for pollution reductions are facilitated.

Reserves of oil and natural gas

Asset accounts for the Danish reserves of oil and natural gas are part of the current environmental accounts. The asset accounts are made up in physical units as well as in monetary units (DKK). The accounts show opening and closing stocks and the changes in-between. The changes shown in the accounts are: Extractions, new discoveries and other economic appearances and disappearances. For the monetary accounts also revaluations of the reserves are included.

The monetary value of the reserves is calculated as the net present value of the physical stocks. Thus, expected extraction profiles, averaged net unit resource rent and a discount factor for the expected future income are applied to obtain the monetary value of the present reserves.

A discount factor of four per cent has been chosen for the net present value calculation of the market value. The size of the discount factor is crucial for the calculation and it is a critical point when it comes to sustainability analysis and the consideration for future generations. Therefore, results of alternative calculations using discounts rates reaching from zero to five per cent are published, together with the market value calculations of the reserves.

Section 2.6 elaborates on the physical and monetary asset accounts for oil and natural gas.

Input-output tables and analysis

A long tradition exists for Statistics Denmark to publish input-output tables, together with multipliers for economic variables like imports, employment and energy use. The multipliers show the direct and indirect effects of private consumption, exports or other kinds of final demand. During recent years also results of input-output modelling of direct and indirect water consumption and air emissions from various groups of private consumption and other types of final demand have been introduced.

The publishing also includes results of direct and indirect global environmental pressures from Danish final demand. This means that *e.g.* the CO_2 "rucksack" of imported products is included in the calculations of the effects from Danish consumption, capital formation, exports etc. The inclusion of the "rucksack" is important when it comes to analysis of sustainability from a wider perspective, for instance, in relation to analysis of whether a country "exports" the environmental pressures to other countries because it imports products from abroad.

While input-output models offer very simple and fast answers to some of the questions concerning global environmental aspects of the Danish economic activities it must be emphasised that there is room for improvement with regard to the assumptions lying behind the calculations of the environmental "rucksacks". In effect, the calculations are based on the assumption that imported products are produced by using the same technology (including energy intensity and energy types) as Danish products are produced by. Clearly, this assumption is problematic when it comes to imports of electricity, for instance, which are produced in quite a different way in Denmark and in the countries from which Denmark imports.

Closer international cooperation on the modelling and calculation of global environmental pressures from national activities and the exchange of data and construction of databases would be a way forward to ensure better consistency and more reliable results in this field.

Besides the calculation of global pressures from Danish economic activities, input-output modelling based on the environmental accounts has been used for decomposition of the development in air emissions by underlying driving forces. This is described in section 2.2.

Figure 1. **The Danish Environmental Accounts**

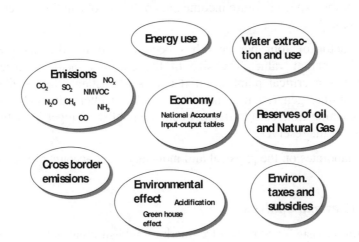

Further development and pilot projects

The Danish Environmental accounts are under further development with regard to both the flow accounts and the asset accounts:

- Pilot projects have been carried out in order to establish economy-wide material flow accounts (MFA) for Denmark. Thus, indicators for direct and total material inputs (DMI and TMR, etc.) have been calculated. Section 2.3 describes how the accounts have been extended to include a breakdown of the material flows by industries and household in such a way that the material flows can be linked with the various activities of the Danish economy.

- In an ongoing project it is examined how far it is possible to use the physical supply and use tables for natural resources and products to establish accounts for certain fractions of waste (e.g. paper and glass). The project is linked to the material flow accounts by industries and previous work on complete physical input-output tables. It is expected that the accounts can be a useful supplement to existing solid waste statistics, and used for analysis of the relation between the input side and output side of the economy.

- The accounts for air emissions are currently being extended by 13 more types of air emissions including particulate matters (TSP, PM10 and PM2.5), priority and other metals (cadmium, lead, mercury and arsenic, chromium, copper, nickel, selenium, zinc) as well as aromatic hydrocarbons, PAH's (pyrene and flourethane). These types of emissions are included in the Danish CORINAIR database and in Denmark's' reporting to the Economic Commission for Europe, Executive Body for the Convention on Long-Range Transboundary Air Pollution. A future extension of the Danish environmental accounts by these types of pollutants should enable analysis of the driving forces behind the specific emissions in the same way as described elsewhere in this paper for the other types of air emissions.

- Physical and monetary asset accounts for the Danish forests are under development. Danish forests are with respect to area as well as economic aspects of minor importance, but it is a political goal to double the forest area within 80-100 years. So far, focus has been on forest area and volume of standing timber as well as on the monetary asset accounts consistent with national accounts principles. However, attempts are now being made to extend the accounts with information on more general sustainability aspects like carbon storage in standing timber and forest ecosystems, recreational areas of forests, recreational visits to forests as well as the protective functions of forests (soil protection). The European Framework for Integrated Environmental and Economic Accounting for Forests (IEEAF) is the starting point for this work.

Examples of the use of the Danish environmental accounts

Decoupling indicators and industrial profiles

A main component of strategies for sustainable development includes decoupling of environmental pressures from economic growth. Subsequently, indicators for decoupling are more or less standard in most sustainability indicator sets.

Elaborated environmental and economic accounts offer one of the best opportunities for the construction of decoupling indicators. The reason is that the accounts include consistent information on the economic and environmental pressure aspects, which are going to be related. Thus, the factors for economy and environment, which are juxtaposed in the decoupling indicators, are based on the same definitions and classification of activities. When, for instance, economic growth (GDP) is contrasted with air emissions, the environmental accounts' air emissions data reflect the economic activities, which create the economic growth. In contrast, it is not always the case that other national emissions inventories (UNFCC and UNECE/CLRTAP) show a consistent connection between the economic dimension and the environmental pressure dimension. The reason is that the conventions have a territorial and not a national economic approach to the emission inventories. This is of importance especially in relation to transport activities. In the Danish case this means that the national emissions inventories underestimate the emissions compared to the environmental accounts. For CO_2 emissions, for instance, the underestimation is approximately 10-15 per cent.

However, in relation to the indicators for decoupling the possibilities for a consistent breakdown of the overall indicators by industries and households are more important. This makes it possible to obtain a broader picture of the underlying trends and thus a more complete picture of the decoupling.

Based on the environmental accounts Figure 2 shows the development of selected economic and environmental indicators from 1998 to 2001. The left topmost figure shows the development for the total economy, while the others show a breakdown by households and main industry groups. In fact, the environmental accounts include information which makes it possible to draw similar figures for each of the 130 industries included in the accounts' classification or relevant aggregations of these. Thus, a detailed picture of the development can be obtained.

Overall, the economic growth and the development in employment have been positive for the period in focus. The indicators for resource use (water and energy) and environmental pressure (greenhouse gasses and acidification has on the other hand shown a decrease. Thus, an absolute decoupling of environmental pressure and economic growth can be seen. However, for the transport services industries it is seen that the absolute pressure has been growing, except for water use, but at a smaller pace than the economic growth. In other words, for the transport services industries there have been a relative decoupling.

It is worthwhile to observe that the use of the national accounts classification means that the transport, which is carried out by the industries (e.g. manufacturing industries operating their own lorries, etc.) is allocated to the industries themselves and not to the transport services. In the light of the importance of transport, it is relevant to include cross-classifications in the environmental accounts in order to facilitate the construction of "classical" sector indicators for transport. In the Danish environmental accounts this facility has been introduced by including information about own-transport emissions from each of the 130 industries. Thus, indicators for transport as such can be constructed from the environmental accounts as well.

Figure 2. **Selected Economic and Environmental Indicators – Percent Change 1998-2001**

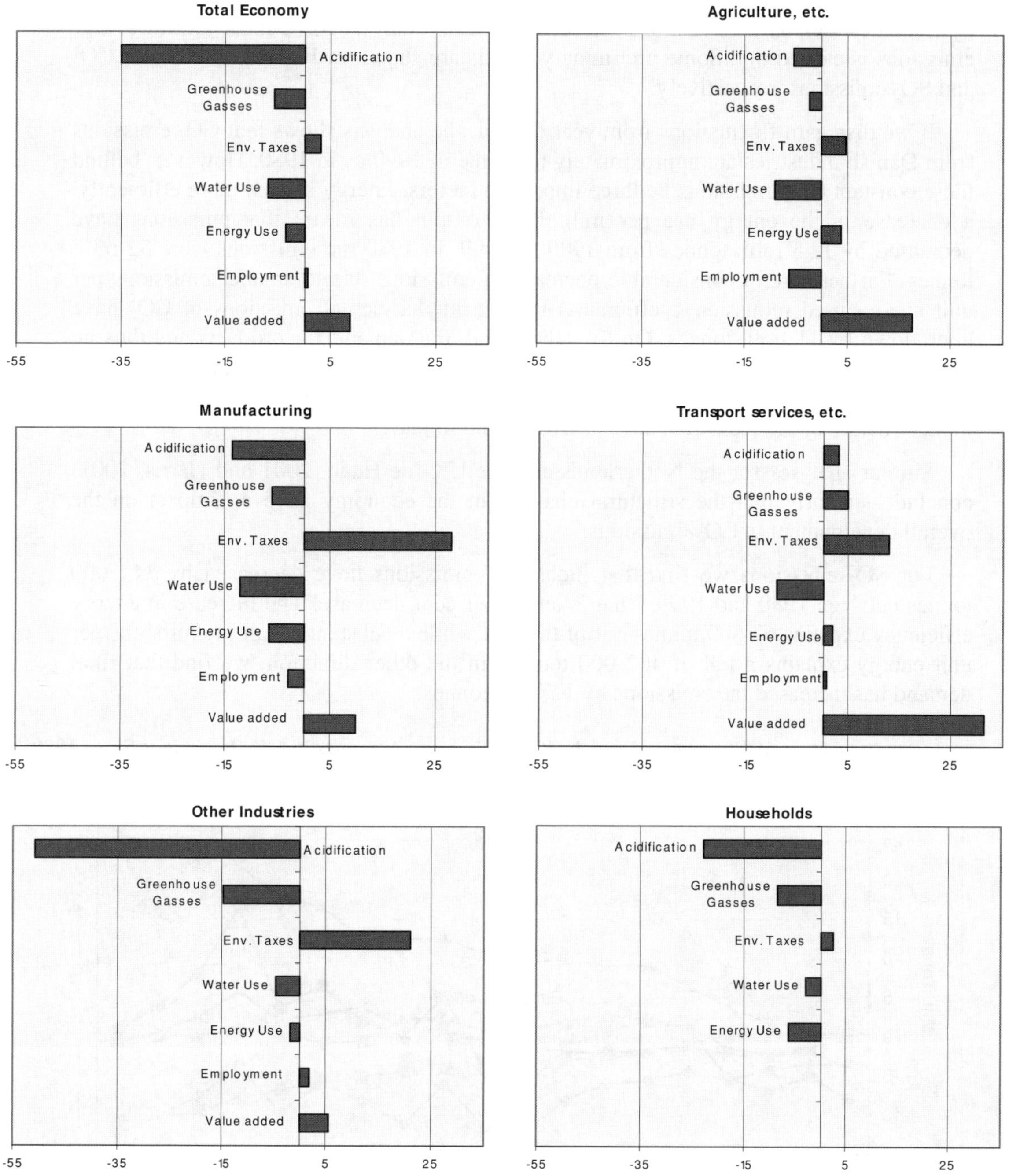

Source: Danish Environmental Accounts, Statistics Denmark

Emissions to air and decomposition analysis

Structural decomposition analysis based on input-output modelling combined with environmental accounts can be used to analyse which underlying factors that have determined the development of environmental pressures.

Many examples exist of the use of structural decomposition analysis (*c.f.* Hoekstra and van den Berg, 2002, which present a good survey). In an ongoing project carried out by Statistics Denmark for Eurostat a decomposition analysis for Danish industries´ air emissions is carried out. Some preliminary results are shown in Figures 3 and 4 for CO_2 and SO_2 emissions, respectively.

If we disregard fluctuations from year to year, the analysis shows that CO_2 emissions from Danish industries are approximately the same in 1999 as in 1980. However, behind these constant CO_2-emissions lie three important factors. Energy is used more efficiently, a decrease in the energy use per mill. DKK output has meant that emissions have decreased by 12.5 mill. tonnes from 1980 to 1999. In 1980 the emissions were 52 mill. tonnes. Furthermore, a considerable decrease in emissions due to smaller emissions per unit energy used (emission coefficients) has meant that actual emissions of CO_2 have gone down by 11 mill. tonnes. On the other hand, the demand for products and thus an increase in production has meant an increase in emissions by 25 mill. tonnes. Changes in the structure of the economy, *i.e.* change in the pattern of demand and changes in the input structure of the industries have almost had no impact.

Similar analyses for the Netherlands and the UK (de Haan, 2001 and Harris, 2001) conclude similarly that the structural changes in the economy have no impact on the overall development in CO_2-emissions.

For SO_2 emissions we find that industries´ emissions have decreased by 344 000 tonnes between 1980 and 1999. That is an 85 per cent decrease. The increase in energy efficiency explains 67 000 tonnes out of the fall, while a substantial fall in emissions per unit energy explains a fall of 402 000 tonnes. In the other direction, we find that final demand has increased the emissions by 127 000 tonnes.

Figure 3. **Decomposition of Changes in Danish CO_2 Emissions - Changes in CO_2 Emissions Since 1980**

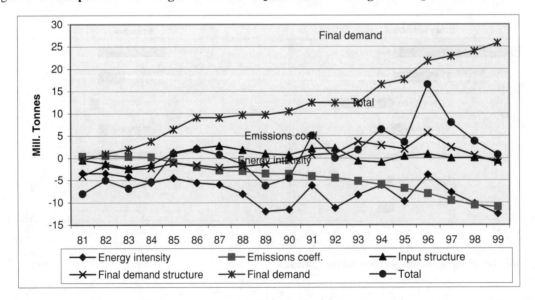

Source: Preliminary modelling results by P. Rørmose and T. Olsen, Statistics Denmark.

Figure 4. **Decomposition of Changes in Danish SO$_2$ Emissions – Changes in SO$_2$ Emissions Since 1980**

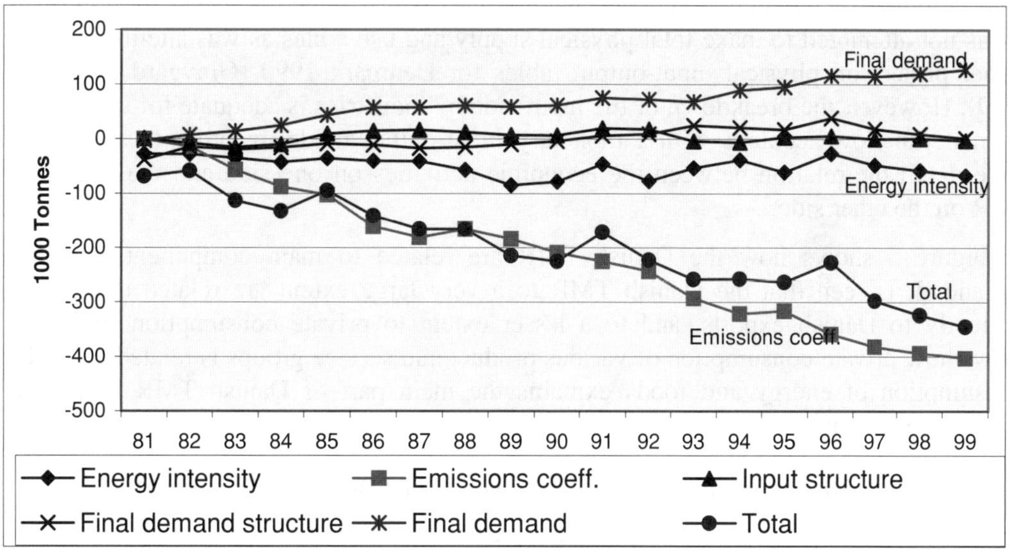

Source: Preliminary modelling results by P. Rørmose and T. Olsen, Statistics Denmark.

MFA, Economy-wide material flow accounts by economic activities

In recent years indicators for the total mass flow of the economy have been developed and constructed for several countries (for example Bringezu and Schütz, 2001), and Eurostat has set up an accounting framework (*c.f.* Eurostat, 2001).

Material input indicators like DMI (direct material input) and TMR (total material requirement) for Denmark 1981, 1990 and 1997 have been estimated by Statistics Denmark as pilot projects. The results have attracted the attention of politicians, the press and green organisations. Furthermore, TMR has been chosen as one of the indicators in the sustainability indicator set, which the Danish Government has published. The popularity of the MFA-indicators is inherent in the fact that TMR and similar MFA-indicators are closely linked with the global aspects of sustainability, ecological rucksacks, etc. because raw material equivalents and indirect flows abroad are counted and included when the material requirements of a country are estimated.

Although many regard the MFA indicators (TMR and DMI) as good sustainability indicators, criticism has also been raised against these indicators. The total weight of materials is often regarded as being to aggregate a measure to assess environmental pressure, resource scarcity or sustainability in a meaningful way. This criticism, which must be taken seriously, means that more work is needed to find ways for extending the MFA accounts with more precise information about the pressures following from the material flows. In a policy context, it seems also relevant to account for the link between the material flows and the economic activities, which lie behind the flows.

The MFA-projects carried out by Statistics Denmark have shown that the SEEA 2003 approach of establishing supply and use tables for physical flows (*c.f.* SEEA 2003, chapter 3) and the MFA-approach can be combined in a useful way, which introduces the economic dimension specifically in the MFA accounts. In the projects, the basic information about resource extraction and foreign trade was combined with the supply and use tables of the Danish national accounts. In this way, a total breakdown of the material inputs by receiving industries and households was obtained. In the MFA-project it was not attempted to make total physical supply and use tables as was attempted in an earlier project on physical input-output tables for Denmark 1990 (Gravgård Pedersen, 1999). However, the breakdown of the input-side by industries is adequate for combining the material flow accounts with a monetary input-output model in order to analyse in some detail the relation between the economic activities on one side and the DMI and TMR on the other side.

Figure 5 shows how the Danish TMR are related to main components of final demand. It is seen that the Danish TMR to a very large extent are related directly or indirectly to Danish exports, and to a lesser extent to private consumption. Figure 6 shows how private consumption of various product and service groups is related to TMR. Consumption of energy and foods explains the main part of Danish TMR related to private consumption.

Figure 5. **Direct and Indirect TMR Caused by Final Demand – Denmark 1997**

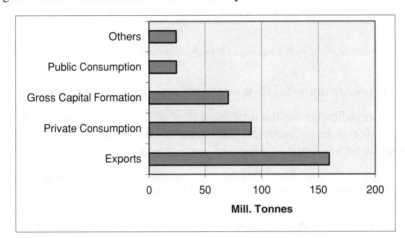

Source: Gravgård Pedersen, 2002.

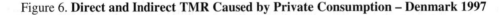

Figure 6. **Direct and Indirect TMR Caused by Private Consumption – Denmark 1997**

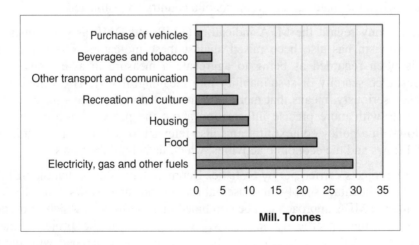

Source: Gravgård Pedersen, 2002.

Some conclusions for the future work on MFA can be offered from the Danish pilot projects: Detailed accounts by industries and households as well as by material groups (energy, biomass, chemicals, etc.) are useful and demanded by the users. Physical supply and use tables for resources and products seem to be a relevant tool for constructing an underlying economic-environment database for the material flows. Still, a lot of work remains as regards the indirect flows (rucksacks, hidden flows, etc.). There is a strong need for international cooperation and exchange of data in this field in order to share and develop knowledge, and ensure harmonised estimation methods.

Environmental performance score by household types

Household consumption and family lifestyle are the subject for an ongoing research project[1], in which the Danish environmental accounts, input-output tables and national consumer survey statistics are used in an integrated modelling framework. In a first step, households´ environmental performance is evaluated using environmental pressure indicators. In a subsequent step, Data Envelopment Analysis (DEA) is used to construct an aggregate score in order to evaluate the relative environmental performance of the various households.

Table 1 shows some preliminary results from the analysis. Households are grouped according to income, age and housing. The consumption of each group of households is evaluated with respect to direct and indirect contributions to eight environmental pressures: Greenhouse effect, acidification, ozone depletion, photochemical oxidation, water use, total material requirement, emissions of cadmium and PAH's. The table shows the average contribution per DKK 1 000 aggregate consumption.

In general, the average environmental pressures per DKK 1 000 spent are smallest for households living in urban flats and largest for households living in rural houses when it comes to pressure types which are closely linked to energy consumption (acidification, greenhouse effect and TMR). For other kinds of pressure by housing type, the pattern is much more diverse. Another tendency is that higher income families contribute less per DKK 1 000 spent. This is partly related to the fact that the share of energy consumption out of total consumption decreases with increasing income.

The information on the households´ various environmental pressures are summarised by using Data Envelopment Analysis (DEA). DEA was introduced by Charnes, Cooper and Rhodes (1978) as a production frontier approach tool for measuring the efficiency of a unit by computing the weighted sum of outputs divided by a weighted sum of inputs. The method can generally be used for productivity measures in cases when inputs or outputs have no observable prices or other weights attached. Instead of assigning more or less arbitrary monetary values or weights to the environmental pressures, DEA is used in the ongoing project to calculate a system of weights for each household group, which - when applied to the environmental pressures - is the best for the household group in terms of less weighted environmental pressures per DKK 1 000 of consumption. The philosophy behind this procedure of assigning weights to the environmental pressures is the following: For each household we choose exactly those weights that give the best possible result (less pressure) for the household. By doing this we present the household in the best possible light. If the household, in spite of this, turns out to have a poorer aggregated environmental performance than the other households, we can convincingly

---

1. The project is carried out by Institute for Local Government Studies, National Environmental Research Institute, University of Copenhagen and Statistics Denmark.

argue that there is room for improvement and that the household might be able to perform better by adopting consumption patterns from other households. The weights are chosen by solving a linear programming problem as an approximation to a non-linear programming problem, which minimises the aggregated environmental pressure relative to the value of consumption. It is worthwhile noticing that this procedure only leads to an assessment of the relative environmental pressure of the households. It is by no means an absolute measure of environmental performance.

Table 1. Environmental Pressures and Performance Score by Family Types, Denmark 1997

	Acidif- ication (mol per 1000 DKK)		Green-house Effect (kg per 1000 DKK)		Ozone depletion (mg per 1000 DKK)		Photo-chemical Oxidation (g per 1000 DKK)		Water Use (m3 per 1000 DKK)		Total Material require-ment (kg per 1000 DKK)		Cadmium (mg per 1000 DKK)		PAH's (mg per 1000 DKK)		Environ-mental Perfor-mance Score (%)	
Low income																		
Young																		
Urban flat	12	(5)	83	(5)	98	(10)	72	(5)	1.00	(12)	293	(4)	0.9	(15)	4.0	(15)	102	(14)
Urban house	13	(17)	91	(14)	96	(7)	89	(11)	1.00	(11)	309	(16)	0.8	(5)	3.3	(7)	101	(15)
Rural house	13	(18)	96	(16)	96	(8)	125	(26)	0.77	(3)	302	(9)	0.9	(11)	3.9	(13)	104	(10)
Middle-aged																		
Urban flat	12	(7)	87	(8)	91	(4)	73	(6)	1.36	(24)	294	(5)	1.1	(23)	5.3	(25)	102	(13)
Urban house	13	(16)	94	(15)	90	(3)	92	(13)	1.09	(16)	307	(13)	0.8	(2)	3.2	(5)	105	(5)
Rural house	14	(24)	110	(23)	92	(6)	101	(20)	0.87	(6)	307	(14)	0.9	(13)	3.4	(9)	104	(7)
Elderly																		
Urban flat	13	(12)	91	(12)	90	(2)	65	(3)	1.40	(25)	307	(12)	1.3	(26)	6.2	(27)	104	(8)
Urban house	14	(22)	109	(22)	87	(1)	92	(12)	1.18	(20)	316	(18)	1.0	(20)	4.3	(19)	103	(12)
Rural house	15	(27)	126	(27)	91	(5)	98	(18)	1.14	(18)	339	(26)	1.2	(25)	5.2	(23)	97	(22)
Middle income																		
Young																		
Urban flat	12	(8)	83	(4)	106	(22)	98	(17)	1.25	(22)	300	(7)	0.9	(10)	4.0	(14)	98	(21)
Urban house	13	(13)	90	(11)	111	(26)	101	(19)	0.87	(5)	323	(22)	0.8	(8)	3.1	(4)	103	(11)
Rural house	15	(26)	110	(24)	104	(18)	137	(27)	0.88	(7)	338	(24)	0.8	(3)	2.9	(2)	104	(9)
Middle-aged																		
Urban flat	12	(10)	84	(6)	98	(11)	81	(9)	1.19	(21)	299	(6)	0.9	(16)	4.2	(16)	99	(19)
Urban house	14	(21)	98	(20)	104	(17)	103	(21)	1.05	(14)	322	(20)	0.8	(9)	3.5	(10)	96	(24)
Rural house	15	(25)	106	(21)	101	(12)	116	(25)	1.02	(13)	334	(23)	0.8	(7)	3.3	(8)	97	(23)
Elderly																		
Urban flat	12	(9)	88	(9)	102	(15)	77	(8)	1.72	(26)	306	(11)	1.1	(22)	5.2	(24)	95	(25)
Urban house	13	(15)	98	(19)	104	(19)	93	(15)	1.07	(15)	318	(19)	1.0	(18)	4.2	(18)	93	(26)
Rural house	14	(20)	113	(25)	107	(23)	111	(23)	1.25	(23)	360	(27)	1.2	(24)	5.5	(26)	89	(27)
High Income																		
Young																		
Urban flat	9	(1)	66	(1)	107	(24)	41	(1)	1.17	(19)	286	(1)	0.9	(14)	3.8	(12)	156	(1)
Urban house	13	(14)	97	(17)	103	(16)	107	(22)	0.86	(4)	304	(10)	1.0	(19)	4.4	(20)	98	(20)
Rural house	11	(3)	85	(7)	115	(27)	97	(16)	0.48	(1)	309	(15)	1.1	(21)	5.1	(22)	139	(2)
Middle-aged																		
Urban flat	12	(4)	81	(3)	105	(21)	77	(7)	1.12	(17)	289	(2)	0.9	(17)	4.2	(17)	99	(18)
Urban house	12	(11)	91	(13)	104	(20)	82	(10)	0.97	(9)	315	(17)	0.8	(1)	2.9	(1)	110	(4)
Rural house	14	(19)	98	(18)	102	(14)	114	(24)	0.93	(8)	322	(21)	0.8	(4)	3.1	(3)	100	(16)
Elderly																		
Urban flat	10	(2)	79	(2)	98	(9)	64	(2)	1.98	(27)	289	(3)	0.8	(6)	3.3	(6)	104	(6)
Urban house	12	(6)	90	(10)	108	(25)	92	(14)	0.97	(10)	300	(8)	0.9	(12)	3.6	(11)	100	(17)
Rural house	14	(23)	113	(26)	102	(13)	70	(4)	0.67	(2)	339	(25)	1.3	(27)	4.9	(21)	110	(3)

Note: Ranking in brackets

Source: Modelling results by M. Wier and L.B. Christoffersen, AKF, Institute of Local Government Studies.

The last column in table 1 presents the DEA environmental performance index based on the eight environmental pressure indices. The ranking of households is presented in brackets. The elderly, middle-income households living in rural houses display the worst performance. Their performance score at 89 means that all types of environmental pressures from the household would have to be reduced to 89 per cent of its actual state if it were to obtain as little pressure as the best of the households.

Young, high-income households living in urban flats show the best performance score. The environmental performance score at 156 per cent means that for this household type all environmental pressures could be increased by 56 per cent per DKK 1 000 consumed, and the other types of households would still not perform better.

The three best performance scores are found among the high-income households while the three poorest performances are found among the elderly, middle-income households.

Obviously, for a full analysis one must also include the absolute levels of consumption and absolute levels of environmental pressures from the various income groups.

The DEA method in combination with environmental accounts and input-output analysis give by no means any final answers to the weighting problems in relation to an assessment of the overall absolute environmental pressures by various groups. However, it might offer a starting point for a discussion of how various socio-economic groups perform relative to other groups. By using sensitivity analysis and by introducing various forms of restrictions on the weighting schemes more in-depth information on the link between the activities and the environmental pressures can most probably be revealed.

Modelling of environmental policy – costs and sustainability

As an example of how information from the environmental accounts can be used as basis for scenarios and analysis of economic consequences of environmental policy the Danish ADAM-EMMA system is mentioned here.

ADAM (**A**nnual **D**anish **A**ggregate **M**odel) is a macro-econometric model developed by the macroeconomic modelling unit of Statistics Denmark. The model gives a simplified description of the interactions of the Danish economy. It is used by Danish government agencies for macroeconomic forecasting and planning. The EMMA system of energy and emission models for ADAM has been developed by National Environmental Research Institute, Risø National Laboratory and Statistics Denmark.

EMMA, which uses the environmental accounts as inputs for its estimations, is in combination with ADAM suitable for answering questions like: Given the economic development, which emissions will be generated? Given specific targets for emissions or emissions reductions, will these be obtained given the projected economic development and present policies? Are the targets obtainable assuming an alternative economic development or with alternative policy options (Andersen and Trier, 1995).

An example of the use of the ADAM-EMMA system is given by the modelling of an implementation of a specific strategy for reaching the Kyoto protocol goal of a reduction of Danish CO_2 emissions by 21 per cent in 2012 compared to 1990. The specific strategy used in the example includes a combination of buying up of international CO_2-quotas, energy savings, more extended use of renewables and the introduction of a CO_2-tax.

Official government plans for economic growth, etc. were introduced into a "doing nothing" scenario, *i.e.* a growth scenario (1.4 per cent economic growth per year) without any specific strategy for a reduction of the CO_2 emissions. This was used as a reference point for the modelling of the reduction strategy. The leftmost figure in figure 7 shows how the combined strategy reduces the emissions compared to the "doing nothing" scenario. It is seen that the strategy reduces emissions by 40 per cent compared to the "doing nothing" scenario in the end of the period (2030). This is necessary in order to keep the CO_2 emissions within the framework of the Kyoto protocol because the general economic growth causes an increasing amount of emissions if nothing is done. The rightmost figure shows how the reduction strategy has an effect on economy each year compared to the "doing nothing" situation. It is seen that most economic variables are moved upwards in the beginning of the period (due to large investments in energy savings, etc.). After this initial period all economic indicators lie below what they would have done if the strategy had not been implemented. From the middle of the period (2015) the effect of the strategy upon the economy seems to stabilise. GDP, for instance, lies approximately 2-3 per cent below the GDP of "doing nothing".

Figure 7. **Effect on CO_2 Emissions and Economy of a CO_2 Reduction Strategy**

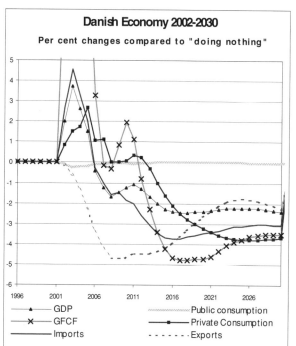

Source: Modelling results by Kenneth Karlsson, The Macroeconomic Model Unit at Statistics Denmark.

So far, the ADAM-EMMA system only includes the possibility to create scenarios and to analyse the link between energy use and energy related emissions on one side and the economy on the other side. However, plans and possibilities exist for extending the modelling complex with other sub-models, which can be used for modelling of other types of emissions, solid waste generation as well as resource inputs to the economy (e.g. DMI and TMR). Unfortunately, financial funding for the implementation of this comprehensive system is lacking for the moment. No doubt, however, a future implementation of such a system will widen the possibilities for analysing the economic consequences of reaching environmental sustainability as well as the consequences for environmental sustainability if measures are not taken to mitigate the effect of economic growth.

Danish oil and natural gas – physical and monetary asset accounts

As an example of how environmental accounts can contribute to a consistent evaluation of economic and (physical) resource aspects of sustainability the development of the Danish reserves of oil and natural gas is shown here. The asset accounts were briefly introduced in section 1.3.

Figures 8 and 9 show the development in the reserves from 1990 to 2000.

The reserves of natural gas and oil measured in physical units (m^3 and tonnes) increased by 15 and 35 per cent, respectively. The larger reserves at the end of the period were obtained in spite of an increasing extraction of both natural gas and oil through the years. The reason for the growing reserves is new discoveries of oil and natural gas through exploration activities. Furthermore, the reserves are defined as the resources which are technical possible and economic profitable to extract. Thus, changes in technology and oil prices had an effect on the physical size of the reserves.

Due to larger physical reserves, but mainly due to large increases in the per unit resource rent, the value of the reserves has increased substantially during the period. The resource rent used in the calculation is based on three-year averages of the actual resource rents in order to smooth the fluctuations in oil prices. Anyhow, the value of the oil and natural gas expresses expectations of how much resource rent the reserves will bring in the future, and these expectations are strongly influenced by previous and present oil prices.

Without doubt, both the physical and monetary asset accounts indicate that the development in the reserves has been sustainable from an economic viewpoint. The monetary asset accounts tell us the important message that we are far better off economically with respect to oil and natural gas. The value of the reserves was in fact many times larger in 2000 compared to 1990. From an economic viewpoint indicators based on the physical asset accounts underestimate how much better off we are.

However, it is probably safer not to rely entirely on the monetary asset accounts. Instead, the monetary and physical asset accounts should be seen in combination. The reason is that the monetary asset accounts build heavily on assumptions about future extraction patterns and expectations of future prices and costs. If these expectations fail to be fulfilled, the future economic welfare and sustainability is overestimated by the asset accounts. The physical asset accounts on the other hand give a more conservative picture of the development, which from a precautionary principle might be more appropriate when it comes to assessment of sustainability. Furthermore, even though the physical asset accounts are based on (market-) economic principles it is much closer to a broader sustainability concept, which includes components like existence values and bequest values. Thus, there are strong reasons too look at the two types of asset accounts in combination.

Figure 8. **Oil and Natural Gas Reserves – Physical Stocks (Cubic Metre, 1990 = 100)**

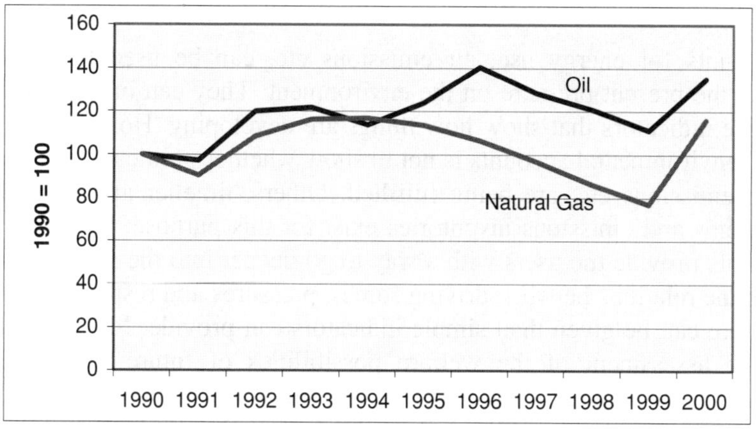

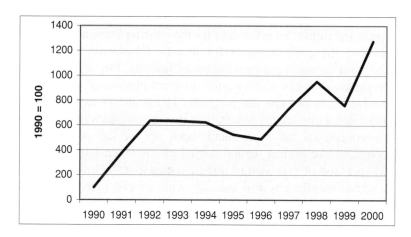

Source: Danish Environmental Accounts, Statistics Denmark.

Figure 9. **Value of Oil and Natural Gas Reserves (Mill. DKK, 1990 =100)**

Source: Danish *Environmental* Accounts, Statistics Denmark.

Conclusion

The present Danish environmental accounts cannot – and don't pretend – to answer the question whether the development is sustainable or not. First of all, an overall agreement about what sustainability means in practice is lacking. Secondly, the environmental aspects, which in practice have been and can be implemented in the accounts, are too limited in numbers for us to obtain a full picture of the development.

However, less can do, and it is just as obvious that the consistent linkage of economic and environment variables is very useful when the development is analysed. As the examples of the use of the Danish environmental accounts have shown, the construction of indicators and the combination of the accounts with modelling and other sets of statistics makes it possible to provide interesting empirical results that can be used as input for a discussion of whether the development is sustainable or not. This is the case even though the accounts themselves don't pretend to say anything about sustainability or rely on a specific definition of sustainability.

Flow accounts for energy use, air emissions etc. can be used to assess the past behaviour and the present pressure on the environment. They can in an efficient way be used to provide indicators that show how things are developing. However, the main aim of the Danish environmental accounts is not to show whether political goals and plans for reductions of emissions etc. are being fulfilled. Others, timelier and more appropriate statistical systems and emissions inventories exist for this purpose. It is more important that the accounts provide the users with a way to go deeper into the structures behind the pressures and the relations between driving forces, pressures and responses. Thus, a more complete picture can be given than simple indicators can provide. Maybe most useful in relation to the assessment of the welfare possibilities of future generations are the physical flow accounts when they are used in combination with economic-environmental models as described, for example, in section 2.5. The trade-offs between economic and environmental policies as well as technological problems can be highlighted in this way. Here, the accounts provide the models with detailed and appropriate data, which no other statistics on energy use and emissions, etc. are able to do.

Physical and monetary asset accounts for environmental assets are by nature directly aimed toward the specific definition of sustainability as something that concerns how much we pass on to the future. So is the case for the existing Danish asset accounts for oil and natural gas and the pilot accounts for forests. Obviously, this is an important question, and the asset accounts can provide useful insights. Physical and monetary asset accounts for the same assets can display quite different pictures of the development, and both have their advantages and specific purposes. The monetary asset accounts show the assets from a pure economic angle, and from a strong sustainability point of view. The physical asset accounts, on the other hand, open up for the possibilities that other sustainability concepts like critical natural capital etc. is taken into account. Besides, it avoids the tricky question of valuation of non-marketed assets. However, it must be born in mind, that in some cases the physical asset accounts are also constructed with a view to the economic aspects of the resources, *c.f.* the example of the accounts for Danish oil and natural gas. Finally, bearing in mind that the monetary asset accounts to a considerable degree are based on assumptions and expectations on future extractions, prices etc. (not to mention the discount rate), it seems reasonable not always to rely entirely on these accounts even when the focus is narrowed to economic sustainability. A presentation of the physical accounts, together with the monetary accounts gives a better ground for an assessment of the possibilities we pass on to the future.

References

Andersen, F.M. and Trier, P.: Environmental satellite models for ADAM - CO_2, SO_2 and NO_x emissions. NERI technical Report No. 148. National Environmental Research Institute, December 1995

Bringezu, S. og Schütz, H. : Total Material requirement of the European Union. Technical report No. 55. European Environment Agency, 2001

Charnes , A., Cooper, W. and E. Rhodes, E: Mesuring the Efficiency of Decision Making Units. Journal of Operational Research, 2: 429-444, 1978 de Haan, M.: A Structural Decomposition Analysis of Pollution in the Netherlands. In *Economics Systems Research*, Vol. 13, No2., 2001

Eurostat: Economy-wide material flow accounts and derived indicators - A methodological guide. European Commission , Eurostat, Theme 2, Economy and Finance, 2001

Gravgård Pedersen, O.: Physical Input-Output Tables for Denmark – Products and Materials 1990, Air Emissions 1990-92. Statistics Denmark, 1999

Gravgård Pedersen, O.: DMI and TMR Indicators for Denmark 1981, 1990 and 1997 – An assessment of the Material Requirements of The Danish Economy. Statistics Denmark, 2002

Harris, R.: The impact of the UK economy upon changes in atmospheric emissions between 1990 and 1998. Mimeograph., 2001

Hoekstra, R. and van den Berg, C.J.: Structural Decomposition Anlaysis of Physical Flows in the Economy. Environmental and Resorce Economics Vol. 23. pp. 357-378. Kluwer, 2002

SEEA 2003: Handbook of National Accounting – Integrated Environmental and Economic Accounting ST/ESA/STAT/SER.F/61/Rev.1 (Final Draft) United Nations et.al., 2003

Material Flow Accounts and Balances to Derive a Set of Sustainability Indicators

F. Alonso Luengo and L. Bailon Chico
INE, Spain

Introduction

Natural resources use and efficiency is one of the key policy issues in the Sixth Environmental Action Programme 2001-2010. Furthermore, natural resources use and/or material consumption parameters should be included in a sustainable development indicators system. An integrated environmental and economic accounting system seems to be the finest tool to achieve this indicators framework.

The integrated environmental and economic accounting system objective is to provide a detailed description of environment and economy relationships. It is essential, to describe this relationships, the availability of environmental and economic data based in similar accounting standards and concepts.

The right interpretation and analysis of the results requires data expressed in physical units, as they are more suitable than monetary units. Therefore, to measure material flows from the environment to the economy and this to the environment, data should be expressed in tonnes, as material flows change their shape and composition across production and consumption processes.

This work is a preliminary implementation of the EUROSTAT methodological guide "Economy-wide material flow accounts and derived indicators", and represents a first approach of the National Statistical Institute (INE) to compile the *material flow accounts and balances* which will be incorporated to develop a *system of sustainable development indicators*.

Objectives

The main purposes of economy-wide material flow accounts implementation are to:

- Provide information over the structure and changes over time of the physical metabolism of the economy.

- Derive a set of aggregated indicators for natural resources use.

- Derive indicators for resources productivity and eco-efficiency, by relating resource use indicators to GDP and other economic indicators.

- Provide indicators for the material intensity of lifestyles, by relating these indicators to population size and other demographic indicators.

- Integrate information into the national accounts.

- Supply statistical data and information to settle any kind of users requests.

Definitions

Material flow accounts show material physical inputs that get into national economic system, and the outputs to other economies or to the environment. They are accounts expressed in physical units (tonnes) that describe extraction, transformation, consumption and final disposal of chemicals, raw materials or products.

The first law of thermodynamics, or the conservation of matter principle, is the conceptual basis of these accounts. It states that matter is neither created nor destroyed by any physical transformation, it just gets transformed. This principle can be applied to specific substances and materials with high environmental impact; including fuels, strategic materials, wood, pesticides, zinc, etc. Next diagram shows input and output flows, and material accumulation in the economic system.

Figure 1. **General scheme of material flows into the economy**

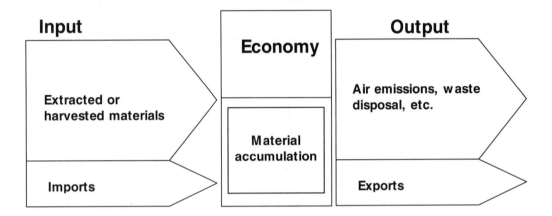

Accounts framework

Accounts scope

Material flow accounts should be consistent with *national* economic *accounts*. National accounts define national economy as a whole of activities and transactions of resident economic agents, these which have a centre of interest in the national economic territory. Some of these transactions carry out outside the national economic territory, and others, inside this territory, are carried out by non resident units.

Therefore, material flow accounts, the same as national accounts, should apply the *residence principle*. According to this principle, material used by resident units away the national territory have to be considered as domestic economy inputs, and materials used by non resident units inside the national territory should be excluded from the accounting framework.

National economic territory, according to national accounts, is constituted by the geographical territory and free zones, national air space, territorial waters, continental shelf placed on international waters over which the country has exclusive rights, territorial enclaves and deposits situated on international waters that are exploited by resident units. National economic territory does not include other countries' or international organisations' extra-territorial enclaves placed into the geographical territory.

Territories out of the boundaries of national economic territory are considered as the "rest of the world".

National environment is defined as the geographical space of national economic territory. Territories out of the boundaries of national environment are named "rest of the world environment".

System boundaries of flows between economic and natural scopes

Material flow accounts show material physical inputs of the national economic system and outputs to other economies or to the environment. These accounts describe extraction, transformation, consumption and final disposal of materials.

It is difficult to succeed a whole material balance of the economy, since not every material input or output have a systematic follow-up. Material flows are classified into three main categories: raw materials, as material inputs extracted from the environment; products, which are the final result of production process; and wastes, not wanted by-products of production and consumption processes.

MFA can provide a detail level depending on material characteristics:

- Extraction/ harvesting (agriculture, forestry, mining and quarrying).

- Transformation/ conversion (refineries, metal industry).

- Intermediate uses (manufacture industry).

- Final uses (household consumption).

- Material stocks (gross capital formation, durable consumer goods).

- Imports/ Exports.

- Wastes (waste disposal, air emissions, waste water).

- Flows and accumulation in nature.

There are counted only flows that cross the system boundary. That means flows from national environment to the economy, flows between national and the rest of the world economy (imports and exports), and flows from the economy to national environment or to rest of the world environment.

Material flows within the economy are not presented in MFA, although they are described in Physical Input-Output Tables (PIOT). There are neither considered natural flows that take place within the environment, or between national and the rest of the world environment (across frontier flows).

Figure 2 shows account flows, including both national and rest of the world economy, as well as national and rest of the world environment. Only flows that cross the national economy boundary (represented with thicker line) are taken into account.

Figure 2. **Physical flows and the scope of physical flow accounting**

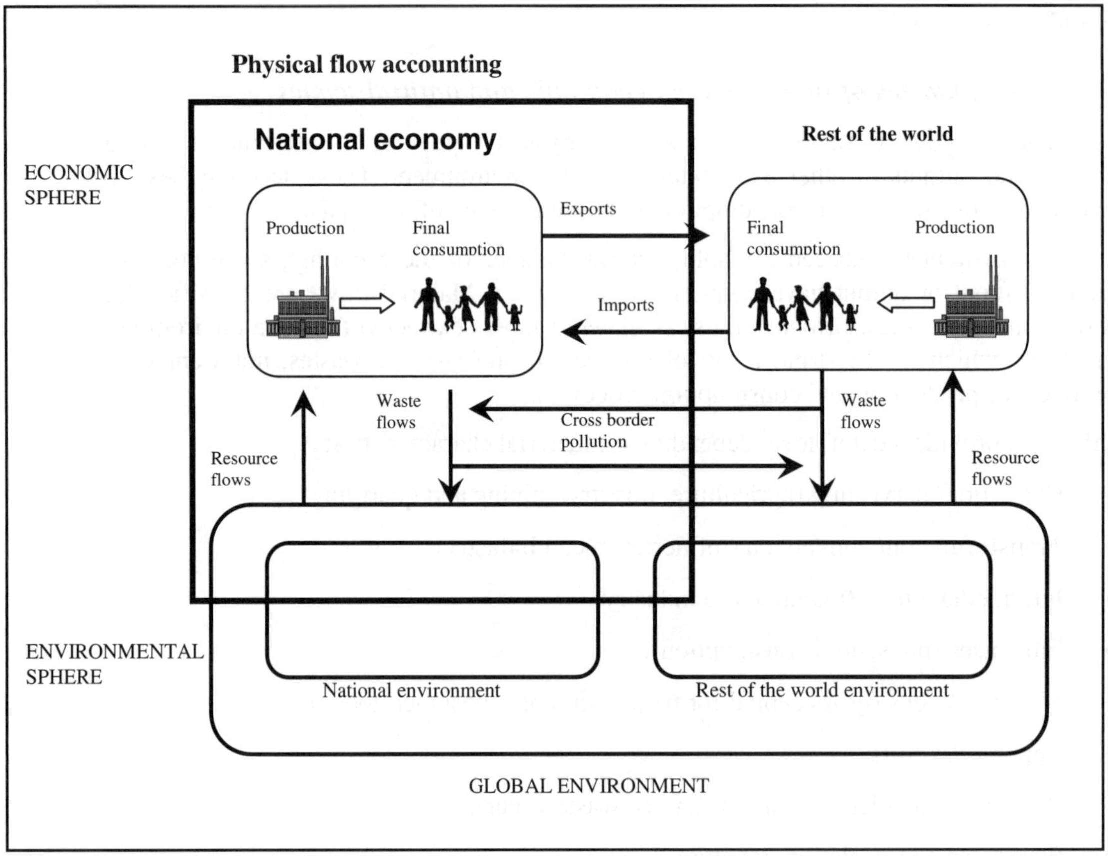

Concepts, definitions and classifications

Material flows from national environment to the economy are called input flows, and they refer to the extraction or movement of natural materials on purpose and by humans or human-controlled means of technology.

Output flows released to the environment means that economic system or society loses control over the location and composition of the materials.

Flows classification

Material flows can be grouped depending on the dimension used to characterise categories of material flows and indicators. Attending to the territorial dimension to indicate the origin and destination of flows, they are classified into *domestic and rest of the world flows*. If it is beard in mind the product-chain or life-cycle dimension, there are two types: *direct and indirect flows* to indicate whether flows are directly observed, or they are obtained as a calculation of up-stream material requirements.

The product dimension indicates whether flows enter the economic system or not, and divides flows into *used and unused*. This classification is only used for inputs. For outputs, terms *processed and not processed* are used to determine flows stemming from an cconomic system or not.

Combining the three dimensions leads to five categories of inputs relevant for economy-wide MFA:

Table 1. **Material input categories**

Product-chain	Used or unused	Domestic or rest of the world	Term used
Direct	Used	Domestic	Domestic extraction (used)
Not applied	Unused	Domestic	Unused domestic extraction
Direct	Used	Rest of the world	Imports
Indirect (up-stream)	Used	Rest of the world	
Indirect (up-stream)	Unused	Rest of the world	Indirect (input) flows associated to imports

Materials extracted or mobilised on purpose and by means of technology which are not fit or intended for use are named *hidden flows*. For materials extracted or moved on a nation's territory, these hidden flows are "unused domestic extraction".

Output flows can be classified into:

Table 2. **Material output categories**

Product-chain	Processed or not	DOMESTIC OR REST OF THE WORLD	TERM USED
Direct	Processed	Domestic	Domestic processed output to nature
Not applied	Not processed	Domestic	Disposal of unused domestic extraction
Direct	Processed	Rest of the world	Exports
Indirect (up-stream)	Processed	Rest of the world	
Indirect (up-stream)	Not processed	Rest of the world	Indirect (output) flows associated to exports

Indirect flows are defined only for economy-wide material flows, and they only refer to imports and exports. They are the material requirements associated to the production of a product or raw material.

On the input side, indirect flows are defined as up-stream material input flows that are associated to imports but are not physically imported. On the output side, indirect flows are up-stream material input flows associated to exports but not physically exported. Therefore, indirect flows are the "cradle to border" inputs necessary to make a product available at the border for import or export, excluding the mass of the product itself. Two types of indirect flows are distinguished: used and unused. Indirect flows can only be calculated after the accounts for direct (used) materials have been completed.

- For economy-wide MFA, two components of indirect flows are distinguished:

- Up-stream indirect flows expressed as the Raw Material Equivalents (RME) of the imported or exported products. The RME is the used extraction that was needed to provide the products.

- Up-stream indirect flows of unused extraction associated to this RME.

Indicators and balances derived from the accounts

MFA derived indicators

A set of indicators can be derived from the material flow accounts so as to provide an aggregate picture of the "industrial metabolism". These indicators can be grouped into input, consumption and output indicators. More indicators could be derived from the accounts, by setting the boundaries of the accounts differently or by compiling indicators per material group.

It is not yet clear which of the indicators will be considered the most relevant and useful in the longer term. Only future use in analysis can provide a sound basis for such recommendations. The choice of the most relevant indicators will depend on the policy focus and on proven usefulness and applicability of indicators in policy analysis. At this stage, only a set of criteria for the selection of indicators can be offered:

- Ease of understanding the meaning of an indicator.

- Ease of compilation.

- Data availability.

- Compatibility with the national accounts.

- Potential for policy uses.

- Completeness of the indicator

Resource use and efficiency has emerged as a major issue for long-term sustainability and environmental policies at the EU member states level. Objectives include to increase substantially the resource efficiency of the economic system, thereby reducing the use of natural resources and related negative impacts on the environment. Two main themes have been identified as policy relevant: the total quantity used and the efficiency in use. Domestic Material Consumption (DMC) or Total Material Requirement (TMR) were considered good indicators to describe those issues.

At present it appears that good candidates for core indicators would be the input indicators Direct Material Input (DMI) and Total Material Requirement (TMR), as well as the consumption indicators Domestic Material consumption (DMC) and, maybe, Total Material Consumption (TMC).

Table 3 shows a composite material balance that allows the derivation of several material flow indicators. It includes all the items important for the full set of economy-wide material flow accounts in a summary form, but is not actually used for balancing purposes, therefore it doesn't represent the full sequence of accounts.

Table 3 - **Economy-wide material balance with derived resource use indicators**

INPUTS (origin)	OUTPUTS (destination)
Domestic extraction Fossil fuels (coal, oil...) Minerals (ores, sand...) Biomass (timber, cereals...) **Imports**	**Emissions and wastes** Emissions to air Waste landfilled Emissions to water **Dissipative use of products and losses** (fertiliser, manure, seeds; corrosion...)
Direct material inputs (DMI)	**Domestic processed output to nature (DPO)**
Unused domestic extraction From mining/quarrying From biomass harvest Soil excavation	**Disposal of unused domestic extraction** From mining/quarrying From biomass harvest Soil excavation
Total material input (TMI)	**Total domestic output to nature (TDO)**
Indirect flows associated to imports	**Exports**
Total material requirements (TMR)	**Total material output (TMO)**
	Net additions to stock (NAS) Infrastructures and buildings Other (machinery, durable goods...)
	Indirect flows associated to exports

Main accounting balances

Direct material inputs are all solid, liquid and gaseous materials that enter the economy for further use, either in production or consumption processes; and they are classified by their origin into domestic extraction (used) and imports. If exports are subtracted from direct material inputs, the result will be *domestic material consumption*, which measures the total amount of material directly used in an economy.

Adding unused domestic extraction and indirect flows associated to imports to direct material inputs, *total material requirement* will be obtained. It measures the total "material base" of an economy. Subtracting exports and indirect flows associated to exports, the result is *total material consumption*, which represents the total material use associated with domestic production and consumption activities.

Domestic processed output is defined as the total weight of materials, extracted from the domestic environment or imported, which have been used in the domestic economy before flowing to the environment. These flows occur at the processing, manufacturing, use, and final disposal stage of the production-consumption chain. Adding the disposal of unused domestic extraction, there is *obtained total domestic output* to nature. Finally, *total material output* measures the total of material that leaves the economy, both to the environment and to the rest of the world (exports).

Material flow accounts estimation for Spain. Statistical data sources

The Spanish Mining Statistics published by the Directorate-General for Energy and Mine Policy of the Ministry of Economics is the statistical source used to estimate most of the direct flows relative to domestic extraction of fossil fuels, minerals, ores and quarrying products.

With regard to biomass, the Agricultural Statistics of the Ministry of Agriculture, Fisheries and Food allows to estimate biomass from agriculture, forestry, hunting and inland fishing. Data from sea fishing biomass were obtained from the FAO statistics.

Imports and exports data were estimated from Foreign Trade Statistics of the Tax Office, which offers detailed information about imported and exported products by raw material, product type, etc. in physical units. Those data have been classified according to EUROSTAT Combined Nomenclature, so they can be related to domestic production.

On the outputs to the environment side, waste landfilled and waste water data were calculated from the statistical survey over industry and services waste generation, and the survey over municipal solid waste collection and processing; both published by the National Statistical Institute (INE). As for emissions to air, NAMEA emission and energy accounts are the most suitable source, as they follow the residence principle. In this case there have been used the air emissions accounts published by INE.

Hidden flows and indirect flows associated to imports and exports are probably the most difficult to establish. They have been estimated from a set of default coefficients published by the Wuppertal Institute, corresponding to each imported or extracted material. Only imported raw materials and semi-manufactured product have been taken into account. For unused domestic extraction, those coefficients have been completed with data from the Spanish Mining Statistics, and they have also been contrasted with waste statistics to prove their reliability.

For unused biomass from harvest, three aspects have been considered: sea fishing discarded by-catch, which represents 25% of the catch according to Greenpeace; wood harvesting losses, from Wuppertal Institute data; and soil losses from agriculture harvesting, which have been calculated from the Agricultural Statistics of the Ministry of Agriculture, Fisheries and Food; and estimations made in the Spanish Forestry Plan.

Preliminary conclusions

Traditional economic system has measured contribution of factors of production, work and capital through their productivity. Data provided by national accounts allow to a detailed research of their productivity evolution over time, and how the introduction of new technologies in the production system has permitted to obtain high growth rates. However, factor of natural resources has been scarcely contemplated in economic analysis and in national accounts development, what shows the scarce interest of economic analysts for these issues.

Nowadays, the new concept of sustainability requires to take this factor into consideration at the same degree as the others, work and capital, in economic development framework. Therefore, natural resources use should be measured, as work and capital, through per capita or productivity terms indicators.

In this sense, direct material input per capita seems to correlate with GDP per capita. Material consumption could also be an appropriate indicator, especially for small economies with a higher dependence on international trade, as it neutralises the effect of economic size on trade.

Preliminary results of this work for Spanish economy show that differences between GDP per capita and material input per capita have increased in the brief period 1996-2000. There could be deduced that on that period a higher proportion of natural resources have been used by production or consumption processes. Those differences are shown in following graphs.

Apparently, direct material input and total material requirements per capita are also correlated. Main differences are due to hidden and indirect flows, which are included in TMR as it measures the real material weight of an economy. In principle, input indicators measure used or mobilised materials to support economic activities (including production for export), and are highly related to each country's means of production.

The development of indictors which measure *material efficiency or productivity* (GDP unit per material indicator unit) or *material intensity* (material indicator unit per GDP unit) has huge significance to compare natural resources use with economic growth. Using efficiency or productivity terms tend to be more common among economists and for comparison with other economic indicators, whereas intensity tends to be more commonly used by environmentalists.

Following graphs show how both indicators change over 1996-2000 period. In 1996, one material input tonne generated 763.0 Euro of GDP, whereas in 2000 it generated only 694.91 Euro; which means a fall in resources productivity of 9%. At the same time, in 1996, 1 310.61 material tonnes were introduced in the economic system to produce one million Euro of GDP. In 2000 there are required 1 439.03 tonnes.

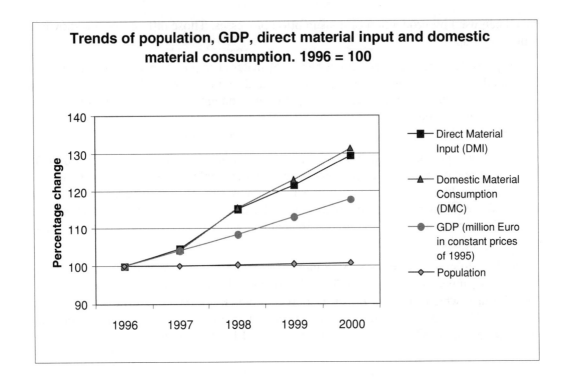

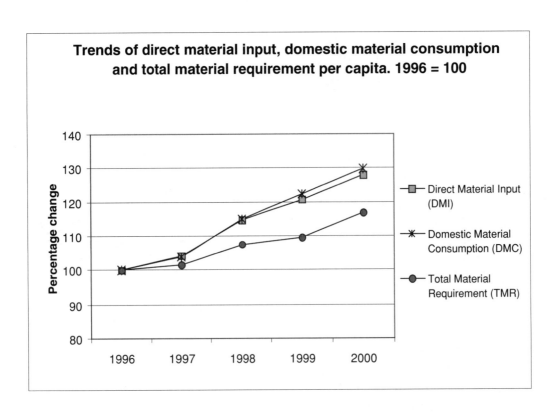

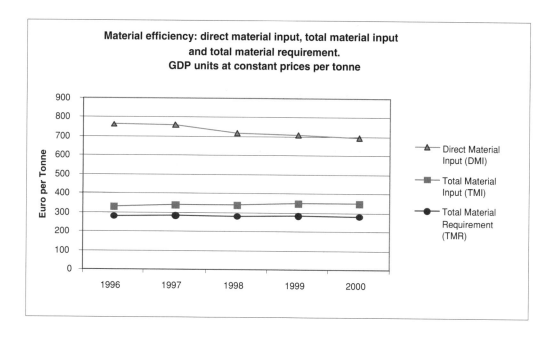

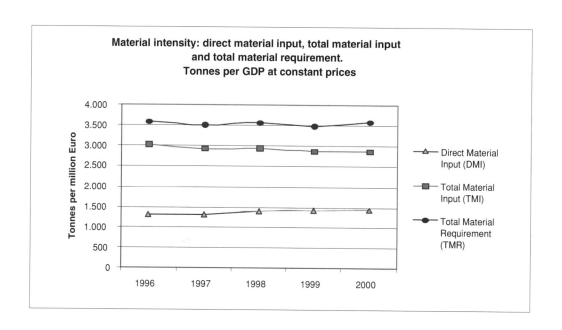

Material flow accounts
(1996 -2000)

Material flows summary account

Unit: tonnes

Inputs (resources)	1996	1997	1998	1999	2000
Domestic extraction	424 135 193	441 623 042	483 521 884	506 270 062	538 527 813
Fossil fuels	28 301 858	26 962 078	26 753 526	24 565 701	23 888 150
Minerals	270 994 790	293 162 727	326 491 197	361 356 542	383 090 198
Metal ores	*1 383 861*	*793 498*	*758 265*	*738 131*	*570 063*
Non-metallic minerals	*9 943 929*	*10 199 229*	*10 112 932*	*10 525 411*	*10 587 135*
Quarry products	*259 667 000*	*282 170 000*	*315 620 000*	*350 093 000*	*371 933 000*
Biomass	124 838 545	121 498 237	130 277 161	120 347 819	131 549 465
From agriculture and forestry	*123 781 808*	*120 385 045*	*129 157 374*	*119 246 142*	*130 620 255*
From fishing and hunting	*1 027 678*	*1 079 863*	*1 085 234*	*1 069 035*	*895 171*
From other activities	*29 059*	*33 329*	*34 553*	*32 642*	*34 039*
Imports	**163 619 225**	**173 007 560**	**194 466 311**	**208 155 981**	**221 911 495**
DMI - Direct material input	**587 754 417**	**614 630 602**	**677 988 195**	**714 426 043**	**760 439 309**
Unused domestic extraction	**768 795 159**	**754 121 658**	**754 777 478**	**738 024 806**	**756 389 689**
Fossil fuels	136 936 055	130 685 088	130 399 170	119 962 967	116 654 568
Minerals	93 142 648	96 764 039	103 354 008	103 808 951	115 722 085
Metal ores	*18 401 060*	*17 318 802*	*16 129 271*	*5 172 072*	*12 769 378*
Non-metallic minerals	*7 338 975*	*6 612 938*	*5 893 465*	*6 729 136*	*5 909 230*
Quarry products	*67 402 613*	*72 832 299*	*81 331 272*	*91 907 743*	*97 043 477*
Biomass from harvest	538 716 456	526 672 531	521 024 300	514 252 888	524 013 036
Soil excavation and dredging	-	-	-	-	-
TMI - Total material input	**1 356 549 576**	**1 368 752 260**	**1 432 765 673**	**1 452 450 849**	**1 516 828 997**
Indirect flows associated to imports	**246 845 940**	**262 576 809**	**300 956 122**	**317 894 051**	**374 702 574**
TMR - Total material requirement	**1 603 395 516**	**1 631 329 069**	**1 733 721 795**	**1 770 344 900**	**1 891 531 571**

-.: not counted

Material flow summary account

Unit: tonnes

Outputs (uses)	1996	1997	1998	1999	2000
Emissions and wastes	283 437 024	292 399 000	315 190 311	343 930 451	352 913 766
Emissions to air	258 546 417	265 567 640	287 775 486	314 474 606	326 856 862
Greenhouse gases	*250 052 417*	*257 061 468*	*279 352 038*	*306 311 480*	*318 843 509*
Acidifying pollutants	*3 394 000*	*3 568 172*	*3 464 448*	*3 437 126*	*3 420 353*
Ozone precursors	*5 100 000*	*4 938 000*	*4 959 000*	*4 726 000*	*4 593 000*
Wastes landfilled	24 117 080	25 971 075	26 465 473	28 442 547	25 065 558
Emissions to water	773 527	860 285	949 352	1 013 298	991 346
Water supply and treatment	*599 477*	*680 074*	*760 578*	*814 906*	*916 617*
Industrial effluents	*174 050*	*180 211*	*188 774*	*198 392*	*74 729*
Dissipative use of products and dissipative losses	**82 562 869**	**84 733 382**	**84 417 287**	**88 682 996**	**88 612 633**
DPO - Domestic processed output to nature	**365 999 893**	**377 132 382**	**399 607 598**	**432 613 447**	**441 526 399**
Disposal of unused domestic extraction	**768 795 159**	**754 121 658**	**754 777 478**	**738 024 806**	**756 389 689**
Fossil fuels	136 936 055	130 685 088	130 399 170	119 962 967	116 654 568
Minerals	93 142 648	96 764 039	103 354 008	103 808 951	115 722 085
Metal ores	*18 401 060*	*17 318 802*	*16 129 271*	*5 172 072*	*12 769 378*
Non-metallic minerals	*7 338 975*	*6 612 938*	*5 893 465*	*6 729 136*	*5 909 230*
Quarry products	*67 402 613*	*72 832 299*	*81 331 272*	*91 907 743*	*97 043 477*
Biomass from harvest	538 716 456	526 672 531	521 024 300	514 252 888	524 013 036
Soil excavation and dredging	-	-	-	-	-
TDO - Total domestic output to nature	**1 134 795 052**	**1 131 254 040**	**1 154 385 076**	**1 170 638 253**	**1 197 916 088**
Exports	**80 778 312**	**86 253 498**	**91 999 060**	**91 054 327**	**95 371 685**
TMO - Total material output	**1 215 573 364**	**1 217 507 538**	**1 246 384 136**	**1 261 692 580**	**1 293 287 773**
NAS - Net additions to stock	**140 976 212**	**151 244 722**	**186 381 537**	**190 758 269**	**223 541 224**
Indirect flows associated to exports	**98 295 414**	**113 837 392**	**113 416 381**	**132 693 813**	**105 094 042**

-: not counted

Economic indicators

Main indicators at constant prices

Unit: million Euro

	1996	1997	1998	1999	2000
Gross domestic product at market prices	448 457	466 513	486 785	507 220	528 439
Gross capital formation	99 498	104 321	115 435	125 711	132 245
Goods and services exports	109 234	125 986	136 281	146 776	161 528
Goods and services imports	107 775	122 054	138 221	155 768	172 223
Total employment. Equivalent jobs	13 183 000	13 596 200	14 153 400	14 657 200	15 156 900

Main indicators at current prices

Unit: million Euro

	1996	1997	1998	1999	2000
Gross domestic product at market prices	464 251	494 140	527 975	565 199	609 319
Gross capital formation	101 683	109 357	122 874	138 733	156 467
Goods and services exports	110 911	132 170	143 852	155 477	173 647
Goods and services imports	108 512	127 144	143 497	162 843	197 509
Total employment. Equivalent jobs	13 183 000	13 596 200	14 153 400	14 657 200	15 156 900

Change indexes of main indicators at constant prices

1996=100

	1996	1997	1998	1999	2000
Gross domestic product at market prices	100	104.03	108.55	113.10	117.83
Gross capital formation	100	104.84	116.02	126.35	132.91
Goods and services exports	100	115.33	124.76	134.37	147.87
Goods and services imports	100	113.25	128.25	144.53	159.80

Change indexes of main indicators at current prices

1996=100

	1996	1997	1998	1999	2000
Gross domestic product at market prices	100	106.44	113.73	121.74	131.25
Gross capital formation	100	107.55	120.84	136.44	153.88
Goods and services exports	100	119.17	129.70	140.18	156.56
Goods and services imports	100	117.17	133.24	150.07	182.02
Total employment. Equivalent jobs	100	103.13	107.36	111.18	114.97

Material flow indicators

Main material flows indicators

Units: tonnes per capita

	1996	1997	1998	1999	2000
Direct material input (DMI)	14.97	15.63	17.20	18.08	19.18
Total material input (TMI)	34.54	34.80	36.36	36.76	38.25
Total material requirement (TMR)	40.83	41.48	43.99	44.80	47.70
Domestic total material requirement	30.38	30.40	31.42	31.49	32.65
Domestic material consumption (DMC)	12.91	13.43	14.87	15.77	16.77
Total material consumption (TMC)	36.27	36.39	38.78	39.14	42.64
Net additions to stock (NAS)	3.59	3.85	4.73	4.83	5.64
Domestic processed output (DPO)	9.32	9.59	10.14	10.95	11.13
Total domestic output (TDO)	28.90	28.76	29.29	29.62	30.21
Direct material output (DMO)	11.38	11.78	12.47	13.25	13.54
Total material output (TMO)	30.95	30.96	31.63	31.93	32.61

Change indexes of main material flows indicators

1996=100

	1996	1997	1998	1999	2000
Direct material input (DMI)	100	104.41	114.90	120.77	128.12
Total material input (TMI)	100	100.75	105.27	106.43	110.74
Total material requirement (TMR)	100	101.59	107.74	109.72	116.83
Domestic total material requirement	100	100.07	103.42	103.65	107.47
Domestic material consumption (DMC)	100	104.03	115.18	122.15	129.90
Total material consumption (TMC)	100	100.33	106.92	107.91	117.56
Net additions to stock (NAS)	100	107.24	131.75	134.54	157.10
Domestic processed output (DPO)	100	102.90	108.80	117.49	119.42
Total domestic output (TDO)	100	99.52	101.35	102.49	104.53
Direct material output (DMO)	100	103.51	109.58	116.43	118.98
Total material output (TMO)	100	100.03	102.20	103.17	105.36

Material intensity indicators

Unit: tonnes per million Euro

	1996	1997	1998	1999	2000
Direct material input (DMI)	1 310.61	1 317.50	1 392.79	1 408.51	1 439.03
Total material input (TMI)	3 024.93	2 934.01	2 943.32	2 863.55	2 870.40
Total material requirement (TMR)	3 575.36	3 496.86	3 561.58	3 490.29	3 579.47
Domestic total material requirement	2 660.08	2 563.15	2 543.83	2 453.17	2 450.46
Domestic material consumption (DMC)	1 130.49	1 132.61	1 203.79	1 229.00	1 258.55
Domestic processed output (DPO)	816.13	808.41	820.91	852.91	835.53
Total domestic output (TDO)	2 530.44	2 424.91	2 371.45	2 307.95	2 266.90
Direct material output (DMO)	996.26	993.30	1 009.91	1 032.43	1 016.01
Total material output (TMO)	2 710.57	2 609.80	2 560.44	2 478.47	2 447.37

Change indexes of material intensity indicators

1996=100

	1996	1997	1998	1999	2000
Direct material input (DMI)	100	100.53	106.27	107.47	109.80
Total material input (TMI)	100	96.99	97.30	94.67	94.89
Total material requirement (TMR)	100	97.80	99.61	97.62	100.11
Domestic total material requirement	100	96.36	95.63	92.22	92.12
Domestic material consumption (DMC)	100	100.19	106.48	108.71	111.33
Domestic processed output (DPO)	100	99.05	100.59	104.51	102.38
Total domestic output (TDO)	100	95.83	93.72	91.21	89.59
Direct material output (DMO)	100	99.70	101.37	103.63	101.98
Total material output (TMO)	100	96.28	94.46	91.77	90.29

Material productivity indicators (eco-efficiency)

Unit: Euro per tonne

	1996	1997	1998	1999	2000
Direct material input (DMI)	763.00	759.01	717.98	709.97	694.91
Total material input (TMI)	330.59	340.83	339.75	349.22	348.38
Total material requirement (TMR)	279.69	285.97	280.77	286.51	279.37
Domestic total material requirement	375.93	390.14	393.11	407.64	408.09
Domestic material consumption (DMC)	884.57	882.92	830.71	813.67	794.56
Total material consumption (TMC)	314.85	325.95	318.51	327.96	312.49

Change indexes of eco-efficiency indicators

1996=100

	1996	1997	1998	1999	2000
Direct material input (DMI)	100	99.48	94.10	93.05	91.08
Total material input (TMI)	100	103.10	102.77	105.64	105.38
Total material requirement (TMR)	100	102.25	100.39	102.44	99.89
Domestic total material requirement	100	103.78	104.57	108.44	108.55
Domestic material consumption (DMC)	100	99.81	93.91	91.98	89.82
Total material consumption (TMC)	100	103.53	101.16	104.16	99.25

Material output intensity indicators

Unit: tonnes per million Euro

	1996	1997	1998	1999	2000
Domestic processed output (DPO)	816.13	808.41	820.91	852.91	835.53
Total domestic output (TDO)	2 530.44	2 424.91	2 371.45	2 307.95	2 266.90
Direct material output (DMO)	996.26	993.30	1 009.91	1 032.43	1 016.01
Total material output (TMO)	2 710.57	2 609.80	2 560.44	2 487.47	2 447.37

Change indexes of material output intensity indicators

1996=100

	1996	1997	1998	1999	2000
Domestic processed output (DPO)	100	99.05	100.59	104.51	102.38
Total domestic output (TDO)	100	95.83	93.72	91.21	89.59
Direct material output (DMO)	100	99.70	101.37	103.63	101.98
Total material output (TMO)	100	96.28	94.46	91.77	90.29

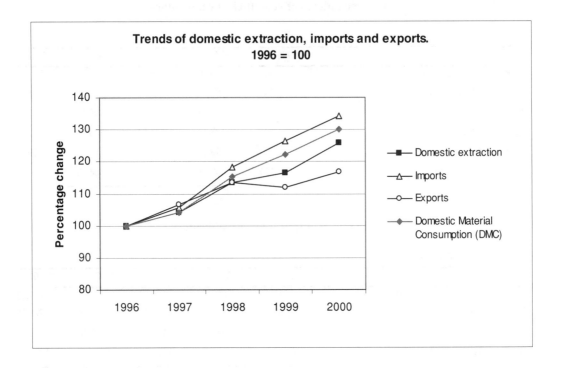

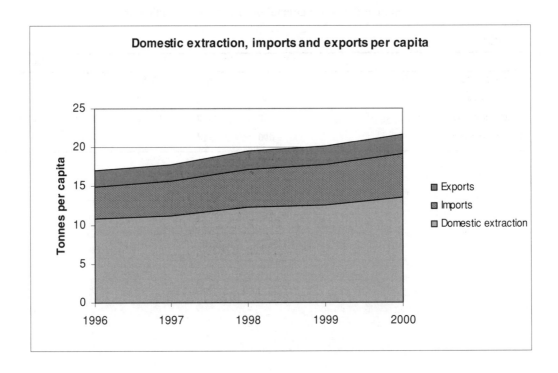

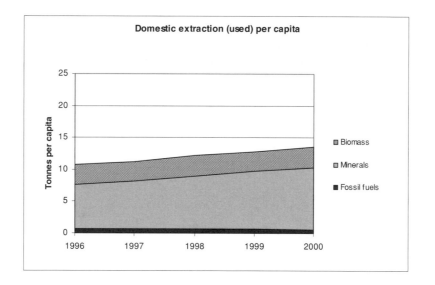

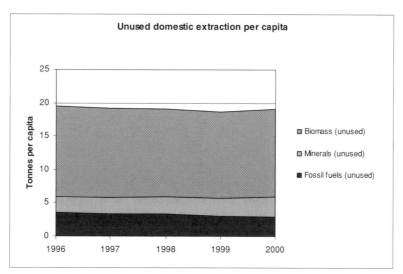

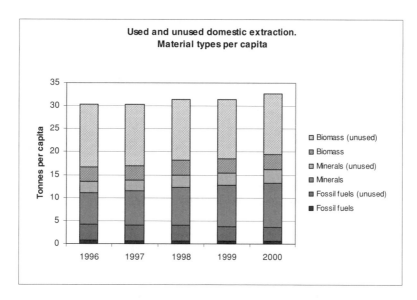

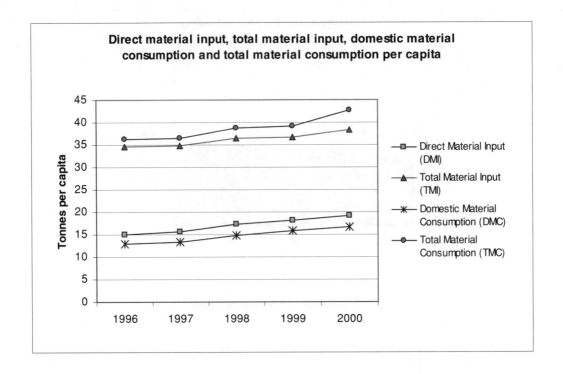

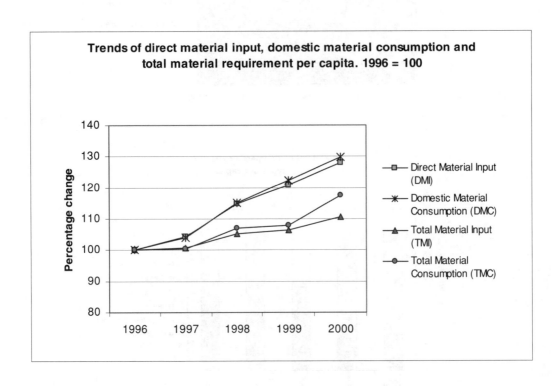

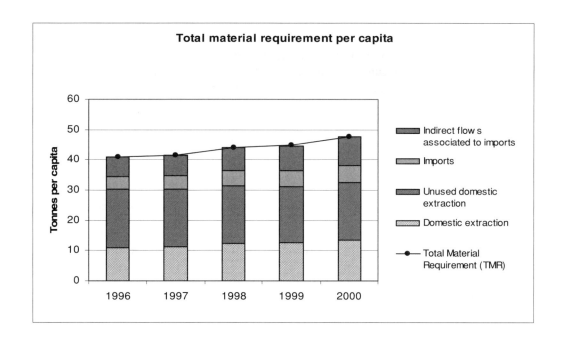

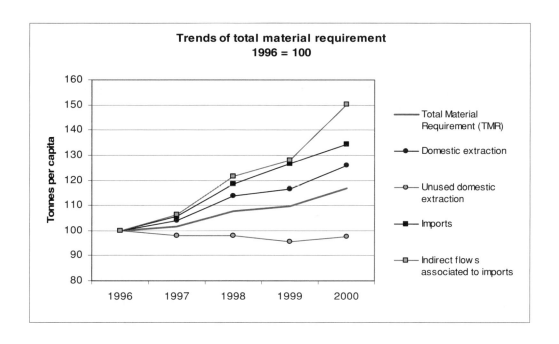

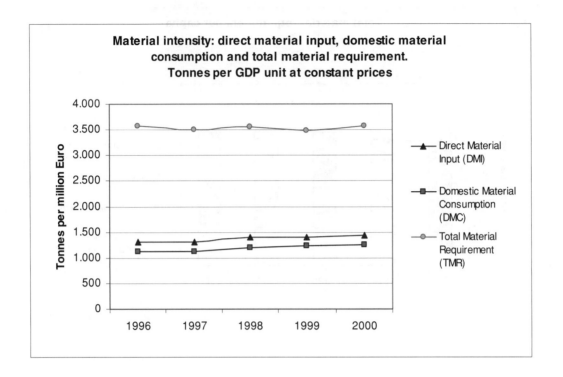

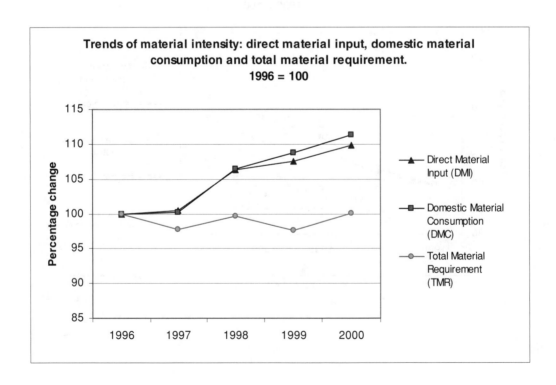

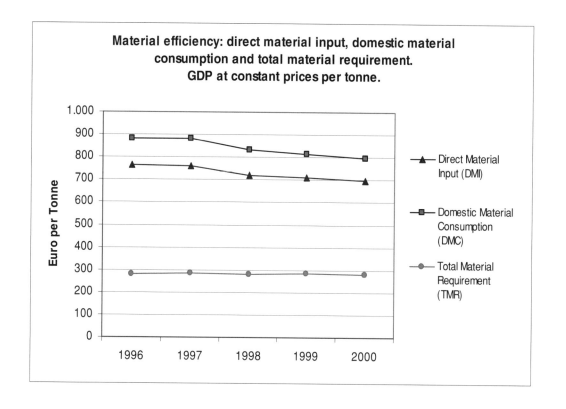

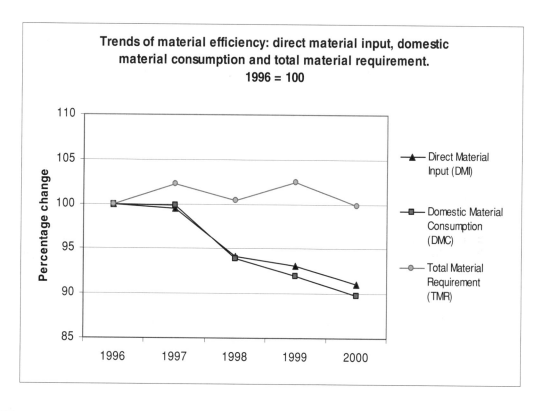

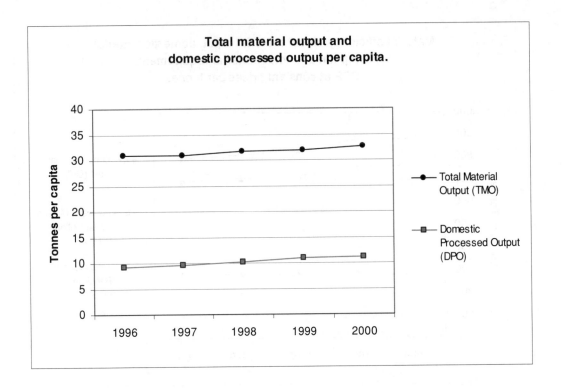

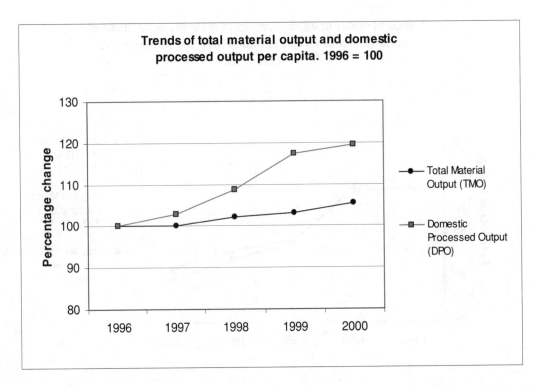

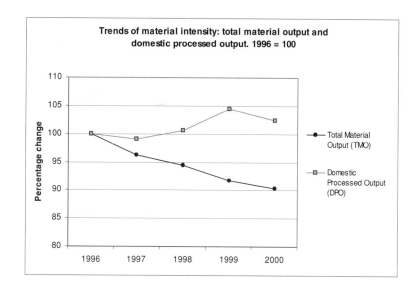

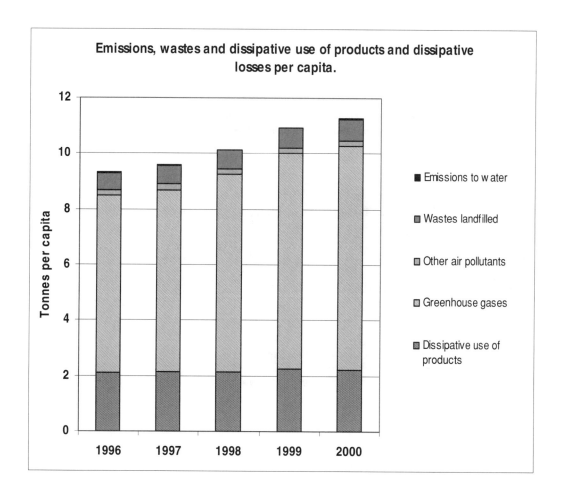

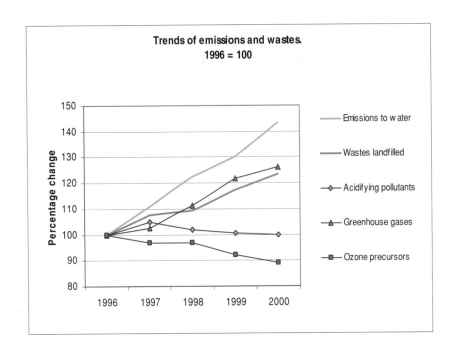

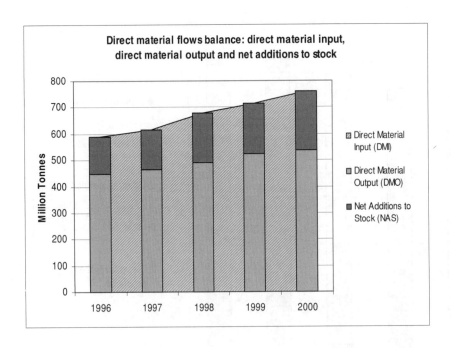

References

EUROSTAT (2001). Economy-wide material flow accounts and derived indicators. A methodological guide. Official Publications of the European Communities, Luxembourg.

EUROSTAT (2002). *Material use in the European Union 1980 – 2000: indicators and analysis.* EUROSTAT Working papers. Publications of the European Communities, Luxembourg.

Bringezu, Stephan and Schütz, Helmut (2001). *Total material requirement of the European Union.* European Environment Agency, Copenhagen.

Bringezu, Stephan and Schütz, Helmut (2001). *Material use indicators for the European Union, 1980 – 1997.* EUROSTAT Working papers. Publications of the European Communities, Luxembourg.

Wuppertal Institut (1998). *MI – Werte (Module).* Wuppertal Institut für Klima, Umwelt, Energie, Wuppertal. www.wupperinst.org/Projekte/mipsonline

D.G. de Política Energética y Minas (2002). *Estadística Minera de España 2000.* Ministerio de Economía, Madrid.

S.D.G. de Estadísticas Agroalimentarias (2002). *Anuario de Estadística Agroalimentaria 2000.* Ministerio de Agricultura, Pesca y Alimentación, Madrid. www.mapya.es

D.G. de Conservación de la Naturaleza (2002). *Plan Forestal Español.* Ministerio de Medio Ambiente, Madrid. www.mma.es

INE (2001). Estadísticas de Medio Ambiente. Estadísticas de Residuos 1999. Instituto Nacional de Estadística, Madrid.

INE (2001). Estadísticas de Medio Ambiente. Estadísticas del Agua 1999. Instituto Nacional de Estadística, Madrid.

INE (2002). *Cuentas Satélite sobre Emisiones Atmosféricas.* Instituto Nacional de Estadística, Madrid. www.ine.es

The Role of the National Accounts and its Satellite Systems for the German National Strategy for Sustainable Development

K. Schoer

Environmental Economic Accounts, Federal Statistical Office Germany

Data requirements for sustainability policy and the role of accounting systems

The general objective of sustainable development (SD) requires a holistic policy approach. Regarding an indicator set for measuring SD in principle two different levels of users and uses have to be distinguished.

The indicators itself are on the first hand a communication tool directed to the general public and the media. They are used for describing important problems under a sustainability perspective and they serve as an instrument for general performance controlling of political measures.

The second level refers to those steps that follow the pure description of a problem. That is the analysis of the underlying mechanisms and reasons for change and the formulation of measures and the assessment of the effects of these measures.

Therefore the individual indicators firstly should be embedded into an underlying, more detailed database from which they can an be derived by aggregation. The disaggregated data for the individual indicators provide the necessary information for a detailed analysis.

Secondly, the underlying data for the individual indicators should be part of a comprehensive framework that ideally integrates all relevant topics, as a policy for SD is characterised by not only looking on how far the goals for the individual indicators can be achieved, but has to have in mind the interdependencies between the topics and the simultaneous achievement of different economic, environmental and social goals. The central point is the integration, *i.e.* the policy for SD cannot be a policy of it's own. The subject of such a policy rather is co-ordination of the different sector policies with the objective of finding a balance between conflicting goals. Decisions on measures aiming at the improvement of one indicator at the same time have to consider the effects that may occur on the other relevant goals of the overall strategy for SD. The rather complex analytical tools required for that type of policy approach demand an a homogeneous and coherent database depicting the interdependencies between the different indicators.

The relationship between the indicator set on top of a data pyramid and the underlying data have to be regarded already in the process of selecting and demarcating the indicators and their database.

The System of National Accounts (SNA) form together with its satellite systems Environmental-Economic Accounts (EEA) and the Socio-economic Accounts (SEA)

an expanded accounting data set. Such an expanded data set is an ideal framework to meet the above mentioned requirements (figure 1).

Figure 1. **National Accounts and its satellite systems**

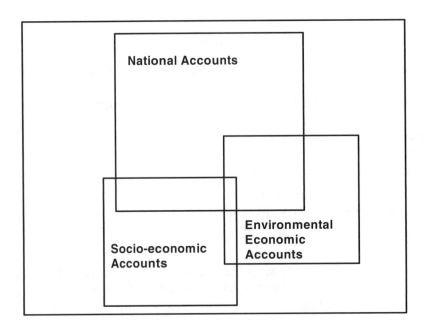

An accounting approach is the most comprehensive and efficient way to provide the required a database. Conceptually as a systems approach the accounts provide a most complete and theoretically sound system description of the relevant stocks and flows. Practically the accounts, as a secondary statistical approach, are a rather cost-efficient tool for generating an underlying database by bringing together and harmonising otherwise scattered, not fully coherent and incomplete primary data in a systematic manner and by providing the basis for estimates to close remaining data gaps.

The SNA is the world wide accepted standard for describing the economic process. The EEA and the SEA extend the economic accounts by a description of the interrelationships of the economic to the environmental and the social system and between the environmental and the social system. The satellite systems in principle use the same concepts, definitions and classifications as the SNA. That guaranties that the data of all three sub-systems can be combined with each other, *i.e.* they form an integrated database that covers the three principal topics of a sustainability approach.

One central classification of the accounting system which is shared commonly by all three sub-systems is the NAMEA-type break down (National accounts Matrices Including Environmental Accounts) by economic activities (homogeneous branches of production or industries and private households). Others are the subdivision of consumption of private households by use categories and of the private households by household-types.

From the data set of the SNA most of the economic and partly also social indicators can be derived. The SNA data set is the basis for already existing and proven analytical tools that are related to the economic process. The extension of this tool for analysing environmental-economic questions has already been put into practice successfully in Germany and other countries.

The relationship between the indicator set for sustainability and the accounting system is shown by the data pyramid in figure 2. The main relationship (bold arrow) exists between the headline indicators (level one indicators) and the accounting data set. Ideally all headline indicators can be derived from the accounting data set by aggregation. Beside that there are a number of further elements and relationships, *i.e.* a set of additional indicators (level two), which supplement the level one indicators, as well as primary and other data, which above all are required for special analysis.

Figure 2. **Data requirement for a strategy on sustainable development**

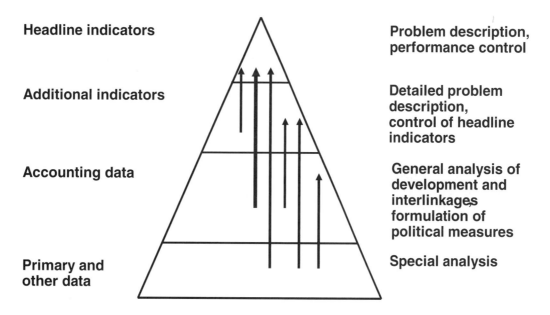

Headline indicators	Problem description, performance control
Additional indicators	Detailed problem description, control of headline indicators
Accounting data	General analysis of development and interlinkages formulation of political measures
Primary and other data	Special analysis

The type of analysis discussed hitherto is directed at deepening. That is, the indicators are disaggregated in order to get an insight into the reasons of the development of the specific indicator and the interrelationship to other topics of the set. However, the indicator set for SD is usually comprised of headline indicators (level one), which were selected for representing a specific topic. Having in mind this it may also be necessary to broaden the scope of the analysis by supplementing the headline indicators by additional indicators (level two indicators) in order to obtain a more comprehensive description of the problem and especially to control whether a headline indicator is representing the problem under consideration in a sufficient manner also in future. In Germany, at least for the environment related indicators, the Ministry of Environment is about to develop such a second level indicator set. Embedding these types of indicators also into the accounting data set could be useful, but seems to be less urgent.

Moreover not all data needs coming up in the course of sustainability analysis can be covered by the accounting data set. Certainly the accounting framework should play a central role for the sustainability indicator set. But the advantage of the accounting framework compared to other data may differ from case to case. It should be noted that there could be politically important indicators for which the integration-aspects do not play an important role. In such cases the embedding into the accounting database is of minor or even without any relevance. Moreover, even with regard to indicators, for which in principle the integration aspect is relevant, there might be analytical approaches and measures related to sustainability policy, which do require more detailed or even other type of data than the accounting data set can provide. An example may be the instrument of legal provisions prescribing the use of certain technical standards. For that type of policy rather data in a breakdown by production techniques than in a breakdown by economic branches are required. In those cases it may be necessary to use appropriate special data in addition to the principal accounting framework.

The role of the German Federal Statistical Office in formulating the national sustainability indicators

The Federal Government adopted the German National Strategy for Sustainable Development in April 2002. The approval was preceded by a discussion of the draft with major groups and institutions of the society. With the approval of the strategy by the government broadly agreed indicators on SD are available. The strategy was developed by the "Committee of State Secretaries for Sustainable Development" which was headed by the advisor to the Federal Chancellor. The strategy has different elements, like defining the key focus points for SD, selecting indicators, formulating quantitative or qualitative goals related to the indicators and a set of measures related to some of the key focus points. The sustainability indicator set is comprised of 21 indicators (figure 3).

Figure 3.

Indicators of the German national stategy for sustainable development

Nb.	Indicator
1	Productivity of energy and raw materials
2	Emissions of the 6 greenhouse gases specified in the Kyoto Agreement
3	The proportion of renewable energy sources in overall energy consumption
4	Increase in land use for housing and transport
5	Development of the stocks of specified animal species
6	Balance of public sector financing
7	Private- and public-sector expenditure on research and development
8	Capital-outlay ratio
9	Educational outcomes for 25-year-olds and number of new students
10	Gross domestic product
11	Transport intensity and share of the railways in providing goods transport
12	Proportion of ecological agriculture and general statement on nitrogen surplus
13	Air pollution
14	Satisfaction with health
15	Number of burglaries
16	Labour force participation rate
17	Full-time care facilities
18	Relationship between male and female gross annual earnings
19	Number of foreign school-leavers who have not completed secondary school
20	Expenditure on development collaboration
21	EU imports from developing countries

By the selection of the indicators the responsible policy makers defined those issues which are particularly relevant under sustainability considerations. By formulating target values the policy side signalises that they are prepared to promote the attainment of the goals by appropriate political measures.

The National Strategy for Sustainable Development contains, beyond the indicators, an identification of a number of priority areas for which political measures where formulated. But many of the measures still have to be put into concrete terms. The first progress report is scheduled for spring 2004. Content and structure of this report is still rather vague. A central point certainly will be the development of the indicators in relation to the target values. As far as the environmental issues are concerned, it is very likely that the tools and practical experiences of environmental-economic analysis that have been developed so far on the basis of the EEA data will play a role in the report.

The role of the German Federal Statistical Office (FSO) in developing the national sustainability indicators was rather limited. Though the statisticians from the FSO took part in different stages as experts, they were not involved in a systematic way with clear responsibilities. Insofar, even in the field of formulating the indicators, there was an obvious dominance of the political side.

Prior to the process of developing the National Strategy for Sustainable Development there were a number of efforts on the national level which also dealt with the issue of SD. Two important initiatives should be referred to, which had a rather direct impact on the final national strategy, the German contribution (national pilot project) to the world wide indicator project of the United Nations Commission on Sustainable Development (UNCSD) and the environmental headline indicator set of the German Ministry of Environment (Environment Barometer), which was published in 1999. Experts from the EEA department of the FSO were involved as statistical advisors in the above mentioned activities which preceded the developing of the final national strategy as well as in the final strategy itself.

Already in the national report to the UNCSD project the interlinkages between the CSD-indicators and the role the EEA database could play in analysing these interrelationships were an important issue. As far as the development of the environment related indicators was concerned the strategy for SD could heavily draw on the work on the German Environment Barometer. The Environment Barometer considerably influenced the public discussions about environmental issues. The indicators of the Barometer became also part of the annual Report of the Federal Government on the economic situation. The development of the Barometer was closely related to the development of the EEA, because the advisory board for the EEA played also an important role in developing the Barometer. Therefore it is not surprising that five out of six indicators of the Barometer (raw material use, the energy use, CO_2 emissions, emissions of acidification gases and land use for housing and transport) were fully embedded into the EEA data-set. That is, these indicators can be derived from the EEA data by aggregation. These five indicators from the Barometer, with a few changes, are also used as the core of environment related indicators of the sustainability indicator set.

German accounting data and the national sustainability strategy

On an international level comprehensive and comparable accounting data for the purpose of sustainability analysis, as far as data beyond the national accounts are concerned, are only available in a fragmentary manner at the moment. Compared to this, in Germany as well as in some other countries the situation is much more favourable.

The German EEA of the FSO from the very beginning was viewed by the Ministry of Environment as a contribution to the sustainability debate and the sustainability paradigm played a central role in developing the concepts and the data of the EEA. In Germany a considerable proportion of the indicators of the National Strategy for Sustainable Development is already embedded into the accounting system. Such there is already available a comprehensive accounting database which is being used for environmental-economic analysis and which can be directly utilised for the sustainability debate. The work on the development of a socio-economic accounting satellite is under progress and will contribute a rather comprehensive coverage of social issues in the accounting data set in near future.

Figure 4 shows which indicators of the national strategy for SD are already integrated into the accounting system. Already covered are especially those sustainability indicators for which the embedding into the accounting system offers high comparative advantages.

Figure 4. **Embedding of the indicators of the German strategy for sustainable development into the accounting data set**

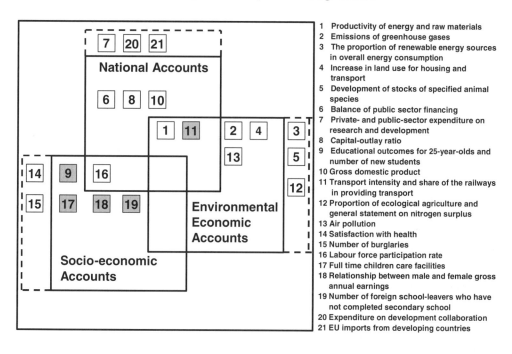

1 Productivity of energy and raw materials
2 Emissions of greenhouse gases
3 The proportion of renewable energy sources in overall energy consumption
4 Increase in land use for housing and transport
5 Development of stocks of specified animal species
6 Balance of public sector financing
7 Private- and public-sector expenditure on research and development
8 Capital-outlay ratio
9 Educational outcomes for 25-year-olds and number of new students
10 Gross domestic product
11 Transport intensity and share of the railways in providing transport
12 Proportion of ecological agriculture and general statement on nitrogen surplus
13 Air pollution
14 Satisfaction with health
15 Number of burglaries
16 Labour force participation rate
17 Full time children care facilities
18 Relationship between male and female gross annual earnings
19 Number of foreign school-leavers who have not completed secondary school
20 Expenditure on development collaboration
21 EU imports from developing countries

Comparative advantages especially appear, if an indicator is strongly related to other indicators of the set or if the accounting framework is needed to generate the required data in a cost-efficient manner. At the moment the indicators public sector financing (6), capital-outlay ratio (8), gross domestic product (10), productivity of energy and raw materials (1), emissions of greenhouse gases (2), increase in land use for housing and transport (4), air pollution (13), labour force participation rate (16) are already embedded into the accounting data set. Disaggregated data regarding the indicator transport intensity and share of railways in providing transport (11) are being compiled and will be included into the data set of the EEA during the year 2003. It is also planned to integrate the indicators educational outcomes and number of students (9), children care facilities (17), relation between male and female earnings (18) and final examination of foreign school leavers (19) into the SEA. These indicators together cover about three third of the total strategy's indicators. The remaining indicators (box with broken line) are expenditure on research and development (7), expenditure on development collaboration (20), imports from developing countries (21), renewable energy sources (3), stocks of specified animals (5), ecological agriculture and nitrogen surplus (12), satisfaction with health (14) and number of burglaries (15). These indicators in principle could also be integrated into the accounting data set. But at least for some of these indicators integration into the accounting system seems to be less urgent.

The NAMEA-type break down, *i.e.* a detailed break down by about 60 homogenous branches of production or industries and private households, is one of the central classifications of the accounting system, which links the economic, environmental and social data. Figure 5 gives an overview on which EEA data for

Germany are available at present or will be available in the course of this year in such a detailed break down.

Figure 5.

Available German EEA data in a NAMEA-type breakdown

	Unit
Primary material by aggregated categories of material	Tonnes
Abstraction of water from nature and water flows within the economy	m^3
Primary energy consumption (total and emission relevant)	Terajoules
Air emissions	Tonnes
Greenhouse gases by type	Tonnes
Air pollution by type	Tonnes
Waste water and other discharge of water into nature	m^3
Waste by waste categories[1]	Tonnes
Land use for housing and transport by land use categories	km^2
Figures on the transport sector by mode of transport	
Transport related energy consumption, fuel consumption, selected air emissions	Terajoules Tonnes
Kilometres driven, person kilometres, tonnes kilometres	km
Transport related environmental taxes by type	Euro
Stock of vehicles by type	Number and Euro

1) Only figures until 1995, old classification

At present NAMEA-type data are provided for Germany on a regular basis for energy flows, air emissions, waste, water and wastewater flows, land use for housing and transport and some partial data on the new sectoral reporting module "transport and environment". Further results on the reporting module "transport and environment" will be available by the end of this year. Around the end of the year also figures in a detailed NAMEA-type breakdown on the supply and use of primary material (raw materials and imported material) and first results of the new sectoral reporting module "agriculture and environment" will be compiled. It is also planned to extend the supply of data on the topic private households and environment considerably in close co-operation with the activities on developing the SEA.

The classic NAMEA-approach concentrates on supplementing the monetary system of national accounts by material flows (physical flow accounts) which are not covered in the monetary description. Especially the reporting modules on land use and transport contain elements which use the basic idea of the NAMEA-framework, but to some extent go beyond the classic approach. They comprise variables in a NAMEA-type break down which do not belong to the material flows. For such variables the same analytical instruments as for material flows can be applied in combination with input-output tables to calculate indirect effects, to carry out decomposition analysis or, above all, the data can be used for multi-sectoral modelling approaches.

The area used for housing and transport is shown in the NAMEA-format in a further breakdown by land use categories. In the international manual SEEA 2000 (System for Integrated Environmental-Economic Accounting) land and land use is not assigned to the physical flow accounts but to the asset accounts. The land use category housing and transport area indicates a particularly intensive structural pressure on the natural assets category land respectively on the eco-systems to be localised there. A number of variables related to transport appear in the German accounts also in the NAMEA-format. In the sense of the SEEA 2000 a part of them can be assigned to the world of physical flow accounting (transport related energy use and air emissions). Some belong to the category of environment related disaggregation of monetary SNA flows or stocks (e.g. environment related taxes, stock of vehicles). Others, like kilometres driven, person kilometres, tonnes kilometres, are not covered in the SEEA-concept up to now.

Further development of the national strategy for sustainable development and the accounting data set

A strategy for the development of an integrated SD policy consists of three elements to be worked on: further adjustment of the indicator set, expansion of the accounting system and development of appropriate tools for integrated SD analysis (see figure 6).

Figure 6. **Strategy for an integrated sustainable development analysis and policy**

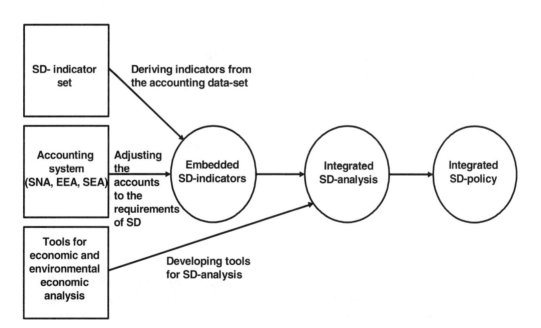

The formulation of an indicator set for SD and the creation of an integrated database required for this purpose necessarily has to be a long-term task. On the one hand policy demands indicators on relatively short notice for describing the sustainability problem. But on the other hand the methodological concepts for approaching the sustainability problem scientifically and politically and, above all, the appropriate database are still under development. This dilemma can be solved only by a stepwise approach.

It is the task of the political side to identify the priority issues to be included into the indicator set for SD. On that basis concrete indicators can be formulated on relative short notice by using already existing data. That was what happened in developing the present national indicator system in Germany. But indicators which were developed in such an ad-hoc manner necessarily run the risk of putting together indicators which are not linked with each other and which therefore can only be of limited use for an integrated policy on SD.

Developing an indicator set for SD that on the one hand perfectly covers the politically important issues and on the other hand is embedded into a coherent and rather comprehensive database can only be an iterative process with a threefold movement.

Firstly, future revisions of the indicator set should, by having in mind the obvious advantages, try to derive as much indicators as possible from the existing accounting data set by aggregation. In any case, in future it will be necessary to review and improve the existing indicator set in the light of new problems, methodological progress and with the goal of attaining better international harmonisation.

Secondly and probably even more important, the accounting system itself has to be adjusted to the new data needs, provided the necessary financial and personal resources are available. It has to be put high priority on extending the accounting data set towards the requirements of a policy for SD. As already mentioned, the accounting framework offers rather good and cost efficient opportunities of generating the required data by reformatting already existing figures. But beyond this, depending on the quality requirement, in the long run it may also be necessary to improve some of the accounting estimates by new primary surveys. As was shown above, in Germany there already exists a broad supply of expanded accounting data that can be used for the purposes of sustainability policy. Therefore the most important task in Germany for the next time will be to intensify the utilisation of these data by politicians and by those institutions which provide scientific policy advisory services in this area.

Thirdly, not only the accounting data set should be expanded. At the same time, also further investment in developing appropriate tools (modelling approaches) for an integrated environmental, social an economic analysis will be necessary. The feedback arising from concrete analytical applications of the data have also proven to be very important for a targeted development of the accounting data set.

Conclusions

The relation between the process of developing the SD indicators set on the one hand and of developing the accounting system as presented in the case study for Germany may at least implicitly give answers to some of the issues of the meeting to be addressed.

In principle the suggested pragmatic national approach towards a strategy for an integrated SD-policy could also be applied on the international level. The national approach is directed on stepwise bringing together the indicator system on SD and the accounting approach. Whereas the indicator system is first of all orientated towards the political demand of providing meaningful information on SD rather quickly, the accounting method follows a strict system orientation and has rather a long-term perspective. For reconciling these two approaches, above all, it will be necessary to provide sufficient resources for developing and extending environmental-economic and socio-economic satellite accounts. The task for the accountants on the international level will be, to work on developing a comparable accounting data set along the priorities formulated by the political decision makers for a policy on SD. The priorities can either be revealed by the politically defined priority areas, or even better, by politically defined indicators.

References

Radermacher, W.: Indicators, green accounting and environment statistics – information requirements for sustainable development, paper for the 51st Session of the International Statistical Institute, Istanbul, 18.-26. August 1997.

Radermacher, W.: Societies' Maneuver Towards Sustainable Development: Information and the Setting of Target Values. In: Müller, F./Leupolt, M. (eds.): Eco Targets, Goal Functions, and Orientors; Berlin 1998.

Radermacher, W.: "Green Stamp" Report on an EU Research Project. In: European Commission (publisher): Proceedings from a Workshop, Luxembourg, 28-29 September 1998.

Schäfer, D.: Interpretation und Verknüpfung von Nachhaltigkeitsindikatoren (Interpretation and interlinking of sustainability indicators). In: Hartard, S./Stahmer, C./Hinterberger, F. (eds.): Magische Dreiecke – Berichte für eine nachhaltige Gesellschaft, vol. 1: Stoffflussanalysen und Nachhaltigkeitsindikatoren; Marburg 2000.

Schoer, K., Flachmann, C., Heinze, A., Schäfer, D., Waldmüller, B.: Environmental-Economic Accounting in Germany 2001, Federal Statistical Office, Wiesbaden 2001.

http://www.destatis.de/allg/e/veroe/e_ugr02.htm

Schoer, K., Räth, N.: Environmental-Economic Accounting in Germany 2002, Federal Statistical Office, Wiesbaden 2002.

http://www.destatis.de/allg/e/veroe/e_ugr02.htm

Stahmer, C.: The Magic Triangle of Input-Output-Tables, 13th International Conference on Input-Output Techniques, 21.-25. August 2000, Macerata, Italy.

The Advisory Committee on " Environmental-Economic Accounting " at the Federal Ministry for the Environment, Nature Conservation and Nuclear Safety: Environmental-Economic Accounting, Fourth and final opinion on the implementation concepts of the German Federal Statistical Office, Berlin 2002.

http://www.destatis.de/allg/e/veroe/e_ugrbeirat.htm

Steurer, Anton: The use of National Accounts in developing SD Indicators, Second Meeting of the ESS Task Force on Methodological Issues for Sustainable Development Indicators, Meeting of 3-4 February 2003.

The Development of Environmental Accounting Frameworks and Indicators for Measuring Sustainability in Japan[1]

N. Ariyoshi, Kumamoto University, Japan

Y. Moriguchi, National Institute for Environmental Studies, Japan

Overview of Research Activities on Environmental Accounting and Indicators in Japan

It was in 1991, more than 10 years ago, when several governmental research institutes in cooperation with researchers in universities started an inter-agency research project on environmental accounting and indicators in Japan. Since then, with some changes of participating institutions, the project has been renewed three times, under funding by the "Global Environmental Research Fund" of the Ministry of the Environment (formerly the Environment Agency of Japan).

The initiation of this research project in the early 1990's was strongly motivated by the worldwide studies on environmental accounting, which had been getting more and more active towards SEEA 1993. The National Institute for Environmental Studies (NIES), which used to belong to the Environmental Agency (Ministry) and later became an independent agency, has been taking a leadership role in organizing the project. The NIES mainly undertook studies on environmental accounting in physical terms. Another key institution in the project has been the Economic Research Institute (ERI) of the Economic Planning Agency (later restructured to be the Economic and Social Research Institute (ESRI) of the Cabinet Office). Apart from the environmental accounting studies, the ERI (ESRI) has been the responsible institution for the System of National Accounts (SNA) in Japan. Thus, both experts in environmental information and statistics and those in national accounting have played key roles in the project.

In the earlier phases of the project, more attention was paid to environmentally-adjusted aggregated indicators to follow up the SEEA 1993. The first trial estimate of the Japanese SEEA, which corresponded to SEEA version 4.2 (maintenance cost approach), was published in 1995. An updated/revised edition, as well as its time-series, was published later in 1998. They were all undertaken by the ERI. In the later phases, the attention of the ERI's study shifted from the SEEA version.4.2 to other components of the SEEA. In particular, it focused on the measurement of environmental protection expenditures and a case study on physical/monetary accounting, in which waste management activities were accounted for. As described later in more detail, the current

---

1. The views expressed in this paper are those of the authors and do not necessarily reflect the views of the authors' institutes. We would like to thank the discussant at the workshop, Robert Smith of Statistics Canada, for providing helpful comments.

focus of the ERI (ESRI)'s study is to compile the Japanese edition of the National Accounting Matrix including Environmental Accounting (NAMEA).

On the other hand, the NIES consistently undertakes empirical studies on physical accounting. Initial attention was directed to international physical flows of natural resources to Japan from the rest of the world, which explained Japan's high dependency on imported natural resources. More in general, Material Flow Accounting (MFA) has been applied to the accounting for international trade flows, total inflows to and outflows from the national economy, as well as inter-industry (inter-sectoral) flows.

Key players of these Japanese studies have also actively participated in international efforts on environmental accounting and indicators, such as the London group and meetings organized by the OECD. Moreover, in 1996 the ERI and United Nations University(UNU) organized the International Symposium on "Integrated Environmental and Economic Accounting in Theory and Practice" in Tokyo, in cooperation with the International Association for Research in Income and Wealth (IARIW).

Physical MFA studies, which are mainly undertaken by the NIES, have been keeping in close collaboration with the OECD and other organisations' international activities. The NIES is one of the collaborators in the international joint publication of 'Resource Flows' (Adriaanse et al., 1997) and 'The Weight of Nations'(Matthews et al, 2000) by the World Resources Institute, which focused on the total material inflows and outflows of industrialized economies. In fact, this joint effort was triggered by an international scientific workshop for indicators of sustainable development at the Wuppertal Institute in Germany, organized by the Scientific Committee on Problems of the Environment (SCOPE). More recently, special sessions and workshops on MFA were organized by the working groups under the OECD Environmental Policy Committee (EPOC), and the NIES consistently contributed to these meetings. The linkage between the accounting framework(s) and the indicators was repeatedly discussed throughout these meetings.

The current Japanese research project in its fourth phase for FY 2001-2003 is being undertaken by the ESRI, the NIES, as well as another new participating institution. It is the National Institute for Advanced Industrial Science and Technology (AIST), which deals with studies on environmental accounting and performance indicators at the company level. The project as a whole aims at the development of environmental/sustainability indicators and accounting at three different levels, namely the national (macro) level, the sectoral (meso) level, and the company (micro) level. The ESRI, the NIES, and the AIST share their roles in these three levels' studies respectively. More ambitiously, possible linkages among these different scales are being considered.

The first author of this paper has been continuously involved in both the ERI (ESRI)'s and the NIES's studies. In the next section, the technical details of the Japanese studies will be described, focusing on the structure of accounting frameworks.

The role of environmental accounting frameworks in the Japanese research project

As denoted in the previous section, in the Japanese research project, the ESRI, the NIES, and the AIST share their roles in the three different levels and undertake the development of environmental accounting frameworks and indicators for measuring sustainable development. In this project, the linkage between the research done at the three levels, as well as the progress of the research, is very important.

In general, the research on sustainable development indicators has resulted in a large number of indicators giving information on developments in the economic, environmental and social areas. Thus, the interrelationships between these indicators are sometimes lost. For example, a little change in one economic area gives some effects to the environment and societal areas, as well as other parts of the economic area. Therefore each of the indicators has to reflect such actual interrelationships. In order to satisfy this requirement, it is necessary to construct a common accounting system that serves as an underlying statistical information system, which adequately represents the interrelationships between the economy, the environment and society, as well as bringing about the linkage between the various indicators. Such a common accounting system enhances the mutual consistency, reliability and comparability of the indicators.

The Japanese research project aims at the construction of a common accounting system and its derived indicator sets at the national economy level, the industrial sector level, and the company level. Figure 1 shows the relationships between the various kinds of accounts and indicators which the Japanese project undertakes. Though figure 1 gives a simple description of each account, more detailed structures of the accounts are shown in tables 1 through 8 at the end of paper.

(1) NAM (National Accounting Matrix)

In the center of figure 1, the National Accounting Matrix (NAM) of the SNA is shown. The NAM denoted here has the stock accounts of the non-financial assets, while the stock accounts of the financial assets are omitted for simplicity. The NAM is a core account of the Japanese system of accounts and indicators for sustainability.

(2) I-O table

To the left of the NAM, the I-O table is shown. It is an analytical accounting framework which is closely related to the NAM.

(3) SEEA93

In the top left of figure 1, the SEEA93 version 4.2 (maintenance cost approach) is shown. The research and trial estimation of the SEEA93 has been conducted by the ESRI (formerly the ERI) since 1991. The distinctive aims of the SEEA93 are to introduce the environmental related activities into the I-O table, to attach the stock account including non-produced natural assets, and to describe the environmental pressures caused by economic activities and the derived depletion of non-produced natural assets by those pressures. In figure 1, the environmental pressures are classified into the use of natural resources (input) and the discharge of residuals (output or negative input). In Japan, the research and trial estimation of the regional edition of the SEEA93 is also being undertaken (Yamamoto et al., 1998).

(4) MAFEE

In the top middle of figure 1, there is an unfamiliar account which is named the "Monetary Accounting Framework for the Environment and Economy" (MAFEE). The MAFEE is a kind of "mediate account" which links the NAM to the SEEA93. It is constructed by introducing the above mentioned distinctive features of the SEEA93 not to the I-O table but rather directly to the NAM.

Figure 1. Interrelationships between environmental accounts and indicators

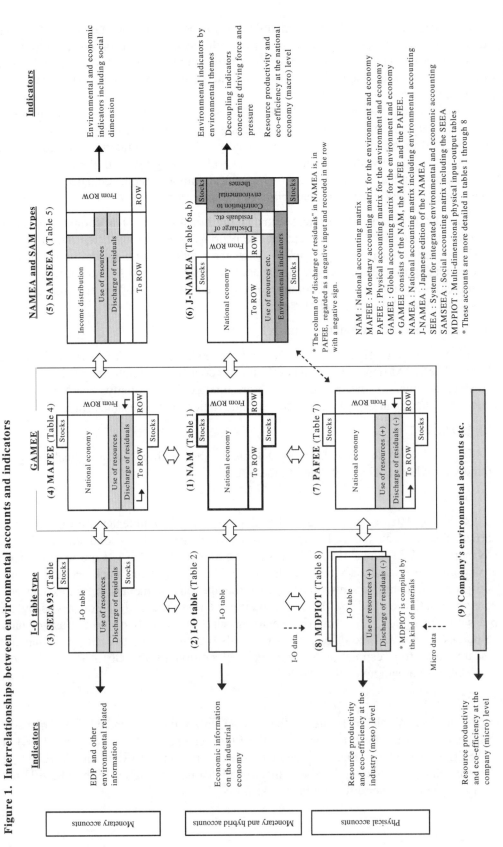

(5) SAMSEEA

In the top right of figure 1, the Social Accounting Matrix including the SEEA (SAMSEEA) is shown. Recently, the first author of this paper started on the construction of the SAMSEEA and CGE analysis based on it along with his colleagues. The progress of this research may bring about a set of indicators including the social dimension as well as policy implications.

(6) NAMEA

To the right of the NAM, the Japanese edition of the NAMEA (J-NAMEA) that has been undertaken by the ESRI, is shown. A more detailed sketch of the J-NAMEA is shown in table 6a, and the first trial estimate of the J-NAMEA is given in table 6b. The J-NAMEA is revised regarding the following points in comparison with the Netherlands' NAMEA.

1） It estimates the emission of pollutions not only by households, but also by the government.

2） It attaches the stock accounts of non–financial assets to capital accounts and records the various social capitals and environmental protection plants. Refer to cell (OA, 8) and (CA, 8) in table 6b.

3） It adds coal, forests, water, and fish to the category of natural resources. Refer to the 11p-11u accounts.

4） It introduces the land use accounts which are closely related to environmental issues. Refer to the 11v-11aa accounts.

5） It records the depletion of natural resources in the rest of the world caused by imports, in order to figure out Japan's high dependency on imported natural resources. Refer to cell (11p-11u, 9).

6） It introduces the hidden material flow account, which records the hidden material flows caused by domestic activities and imports. Refer to the 11ab account.

7） It attaches the stock accounts to parts of the environmental theme accounts.

The ESRI adopts the Driving Force–Pressure–State–Effect–Response (DPSER) indicator framework which is an extension of the PSR framework and covers the economic and environmental dimensions. Thus, the J-NAMEA gives not only the indicators based on environmental themes, but also the decoupling indicator concerning the driving force and pressure in the DPSER framework. Moreover, it also gives the resource productivity and eco-efficiency indicators at the national economy (macro) level.

(7) PAFEE (Physical Accounting Framework for the Environment and Economy)

In the bottom middle of figure 1, there is another unfamiliar account which is named the "Physical Accounting Framework for the Environment and Economy" (PAFEE). The PAFEE is another kind of "mediate account" which links the NAM to the MDPIOT denoted shortly hereafter. It basically has the same accounting structure as the MAFEE. However, it is an account with physical terms and the discharge of residuals is recorded as negative inputs with physical terms. The PAFEE and the MAFEE along with the NAM compose a core framework which is named the "Global Accounting Matrix for Environment and Economy" (GAMEE) (Ariyoshi, 1998).

(8) MDPIOT (Multi-Dimension Physical Input Output tables)

To the left of the PAFEE, the Multi-Dimension Physical Input Output tables (MDPIOT) is shown, which has been developed by the NIES. The distinctive features of the MDPIOT are denoted as follows:

1) It records not only the use of resources from the environment and discharge of residuals to the environment, but also the material flows between industrial sectors according to the kind of materials.

2) Data for the MDPIOT can be compiled in two ways, either top-down from I-O data or bottom-up from the company's data.

3) It gives indicators such as resource productivity and eco-efficiency at the industrial sector (meso) level.

4) The MDPIOT including the material flows induced by imports to Japan is being undertaken (reference table 8).

5) It has a sub-module to calculate the intersectional material flows induced by final demands.

(9) Company's environmental accounts

The data from the company's environmental accounts provide the information needed to calculate resource productivity and eco-efficiency at the industrial sector and company levels.

Among the accounts (1) – (9), the I-O table (2) and the J-NAMEA (6) are directly related to the NAM. Moreover, the SEEA93 (3) and the SAMSEEA (5) are indirectly related to the NAM via the MAFEE, and the MDPIOT (8) is indirectly related to the NAM via the PAFEE. Therefore, the indicators based on these accounts are considered to satisfy the requirements for indicators, such as mutual consistency, reliability and comparability. However, the company's environmental account (9) is not related to the NAM.

Thus, the establishment of the relationship between macro environmental accounting and the company's micro environmental accounting is considered an important task in achieving a consistent system of accounting frameworks and indicators for sustainable development.

Policy application of environmental accounting and derived indicators

There is no inter-agency activity in Japan to establish a comprehensive set of indicators covering the whole scope (environmental, economic and social pillars) of sustainable development. However, some efforts have been made to incorporate a harmonized set of indicators into the national environmental policy. In 1994, the first "Basic Environmental Plan" was established by the cabinet decision based on "Basic Environment Law". The plan mandated the government to develop comprehensive indicators for implementing the plan and for reviewing policy performance towards four long-term policy goals set by the plan. An expert advisory committee was established in the Environment Agency to elaborate the concept and to show options of the indicators, drawing upon related activities in international organisations such as the OECD and the UNCSD, as well as those in other countries. The committee published "A draft set of comprehensive environmental indicators" in 1997, and then submitted a revised report to the Central Environmental Council in 1999. Several indicators based on the MFA were adopted in the report as a sub-set of indicators representing the "sound material cycle" (Moriguchi, 2000).

Very recently, indicators derived from physical material flow accounting were adopted more formally and clearly, with quantitative targets within another national environmental policy framework. The Government of Japan formulated "The Basic Plan for Establishing a Recycling-Based Society" in a Cabinet decision on March 14th, 2003, based on the provisions of Article 15 of "The Basic Law for Establishing a Recycling-Based Society". The purpose of the plan is to promote comprehensive and systematic policies for establishing a recycling-based society. Furthermore, the plan serves as a ten-year program aimed at changing unsustainable patterns of production and consumption into sustainable ones based on the "Plan of Implementation of the World Summit on Sustainable Development" held in September 2002.

For establishing a recycling-based society, the plan set quantitative targets for indicators based on Material Flow Accounts, which are used to understand the entire flow of materials in a national economy. More specifically, the plan set a target for each of the three indicators that represent the three aspects of the material flows in our society. They are indicators of input, cyclical use and output. As the input indicator, a so-called "resource productivity" indicator was adopted.

Resource Productivity = GDP / DMI (Direct Material Input)

This formula is completely identical to the material use indicator in the OECD's indicator set for measuring decoupling of environmental pressure from economic growth (OECD, 2002). The plan set a target that Resource Productivity should be about 390 thousand JPY per ton in FY 2010 (almost double that of about 210 thousand JPY per ton in FY 1990, and about a 40 per cent improvement from about 280 thousand JPY per ton in FY 2000).

Whereas the other two indicators on material cycle (cyclical use rate) and material output (final disposal amount of waste) stand for a more conventional view of waste management and recycling, this input indicator reflects a holistic view of the relationship between economic activities and material use.

Needless to say, statistical basis and analytical soundness have to be ensured and further improved, in order to meet the policy needs and to support the actual measurement of the indicators. It should also be kept in mind that a typical criticism against over-simplification (everything should not be equally measured by mass) has been repeatedly directed to this simple indicator. Physical material flow accounting, if classified by the type of material, enables us to not only weigh materials as the simple sum of the mass, but also to weigh with some weight reflecting economic, social or environmental values. We may seek further elaboration of the accounting framework and derived indicators through international joint studies.

References

Adriaanse, A., Bringezu, S., Hammond, A., Moriguchi, Y., Rodenburg, E., Rogich, D., and Schuetz, H. (1997): *Resource Flows: The Material Basis of Industrial Economies*, World Resources Institute, Washington D.C., 66pp.

Ariyoshi, N., (1998): Global Accounting Matrix for Environment and Economy (GAMEE): A Proposal for the SEEA Revision, *The Fifth Meeting of the London Group on Environmental Accounting: Proceedings and Papers*, pp.91-104.

Keuning, S. J., van Dalen, J., and de Haan, M. (1999): Netherlands' NAMEA: presentation, usage and future extensions, *Structural Change and Economic Dynamics*, 10, pp.15-37.

Matthews E., Amann, C., Bringezu, S., Fischer-Kowalski, M., Huettler, W., Kleijn, R., Moriguchi, Y., Ottke, C., Rodenburg, E., Rogich, D., Shandl, H., Schuetz, H., van der Voet, E., and Weisz, H. (2000): *The weight of nations –Material outflows from industrial Economies-*, World Resources Institute, Washington D.C., 125pp.

Moriguchi, Y. (2000): Material Flow Accounting and its application in Japan, presented at Special session on Material Flow Accounting, OECD/WGEIO, October 24, 2000, Paris.

OECD (2000): Indicators to measure decoupling of environmental pressure from economic growth, SG/SD (2002)1.

United Nations (1993): Handbook of National Accounting: Integrated Environmental and Economic Accounting, Interim version, United Nations, 182pp.

United Nations (2003): *The Handbook of National Accounting: Integrated Environmental and Economic Accounting 2003*, United Nations (http://unstats.un.org/unsd/environment/ seea2003.htm).

Uno, K. (1998): Identifying Research Priority, Uno, K. and Bartelmus, P. eds., *Environmental Accounting in Theory and Practice*, Kluwer Academic Publishers, pp.409-419.

Yamamoto, M., Hayashi, T., and Demura, K. (1998): Estimation of Integrated Environmental and Economic Accounting in Hokkaido, *Studies in Regional Science*, 29 (1), pp.25-40.

Table 1. Basic structure of the NAM (National Accounting Matrix)

(Monetary term)

		Nation A				Rest of the world (ROW)	
		Goods & services (product groups)	Production (activity groups)	Distribution & use of income	Capital	Current account	Capital account
		1	2	3	4	5	6
Opening assets	0				Opening assets		
Nation A — Goods & services (product groups)	1		Intermediate consumption	Final consumption	Capital formation	Export	
Nation A — Production (activity groups)	2	Output					
Nation A — Distribution & use of income	3		Value added				
Nation A — Capital	4			Saving			Net lending from ROW
Rest of the world — Current account	5	Import					
Rest of the world — Capital account	6					Current external balance of ROW	
Closing assets	7				Closing assets		

──────▶ : SNA's monetary flows

Table 2. Basic structure of the I-O table

(Monetary term)

		Nation A			Rest of the world (ROW)	
		Production activities (activity groups)	Final consumption	Capital formation	Export	Import
		1	2	3	4	5
Use of products (activity groups)	1	Intermediate consumption	Final consumption	Capital formation	Export	Import
Value added	2	Value added				
Output	3	Output				

Table 3. Basic structure of SEEA93 (version 4.2)

(Monetary term)

		Nation A		Non-financial assets (uses and stocks of assets)		Rest of the world	
		Production (activity groups)	Final consumption	Produced assets	Non-produced assets	Export	Import (negative sign)
		1	2	3	4	5	6
Opening assets	0	Opening assets					
Use of products (activity groups)	1	Intermediate consumption	Final consumption	Capital formation		Export	Import(-)
Use of natural resorces (types)	2	Use of resources (+)	Use of resources (+)	Depletion of natural resources (-)			
Discharge of residuals (types)	3	Discharge of residuals (+)	Discharge of residuals (+)	Deterioration by residuals (-)		Discharge of residuals (+)	
Eco-margin (negative sign)	4	Sum of the above pressures (-)	Sum of the above pressures (-)	Sum of the above pressures (+)		Sum of the above pressures (-)	
Value added	5	Value added					
output	6	Output					
Closing assets	7	Closing assets					

(Nation A; Use of non-produced natural assets applies to rows 2, 3, 4)

⬜ : Cells for environmental flow data

Table 4. Basic structure of the MAFEE (Monetary Accounting Framework for Environment and Economy)

(Monetary term)

		Nation A			Capital		Rest of the world	
		Goods & services (product groups)	Production (activity groups)	Disribution & use of income	Sectors	Non-financial assets (types)	Current	Capital
		1	2	3	4	5	9	10
Opening assets	0				Opening assets			
Goods & services (product groups)	1		Intermediate consumption	Final consumption		Capital formation	Export	
Production (activity groups)	2	Output						
Distribution & use of income	3		Value added					
Sectors	4			Saving				Net lending from ROW
Natural Assets (types)	5				Capital formation			
Use of natural resorces (types)	6		Use of resources(+)	Use of resources(+)		Depletion of resources (-)		
Discharge of residuals (types)	7		Discharge of residuals (+)	Discharge of residuals (+)		Deterioration by residuals (-)	Discharge of residuals (+)	
eco-margin (negative sign)	8		Sum of the above pressures (-)	Sum of the above pressures (-)		Sum of the above pressures (+)	Sum of the above pressures (-)	
Current account	9	Import					(Production etc. in ROW)	
Capital Account	10						Current external balance of ROW	
Discharge of residuals (types)	11		Discharge of residuals (+)	Discharge of residuals (+)			Discharge of residuals (+)	Deterioration by residuals(-)
Sum of pressures	12		Sum of the above pressures (-)	Sum of the above pressures (-)			Sum of the above pressures (-)	Sum of the above pressures (+)
Closing assets	13				Closing assets			

(Nation A: Capital applies to rows 4, 5; Use of non-produced natural assets applies to rows 6, 7, 8. ROW applies to rows 9–12.)

- - - - - - ▶ : Monetary flows (including imputed environmental cost flows)

⬜ : Cells for environmental flow data

Table 5. Basic structure SAMSEEA

(Monetary term)

	Nation A											Rest of the world	
	Primary distribution of income	Secondary distribution of income (sectors)	Use of income (sectors)	Capital: Sectors	Capital: Non-financial assets (types)	Capital: Use of natural resources (types)	Capital: Discharge of residuals (types)	Capital: eco-margin (negative sign)	Final consumption (purposes)	Production (activity groups)	Goods & services (product groups)	Current	Capital
	1	2	3	4	5	6	7	8	9	10	11	12	13
Primary distribution of income (value added categories) — 1										Value added		Compensation of employees from ROW	
Secondary distribution of income (sectors) — 2	National income											Property income and current transfers from ROW	
Use of income (sectors) — 3		Disposable income											
Capital: Sectors — 4			Saving										Net lending from ROW
Capital: Natural Assets (types) — 5				Capital formation									
Capital: Use of natural resources (types) — 6					Depletion of resources (-)				Use of resources	Use of resources			
Capital: Discharge of residuals (types) — 7					Deterioration by residuals (-)				Discharge of residuals	Discharge of residuals			
Capital: eco-margin (negative sign) — 8					Sum of the above pressures				Sum of the above pressures (-)	Sum of the above pressures (-)			
Final consumption (purposes) — 9			Final consumption										
Production (activity groups) — 10											Output		
Goods & services (product groups) — 11					Capital formation				Final consumption	Intermediate consumption		Export	
Current account — 12	Compensation of employees to ROW	Property income and currnt transfers from ROW									Import		
Capital Account — 13				Capital transfers to ROW (net)								Current external balance of ROW	

∎ : Cells for environmental flow data

Table 6a. Basic structure of the Japanese edition of NAMEA

	Nation A (Monetary term)					Rest of the world (ROW) (Monetary term)		Substances (Physical term)		Environmental themes (Physical term)			
	Goods & services (product groups)	Production (activity groups)	Final consumption (purposea)	Distribution & use of income	Capital	Current	Capital	Pollutants	Natural resources	Global	Regional	Natural resources	Land use
	1	2	3	4	5	6	7	8	9	10			
0 Opening assets					Opening assets					Opening stocks			
1 Goods & services (product groups)		Intermediate consumption	Final consumption		Capital formation	Export							
2 Production (activity groups)	Output							Emission of pollutants by producers					
3 Final consumption (purposes)				Final consumption				Emission of pollutants by consumers					
4 Distribution & use of income		Value added											
5 Capital				Saving			Net lending from ROW	Other domestic emission of pollutants and changes in natural resources					
6 Current account	Import					(Production, etc. in ROW)		Cross border flow of pollutants from ROW					
7 Capital Account						Current external balance of ROW							
8 Pollutants		Absorption of substances in the production process				Cross border flow of pollutants to ROW				Contribution of pollutants to environmental themes			
9 Natural resources													
10 Environmental themes					Environmental indicators								
11 Closing assets					Closing assets					Closing stocks			

- - - - - - : SNA's monetary flows
⇧ : Physical flows

(light grey) : Cells for environmental flow data
(dark grey) : Cells for environmental indicator

Table 6b. First Trial Estimate of the Japanese NAMEA (1995)   (The top left of the J-NAMEA)

◄------ Monetary flows   ◄------ Material flows   : Cells for environmental flow data   : Cells for environmental indicator

Account (classification)		Goods and services (product groups) 1	Production (kind of economic activity) 2	Final consumption (purposes) 3	Generation of income (value added categories) 4	Distribution and use of income (sectors) 5	Taxes (tax categories) 6	Capital (sectors) 7	Environmental protection facilities (types) 8a	Social capital (types) 8b	Others 8c	Current 9	Capital 10	CO2 11a	N2O 11b	CH4 11c	HFCs 11d	PFCs 11e	SF6 11f	CFCs Ozon layer 11g	NOX 11h	SO2 11i	NH3 11j
									Non-financial assets (types)			Rest of the world		Substances / Pollutants / Air									
										Opening stocks 42,678.4 / 601,149.3 / 2,475,490.6									Greenhouse effects					Acidification
Opening stocks	OA																						
Goods and services (product groups)	1	Intermediate consump. 430,940.5		Final consump. 351,564.2					Gross capital formation 6,105.6	38,907.1	95,337.6	Exports 45,230.1		969,670	61	1,208	19,611	10,667	16,533	–	1,300	782	–
Production (kind of economic activity)	2	Output 924,849.6												248,094	10	36	0	0	0	–	708	123	
Final consumption (purposes)	3	Final consump. 351,564.2																					
Generation of income (value added categories)	4		Gross value added 460,552.7			Net national income 371,540.0				Consumption of fixed capital (-) -204.2 / 0.0 / -88,745.4			Compensation of employees from ROW 108.7										
Distribution and use of income (sectors)	5				Net national income 371,540.0		Taxes, receivable 82,589.9						Property income and current transfers from ROW 19,372.2										
Taxes (tax categories)	6	Taxes on imports 900.8	Taxes on production 33,356.5			Current tax on income, wealth etc. 48,242.6																	
Capital (sectors)	7	Statistical discrepancy 3,972.3				Net saving 57,814.6		Net capital formation 5,901.4 / 38,907.1 / 6,592.2				Capital transfers from ROW, net -214.4											
Non-financial assets / Environmental protection facilities (types)	8a																							
Social capital (types)	8b																		Other domestic emission of pollutants				
Others	8c														0	0	160	433	762	197	–	0	0	–
Rest of the world (ROW) / Current	9	Imports 38,272.4			Compensation of employees to ROW 171.8	Property income and current transfers to ROW 15,880.6							Current external balance -10,386.2		0	0	0	0	0	0	–	0	0	–
Capital	10							Changes in claims to ROW 10,171.8													Cross border flow of pollutants from ROW			

National economy

Emission of pollutants by producers

Emission of pollutants by consumers

ROW

(The bottom left of the J-NAMEA)

			Supply of purchaser's price	Input of basic price	Final consumption	Destination of generated income	Current expenditures	Tax receipts, net	Capital expenditure	Non-financial assets			Current receipts from ROW	Capital receipts from ROW	Origin of substances							
Substances	**Pollutants** / **Air**	Greenhouse effects	CO2	11a																			
			N2O	11b																			
			CH4	11c																			
			HFCs	11d																			
			PFCs	11e																			
			SF6	11f																			
		Ozon layer	CFC	11g																			
		Acidifi-cation	NOX	11h																			
			SO2	11i																			
			NH3	11j																			
	Quality of water		T-P	11k	0																		
			T-N	11l	0																		
			Wastewater	11m	0																		
	Waste	Final disposal		11n	212,310																		
		Reuse		11o	149,782																		
	Natural resources	Energy resources	Natural gas	11p	92																		
			Crude oil	11q	34																		
			Coal	11r	153																		
			Forests (volume)	11s	22,915																		
			Waters	11t	88,900																		
			Fish	11u	6,768																		
	Land uses		Agricultural land	11v																			
			Forests etc.	11w																			
			Water of rivers etc.	11x																			
			Roads	11y																			
			Land for housing etc.	11z																			
			Other land	11aa																			
Hidden material flows				11ab																			
Total					968,085.1	924,849.7	351,564.2	371,711.8	473,502.0	82,589.9	61,572.5	5,001.4	38,907.1	6,592.2	54,324.8	-214.4	1,217,764	70	1,404	20,044	11,433	16,730	2,008	906	-

Absorption of substances in the production process

Cross border flow of pollutants to ROW

Depletion of ROW's natural resources caused by import

Domestic hidden flows 1,218

Hidden flows caused by import 2,520

2,375
10,261
3,610
89,015
0
6,755

Reconciliation accounts	R	Other changes and revaluation	-4,019.4	-3,237.4	-117,852.8

Closing stocks	CA	Closing stocks	44,560.4	636,818.9	2,364,737.4

Unit		Billion Yen	1000 t

(The top right of the J-NAMEA)

Substances

Pollutants
- Quality of water: T-P (11k), T-N (11l)
- Wastewater (11m)
- Waste: Finaldisposal (11n), Reuse (11o)

Natural resources
- Energy: Natural gas (11p), Grade oil (11q), Coal (11r)
- Forests (volume) (11s)
- Water (11t)
- Fish (11u)
- Agricultural land (11v)
- Forests etc. (11w)
- Water of rivers (11x)
- Land uses: Road (11y), Land for housing (11z), Other land (11aa)
- Hidden material flows (11ab)

Environmental themes

- Global: Greenhouse effects (12a), Ozone layer depletion (12b)
- Regional: Acidification (12c), Eutrophication (12d), Wastewater (12e), Waste (12f)
- Changes in natural resources: Energy resources (12g), Forests (12h), Water (12i), Fish (12j)
- Changes in land uses: Agricultural land (12k), Forests etc. (12l), Water of river etc. (12m), Road (12n), Land for housing (12o), Other land (12p)
- Hidden material flows (12q)

X1 – Accumulation of substances to the environment
X2 – Changes of natural resources in ROW caused by import

Emission of pollutants by producers: 31 | 503 | 391 | 247,000 | 147,000

Emission of pollutants by consumers: 26 | 321 | 468 | 47,912 | 2,782

Other domestic emission of pollutants

Changes in natural resources: 0 | 0 | 0 | 73,658 | 0 | 0

Restoration of ROW's natural resources by national economy

Changes in Land use: -40 | -20 | 20 | 20 | 30

Total	
Opening stocks	3,119,318.3
Use at purchaser's prices	
Output an basic prices	968,085.1 / 924,849.6
Final consump.	351,564.2
Origin of generated income	371,711.8
Current receipts	473,502.1
Tax payments, net	82,889.9
Capital receipts	61,572.5
Capital formation	5,901.4
	38,907.1
	6,922.2
Current payments to ROW	54,324.8
Capital payments to ROW	-214.4

Opening stocks: 22,597 | 5,170 | 25,420 | 1,320 | 1,190 | 1,680 | 3,000

(The bottom right of the J-NAMEA)

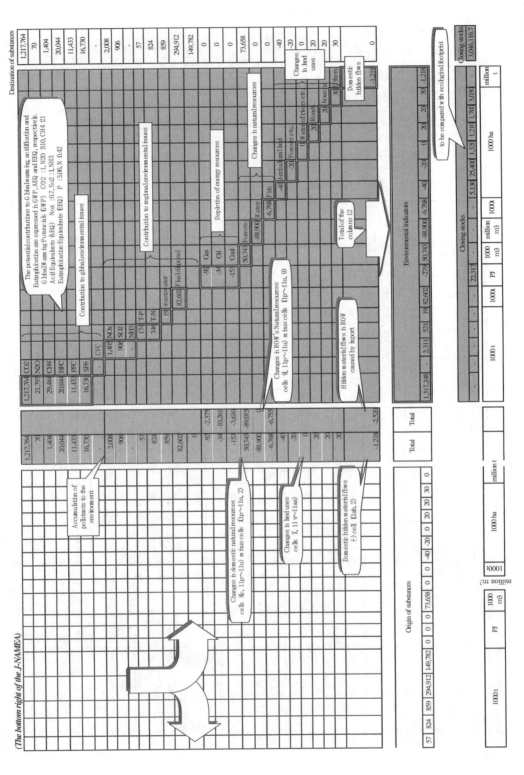

Table 7. Basic structure of the PAFEE (Physical Accounting Framework for Environment and Economy)

(Physical term)

			Nation A						Rest of the world (ROW)		
			Goods & services (product groups)	Production (activity groups)	Distribution & use of income (sectors)	Capital — Sectors	Capital — Natural assets (types)	Material balance in A	Current account	Capital account	Material balance
			1	2	3	4	5	8	9	11	14
Opening assets		0					Opening assets				
Nation A — Goods & services (product groups)		1		Intermediate consumption	Final consumption		Capital formation		Export		
Nation A — Production (activity groups)		2	Output								
Nation A — Distribution & use of income (sectors)		3		(Value added)		(Saving)		Final consumption			
Nation A — Capital — Sectors		4			(Capital formation)			Capital formation, Total use of resources(-) & total discharge of residuals(+)		(Net lending from ROW)	
Nation A — Capital — Natural Assets (types)		5									
Nation A — Pressure on environment — Use of natural resources (types)		6		Use of resources(+)	Use of resources(+)		Total use of resources(-)				
Nation A — Pressure on environment — Discharge of residuals (types)		7		Discharge of residuals(-)	Discharge of residuals(-)		Total discharge of residuals(+)		Discharge of residuals(-)		
Nation A — Material balance in A		8	Import								Material balance in A
Rest of the world (ROW) — Current account		9							(Production etc. in ROW) / (Current/external balance of ROW)	(Capital formation in ROW)	Final consumption
ROW — Capital — Sectors		10									
ROW — Capital — Natural Assets (types)		11									
ROW — Pressure on environment — Use of natural resources (types)		12							Use of resources(+)	Total use of resources(-)	
ROW — Pressure on environment — Discharge of residuals (types)		13			Discharge of residuals(-)				Discharge of residuals(-)	Total discharge of residuals(+)	
Material balance		14						Material balance in A			Capital formation, Total use of resources(-) & total discharge of residuals(+)
Closing assets		15					Closing assets				

→ : Physical flows

▨ : Cells for environmental flow data

Table 8. Basic structure of the MDPIOT (Multi-dimensional physical input-output tables)

Sheets for resource type as 3rd dimension

Resource total

Resource B

Resource A

			Nation A									Nation B (Major trade partners)									The rest of the world (ROW)	Other resources
			Production				Accumulation		Environment		Production				Consump-tion	Accumulation		Environment				
Use (output) Supply/(input)			Base material	Manufac-turing	Service	Waste man-agement	Consump-tion	Capital formation	Waste storage	Env. as source	Env. as sink	Base material	Manufac-turing	Service	Waste man-agement		Capital formation	Waste storage	Env. as source	Env. as sink	Exports from A to ROW (+)	
Lev.1	Level 2		1	2	3	4	5	6	7	8	9	10	11	12	13	14	15	16	17	18	19	20
Nation A — Production	Base material	1	(-,+)*	Flow of intermediate products (-,+)*	Flow of intermediate products (-,+)*	Interm. inputs for waste manag (+)	Material flows to final demand sectors (+)					Exports from A to B (+)									Exports from A to ROW (+)	
	Manufacturing	2																				
	Service	3																				
	Waste management	4	Material flows other than wastes accompanied by waste management activities (+)																			
Nation A — Accumu-lation	Recovered material	5	Recovery of by-products(-) and outputs to recycle/treatment/disposal(+)				Recovery of materials (-)		(-)													
	Intermediate products	6	Apparent intermediate flows				Stock (+)															
	Waste storage	7				Final disposal (-)			Stock (+)													
Nation A — Environ-ment	Environment as source	8	Resource extraction, oxygen input for combustion , etc (+)					Erosion (-,+)		Extractio n total (-)												
	Environmet as sink	9	Direct emission of substances (CO₂, etc.) from economic activities to the environment (-)								Emission total (+)										
Nation B — Production	Base material	10	Imports into A from B (+)									Flows of intermediate products				Material flows to final demand sectors (+)					Exports from B to ROW (+)	
	Manufacturing	11																				
	Service	12																				
	Waste management	13																				
Nation B — Accumu-lation	Recovered material	14										Recovery of by-products(-) and outputs to recycle/treatment/disposal (+)				Recovery of materials (-)		(-)				
	Intermediate products	15										Apparent intermediate flow				Stock (+)						
	Waste storage	16													Final disposal (-)			Stock (+)				
Nation B — Environ-ment	Environment as source	17										Resource extraction, oxygen input for combustion, etc (+)								Extractio n total (-)		
	Environmet as sink	18										Direct emission of substances (CO₂, etc.) from economic activities to the environment (-)					Erosion (-,+)				Emission total (+)		
The rest of the world (ROW)		19	Imports into A from ROW (+)									Imports into B from ROW (+)										(ROW)	
Internal transformation		20	Internal transformation across type of resources (-,+)									Internal transformation across type of resources (-,+)											Balance (+,-)

*) For diagonal elements in production activities, gross production should be indicated with negative sign and self-consumption should be indicated with positive sign.

▨ : Cells for environmental flow data

☐ : In the short term, these cells will be filled by incomplete accounts to record the material flows induced by imports into A

Sustainable Development Indicators for Sweden: Concepts and Framework

M. Nyman

Statistics Sweden

Background

A first set of Swedish Sustainable Development Indicators was published 2001[1]. The publication was made by Statistics Sweden in co-operation with the Swedish Environmental Protection Agency for the Ministry of the Environment. Work with the publication was under direction of a steering committee composed of representatives from the Ministries of the Environment, Health and Social Affairs, Industry and Trade and Finance as well as Statistics Sweden and the National Environmental Protection Agency. An open seminar was held in December 2000 with some 50 participants from government, industry, universities and NGOs, who discussed a first draft of the report and provided valuable input.

This first set was compiled before Sweden had a strategy for sustainable development and were therefore an important underlying document when building up the strategy. Sweden's National Strategy for Sustainable Development was published in April 2002. As the strategy will continue to develop, new indicators will also be developed in the coming years.

Sustainable development indicators

The development toward sustainability in Sweden is reflected by a set of 30 indicators structured along four themes[2]. This is a somewhat different approach than others[3] have taken, both according to number of indicators and the way of structuring them. However, most of the finally selected indicators as well as the indicators discussed during our work are commonly used in other SDI-reports. This makes the Swedish indicators fairly comparable with the others. There is also a strong connection between the environmental indicators chosen and the Swedish "Gröna Nyckeltal" (Key indicators in Swedish only) provided by the Swedish Environmental Advisory Council. The social and economic indicators chosen should also be familiar to readers from these disciplines.

The present set of Swedish indicators is mainly presented in the form of time series. The criteria used for selecting indicators are fairly pragmatic. An indicator should be informative and relevant in terms of sustainability. The data should be readily available in official statistical datasets and, if possible and appropriate, be annual data covering a long time period. A reasonable balance between social, economic and environmental

---

1.   The report is available on the web at www.scb.se/eng/omscb/eu/eu.asp

2.   Please find a list of indicators in the Appendix

3.   For example, Belgium, Finland, United Kingdom.

indicators was also desired. As requested by the steering committee, the total number of indicators should be kept as low as possible, preferably around 30. The main target groups of the report are politicians and civil servants who need brief and focused reports rather than detailed in depth studies. The work with the indicator report thus generates a lot of interesting data and analysis that never makes it into the final report.

The work process is similar to what is usually done in forecasting. The work has to begin with examining which parts of the development that has the largest influence on sustainability. To do this, it is necessary to develop a very broad mapping or conceptual model of all the parts influencing future sustainability, for example transport, manufacturing and heating that all influencing the total carbon dioxide emissions.

The choices involved in minimising the number of indicators are difficult. It is necessary to determine what measures are most important as well as cater for indicators that relates to choices and concerns in everyday life. An example of this type of indicator is prevalence of allergic asthma among school children. We choose to include this indicator because it is an often debated issue which concerns many people. Arguments against this indicator is that there is no clear evidence of what causes these problems (we do not know exactly how and what kind of emissions to air worsens the symptoms). It is also, at least so far, a minor problem in proportion to the total health situation among the population. However, it is an increasing problem, and including this indicator could serve as a warning bell.

Many indicators were discussed but not included in this report despite the fact that they added valuable information about the transition towards sustainability *e.g.* the Households saving ratio, Benzene in urban air. Some of the desired indicators were excluded because of lack of data *e.g.* Noise Share of adults per pupil. Other indicators need to be further developed and relationships between indicators should be worked out. However, in the continuing work with SD indicators a more detailed set may be developed where these discussed indicators can be used.

A better use of the environmental accounts in developing SD indicators was desired after this first report. In a coming report this spring, Statistics Sweden will present SD indicators divided by sector using both the environmental accounts and other sources, *e.g.* health statistics divided by sector. Decoupling indicators will also be used by sector.

Our approach

The work of the Brundtland Commission and others provides the background for the approach we have chosen to structure the indicators. Sustainability indicators are generally designed to illustrate the economic, environmental and social dimensions of sustainable development. There is a danger in categorising a set of indicators with these dimensions since the same phenomena can often be viewed from several perspectives. We have chosen to structure our indicators under themes that we have named **Efficiency**, **Equality/Participation**, **Adaptability** and **Values and resources for coming generations**. Within these themes, the indicators encompass economic, environmental and social dimensions. We hope this approach will serve interdisciplinary and help avoid categorisation. The aim is to bring a focus to the different facets of the transition towards sustainability, rather than serving as a judgment on the present state of sustainability.

- Indicators on **Efficiency** focus on resource use from different perspectives. Resource productivity is undoubtedly one of the key issues in a transition to a sustainable society.

- Indicators on Equality and participation encompass the distributional aspects of development, in terms of sharing both the burdens and benefits in different areas. Many of these indicators deal with traditional economic and social welfare issues; additional data reflect the interest in promoting changes in production and consumption patterns in a more sustainable direction.

- Indicators on Adaptability illustrate actions today that will influence the situation in coming years. These indicators represent different views of the current composition of investments in relation to achieving greater flexibility and efficiency tomorrow.

- The last set of indicators focus on Values and resources for coming generations, or what might be termed manoeuvrability. These indicators emphasise the economic, ecological and human resources we pass on to future generations. Another way of viewing this theme is to say that it concerns the avoidance of debts that tie up (or deplete) resources that could be put to better use tomorrow.

We present and discuss these indicators separately, knowing full well that in terms of sustainability, few if any of them make sense on their own. The reader is left to make his/her own weighting of, for example growth in GDP *versus* changes in levels of emissions or changes in resources spent on education or health care. Obviously, there are trade-offs as well as synergy effects, within and among the variables composing the different indicators – especially over longer time periods.

We do not provide a weighting scheme or specific dependencies among the variables presented in the indicators. We do, however, illustrate some of the linkages among the different indicators by cross-referencing where possible. Future reports on sustainability might proceed in a different, more analytical, direction if there is a demand for it. This would involve a more explicit analysis of dependencies among indicators as well as different schemes for weighting them as components of a type of metaindicator. It is possible that a Green GDP would be included among indicators.

Diagram 1: **Indicators of sustainable Development**

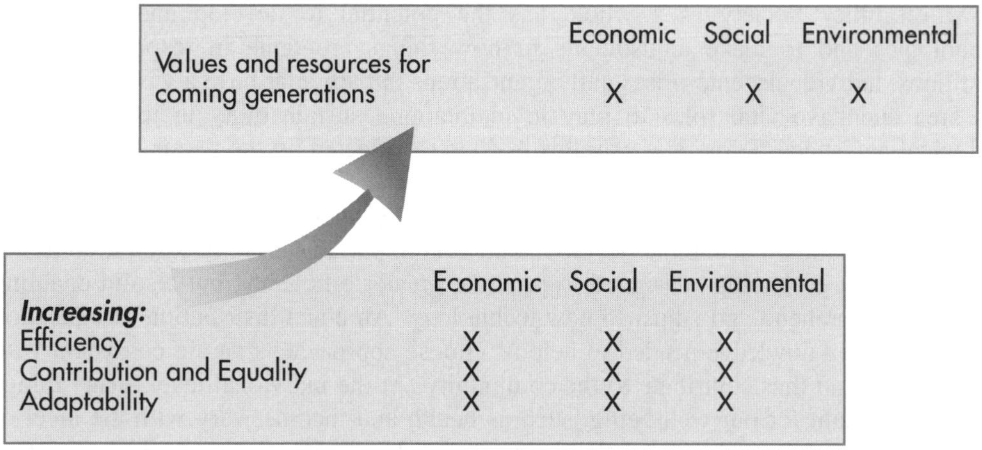

Results

The Sustainable Development Indicators for Sweden show that we are improving our performance in a lot of areas, but still, we are not yet so good at making sustainable choices. We make better cars with less fuel consumption and less emissions. The environmental gain however diminishes because we tend to choose cars with higher performance and travel more by car. Improvements are made in education because of new pedagogical methods and the use of computers. However, fewer pupils are qualifying for upper secondary school. Decreasing expenditures in education resulting among other things in more pupils per teacher could be one explanation.

Efficiency can pave the way for development towards sustainability. Much progress up to now has relied on technological achievements or changes in our ways of doing things that have led to a more rational use of resources. We can now produce more goods and services with less input of energy and labour. The increase in production has resulted in more waste, which we are, however, able to manage better. Measurements of efficiency in social developments pose problems of interpretation because qualitative effects are difficult to measure. Students' results in the school system have deteriorated with an increase in the share of students who are not qualified for upper secondary school.

Contribution and Equality An equal distribution of prosperity enables a broader-based contribution and can also influence the development of both the economy and the environment. The contributions from all sections of the population are important because many of the changes that need to be made affect people's everyday lives and because broad understanding and responsibility are keys to changing consumption patterns and behaviour. The economic recession in the early 1990s and a growing market orientation in Sweden have led to negative development in some of the traditional welfare indicators. However, in Sweden there is great involvement in the ongoing local process with Agenda 21, which has also led to increased responsibility and actions for sustainable development among NGOs, enterprises, municipalities and consumers. This has also led to an increase in the number of environmentally certified enterprises and in the sale of ecolabelled products. The increase in trade has resulted in increased transport. The share of those means of transport that have a negative effect on the environment has increased.

Adaptability Society as a whole has the potential to develop and adapt new technologies and to make adjustments in how things are done in response to new conditions. Individuals, enterprises and organisations in particular have a vast potential in this area and have vital roles to play in maintaining sustainability in the economic, ecological and social fields. The way this is done is reflected by the theme Adaptability. This theme interacts with the themes of Efficiency and Contribution and Equality. For example, a high educational level among the population is considered to be one of the key factors for a country's economic development. It is important not only when it comes to developing new technology designed to promote greater efficiency, but also in enabling people to comprehend and adjust to new technology. An equal distribution of education can provide the knowledge needed to help us choose approaches that are consistent with sustainability and thus contribute to the community. At the individual level, many things that are important for our well being, such as health and income, vary with the level of education. Sweden has a high and slowly increasing level of education in the population and a large and increasing share of GDP is invested in research. This characterizes a dynamic economy. A rising interest for entrepreneurship contributes to increased potential for economic diversity. Adaptation to the use of renewable resources proceeds slowly. Nevertheless, there has been an adaptation in energy usage. For example, the housing sector today is much more energy efficient than previously. Sweden has the highest proportion of renewable energy/total energy among the member states of the EU. A considerable quantity of energy is used for heating purposes, although great progress has been made in efficiency in recent decades. We also note a significant increase in the area under cultivation for organic farming.

Values and resources for coming generations The predominant impression is that Sweden is not passing on to coming generations a similarly large or greater set of values and resources than that inherited by the previous generation. For example, the use of non-renewable resources declined for a period, but it is now increasing again. Asthma allergies are increasing among children, the Baltic Sea is polluted and over fished, and the number of endangered species is increasing. However, there are some positive developments. The central government deficit has fallen and there has been an increase in land and water areas reserved for conservation of wildlife. The total emissions of carbon dioxide show no clear trend. This indicator illustrates one of the most burning issues today that will influence prosperity for coming generations. Adaptation toward sustainability is under way, but much work remains.

Appendix

List of indicators:

Toward sustainability: Efficiency

7. Total energy supply by GDP

8. GDP per hour worked

9. Waste

10. State of health; Expenditure on health

11. Proportion of pupils not qualifying for upper secondary schools

Toward sustainability: Contribution and Equality

12. Population by age group

13. Gross regional product

14. Passenger and freight transport

15. Disposable income per consumption unit

16. Women's salaries as percentage of men's salaries

17. Electoral participation

18. Ratio of the population exposed to violent crime or threat of violence

19. Enterprises with EMAS or ISO 14001 certification, certified eco-schools; area with certified forestry

20. Purchases of eco-labelled products and services

Toward sustainability: Adaptability

21. Primary energy supply mix

22. Investments in share of GDP

23. Newly started enterprises and bankruptcies

24. Level of education

25. Research and development expenditure in relation to GDP

26. Employment: Women and men by activity status

27. Organic farming, grazed pastures and hay meadows

Toward sustainability: Values and resources for coming generations

28. General Government and Central Government Net Debt in per cent of GDP

29. Share of GDP spent on health, education, welfare and social security

30. Direct Material Consumption

31. Quantities of chemicals hazardous to health and/or the environment

32. Prevalence of allergic asthma among school children

33. Protected area

34. Exploitation of Baltic herring

35. Extinct and endangered species

36. Emissions of carbon dioxide

Social Accounting Matrices and Extended Input-Output Tables

C. Stahmer

Federal Statistics Office Germany

Introduction

This paper summarises the historical development of Social Accounting Matrices (SAM) related to input-output tables and describes the linkages between SAM and the input-output framework in the European System of National Accounts. After these introductory remarks, an example of a SAM based on input-output analysis is given which might encourage cooperation projects of statisticians working in these two fields.

SAM and input-output framework

At the end of the forties and beginning of the fifties, Richard Stone already proposed a presentation of the results of national accounting not only in T-accounts but also in a matrix format.[1] He called such matrix a *Social Accounting Matrix* (SAM) and demonstrated that input-output tables could be interpreted as a special case of a SAM: "I propose to use the term input-output table to mean a statement in current money terms of the flow of goods and non-factor services between the operating accounts of the system and between these and all other accounts combined. All other transactions in the system are aggregated and appear as the elements in the final row of the matrix."[2]

In the sixties, Richard Stone and his team developed the Cambridge Growth Model.[3] In this context, he also published a first SAM for Great Britain 1960[4] and improved the conceptual framework of such matrix presentation. He especially stressed the importance of using different statistical units (e.g. commodities, establishments, institutional units) in the system for describing the variety of economic activities in a most suitable way. According to this concept, it is necessary to link the different parts of the accounting system by special transition matrices from one statistical unit to another.[5] These considerations were the starting point for the concepts of the *System of National Accounts (SNA)* 1968.[6] The supply and disposition tables of the input-output framework became an integral part of the national accounting matrix.[7]

---

1.   See Stone 1949, Stone 1951-52, Stone 1955a and 1955b. Cf. also Stone 1961. Comments to this work were made by Hill 1995, p. 27. See also Stahmer 2002 with further references.

2.   Stone 1955b, p. 158 f.

3.   See the overview in Stone 1981a, pp. 77-96.

4.   Stone 1962b.

5.   Stone 1962a.

6.   United Nations 1968.

7.   United Nations 1968, Chapter II and Chapter III, cf. especially the famous table 2.1 of the complete system, p. 18 passim. See also later comments of Richard Stone in Stone 1979 and Stone 1981b.

In the seventies, the term social accounting matrix changed its meaning. It was now used for a type of national accounting matrix especially describing the interrelationships of income and transfer flows between the different institutional units: "The pattern of these transfers conditions the distribution of income in exactly the same way as the pattern of interindustry transactions conditions the structure of production."[8] Such special emphasis on socio-economic analysis was strongly supported by Richard Stone: "We already have a disaggregation of the productive system in input-output tables and, for a more restricted number of countries, a disaggregation of the financial system in flow-of-funds tables. The missing peace is the disaggregation of income and outlay."[9]

In the seventies and eighties, these concepts were especially used in developing countries.[10] The promising experiences in these countries encouraged national accountants to propose socio-economic analysis as integral part of the revised concepts of national accounting.[11] This strategy has been successful: SNA 1993 as well as ESA 1995 contain chapters on SAM which show its usefulness and the great variety of its applications.[12] In the next section, the proposals of the international system of national accounts regarding the linkages between input-output and SAM are described in detail.

Great support for implementing the SAM concepts not only in developing but also in developed countries was given by the work done by Steven Keuning and his team at Statistics Netherlands. They presented the concepts and numerical examples of a *System of Economic and Social Accounting Matrices and Extensions* (SESAME) which comprises a whole family of SAM modules.[13] *Table 1* gives an overview on the different parts of the system which is able to describe economic, social and environmental aspects of human activities in an integrated framework. Eurostat together with several European countries is now preparing a handbook on the concepts of SAM especially based on these experiences.[14]

Linkages of SAM and input-output in the ESA

In the chapter on the sequence of accounts and balancing items (Chapter 8), the ESA also describes different types of matrix presentation of national accounts data (par. 8.100 - 8.155). In the introductory remarks, it is mentioned that the input-output table is a well-known example of such a presentation: "The input-output table is a widely

---

8.   Pyatt 1999, p. 366.

9.   Stone 1985, p. 181.

10.   See Pyatt, Roe 1977 and Pyatt, Round 1985.

11.   Keuning, de Ruijter 1988, Keuning 1991, Pyatt 1985, 1991a and 1991b.

12.   Commission of the European Communities et al. 1993, pp. 461-488, Eurostat 1995, pp. 195-206.

13.   See the overview in Keuning 2000 and Timmerman, van de Ven 2000 with further references.

14.   Eurostat 2002.

Table 1. **System of Economic and Social Accounting Matrices and Extensions (SESAME)**

used matrix framework to supply detailed and coherently arranged information on the flow of goods and services and on the structure of production costs (par. 8.101)."

In the following paragraphs of ESA, it is shown how the full sequence of ESA accounts and balancing items could be presented in a matrix format (8.104 - 8.125 and table 8.19). Each entry in an aggregate matrix can be considered as the grand total of a submatrix which shows detailed information by different types of transactors or other groupings (par. 8.126). A more detailed matrix reveals the economic flows at a meso-level which allows an analysis of the interrelations between the different groups of economic actors. The SAM is described as a special type of matrix presentation which allows a further elaboration on the interrelations between the social and economic aspects of the system. Some information on the SAM is given in the last part of Chapter 8 of the ESA (par. 8.133 – 8.155 and tables 8.20, 8.21).

In the introductory paragraphs of the description of the SAM, the close linkages between SAM and input-output tables are stressed: "The supply and use tables opt for a classification of rows and columns which is most suitable to describe the economic processes under consideration, namely the processes of production and use of products. However, those matrices do not incorporate the interrelations between value added and final expenditure. By extending a supply and use table, or an input-output table, to show the entire circular flow of income at a meso-level, one captures an essential feature of a Social Accounting Matrix (SAM) (par. 8.133)."

According to these considerations, the SAM is defined as a presentation of ESA-accounts in a matrix which elaborates on the linkages between a supply and use table and sector accounts (par. 8.134). Special emphasis is laid on the role of people in the economy which implies a further breakdown of the household sector and a disaggregation of the persons employed. In this context, two parts of the use table of the input-output framework are especially disaggregated: the components of net value added, shown in the third quadrant of the table, and the final uses which are presented in the second quadrant.

Table 8.22 of the ESA gives an example of a detailed matrix of net value added. The compensation of employees is subdivided by resident and non-resident employees. Resident employees are further disaggregated by sex, category of occupation and place of residence. Net operating surplus is shown in a breakdown by the (sub) sector of the enterprises to which the establishment belongs, and net mixed income according to the location of the household enterprises (par. 8.153). Employees could further be subdivided by level of schooling, age and type of job contract (full-time/part-time, permanent/temporary) (par. 8.136). It is recommended that labour income is also decomposed into hours worked and average wage rates per hour (par. 8.138).

In the input-output framework, final uses are shown in a breakdown by product group. The SAM concepts recommend a further breakdown of final consumption expenditures by institutional sectors (e.g. types of households). Changes in inventories should be shown in a cross classification by product group and institutional sector, gross fixed capital formation by product group and investing industries. For socio-economic analysis, the proposed breakdown of final consumption expenditures by product group and household (sub) sectors would have higher priority than the disaggregation of capital formation.

Example of a SAM based on input-output analysis (SAMIO)

In this section, an example is given for using extended input-output tables and SAM modules to compile a SAM which is based on results of input-output analysis. This matrix is called SAMIO to stress the linkages between SAM and the I-O framework. The example shall encourage common research and analysis of input-output and SAM specialists. Such cooperation is urgently needed for improving the data base for developing strategies towards sustainable development.

By applying input-output models, the SAMIO gives a very condensed picture of the production and consumption activities of certain groupings of the population. The SAM data on value added and labour inputs by socio-economic group are directly linked with the SAM modules on final uses by socio-economic group. Such linkages of labour and consumption were already proposed by Utz-Peter Reich, Philipp Sonntag and Hans-Werner Holub twenty-five years ago.[15] They presented a Labour-Consumption Accounting which has several similarities with the approach presented in this section.

The SAMIO concepts allow a new type of operating surplus: Each socio-economic group is not only delivering results of their production activities to themselves or to other persons but also receiving such results from themselves or from others. The balancing items of these flows show for each socio-economic group who is the "net recipient" or "net supplier" of these interrelationships. The total amount of received production values could be treated as a variable of the welfare function of these persons.

Following the concepts of the "magic triangle" of input-output tables, the SAMIO is compiled in time units, in monetary units and in physical term (tons).[16] Differing from traditional concepts, the concepts of SAMIO are derived from considerations on the time use of the population. In this context, the pioneering work of Gary Becker and Graham Pyatt was very stimulating for developing suitable concepts.[17] A broader approach which is also based on welfare considerations was proposed by Gerhard Scherhorn.[18] He also distinguishes welfare caused by goods and services, welfare connected with time use and welfare related to environmental conditions.

Data base for compiling SAMIO

An extended monetary input-output table - similar to the table described in the context of the "magic triangle" - is the starting point for the computation.[19] *Table 2* shows this table based on 1990 data for Germany. The main differences refer to the treatment of education services, the concepts of household services and the disaggregation of the private consumption.

Education services (column/row 7) are treated in a more conventional way. The gross output does not become part of fixed capital formation but is treated as government consumption. This concept also implies that the consumption of fixed produced assets

---

15.   Reich et al. 1977, see also Horz, Reich 1982 and Reich 1986.

16.   See Stahmer 2000.

17.   See Becker 1965 and Pyatt 1990. Cf. also Kazemier, Exel 1992.

18.   Scherhorn 2002 with further references.

19.   See the detailed information in Stahmer et al. 2002 and Stahmer 2000.

does not include the consumption of educational capital. Furthermore it is not necessary to introduce the margin of education as a balancing item.

The treatment of all household services as production activities has not changed.[20] According to this concept, consumer durables are investment goods which are depreciated. Differing from the monetary I-0 table of the "magic triangle", the labour inputs of household production (defined with the so-called third-person criterion) get no monetary value. Some changes have also been made with regard to the uses of household services. Household services related to employment (column/row 10) are not treated as intermediate consumption but as private consumption. According to this concept, the balancing item of the margin of labour was not necessary. Corresponding with the treatment of education services, the household services related to studying (column/row 11) are not treated as fixed capital formation but as private consumption. No changes have been made in the cases of the use of household production services (column/row 9) and other household services (column/row 12). Household production services are mainly intermediate inputs, other household services represent the main part of private consumption.

The column of private consumption is further subdivided by specific socio-economic groups of the population. The example in *table 2* only shows a disaggregation by young people (0 - 17 years old), adults except aged persons (18 - 64 years old) and aged persons (65 years and older). The detailed breakdown of private consumption compiled for Germany 1990 comprises 32 types of households with further subdivisions by the persons living in the households (2 to 5 groups of persons). The basic data only deliver monetary information on the households as a whole. The further breakdown by person could partly be estimated by applying specific weighting procedures and partly by using simplified weighting systems (e.g. equivalent scales). Following this two-stage procedure, the whole population was finally disaggregated by 120 groups of persons. Main emphasis has been laid on the situation of young people in different types of families. These data were compiled in the context of a research project sponsored by the "Deutscher Arbeitskreis für Familienhilfe (German Association for Supporting Families)", Kirchzarten.

As memorandum items, *table 2* also shows the direct time inputs of the different activities. In the case of employment (columns 1 – 8), the time inputs show the hours at the working place.

For socio-economic analysis, it is preferable to endogenize the consumption of fixed produced assets. Finally, the use of fixed assets has also an intermediate character.[21] Investment goods are directly or indirectly inputs for producing private or government consumption goods and services, other investment goods or exports. Input-output models can reveal these linkages between inputs and final uses. As a necessary data base for input-output analysis, the depreciation items of the different industries (branches) are subdivided by the type of investment goods. For modelling purposes, these data are treated as additional intermediate inputs. In accordance with this concept, the primary inputs (third quadrant of the I-O table) will only comprise imports for intermediate uses and net value added. An additional correction has to be made in the second resp. fourth quadrant. The columns of fixed capital formation are reduced by the corresponding items of depreciation showing only net capital formation. Thus, the row sums of total uses of depreciation will become zero. *Table 3* shows such a matrix for the consumption of

20. See Becker 1964 and Lancaster 1966.

21. See Stahmer, Strassert 2002.

domestically produced assets and the corresponding corrections. Row 13 of *table 3* corresponds with row 19 of *table 2*.

Socio-economic activities are not only based on the use of domestic product but also directly or indirectly linked with imported goods and services. For analyzing the impacts of foreign trade in the countries of origin it is necessary to endogenize not only the consumption of fixed assets but also the intermediate inputs of imports. A thorough analysis of the production activities abroad would only be possible if input-output tables of all important countries delivering import goods would be available. For getting first estimates, it is possible to apply the domestic input structures also for describing foreign production activities. Of course, such assumption neglects the fact that many imported products are not domestically produced. *Table 3* also shows an import matrix which is used for input-output analysis in the following sections. It should be mentioned that this import matrix also contains a depreciation matrix for the imported investment goods with corresponding corrections in the columns of fixed capital formation. The data on imports correspond with the figures in *table 2*, rows 20, 22 and 23.

Table 2. **Extended monetary Billion**

Row No. / Supply	Input of agri-culture, forestry, fishing	mining, water and energy supply	manu-facturing	con-struc-tion	market services	environ-mental protec-tion ser-vices	edu-cation services	non-market services	house-hold produc-tion
	1	2	3	4	5	6	7	8	9
Product output by product group									
1 Products of agriculture, forestry, fishing	7.5	0.1	43.4	0.1	5.9	-	0.1	1.1	6.0
2 Prod.of mining, water and energy supply	1.8	30.8	45.0	0.5	20.7	0.7	1.6	5.7	15.4
3 Products of manufacturing	14.8	13.1	571.1	72.0	109.0	2.4	2.7	41.3	109.1
4 Construction work	0.7	3.9	7.1	4.2	23.4	1.8	1.3	7.2	1.0
5 Market services	8.2	15.9	288.6	39.6	424.5	1.7	7.8	109.1	127.9
6 Environmental protection services	0.1	0.9	5.2	2.0	1.8	4.9	0.5	1.1	2.5
7 Education services	-	-	-	-	-	-	-	-	-
8 Non-market services	0.4	0.5	5.8	0.7	4.9	1.3	0.1	66.5	2.8
9 Household production services	-	-	-	-	-	-	-	-	42.3
10 Househ. services related to employment	-	-	-	-	-	-	-	-	-
11 Household services related to education	-	-	-	-	-	-	-	-	-
12 Other household services	-	-	-	-	-	-	-	-	-
13 **Domestic products, totals**	**33.5**	**65.1**	**966.0**	**119.1**	**590.1**	**12.9**	**14.1**	**232.1**	**307.0**
14 Compensation of employees	7.0	35.4	486.3	85.4	405.7	6.2	77.8	211.6	-
15 Net operating surplus	21.9	12.3	94.9	34.6	388.1	- 0.7	0.4	-	-
Revenues on products									
16 Non-deductible value added tax	-	-	-	-	11.6	1.0	1.3	14.3	23.3
17 Taxes less subsidies on products	- 4.5	- 2.6	54.5	2.3	23.3	-	0.2	0.3	-
18 **Net value added**	**24.4**	**45.2**	**635.6**	**122.3**	**828.7**	**6.4**	**79.7**	**226.2**	**23.3**
Consumption of fixed produced assets 2)									
19 Domestic investment goods	10.3	17.6	61.5	4.6	141.3	6.2	7.5	8.4	22.9
20 Imported investment goods	1.5	2.7	11.4	0.7	18.3	0.3	0.9	0.9	6.8
21 Non-deductible value added tax	-	-	-	-	11.2	-	-	2.6	3.6
Imports from the rest of the world									
22 Goods	5.9	13.4	225.2	13.0	29.5	0.7	0.6	13.6	42.1
23 Services	0.4	0.7	8.6	1.0	22.9	0.0	0.9	5.7	4.8
24 **Primary inputs, totals**	**42.6**	**79.6**	**942.3**	**141.7**	**1 051.8**	**13.6**	**89.5**	**257.5**	**103.6**
25 **Gross output, final uses**	**76.0**	**144.7**	**1 908.3**	**260.8**	**1 642.0**	**26.6**	**103.6**	**489.6**	**410.6**
Memorandum item:									
26 Time inputs (Mill.hours)	2 035	743	13 821	3 333	17 404	262	1 828	6 841	82 320

1) Including consumption of private non-profit organisations serving households (18.7 Bill..DM).
2) Including consumer durables.

input-output table - Germany 1990 - Deutsch marks

branches				Final uses									
household services (except household production)				private consumption				fixed capital formation					
services related to employ-ment	services related to studying	other services	totals	young persons	adults (except aged persons)	aged persons	govern-ment con-sump-tion[1]	fixed assets (except consumer durables incl. change in stocks)	con-sumer durables	exports to the rest of the world	totals	Total uses	Row no.
10	11	12	13	14	15	16	17	18	19	20	21	22	
0.1	0.0	3.2	**67.3**	-	-	-	-	2.8	-	5.9	**8.7**	**76.0**	1
0.4	0.2	18.4	**141.3**	-	-	-	-	- 0.7	-	4.1	**3.4**	**144.7**	2
7.6	1.5	116.1	**1 060.6**	-	-	-	-	184.7	73.3	589.7	**847.7**	**1 908.3**	3
0.1	-	2.4	**53.1**	-	-	-	-	205.1	-	2.5	**207.7**	**260.8**	4
20.1	10.1	403.4	**1 457.1**	-	-	-	-	32.6	40.7	111.6	**184.9**	**1 642.0**	5
0.2	0.1	7.2	**26.5**	-	-	-	0.1	-	-	-	**0.1**	**26.6**	6
-	-	-	**-**	-	-	-	103.6	-	-	-	**103.6**	**103.6**	7
0.3	2.2	20.7	**106.2**				380.6	1.1	-	1.8	**383.4**	**489.6**	8
-	5.6	297.7	**345.6**	32.7	25.2	6.9	-	-	-	-	**64.8**	**410.4**	9
-	-	-	**-**	0.6	51.3	1.1	-	-	-	-	**53.0**	**53.0**	10
-	-	-	**-**	17.0	7.6	1.2	-	-	-	-	**25.8**	**25.8**	11
-	-	-	**-**	97.8	824.8	177.4	-	-	-	-	**1 099.9**	**1 099.9**	12
28.7	**19.8**	**869.2**	**3 257.7**	**148.1**	**908.9**	**186.7**	**484.2**	**425.6**	**114.0**	**715.6**	**2 983.0**	**6 240.7**	13
-	-	-	**1 315.5**								**-**	**1 315.5**	14
-	-	-	**551.4**								**-**	**551.4**	15
3.0	1.1	50.3	**106.0**	-	-	-	-	27.7	17.9	3.4	**49.0**	**155.0**	16
-	-	-	**73.4**								**-**	**73.4**	17
3.0	**1.1**	**50.3**	**2 046.3**								**-**	**2 046.3**	18
9.6	1.6	53.5	**345.1**	-	-	-	-	- 257.4	- 87.7	-	**- 345.1**	**-**	19
2.9	0.6	14.4	**61.3**	-	-	-	-	- 36.6	- 24.7	-	**- 61.3**	**-**	20
1.5	0.3	8.3	**27.5**	-	-	-	-	- 13.8	- 13.7	-	**- 27.5**	**-**	21
5.0	1.0	70.2	**420.1**					66.3	31.9	47.4	**145.6**	**565.7**	22
2.2	1.4	34.0	**82.7**					0.1	0.1	0.4	**0.6**	**83.3**	23
24.2	**6.0**	**230.6**	**2 983.0**	-	-	-	-	**- 241.5**	**- 94.0**	**47.8**	**- 287.7**	**2 695.3**	24
53.0	**25.8**	**1 099.8**	**6 240.7**	**148.1**	**908.9**	**186.7**	**484.2**	**184.1**	**20.0**	**763.4**	**2 695.3**		25
12 255	15 430	397 824	**554 097**										26

Table 3. Additional Billion

Row No.	Uses / Supply	Input of agri-culture, forestry, fishing	mining, water and energy supply	manu-facturing	con-struc-tion	market services	environ-mental protec-tion ser-vices	edu-cation services	non-market services	house-hold produc-tion
		1	2	3	4	5	6	7	8	9

Consumption of fixed domestically produced assets

Row No.	Product group	1	2	3	4	5	6	7	8	9
1	Products of agriculture, forestry, fishing	-	-	-	-	0.2	-	-	-	-
2	Prod. of mining, water and energy supply	-	-	-	-	-	-	-	-	-
3	Products of manufacturing	7.1	11.7	46.4	3.5	56.1	0.7	2.7	2.7	15.0
4	Construction work	2.3	4.9	9.5	0.6	71.7	5.4	4.2	5.2	-
5	Market services	0.9	1.0	5.5	0.5	12.8	0.1	0.5	0.5	7.9
6	Environmental protection services	-	-	-	-	-	-	-	-	-
7	Education services	-	-	-	-	-	-	-	-	-
8	Non-market services	-	-	0.1	-	0.4	-	-	-	-
9	Household production services	-	-	-	-	-	-	-	-	-
10	Househ. services related to employment	-	-	-	-	-	-	-	-	-
11	Household services related to education	-	-	-	-	-	-	-	-	-
12	Other household services	-	-	-	-	-	-	-	-	-
13	**Totals**	**10.3**	**17.6**	**61.5**	**4.6**	**141.3**	**6.2**	**7.5**	**8.4**	**22.9**

Imports from the rest of the world

Row No.	Product group	1	2	3	4	5	6	7	8	9
1	Products of agriculture, forestry, fishing	1.5	0.0	15.6	0.0	1.8	-	0.0	0.7	8.9
2	Prod. of mining, water and energy supply	0.1	9.0	25.6	0.0	0.2	0.0	0.0	0.1	0.2
3	Products of manufacturing	5.8	7.0	195.4	13.7	45.5	0.9	1.4	13.7	39.8
4	Construction work	0.0	0.0	0.0	0.1	0.3	0.0	0.0	0.0	0.0
5	Market services	0.4	0.7	8.7	1.0	22.9	0.0	0.7	4.0	4.6
6	Environmental protection services	-	-	-	-	-	-	-	-	-
7	Education services	-	-	-	-	-	-	-	-	-
8	Non-market services	-	-	-	-	-	-	0.1	1.7	0.2
9	Household production services	-	-	-	-	-	-	-	-	-
10	Househ. services related to employment	-	-	-	-	-	-	-	-	-
11	Household services related to education	-	-	-	-	-	-	-	-	-
12	Other household services	-	-	-	-	-	-	-	-	-
13	**Totals**	**7.8**	**16.8**	**245.3**	**14.8**	**70.7**	**1.0**	**2.3**	**20.2**	**53.7**
14	Goods	5.9	13.4	225.2	13.0	29.5	0.7	0.6	13.6	42.1
15	Services	0.4	0.7	8.6	1.0	22.9	0.0	0.9	5.7	4.8
16	Consumption of imported fixed produced assets 1)	1.5	2.7	11.4	0.7	18.3	0.3	0.9	0.9	6.8

1) Including consumer durables.

use tables 1990 – Deutsche marks

branches	Final uses		Total	Row

household services (except household production)			totals	private consumption			government consumption[1]	fixed capital formation			totals	uses	no.
services related to employment	services related to studying	other services		young persons	adults (except aged persons)	aged persons		fixed assets (except consumer durables incl. change in stocks)	consumer durables	exports to the rest of the world			
10	11	12	13	14	15	16	17	18	19	20	21	22	
domestic ally produced assets													
-	-	-	**0.2**	-	-	-	-	- 0.2	-	-	**- 0.2**	-	1
-	-	-	**0.0**	-	-	-	-	-	-	-	**·**	-	2
7.4	1.0	33.1	**187.6**	-	-	-	-	- 131.0	- 56.5	-	**- 187.6**	-	3
-	-	-	**103.9**	-	-	-	-	- 103.9	-	-	**- 103.9**	-	4
2.2	0.6	20.4	**52.9**	-	-	-	-	- 21.8	- 31.1	-	**- 52.9**	-	5
-	-	-	**·**	-	-	-	-	-	-	-	**·**	-	6
-	-	-	**·**	-	-	-	-	-	-	-	**·**	-	7
-	-	-	**0.6**	-	-	-	-	- 0.6	-	-	**- 0.6**	-	8
-	-	-	**·**	-	-	-	-	-	-	-	**·**	-	9
-	-	-	**·**	-	-	-	-	-	-	-	**·**	-	10
-	-	-	**·**	-	-	-	-	-	-	-	**·**	-	11
-	-	-	**·**	-	-	-	-	-	-	-	**·**	-	12
9.6	**1.6**	**53.5**	**345.1**	-	-	-	-	- 257.4	- 87.7	-	**- 345.1**	-	13
rest of the world													
0.1	0.0	4.1	**32.8**	-	-	-	-	0.8	-	1.1	**1.9**	34.7	1
0.0	0.0	0.2	**35.3**	-	-	-	-	- 0.1	-	0.0	**0.0**	35.3	2
7.8	1.6	80.1	**412.7**	-	-	-	-	28.6	7.3	46.4	**82.4**	495.0	3
0.0	-	0.0	**0.5**	-	-	-	-	0.4	-	0.0	**0.4**	0.9	4
2.2	1.2	32.8	**79.3**	-	-	-	-	0.0	0.0	0.2	**0.2**	79.5	5
-	-	-	**·**	-	-	-	-	-	-	-	**·**	-	6
-	-	-	**·**	-	-	-	-	-	-	-	**·**	-	7
0.0	0.2	1.4	**3.6**	-	-	-	-	-	-	-	**·**	3.6	8
-	-	-	**·**	-	-	-	-	-	-	-	**·**	-	9
-	-	-	**·**	-	-	-	-	-	-	-	**·**	-	10
-	-	-	**·**	-	-	-	-	-	-	-	**·**	-	11
-	-	-	**·**	-	-	-	-	-	-	-	**·**	-	12
10.1	**3.0**	**118.6**	**564.2**	-	-	-	-	29.8	7.4	47.8	**84.9**	649.1	13
5.0	1.0	70.2	**420.1**	-	-	-	-	66.3	31.9	47.4	**145.6**	565.7	14
2.2	1.4	34.0	**82.7**	-	-	-	-	0.1	0.1	0.4	**0.6**	83.3	15
2.9	0.6	14.4	**61.3**	-	-	-	-	- 36.6	- 24.7	-	**- 61.3**	-	16

For linking environmental aspects with the socio-economic data base of I-O tables, material balances are used which give a complete description of all physical inputs and outputs of the different industries (branches). The data used in the context of describing ecological aspects of the SAMIO in section 3.4 are shown in *table 4*.

In linking physical flows with the monetary data of the extended I-O table, only parts of the material balances are used. Physical flows, which are not further taken into account, are indicated by italic letters. With regard to the *product flows*, all intermediate domestic products (rows 2 and 17) will be excluded. Remaining product flows are only the imports of intermediate products (row 3), exports of goods (row 19) and the physical flows of investment goods (row 18). In the case of *raw materials and residuals*, all throughput materials (rows 8 and 20) are excluded. These materials comprise cooling water or soil excavation for structures which are used as raw materials and which are given back to the nature as residuals without any further economic treatment. Furthermore, residuals which are still treated or re-used for economic purposes (rows 5 and 21), are excluded. The remaining residuals (rows 23 to 28) which are linked with socio-economic data in the model described in section 3.4, are stored in controlled landfills (like waste) or are disposed back into the nature (e.g. air pollution or treated waste water). In the case of natural resources, only those are taken into account in socio-economic modelling which are used as inputs of economic activities (rows 9 to 14).

SAMIO in time units

The social accounting matrix based on input-output analysis (SAMIO) focusses on the activities of the population disaggregated by socio-demographic or socio-economic groups of persons. A very simple disaggregation of the population is used as example in this chapter: The persons are only subdivided according to their age. The chosen three groupings of the population are young people (0 to 17 years old), adults except seniors (18 to 64 years old) and aged persons (65 years and older). In Germany 1990, 11.6 million persons belonged to the young people, 42.0 to the adults except seniors and 9.7 to the aged people. Other possible classifications could be types of households, education levels or sex.

Table 4. Material balances 1990
Million tons

Columns 1–12 are grouped under **Input of branches**. Columns 10–12 fall under the sub-group **household services (except household production)**. Values shown per million tons; "-" denotes nil.

Row No.	Supply	(1) agriculture, forestry, fishing	(2) mining, water and energy supply	(3) manufacturing	(4) construction	(5) market services	(6) environmental protection services	(7) education services	(8) non-market services	(9) household production	(10) services related to employment	(11) services related to studying	(12) other services	(13) Totals
	Inputs													
1	**Product inputs**	*199*	*2 141*	*2 202*	*618*	*148*	*17*	*52*	*333*	*802*	*75*	*37*	*2 201*	*8 825*
2	*Domestic origin*	188	2 092	1 963	590	134	17	52	331	783	71	36	2 180	8 438
3	*Imported*	10	49	239	28	13	0	0	2	19	4	1	21	387
4	**Residual inputs for economic treatment or re-use**	-	1	13	9	104	4 461	0	0	1	0	0	2	4 591
5	*Current production*	-	-	3	0	104	4 461	0	0	1	0	0	0	4 569
6	*Fixed produced assets*	-	1	10	9	0	-	0	0	0	0	0	2	22
7	**Natural resource inputs of throughput materials**	-	32 386	5 346	113	-	3 500	-	-	-	-	-	-	41 345
8	**Other natural resource inputs**	607	5 839	1 139	68	118	10	15	90	94	29	5	152	8 165
9	Energy carries	-	193	-	-	-	-	-	-	-	-	-	-	193
10	Other solid materials	1	25	591	56	-	-	-	1	-	-	-	-	673
11	Water raised	262	5 361	373	4	28	-	13	77	15	1	1	42	6 177
12	Oxygen	33	258	175	8	90	10	2	12	79	28	4	110	810
13	Carbon dioxide	311	-	-	-	-	-	-	-	-	-	-	-	311
14	Other air components	-	1	-	-	-	-	-	-	-	-	-	-	1
15	*Totals*	806	40 367	8 699	808	370	7 988	67	423	897	105	42	2 354	62 926
	Outputs													
16	**Domestic product outputs**	*251*	*6 961*	*1 361*	*540*	*99*	*0*	-	*17*	*36*	-	-	-	*9 266*
17	*Intermediate products*	194	6 935	1 187	6	80	0	-	-	36	-	-	-	8 438
18	*Gross capital formation*	47	-	18	534	7	-	-	17	-	-	-	-	622
19	*Exports*	10	27	156	0	13	-	-	-	-	-	-	-	206
20	**Residual outputs of throughput materials**	-	32 386	5 346	113	-	3 500	-	-	-	-	-	-	41 345
21	**Residual outputs for economic treatment or re-use**	27	102	1 237	80	114	13	49	299	660	60	32	1 896	4 569
22	**Other residual outputs**	527	918	755	75	157	4 475	18	107	201	45	10	459	7 746
23	Waste	253	18	116	58	20	44	0	2	3	0	0	27	541
24	Waste water	-	18	184	-	-	4 395	-	-	1	0	0	3	4 600
25	Water vaporised	13	606	283	8	54	22	15	93	126	20	6	321	1 567
26	Oxygen	226	-	-	-	-	-	-	-	-	-	-	-	226
27	Carbon dioxide	34	274	161	7	80	12	2	12	68	24	4	99	778
28	Other air emissions	2	2	11	1	4	1	0	0	3	1	0	9	34
29	*Totals*	806	40 367	8 700	808	370	7 988	67	423	897	105	42	2 354	62 926

Starting point for constructing a SAMIO is the total amount of hours available in one year to the different groups of population. It is easy to compile these data because the yearly time budget is fixed (8 760 hours per person, in leap years 8 736 hours). In row 14 and columns 1 to 3 of *table 5*, the available time of the three groups of population is recorded. These figures could be interpreted as the total supply of time.

The use of the time budget of the age groups is shown in the first three rows of *table 5*. Three different types of time use are distinguished:

- personal activities which are undertaken for own purposes only (columns 1 to 3),

- unpaid household production activities done not only for own purposes but also for other members of the same household or for members of other households (columns 4 to 6) and

- paid employment activities which aim at producing marketed or non-marketed products.

The figures of the first two mentioned categories were estimated using the data of the time budget survey 1991/92. In the case of employment, the totals are also recorded in the time budget survey. The disaggregation of hours worked according to the different types of final uses and the age groups can only be made by input-output analysis. The directly and indirectly necessary labour hours of the different socio-economic groups of the population to produce the different types of final uses can be estimated by the following equations:

(1) $\quad T_{dom}^P = T_{SAM} B_{dom} Y_{dom}$ $\qquad$ with

(2) $\quad T_{SAM} = \begin{pmatrix} t_1 \\ . \\ . \\ . \\ . \\ t_n \end{pmatrix}$ $\qquad i = 1,...,n$

(3) $\quad B_{dom} = (I - A_{dom} - D_{dom})^{-1}$

t_i $\quad$ row vector of labour hour coefficients (including traveling time to the working place) of the socio-economic group i related to the monetary gross output by branch[22]

A_{dom} coefficient matrix of (monetary) intermediate inputs of domestic products related to (monetary) gross output by product group and branch

D_{dom} coefficient matrix of (monetary) consumption of fixed produced assets (domestic production) related to (monetary) gross output by investment good and branch

Y_{dom} matrix of (monetary) final uses of domestic products by product group and category of final uses

---

22. The time inputs of private activities are not taken into account. The row vector contains zeros for these branches.

Table 5. **Social accounting matrix in time units based on input-output analysis (SAMIO - T) 1990**
Billions hours

Supply \ Uses	Row No.	Personal activities			Household production		Final consumption (Employment)					Net fixed capital formation	Exports of products	Total uses
		Young persons	Adults (except aged persons)	Aged persons	Services within households	Services between households	Private consumption	Services of NPISH[1]	Education services	Health services	Other government services			
		(1)	(2)	(3)	(4)	(5)	(6)	(7)	(8)	(9)	(10)	(11)	(12)	(13)
Young persons (until 17 years old)	1	97.7			2.5	0.1	0.7				0.1		0.1	101.2
Adults (excl. aged persons) (18 to 64 years old)	2		249.4		57.9	4.1	21.2	0.7	3.0	3.9	6.9	4.9	16.0	368.0
Aged persons (65 years and older)	3			66.1	16.7	1.0	0.9			0.1	0.1			84.9
Unpaid services within households	4	15.2	45.2	16.7										77.1
Unpaid services between households	5	1.3	2.1	1.8										5.2
Private consumption	6	2.7	16.7	3.4										22.8
Services of NPISH[1]	7	0.1	0.5	0.1										0.7
Education services	8	1.8	1.1	0.1										3.0
Health services	9	0.4	2.2	1.4										4.0
Other government services	10	1.3	4.7	1.1										7.1
Net fixed capital formation	11													0.0
Imports of products	12	1.4	8.2	1.8								1.9	5.6	18.9
Balances	13	-20.7	37.9	-7.6								-6.8	-2.8	0.0
Total Supply	**14**	**101.2**	**368.0**	**84.9**	**77.1**	**5.2**	**22.8**	**0.7**	**3.0**	**4.0**	**7.1**	**0.0**	**18.9**	

Memorandum item:
Population (1 000 persons)   11 551   42 006   9 693   63 250

[1] Non-profit institutions serving households.

It has to be mentioned that the labour hours necessary to produce investment goods are shown in *table 5* for net investment only. Labour hours directly and indirectly necessary for reproducing depreciated investment goods are associated with the other final uses (private consumption, government consumption, exports).

The breakdown of labour hours by age group and branch is part of a SAM module describing the paid working hours disaggregated according to different socio-demographic and socio-economic criteria (see the module time accounts (TA) in *table 1*). In the case of the chosen age groups, it was only necessary to distribute a few labour hours of young and aged persons among the different branches because their participation in paid employment is low. *Table 5* reveals the expected result that most of the hours spent for paid employment are associated with persons aged from 18 to 65 years.

The first three columns of *table 5* show the beneficiaries of the time spent. The three age groups of the population receive

- hours of personal activities from themselves (rows 1 to 3),

- hours of household production from themselves, from other members of the same household or from members of other households (rows 4 and 5) and

- hours of paid employment activities as far as they consume products which are directly or indirectly produced by these labour hours.

The distribution among the beneficiaries of the hours of household production activities could partly be compiled by the results of specific questions of the time budget survey. In several cases, the distribution could only be roughly estimated using suitable ratios of distribution (e.g. number of persons in the different types of household).

The distribution of the labour hours directly and indirectly necessary for producing consumption goods and services (row 6) for the different age groups of population could be estimated by using equation (4):

(4) $\quad t_{dom}^{u} = t \ B_{dom} \ Y_{SAM}$ \quad with

(5) $\quad Y_{SAM} = (C_1 \ ... \ C_m \ inv' \ ex')$ \quad and

$\quad\quad i = 1, ..., n$

(6) $\quad t = \sum_{i=1}^{n} t_i$

Y_{dom} and Y_{SAM} are related in the following way:

(7) $\quad Y_{dom} = (C \ inv' \ ex')$ \quad with

(8) $\quad C = \sum_{i=1}^{n} C_i$

$\quad C_i$ matrix of (monetary) final consumption of the socio-economic group i by product group and category of final consumption

$\quad\quad$ inv' $\quad$ column vector of net fixed capital formation by product group

$\quad\quad$ ex' column vector of exports of goods and services by product group

---

According to equation (5), the disaggregation of final uses by socio-demographic/economic groups not only contains a breakdown of private consumption (as it is done in *table 2*) but is also extended to the consumption of non-profit institutions serving households (NPISH) and government consumption. For a comprehensive socio-economic analysis, the beneficiaries of non-market services should be identified. These services comprise parts of individual consumption which could be associated with specific groups of persons without greater difficulties and collective consumption which are provided simultaneously to all members of the community (see ESA, par. 3.83).

In our numerical example, private consumption (row 7) can be subdivided by 120 groups of persons in 32 types of households. For calculating *table 5*, the socio-economic classification was aggregated to the three age groups. The distribution of education services (row 8) among the age groups of pupils was relatively easy. In the input-output table used as data base, ten different types of institutions delivering education services were distinguished (from "kindergarten" up to university)[23]. The distribution of the other services of government and of the non-profit institutions serving households among the age groups of population was estimated based on quota which was derived from different sources. In the case of health services (row 9), detailed data of the health insurance companies could be used. It should be mentioned that the health services only comprise the non-marketed part. Services directly paid by households are recorded as private consumption. As far as no special key was available, the final consumption items were distributed according to the number of persons in each age group.

The population is not only consuming domestic products but also imported goods and services. Thus, labour hours abroad are necessary to produce directly or indirectly the products which are delivered to the importing country. If no information on the input-output relations in countries producing import products were available, it seems acceptable to use the assumption of same input coefficients for producing domestic and imported products. The results could be interpreted as the opportunity costs of producing in the own country instead of importing these products.

The calculation of the labour hours directly and indirectly necessary to produce imported products abroad follows the following equation:

$$(9) \qquad t_{imp} = t \; B \; A_{imp} \; B_{dom} \; Y_{SAM} + t \; B \; Y_{imp}$$

with

$$(10) \qquad B = (I - A_{dom} - D_{dom} - A_{imp})^{-1}$$

> A_{imp} coefficient matrix of (monetary) intermediate inputs of imported products (including consumption of imported investment goods) related to (monetary) gross output by product group and branch
>
> Y_{imp} matrix of (monetary) final uses of imported products by product group and category of final uses

In equation (9) the first term on the right side comprises the labour hours directly and indirectly necessary to produce imported intermediate products (including also imported products for private consumption). The second term denotes the labour hours necessary

---

23.   See Ewerhart 2001.

for producing directly imported products for final uses which comprise investment goods and directly re-exported import products.

The indirectly imported labour hours which are associated with the three age groups of population (row 12 of *table 5*) only comprise hours necessary for producing imported intermediate inputs which are directly or indirectly used for the production of final consumption. Differing from the domestic production (see rows 6 to 10 of *table 5*), no breakdown by type of final consumption is shown in the table.

The data for (net) capital formation and exports (row 12, columns 11 and 12 of *table 5*) are an addition of the labour hours of intermediate imports indirectly necessary for producing these types of final uses and the labour hours necessary for the directly imported products of final uses.

The totals of all hours received by the different socio-economic groups could be interpreted as inputs of their welfare function. Young people benefitted from 122 billion hours, adults (except seniors) from 330 billion hours and aged people from 93 billion hours (rows 1 to 12, columns 1 to 3 of *table 5*). In comparison with the number of persons belonging to the age groups, young people receive 10 550 hours per head, adults (except aged persons) only 7860 and aged people 9540 hours per head. These figures could be compared with the annual hours of each person (8760).

In row 13 of *table 5*, the time delivered and the time received are balanced. This balancing procedure is shown for the different age groups of the population, for the foreign trade and for fixed capital formation.

In the case of the socio-economic groups, the balancing items reveal the social position of the respective group. Because of the great amount of their employment work and their unpaid household production, the adults (younger than 65 years) are delivering much more time than they are receiving. Apart from their personal time of 250 billion hours, they are spending 118 billion hours for work others are also benefitting from. On the other hand, they are only receiving 80 billion hours from others. Thus, they have a net spending of 38 billion hours.

In our highly aggregated example, the other two age groups are the beneficiaries. Young people are only spending less than 4 billion hours for others but are receiving nearly 25 billion hours: They have a "deficit" of about 21 billion hours. This amount represents the investment of the society in the young generation.

In the case of aged persons, their "time account" has also a negative balancing item (8 billion hours). Apart from their private time (66 billion hours), the time of their own social work amounts to 19 billion hours which especially contains hours of household work. On the other hand, they are receiving 27 billion hours which also contain the hours necessary for producing goods and services consumed by aged persons.

The society is not only investing in the young generation but also in extended production facilities. In our example, net capital formation has a positive amount (7 billion hours). This amount is balanced in row 13 of *table 5* by the corresponding negative item.

In the case of Germany, the foreign trade with products shows a surplus of exports in comparison with the imports (exports: 22 billion hours, imports: 19 billion hours). This surplus (3 billion hours) is balanced by the corresponding negative item in row 13 of *table 5* which is lastly delivered by the age group actively involved in economic production (18 to 65 years old).

SAMIO in monetary units

The SAMIO in time units also delivers the basic scheme for the SAMIO in monetary units. For socio-economic analysis, it seems to be preferable to apply specific concepts which do not automatically accept the dominance of economic monetary thinking. The time use data of the population could be used as a suitable starting point.

Starting point of the monetary SAMIO which is presented in *table 6* are the figures for net value added (including the value of household work) which are distributed among the three age groups of population according to their participation in the different production activities (row 14, columns 1 to 3). Differing from the SAMIO in time units, these values could only be determined by firstly estimating the uses of the monetary values (rows 1 to 3 in *table 6*).

The time used for personal activities (rows 1 to 3, columns 1 to 3) does not get a monetary value. The values of household work (rows 1 to 3, columns 4 and 5) are easily compiled by multiplying the figures of time use by a suitable wage rate. In the German case, the wage rate of a domestic servant (the so-called generalist) has been used. Of course, other types of valuation (e.g. the wage rates of specialists) could easily be introduced.

Similar to the procedure in the case of time units, the monetary values of the different final uses associated with the socio-economic groups as employed persons (rows 1 to 3, columns 6 to 12 of *table 6*) are estimated by linking net value added and final uses within an input-output model:

$$(11) \quad M_{dom}^P = NVA_{SAM}\, B_{dom}\, Y_{dom} \qquad \text{with}$$

$$(12) \quad NVA_{SAM} = \begin{pmatrix} nva_1 \\ \vdots \\ nva_n \end{pmatrix} \qquad i = 1,\ldots n$$

nva_i row coefficient vector of net value added produced by the employed persons of socio-economic group i related to the monetary gross output by branch (with zeros in the case of the branches of private activities)

Table 6. Social accounting matrix in monetary units based on input-output analysis (SAMIO - M) 1990
Billions Deutsche Marks

Uses \ Supply (Row No.)	Personal activities			Household production		Final consumption		Employment			Net fixed capital formation	Exports of products	Total uses
	Young persons	Adults (except aged persons)	Aged persons	Services within households	Services between households	Private consumption	Services of NPISH[1]	Education services	Health services	Other government services			
	(1)	(2)	(3)	(4)	(5)	(6)	(7)	(8)	(9)	(10)	(11)	(12)	(13)
1 Young persons (until 17 years old)	0			25.4	1.3	28.1				2.9		3.5	61.2
2 Adults (excl. aged persons) (18 to 64 years old)		0		598.8	46.0	846.9	17.1	97.8	117.6	195.2	164.5	556.3	2 640.2
3 Aged persons (65 years and older)			0	170.7	10.9	37.2			3.9	2.8			225.5
4 Unpaid services within households	158.8	465.4	170.7										794.9
5 Unpaid services between households	14.5	23.8	19.9										58.2
6 Private consumption	108.5	666.0	137.7										912.2
7 Services of NPISH[1]	3.1	11.4	2.6										17.1
8 Education services	61.8	35.0	1.0										97.8
9 Health services	11.8	67.5	42.2										121.5
10 Other government services	36.7	133.4	30.8										200.9
11 Net fixed capital formation													0.0
12 Imports of products	49.2	270.8	58.3								67.1	203.6	649.0
13 Balances	- 383.2	966.9	- 237.7								- 231.6	- 114.4	0.0
14 Total Supply	**61.2**	**2 640.2**	**225.5**	**794.9**	**58.2**	**912.2**	**17.1**	**97.8**	**121.5**	**200.9**	**0.0**	**649.0**	

Memorandum item:
Population (1 000 persons)   11 551   42 006   9 693   63 250

[1] Non-profit institutions serving households.

In our example, the contribution of the employed persons of the different socio-economic groups to the production of the branch where they are employed is estimated using the ratios of distribution of the labour hours of the employed persons. Of course, other quota could also be applied.

In the rows 4 and 5 of *table 6* the valued hours of household production are distributed among the age groups benefitting from these services. Because of the unique type of monetarization (only "generalists"), the quota of the age groups are very similar to those of *table 5*.

In the rows 6 to 10 of *table 6*, the net value added associated with the final uses is distributed among the beneficiaries of these products. The compilation method corresponds with the procedure already described in equation (4):

$$(13) \quad m^u_{dom} = nva \; B_{dom} \; Y_{SAM} \quad \text{with}$$

$$(14) \quad nva = \sum_{i=1}^{n} nva_i$$

The monetary values of imported products are linked with the final consumption of the age groups of population, with net capital formation and with exports in row 12 of *table 6*. In this case, it is not necessary to take into account the production facilities abroad. The imported values are directly associated with the final uses by the following equation (15):

$$(15) \quad m^u_{imp} = (1...1) \, (A_{imp} \; B_{dom} \; Y_{SAM} + Y_{imp})$$

The total monetary values received by the different socio-economic groups (rows 1 to 12, columns 1 to 3 of *table 6*) could be interpreted as a monetary contribution to their welfare functions. The young persons receive 444 billion Deutsche Mark (38 480 DM per head), the adults (except seniors) 1 673 billion Deutsche Mark (39 830 DM per head) and the aged persons 464 billion Deutsche Mark (47 790 DM per head). In the case of young people, the high costs of education within and outside the households are strongly influencing the result. In the case of aged persons, the high amount of care within the households and the high health expenditures are determining the level of total costs.

The balancing items shown in row 13 of *table 6* could be interpreted in the same way as already done in the case of time units. The adults (with age from 18 to 65 years) deliver values of 967 billion Deutsche Mark to the other two age groups (383 and 238 billion Deutsche Mark respectively), to future economic activities (net investment: 232 billion Deutsche Mark) and to other countries (export surplus: 114 billion Deutsche Mark).

The description of the compilation methods may have revealed already the close linkages between the SAMIOs in time and monetary units. Apart from the time used for personal activities (rows 1 to 3, columns 1 to 3), monetary and time data could also be interpreted simultaneously: The time data represent the direct and indirect time inputs to produce the monetary values. On the other side, the monetary data can be interpreted as the values given to the time received or spent by the different groups of population.

SAMIO in physical units

Comprehensive studies on possibilities to achieve paths of sustainable development imply an integrated social, economic and environmental analysis. Very similar to the concepts applied in SESAME, data on natural resources and residuals could be linked with the social and economic information given in SAMIO.

These linkages are based on the complete material balances which have already been described (see *table 4*) and the consistent presentation of physical flows in physical input-output tables presented in the context of the "magic triangle".[24] Differing from the approach chosen in these tables, only specific physical flows which belong either to the primary inputs or to the final uses, are chosen for further analysis. These physical flows comprise natural resources which are used as intermediate inputs of economic activities and residuals which are leaving the economic circuit and are stored in controlled landfills (e.g. waste) or disposed again into the nature (e.g. air emissions or treated waste water). In *table 4*, these physical flows have already been indicated.

Apart from the mentioned flows of natural resources and residuals, specific physical product inputs and outputs could be taken into account: Imported intermediate inputs are part of the primary inputs, investment goods and exports of goods are part of the final uses in physical accounting. Nevertheless, these physical flows were excluded because they are represented in the SAMIO by the natural resources directly or indirectly necessary to produce them. This treatment does not exclude a supplementary analysis of these flows in the context of balancing transboundary flows or accounting the changes of physical assets. For such studies, the figures of *table 4* deliver a suitable data base.

The physical flows are associated with the activities of the different age groups of population in the **tables 7a and 7b**. *Table 7a* shows the use of natural resources, *table 7b* the mentioned residuals flows.

---

24. See Stahmer 2000, pp. 145 - 147.

Table 7. Social accounting matrix in physical units based on input-outut analysis (SAMIO - P) 1990
a) Natural resource inputs - Million tons

Row No.	Uses / Supply	Personal activities			Household production		Final consumption					Net fixed capital formation	Exports of products	Total uses
		Young persons	Adults (except aged persons)	Aged persons	Services within households	Services between households	Private consumption	Services of NPISH[1]	Education services	Health services	Other government services			
		(1)	(2)	(3)	(4)	(5)	(6)	(7)	(8)	(9)	(10)	(11)	(12)	(13)
1	Young persons (until 17 years old)	17			3	0	137				7		12	176
2	Adults (excl. aged persons) (18 to 64 years old)		143		66	6	4 119	37	175	240	496	535	1 930	7 747
3	Aged persons (65 years and older)			26	20	0	181			8	7			242
4	Unpaid services within households	18	57	14										89
5	Unpaid services between households	1	2	3										6
6	Private consumption	537	3 222	678										4 437
7	Services of NPISH[1]	7	24	6										37
8	Education services	108	64	3										175
9	Health services	24	138	86										248
10	Other government services	93	339	78										510
11	Net fixed capital formation													
12	Imports of products	264	1 464	314								280	1 033	3 355
13	Balances	- 893	2 294	- 966								- 815	380	0
14	**Total Supply**	**176**	**7 747**	**242**	**89**	**6**	**4 437**	**37**	**175**	**248**	**510**	**0**	**3 344**	

63 250

Memorandum item:
Population (1 000 persons)   11 551   42 006   9 693

[1] Non-profit institutions serving households.

Table 7a. **Social accounting matrix in physical units based on input-outut analysis (SAMIO - P) 1990**
b) Residual outputs - Million tons

Row No.	Uses / Supply	Personal activities			Household production		Final consumption / Employment					Net fixed capital formation	Exports of products	Total uses
		Young persons (1)	Adults (except aged persons) (2)	Aged persons (3)	Services within households (4)	Services between households (5)	Private consumption (6)	Services of NPISH[1] (7)	Education services (8)	Health services (9)	Other government services (10)	(11)	(12)	(13)
1	Young persons (until 17 years old)	48			38	1	140				6		9	242
2	Adults (excl. aged persons) (18 to 64 years old)		390		124	3	4 226	18	159	155	391	267	1 463	7 196
3	Aged persons (65 years and older)			76	28	7	186			5	6			308
4	Unpaid services within households	38	124	28										190
5	Unpaid services between households	1	3	7										11
6	Private consumption	554	3 303	695										4 552
7	Services of NPISH[1]	3	12	3										18
8	Education services	99	58	2										159
9	Health services	15	89	56										160
10	Other government services	73	268	62										403
11	Net fixed capital formation													
12	Imports of products	184	1 020	222								198	771	2 395
13	Balances	- 773	1 929	- 843								- 465	152	0
14	**Total Supply**	242	7 196	308	190	11	4 552	18	159	160	403	0	2 395	

Memorandum item:
Population (1 000 persons)   11 551   42 006   9 693   63 250

[1] Non-profit institutions serving households.

The input-output models used for estimating these linkages correspond with the models already described in section 3.2 (SAMIO in time units). For calculating the physical flows connected with the groups of population as producers, the following equation can be used:

$$(16) \quad P_{dom}^p = \begin{pmatrix} NR_{SAM} \\ RS_{SAM} \end{pmatrix} B_{dom} \ Y_{dom}$$

with

$$(17) \quad NR_{SAM} = \begin{pmatrix} NR_1 \\ \vdots \\ \dot{NR}_n \end{pmatrix} \quad i = 1,...,n$$

and

$$(18) \quad RS_{SAM} = \begin{pmatrix} RS_1 \\ \vdots \\ \dot{RS}_n \end{pmatrix} \quad i = 1,...,n$$

> NR_i coefficient matrix of physical inputs of domestic natural resources used by the socio economic group i related to (monetary) gross output by type of natural resources and branch
>
> RS_i coefficient matrix of residuals produced by the socio-economic group i related to (monetary) gross output by type of residuals and branch

Differing from the distribution of time units among the different socio-economic groups, complete matrices of natural resource inputs and residual outputs have to be estimated for each socio-economic group. In our numerical example, the calculation of the distribution of the physical flows among the socio-economic groups as producers is based on very simple assumptions (e.g. quota of labour hours by branch). In the case of private activities, two types of environmental impacts have to be distinguished: Impacts of producing the intermediate inputs of private activities and impacts of the production processes of the private activities themselves. In the first case, households arc only ind bvirectly responsible for, in the second case they are immediately producing residuals and using natural resources. In *table 7a/b*, the direct environmental impacts are shown in the rows 1 to 3 of the columns 1 to 5, the indirect impacts which are connected with employment work, are recorded in the rows 1 to 3 of column 6. For achieving this breakdown, submatrices of NR_{SAM} and RS_{SAM} were used which only contain data on the activities which are intended to be shown separately.

A similar procedure was necessary in the case of identifying the environmental impacts of the socio-economic groups as users. The basic equation has been

$$(19) \quad M_{dom}^U = \begin{pmatrix} NR \\ RS \end{pmatrix} B_{dom} \ Y_{SAM}$$

with

$$(20) \quad NR = \sum_{i-1}^{n} NR_i \quad \text{and}$$

$$(21) \quad RS = \sum_{i-1}^{n} RS_i$$

For separating the direct from the indirect environmental impacts of private activities, submatrices of NR and RS were necessary. The rows 1 to 5 of columns 1 to 3 of *table 7a/b* show the direct impacts connected with private activities, row 6 of columns 1 to 3 the indirect impacts of private consumption. The rows 7 to 10 of columns 1 to 3 show the environmental impacts of the other final consumption distributed among the age groups of the population as users.

The SAMIO in physical units not only describes the domestic physical flows but also the use of natural resources and the production of residuals abroad which is connected with the production of imported goods and services. In studies of the Wuppertal Institute, these flows are indicated as "rucksacks" of the domestic production. Detailed analysis is necessary for estimating these rucksacks in a suitable manner. For simplifying the compilation procedure, the presented example is based on the assumption that the production processes in the own country and abroad are identical. Following this simple approach, equation (22) could be applied:

$$(22) \quad M_{imp}^{U} = \begin{pmatrix} NR \\ RS \end{pmatrix} B \, A_{imp} \, B_{dom} \, Y_{SAM}$$

$$+ \begin{pmatrix} NR \\ RS \end{pmatrix} B \, Y_{imp}$$

The results of this calculation of the uses of natural resources are shown in row 12 of *table 7a*. The data on the production of residuals linked with the socio-economic groups, the net investment and the exports are presented in row 12 of *table 7b*.

In the **tables 8a** and **b**, the information on natural resources and residuals is shown in a breakdown by different types of materials using a simplified version of the *tables 7a* and *7b*. Such differentiation is especially necessary to separate the huge amounts of water raised and waste water from the other flows. Furthermore, detailed information on specific natural resources and emissions is necessary for further analysis of environmental themes as it is proposed in the NAMEA framework mentioned.

The flows of natural resources and residuals are recorded as flows between the domestic economy and the natural environment of the own country and of the rest of the world. The totals of the rows 9 and 11 of the columns 1 to 3 in *table 8a* correspond with the totals of the rows 1 to 10 and 12 respectively of the columns 1 to 3 in *table 7a*. In the same way, the totals of the rows 10 and 12 of the columns 1 to 3 in *table 8b* could be found as totals of the rows 1 to 10 and 12 respectively of the columns 1 to 3 in *table 7b*.

The balances of natural resources and residuals are shown in row 13 of the *tables 7a* and *table 7b* respectively. In the case of physical flows, the imports play a more important role than the exports. Thus, the balance of exports and imports shows a surplus of foreign natural resources (380 million tons) and of foreign residuals (152 million tons).

Outlook

The concepts of SAMIO presented could only provide a starting point for further discussions. One field of research could be the integration of such data with econometric and general equilibrium models.[25] Furthermore, it could be analysed to which extent such tables could be applied for welfare analysis.

Nevertheless, future work has to focus on an improvement of the data base available. The implementation of the SESAME concepts in an increasing number of countries is an important and encouraging step towards this aim. A closer cooperation of the "input-output people" with the statisticians calculating SAM modules will be a further precondition for future progress.

---

25.   See Frohn 2001 and 2002.

Table 8: Social accounting matrix in physical units based on input-outut analysis (SAMIO - P) 1990
a) Natural resource inputs by type of resource - Million tones

Row No.	Supply / Uses	Personal activities			Household production		Final consumption	Employment		Domestic environment		Exports of		Total uses
		Young persons (1)	Adults (except aged persons) (2)	Aged persons (3)	Services within households (4)	Services between households (5)	(6)	Net fixed capital formation (7)	Exports of products (8)	Natural resources (9)	Residuals (10)	Natural resources (11)	Residuals (12)	(13)
1	Young persons									176				176
2	Adults (excl. aged persons)									7 747				7 747
3	Aged persons									242				242
4	Services within households													
5	Services between househ.													
6	Final consumption													
7	Net fixed cpaital formation													
8	Exports of products													
9	Domestic natural resources	805	3 989	894				535				1 942		8 165
	Energy carriers	15	73	16				3				87		194
	Other solid materials	43	195	44				214				176		672
	Water raised	641	3 170	714				272				1 380		6 177
	Oxygen	77	396	86				37				212		808
	Carbon dioxide	29	154	34				9				86		312
	Other air components	0	1	0				0				1		2
10	Domestic residuals													
11	Foreign natural resources	264	1 464	314				280				1 033		3 355
	Energy carriers	27	145	30				20				102		324
	Other solid materials	20	102	22				50				135		329
	Water raised	163	922	199				172				632		2 088
	Oxygen	24	130	28				29				109		320
	Carbon dioxide	30	164	35				9				54		292
	Other air components	0	1	0				0				1		2
12	Foreign residuals													
13	Balances	- 893	2 294	- 966				- 815				380		0
14	Total supply	176	7 747	242				0		8 165		3 355		0

Table 8: **Social accounting matrix in physical units based on input-outut analysis (SAMIO - P) 1990**
b) Residual outputs by typ of residuals - Million tones

Row No.	Supply \ Uses	Personal activities			Household production		Employment			Domestic environment		Exports of		Total uses
		Young persons	Adults (except aged persons)	Aged persons	Services within households	Services between households	Final consumption	Net fixed capital formation	Exports of products	Natural resources	Residuals	Natural resources	Residuals	Total uses
		(1)	(2)	(3)	(4)	(5)	(6)	(7)	(8)	(9)	(10)	(11)	(12)	(13)
1	Young persons										242			242
2	Adults (excl. aged persons)										7 196			7 196
3	Aged persons										308			308
4	Services within households													
5	Services between househ.													
6	Final consumption													
7	Net fixed cpaital formation													
8	Exports of products													
9	Domestic natural resources													
10	Domestic residuals	831	4 247	929				267					1 472	7 746
	Waste	46	243	53				48					152	542
	Waste water	523	2 677	583				115					702	4 600
	Water vaporized	164	821	184				59					338	1 566
	Oxygen	21	112	24				6					62	225
	Carbon dioxide	74	378	82				37					208	779
	Other air emissions	3	16	3				2					10	34
11	Foreign natural resources													
12	Foreign residuals	184	1 020	222				198					771	2 395
	Waste	33	183	40				20					90	366
	Waste water	69	388	85				90					345	977
	Water vaporized	37	201	44				51					187	520
	Oxygen	21	119	26				7					40	213
	Carbon dioxide	23	123	26				29					104	305
	Other air emissions	1	6	1				1					5	14
13	Balances	- 773	1 929	- 843				- 465					152	0
14	**Total supply**	**242**	**7 196**	**308**							**7 746**		**2 395**	

References

Becker, Gary S. (1964): *Human Capital*, Columbia University Press: New York, London

Becker, Gary S. (1965): A Theory of the Allocation of Time, in *Economic Journal*, Vol. 75, pp. 493 – 517

Commission of the European Communities - Eurostat, International Monetary Fund, Organisation for Economic Co-operation and Development, United Nations, World Bank (1993): *System of National Accounts 1993*, Brussels/Luxemburg/ New York/Paris/Washington, D.C.

Eurostat (1995): European System of Accounts - ESA 1995, Luxembourg

Eurostat (2002): Draft Handbook on Social Accounting Matrices and Labour Accounts, preliminary version presented at the Voorburg Seminar, 17 - 18 June, Luxemburg

Ewerhart, Georg (2001): *Humankapital in Deutschland - Bildungsinvestitionen, Bildungsvermögen und Abschreibungen auf Bildung*, Beiträge zur Arbeitsmarkt- und Berufsforschung, No. 247, Bundesanstalt für Arbeit: Nürnberg

Frohn, Joachim (2001): Ökonometrische Modelle zur Analyse von Umweltstrategien, in Susanne Hartard, Carsten Stahmer (eds.), *Bewertung von Nachhaltigkeitsstrategien*, Metropolis: Marburg, pp. 139 – 158

Frohn, Joachim (2002): Zur Erweiterung von ökonometrischen Umweltmodellen um soziale Komponenten, in Susanne Hartard, Carsten Stahmer (eds.), *Magische Dreiecke - Berichte für eine nachhaltige Gesellschaft*, Band 3: *Sozio-ökonomische Berichtssysteme*, Metropolis: Marburg

Horz, Kurt, Utz-Peter Reich (1982): Dividing Government Product between Intermediate and Final Uses, in *Review of Income and Wealth*, Series 28, No. 3, pp. 325 – 343

Hill, Peter (1995): Richard Stone's Contribution to National Accounting, in Annali di Statistica, Series X, vol. 6: *Social Statistics, National Accounts and Economic Analysis*, International Conference in Memory of Sir Richard Stone, Certosa di Pontignano, Siena, October 1993, pp. 23 – 30

Kazemier, Brugt and Jeanet Exel (1992): *The Allocation of Time in the Netherlands in the Context of the SNA; A Module*, Netherlands Central Bureau of Statistics, National accounts, occasional paper, NA-052

Keuning, Steven J. (1991): Proposal for a Social Accounting Matrix which fits into the Next System of National Accounts, in *Economic Systems Research*, Volume 3, Number 3, pp. 233 – 248

Keuning, Steven J. (2000): Accounting for Welfare with SESAME, in: United Nations, Handbook of National Accounting, Household Accounting: Experience in Concepts and Compilation, Volume 2: Household Satellite Extensions, Studies in Methods, Series F, No. 75, New York, pp. 273 – 307

Keuning, Steven J. and Willem A. de Ruijter (1988): Guidelines to the Construction of a Social Accounting Matrix, in *Review of Income and Wealth*, Series 34, Number 1, March, pp. 71 – 100

Lancaster, Kelvin (1966): A New Approach to Consumer Theory, in *Journal of Political Economy*, Vol. 74, pp. 132 – 157

Lützel, Heinrich (1989): Household Production and National Accounts, in *Statistical Journal of the United Nations ECE*, Vol. 6, No. 4, pp. 337 – 348

Pyatt, Graham (1985): Commodity Balances and National Accounts - A SAM Perspective, in *Review of Income and Wealth*, Series 31, No. 2, pp. 155 – 169

Pyatt, Graham (1990): Accounting for Time Use, in *Review of Income and Wealth*, Series 36, No. 1, pp. 33 – 52

Pyatt, Graham (1991a): Fundamentals of Social Accounting, in *Economic Systems Research*, Volume 3, Number 3, pp. 315 – 341

Pyatt, Graham (1991b): SAMs, the SNA and National Accounting Capabilities, in *Review of Income and Wealth*, Series 37, No. 2, June, pp. 177 – 198

Pyatt, Graham (1999): Some Relationships between T-Accounts, Input-Output Tables and Social Accounting Matrices, in *Economic Systems Research*, Vol. 11, Number 4, December, pp. 365 – 389

Pyatt, Graham, Alan R. Roe and associates (1977): *Social Accounting Matrices for Development Planning: With Special Reference to Sri Lanka*, Cambridge University Press: Cambridge

Pyatt, Graham and Jeffery I. Round (eds.) (1985): *Social Accounting Matrices, A Basis for Planning*, A World Bank Symposium, Washington, D.C.

Reich, Utz-Peter (1986): Treatment of Government Activity on the Production Account, in *Review of Income and Wealth*, Series 32, No. 1, pp. 69 – 85

Reich, Utz-Peter, Philipp Sonntag and Hans-Werner Holub (1977): Arbeit - Konsum - Rechnung, Axiomatische Kritik und Erweiterung der Volkswirtschaftlichen Gesamtrechnung, Bund: Köln

Schäfer, Dieter and Norbert Schwarz (1995): *The Value of Household Production in the Federal Republic of Germany 1992*, 30 pages, unpublished paper

Scherhorn, Gerhard (2002): Zur Messung des Wohlstands, in Susanne Hartard, Carsten Stahmer (eds.), *Magische Dreiecke - Berichte für eine nachhaltige Gesellschaft*, Band 3: *Sozio-ökonomische Berichtssysteme*, Metropolis: Marburg

Stahmer, Carsten (2000): The Magic Triangle of Input-Output Tables, in: Sandrine Simon and John Proops (eds.), *Greening the Accounts*, Edward Elgar: Cheltenham, UK, Northampton, MA, USA, pp. 123 - 154

Stahmer, Carsten (2002): Das Unbekannte Meisterwerk – Sir Richard Stone und sein System of Social and Demographic Statistics, in Susanne Hartard, Carsten Stahmer (eds.), *Magische Dreiecke - Berichte für eine nachhaltige Gesellschaft*, Band 3: *Sozio-ökonomische Berichtssysteme*, Metropolis: Marburg

Stahmer, Carsten, Georg Ewerhart, Inge Herrchen (2002): Monetäre, Physische und Zeit-Input-Output-Tabellen 1990, Metzler-Poeschel: Stuttgart

Stone, Richard (1949): Social Accounting, Aggregation and Invariance, in *Cahiers du Congrès International de Comptabilité, 1948*, French translation: Economie Appliquée, vol. II, No. 1, pp. 26 – 54

Stone, Richard (1951-52): Simple Transaction Models, Information and Computing, paper presented at a conference on Automatic Control, Cranfield, 1951, in *The Review of Economic Studies*, Vol. XIX, No. 2, pp. 67 – 84

Stone, Richard (1955a): Model-Building and the Social Accounts: A Survey, in International Association for Research in Income and Wealth (ed.), *Income and Wealth*, Series IV, Bowes and Bowes: Cambridge

Stone, Richard (1955b): Input-Output and the Social Accounts, in University of Pisa (ed.), *The Structural Interdependence of the Economy, Proceedings of an International Conference on Input-Output Analysis*, Varenna, J. Wiley: New York, Giuffre: Milan, pp. 155 – 172

Stone, Richard (1961): *Input-Output and National Accounts*, OEEC, Paris

Stone, Richard (1962a): Multiple Classifications in Social Accounting, in *Bulletin of the International Statistical Institute*, Volume XXXIX, No. 3, pp. 215 - 233, reprint: University of Cambridge, Department of Applied Economics, Reprint Series, No. 220, 1964

Stone, Richard (1962b): A Social Accounting Matrix for 1960 (with Alan Brown and others), in *A Programme for Growth*, No. 2, Chapman and Hall: London

Stone, Richard (1979): *Where are we now? A Short Account of the Development of Input-Output Studies and their Present Trends*, paper presented at the 7th International Conference on Input-Output Techniques, Innsbruck, April

Stone, Richard (1981a): *Aspects of Economic and Social Modelling*, Librairie Droz: Genève

Stone, Richard (1981b): *Input-Output-Analysis and Economic Planning: A Survey*, presented June 1978, in *Mathematical Programming and its Applications*, Angeli: Milan

Stone, Richard (1985): The disaggregation of the Household Sector in the National Accounts, in Graham Pyatt and Jeffery I. Round (eds.), *Social Accounting Matrices, A Basis for Planning*, The World Bank, Washington, D.C., pp. 145 - 185

Stone, Richard and Giovanna Croft-Murray (1959): *Social Accounting and Economic Models*, Bowes and Bowes: London

Strassert, Günther, Carsten Stahmer (2002): Sachkapital und Physische Input-Output-Rechnung, in Susanne Hartard, Carsten Stahmer (eds.), *Magische Dreiecke - Berichte für eine nachhaltige Gesellschaft*, Band 3: *Sozio-ökonomische Berichtssysteme*, Metropolis: Marburg

Timmerman, Jolanda and Peter van de Ven (2000): The SAM and SESAME in the Netherlands. A Modular Approach, in: United Nations, Handbook of National Accounting. Experience in Concepts and Compilation, Volume 2: Household Satellite Extensions, Studies in Methods, Series F, No. 75, New York, pp. 309 - 354

United Nations (1968): *A System of National Accounts*, Studies in Methods, Series F, No. 2, Rev. 3, New York

On SAMs According to ESA95

H.N. Kal

Statistics Netherlands

Introduction

The increasing integration of economic and social policies in Europe, and across the world, requires increased integration of economic and social statistics. The Handbook on Social Accounting Matrices and Labour Accounts has been written to help the Statistics Offices of EU member states (and, indeed, any other country) to meet this requirement.

It is generally acknowledged that human capital is in Europe the most critical factor for the generation of social welfare. Yet, traditional National Accounts do not distinguish between low-skilled and high-skilled labour, or any other type of labour. This serious shortcoming is remedied in Social Accounting Matrices (SAMs), which also have various other features that augment to their usefulness. SAMs use the very powerful (matrix) framework of national accounts, by integrating into a single (matrix) format supply and use tables or an input-output table and institutional sector accounts. In general, social statistics lack a framework that ensures consistency across a range of statistics from different sources. SAMs provide this, ensuring consistency not just between social statistics in the matrix, but also between these social statistics and national accounts. The focus on households and employment categories means a greater emphasis on the role of people in the economy.

The Handbook on Social Accounting Matrices and Labour Accounts concentrates on labour statistics and their links with national accounts. This can be seen as one of the most important sets of relationships that concern policy makers today. Studying a labour-oriented SAM enables policy makers better to understand relationships between output, labour (and therefore productivity), households, income, and expenditure at very detailed levels.

The manual explains how SAMs can be derived from an expansion of national accounts matrices (NAMs), what data are needed, and what methodologies can be applied, for example, to ensure consistency and coherence in the system. It is a document designed for both users and producers. For users, it explains what SAMs can do to answer policy and research questions. For producers, it provides background to explain how SAMs can be compiled. It is written entirely in conformance with the world (SNA) and European (ESA) systems of accounts.

Background

Preparation and publication of the Handbook on Social Accounting Matrices and Labour Accounts is one of the responses to the 1999 ECOFIN Council document on the statistical requirements for the implementation of Stage 3 of Economic and Monetary Union (EMU). This saw "effective surveillance and co-operation of economic policies" as of "major importance". It requires "a comprehensive information system providing policy makers with the necessary data on which to base their decisions". ECOFIN commended the national accounts because they are "based on harmonised concepts", and they "provide both mutually consistent aggregate indicators and a detailed statistical information system". It emphasised the need to develop more comprehensive and comparable indicators and accounts for labour, and to ensure their consistency with national accounts. This is what Social Accounting Matrices (SAMs) do.

A SAM is basically a matrix that incorporates a combination of:

- the national accounts (showing, in addition, for all transactions who pays what to whom; cf. flow-of-funds matrices), and

- detailed labour accounts (both earnings, employment and average wage rate) by industry, by type of labour (male/female, skill level, etc.), and by household subsector.

Because of its matrix format, the SAM also elaborates the national accounts' information on income and expenditure distributions. For instance, a SAM presents expenditure patterns by product group and by household subsector, and commonly also breaks down investment, by sector of origin and industry of destination, and as well by industry of destination and by product group. The SAM is, however, a flexible format that can be adjusted to the policy priorities at hand, and to the basic statistics and other resources that are available. It is an analytical information system with which for example the interrelations between conventional EMU objectives (e.g. growth and government deficits) and labour market developments can be monitored and analysed.

The EU Statistical Programme Committee (SPC) approved the Leadership Group on Social Accounting Matrices (LEG SAM) during its 33rd session on 25 May 1999 (document CPS 99/33/14). The LEG SAM is a partnership in the framework of the European Statistical System, approved by the SPC.

The objectives of the LEG SAM were threefold:

1. Designing a methodology for the compilation of SAMs and a set of standard classifications to be used. These items will be described in a handbook on SAMs.

2. Exploring the possibilities for compiling SAMs in all (participating) European countries, using existing data sources. Although there are other subjects that can be described in detail in a SAM (e.g. income (re-)distribution and consumption patterns), this SAM will focus on labour market information;

3. Compiling a pilot-SAM for each of the participating countries for the year 1997 if possible. In addition, some information on the compilation of a "European SAM" or some comparative analysis of the pilot-SAMs and Labour accounts will be produced.

The SAM LEG started in October 1999. In addition to Eurostat, the statistical offices of the following countries participate in this LEG: Belgium, Finland, Greece, Italy, Netherlands, Norway, Portugal, and United Kingdom. From each country two representatives attend the meetings: one labour statistics expert and one expert on national accounts. The Netherlands had the co-ordinating responsibility of the SAM LEG.

Procedure

Meetings have taken place in Lisbon (20-10-1999), London (7/8-3-2000), Brussels (15/16-6-2000), Luxembourg (9/10-10-2000), Athens (26/27-3-2001), Helsinki (14/15-6-2001) and Rome (12/13-11-2001).

The Draft Handbook of Social Accounting Matrices and Labour Accounts has been presented and discussed during a Workshop in Voorburg at Statistics Netherlands on 17/18 June 2002. At this meeting 55 people representing 22 countries have actively participated in the discussions. After the Workshop, an additional LEG meeting has been organised to co-ordinate the work to be done with regard to the final version of the handbook. In November 2002, the Draft Handbook has been presented before the National Accounts Working Group.

A Network group has been founded of several non-participating institutions who have expressed an interest in the ongoing work (ECB, ILO, UN, IMF, OECD, universities and NSI's). In total 64 persons have received the draft versions of the chapters of the handbook. Valuable comments have been received and incorporated in the text.

The final report of the LEG SAM consists of a manual on the compilation of SAMs and labour accounts and pilot matrices for seven participating countries. The final report was presented to the SPC by Statistics Netherlands during the 50th SPC in September 2003.The SPC expressed the following opinions:

• The SPC welcomed the work done by the LEG SAM and congratulated Statistics Netherlands for leading this group.

• Some delegates requested a position of Eurostat concerning the Community funding to be allocated for the development of this project. Eurostat confirmed that a commitment on this issue cannot be taken at present, given the increasing demand in social statistics. If some countries decide to develop SAMs, Eurostat is ready to act as a focal point.

The Handbook on SAMs and Labour Accounts is published as Eurostat Working Paper 3/2003/E/N 23 and is available on request at the Eurostat secretariat - Unit E3, Bech Building D2/727 – 5, rue Alphonse Weicker – L – 2721 Luxembourg, tel: (352) 4301-33293, fax: (352) 4301-35399, e-mail: Renata.Passarella@cec.eu.int.

The electronic version of the handbook is available at the web-site of the Employment Statistics Experts Working Group:
http://forum.europe.eu.int/Members/irc/dsis/employ/home.

Handbook on SAMs and Labour Accounts

A Social Accounting Matrix (SAM) elaborates the interrelationship between economic and social statistics by linking together the (mainly) macro-statistics of national accounts with the (mainly) micro- statistics of the labour market and of households. Both ESA95 (8.134) and SNA93 (20.4) in their definitions of SAMs, emphasise the linkages between supply and use tables and sector accounts, and their focus on the role of people in the economy. As examples, the two international guidelines refer to "extra breakdowns of households and disaggregated representations of labour markets". With these links and extra breakdowns, it is possible for the analyst to investigate economic and social policy issues within an integrated framework.

The aim of the handbook is to provide member states of the European Union and, indeed, other countries, with sufficient information to enable them to understand what SAMs are, how they can be compiled, and how they can be used. The handbook takes ESA95 as its starting point, and is entirely consistent with it and with SNA93. Parts of the manual are extracts from ESA95 and SNA93.

Although this handbook is a general guidance on SAMs, it concentrates on a labour-oriented SAM, *i.e.* its main purpose is to describe a SAM that provides detailed information on the met demand for and used supply of labour in monetary terms.

The introductory chapter sets the scene by outlining the general principles and characteristics of accounting. It gives a brief overview of the different statistical systems (accounts, national accounts, and labour accounting systems) that need to be brought together in order to construct a SAM. The structure is as follows: it begins with a definition of SAMs, briefly describes their use, and the purpose of the handbook; a road map describes the content of each chapter of the handbook, and provides the reader with alternative routes through the handbook according to their interests and expertise; general principles of accounting – illustrates the advantages arising from constructing economic accounting systems by outlining some important principles and characteristics; overview of national accounts – provides a very brief introduction to the system of national accounts; overview of labour accounts – provides a brief introduction to labour accounts, and the Labour accounting System of the International Labour Organisation (ILO), which provide a framework for integrated labour market statistics; and classifications – describes the units and the classification of units that are used within the individual accounts to show who paid what to whom.

National Accounts Matrices - NAMs

Next is described how national accounts can be expressed in matrix format. The advantages and limitations of this alternative presentation are assessed. Then the aggregate National Accounts Matrix (NAM) is introduced followed by the eleven individual accounts that together make up the NAM. After explaining how NAMs can be used to show the circular flow of income the detailed NAM is presented with descriptions of the detailed component accounts (the level of detail of this NAM gives the basic framework for SAMs). Some methods for compiling a number of specific cells in these accounts are outlined.

The way to produce the different sub-matrices is explained and demonstrated all over the handbook, with the help of detailed examples. These numerical examples are based on figures in the ESA95 manual. Examples on the methods used to breakdown the NAM figures are also given.

Elaboration of a Social Accounting Matrix - SAM

A SAM is built within the detailed NAM framework, with each control total of the national accounts matrix being expanded into a sub-matrix whose rows and columns use more detailed breakdowns of transactors and transactions. The expansions provide a coherent set of sub-matrices. The expansions focus on the role of people in the economy. For example, the household sector may be broken down into categories of households to show a detailed presentation of the labour market. Alternatively, households may be grouped by size or according to the education attainment of the head of the household. It is possible to apply several different classifications to the same group of transactors. For example, households may be grouped by income class in the allocation of primary income account, and by main source of income in the use of income account. The choice of the classification depends on the analytical purposes of the proposed SAM.

One of the main purposes of the SAM presented in the manual is to provide detailed information on the (met) *demand and supply of labour* in monetary terms, where this labour is employed in the production system. This is called a labour-oriented SAM.

The *demand for labour* is linked to the value added sub-matrix, and to the sub-matrix showing the compensation of employees paid by the rest of the world. The transition to the detailed NAM transforms the value added cell of the aggregate NAM into a sub-matrix where columns correspond to industries and rows to components of value added. The labour-oriented SAM focuses on the value added categories that remunerate labour, *i.e.* on compensation of employees and on mixed income. Compensation of employees is broken down according to demographic, social or economic characteristics of employees. Mixed income may be analysed by characteristics of the self-employed. The expansion of these sub-matrices shows the amount of money paid by industries to the categories of labour used (*demanded*) in the production process.

The *supply of labour* in monetary terms is shown by the generated income sub-matrix and by the sub-matrix that records the compensation of employees paid to non-resident workers. The SAM requires an expansion of compensation of employees by both the characteristics of employees, and by the group of households to which the workers belong. The sub-matrices generated by these disaggregations show the amount of money received by each household group for having *supplied* different kinds of labour in the production process.

The detailed NAM serves as a conceptual reference matrix, and, at the same time, provides numerical constraints. The following figure synthesises the transition from the NAM sub-matrices to the detailed tables of the SAM where the demand and supply of labour in monetary terms are described. The key element is the introduction of social and demographic characteristics into the NAM sub-matrices.

The division of households into sub-groups affects all the sub-matrices of the detailed NAM where households are included as a sector. Particularly relevant are the sub-matrices that describe the allocation of primary income, the secondary distribution of income, and the derived balancing items. The sub-matrices generated by the division of households into sub-groups are described in detail. The distribution of property income and the secondary distribution process are brought into focus.

An important part of the SAM, especially when it comes to analysing welfare issues, is final consumption expenditure for different household types. The final consumption expenditure sub-matrix of the SAM analyses national consumption not only by groups of products but also by groups of households.

Theoretical concepts with numerical examples based on figures in the ESA95 manual are supported in the handbook. Examples on the methods used to breakdown the NAM figures are also given. In most countries, data are not always available for a full breakdown of the flows from and to the rest of the world, especially when the flows are negligible. This is particularly evident for the secondary distribution of income flows. The elaboration of SAMs requires a considerable use of concepts and definitions of labour.

Transition from the NAM sub-matrices to the SAM tables

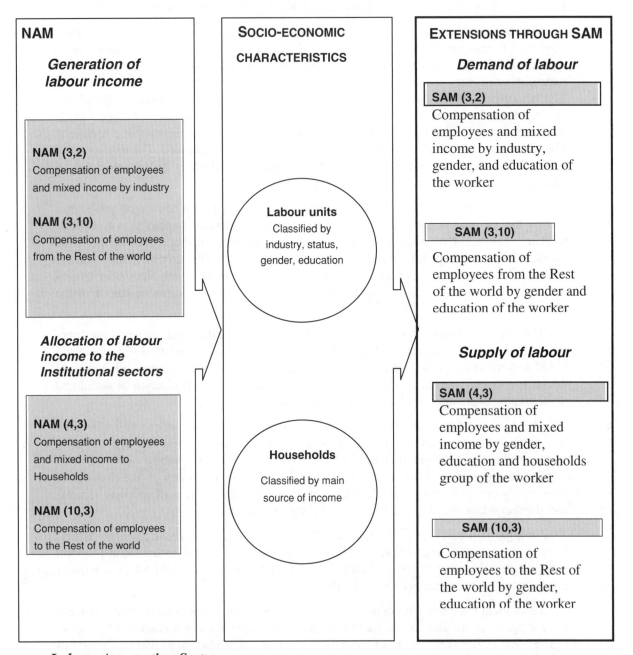

Labour Accounting System

Economic and social statistics meet in the area of labour statistics. Expanding sub-matrices in the NAM with socio-economic variables introduces variables and characteristics which, for most countries, have to be gathered from a variety of sources. The handbook focuses (in a separate chapter) on the labour market. It describes the possibilities and advantages of integrating labour market statistics in a labour accounting system (LAS), and in a socio-demographic oriented NAM - the SAM. SAMs and labour accounts partly overlap. This is where supply of and demand for labour meet. The monetary part of the overlap has been described in the chapter that deals with the elaboration of a SAM, and the non-monetary (or labour volume) part is described in the chapter about the LAS.

Most developed countries have been collecting labour market data since the beginning of the 20th century. Population and establishment censuses, household and enterprise surveys on the labour force, hours of work, earnings and labour costs, as well as registers of population, taxes and social security provide data for monitoring labour market development on a regular basis.

Despite the availability of a large amount of statistical information, researchers, statisticians and politicians encounter major problems in obtaining a complete picture of the labour market. According to Buhmann *et al.* (2000)[1] these difficulties are due to:

- contradictory results between data sources

- incomplete coverage

- difficulties and limitations in describing labour market dynamics

- absence of links between labour market statistics and other social and economic statistics.

  In the manual is described:

- how these problems affect labour market statistics in the EU;

- how they led to the development of a labour accounting system;

- the conceptual framework for LAS that was developed in the 1980s;

- how this framework is used in practice;

- the inter-connections between national accounts, SAMs and LAS;

- the compilation of the non-monetary part of these systems which complements the description of the monetary part in the chapter that deals with the elaboration of a SAM.

Compilation Procedures and Techniques

SAMs and labour accounts bring together a variety of data. These include the integrated estimates from national accounts, basic statistics from central registers and censuses, and results from household surveys (labour force survey, household budget survey etc.), and establishment surveys (structure of earnings survey, labour cost survey, etc.). They are brought together, in a consistent way, using statistical integration procedures. The handbook looks at the principles underlying these procedures.

The process of building a labour-oriented SAM usually involves the following steps:

1. identification and preparation of appropriate data sources. This may include *matching* of several micro-data files to obtain the set of variables of interest for each individual,

---

1. Buhmann, B., W.P. Leunis, L. Sølling, A. Vuille, and K. Wismer, *Labour Accounts: A Step Forward to a Coherent and Timely Description of the Labour Market,* Paper presented at the Siena Group Meeting on Social Statistics, Maastricht, May 22-24, 2000.

and the complex task of *harmonising* the variables with the national accounts concepts;

2. combination of data sets to enable decomposition of the traditional national accounts figures into more detailed socio-economic variables (e.g. gender and level of education). *Calibration* techniques for micro-data are often useful to reduce the impact of sampling variation and non-response bias etc. in surveys; and

3. *error detection* and *regularisation* or *balancing*. Inconsistencies between estimates obtained by aggregation of micro-data and the national accounts figures may still be present after step 1 and 2. For example, identity relations may not hold. These inconsistencies should be investigated to discover errors in the data etc., and corrections made. Regularisation or balancing techniques can then be used to obtain strict numerical consistency in the macro-data. (This process can also provide feedback to survey statisticians (and national accountants) to improve estimates from surveys or registers (or in national accounts)).

To integrate different sources, top-down or bottom-up approaches can be used. The manual describes these approaches, discusses the advantages of combining the two approaches, gives examples of the adjustments needed to combine the various sources available in labour accounts and SAMs, and describes some specific techniques that can be used in the integration process.

Applications of Social Accounting Matrices

The area covered by SAMs is the link between two often distinct worlds of statistics: economic statistics and social statistics. The integration of these fields of statistics enables a wider range of policy issues to be monitored and analysed. Even linking labour market and income distribution issues to macro-economic policy objectives such as economic growth, low inflation, and government fiscal balance becomes a real possibility. Labour markets are covered only sketchily in national accounts. The lack of information, for example, on labour and pay by educational level and by gender is a serious omission. A SAM-framework increases the opportunities for a more complete analysis, either directly by inclusion of a breakdown by labour categories in the relevant accounts, or indirectly by presenting and quantifying the link with underlying micro and meso data.

Their usefulness to producers of statistics (compilers of basic statistics, and national accountants) is addressed in the handbook, which looks at the advantages of more integration of basic data. Their usefulness to users is addressed and SAMs as tools for policy analysis are discussed.

Although SAMs and labour accounts have been produced in a number of countries, their use in developed countries is still not widespread. One reason for this is that there is still no country where SAMs are being produced both regularly and speedily. Until recently, the timeliness of SAMs was not seen as a high priority, because there was greater emphasis on structural analysis.

The types of analyses that are possible with SAMs are presented in the manual. As an illustration, the SAM figures, for 1999, for the Netherlands are combined with similar figures for previous years. Another type of analysis is the comparison of the structure of the labour market in eight European countries. The figures for the countries participating in the LEG are used to make this comparison. A large part of SAM analysis uses modelling approaches, which are described in more detail.

Pilot-SAMs

One of the objectives of the LEG was the compilation of a pilot-SAM for each of the participating countries for the year 1997 if possible. Five countries have compiled a SAM for 1997, one for 1996 and one for 1995.

The classifications used in the pilot SAMs are the following:

Classification of labour

Labour is classified by gender, status in employment and educational attainment in the pilot SAMs. As a result, the following minimum of 12 types (2x2x3) of labour will be distinguished:

Gender

- Male

- Female

Status in employment

- Paid employment

- Self-employed

Level of education

- Primary or lower secondary education (ISCED '97 levels 1-2)

- Upper secondary or post secondary education (ISCED '97 levels 3-4)

- Post secondary education (ISCED '97 levels 5-6)

Classification of households

Households are classified by the main source of income of the household. As a minimum, the following four groups are distinguished (households with their main source of income from):

- Wages and salaries

- Mixed income (including property income)

- Income in connection with old age (retirement)

- Other transfer income

Classification of activities

For the pilot SAMs at least a subdivision in the following six NACE groups is:

- Agriculture, hunting and forestry; Fishing   A/B

- Mining and quarrying; Manufacturing; Electricity, gas
  and water supply   C/D/E

- Construction   F

- Wholesale and retail trade, repair of motor vehicles,
  motorcycles and Personal and household goods; Hotels
  and restaurants; Transport, storage and communication   G/H/I

- Financial intermediation; Real estate, renting and
  business activities   J/K

- Public administration and defence, compulsory social
  security; Education; Health and social work, Other
  community, social and personal services activities;
  Private households with employed persons   L/M/N/O/P

In the annex of the handbook, each country (Belgium, Finland, Greece, Italy, Netherlands, Portugal, United Kingdom) describes the background of their pilot-SAM, the sources used for the compilation, the pilot-SAM itself and the perspectives for the future.

SAM-viewer

A SAM is usually presented through subsequent tables, as shown by the ESA95 examples. The more the detail of the matrix grows, the more the reading of the matrix is difficult (the matrix being necessarily printed on several pages). In order to overcome this problem, the LEG has developed an electronic presentation of the SAM, the *SAM-viewer*, working under Excel 97 and subsequent versions.

The SAM-viewer consists of the ESA95 SAM (based on the numerical example used in ESA95) and a set of linked files each showing one of the full-fledged pilot-SAMs compiled by the participating countries of the LEG. On the "home-page" of the ESA95 SAM there are buttons leading the user to one of the seven available pilot-SAMs (Belgium, Finland, Greece, Italy, Netherlands, Portugal, United Kingdom).

The "home page" of each pilot-SAM corresponds to the aggregate NAM/SAM of the concerned country. By clicking on a sub-matrix the user can reach a deeper level of detail. For some sub-matrices there are buttons at the user's disposal to go even one or more levels deeper.

The screen views on the next pages show what the user can see on the screen by:

- clicking a country button (in screen view 1 the aggregate NAM/SAM of the Netherlands is shown).

- clicking on the sub-matrix (3,2) Net Value Added (screen view 2).

- clicking the button "To a more detailed Value Added matrix" (screen view 3).

- clicking the button "To the underlying labour matrix in fte" (screen view 4). Clicking the button "Back to the SAM" brings you back to the aggregate NAM/SAM (screen view 1).

- clicking on sub-matrix (4,3) Net Generated Income (screen view 5).

- clicking the button "To a more detailed Generated Income matrix" (screen view 6).

- clicking the button "To the underlying labour matrix in fte" (screen view 7). Clicking the button "Back to the SAM" brings you back to the aggregate NAM/SAM (screen view 1).

- clicking on the sub-matrix (1,6) "Final Consumption Expenditure" (screen view 8).

- clicking the button "To a more detailed Use of Income matrix" (screen view 9).

Screen views

1. The Aggregate Social Accounting Matrix of the Netherlands, 1997

2. Sub-matrix (3,2): Net value added

3. Sub-matrix (3,2): A detailed net value added matrix

4. Labour matrix underlying the value added matrix (in fte)

5. Sub-matrix (4,3): Net generated income

6. Sub-matrix (4,3): A detailed generated income matrix

7. Labour matrix underlying the generated income matrix (in fte)

8. Sub-matrix (1,6): Final consumption expenditure

9. Sub-matrix (1,6): A detailed final consumption expenditure matrix

Screen view 1

THE DUTCH SOCIAL ACCOUNTING MATRIX

BACK TO THE ESA95 SAM

1997 -current million euro -

Account	codes	1 Goods and services	2 Production	3 Generation of income	4 Allocation of primary income	5 Secondary distribution of income	6 Use of income	7 Capital	8 Fixed capital formation	9 Financial	10 RoW (current)	11 RoW (capital)	12 Total
Goods and services	1	TRADE AND TRANSPORT MARGINS 0	INTERMEDIATE CONSUMPTION 320 674				FINAL CONSUMPTION 241 415	CHANGES IN INVENTORIES (1) 839	GROSS FIXED CAPITAL FORMATION 71 680		EXPORTS OF GOODS AND SERVICES (2) 204 152		838 760
Production	2	OUTPUT 619 059											619 059
Generation of income	3		NET VALUE ADDED 248 550	VAT NOT HANDED OVER TO THE GOVERNMENT 614							COMPENSATION OF EMPLOYEES FROM THE R.O.W. 584		249 749
Allocation of primary income	4	TAXES ON PRODUCTS LESS SUBSIDIES 33 051		NET GENERATED INCOME 249 036	PROPERTY INCOME 107 136						PROPERTY INCOME FROM THE R.O.W. 35 117		424 340
Secondary distribution of income	5				NET NATIONAL INCOME 287 625	CURRENT TRANSFERS 269 682					CURRENT TRANSFERS FROM THE R.O.W. 3 499		560 807
Use of income	6					NET DISPOSABLE INCOME 284 649	ADJUSTMENT FOR CHANGE IN NET EQUITY ON PENSION FUNDS 16 092						300 742
Capital	7						NET SAVING 43 379	CAPITAL TRANSFERS (3) 7 790		BORROWING 186 706		CAPITAL TRANSFERS FROM THE R.O.W. 1 101	238 976
Fixed capital formation	8		CONSUMPTION OF FIXED CAPITAL 49 835					NET FIXED CAPITAL FORMATION 21 845					71 680
Financial	9							LENDING 205 964				NET LENDING OF THE R.O.W. -19 258	186 706
RoW (current)	10	IMPORTS OF GOODS AND SERVICES (4) 186 650		COMPENSATION OF EMPLOYEES TO THE R.O.W 98	PROPERTY INCOME TO THE R.O.W. 29 579	CURRENT TRANSFERS TO THE R.O.W. 6 475	ADJUSTMENT FOR CHANGE IN NET EQUITY ON PENSION FUNDS TO THE R.O.W -145						222 657
RoW (capital)	11							CAPITAL TRANSFERS TO THE R.O.W 2 538			-20 695		-18 157
Total	12	838 760	619 059	249 749	424 340	560 807	300 742	238 976	71 680	186 706	222 657	-18 157	

(1) Including acquisition less disposable of valuables
(2) Including purchases in domestic market by non-residents
(3) Including acquisitions less disposable of non-produced non-financial assets
(4) Including purchases abroad by residents and imports paid on products and taxes on products paid to the Rest of the World

Screen view 2

Net value added **SUB-MATRIX (3,2) NET VALUE ADDED**

Generation of income (value added categories)	codes	Production (NACE-rev. 1 Industries)						Total
		Agriculture, forestry, fishing (NACE A/B)	Mining, quarrying, manufacturing, electricity, gas and water supply (NACE C/D/E)	Construction (NACE F)	Trade, repair, hotels and restaurants, transport, storage and communication (NACE G/H/I)	Financial intermediation, real estate, renting and business activities (NACE J/K)	Public administration and defense, education, health and social work, services n.e.c. (NACE L/M/N/O/P)	
		1	2	3	4	5	6	8
Compensation of employees	1	1 963	32 795	11 662	37 891	33 770	49 954	168 035
Net mixed income	2	5 848	942	1 937	7 287	5 512	6 241	27 766
Net operating surplus	3	332	21 947	1 992	13 149	12 207	2 918	52 544
Other taxes less subs. on pr.	4	-924	201	-55	208	867	-92	205
Total	5	7 218	55 884	15 536	58 535	52 356	59 022	248 550

248 550

Screen view 3

Net value added

248 550

SUB-MATRIX (3,2) A DETAILED VALUE ADDED MATRIX

				Production (NACE-rev. 1 Industries)						Total
Generation of income (value added categories)			codes	Agriculture, forestry, fishing (NACE A/B)	Mining, quarrying, manufacturing, electricity, gas and water supply (NACE C/D/E)	Construction (NACE F)	Trade, repair, hotels and restaurants, transport, storage and communication (NACE G/H/I)	Financial intermediation, real estate, renting and business activities (NACE J/K)	Public administration and defense, education, health and social work, services n.e.c. (NACE L/M/N/O/P)	
				1	2	3	4	5	6	7
Wages and salaries	Male	Primary/lower secondary (ISCED 1-2)	1	715	8 199	4 168	8 642	3 206	2 751	27 682
		Upper or post secondary (ISCED 3-4)	2	662	11 527	4 564	12 454	8 038	7 664	44 910
		Tertiary (ISCED 5-6)	3	81	5 356	672	4 526	10 389	13 753	34 777
	Female	Primary/lower secondary (ISCED 1-2)	4	141	1 314	83	2 632	1 894	2 007	8 072
		Upper or post secondary (ISCED 3-4)	5	102	1 437	216	3 896	3 489	7 242	16 381
		Tertiary (ISCED 5-6)	6	19	848	63	1 416	2 719	7 751	12 816
Employers' social contributions			7	242	4 115	1 895	4 324	4 035	8 787	23 397
Net mixed income			8	5.848	942	1 937	7 287	5 512	6 241	27 766
Net operating surplus			9	332	21.947	1 992	13 149	12 207	2 918	52 544
Other taxes less subsidies on production			10	-924	201	-55	208	867	-92	205
Total			15	7 218	55 884	15 536	58 535	52 356	59 022	248 550

Screen view 4

Total labour **The Labour matrix underlying the value added matrix (in fte)**
units

5 992

Type of labour			codes	Economic activity (NACE-rev. 1 Industries)						Total
				Agriculture, forestry, fishing (NACE A/B)	Mining, quarrying, manufacturing, electricity, gas and water supply (NACE C/D/E)	Construction (NACE F)	Trade, repair, hotels and restaurants, transport, storage and communication (NACE G/H/I)	Financial intermediation, real estate, renting and business activities (NACE J/K)	Public administration and defense, education, health and social work, services n.e.c (NACE L/M/N/O/P)	
				1	2	3	4	5	6	7
Employees	Male	Primary/lower secondary (ISCED 1-2)	1	34	297	169	316	138	100	1 052
		Upper or post secondary (ISCED 3-4)	2	29	367	174	425	259	255	1 508
		Tertiary (ISCED 5-6)	3	3	130	21	114	243	367	878
	Female	Primary/lower secondary (ISCED 1-2)	4	10	70	5	164	110	104	462
		Upper or post secondary (ISCED 3-4)	5	7	69	11	218	174	351	829
		Tertiary (ISCED 5-6)	6	1	31	3	57	99	281	471
Self-employed	Male	Primary/lower secondary (ISCED 1-2)	7	63	16	26	59	16	11	190
		Upper or post secondary (ISCED 3-4)	8	67	16	30	81	35	24	254
		Tertiary (ISCED 5-6)	9	7	5	4	18	40	35	109
	Female	Primary/lower secondary (ISCED 1-2)	10	13	4	1	24	7	64	113
		Upper or post secondary (ISCED 3-4)	11	9	4	2	25	8	47	96
		Tertiary (ISCED 5-6)	12	1	1	0	5	6	16	30
Total			15	242	1 009	445	1 505	1 136	1 655	5 992

Screen view 5

Net generated income **SUB-MATRIX (4,3) NET GENERATED INCOME**

249 036

		Generation of income (value added categories)				Total
Allocation of primary income (Institutional sectors)	codes	Compensation of employees	Net mixed income	Net operating surplus	Other taxes less subsidies on production	
		1	2	3	4	5
Non-financial corporations	1			50 630		50 630
Financial corporations	2			-3 156		-3 156
General government	3				153	153
Households	4	167 958	27 766	5 685		201 409
Non-profit inst. serving hh	5					0
Total	6	167 958	27 766	53 159	153	249 036

Screen view 6

Net generated **SUB-MATRIX (4,3) A DETAILED GENERATED INCOME MATRIX** income

			Generation of income (value added categories)										Total
Allocation of primary income (Institutional sectors)			Wages and salaries						Employers' social contributions	Net mixed income	Net operating surplus	Other taxes less subsidies on production	
			Male			Female							
			Primary/lower secondary (ISCED 1-2)	Upper or post secondary (ISCED 3-4)	Tertiary (ISCED 5-6)	Primary/lower secondary (ISCED 1-2)	Upper or post secondary (ISCED 3-4)	Tertiary (ISCED 5-6)					
		codes	1	2	3	4	5	6	7	8	9	10	15
Non-financial corporations		1									50 630		50 630
Financial corporations		2									-3 156		-3 156
General government		3										153	153
Households classified by main source of income	Wages and salaries	4	26 024	42 809	33 504	6 879	14 186	10 787	22 206	6 766	3 810		166 971
	Mixed income (including property income)	5	742	1 299	789	779	1 832	1 772	694	18 506	632		27 045
	Income in connection with old age (retirement)	6	478	372	229	137	105	79	212	1 402	1 012		4 025
	Other transfers income (including other households)	7	423	407	236	273	249	171	285	1 093	231		3 368
Non-profit institutions serving households		8											0
Total		9	27 667	44 886	34 758	8 068	16 372	12 809	23 397	27 766	53 159	153	249 036

249 036

Screen view 7

Total labour **The Labour matrix underlying the generated income matrix (in fte)**
units

5 993

Type of Households (by main source of income)	codes	Type of labour												Total
		Employees						Self employed						
		Male			Female			Male			Female			
		Primary/lower secondary (ISCED 1-2)	Upper or post secondary (ISCED 3-4)	Tertiary (ISCED 5-6)	Primary/lower secondary (ISCED 1-2)	Upper or post secondary (ISCED 3-4)	Tertiary (ISCED 5-6)	Primary/lower secondary (ISCED 1-2)	Upper or post secondary (ISCED 3-4)	Tertiary (ISCED 5-6)	Primary/lower secondary (ISCED 1-2)	Upper or post secondary (ISCED 3-4)	Tertiary (ISCED 5-6)	
		1	2	3	4	5	6	7	8	9	10	11	12	13
Wages and salaries	1	991	1 439	844	395	718	397	158	205	90	86	78	25	5 425
Mixed income (including property income)	2	28	44	19	44	93	64	25	41	14	13	12	4	401
Income in connection with old age (retirement)	3	18	13	6	8	6	3	3	2	1	6	2	0	67
Other transfers income (including other households)	4	17	14	6	16	13	6	5	6	4	8	4	1	99
Total	5	1 054	1 509	876	462	830	471	190	254	109	113	96	30	5 993

Screen view 8

National final expenditure

SUB-MATRIX (1,6) FINAL CONSUMPTION EXPENDITURE

Goods and services (CPA groups)		codes	Use of income (Institutional sectors)					Total
			Non-financial corporations	Financial corporations	General government	Households	Non-profit institutions serving households	
			1	2	3	4	5	6
Products of agriculture, hunting, forestry, fisheries and aquaculture (CPA A/B)	1	1				3 870		3 870
Products from mining and quarrying, manufactured products and energy products (CPA C/D/E)	2	2			2 497	79 102		81 598
Construction work (CPA F)	3	3			468	354		822
Wholesale and retail trade services; repair services, hotel and restaurant services, transport and communication services (CPA G/H/I)	4	4			710	18 653		19 362
Financial intermediation services, real estate, renting and business services (CPA J/K)	5	5			4 489	36 537		41 025
Other services (CPA L to P)	6	6			68 256	24 668	1 813	94 737
Total		7			76 420	163 183	1 813	241 415

241 415

Screen view 9

National final **SUB-MATRIX (1,6) A DETAILED FINAL CONSUMPTION MATRIX**
expenditure

241 415

Goods and services (CPA groups)	codes	Use of income (Institutional sectors)								Total
		Non-financial corporations	Financial corporations	General government	Households (by main source of income)				Non-profit institutions serving households	
					Wages and salaries	Mixed income (including property income)	Income in connection with old age (retirement)	Other transfers income (including other households)		
		1	2	3	4	5	6	7	8	9
Products of agriculture, hunting, forestry, fisheries and aquaculture (CPA A/B)	1				2 388	329	859	293		3 870
Products from mining and quarrying, manufactured products and energy products (CPA C/D/E)	2			2 497	50 577	6 882	14 466	7 176		81 598
Construction work (CPA F)	3			468	249	27	65	13		822
Wholesale and retail trade services; repair services, hotel and restaurant services, transport and communication services (CPA G/H/I)	4			710	11 695	1 529	3 583	1 846		19 362
Financial intermediation services, real estate, renting and business services (CPA J/K)	5			4 489	21 206	3 554	7 224	4 552		41 025
Other services (CPA L to P)	6			68 256	15 698	2 744	4 654	1 572	1 813	94 737
Total	7			76 420	101 814	15 065	30 852	15 452	1 813	241 415

A Pilot SAM for Italy: Methodology and Results

F. Battellini, A. Coli, F. Tartamella

ISTAT, Italy

Introduction

SAMs are an important analysis tool, not only as a coherent accounting structure for National Accounts data, but also as a base for economic modelling since "the structure of each SAM already reflects the relationships represented in an economy-wide model" (SNA93, 20.130).

The distinctive feature of a SAM, which makes it an attractive tool also from an economic point of view, is the fact that the whole economic system is represented, with its complexity and with its interrelations. Social Accounting Matrices were in fact elaborated as a tool to improve economic analysis, before than as an accounting apparatus.

The traditional macro economic aggregates were able to measure the whole economic growth which followed the Second World War, but they were not able to capture the inequalities in the change of living conditions. SAMs were conceived as a distributive analysis tool to investigate how economic aggregates growth is distributed among institutions and especially within families. In fact, SAM analysis allows linking the primary to the secondary distribution of income, so that it is possible to connect the degree of household income inequality (secondary income distribution) to value added generation (primary income distribution). The full economic cycle is shown in a matrix format: national accounts are therefore displayed in a way that easily allows for modelling and analysis of transmission mechanism.

Building a SAM is not trivial since the accounts (in particular those referred to primary and secondary income distribution) have to be further subdivided into subcategories according to the socio-economic aspects under investigation. This has to be done adopting the same definitions, starting from the same classifications and following, as far as possible, the same methodology used to build national accounts. Istat has started a project for the compilation of a labour oriented SAM in the context of an international working group[1]. This group identified gender and education level as the key variables which, in addition to the traditional ones of national accounts (such as industries and institutional sectors), are more suited to study the labour market. This detail in the analysis shows how the worker's characteristics both the ones due to individual choices

---

1.   Leadership Group on Social Accounting Matrices. The group is coordinated by the Dutch Statistical office. Its aim is the drafting of a handbook for the compilation of SAMs and the construction of a pilot SAM for each participating country: Belgium, Finland, Greece, Italy, Netherlands, Norway, Portugal, United Kingdom.

(such as the education level) and those predetermined (as gender) are linked to the productive structure (analysed by industry) and influence the remuneration of labour.

Factor remuneration is the crucial linking pin between industries and institutional sectors. Through it, industries pay institutional sectors for having supplied factors in the production process. In national accounts (NA) this linkage is not completely elaborated. In fact, in the standard accounts, the generation of income account plays the role of an intermediate account mainly "serving to derive surplus/mixed income as balancing item" (see SNA93 § 20.49). Standard national accounts do not provide detailed information on the quality of factors employed in the production process. Nor it is possible to know what kind of household is endowed with specific types of factors. In short, the accounts do not clearly show the interrelationships between production units (local kinds of activity units, LKAUs for short) and institutional units.

SAMs overcome this shortcoming by deepening the analysis of the income distribution process. Namely, a SAM gives details on processes involving households: "The allocation of primary income account of a detailed SAM presents households labour income(s) as a contribution by one or more (self-) employed household members. Among other things, this will indicate to what extent each household group depends on multiple sources of labour income. Apart from this, the transaction categories shown in the distribution and use of income accounts of a SAM are typically about the same as in the central framework" (see SNA93 § 20.56).

Data on labour can be reconciled to the SAM figures through the decomposition of value added categories into volume and price components, namely labour (persons employed, jobs, full time equivalent units (FTEU), hours worked) and earnings (wage rates, mixed income per self-employed). Both volume and price measures are disaggregated according to the SAM socio-demographic criteria.

Labour is the volume component both of the value added cell and the generated income cell. The former (demand side of labour) analyses labour input according to the employing industry *and* the socio-economic characteristic of the worker. The latter (supply side of labour) analyses labour according to the individual characteristics (gender and education level) of the worker *and* the characteristics of his/her household.

In fact, the input of labour underlying the SAM figures can be considered from two different perspectives: on the production side as one of the inputs used to produce GDP; from the income perspective, as a source of income for household. This double reading reflects the main macro-economic identity underlying national accounts according to which GDP is at the same time a measure of output and of income.

The analysis of the labour factor in a SAM format represents a further impulse to the estimation of the input of labour on the basis of national accounts concepts. This allows to enhance the reliability of the macro-economic indicators (such as performance indicators, per capita values) conventionally used by policy makers for economic analysis, time series analysis and international comparisons.

The SAM and the integrated set of labour tables are an example of the so called SESAME (System of Economic and Social Accounting Matrices and Extensions). Here national accounts variables are dis-aggregated according to economic, social and demographic criteria and/or decomposed into volume and price measures.

This paper focus on *the value added cell*, *i.e.* on the factor remuneration process. The first paragraph is devoted to an overview on the national accounts matrix. Subsequently we focus on the theoretical aspects of the value added cell and the underlying labour input. The examples presented in these sections are taken from the Europeland SAM[2]. We then describe the Italian method used to estimate the value added matrix and the related labour matrix based on the LEG directives. Finally we present some analysis on the results of the pilot SAM of three countries participating to the group. The analysis is limited to the value added matrix and in particular to employees' figures. Data refer to 1996 for Italy and to 1997 for Belgium and the Netherlands.

An overview on the National Accounts Matrix

A national account matrix (NAM) is the presentation of the national accounts variables in a matrix format. Rows show entries whereas columns record outlays.

The simplest version is the National Accounts Matrix for the whole economy (aggregated NAM). The construction of such a matrix is easy, the only relevant question being the choice of the accounts. The NAM displayed in table 1 includes the accounts suggested by ESA95. Figures are taken from The Europeland SAM (see footnote 2).

We can get more detailed national accounts matrices by subdividing each account according to groups of actors and/or transactions. As a result the NAM cells become matrices and vectors.

The first step towards a detailed NAM is the subdivision of the accounts according to the NA definitions and classifications. This operation is not always straightforward due to the lack of detailed enough data. For example, in the Italian NAM we have to consider an *ad hoc* account for "Taxes and subsides". Besides, it is not possible to separate out the consumption of fixed capital from the operating surplus and the mixed income.

The cells where the income distribution process takes place are the following:

- the value added cell (see table 1 cell 3,2) which transfers value added from the production units to the   primary inputs employed in production;

- the generated income cell and the property income cell (see table 1 cells 4,3 and 4,4) which transfer value added from primary inputs to the institutional sectors whom they belong to;

- the current transfer cell (see table 1 cell 5,5) which completes the income distribution process leading to disposable income.

In this paper we focus on *the value added matrix, i.e.* on the passage of primary income from industries to production factors.

2.   The European Leadership Group on Social Accounting Matrices has developed a SAM viewer called Europeland SAM. It is an electronic sheet which displays the pilot SAMs of the LEG countries and a SAM based on ESA95 figures. The tables of section 3 are taken from the ESA95 SAM.

Table 1. An aggregated National Accounts Matrix

Euroland SAM figures (see footnote 2)

Account	codes	Goods and services (1)	Production (2)	Generation of income (3)	Allocation of primary income (4)	Secondary distribution of income (5)	Use of income (6)	Capital (7)	Gross fixed capital formation (8)	Financial (9)	RdM (current) (10)	RdM (capital) (11)	Total (12)
Goods and services	1	TRADE AND TRANSPORT MARGINS — 0	INTERMEDIATE CONSUMPTION — 1 904				FINAL CONSUMPTION — 1 371	CHANGES IN INVENTORIES (1) — 38	GROSS FIXED CAPITAL FORMATION — 376		EXPORTS OF GOODS AND SERVICES (2) — 535		4 225
Production	2	OUTPUT — 3 595											3 595
Generation of income	3		NET VALUE ADDED — 1 469								COMPENSATION OF EMPLOYEES FROM R.O.V. — 6		1 475
Allocation of primary income	4	TAXES ON PRODUCTS LESS SUBSIDIES — 133		NET GENERATED INCOME — 1 473	PROPERTY INCOME — 341						PROPERTY INCOME FROM THE R.O.V. — 66		2 013
Secondary distribution of income	5				NET NATIONAL INCOME — 1 633	CURRENT TRANSFERS — 1 096					CURRENT TRANSFERS FROM THE R.O.V. — 10		2 739
Use of income	6					NET DISPOSABLE INCOME — 1 604	ADJUSTMENT FOR CHANGE IN NET EQUITY ON PENSION — 11						1 615
Capital	7						NET SAVING — 233	CAPITAL TRANSFERS (3) — 62		BORROWING — 603		CAPITAL TRANSFERS FROM THE R.O.V. — -1	897
Gross fixed capital formation	8		CONSUMPTION OF FIXED CAPITAL — 222					NET FIXED CAPITAL FORMATION — 154					376
Financial	9							LENDING — 641				NET LENDING OF THE R.O.V. — -38	603
RdM (current)	10	IMPORTS OF GOODS AND SERVICES (4) — 497		COMPENSATION OF EMPLOYEES TO R.O.V. — 2	PROPERTY INCOME TO THE R.O.V. — 39	CURRENT TRANSFERS TO THE R.O.V. — 39	0				-41		577
RdM (capital)	11							CAPITAL TRANSFERS TO THE R.O.V. — 3					-39
Total	12	4 225	3 595	1 475	2 013	2 739	1 615	897	376	603	577	-39	-39

* The matrix is based on table 8.20 of ESA95.
(1) Including acquisition less disposable of valuables
(2) Including purchases in domestic market by non-residents
(3) Including acquisitions less disposable of non-produced non-financial assets
(4) Including purchases abroad by residents and imports paid to the Rest of the World

Focus on the value added matrix

From a standard to a labour-oriented value added matrix

The *value added cell* is the interception of the production account (column) and the generation of income account (row). This means that a monetary flow moves from production units to kinds of primary inputs (labour, capital).

The sub-matrix in Table 2 is obtained by applying national accounts standard classifications to the NAM Production and Generation of income accounts.

Value added is classified by (net/gross) primary input categories: compensation of employees, mixed income, operating surplus and other taxes and subsidies on production.

Industries are grouped into six branches:

1.   Agriculture, hunting, forestry and fishing (NACE-Rev.1 A/B)

2.   Mining, quarrying, manufacturing, electricity, gas and water supply (NACE-Rev.1 C/D/E)

3.   Construction (NACE-Rev.1 F)

4.   Trade, repair, hotels and restaurants etc. (NACE-Rev.1 G/H/I)

5.   Financial intermediation, real estate, renting and business activities (NACE-Rev.1 J/K)

6.   Public administration and defence, education, health and social work, services n.e.c. (NACE-Rev.1 L/M/N/O/P)

Starting from this sub-matrix we can further detail the compensation of factors. Particularly, LEG members have decided to subdivide compensation of employees by gender and education level. In particular we distinguish workers according to three levels of education attained:

*   Lower: this includes primary and lower secondary school (ISCED 1-2)

*   Medium: this includes upper or post secondary school (ISCED 3-4)

*   Higher: this corresponds to tertiary education (ISCED 5-6)

Table 2- **A standard value added sub-matrix**

Figures from ESA95 SAM (see footnote 2)

Generation of income account	Production account						FISIM	Total
	Agriculture etc.	Mining, quarrying, manufac. etc.	Construc.	Trade, repair, hotels, etc	Financial intermediation etc.	Public administration etc.		
Compensation of employees	9	349	58	60	54	232		762
Net mixed income	14	227	35	39	99	18		432
Net operating surplus	9	30	18	7	160	41	-48	217
Other taxes less subsidies on production	-2	44	5	-6	12	5		58
Total	30	650	116	100	325	296	-48	1 469

We can analyse mixed income according to the gender and the education level of the self-employed as well. In this case, however, the ratio between this amount and the underlying volume of labour does not represent a per capita compensation of self-employed labour, but mixed income per self-employed labour units.

Table 2a shows a value added sub-matrix where such classifications have been applied.

In order to get a proper *labour-oriented SAM*, we should separate out the remuneration of labour from the other remuneration of primary inputs. This means estimating an imputed labour compensation for the self-employed which is then separated and subtracted from mixed income.

In this case we would get a value added sub-matrix as the one displayed in table 3. Compensation of labour now reflects the remuneration of *all* labour provided in the production process, which is made of self-employed and employee labour. The net operating surplus of self-employed records the remuneration of self-employed, *other* than labour compensation.

Table 2a - **A more detailed value added sub-matrix**

Figures from ESA95 SAM (see footnote 2)

Generation of income account			Production account						FISIM	Total
			Agriculture etc.	Mining, quarrying manufacturin g etc.	Construction	Trade, repair, hotels, etc.	Financial intermed. etc.	Public administ.		
Compensation of employees	Male	Lower	6.4	179.9	49.0	30.8	13.0	34.4		313
		Medium	0.2	29.7	3.5	5.7	10.5	10.1		60
		Higher	0.4	34.6	3.2	5.6	14.5	70.7		129
	Female	Lower	1.9	82.0	1.0	11.2	6.4	40.6		143
		Medium	0.2	12.4	0.7	3.6	5.1	10.6		33
		Higher	0.0	10.6	0.7	3.2	4.6	65.6		85
Net Mixed income	Male	Lower	8.6	128.5	31.4	21.8	21.5	5.0		217
		Medium	0.3	28.0	2.0	5.0	23.2	1.9		60
		Higher	0.0	12.0	1.5	1.5	35.0	1.9		52
	Female	Lower	5.1	47.9	0.1	8.2	5.7	5.8		73
		Medium	0.1	8.7	0.0	2.2	4.8	2.4		18
		Higher	0.0	2.0	0.0	0.4	8.8	1.0		12
Net operating surplus			8.8	29.9	18.4	7.0	159.6	41.3	-48	217
Other taxes less subsidies on production			-2.0	44.0	5.0	-6.0	12.0	5.0		58
Total			30	650	116	100	325	296	-48	1 469

Table 3 - **A labour-oriented value added sub-matrix**

Figures from ESA95 SAM (see footnote 2)

Generation of income account		Production account						FISIM	Total
		Agriculture etc.	Mining, quarrying, manufac.	Construction	Trade, repair, hotels, etc	Financial intermed. etc	Public administr. etc.		
Compensation of labour	Employees	9	349	58	60	54	232		762
	Self Employed	7	120	19	21	52	10		229
Net operating surplus of self-employed		7	107	16	18	47	8		203
Net operating surplus		9	30	18	7	160	41	-48	217
Other taxes less subsidies on production		-2	44	5	-6	12	5		58
Total		30	650	116	100	325	296	-48	1 469

The labour-oriented value added sub-matrix has the following advantages:

- It shows the labour income share of GDP (NDP).

- It allows calculating the labour compensation per unit of output. This index can be useful for measuring the actual labour intensity of each industry.

We can analyse both self-employed and employee compensation of labour according to the gender and education level of labour units. The result is displayed in table 3a.

Table 3a - **A more detailed version of the labour-oriented value added sub-matrix**

Figures from ESA95 SAM (see footnote 2)

Generation of income account			Production account						FISIM	Total
			Agriculture etc.	Mining, quarrying, manufacturing etc.	Construction	Trade, repair, hotels, etc	Financial intermediate. etc	Public administration etc.		
Employees	Male	Lower	6.4	179.9	49.0	30.8	13.0	34.4		313
		Medium	0.2	29.7	3.5	5.7	10.5	10.1		60
		Higher	0.4	34.6	3.2	5.6	14.5	70.7		129
	Female	Lower	1.9	82.0	1.0	11.2	6.4	40.6		143
		Medium	0.2	12.4	0.7	3.6	5.1	10.6		33
		Higher	0.0	10.6	0.7	3.2	4.6	65.6		85
Self-employed	Male	Lower	5	62	16	11	13	1		108
		Medium	0	10	1	2	10	0		24
		Higher	0	12	1	2	14	3		32
	Female	Lower	2	28	0	4	6	2		42
		Medium	0	4	0	1	5	0		11
		Higher	0	4	0	1	5	3		12
Net operating surplus of self-employed			7	107	16	18	47	8		203
Net operating surplus			9	30	19	7	160	41	-48	217
Other taxes less subsidies on production			-2	44	5	-6	12	5		58
Total			30	650	116	100	325	296	-48	1 469

Most of the objections against this framework are due to the difficulty of estimating self-employed labour compensation which, in fact, is not paid out separately from the compensation of self-employed capital. Therefore, such a separation can only be imputed with the help of a specific estimation method. For the same reason ESA95 has established to consider a mixed income category through which all the factors supplied by self-employed are remunerated.

Nevertheless there are countries (like Italy) where self-employed labour is dominant and so peculiarly organised that such an approach is particularly favoured.

The methods used to construct a value added sub-matrix

Though the labour-oriented value added matrix may have some advantages, it may be advisable to start with a simpler framework, such as the one shown in Table 2a.

From a practical point of view this means estimating the compensation of 36 kinds of employee as well as the net mixed income generated by 36 kinds of self-employed.

We can identify two methods. The former consists in applying proper per capita wage rates to the volume of labour employed in the production process. We can call this approach as the "labour-funded method". The latter consists in subdividing directly national accounts compensation of employees and net mixed income by proper indicators.

In the first case we have to estimate a matrix of per capita values as well as a labour matrix. Both of them have to respect national accounts constraints: particularly, the weighted average of per capita values must equal averages in the national accounts and the sum of labour units must be equal to national accounts totals. Reconciliation with national accounts data can be reached through iterative processes aimed at distributing discrepancies.

In the second case we estimate directly compensation of employees and net mixed income sub-matrices.

Both the methods belong to the general class of top-down methods. The choice between the mentioned methods depends on the availability of data, especially on the existence of labour accounts coherent with national accounts.

The LEG countries which apply the labour-funded method are Italy, Netherlands and Portugal, i.e. those countries where employment data are consistent with national accounts. The estimation process follows more or less the same steps.

The labour input underlying the value added sub-matrix

The estimation of the input of labour within national accounts is aimed at measuring the volume of labour underlying the output produced by the economic system in the reference period. Therefore the measure of the input of labour is strictly linked to the production boundaries set by ESA 95 (see ESA95 §§ 11.11-11.16), this requiring the estimates on the input of labour to be exhaustive as the estimates on production, income and expenditure are. The strict link between the production boundaries and the definition of the input of labour in national accounts explains the difference between the latter and the definition of employment set by statistical surveys (both by surveys on households and surveys on firms). In particular this difference concerns two main aspects: the first one is related to the reference population; the second one regards the coverage of the activities included. These aspects are strictly linked but it is possible to schematically separate them.

As mentioned at the beginning of this paragraph, the reference population in national accounts is represented by all the labour units who have provided labour to production units taking part in the realisation of production and income as defined in national accounts. In this respect it differs from the population measured by statistical surveys or administrative archives which respond to specific purposes different from the measurement of the input of labour in the national accounts context; in particular they all survey a specific economic or social phenomenon, thus determining the reference population and the survey boundaries. For example, as far as the residence is concerned, surveys on households generally refer to the resident population and, therefore, they register employment (in terms of number of persons employed) referring to the legal residence of persons surveyed; on the contrary the national accounts allows two different measures of employment: domestic employment and national employment. In particular domestic employment is defined with respect to the residence of the production unit since the objective is that of measuring the input of labour contributing to the final output of the economic system. In ESA95 a complete list of the categories of workers to be included and excluded from the domestic concept of employment is presented (see ESA95 §§ 11.17-11.19)[3].

Therefore the use of different statistical and administrative sources in order to estimate the input of labour in national accounts requires a series of adjustments first of all aimed at harmonising definitions adapting those of basic statistics to the national accounts ones.

With respect to the second aspect explaining the diverging concepts of employment in national accounts and in surveys (i.e. the coverage of the activities to be included), it has been assumed that the ESA95 production boundaries include "… production, primary income and expenditures that are directly and non-directly observed in statistical surveys or administrative files"[4]. In particular the non observed economy includes:

1. the underground economy (SNA93, §§ 6.34), illegal activities (SNA93, §§ 6.31-6.33), the informal sector (SNA93, Annex to Chapter 4)[5]: in particular the activities classified as "underground economy" are characterised by the deliberate intention of an economic agent to avoid paying taxes, social security contributions, to ignore minimum wages, work schedules, safety standards;

2. other productive activities not surveyed because of inefficiencies of the statistical information system (caused, for example, by failure to up-date statistical archives or registers on existing employment which complies with law) or because of lack of sensitivity of those who are responsible for the compilation of the questionnaires (non response).

---

3. A detailed analysis of all the differences among surveys concepts and between surveys and national accounts ones is presented in chapter 4 of the Handbook of the SAM and in the documents produced by the Eurostat Task Force on ESA employment. (in particular see "Annex to CN 427. Employment in National Accounts", Eurostat B1/Annex CN 427e ; "Employment in national accounts. Italian comments to annex CN 427", document presented at the meeting of the Working Party "National Accounts", Luxembourg 16-17 December 1999).

4. See Decision of the European Commission 94/168/EC, Euratom 22 February 1994, art. 2.

5. EU member states have agreed on postponing the inclusion of illegal activities in the current estimates, at least in the first phase of ESA95 implementation. With respect to informal activities, the definition of this sector has just been set in details by a Handbook on the Non Observed Economy edited by OECD.

Different methodologies have been proposed and implemented by countries in order to measure the non observed economy. Part of the techniques allowing to integrate information in order to fill the gap due to statistical reasons (point b.) are presented in chapter 4 of the Handbook on SAM, while the Italian approach for the estimation of labour input can be assumed as an example of the methodologies used in order to estimate the input of labour including the underground economy.

Both chapter 4 of the Handbook on SAMs and the paragraph in this paper describing the Italian approach for the estimation of the input of labour show that generally no survey is specifically aimed at the measurement of underground activities and the related employment. In this respect comparing figures derived from different sources allows to point out discrepancies which can assume very different meanings: in particular when definitional aspects have been solved and when all the "statistical" causes of discrepancies among sources have been removed, discrepancies can help in the measurement of economic phenomena. As cited in the Italian case, for example, the basic assumption for the estimation of the "underground input of labour" is that establishment survey data do not incorporate the underground economy while surveys on households do; therefore the estimations for this can be made by comparing data from households and data from establishments, after adjustments for all other differences caused by "non-economic" reasons (see point b. above) have been made.

In order to respond to the objective of measuring the amount of labour underlying GDP and income, the measurement of employment in national accounts is not limited to the number of employed persons. Actually ESA95 indicates four different measures of employment in the National Accounts context: employed persons, jobs, full-time equivalent units (FTEU) and hours worked. Jobs result as the summing up of the number of persons employed and their multiple jobs (see §§ 11.22 and 11.23). The amount of hours worked should refer to the production boundaries, i.e. to exhaustiveness requirements: a detailed description of what to include and exclude in order to estimate such an indicator is presented in ESA95 (see § 11.27-11.31). Finally FTEU can be obtained in two different ways. When exhaustive estimates on the number of hours actually worked is available, FTEU are calculated as the ratio between the number of hours worked and the number of hours worked by full-time jobs (see ESA95 § 11.32-11.34). When exhaustive estimates on the amount of hours actually worked (representing the numerator in the calculation of FTEU) are not available, FTEU can be indirectly estimated through coefficients. In this latter case available data on hours worked (captured by surveys or recorded by administrative registers) can be used in order to calculate indicators through which jobs can be transformed into full-time equivalents units.

When the national accounts provide such estimates on the input of labour, indicators can be calculated and used for international comparisons and economic analysis. In particular at the international level the economic aggregates can be homogeneously compared through per capita values if employment figures provided by countries respond to the same definitions and if they are coherent with the definitions of the economic aggregates considered. Furthermore estimates on the input of labour represent important variables for economic analysis purposes. For example the input of labour is the variable used in the building up of performance indicators (productivity of labour in terms of value added or production); it allows to elaborate indicators on the intensity of labour or intensity of capital; it is a volume component of economic aggregates, such as compensation of employees, allowing to analyse separately the volume effect and the price effect in time series perspective: in the latter case, for example, ESA95 suggests the calculation of employee labour input at constant compensation which allows to calculate implicit price indices for labour to be compared with implicit price indices on final uses (see ESA95 § 11.36-11.37).

According to ESA 95, the input of labour should be estimated adopting the following classifications: by economic activity or by institutional sector. When the input of labour is integrated into a SAM, it must be reported into a matrix format where figures can be dis-aggregated and cross-classified according to the same classifications used in the SAM. In particular the labour matrix underlying the value added matrix is supposed to analyse labour by the employing industries and by labour factor categories (identified by status in employment, gender and education level).

The compilation of a matrix presenting the input of labour dis-aggregated by economic activity and labour categories allows to measure the volume of work provided by each category of labour factor to each industry and it can be directly linked to the value added matrix showing the flow of value added produced by each industry and the labour category which is remunerated by it. The labour matrix underlying the value added matrix is represented in table 4. The input of labour registered in this matrix refers to the domestic concept, which means that labour provided by resident workers to non resident production units are excluded while labour provided by non resident persons to resident production units are included (ESA95 §§ 11.17-11.19). This is shown in table 4 where column 7 is blank. Table 4 reports figures referring to the Europeland SAM, where domestic employment (i.e. including non resident workers) is cross classified by industry, gender and level of education.

Table 4 - **The labour matrix underlying the value added matrix**

Figures from ESA95 SAM (see footnote 2)

	Labour categories			Industries						
				Agriculture etc.	Mining, quarrying manufac. etc	Construction	Trade, repair, hotels, etc	Financial intermed. etc.	Public administr. etc.	Total
				1	2	3	4	5	6	
1	Employees	Male	Lower	24.0	156.7	58.9	94.3	14.6	71.0	419
2			Medium	1.0	16.9	3.0	13.4	10.9	16.7	62
3			Higher	0.8	10.0	1.4	5.7	9.2	31.9	59
4		Female	Lower	11.2	118.2	1.3	53.0	12.2	119.0	315
5			Medium	0.7	11.1	0.9	12.9	8.2	23.3	57
6			Higher	1.0	5.1	0.6	6.2	5.4	69.7	88
7	Self-employed	Male	Lower	32.1	111.9	37.8	66.8	24.1	10.3	283
8			Medium	1.9	15.9	1.7	11.7	24.2	3.2	59
9			Higher	0.0	3.4	0.7	1.5	22.1	0.8	29
10		Female	Lower	30.2	69.1	0.1	38.7	10.8	17.1	166
11			Medium	0.3	7.8	0.0	7.8	7.7	5.2	29
12			Higher	0.3	1.0	0.0	0.7	10.4	1.1	13
			Total	104	527	106	313	160	369	1 579

Implementing a labour-oriented value added matrix in Italy

The value added matrix

Our target is the estimation of the value added matrix shown in table 3a where compensation of self-employed labour is separated out from mixed income.

The first step is the estimation of the standard value added sub-matrix (table 5).

The standard value added sub-matrix simply arranges data currently produced in the national accounts.

According to ESA95, mixed income is the balancing item of the generation of income account of unincorporated enterprises owned by households, excluding quasi-corporations and excluding the owner-occupiers as producers of housing services for own final consumption. In the Italian national accounts these enterprises identify the Production Households sector which is namely composed by unincorporated enterprises owned by households, with less than five workers[6].

Differently from the theoretical framework, we cannot separate out fixed capital consumption from operating surplus and mixed income. As a consequence the matrix records *gross operating surplus* and *gross* mixed *income*.

Finally, it is worth stressing how the matrix shows value added at basic prices. The only taxes remaining to be paid out of gross value added at basic prices consist of "other taxes on production". These taxes mainly consist of current taxes (or subsidies) on the labour and capital employed in the enterprises as payroll taxes or taxes on vehicles or buildings. National accounts analyse such taxes by 101 industries.

Table 5 - **The standard value added sub-matrix for Italy**

Current millions euro, 1996

Generation of income account	Production account						FISIM	Total
	Agriculture etc.	Mining, quarrying, manufacturing etc.	Construction	Trade, repair, hotels, etc	Financial intermediation etc.	Public administr. etc.		
Compensation of employees	7 428	118 598	18 740	81 088	54 434	137 427	0	417 714
Gross mixed income	19 468	11 088	11 703	60 676	30 563	20 858	0	113 638
Gross operating surplus	4 056	92 517	17 126	80 803	133 624	19 623	-40 720	347 748
Other taxes less subsidies on production	-1 178	25	167	1 630	5 258	68	0	5 970
Total	29 774	222 228	47 736	224 197	223 879	177 976	-40 720	885 070

In the standard matrix, compensation of labour is included both in compensation of employees and in mixed income.

In order to construct a labour-oriented SAM, it is preferable, in our view, to separate out self-employed labour compensation from mixed income thus getting a value added matrix where compensation of labour remunerates both employees and self-employed.

We compensate self-employed labour exactly as the labour supplied by employees, provided they work in the same kind of activity and in enterprises of similar dimension,

6. In the Italian national accounts, self-employed labour underlying mixed income is only a part of self-employed labour engaged in the production process. In fact, in Italy there are self-employed working in corporations and quasi-corporations who cannot be considered strictly neither employees nor capital earners. These persons are remunerated through operating surplus in the generation of income account, and through capital income in the allocation of primary income account.

taking into account the different (generally higher) number of hours worked by self-employed. The results are in table 6.

Table 6 - **The labour-oriented value added sub-matrix for Italy**

Current millions euro, 1996

Generation of income account		Production account						FISIM	Total
		Agriculture etc.	Mining, quarrying, manufact.	Construction	Trade, repair, hotels, etc	Financial intermed. etc	Public administr. ecc.		
Compensation of labour	Employees	7 428	118 597	18 741	81 088	54 434	137 427	0	417 714
	Self-employed	12 963	7 179	5 679	37 517	13 098	7 028	0	83 465
Gross operating surplus*		10 562	96 426	23 151	103 961	151 089	33 452	-40 720	377 921
Other taxes less subsidies on production		-1 178	25	167	1 630	5 258	68	0	5 970
Total		29 774	222 228	47 736	224 197	223 879	177 976	-40 720	885 070

* This aggregate is equal to the operating surplus and mixed income less imputed self-employed compensation of labour

Italy applies a labour-based method in order to estimate compensation of employees, the variable being estimated by multiplying compensation of employee rates by full time equivalent labour units.

For the time being, national accounts analyse compensation of employees by industry (101 branches), class size (8 classes), and separating out workers employed in the underground economy (non-registered) from the others (registered).

Our objective is to further analyse compensation of employees/self-employed labour by gender and education.

The exercise presented here refers to 1996. Monetary variables are measured in current lire, labour in full time equivalent units.

The first step is the estimation of a labour matrix where both employee and self-employed labour are analysed by gender and education (table 9).

As a second step we estimate the per capita remuneration of labour, both for employees and self-employed. Such values are multiplied by the underlying labour units in order to get a first estimate of compensation of labour and the corresponding per capita values (tables 11, 12).

Finally estimates have to be reconciled to the NA data on compensation of employees and mixed income by industry (table 13).

The labour matrix

The Italian approach for the estimation of the input of labour

ISTAT has a long tradition about the integration of labour statistics within the national accounts framework. Actually, national account estimates move from this integration which guarantees on the exhaustiveness of Italian GDP. In fact, almost 70% of Italian GDP is estimated through the following method: per capita values (value added, production, wages and salaries) are multiplied by the estimated input of labour, after having corrected the per capita values for underreporting and after having estimated the overall labour underlying product (registered and non-registered).

Labour input estimates aim at measuring exhaustively both observed and non observed labour.

The labour input is estimated for the benchmark year[7] applying the technique described hereafter; for the following years, estimates are obtained updating benchmark estimates through a set of indicators. The estimation technique for the benchmark year is based on the collection of all the available sources of information and proceeding on the following steps (schematically presented in the box):

A1 harmonisation of the reference period and territory;

A2 conceptual harmonisation to national accounts definitions (with reference to "domestic employment" as a production factor of GDP);

B1 estimation of labour demand through the integration of sources on enterprises (for example *ad hoc* estimation of employment in some economic activities for which exhaustive data sources exist, like General Government; integration of administrative data on special categories of workers like own account workers, if under-covered);

B2 estimation of labour supply through the integration of sources on households (Census of the Population and Labour Force Survey) and correction of main errors within the sources on the side of labour supply (for example classification of economic activity).

The objective of steps A and B, is to achieve the exhaustiveness of sources measuring in the households the number of primary jobs, both registered and non registered, and in the enterprises the number of registered jobs. These steps aim at filling statistical gaps due to non-response or lack of up-dated registers, or due to differences in the reference population of surveys.

C comparison of labour supply and labour demand to identify primary and multiple registered jobs and most of the non-registered primary jobs.

Comparison of data sources is made at a very detailed level. In particular estimates are made separately for three status in employment (employees, own-account workers/employers, family workers: I=1, 2, 3; consistently with ESA95 definitions), economic activities (5 digit of ATECO91[8]: J=1… 873) and regions (2 digit of NUTS: N=1… 20)[9]. The process is displayed in the box which follows:

D estimation of other components of the underground economy: non registered foreign workers (through indirect estimates based on administrative and other sources), non registered multiple jobs (indirectly estimated through monetary aggregates or other indicators), persons declaring themselves as non-employed but declaring also to have worked in the reference week (surveyed by the labour force survey -LFS), informal jobs (in the agriculture and construction sectors);

---

7.   The last benchmark refers to 1991, when the last available Population and Enterprises Census was performed.

8.   The first four digits of ATECO91 correspond directly to NACE Rev1.

9.   We build two matrices, one with the data integrated from the supply side and one from the demand side, each matrix of 20x3x873=52380 cells (regionsxstatusxATECO). Each cell identifies the number of workers of region N, status I and ATECO J.

E transformation of jobs into full-time equivalent units through a coefficient resulting as the ratio between the average number of hours actually worked and the number of hours to be worked according to National Contracts[10].

Italian approach to the estimation of the input of labour

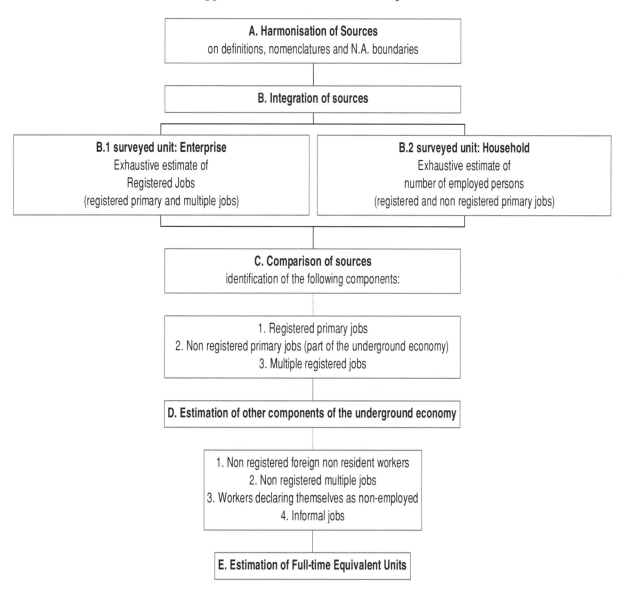

The updating reflects the benchmark principles since different sources are used in order to derive indicators which are directly applied to update the different segments of employment. For example households surveys (like LFS) provide the indicators applied to primary registered and non- registered jobs, while administrative data and registers of enterprises provide the indicators applied to registered jobs.

---

10.   Note that the number of hours actually worked used to calculate the coefficient to transform jobs into FTEU is not the exhaustive estimate of the total amount of hours worked (as defined by ESA95) but it represents an average indicator separately estimated by status in employment, economic activity and segment of labour, derived from the available sources of information.

Table 7 reports the sources of data used both for the estimation of the input of labour in the benchmark year and for the updating in the following years. In particular census data were available only in 1991, while administrative data and sample surveys are available every year.

Table 7 - **Main Sources of Information used for the purpose of the estimation of the input of labour**

	Sources	Typology of Information	1991	Current Years
Households and Enterprises:				
A	Population Census	Resident employed persons by working place	X	
B	Labour-Force Survey	Resident employed persons	X	X
C	Multipurpose Survey	Persons employed by households		X
D	Manufacture, Services and Institution Census	Registered employment, main and multiple activities	X	
E	Agriculture Census	Agricultural sector, main and multiple activities	X	
F	Tax Register	Enterprises and employed persons with VAT code	X	X
G	Register of Production Enterprises (A.S.I.A.)	Number of people employed by economic activity		X
H	INPS (National Institute for Social Security) data on employees and coadjutants	Employees from households and enterprises, co-ordinated and continual co-operators, foreigners	X	X
I	ISTAT statistic surveys on the accounts of enterprises	Employees, up to 19 people, more than 20, more than 500 people in bigger-sized enterprises		X
L	Balance date per specific economic activity	Energy, tobacco, railways, post offices, telecommunications, credit, insurance	X	X
M	Periodical statistic surveys on activities sensitive to underground works	Ordinary and extraordinary maintenance of homes, holidays		Casual
N	Administrative data and statistic surveys on specific typologies of employees	Non-resident foreigners, temporary lay-off, part-time workers	X	X
O	Administrative data on specific economic activities	Transport of goods and passengers on the road, research and development, private education	X	X
Institutions				
P	State General Accounting Office, Ministries and other Bodies	Employees of the General Government	X	X
Q	ISTAT statistic surveys on public institutions	Municipalities, Mountain communities, provinces, regions		X
R	INPS Data for Private Social Institutions	Associations, Organisations and others	X	X

The labour matrix underlying the value added matrix

As explained above, ISTAT estimates full time equivalent units integrating and comparing different data sources, from the supply and the demand side of labour. This process is conceived in a way that makes impossible to associate to each labour unit the characteristics of the worker underneath it which have not been used as classification variables throughout all the benchmark steps. Therefore in order to derive a classification of labour by gender and education level we had to replicate the benchmark process considering from the beginning gender as one of the classification variables. With respect to education, no information is available from the demand side sources so that the disaggregation of labour by education level is carried out applying to the whole amount of labour the coefficients derived from the supply side sources.

Although we replicated the benchmark process, the already disseminated national accounts estimates represent a constraint. Therefore the results of the re-benchmarking process are used as indicators to split through a top-down approach the official data on labour. The advantage of this approach with respect to a mere application of coefficients derived from one source of information (for example the LFS), is that it is based on the same procedure and data sources used to estimate the official data: *i.e.* for each segment of labour estimated for the benchmark year, we estimated separately the corresponding indicators by gender.

We replicated the process with a less detailed classification of the economic activities. The purpose is twofold: first we decided to rely more upon a variable which less suffers from classification errors (gender) and to rely less upon the detailed classification of economic activity, which is often mistaken in the supply side sources. Secondly to overcome, at least partially, the impossibility to replicate the too onerous *filières[11]* process which, in the benchmark, allowed to correct classification errors related to economic activities in the population census.

The re-benchmarking process has been carried out by gender, three statuses in employment, twenty regions, sixteen economic activities[12]. The steps followed are the same described for the benchmark process (see box). The main aspects to be pointed out are the following.

1. Independent workers.

As stated in note 6, the self-employed included in the labour matrix are those employed in the Production Households sector which is namely composed by unincorporated enterprises owned by households, with less than five workers. Since the information needed in order to separate self-employed by institutional sector are not available in the Census of the Population and in the surveys on households in general, the break-down of self-employed by gender is based on indicators derived from the Census on Manufacture, Services and Institutions (which is also the main input for the estimation of labour by institutional sector). These indicators by gender have been differentiated for registered and non registered jobs using the information obtained from the re-benchmarking process[13].

2. The sources of information used in order to estimates the indicators to split national accounts estimates on the input of labour by gender and education are described in table 8 (letters in the first column refer to the corresponding source in table 7).

---

11. A *filière* is a group of economic activities describing the whole process through which a raw material is extracted, transformed into a finished product and sold on the market. The *filière* approach is based on the grouping of data from households survey (Census of the Population) in *filières*. Each macro-*filière* contains data classified by economic activity. The basic assumption is that economic activity classification errors resulting from information given by individual workers in the Census of Population will, in all probability, remain within the same *filière* of production thus nullifying the error. (Istat, 1993).

12. 1 agriculture (NACE divisions 01-05); 2 mining, quarrying, extraction and transformation of raw materials and electricity, gas and water supply (NACE divisions 10-14, 23-28, 40-41); 3 manufacturing (NACE divisions 15-22, 36-37); 4 manufacture of machinery and equipment (NACE divisions 29-35); 5 construction (NACE division 45); 6 trade (NACE divisions 50-52); 7 hotels and restaurants (NACE division 55); 8 transport and communications (NACE divisions 60-64); 9 credit (NACE division 65); 10 insurance (NACE division 66); 11 auxiliary to financial intermediaries and business activities (NACE divisions 67-74); 12 Public Administration (NACE division 75); 13 Education (NACE division 80); 14 Health and social work (NACE division 85); 15 Other Social and Personal activities (NACE divisions 90-93); 16 Private Households with employed persons (NACE division 95)

13. The underlying assumption is that once self-employed of Production Households sector are broken down by gender, the quota of registered for males and the quota of registered for females is the same in the Production Households sector and in the Corporations and Quasi-Corporations sector.

Table 8 - **Main Sources of Information used for the purpose of the estimation of the input of labour**

	Sources	Typology of Information	Gender	Education
		Households and Enterprises:		
A	Population Census	Resident employed persons by working place	X	X
B	Labour-Forces Survey	Resident employed persons	X	X
D	Manufacture, Services and Institution Census	Registered employment, main and multiple activities	X	
E	Agriculture Census	Agricultural sector, main and multiple activities	X	
L	Balance date of specific economic activities	Credit, insurance	X	X (credit only)
N	data on specific typologies of employees	Non-resident foreigners	X	
Institutions				
P	State General Accounting Office, Ministries and other Bodies	Employees of the General Government	X	X

3. Estimation of indicators for the different segments of labour. Summarising what we explained above, the indicators by gender for each of the different segments of labour have been calculated as follows:

1. registered primary jobs, registered multiple jobs, non registered primary jobs.

For 1991, comparison of census data (integrated as described above) is made separately for gender (K=1,2), three status in employment (employees, own-account workers/employers, family workers: I=1, 2, 3; consistently with ESA95 definitions), economic activities (macro-industries: J=1, …, 16) and regions (2 digit of NUTS: N=1, …, 20) [14]. The process is displayed in the box which follows:

A) $Ls_{nijk} \cap Ld_{nijk}$ = registered primary jobs

B) $|Ls_{nijk} - Ld_{nijk}| > 0$: B1) $Ls_{nijk} > Ld_{nijk} \rightarrow Ls_{nijk} - Ld_{nijk}$ = non registered primary jobs

---

Once 1991 indicators by gender are obtained, they are updated through the rates of change of the gender structure derived from the LFS.

2. *Workers declaring themselves as non-employed* (see previous paragraph, point D).

This segment of labour is estimated using LFS and the Population Census and currently updating on the basis of LFS; therefore the dis-aggregation by gender and education is directly obtained from LFS for the year 1996.

3. *Non-registered and non-resident foreign workers are broken down through indicators derived from data provided by ISTAT and Caritas (a private non profit institution) which publishes a yearbook on immigration in Italy.*

4. *Non-registered multiple jobs* are broken down by gender applying the same coefficients calculated for the non registered primary jobs (see point a.)

---

14. We build two matrices, one with the data integrated from the supply side and one from the demand side, each matrix of 20x2x3x16=1920 cells (regions x gender x status x macro-industries). Each cell identifies the number of workers of region N, gender K, status I and macro-industry J.

A further analysis can be made for some sectors of economic activities, for which specific and exhaustive sources of information are available.

5. *Agriculture* (NaceRev.1 division 01 - 05)

The Census of Agriculture carried out in 1990 is the base for the calculation of indicators by gender for all the segments of labour of this sector (registered and non registered primary and multiple jobs, excluding non-registered and non-resident foreign workers, the estimation of which is described at point c). The updating method is the same described in point a.

6. *Public Administration* (NaceRev.1 division 75)

The Public Administration Yearbook provides detailed data on labour by gender and education level. The Yearbook is the main source used in the current estimation of labour in the GG sector. Data are estimated and broken down by gender and education directly for 1996.

7. *Credit and Insurance sectors*. (NaceRev.1 division 65 and 66)

The National Associations of Companies engaged in the credit and insurance sectors provide yearly detailed statistics on registered workers. This allowed to estimate directly for 1996 labour by gender and education (in the credit sector) or gender only (in the insurance sector).

8. *Private Households with employed persons* (NaceRev.1 division 95)

The INPS (National Institute for Social Security) yearly provides data on registered workers employed by Households and the ISTAT Multipurpose survey provides data on the registered and non-registered workers. Data are available by gender.

Where not stated differently, the break-down by education level (ISCED 1-2, ISCED 3-4, ISCED 1-2) is carried out through a mere top-down approach, applying indicators derived from the LFS, estimated separately for status in employment, six industries[15], gender.

Following the steps described so far, it was possible to estimate jobs by gender and education. Next step focus on the estimation of full-time equivalents. As explained in par.3.2, this implies the estimation of coefficients to transform part-time jobs (both registered and non-registered) into FTEU, taking into account the amount of hours worked. When the input of labour is analysed also by gender and education, coefficients to transform jobs into FTEU should be estimated separately for gender and education, in addition to the economic activity. In this respect the current coefficients used, have been differentiated by gender and education using the information on hours worked derived from the LFS.

Table 9 reports the input of labour by industry, status in employment, gender and education. Data refer to FTEU for 1996. Tables A.1-A.3 in the Annex report some analysis on the distribution of labour by status in employment, macro-industries, gender and education level.

---

15. The six industries are those used in the pilot SAM.

Table 9 - **The labour matrix underlying the value added matrix**

Full time equivalent units, 1996

Labour categories			Industries						
			Agriculture etc.	Mining, quarrying, manufac. etc.	Construction	Trade, repair, hotels, etc	Financial intermed. etc.	Public administr. etc.	Total
Status	Gender	Education							
Employees	male	low	306 767	1 907 648	659 330	1 313 372	191 088	948 608	5 326 813
		medium	48 044	902 975	129 428	654 357	513 446	705 231	2 953 481
		high	2 240	101 973	9 107	71 292	157 473	441 196	783 281
		total	357 051	2 912 596	797 865	2 039 021	862 007	2 095 035	9 063 575
	female	low	187 395	874 915	18 799	658 578	202 374	1 067 412	3 009 473
		medium	13 825	426 408	38 747	532 651	439 477	1 377 677	2 828 785
		high	597	39 375	804	41 441	47 995	622 412	752 624
		total	201 817	1 340 698	58 350	1 232 670	689 846	3 067 501	6 590 882
	total employees		558 868	4 253 294	856 215	3 271 691	1 551 853	5 162 536	15 654 457
Self-employed[*]	male	low	562 776	193 602	184 595	797 809	47 087	131 800	1 917 667
		medium	72 069	88 871	91 115	380 200	129 320	83 106	844 681
		high	4 553	10 453	27 905	36 989	356 113	89 161	525 175
		total	639 398	292 926	303 615	1 214 998	532 520	304 067	3 287 523
	female	low	159 000	75 612	14 413	400 975	44 488	108 060	802 549
		medium	19 723	39 827	3 006	194 775	33 884	76.111	367 326
		high	1 152	4 604	1 009	17 300	29 667	43 808	97 540
		total	179 875	120 043	18 428	613 050	108 039	227 979	1 267 415
	total self-employed		819 273	412 969	322 043	1 828 048	640 559	532 046	4 554 938
Total FTEUs			1 378 141	4 666 263	1 178 258	5 099 739	2 192 412	5 694 582	20 209 395

(*) FTEUs of self-employed included in the table relate to self-employed working in unincorporated enterprises. In order to get the total amount of FTEUs of self-employed estimated as labour input in National Accounts it is necessary to sum up 1) self-employed producing for own final consumption and 2) self-employed working in corporations.

Compensation of labour by industry, gender and education

The monetary counterpart of the labour matrix is a matrix containing *compensation of labour per capita values* for each category of employment.

The data sources

The main data sources used for the estimates are national accounts, sample surveys and administrative data sources.

National accounts

Particularly we have used the following NA statistics:

- Wages and salaries (D.11) paid to registered employees, cross-classified by 101 industries and 8 size classes;

- Wages and salaries (D.11) paid to non-registered employees, cross-classified by 101 industries and 8 size classes;

- Employers' actual social contributions (D.121) cross-classified by 101 industries and 8 dimensional classes;

- Employers' imputed social contributions (D.122) cross-classified by 101 industries and 8 size classes

- Full time equivalent units of registered employee labour cross-classified by 101 industries and 8 size classes

- Full time equivalent units of non-registered employee labour cross-classified by 101 industries and 8 size classes

Sample surveys

In Italy, there are only few surveys which collect data on wages and salaries simultaneously by industry, gender and education. For this exercise, we have used the Bank of Italy survey on households' income and wealth (SHIW) for the year 1995 and the ISTAT survey on wages and salaries (ESES) for the year 1995.

The SHIW collects data on the net income earned by each component of the household, by pointing out each single source of income. The survey collect also demographic, social and economic characteristics of the earner. The surveyed unit is the household. The sample is about 8000 households and 25000 persons. The SHIW is carried out every two years.

The ESES collects data on the structure of wages and salaries by social and demographic characteristics of the employee and according to the industry where he/she is employed.

According to the European statistical program the survey is carried out every four years. The survey focuses on local units with more than 10 workers and belonging to the manufacturing and service economic activities (namely, NACE rev.1 C-K). In 1995, the sample was 7500 local units and about 103000 employees.

Administrative data

We have used statistics on wages and salaries by professional level, collected by the Italian Bank Association on the employees of the credit and insurance sectors. Moreover we have used Government statistics on the wages and salaries of the public sector employees. Both the data sources provide only the professional level detail.

Method and results

We apply different methods for each industry, depending on the availability and reliability of data.

As a first common step, we calculate compensation of employees per capita values for each industry, separating registered employees from non-registered employees. The difference is equal to the employers' actual and imputed social contributions.

On the basis of available data sources we calculate wage differentials by gender and education for each industry.

For what concerns the agriculture sector, we can only use the SHIW data. Due to the very small size of the sample, some cells record only a few number of cases, especially for the less frequent typologies like high education. For this reason, at first we differentiate wages by gender, and only as a second step we differentiate them by education. The assumption is that wage differences due to education are independent from the gender of the worker. Another problem is connected with the use of the SHIW.

As a matter of fact, the survey collects *net* incomes whereas we need a proxy variable of wages and salaries. A micro simulation model developed at ISTAT allows estimating social contributions and taxes charging on each income. Differentials on wages and salaries are calculated using these "gross" values. Nevertheless, we have verified that social contributions and taxes are proportional to the net compensation of labour and do not affect significantly the differentials by gender and education.

The differentials for Manufacturing, Construction, Trade and Financial sectors are calculated on the basis of the ESES. The population surveyed does not include enterprises with less than 11 workers. This fact may affect the results for the industries characterised by small enterprises, namely construction and trade. The assumption is that differentials by gender and education are not affected by the size of the enterprise. Differentials for the Financial sector have been calculated also taking into account administrative data on wages and salaries by professional level.

Finally, for the sixth industry (Public administration etc) we have used mainly the SHIW and General Government administrative data on wages and salaries analysed by professional category. Table 10 displays the differentials estimated for each industry.

Table 10 - **Wage differentials by gender and education (industry average=1)**

Percentages

Kind of labour	Industries					
	Agriculture etc.	Mining, quarrying, manufacturing	Construction	Trade, repair, hotels, etc	Financial intermediation. etc	Public administration etc.
Male-Low	0.99	1.00	0.94	1.01	0.84	0.95
Male-Medium	1.49	1.28	1.28	1.24	1.27	1.07
Male-High	2.21	2.26	1.70	1.72	1.71	1.66
Female-Low	0.73	0.79	0.87	0.80	0.65	0.63
Female- Medium	1.10	0.96	1.01	0.89	0.84	0.89
Female-High	1.64	1.28	1.01	1.33	1.07	1.05

We apply wage differentials to the compensation of employee per capita values of each industry, separating registered from non-registered employees. We assume that wage differentials do not change in the underground economy. The estimates are shown in table 11.

Table 11 - **Per capita compensation of employees – first estimates**

Current thousand euros, 1996

Kind of labour	Industries					
	Agriculture etc.	Mining, quarrying, manufacturing	Construction	Trade, repair, hotels, etc	Financial intermediation. etc	Public administration etc.
Male-Low	13.15	27.94	20.60	25.04	29.51	25.40
Male-Medium	19.75	35.62	27.96	30.68	44.49	28.45
Male-High	29.38	62.90	37.26	42.71	60.11	44.20
Female-Low	9.76	22.04	19.05	19.78	22.68	16.69
Female- Medium	14.66	26.85	22.04	22.06	29.34	23.76
Female-High	21.81	35.76	22.20	33.01	37.69	28.01
Total	13.29	27.88	21.89	24.78	35.08	26.62

We apply also the same differentials to the self-employed compensation of labour, thus getting the following *imputed wages and salaries rates*.

Table 12 - **Per capita compensation of self-employed labour – first estimates**

Current thousand euros, 1996

Kind of labour	Industries					
	Agriculture etc.	Mining, quarrying, manufacturing	Construction	Trade, repair, hotels, etc	Financial intermediation. etc	Public administration etc.
Male-Low	15.65	17.42	16.60	20.73	17.20	12.61
Male-Medium	23.51	22.21	22.53	25.41	25.93	14.12
Male-High	34.98	39.21	30.02	35.37	35.04	21.94
Female-Low	11.62	13.74	15.35	16.38	13.22	8.28
Female- Medium	17.45	16.74	17.76	18.27	17.10	11.79
Female-High	25.96	22.29	17.88	27.33	21.97	13.90
Total	15.82	17.38	17.63	20.52	20.45	13.21

Reconciliation with national accounts

The remuneration of labour rates are applied to the corresponding full time equivalent units. The result is a first estimate of compensation of labour by branch, gender and education. Such data have to be reconciled to National accounts constraints (namely to the compensation of employees by industry) and to the imputed compensation of self-employed: discrepancies are allocated in proportion to compensation of employees/self-employed recorded by each category of employment.

In the following figure we make a comparison between the first estimates (FE) and the post-reconciliation estimates (NA). Comparisons are made for employees (E) and self-employed (SE).

Fig. 1 **Comparison between "First estimates" and "Post-reconciliation estimates"**

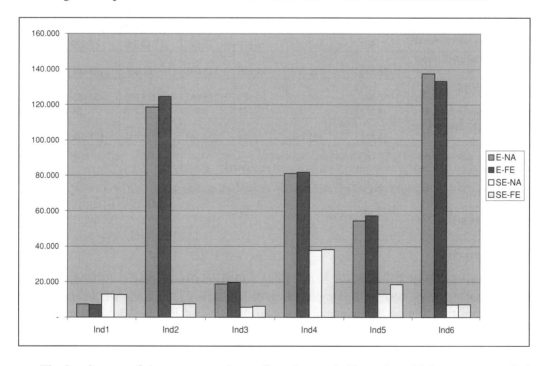

Final estimates of the compensations of employees/self-employed labour are recorded in the value added sub-matrix as shown in table 13, while implicit per capita compensation of labour is shown in table A4 in the annex.

Table 13 - **The final value added matrix**

Current million euros, 1996(*).

Generation of income account			Production account						FISIM	Total
			Agriculture etc.	Mining, quarrying, manufact. etc.	Construct.	Trade, repair, hotels, etc	Financial intermediat. etc	Public administr. etc.		
Employees	male	low	4 307	50 601	13 292	31 823	5 482	25 093	0	130 598
		medium	1 021	31 325	3 753	20 563	21 359	21 990	0	100 011
		high	76	6 277	351	3 064	9 362	21 285	0	40 416
		total	*5 403*	*88 204*	*17 396*	*55 451*	*36 203*	*68 368*	*0*	*271 025*
	female	low	1 807	18 089	376	12 387	4 292	16 599	0	53 550
		medium	203	10 922	947	11 853	12 031	34 340	0	70 296
		high	15	1 383	20	1 398	1 908	18 119	0	22 843
		total	*2 024*	*30 395*	*1 343*	*25 638*	*18 231*	*69 059*	*0*	*146 689*
	total employees		**7 428**	**118 598**	**18 740**	**81 088**	**54 434**	**137 427**	**0**	**417 714**
Self-employed	male	low	8 957	3 203	2 814	16 361	574	1 640	0	33 549
		medium	1 718	1 875	1 864	9 545	2 379	1 157	0	18 538
		high	151	388	753	1 216	8 850	1 933	0	13 289
		total	*10 827*	*5 465*	*5 430*	*27 121*	*11 803*	*4 730*	*0*	*65 377*
	female	low	1 767	983	187	6 435	419	855	0	10 646
		medium	341	635	48	3 509	412	860	0	5 805
		high	28	95	14	452	463	583	0	1 636
		total	*2 136*	*1 714*	*248*	*10 396*	*1 295*	*2 299*	*0*	*18 088*
	total self-employed		**12 963**	**7 179**	**5 679**	**37 517**	**13 098**	**7 029**	**0**	**83 465**
Total compensation of labour			**20 390**	**125 777**	**24 418**	**118 606**	**67 531**	**144 455**	**0**	**501 179**
Operating surplus(**)			10 562	96 426	23 151	103 961	151 089	33 453	-40 720	377 921
Other taxes less subsidies on production			-1 178	25	167	1 630	5 258	68	0	5 970
Total Value Added (basic prices)			29 774	222.228	47 736	224 197	223 879	177 976	-40 720	885 070

(*) This table has been originally estimated in Italian lire and then transformed into euro values, thus determining very small discrepancies among the data reported in this table and the published national accounts data (in euros).

(**)This aggregate is equal to the operating surplus and mixed income less imputed self-employed compensation of labour

Analysis of the results[16]

The Italian case

The final result of the exercise is the value added matrix displayed in table 13. As shown in table 14, the weight of compensation of labour is 57% for the whole economy, ranging from the 30% of the financial sector to the 81% of Public Administration and other services.

---

16.   This section is mainly based on Battellini F., Coli A., Tartamella F. (2002).

Table 14 - **Distribution of value added among primary inputs**

Percentages

			Agriculture etc.	Mining, quarrying, manufact. etc.	Construction	Trade, repair, hotels, etc	Financial intermediat.et c.	Public administrat etc.	Total
Labour	male	low	0.45	0.24	0.34	0.21	0.03	0.15	0.19
		medium	0.09	0.15	0.12	0.13	0.11	0.13	0.13
		high	0.01	0.03	0.02	0.02	0.08	0.13	0.06
		total	*0.55*	*0.42*	*0.48*	*0.37*	*0.21*	*0.41*	*0.38*
	female	low	0.12	0.09	0.01	0.08	0.02	0.10	0.07
		medium	0.02	0.05	0.02	0.07	0.06	0.20	0.09
		high	0.00	0.01	0.00	0.01	0.01	0.11	0.03
		total	*0.14*	*0.14*	*0.03*	*0.16*	*0.09*	*0.40*	*0.19*
		total	**0.68**	**0.57**	**0.51**	**0.53**	**0.30**	**0.81**	**0.57**
*Operating surplus**			*0.35*	*0.43*	*0.48*	*0.46*	*0.67*	*0.19*	*0.43*
Other taxes less subsidies			*-0.04*	*0,00*	*0.00*	*0.01*	*0.02*	*0.00*	*0.01*
Total			1.00	1.00	1.00	1.00	1.00	1.00	1.00

* This aggregate is equal to the operating surplus and mixed income less imputed self-employed compensation of labour

Table 15 shows as the case of Public administration and other services sector is a striking example of how the analysis of value added composition, and in particular of labour compensation, can be enriched by the joint analysis of prices (per capita compensations) and volumes (FTEUs). In this sector females count for 58% of FTEUs. Since their per capita compensation is 85% when compared to the branch average, their quota of compensation reduces to 49%. On the contrary, males in the same sector counts for the 42% of the branch FTEUs: thanks to their per capita compensation which is 120% with respect to the branch average, their quota in terms of compensation reaches 51%. On the contrary, in the construction sector, where there is no gender wage differential, 93% of FTEUs are males, as well as 93% of sector remuneration is received by males. Analogously, per capita education differentials act on compensation shares. For example, in the Public administration and other services sector the quota of low educated FTEUs is twice as much the quota of high educated FTEUs (40% the former *versus* 21% the latter); per capita compensation of low educated is 77% and the one of high educated is 138% with respect to the branch average. As a result, the share of compensation is almost the same: 31% is perceived by low educated and 29% by high educated.

Table 15 – **Analysis of labour compensation**

Percentages (branch=100)

		Agriculture etc.	Mining, quarrying, manufact. etc.	Construction	Trade, repair, hotels, etc	Financial intermediat.e tc.	Public administrat etc.	Total
Total FTEUs	male	72.30	68.70	93.48	63.81	63.61	42.13	61.12
	female	27.70	31.30	6.52	36.19	36.39	57.87	38.88
		100	100	100	100	100	100	100
	low	88.23	65.40	74.44	62.17	22.12	39.61	54.71
	medium	11.15	31.25	22.26	34.55	50.91	39.37	34.61
	high	0.62	3.35	3.30	3.28	26.97	21.01	10.68
		100	100	100	100	100	100	100
Total labour compensation	male	79.60	74.47	93.48	69.62	71.09	50.60	67.12
	female	20.40	25.53	6.52	30.38	28.91	49.40	32.88
		100	100	100	100	100	100	100
	low	82.58	57.94	68.26	56.49	15.94	30.59	45.56
	medium	16.10	35.58	27.08	38.34	53.58	40.39	38.84
	high	1.32	6.47	4.66	5.17	30.48	29.02	15.60
		100	100	100	100	100	100	100
Labour compensation differentials [*]	male	110	108	100	109	112	120	110
	female	74	82	100	84	79	85	85
		100	100	100	100	100	100	100
	low	94	89	92	91	72	77	83
	medium	144	114	122	111	105	103	112
	high	213	193	141	158	113	138	146
		100	100	100	100	100	100	100

[*] Labour compensation differentials are obtained as the percentage ratio between per capita compensation of each labour category and the average per capita compensation of the branch.

We concentrate now on the analysis of employees. Table 16, based on table 9, displays the percentage distribution of employees of the six labour categories in each branch. The last row gives the incidence of each branch over the total economy in terms of employment.

Table 16 shows that in Italy employees in FTEUs are mainly men (57,9% of FTEUs). This is particularly evident in the construction sector where men represent 93,2% of total FTEUs. Only the Public administration and other services sector employ more women than men. With respect to the education level, 53,3% are low educated ad 63,9% of the low educated are men. Considering the quota of low educated within the same branch, the agricultural sector is the one registering the highest quota (88,4%) while the smallest quota is registered in the financial sector (25,4%). On the opposite the highest quota of high educated within the same branch is registered in the Public administration and other services sector (20,6%).

Table 16 – **Employees' labour by gender and education**

Percentage values

			Agriculture etc.	Mining, quarrying, manufacturing etc.	Construction	Trade, repair, hotels, etc	Financial intermediation etc.	Public administration etc.	Total
employees	male	low	54.9	44.9	77.0	40.1	12.3	18,4	34,0
		medium	8.6	21.2	15.1	20.0	33.1	13,7	18,9
		high	0.4	2.4	1.1	2.2	10.1	8,5	5,0
		total	63.9	68.5	93.2	62.3	55.5	40,6	57,9
	female	low	33.5	20.6	2.2	20.1	13.0	20,7	19,2
		medium	2.5	10.0	4.5	16.3	28.3	26,7	18,1
		high	0.1	0.9	0.1	1.3	3.1	12,1	4,8
		total	36.1	31.5	6.8	37.7	44.5	59,4	42,1
Total employees			**100.0**	**100.0**	**100.0**	**100.0**	**100.0**	**100.0**	**100.0**
total low			88,4	65,4	79.2	60.3	25.4	39.1	53.3
total medium			11,1	31,3	19.6	36.3	61.4	40.3	36.9
total high			0,5	3,3	1.2	3.4	13.2	20.6	9.8
Total employees			**100.0**	**100.0**	**100.0**	**100.0**	**100.0**	**100.0**	**100.0**
FTEU branch / FTEU total economy			3,6	27,2	5.5	20.9	9.9	33.0	100.0

Figure 2 pictures compensations differential by gender and education level for each branch. Each point coordinates correspond to percentages, with respect to the branch average, of male compensation (x axis) and female compensation (y axis) with the same education level working in the same branch. The value of 100 on both axes corresponds therefore to the branch average compensation. Points on the bisector represent cases in which average male compensation equals the female one. Points at the right (left) hand side of the vertical axis placed at value 100 represent men labour categories whose compensation is higher (lower) than the branch average. Correspondingly points above (below) the horizontal axis placed at value 100 represent women labour categories whose compensation is higher (lower) than the branch average. The figure shows as all points are below the bisector, proving that male work is more remunerated than the female one. The distance grows with the education level. Moreover figure 2 illustrates how for males medium education levels and in many cases even low education level assure, on average, an income which is equal or higher than the branch average, since it is, in percentage, equal or higher than 100. Female average compensation, instead, is higher than the branch average only when the education level is high. The only exception is in the agriculture and construction sectors where, presumably, women have higher professional status, even for medium education level. Within the same branch, differences in compensations among different work typologies can be also ascribed to differences in hours worked[17], in professional status, in years of service, or to productivity premia. Also the composition in terms of registered and non-registered work in the different work typologies can explain gender and education compensation differentials. Non-registered workers compensation does not include in fact social contributions. It is therefore, *ceteris paribus*, lower than registered workers compensation. Some branches record a higher occurrence of the non-registered work for women. This brings female average compensation to be lower than that of males, for the same branch and education level.

---

17.   FTEUs are computed taking into account part-time work, but not overtime. This is why compensation differentials can not be explained by the prevalence of part-time work in some categories. It is possible instead to ascribe them to overtime work.

Figure 2. **Compensation of employees gender differentials by education level (branch average=100) ,
Italy -1996**

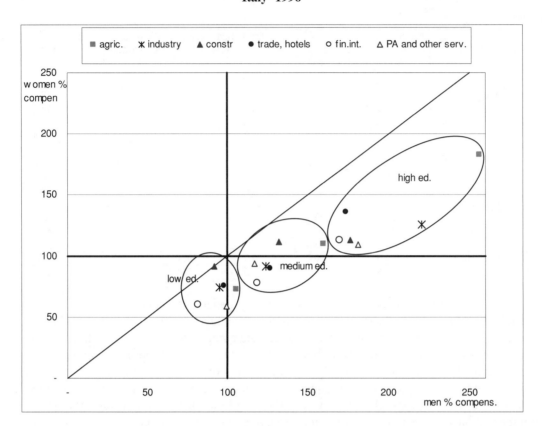

The situation pictured in figure 3 is more complex. It shows differentials with respect to the average national compensation. In this case compensation differentials can be also explained by a branch effect. Figure 3[18] therefore allows explaining differentials jointly with branch, gender and education effect. Moreover, the comparison with figure 2 highlights the sole branch effect. For example, figure 3 illustrates that the manufacturing and financial intermediation sectors record higher compensation than the national average, for each gender and education level, since they are always pictured in a high-right position with respect to the other points in the same circle. If we compare the same points in figure 2, it is possible to notice as they are placed at the opposite extreme in the same education circle. This proves that the male comparative advantage is mainly due to the branch more than to the education level. The joint effect branch-education-gender is more evident in the case of agriculture and construction. In these sectors for women a high education level is not enough to perceive a remuneration above the national average (figure 3), while it allows overcoming the branch average (figure 2).

---

18.   Criteria for the construction of the picture are the same as those described for figure 2: therefore bisector and vertical and horizontal axis can be interpreted in the same way.

Figure 3. **Employees compensation gender differential for each education level (national average=100), Italy – 1996**

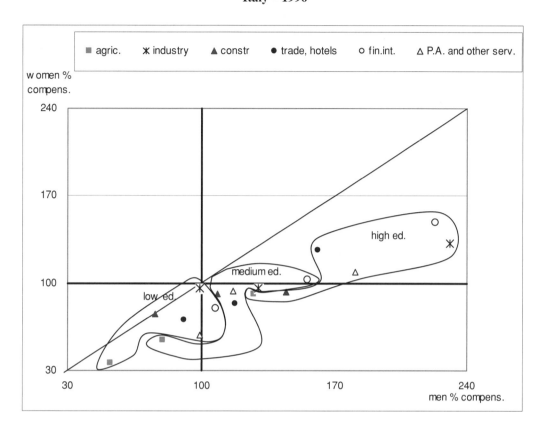

In the Annex, some elaboration on the weight of each labour category in terms of FTEU and the wage gaps are presented.

International comparisons[19]

Figures 4 and 5 picture the education gap, *i.e.* they show how much, for the same gender, wages[20] vary by education level in each branch. The analysis is carried out separately for males (figure 4) and females (figure 5). Values are obtained as the ratio between the average wage of each education level and the corresponding branch average wage. Figures are in percentages.

The Italian education gap is higher than the one recorded in the other countries: this may imply that in Italy education "pays" more and that a high education level increases the probability to have a higher compensation. In the three countries the "gain" due to education is in the average higher for males.

In Italy the "gain" due to education is more evident in the agricultural sector (where the number of non-registered workers with low education is particularly high), both for

---

19. Evaluations are restricted to countries having comparable FTEUs estimates.

20. In international comparisons we analyse wages, while examining the sole Italian case we referred to compensation of employees. We remind that the latter are obtained summing social contributions to wages.

males and females; this sector is followed by the manufacturing industries for males and by the services sector for females.

Figure 6 reports the *gender gap*, *i.e.* the percentage ratio between the remuneration of females and the remuneration of males, given the education level and the industry: when the ratio equals 100 the remuneration of females is equal to that of males with the same education level and in the same industry. On the contrary, when the ratio is lower (higher) than 100, the remuneration of females is lower (higher) than that of males with the same education level and in the same industry.

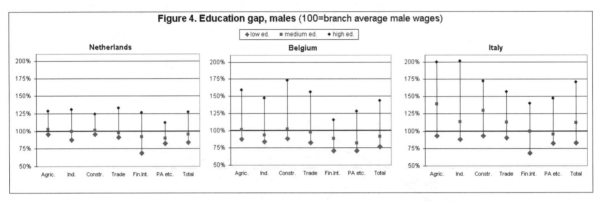

Figure 4. Education gap, males (100=branch average male wages)

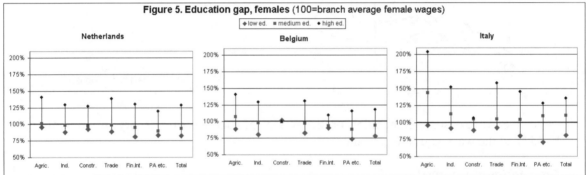

Figure 5. Education gap, females (100=branch average female wages)

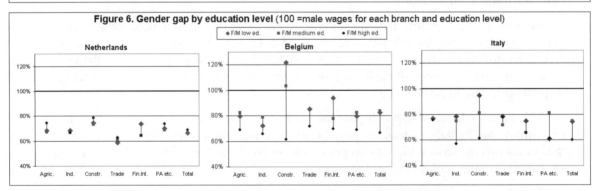

Figure 6. Gender gap by education level (100 =male wages for each branch and education level)

In the three countries females are paid less than men, for each education level and in each industry. The only exception is the construction sector in Belgium where low and medium educated females receive a higher remuneration than men with the same education level in the same sector. Remember that, in this sector, women presumably carry out jobs in higher professional status even when they are low educated. The same phenomenon in Italy does not allow women to gain higher remuneration than men but it reduces the gap between males and females wages.

Figure 6 also tells that in the Netherlands the gender gap does not vary with the education level as shown by the proximity of the points in the graph. The gap increases with the education level in the case of Belgium and Italy: highly educated women receive a remuneration which in the average is higher than that received by low educated women; but this gain is lower than that registered by males in the same sector and with the same education level. Therefore for high level of education the gender gap is higher than that for low educated workers.

Analogously to figures 2 and 3, figure 7 shows, for each country and for the total economy, wage differentials due to gender and education (average national wages =100).

Figure 7. **Gender wage differential by education level (national average=100) - Italy (1996), Belgium and the Netherlands (1997)**

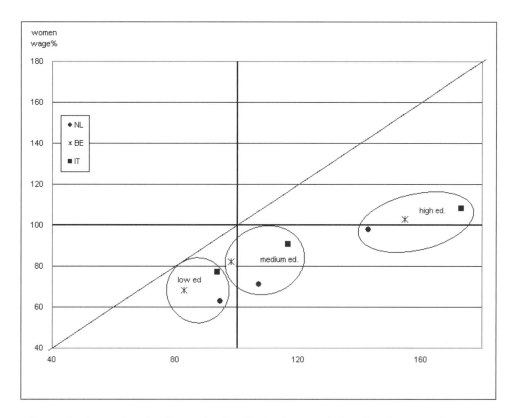

It synthesises what is shown in details in figures 4-6 and points out that wages are positively correlated with the education level. Moreover it shows that females' wages are systematically lower than males ones and the gap increases with the education level. Note the case of the Netherlands where highly educated women receive a lower wage than the national average.

Conclusion

In most of the European countries labour data are not integrated with national accounts statistics. On the contrary, Italy has a long tradition in this field, GDP estimates being based on an exhaustive estimation of the units of labour employed in the production process. This is essential in the compilation of a labour-oriented SAM. One of the objectives of the European LEG on SAMs was, in fact, to favour the estimation of labour input in the national accounts context by developing a labour-oriented SAM. Therefore the group decided to design a SAM where all monetary flows related to labour and the corresponding labour units are analysed by industry, status in employment (employees, self-employed), gender and education level.

In order to compile the pilot SAM for Italy, we took into account gender and education to estimate both labour units and compensation of labour. In this respect we replicated as far as possible the national account method, where traditionally the background characteristics of the workers like gender and education are not taken into account for the estimation of labour units and compensation of employees.

For what concerns employment we replicated the benchmark process adding gender as an input variable. The total amount of persons employed and jobs summed up to the same figures obtained in the benchmark of national accounts: in fact they are determined respectively by the amount of persons employed surveyed by the Census of the Population (integrated with LFS) and the number of jobs surveyed by the Manufacturing and Services Census, which represented the input sources in the benchmark and in the re-benchmark process. Nevertheless some differences have arisen. Since this method gives results which crucially rely on the disaggregation adopted, the use of a different breakdown (gender, three status in employment and only 16 industries instead of 873), determined a different distribution of employment among registered, non-registered and multiple jobs. In particular the weight of registered primary jobs over total amount of jobs resulting from the comparison of demand side and supply side sources was 1% lower in the re-benchmarking with respect to the benchmark. This difference is not significant thus validating the estimates made in the benchmark. But, at the same time, it proves that the level of detail in the analysis affects the results obtained and therefore it requires a deep investigation in order to determine the appropriate and reliable level of analysis.

For what concerns compensation of employees, we differentiated the NA per capita values according to proper wage differentials. This means that NA constraints are an input of the method. As a result we cannot clearly point out the changes induced by the inclusion of the worker's background characteristics in the estimation process. For this purpose we ought to estimate *ex novo* per capita values on the basis of both currently used data sources and the ones we have used for this exercise. This exercise has pointed out the lack of appropriate data sources for the estimate of reliable wage differentials, especially for workers employed in agriculture. Existing data sources do not cover all the economic activities or have too small sub-samples for the cross-classification of interest.

These considerations show how the application of the same methodology can lead to different estimates when different variables of analysis are used. In general this shows how relevant is the choice of variables of analysis for the estimation procedure. In particular for SAMs, this makes evident the relevance of choosing a top-down rather than a bottom-up approach for the compilation process, especially when the SAM variable of analysis are not used for national accounts estimates.

The results presented here show the existence of compensation differentials due to gender and education level, not only in Italy but also in other two countries in the EU. Also in this perspective, *i.e.* when analysing the results and investigating on their causes, the role of the variables used in order to disaggregate the data is important. For example many times it has been pointed out that compensation differentials due to gender may be explained, among other reasons, by the real capacity and/or possibility of the worker to get to a professional status adequate to his/her education level. It would be necessary and it is desirable to further develop the level of analysis of this study, including, for example, the professional status.

In this paper the analysis of the results has been limited to compensation differentials at the national and international level. Many studies can be carried out within a SAM system. It is worth noting here that every kind of analysis which, differently than SAM, is carried out outside the macroeconomic framework of the national accounts would not allow to catch the link between the labour market dynamic and the macroeconomic variables. On the contrary in a SAM the links between the economic actors in all the phases of the economic process are made explicit. In particular the worker is considered both as labour factor and as income recipient within his/her household. This allows, for example, to measure the effects on the household income of an increase of women participation in the labour market, of retirement of wide cohorts in a certain time lag, of an increase in the education level of workers, etc.

This issue assumes a particular relevance not only at the national level but especially in the European context where planning and evaluating of European policies on the labour market requires more and more the availability of integrated information systems where analytical data on the structure and dynamics of the labour market are linked to economic fundamentals such as the GDP, public debt, the inflation rate, etc. The compilation of SAMs represents an important step towards this kind of integrated analysis.

For this purpose it would be important to elaborate SAMs timely and regularly in order to be provided with time series. This allows analysing how the distribution of income changes in time and evaluating the efficacy of policies towards the achievement of social sustainability.

Annex

Tables A.1 - A.3 are based on data reported in table 9: they show the percentage composition of labour input by gender, education and industries. In particular table A.1 analyses the distribution of labour by education in each industry and status in employment (first block of rows) and the distribution by gender in each industry and status in employment (second block of rows). Table A.2 points out the distribution of labour by education level separately for males and females in each industry and status in employment. Table A.3 shows how labour by gender and labour by education are distributed by industries.

Tables A.4 - A.6 refer to compensations of labour categories. In particular table A.4 displays implicit per capita compensation of labour by industry, status, gender and education. Table A.5 reports wage differentials due to education level, by industry, status and gender. Finally, table A.6 shows, for each education level, the ratio between per capita compensation of females and per capita compensation of males: the analysis is performed for each industry and separating out employees and self-employed.

Table A.1 - **Labour by education and by gender**

Full time equivalent units, % - 1996

Status	education	Agriculture etc.	Mining, quarrying, manufac. etc.	Construc.	Trade, repair, hotels, etc	Financial intermediation etc.	Public administration etc.	Total
Employees	Low	0.88	0.65	0.79	0.60	0.25	0.39	0.53
	medium	0.11	0.31	0.20	0.36	0.61	0.40	0.37
	High	0.01	0.03	0.01	0.03	0.13	0.21	0.10
	Total	1.00	1.00	1.00	1.00	1.00	1.00	1.00
Self-employed	Low	0.88	0.65	0.62	0.66	0.14	0.45	0.60
	medium	0.11	0.31	0.29	0.31	0.25	0.30	0.27
	High	0.01	0.04	0.09	0.03	0.60	0.25	0.14
	Total	1.00	1.00	1.00	1.00	1.00	1.00	1.00
Total	Low	0.88	0.65	0.74	0.62	0.22	0.40	0.55
	medium	0.11	0.31	0.22	0.35	0.51	0.39	0.35
	High	0.01	0.03	0.03	0.03	0.27	0.21	0.11
	Total	1.00	1.00	1.00	1.00	1.00	1.00	1.00
Status	Gender							
Employees	Male	0.64	0.68	0.93	0.62	0.56	0.41	0.58
	Female	0.36	0.32	0.07	0.38	0.44	0.59	0.42
	Total	1.00	1.00	1.00	1.00	1.00	1.00	1.00
Self-employed	Male	0.78	0.71	0.94	0.66	0.83	0.57	0.72
	Female	0.22	0.29	0.06	0.34	0.17	0.43	0.28
	Total	1.00	1.00	1.00	1.00	1.00	1.00	1.00
Total	Male	0.72	0.69	0.93	0.64	0.64	0.42	0.61
	Female	0.28	0.31	0.07	0.36	0.36	0.58	0.39
	Total	1.00	1.00	1.00	1.00	1.00	1.00	1.00

Table A.2 - **Labour by gender and education**

Full time equivalent units, % - 1996

Status	gender	education	Agriculture etc.	Mining, quarrying, manufac. etc.	Construc.	Trade, repair, hotels, etc	Financial intermediation etc.	Public administr. etc.	Total
Employees	Male	low	0.86	0.65	0.83	0.64	0.22	0.45	0.59
		medium	0.13	0.31	0.16	0.32	0.60	0.34	0.33
		high	0.01	0.04	0.01	0.03	0.18	0.21	0.09
		Total	1.00	1.00	1.00	1.00	1.00	1.00	1.00
	Female	low	0.93	0.65	0.32	0.53	0.29	0.35	0.46
		medium	0.07	0.32	0.66	0.43	0.64	0.45	0.43
		high	0.00	0.03	0.01	0.03	0.07	0.20	0.11
		Total	1.00	1.00	1.00	1.00	1.00	1.00	1.00
Self-employed	Male	low	0.88	0.66	0.61	0.66	0.09	0.43	0.58
		medium	0.11	0.30	0.30	0.31	0.24	0.27	0.26
		high	0.01	0.04	0.09	0.03	0.67	0.29	0.16
		Total	1.00	1.00	1.00	1.00	1.00	1.00	1.00
	Female	low	0.88	0.63	0.78	0.65	0.41	0.47	0.63
		medium	0.11	0.33	0.16	0.32	0.31	0.33	0.29
		high	0.01	0.04	0.05	0.03	0.27	0.19	0.08
		Total	1.00	1.00	1.00	1.00	1.00	1.00	1.00
Total	Male	low	0.87	0.66	0.77	0.65	0.17	0.45	0.59
		medium	0.12	0.31	0.20	0.32	0.46	0.33	0.31
		high	0.01	0.04	0.03	0.03	0.37	0.22	0.11
		Total	1.00	1.00	1.00	1.00	1.00	1.00	1.00
	Female	low	0.91	0.65	0.43	0.57	0.31	0.36	0.49
		medium	0.09	0.32	0.54	0.39	0.59	0.44	0.41
		high	0.00	0.03	0.02	0.03	0.10	0.20	0.11
		Total	1.00	1.00	1.00	1.00	1.00	1.00	1.00

Table A.3 - **Labour by gender and education**

Full time equivalent units, % - 1996

Status	Education	Agriculture etc.	Mining, quarrying, manufac. etc.	Construc.	Trade, repair, hotels, etc	Financial intermediation etc.	Public administration etc.	Total
Employees	Low	0.06	0.33	0.08	0.24	0.05	0.24	1.00
	Medium	0.01	0.23	0.03	0.21	0.16	0.36	1.00
	High	0.00	0.09	0.01	0.07	0.13	0.69	1.00
	Total	0.04	0.27	0.05	0.21	0.10	0.33	1.00
Self-employed	Low	0.27	0.10	0.07	0.44	0.03	0.09	1.00
	Medium	0.08	0.11	0.08	0.47	0.13	0.13	1.00
	High	0.01	0.02	0.05	0.09	0.62	0.21	1.00
	Total	0.18	0.09	0.07	0.40	0.14	0.12	1.00
Total	Low	0.11	0.28	0.08	0.29	0.04	0.20	1.00
	Medium	0.02	0.21	0.04	0.25	0.16	0.32	1.00
	High	0.00	0.07	0.02	0.08	0.27	0.55	1.00
	Total	0.07	0.23	0.06	0.25	0.11	0.28	1.00
Status	*Gender*							
Employees	Male	0.04	0.32	0.09	0.22	0.10	0.23	1.00
	Female	0.03	0.20	0.01	0.19	0.10	0.47	1.00
	Total	0.04	0.27	0.05	0.21	0.10	0.33	1.00
Self-employed	Male	0.19	0.09	0.09	0.37	0.16	0.09	1.00
	Female	0.14	0.09	0.01	0.48	0.09	0.18	1.00
	Total	0.18	0.09	0.07	0.40	0.14	0.12	1.00
Total	Male	0.08	0.26	0.09	0.26	0.11	0.19	1.00
	Female	0.05	0.19	0.01	0.23	0.10	0.42	1.00
	Total	0.07	0.23	0.06	0.25	0.11	0.28	1.00

Table A.4 - **Implicit per capita (compensation of labour/fteu) by industry, status, gender, education**

Current thousands euro, 1996

			Agriculture etc.	Mining, quarrying, manufacturing etc.	Construction	Trade, repair, hotels, etc	Financial intermediation etc.	Public administration etc.	Total
Employees	male	Low	14.04	26.53	20.16	24.23	28.69	26.45	24.52
		Medium	21.24	34.69	29.00	31.43	41.60	31.18	33.86
		high	34.04	61.56	38.54	42.98	59.45	48.24	51.60
		Total	15.13	30.28	21.80	27.19	42.00	32.63	29.90
	female	Low	9.64	20.68	20.01	18.81	21.21	15.55	17.79
		Medium	14.65	25.61	24.45	22.25	27.38	24.93	24.85
		high	24.34	35.14	24.78	33.73	39.75	29.11	30.35
		total	10.03	22.67	23.02	20.80	26.43	22.51	22.26
		total	13.29	27.88	21.89	24.78	35.08	26.62	26.68
Self-employed	male	low	15.92	16.55	15.24	20.51	12.20	12.44	17.49
		medium	23.84	21.09	20.46	25.10	18.40	13.92	21.95
		high	33.15	37.08	26.97	32.88	24.85	21.67	25.30
		total	16.93	18.66	17.89	22.32	22.16	15.56	19.89
	female	low	11.11	13.00	12.95	16.05	9.42	7.92	13.27
		medium	17.29	15.96	15.82	18.01	12.17	11.30	15.80
		high	24.00	20.72	14.05	26.14	15.62	13.32	16.77
		total	11.87	14.28	13.48	16.96	11.99	10.08	14.27
		total	15.82	17.38	17.63	20.52	20.45	13.21	18.32
Total	male	low	15.25	25.61	19.08	22.82	25.43	24.74	22.66
		medium	22.80	33.47	25.47	29.10	36.93	29.36	31.21
		high	33.44	59.28	29.82	39.53	35.46	43.78	41.04
		total	16.29	29.22	20.72	25.38	34.42	30.47	27.24
	female	low	10.32	20.06	16.94	17.76	19.08	14.85	16.84
		medium	16.21	24.79	23.82	21.12	26.29	24.21	23.81
		high	24.12	33.63	18.81	31.49	30.53	28.07	28.79
		total	10.90	21.98	20.73	19.52	24.47	21.65	20.97
		total	14.80	26.95	20.72	23.26	30.80	25.37	24.80
Employees		low	12.37	24.69	20.16	22.42	24.84	20.68	22.09
		medium	19.77	31.78	27.95	27.31	35.04	27.04	29.45
		high	32.00	54.20	37.43	39.58	54.85	37.05	41.19
Self-employed		low	14.86	15.55	15.08	19.02	10.85	10.40	16.25
		medium	22.44	19.50	20.31	22.70	17.10	12.67	20.09
		high	31.30	32.08	26.52	30.73	24.14	18.92	23.97
Total		low	13.85	23.88	19.00	21.13	22.20	19.59	20.65
		medium	21.36	30.70	25.21	25.81	32.42	26.02	27.83
		high	31.53	52.07	29.30	36.70	34.81	35.03	36.22

Table A.5 - **Education gap**

Percentage values

			Agriculture etc.	Mining, quarrying, manufacturing etc.	Construction	Trade, repair, hotels, etc	Financial intermediation etc.	Public administration etc.	Total
employees	male	low	93	88	92	89	68	81	82
		medium	140	115	133	116	99	96	113
		high	225	203	177	158	142	148	173
		total	*100*	*100*	*100*	*100*	*100*	*100*	*100*
	female	low	96	91	87	90	80	69	80
		medium	146	113	106	107	104	111	112
		high	243	155	108	162	150	129	136
		total	*100*	*100*	*100*	*100*	*100*	*100*	*100*
		Low	93	89	92	90	71	78	83
		Medium	149	114	128	110	100	102	110
		High	241	194	171	160	156	139	154
		total	*100*	*100*	*100*	*100*	*100*	*100*	*100*
self-employed	male	low	94	89	85	92	55	80	88
		medium	141	113	114	112	83	90	110
		high	196	199	151	147	112	139	127
		total	*100*	*100*	*100*	*100*	*100*	*100*	*100*
	female	low	94	91	96	95	79	79	93
		medium	146	112	117	106	102	112	111
		high	202	145	104	154	130	132	118
		total	*100*	*100*	*100*	*100*	*100*	*100*	*100*
		low	94	89	85	93	53	79	89
		medium	142	112	115	111	84	96	110
		high	198	185	150	150	118	143	131
		total	*100*	*100*	*100*	*100*	*100*	*100*	*100*
Total	male	low	94	88	92	90	74	81	83
		medium	140	115	123	115	107	96	115
		high	205	203	144	156	103	144	151
		total	*100*	*100*	*100*	*100*	*100*	*100*	*100*
	female	low	95	91	82	91	78	69	80
		medium	149	113	115	108	107	112	114
		high	221	153	91	161	125	130	137
		total	*100*	*100*	*100*	*100*	*100*	*100*	*100*
		low	94	89	92	91	72	77	83
		medium	144	114	122	111	105	103	112
		high	213	193	141	158	113	138	146
		total	*100*	*100*	*100*	*100*	*100*	*100*	*100*

Table A.6 - **Gender gap**

Percentage values

		Agriculture etc.	Mining, quarrying, manufacturing etc.	Construction	Trade, repair, hotels, etc	Financial intermediation etc.	Public administration etc.	Total
employees	*F/M*	66	75	106	76	63	69	74
	F/M low	69	78	99	78	74	59	73
	F/M medium	69	74	84	71	66	80	73
	F/M high	71	57	64	78	67	60	59
self-employed	*F/M*	70	77	75	76	54	65	72
	F/M low	70	79	85	78	77	64	76
	F/M medium	73	76	77	72	66	81	72
	F/M high	72	56	52	79	63	61	66
Total	*F/M*	67	75	100	77	71	71	77
	F/M low	68	78	89	78	75	60	74
	F/M medium	71	74	94	73	71	82	76
	F/M high	72	57	63	80	86	64	70

References

BANCA D'ITALIA (1991,1993,1995) "I bilanci delle famiglie italiane", in *Supplementi al Bollettino Statistico*.

Battellini F. (2001) "Supply and demand of labour" draft of section 3.2 of the LEG Manual on the SAM.

Battellini F., Caricchia A., Coli A., (1997), 'La matrice de compatibilité sociale et les comptes satellites comme instruments d'intégration des statistiques économiques et sociales' in: E. Archambault and M. Boeda (eds), Compatibilité nationale - Développements récents, Economica, Paris.

Battellini F., Coli A., Tartamella F. (2001), "The construction of a value added matrix: the Italian experience", paper presented at the *SAM users workshop*, November 2001, Rome.

Battellini F., Coli A., Tartamella F. (2002), "Differenziali di remunerazione nel quadro macroeconomico dei conti nazionali", in ISTAT *Rapporto Annuale. La situazione del Paese nel* 2001 Roma.

Calzaroni, M., The exhaustiveness of production estimates: new concepts and methodologies, International Conference on Establishment Surveys, Buffalo, USA, 17-21 June, 2001.

CARITAS (1997) "Immigrazione", Dossier statistico.

Carlucci M., and R. Zelli, A sam-based system focused on labour market: perspectives and utilizations, Paper presented at the SAM User Workshop, Rome, November 2001.

Cimino E., Coli A. (1998), The compilation of a social accounting matrix for Italy, Paper prepared for the 25th General Conference of The International Association for Research in Income and Wealth, Cambridge.

Coli A. (2001) "The demand side of the labour market in a SAM" draft of section 2.2 of the LEG Manual on the SAM.

Coli A. (2001) "La remunerazione del fattore lavoro in una SAM" terzo rapporto per il gruppo di lavoro ISCONA sulla "Stima di matrici di contabilità sociale".

Coli A., Tartamella F. (2000), The link between national accounts and households micro data, Paper prepared for the 2000 meeting of the Siena group on social statistics, Maastricht.

Coli A., Tartamella F. (2000), 'A Pilot Social Accounting Matrix for Italy with a Focus on Households', Paper prepared for the 26th General Conference of the IARIW in Cracow, Poland.

EUROSTAT (1996) "European System of Accounts: ESA 1995".

EUROSTAT (forthcoming) "Handbook on Social Accounting Matrices and Labour Accounts".

Hayes K. (1996) "The Exhaustiveness of the GNP Estimates in the EU Member States", paper submitted by Eurostat at the Joint UNECE/Eurostat/OECD Meeting on National Accounts, Geneva: 30 April-3 May 1996

ILO (1993), "Resolution of the fifteenth International Conference of Labour Statisticians".

ISTAT (1991) "Classificazione delle attività economiche", in Metodi e norme, Roma.

ISTAT (1993), "The underground economy in Italian economic accounts", Annali di Statistica, Serie X, vol.2., Roma.

ISTAT (1996) "Verso il nuovo sistema di contabilità nazionale", in Annali di statistica, Roma.

ISTAT (1997) "Conti Nazionali Economici e Finanziari dei Settori Istituzionali" - Anni 1980-1995, Contabilità nazionale, tomo 2 in Annuari.

ISTAT (2000) "Tavola intersettoriale dell'economia italiana, anno 1992", in Informazioni, Roma.

ISTAT (2000) "La struttura del costo del lavoro e delle retribuzioni nella seconda metà degli anni '90", in Informazioni, Roma.

ISTAT(anni vari) "Indagine campionaria trimestrale sulle Forze di lavoro", in Annuari, Roma.

Leunis Wim (2000), "The description of ESA'95 employment; relation between Labour Force Survey and National Accounts in the Netherlands", interim summary report for Eurostat Task Force ESA Employment, Statistics Netherlands.

Keuning S.J,. De Ruijter Willem A. (1988) "Guidelines to the construction of a social accounting matrix", in Review of Income and Wealth.

OECD et al.(2002), "Measuring the Non-Observed Economy: a Handbook", Paris

Rey, G.M. (1997) "Economic Analysis and Empirical Evidence of Illegal Activity in Italy", in Contributi ISTAT, 6/1997, ISTAT, Roma

Skoglund Tor (2001), "Employment in the Norwegian National Accounts", Statistics Norway

UNITED NATIONS ET AL. (1993) "System of National Accounts: SNA93".

Using Environmental Accounts to Promote Sustainable Development: Experiences in Southern Africa[12]

A. Alfieri, United Nations Statistical Division

R. Hassan, Centre for Environment and Economic Policy in Africa

G. Lange, Institute for Economic Analysis

Abstract

Environmental accounts bring together economic and environmental information in a common framework to measure the contribution of the environment to the economy and the impact of the economy on the environment. They enable governments to set priorities, monitor economic policies more precisely, enact more effective environmental regulations and resource management strategies, and design more efficient market instruments for environmental policies. This article uses examples from the regional environmental accounting program in Southern Africa to demonstrate the usefulness of environmental accounts to policy making and natural resource management. The examples address 1) the contribution of natural capital endowments (minerals and fisheries) to sustainable development in Botswana and Namibia; 2) the economic importance of non-market forest goods and services in South Africa; and 3) the socio-economic impact of current water allocation and pricing policies in Botswana, Namibia and South Africa. While there are many additional policy applications, these few provide a powerful argument for the use of environmental accounts in all countries.

Overview of Environmental Accounts

Over the past few decades countries have embraced the notion of sustainable development, popularly expressed by the Brundtland Commission Report, *Our Common Future*, as '…development that meets the needs of the present without compromising the ability of future generations to meet their own needs' (World Commission on Environment and Development, 1987). The search for ways to operationalise this notion has focused, in part, on national economic accounts: incorporating the role of the environment and natural capital more fully into the conventional system of national accounts (SNA) through a system of satellite accounts for the environment.

The SNA (CEC *et al.*, 1993) is particularly important because it constitutes the primary source of information about the economy and is widely used for analysis and decision-making in all countries. However, the SNA does not cover the environment in a comprehensive manner. For example, while the income from extracting minerals is recorded in the national accounts, the simultaneous depletion of mineral reserves is not. Wild, uncultivated fisheries and forests have received similar treatment. This can result in quite misleading economic signals about sustainable national income. Indeed, one of the primary motivations for the early environmental accounting efforts in the mid-1980s was concern that rapid economic growth in some developing countries was achieved

---

1. This paper represents the views of the authors and not necessarily the views of the organizations they authors are affiliated with.

2. A previous version of this paper was published in *Natural Resources Forum* Vol. 27, No.1, February 2003, pag. 19-31.

through liquidation of natural capital (Repetto et al., 1987, 1989). In the long run, this practice is unsustainable; once the resources are exhausted, the economy will decline.

The 1993 revision of the SNA addresses some of these problems, notably by expanding the asset boundary to include a broader range of natural assets such as natural forests. But relatively few countries have fully implemented this module of the 1993 SNA, and even with this expanded coverage, significant gaps remain. Non-marketed environmental goods and services, which are especially critical to rural livelihoods in many developing countries, have very limited representation in the national accounts. Ecosystem services such as absorption of pollution, watershed protection and carbon storage are not included at all.

A system of SNA satellite accounts for the environment, known as the System of integrated Environmental and Economic Accounts (SEEA), was developed to address these gaps (UN, 1993 and UN et al. 2003). The SEEA assesses the economic value of a country's environmental resources and how they are used. It provides better measures of economic performance that take into account the environment, and link problems such as land degradation, groundwater depletion, or deforestation to the economic activities that cause them, as well as to the activities that are affected by them. This promotes sound economic decision-making by demonstrating to policy makers that the nation's natural resources are capital assets rather than unlimited "free goods".

Environmental accounts have evolved since the 1970s through the efforts of national statistical offices and individual practitioners, each developing their own frameworks and methodologies. Since the late 1980s, a concerted effort to standardize the framework and methodologies was undertaken by the London Group–a group of countries and international organizations, namely United Nations Statistics Division, Eurostat, OECD, the World Bank, and the IMF, established by the UN Statistical Commission[3]. The United Nations published an interim handbook on environmental accounting in 1993 (UN, 1993) which was complemented by an operational manual (UN and UNEP, 2000) and has since been revised (UN et al., 2003). The SEEA-2003 is a manual of best practices and represents a major step towards the harmonization of concepts and definitions in environmental accounting.

As satellite accounts, the SEEA has a similar structure to the SNA, consisting of both stocks and flows of environmental goods and services. The SEEA has four major components, which are constructed wherever possible in both physical and monetary units:

• Asset accounts, which record stocks and changes in stocks of natural resources. These accounts provide information about the value of natural capital and whether it is being depleted;

• Flow accounts for materials, energy and pollution, which provide information at the industry level about the use of energy and materials as inputs to production and final demand, and the generation of pollutants and solid waste.

These accounts show the dependence of the economy and specific households on environmental goods and services, and the cost of environmental degradation. They are

3. Members of the London Group include Statistical Offices from developed countries, with experience in the field. However, many developing countries and NGOs with a strong interest and experience in environmental accounting have participated in the meetings.

used extensively with input-output (IO) tables and social accounting matrices (SAMs) for environmental-economic modelling;

- Environmental protection and resource management expenditure accounts. These accounts reorganize information already in the SNA to make expenditures incurred to protect the environment and manage natural resources more explicit and easier to analyse;

- Environmentally-adjusted indicators of macroeconomic performance, which include indicators of sustainability such as environmentally-adjusted Gross Domestic Product (GDP), Net Domestic Product (NDP), National Savings and national wealth.

Environmental accounts improve policy-making by providing aggregate indicators for monitoring environmental-economic performance, as well as a detailed set of statistics to guide resource managers toward policy decisions that will improve environmental-economic performance in the future.

Indicators for improved monitoring of sustainability include

- Macroeconomic indicators of sustainability

- Sectoral indicators of sustainability

- Indicators of the impact of economic policies on the environment

- Indicators of progress toward meeting specific environmental-economic goals

Detailed statistics for improved policy analysis and environmental management support the:

- Design of more effective environmental regulation and economic instruments;

- Design of more effective resource management policies;

- Assessment of alternative development paths and their impact on the environment;

- Understanding linkages between environment and poverty.

There are two features that distinguish the SEEA from other databases about the environment: integration of environmental data with economic accounts, and comprehensive treatment of all important natural resources, linking them with the economic sectors that rely on them, directly and indirectly, and those sectors that affect them.

In contrast to other environmental databases, the purpose of the SEEA is to directly link environmental data to the economic accounts. The SEEA achieves this by sharing structure, definitions and classifications with the SNA. The flow accounts become, in effect, an extension of the input-output table commonly used for multi-sectoral economic analysis. The advantage of the SEEA is that this kind of database provides a tool to overcome the tendency to divide issues along disciplinary lines, in which analyses of economic issues and of environmental issues are carried out independently of one another.

While there has been a great deal of progress with environmental accounting in industrialised countries, sustained efforts in developing countries have been more limited. One exception is a regional program in Southern Africa, initiated in 1995 and directed by eight government and non-governmental organisations. This program, now based at the

Centre for Environment and Economic Policy in Africa (CEEPA) at the University of Pretoria, grew out of the recognition that environmental constraints pose an increasing challenge to economic development and that economic principles are increasingly important for sustainable resource management. A framework that integrated environmental and economic information was needed to support sustainable development, and environmental accounts provide such a framework.

Based on the SEEA, environmental accounts were constructed for the three core countries of the program, Namibia, Botswana and South Africa. The environmental accounts for Southern Africa reflect the priorities of each country. Mineral and water accounts were constructed for all three countries. Namibia and Botswana both constructed accounts for livestock, wildlife, and energy. Namibia constructed fisheries accounts and South Africa constructed forestry accounts. No accounts for pollution have been constructed yet mainly because it is not a serious national problem.

The purpose of this paper is to show how the environmental accounts have actually been used to influence policy, based on the experiences in Southern Africa. The examples presented here were chosen to show the breadth of the potential uses of environmental accounts. This paper is intended for a non-technical readership, so discussion of the underlying theory is quite brief. A comprehensive technical description of the compilation of the accounts in Southern Africa and the policy applications can be found in Lange, Hassan and Hamilton (2002).

As background, Section 2 describes the role of natural resources in the economies of Botswana, Namibia, and South Africa. The following two sections present the policy applications of the environmental accounts in these countries. Section 3 uses the asset accounts to address how some conventional indicators of macroeconomic performance can be revised to reflect natural capital. Section 4 uses the flow accounts to provide an example of the economic importance of non-market environmental goods and services (forests in South Africa) and an economic perspective on the supply and use of a scarce resource–water–in each of the three countries. Section 5 presents concluding comments and discusses future directions for this work.

Economic Dependence on Natural Resources in Southern Africa

Botswana, Namibia, and South Africa are neighbouring countries with quite different economic and political histories. Under apartheid, South Africa developed two distinct economies: a traditional sector, in which the majority of the people were restricted to a disproportionately small and low quality land area and practiced mostly subsistence agriculture, and a modern, commercial economy based on manufacturing and export-oriented mining and farming of high potential land, which was controlled by a minority. Namibia, colonized by Germany in the 19th century and administered by South Africa after the First World War, developed a similar, dualistic economy. In both countries, this system ended in the 1990s and they now face the enormous task of integrating the traditional and the commercial economies. Rapid economic growth is a primary objective of virtually all countries, but this goal has added significance in Namibia and South Africa because of the urgency of reducing the great social and economic inequalities.

By contrast, Botswana, with the highest per capita income in 1999 (Table 1), was never formally colonized, although it was a British protectorate until 1966. At independence the economy was based on extensive livestock grazing, but several years later diamonds were discovered. A remarkable example of prudent management of natural capital, Botswana has developed from one of the poorest countries to one of the fastest growing in the world. Botswana continues to suffer from income inequality, but not as severely as in Namibia and South Africa.

Botswana and Namibia are rather similar in size and population; South Africa is larger by an order of magnitude. All countries are highly dependent on natural resources. Primary sector activity is important in all three countries, but there is more processing of primary resources in South Africa than in the other two. Primary sector activity combined with the processing of primary products accounts for 38%, 28%, and 26% of GDP in Botswana, Namibia, and South Africa, respectively.

Raw and processed primary products dominate exports in all countries, accounting for 76%, 79%, and 46% of total exports in Botswana, Namibia and South Africa, respectively. Minerals are clearly the most important sector of the Botswana economy. Agriculture, fish, and minerals are all important in Namibia. Agriculture, forest products, and minerals are the primary sector drivers in South Africa. High economic dependence on primary products makes efficient management of natural capital critical both for current economic performance as well as for sustainability.

Table 1. **Structure of the economies of Botswana, Namibia, and South Africa in 1999**

	Botswana	Namibia	South Africa
Area of country (thousands of km²)	582	842	1,221
Population (millions)	1.61	1.80	42.1
Land/capita (Km²/capita)	0.36	0.47	0.03
GDP (in millions of currency units)	Pula 25 208	N$ 21 124	Rand 723 247
GDP (millions of US$)	5 458	3 469	118 757
GDP (US$ per capita)	3 390	1 927	2 821
Structure of GDP (percent of total)			
Primary sectors	**35.9**	**20.1**	**9.4**
Agriculture, forestry, fisheries	2.6	10.4	3.5
Mining	33.3	9.7	5.9
Non-primary sectors	**64.1**	**79.9**	**90.6**
Food processing	2.0	8.0	8.5
Wood products	*	*	3.2
Mineral and metal processing	*	*	5.1
Manufacturing	4.9	10.2	27.1
Other manufacturing	2.9	2.2	1.1
Services and other	59.2	67.6	45.7
Exports as % of GDP	56.0%	46.8%	25.9%
Structure of exports (percent of total)			
Agricultural and processed food products	1.9	16.0	8.9
Fish and fish products	*	23.0	*
Forest and wood products	*	*	3.3
Minerals	73.7	40.1	34.3
Other (non-primary)	24.4	20.9	53.7

* Less than 1%

Notes: Foreign exchange rates used: Pula = 0.2165 US$. Rand and Namibia $ = 0.1642 US$

Source: Based on Bank of Botswana, 2001; Central Bureau of Statistics, 2001; South Africa Reserve Bank, 2001; Statistics South Africa, 2001

Asset accounts: managing natural capital to build total national wealth

One of the fundamental indicators of a country's well being is the trend in per capita wealth over time, where wealth is defined in the broadest sense to include produced, natural and human capital. In many developing countries, natural capital is a significant, and sometimes the largest, component of national wealth. Yet, in the past, this wealth has not been valued or monitored. Sustainable development requires non-declining levels of per capita wealth.[4]

Implementation of this indicator of sustainability raises two major challenges 1) total wealth must include all forms of capital and 2) correct prices must be used to value each

---

4. For a review of this subject and problems associated with implementation, see Dasgupta and Maler, 2000; Heal and Kristrom, 2001; Pearce and Atkinson, 1993.

type of capital. Human capital, a very significant component of wealth, is often omitted because there is no agreement yet about how to measure it. Ecosystem services provided by natural capital are also underestimated in the measure of wealth because there is a great deal of uncertainty about how to measure (in physical terms) and value these services. While much work remains to be done in the area of asset valuation, the SEEA takes a reasonable first step toward implementation of the non-declining per capita wealth indicator of sustainability. This indicator can be expressed as:

$$(1) \quad \frac{K_{t+1}}{P_{t+1}} \geq \frac{K_t}{P_t}$$

where P is population and K is the value of total wealth defined to include produced capital, natural capital, human capital, and net foreign financial assets:

$$(2) \quad K = K_P + K_N + K_H + K_F$$

In fact, for developing countries with aspiration for higher material standards of living, per capita wealth must increase. Resource abundance potentially provides countries with a unique opportunity to finance rapid economic development. However, the resource-rich developing countries have fared significantly worse than resource-poor countries over the past few decades, a surprising outcome known as the 'resource curse' (Auty and Mikesell, 1998; Sachs and Warner, 1995). What has gone wrong?

From equation 2, it is clear that if one form of wealth, for example, natural capital, is being depleted, total wealth will decline unless this depletion is offset by investment in other forms of capital. Based on this relationship, the economic rule for sustainability, known as the Hartwick-Solow rule, requires that depletion of natural capital, K_N, be offset by a compensating increase in other forms of capital (Solow, 1974, 1986; Hartwick, 1977). The process of building national wealth in resource-rich developing countries requires transforming natural capital into other productive assets, such as human capital (education, health), public infrastructure, improved environment, or other types of wealth. In this way, utilization of natural resources can be economically sustainable–because it creates a permanent source of income–even for resources, like minerals that are not biologically sustainable.

Many resource rich countries have not been successful in transforming natural capital into other forms of wealth; natural capital has often been liquidated to fund current consumption rather than investment. While there are many reasons for such an outcome, we will focus on the process that is necessary for the transformation of natural capital and the information that environmental accounts now offer to better monitor whether this process is taking place, and where it may have gone wrong.

There are three components to the successful transformation of natural capital into other forms of wealth:

1. managing natural resources to maximize the generation of resource rent

2. recovery of resource rent by an agent capable of reinvesting it

3. reinvestment of resource rent in productive assets

Environmental accounts first of all provide measures of natural capital that can be used to monitor total wealth over time and whether depletion of resources is compensated for by investment in other assets. The environmental accounts also provide more detailed statistics to assess whether natural capital is being used to build national wealth: maximizing income from natural capital, recovering resource rent, and reinvestment of resource rent. This section provides shows how the environmental accounts can be used to monitor recovery and reinvestment of rent. [5]

Monitoring natural capital and total national wealth

The SEEA physical asset accounts provide indicators of ecological sustainability and detailed information for the management of resources. The volume of mineral reserves, for example, is needed to plan extraction paths and indicates how long a country can rely on its minerals. The volume of fish or forestry biomass helps to determine sustainable yields and appropriate harvesting policies. The asset accounts track the changes in stock over time and indicate whether depletion is occurring. They can, thus, show the effects of resource policy on the stock and can be used to motivate a change in policy.

The biological depletion of Namibia's fish stocks since the 1960's, for example, has provided a very clear picture to policy-makers of the devastating impact of uncontrolled, open-access fishing (Figure 1) prior to independence. The combined fishable biomass of the three major species fell from 14 million tons in the late 1960s to around 2 million tons in the 1990s; only stocks of horse mackerel–the lowest value fish–increased. At independence in 1990, the new government reversed previous policies and has established policies to prevent further depletion, but there has been no recovery to previous levels.

---

5.   This paper is too brief to address the first issue, maximizing income from natural capital. However, this issue is discussed in Lange2002b

Figure 1. **Biomass of major commercial fish species in Namibia, 1963 to 2001**

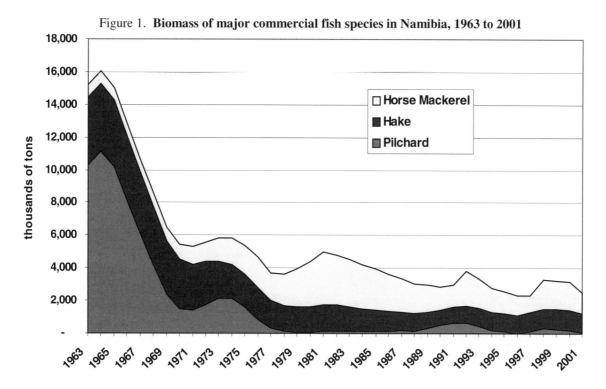

Source: Based on Marine Research and Information Centre, 2001

Figure 2. **Total national wealth of Botswana and Namibia, 1980 to 1998**

A. Botswana (million pula, constant 1993/94 prices)

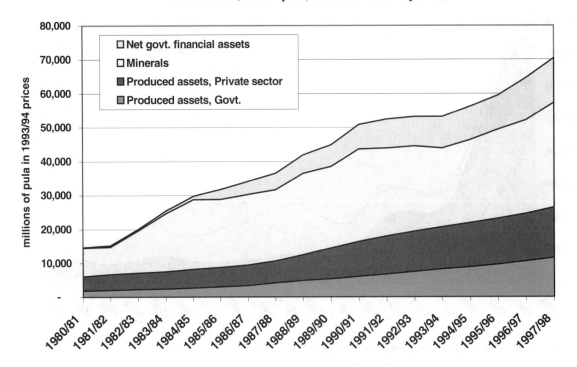

B. Namibia (million Namibia $, constant 1990 prices)

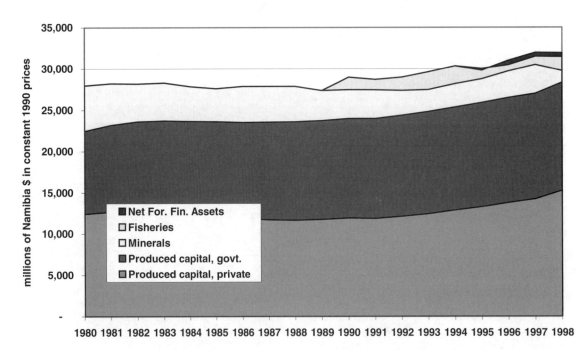

Source: Adapted from Lange, 2002b

While the physical accounts for individual assets can be used to monitor ecological sustainability, a more complete assessment of sustainability requires calculation of the economic value of a resource. From this, trends in per capita national wealth can be derived. These trends can also bc analyzcd to assess characteristics important to economic development, such as the diversity of wealth, ownership distribution, and volatility due to price fluctuations, an important feature for economies dependent on primary commodities (See Lange, 2001 for a discussion of this issue and some examples).

Figures from the environmental accounts for Botswana and Namibia are shown in Figure 2 (comparable national figures are not available for South Africa at this time). The natural capital assets of Botswana include minerals only, while Namibia's natural capital includes both minerals and fisheries[6]. Other forms of national wealth include produced capital (public and private sector) and net foreign financial assets. Human capital is not included because there is not consensus at this time about how to measure it.

Total wealth in constant prices increased for both countries over the past two decades, by about 500% in Botswana from pula 12 billion to pula 72 billion, but only 14% in Namibia from N$28n billion to N$32 billion. Adjusted for population growth, Botswana's real, per capita wealth increased by about 250%, while Namibia's per capita wealth declined roughly by 25% (Figure 3). Only Botswana has been successful using its natural capital to build national wealth.

Figure 3. **Index of per capita, real wealth in Botswana and Namibia, 1980 to 1998**

Source: Adapted from Lange, 2002b

---

6. While other important types of natural capital, notably land, are not yet included, this is not expected to seriously affect the trends in per capita wealth for the two countries. This is discussed further in (Lange et al. 2002).

In Botswana, total wealth grew steadily over the period. The growth of government's net foreign financial assets is especially striking, increasing from less than 1% of national wealth in 1980 to 18% by 1997. The rapid growth of national wealth is consistent with Botswana's development policy, which set a goal of improving living standards and reducing poverty based on investment of mineral revenues. Physical depletion of mineral assets was offset by management changes to speed up extraction thereby increasing the value of minerals, and by investing all resource rent in other assets (on these points, see (Lange and Wright, 2002)).

Prior to independence in 1990, an occupying country, South Africa, exploited Namibia's resources with relatively little concern for Namibia's own national development. There was no policy of reinvestment of revenues from natural capital and by the time Namibia had achieved independence in 1990 its natural resources were vastly depleted. There was almost no growth in produced capital in the decade before independence and mineral wealth declined as minerals were depleted. Namibia's most lucrative fisheries were located in its 200-mile Exclusive Economic Zone (EEZ), but outside its 12-mile territorial limits. Under South African rule, Namibia's claim to the EEZ was not recognized internationally, and its fisheries were exploited mostly by foreign operators under what was effectively an open access regime. Consequently, fish stocks were not considered part of Namibia's national wealth. Only with independence was Namibia able to gain control over fisheries in its EEZ and fisheries became part of its national wealth. After independence there was also an increase in investment in Namibia, increasing produced capital; mineral wealth continued to decline. Net foreign financial assets form an insignificant share of national wealth.

Management of natural resources for sustainable development

As discussed earlier in this section, sustainable development requires the transformation of natural capital into other forms of wealth. This is achieved by recovering the resource rent and reinvesting it in productive assets. When government is the owner of resources, as is the case in Botswana and Namibia, government bears this responsibility for reinvestment. This requires establishing taxes to recover resource rent and a commitment to reinvest the rent.

Regarding recovery of resource rent, Botswana has been rather successful in recovering rent, averaging 76% (Table 2). Namibia has had much more volatile rent. The Namibian mining industry has paid on average at least 50% of the rent in taxes. By contrast, government has not recovered most rent from fisheries. There was no rent recovery prior to independence in 1990; when quota levies were first introduced, more than 50% of the rent was recovered, but the rate of recovery has since diminished significantly. This is the result, mainly, of the failure to increase quota levies for inflation; quota levies are set as a fee per ton of quota rather than a percentage of profits. A contributing factor is the increasing Namibian participation and ownership in the fishing industry, which is awarded a subsidy up to 50% of the quota levy.

As long as fisheries are not being depleted, recovery and reinvestment of resource it is not necessary for sustainable development. When managed sustainably, fisheries will continue to generate income and employment for future generations. However, exploitation of fisheries cannot be sustainably increased; hence, income will not increase as population grows[7]. For a country with a growing population and aspirations for higher standards of living, its natural resources provide revenues, which could be used to build national wealth. Failure to reinvest the rent represents a lost opportunity to build national wealth.

Table 2. **Resource rent and government appropriation of rent in Botswana and Namibia 1980 to 1997**

| | Botswana (millions of pula) | | Namibia (millions of N$) | | | |
| | Minerals | | Fisheries | | Minerals | |
	Rent	Taxes	Rent	Taxes	Rent	Taxes
1980	118	101			341	183
1981	57	77			97	151
1982	186	100			71	55
1983	276	194			37	48
1984	555	376			67	110
1985	893	581			355	134
1986	950	845			358	242
1987	1 380	1 034			162	317
1988	2 546	1 508			408	315
1989	2 403	1 596			513	322
1990	2 458	2 005	153	44	57	199
1991	2 406	1 888	125	64	33	140
1992	2 282	1 866	192	87	10	211
1993	3 030	2 279	306	96	-256	302
1994	3 129	2 349	429	115	116	309
1995	3 779	2 591	449	98	-70	188
1996	5 263	3 640	243	53	85	231
1997	6 409	4 681	406	79	329	249

Notes:

[1] Blank means no entry.

[2] Taxes include all forms of taxes, royalties, licensing fees and other levies on the exploitation of the resource.

Source: Adapted from Lange, 2002a; Lange and Hassan, 2002.

Regarding the second requirement for using natural capital to build national wealth, reinvestment of resource rent, the policies of Botswana and Namibia are quite different. Botswana developed an explicit policy of reinvestment of all resource rent and an indicator to monitor this policy, the Sustainable Budget Index (SBI). Namibia has had no explicit policy regarding reinvestment of revenues from natural capital. Botswana's SBI measures the ratio of government's recurrent expenditures to its recurrent revenues, which are defined as non-mineral revenues. (See Lange, and Wright, 2002 for discussion of the SBI). An SBI value equal to or less than 1 indicates sustainability, while a value

7. After a decade's effort to rebuild fish stocks to previous levels there is little evidence that this can be achieved. Even with constant levels of stocks, it may be possible to increase the value and the income generated from fish by developing more valuable fish products, but this source of income growth cannot continue indefinitely.

greater than 1 indicates unsustainable reliance of public consumption on non-renewable sources of revenue (i.e., minerals).

The SBI rule in effect requires that all mineral revenues be used for public sector investment. It was recognized that conventional budget categories do not adequately reflect investment in human capital, so, in order to better represent total investment the portion of the recurrent budget used for human capital (education and health), about 30% of the budget, is redefined as a development expenditure for the calculation of the SBI. Figure 4 shows that Botswana's SBI has been well under 1 for most of the past 20 years, indicating the government's sustainable use of mineral revenues, although in 2000 government has started to use mineral revenues to fund some public consumption.

Figure 4. **The Sustainable Budget Index of Botswana, 1980 to 2002**

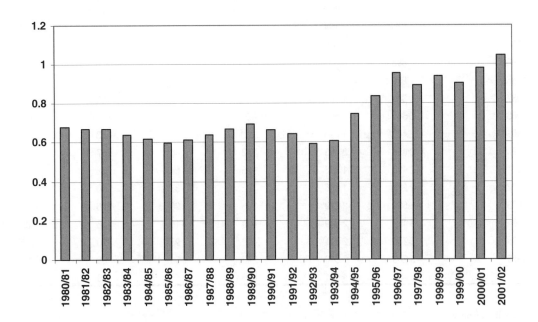

Note:

[1] The SBI measures the ratio of recurrent government expenditures (excluding spending for education and health) to non-mineral government revenues

[2] A value equal to or less than 1 indicates sustainable reliance of public consumption on non-renewable sources of revenue (minerals); a value greater than 1 indicates unsustainable reliance

[3] The values in the graph are calculated as a 3-year moving average of the SBI

Source: Adapted from Lange and Wright, 2002

In sum, the comparison of the asset accounts for Botswana and Namibia indicate that both countries have significant natural capital, but that only Botswana has been successful in using its natural capital to build national wealth. Botswana has recovered most of the resource rent generated by its minerals and has consistently reinvested all of it. Namibia has not been able to recover as much of the resource rent, partly due to external factors such as the lack of control over its marine fisheries until recently, but partly due to domestic policy decisions. Not surprisingly, Namibia has failed to build national wealth. The effect is significant: Botswana's per capita, real GDP has grown at an annual rate of

5%, while Namibia's per capita, real GDP has stagnated, declining at an annual rate of – 0.025% (Lange, 2002b).

Flow accounts: improving natural resource management

Two examples of the use of environmental flow accounts are presented here, one for forestry and the other for water. Forestry accounts address the issue of valuation of non-market environmental goods and services. Deforestation is a serious problem with both local and global consequences. Yet sustainable forestry has often failed in part because of a lack of understanding of the true economic value of forests, a value that would take into account not just the timber values, but all the other non-timber goods and services provided by a forest. The forestry accounts can support sustainable forestry by providing a measure of the total value of forests, and who benefits from the different values.

The water accounts presented here for Botswana, Namibia, and South Africa provide a unique perspective on the economics of water supply and use. Water accounts are used to monitor both the physical and the socio-economic implications of water supply and water allocation. The water accounts enable policy makers to design more efficient and equitable water policies, and to make more informed decisions regarding the efficient allocation of water to different economic activities. In addition, the water flow accounts can be combined with economic models to explore the impacts of alternative water policies, such as the impact on water demand of price increases, or the introduction of water conservation technologies.

Forest accounts: measuring non-marketed environmental benefits

Forest management and land use planning, especially in developing countries, are often based on information about a limited range of economic values, usually just timber value. Better understanding of the value of the full range of goods and services supplied by forests, and who benefits from these goods and services, is essential for optimal utilization of forests, and may provide an economic rationale for conserving forests. Forest accounts have been used by policymakers, such as those in South Africa, to provide a better estimate of the total economic value of goods and services provided by forests and to understand the impact of policies that affect forest resources.[8]

South African environmental accounts classify forests into three major categories: cultivated forest plantations which provide most of the country's commercial timber and tree products, natural forests and woodlands which are used by rural communities, and fynbos woodlands, which is a unique biome in South Africa, the Cape Floral Kingdom (Hassan, 2002). Forests in national parks and protected areas have not yet been included in the accounts. The forest accounts include asset accounts for standing timber in cultivated forests, and the production of timber and non-timber goods and services from all three types of forests. The information about production from natural forests and fynbos woodlands is especially useful because many of these values were not previously included in the national accounts of South Africa.

---

8. Estimating the asset value of forests would require information (or assumptions) about future uses of forests. Such estimation can be quite complex since some uses may exclude or limit others, e.g., watershed protection *v* logging. Most asset valuation has therefore been limited so far to timber values and carbon storage values. However, the forest flow accounts provide the initial information for further analysis of potential trade-offs among competing, alternative uses of forests.

Timber products in natural forests include fuel wood and wood for construction used mainly by rural communities. The major non-timber goods are honey, flowers, traditional foods and medicines. Non-timber services include carbon storage, livestock grazing in natural forests and fynbos, recreational services of fynbos woodlands, and the pollination service provided to agriculture by wild bees in fynbos woodlands. The forestry accounts also measure an important environmental externality: the cost of water abstraction by cultivated forests. Cultivated forest plantations of exotic species (mainly pines and gums) absorb much more rainfall than native species, thus reducing runoff. South Africa is a water-scarce country so this reduced runoff has a cost in terms of foregone use of water by downstream users. In South Africa, this externality is being treated quite seriously. The new South African water policy has proposed charging forest plantations for this water abstraction externality.

In South Africa, commercial timber harvest accounts for well under a third of forest value (Table 3). The largest single forest value is non-market goods from natural forests, which are used mainly by traditional rural communities. Combined with livestock grazing, the goods and services in natural forests account for over half of total forest value. In contrast to some developed countries, recreational use of forests is very small and limited to fynbos woodlands; tourism in cultivated forests and natural woodlands is negligible. However, the recreational value of forests in national parks and protected areas, which are major domestic and international tourism sites, have not yet been included in the forest accounts. Carbon storage is significant in cultivated and natural forests. The water abstraction externality by cultivated forests accounts for about 12% of the value of commercial timber harvest.

The question of who benefits from forests is increasingly important for development policy. Commercial timber mainly benefits large-scale commercial timber producers, while the natural woodlands, making a far larger economic contribution, benefit poor rural communities.

Table 3. **Value of forest goods and services produced by different types of forests in South Africa, 1998**

(millions of rands)

	Cultivated forests	Natural forests	Fynbos woodlands	Total
Commercial timber harvest	1 856	NA	NA	1 856
Non-market timber and non-timber goods	NA	2 613	79	2 692
Forest services				
Recreation	NA	NA	29	29
Livestock grazing	NA	1 021	NA	1 021
Pollination services	NA	NA	786	786
Reduction of rainfall runoff	-225	NA	NA	-225
Carbon storage	120	360	NAV	480
Subtotal	-105	1 381	815	2 091
Total value of forests	**1 751**	**3 994**	**894**	**6 639**

NA: not applicable

NAV: not available

Source: Adapted from Hassan, 2002

Water accounts: assessment of water allocations in Botswana, Namibia, and South Africa

Water is a major constraint to development in a number of Southern African countries. Except for a few, relatively small areas, average rainfall in Namibia, Botswana and South Africa is well below the minimum required for dryland farming. Highly variable rainfall makes even the wet areas drought-prone. Water use in all three countries has grown rapidly over the past 25 years and there is concern that water supplies are not being used sustainably. South Africa is expected to face acute water scarcity in the coming decades. Water scarcity has international repercussions because every country in Southern Africa relies to varying degrees on shared international rivers.

In the past, all three countries viewed water scarcity as a problem of supply to be solved by feats of engineering. Water policy in South Africa and Namibia favored the minority populations and commercial sectors with little regard for economic efficiency or equity. Heavily subsidized commercial irrigation, concentrated in the hands of the minority, was the main beneficiary, while the majority rural population did not have ready access to safe drinking water. However, new policies in all three countries have raised the issues of sustainable use of water and of economic efficiency, which are gradually changing the way water is priced and allocated. In designing a new water policy, it is essential to know the economic value of water, and the economic and social implications of changing water pricing and allocation. Water accounts provide this information. The water accounts provide information about the current pattern of water use, its socio-economic benefits, and the potential impact of policy changes, such as water pricing and property rights, on the allocation of water among competing users, and on the macroeconomy.

This section provides an international comparison of water use in 1996 by natural source and by end user, the socio-economic benefits of water under the present allocation by sector, and the extent of water subsidies by sector. The figures presented in this article are highly aggregated; more detailed water accounts can be found in Lange, Hassan, and Jiwanji, 2002.

South Africa is the major user of water in the region, which is not surprising, given its much larger population and economy (Table 4). However, even after adjusting water use for population, South Africa still has the highest water use at 365 cubic meters per capita, more than twice that of Namibia (157 cubic meters) and more than three times that of Botswana (95 cubic meters).

Throughout the world, agriculture is a major user of water, and that is true for southern Africa as well. Agricultural use accounts for 73% of all water use in South Africa, but only 48% in Botswana and 58% in Namibia. Per capita water use excluding agriculture brings the water use figures closer together for the three countries, but South Africa still uses twice as much as Botswana.

Table 4. **Water use by sector in Botswana, Namibia, and South Africa, 1996**

	Botswana	Namibia	South Africa
Total water use (million m³)	142	256	14 830
Per capita water use (m3 per person)	95	157	365
Per capita water use excluding agriculture (m3 per person)	49	69	98
Percentage Distribution by Sector			
Agriculture	48	58	73
Mining	11	10	3
Manufacturing	1	2	1
Trade, Services, Government	9	3	9
Households	31	29	13
Total	100	100	100

Source: Adapted from CSIR, 2001; Lange and Hassan, 1999; Lange et al, 2001

Botswana and Namibia rely on groundwater for half or more of their water supply (Table 5). There is special concern over use of fossil groundwater, aquifers that cannot be recharged significantly over a time scale meaningful to human activity. There are indications that Botswana and Namibia are relying, in part, on fossil groundwater, but there is not sufficient information about reserves or recharge rates for all the aquifers to make a clear assessment. South Africa relies mainly on rivers and has an extensive system of inter-basin transfers, including the controversial Lesotho Highlands Project; only 2% of its water is presently obtained from groundwater sources.

Table 5. **Water use by natural source in Botswana, Namibia and South Africa in 1996 (in percent)**

	Botswana	Namibia	South Africa
Groundwater	59	50	2
Perennial rivers	20	30	59
Dam storage of ephemeral surface water	21	20	39
Total	100	100	100

Source: Adapted from CSIR, 2001; Lange 1998, 2002c;Lange *et al.* 2001

There are various indicators of the socio-economic benefits of water use, such as sectoral value-added (GDP) per cubic meter of water input, or employment per cubic meter of water input. Botswana and Namibia's lower per capita water use is reflected in systematically higher economic value-added per cubic meter of water input (Table 6). For the economy as a whole, Botswana's GDP per cubic meter of water input is nearly five times as great as South Africa's. This gap is reduced considerably when agricultural water use is excluded, but is still very large. Furthermore, Botswana generates consistently higher value-added than the other two countries in all sectors. The higher returns to water use in Botswana represent a combination of two factors: difference in water efficiency, and different choices of economic activity. The relative importance of water efficiency and output mix can only be assessed with much more detailed water accounts.

Table 6. **National income generated per cubic metre of water used by sector in Botswana, Namibia, and South Africa, 1996 (pula per cubic metre of water used)**

	Botswana	Namibia	South Africa
GDP per m³ of water input	124	45	25
GDP per m³ of water input excluding agriculture	158	108	87
Agriculture	9	6	2
Mining	420	54	61
Manufacturing	437	189	98
Trade, Services, Government	724	542	155

Note: The figures in rands for Namibia and South Africa were converted to pula at a rate of 0.75 pula per rand

Source: Adapted from CSIR, 2001; Lange and Hassan, 1999; Lange *et al*, 2001

A partial explanation for differences in water use among the three countries may be found in the price of water in each country. Despite having reached the limits of domestically available water, no country has implemented full-cost recovery pricing in all sectors (Table 7). However, in 1996 subsidies were lowest in Botswana, an estimated economy-wide average of less than 26%, and highest in South Africa where the economy-wide subsidy reached 86% of costs. South African subsidies were extremely high for agriculture, 97%, which may partly explain the much greater amount of irrigated agriculture than in the other two countries. Namibia had similarly low water tariffs until independence when a policy to gradually introduce full-cost pricing was introduced. South Africa has also adopted full-cost pricing, and in both countries charges for agricultural users have risen since 1996, although full-cost recovery has not yet been achieved.

Table 7. **Water subsidies by economic sector in Namibia and South Africa in 1996 (Subsidy as per cent of total cost)**

	Botswana	Namibia	South Africa
Economy-wide average	**Less than 26%**	**34%**	**86%**
Agriculture	NA	41	97
Mining	NA	7	56
Trade and Services	NA	41	56
Manufacturing	NA	45	56
Households	NA	38	56

NA: not available

Source: Based on CSIR, 2001; Lange *et al*., 2001; Lange and Hassan, 1999; Lange, 2002c

Conclusions and future directions

This paper reports on a few of the policy applications from the environmental accounting initiative in Southern Africa. The asset accounts can provide more accurate indicators of national wealth, and information for management of national wealth. Although not discussed here, these accounts can also be used to provide other improved indicators of macroeconomic performance, such as Genuine Saving, and Environmentally Adjusted ('green') Gross Domestic Product and Net Domestic Product. The flow accounts demonstrated the importance of non-market forest goods and services, and the socio-economic implications of current patterns of water allocation and pricing in southern Africa. Environmental accounts improve policy-making by providing better technical information for analysis and indicators, but the accounts also contribute in a much broader way to global dialogue about the environment and sustainable development.

Environmental accounts provide a framework for a new way of thinking about environmental and natural resource management. Environmental accounts are based on a systems approach in which the key feature is to understand the interdependence of the economy and the environment. This supports integration of environmental considerations into macro-level economic policy analysis in a formal and consistent way which, in turn, provides a concrete basis for productive dialogue among line Ministries about alternative, cross-sectoral development strategies and the associated policy tradeoffs.

The environmental accounts provide a transparent system of information which can be used by government policy-makers, businesses, NGO's and private citizens. The power of the SNA for economic information stems from the fact that it has become an information system to which all stakeholders agree (despite recognized limitations). Environmental accounts play a similar role in searching for common ground to describe the environment-economic linkages and to promote constructive dialogue in a potentially conflict-ridden situation.

The regional program in environmental accounting is now embarking on its third phase; much additional work remains to be done especially in the area of policy analysis and indicators. During the next phase, the program will expand to several additional countries in East and Southern Africa, and advance policy applications of the environmental accounts in several new directions. One direction is the development of a framework based on environmental accounts to monitor the linkages between poverty and the environment, providing indicators of poverty and the environment, as well tools for designing more effective policies to jointly address poverty and sustainable environmental management. Another direction is the use of environmental accounting to improve trans-boundary resource management in key areas such as water, wildlife and tourism.

Acknowledgements

We would like to thank our many professional collaborators. We also want to express our gratitude for several international donors who provided much of the financial support for this work, notably the Swedish International Development Cooperation Agency, United States Agency for International Development and the World Bank.

References

Auty, R.M. and R. Mikesell, 1998. *Sustainable Development in Mineral Economies*. Clarendon Press, Oxford.

Bank of Botswana, 2001. *Annual Report 2000*. Bank of Botswana, Gaborone, Botswana.

Central Bureau of Statistics, 2001. *National Accounts 1993-2000.* National Planning Commission, Windhoek, Namibia.

Commission of the European Communities, International Monetary Fund, Organisation for Economic Co-operation and Development, United Nations, World Bank, 1993. *System of National Accounts 1993*, Brussels/Luxembourg, New York, Paris, Washington, D.C..

CSIR (Council on Scientific and Industrial Research), 2001. Water resource accounts for South Africa, 1991-1998. Final report to the Natural Resource Accounting Programme of Southern Africa.

Das Gupta, P. and K.-G. Maler, 2000. Net national product, wealth, and social well-being. *Environment and Development Economics.* 5(1): 69-94.

Hartwick, J. M., 1977. Intergenerational equity and the investing of rents from exhaustible resources. *American Economic Review*, 67 (5): 972-974.

Hassan, R., 2002. Forestry accounts: capturing the value of forest and woodland resources, in G. Lange, R. Hassan, and K. Hamilton, 2002

Heal, G. and B. Kristrom, 2001. National income and the environment. Unpublished paper.

Lange, G., 2002a. Fisheries accounts: managing a recovery fishery, in G. Lange, R. Hassan, and K. Hamilton, 2002

Lange, G., 2002b. Natural capital, national wealth and sustainable development: contrasting examples from Botswana and Namibia. Unpublished Working Paper.

Lange, G., 2002c. Water accounts for Namibia, 1993 to 2000. Draft working paper.

Lange, G., 2001. Environmental accounts: uses and policy applications. Working Paper for the Environment Department, The World Bank.

Lange, G., 1998. An approach to sustainable water management in Southern Africa using natural resource accounts: the experience in Namibia. *Journal of Ecological Economics*, 26(3): 299-311.

Lange, G., J. Arntzen, S. Kabaija, and M. Monamati, 2001. Botswana's Natural Resource Accounts: The Case of Water. Report to the Botswana Natural Resource Accounting Programme, National Conservation Strategy Agency and Ministry of Finance, Central Statistics Office. Gaborone, Botswana.

Lange, G. and R. Hassan, 2002. Mineral accounts: managing an exhaustible resource, in G. Lange, R. Hassan, and K. Hamilton, 2002

Lange, G. and R. Hassan, 1999. Natural resource accounting: a tool for sustainable macroeconomic policy in Southern Africa. IUCN Policy Brief, IUCN/ROSA: Harare, Zimbabwe.

Lange, G., R. Hassan, and M. Jiwanji, 2002. Water accounts: an economic perspective on managing water scarcity, in G. Lange, R. Hassan, and K. Hamilton, 2002

Lange, G., R. Hassan, and K. Hamilton, 2002 in press. *Environmental Accounting in Action: Case Studies from Southern Africa.* Edward Elgar Publishers, Cheltenham, UK.

Lange, G. and M. Wright, 2002. Sustainable Development in Mineral Economies: The Example of Botswana. Paper presented at the Biennial Conference of the

International Society for Ecological Economics. 6-9 March, 2002. Souse, Tunisia. Submitted for publication to *Environment and Development Economics*.

Marine Research and Information Centre, 2001. unpublished database of fish stocks, catch and TAC. MRIC, Swakopmund, Namibia.

Pearce, D.W., and G., Atkinson, 1993. Capital theory and the measurement of sustainable development: an indicator of weak sustainability. *Ecological Economics* 8: 103-108.

Repetto, R. M. Wells,C. Beer and F. Rossini 1987. *Natural Resource Accounting for Indonesia.* World Resources Institute, Washington, D.C.

Repetto, R., W. Magrath, M. Wells, C. Beer and F. Rossini, 1989. *Wasting Assets: Natural Resources in the National Accounts.* World Resources Institute, Washington, D.C.

Sachs, J. and A. Warner, 1995. Natural resource abundance and economic growth. Development Discussion Paper No. 517a, Harvard Institute for International Development, Cambridge.

Solow, R., 1974. Intergenerational equity and exhaustible resources. *Review of Economic Studies*. 41:29-45.

Solow, R., 1986. On the intergenerational allocation of natural resources. *Scandinavian Journal of Economics*. 88:141-149.

Statistics South Africa, 2001. *The 1998 Social Accounting Matrix.* SSA, Pretoria, South Africa.

South Africa Reserve Bank, 2001. *Quarterly Bulletin.* March, 2001. SARB, Pretoria.

United Nations, European Commission, International Monetary Fund, Organisation for Economic Co-operation and Development, World Bank, 2003. *Integrated Environmental and Economic Accounting 2003.* Final draft. Available at the UNSD website: http://unstats.un.org/unsd/environment/seea2003.htm

United Nationsand United Nations Environment Programme, 2000. *Integrated Environmental and Economic Accounting – An Operational Manual.* Series F, No. 78. United Nations, New York.

United Nations, 1993. *Integrated Environmental and Economic Accounting.* Series F, No.61.United Nations, New York.

World Commission on Environment and Development (WCED). 1987. *Our Common Future.* Oxford University Press, Oxford.

OECD PUBLICATIONS, 2, rue André-Pascal, 75775 PARIS CEDEX 16
PRINTED IN FRANCE
(30 2004 04 1 P) ISBN 92-64-02012-8 – No. 53567 2004